THE ULTIMATE GUIDE TO GREAT REGGAE

Popular Music History

Series Editor: Alyn Shipton, Royal Academy of Music, London, and City University, London

This series publishes books that challenge established orthodoxies in popular music studies, examine the formation and dissolution of canons, interrogate histories of genres, focus on previously neglected forms, or engage in archaeologies of popular music.

Published

Handful of Keys
Conversations with Thirty Jazz Pianists
Alyn Shipton

Lionel Richie
Hello
Sharon Davis

The Last Miles
The Music of Miles Davis, 1980–1991
George Cole

Mr P.C.
The Life and Music of Paul Chambers
Rob Palmer

Jazz Visions
Lennie Tristano and His Legacy
Peter Ind

Trad Dads, Dirty Boppers and Free Fusioneers
A History of British Jazz 1960–1973
Duncan Heining

Chasin' the Bird
The Life and Legacy of Charlie Parker
Brian Priestley

Soul Unsung
Reflections on the Band in Black Popular Music
Kevin Le Gendre

Out of the Long Dark
The Life of Ian Carr
Alyn Shipton

Jazz Me Blues
The Autobiography of Chris Barber
Chris Barber with Alyn Shipton

Bill Russell and the New Orleans Jazz Revival
Ray Smith and Mike Pointon

An Unholy Row
Jazz in Britain and Its Audience, 1945–1960
Dave Gelly

Lee Morgan
His Life, Music and Culture
Tom Perchard

Being Prez
The Life and Music of Lester Young
Dave Gelly

The Godfather of British Jazz
The Life and Music of Stan Tracey
Clark Tracey

THE ULTIMATE GUIDE TO GREAT REGGAE

THE COMPLETE STORY OF REGGAE TOLD THROUGH ITS GREATEST SONGS, FAMOUS AND FORGOTTEN

MICHAEL GARNICE

SHEFFIELD UK   BRISTOL CT

Published by Equinox Publishing Ltd.

UK: 415 The Workstation, 15 Paternoster Row, Sheffield, S1 2BX
USA: ISD, 70 Enterprise Drive, Bristol, CT 06010

www.equinoxpub.com

First published 2016

British Library Cataloguing-in-Publication Data
A catalogue record for this book is available from the British Library.

Library of Congress Cataloging-in-Publication Data
Garnice, Michael, 1959-
  The ultimate guide to great reggae : the complete story of reggae told
through its greatest songs, famous and forgotten / Michael Garnice.
      pages cm. — (Popular music history)
  Includes bibliographical references and index.
  ISBN 978-1-78179-095-3 (hardback)
  1. Reggae music—History and criticism. 2. Reggae music—Discography. I.
Title.
  ML3532.G37 2014
  781.646—dc23
                                2014011972

ISBN: 978 1 78179 095 3   (hardback)

Typeset by CA Typesetting Ltd, www.sheffieldtypesetting.co.uk
Printed and bound by Bell & Bain Ltd., 303 Burnfield Road, Thornliebank, Glasgow,
G46 7UQ, United Kingdom

Contents

Acknowledgments   vii
Introduction   1

1 Jamaica's history of great records   5
2 Great songs from the golden age of mento singles   34
3 Count Lasher   55
4 Chin's Calypso Sextet   60
5 Great Jamaican R&B   70
6 The Skatalites   76
7 Bob Marley & The Wailers, Part 1:
     Ska and more at Studio One   90
8 More great ska songs   111
9 Prince Buster   119
10 Great Treasure Isle rock steady songs   123
11 Great rock steady from other studios   134
12 Desmond Dekker & The Aces with The Dynamites at Beverly's   145
13 Toots & The Maytals   153
14 The Ethiopians   162
15 Great Studio One rock steady and reggae instrumentals   168
16 More great Studio One rock steady and pre-roots reggae songs 182
17 Bob Marley & The Wailers, Part 2:
     Self-produced singles in their middle period   189
18 Bob Marley & The Wailers, Part 3:
     The JAD productions in their middle period   201
19 Bob Marley & The Wailers, Part 4:
     An LP produced by Leslie Kong in their middle period   207
20 Bob Marley & The Wailers, Part 5:
     Produced by Lee Perry in their middle period   211
21 Bob Marley & The Wailers, Part 6:
     Work with sundry other producers in their middle period   224
22 More great early reggae   227
23 Jimmy Cliff   232
24 Nora Dean   236
25 Augustus Pablo   245
26 Lee Perry before the Black Ark   255
27 Lee Perry and the Black Ark sound   263

28 Junior Murvin at the Black Ark   274
29 The Congos at the Black Ark and elsewhere   284
30 More great dub   291
31 Great mento-reggae by Stanley Beckford and others   299
32 Great mento after the golden age   304
33 More great reggae instrumentals   312
34 The Abyssinians   317
35 Burning Spear   321
36 More great Nyabinghi and Nyabinghi-reggae songs   324
37 Dennis Brown   330
38 Gregory Isaacs   338
39 Black Uhuru and Michael Rose   344
40 More great Sly & Robbie songs   366
41 Black Slate   370
42 Steel Pulse   374
43 More great roots reggae   381
44 Big Youth   410
45 More great DJ songs   417
46 Bob Marley & The Wailers, Part 7:
        The internationally released LPs   448
47 Bunny Wailer, after The Wailers   514
48 Peter Tosh, after The Wailers   520
49 Great dub poetry   529
50 Great Jamaica Jazz   533
51 Barrington Levy and the birth of dancehall   537
52 Johnny Osbourne   542
53 More great dancehall   548
54 Coda: More great songs, but difficult to categorize   577

Bibliography   589
Index of names   590
Index of songs   594

Acknowledgments

Two invaluable references on Jamaican music were at my elbow as I wrote this book. The first is *Roots Knotty Roots* by Michael Turner and Robert Schoenfeld. I frequently consulted this ambitious database of every Jamaican single from 1952 through 1985 to find the producer's name and the year of release for many of the songs I describe. The second is *Bob Marley and the Wailers: The Definitive Discography* by Roger Steffens and Leroy Jodie Pierson. This equally ambitious work documents the details of every recording session by The Wailers. It was particularly helpful in clarifying the band line-up on a given song. Two websites proved to be important references and can be recommended to anyone who wants to explore their subjects further: Jamaican Riddim Directory (www.jamrid.com) and Roots Archives (http://www.roots-archives.com). Other general reference sources were consulted for biographical facts on the artists described.

I'd like to thank ethnomusicologist and subject-matter expert Dr. Daniel Neely for our ongoing and lopsided conversation about mento that has corrected and greatly enriched my own website www.mentomusic.com. I am also grateful to Gaël Doyen, who helped me fill in the gaps in my Bob Marley & The Wailers collection.

I'd also like to thank my copyeditor, Sandra Margolies, for her tireless and invaluable input. Thanks are due to Jah Lounge, the cornerstone of the interest in reggae that developed in Ithaca, New York, from the late 1970s into the 1980s and which had a great impact on me and others.

I'd also like to thank my brother Eric Garnice, music-lover, multi-instrumentalist, and general good guy for our decades-long continuous dialog about music. Thanks, too, to my mother for volunteering to proofread a book that she had only marginal interest in. Without her diligence, this book might have embarrassingly described a singer's gentle voice as being genital. And thanks to Dad as well for his support. Most of all, thank you to my supportive wife Grace, who has the good taste to love Jamaican music. She gave me the freedom to write this book over the course of years of weekends.

Introduction

Why this book?

There were a number of reasons for writing this book. Taken together, they made it a necessity.

First and foremost was my wish to provide a guide that, honoring I-Roy's famous edict, *won't waste your time with any 'lightweight stuff.'* This book will write about the great songs amidst the tremendous amount of reggae that has been released, and won't waste time on anything less. As you will see, Jamaica's output of reggae is huge (and that's without even considering the rest of the world). This book will ensure that you don't miss out on great reggae and wind up spending your time and money on lesser material. We will explore how, until fairly recently, most reggae tracks were released as singles. As time goes on, more and more of these tracks are appearing on new CD collections and are available as single-song purchases on line. Fire up your favorite digital music service, take this book in hand, and you're set for some prime cherry-picking.

Along the way, you will see examples of great songs that cannot be acquired on CD or digitally, leaving the original vinyl as the only non-pirated source. By shining a spotlight on these glaring omissions, I hope to encourage record companies and digital music services to fill these gaps in reggae availability.

A crucial reason for writing this book was to tell the history of recorded Jamaican music. It's a fascinating story of creativity, fierce rivalries, resourcefulness, unlikely heroes and an abundant talent. It has resulted in a continuous six-decade flow of music that is of impressive quantity, quality and diversity. Too often, only part of this story is told. This book covers the entire story of reggae, with equal love for mento, ska, rock steady, reggae proper, DJ, dub, Nyabinghi, roots, Jamaica Jazz, dub poetry, dancehall and more.

There was no more important reason for writing this book than to give these great songs their due and to celebrate the people responsible for them. It's my hope not only that this book will help you find the best reggae, but also that the descriptions will enhance your enjoyment of the songs.

The final reason I wrote this book was to set right the three common misconceptions listed below.

The Three Most Common Misconceptions about Reggae

Misconception #1: "All reggae sounds alike."

I hear this too often from my fellow Americans. I assume that it is heard less frequently in the UK, which has had a longer and deeper appreciation of reggae, and it would be anathema in Jamaica. When I hear this assertion, the responses that first come to mind are "You mustn't have heard very much reggae" and "There may be something wrong with your auditory cortex; have it checked." But I actually respond more kindly, as the speaker is obviously someone who has been missing out on droves of wonderful songs. This book will illustrate the distinctly different styles of reggae and their diverse sounds.

The songs in this book range from polished to ragged, from spartan to ornate, from earthy to spacey. Their sound can be monochrome flat or peacock-hued psychedelic; burn white-hot or sooth ocean-blue cool. The germ of the song may come from Jamaica's folk music past, from an overseas song or have emerged new from the mind of the songwriter. There are songs of love and songs of pain; songs that range from the devoutly sacred to the explicitly violent or downright pornographic. In short, all reggae does not sound alike.

Misconception #2: "Reggae started with and/or died with Bob Marley", or, alternately, "The only reggae I know/need is Bob Marley."

Bob Marley is the reggae colossus – Jamaica's greatest musical light. Through his live shows he touched more people around the world than any other reggae performer, and in both quantity and quality his recorded body of work is unsurpassed in Jamaica and compares favorably with that of any other international music superstar. Seven chapters in this book are devoted to giving the music of Bob Marley the deep and comprehensive review it deserves.

But reggae did not begin with Bob Marley, end with his passing, or otherwise cease while he was recording. In fact, the sum total of great records by the other artists in this book easily outdistances that from him. But if Bob Marley is by no means the whole story of reggae, he can be your gateway into the greater story, as he was for me and so many others. This book will not only celebrate Bob Marley's entire body of work, but will put him into perspective with the many other reggae artists who made great records before, during and after his reign.

Misconception #3: "The story of reggae begins with ska", or, alternately, "The story of reggae begins with Jamaican R&B."

If only we could go back and fix every account of reggae's history that begins with these old canards. A reggae history that ignores mento is like a biography that ignores the subject's childhood. The nearly forgotten mento records of the 1950s show a clear lineage to the reggae that followed. This book will put the great records of mento's golden age into perspective as the seed from which all other reggae grew.

Frequently asked questions

Q: What is reggae?

A: This book employs two uses of the word "reggae." First, as in the title, there is the broad usage that describes a line of Jamaican music that runs from rural mento, through Jamaican R&B, ska, rock steady, reggae proper, Nyabinghi, roots reggae, DJ, dub, mento-reggae, Jamaica Jazz, dancehall and ragga. Second, it is used to describe reggae proper, the music that followed the similar ska and rock steady styles that emerged in 1969. I have endeavored to make it clear from the context which meaning I'm using.

Q: I noticed that you have twice as many songs by artist A as by artist B. Are you saying that A is better than B? There would not have been a B if not for A. B is not fit to light A's spliff! Are you crazy?

A: It's folly to apply that kind of math to this book. In the above case, I am not saying that artist B is "better" than A. All this means is that B had more songs that were special than A. A may have many more good songs than B, and B might not have had a career if not for A. And, yes, I probably am crazy. For years, I've had a passion for Jamaican music, and listened to thousands upon thousands of reggae songs. I felt compelled to use a portion of my life to identify and describe reggae's crème de la crème for anyone interested.

Q: Why no songs by so and so? They are great and/or have put out a large number of releases.

A: There are some acts that have contributed significantly to the sum of reggae but are not a significant part of this book. That's because, although they may have recorded a large number of perfectly good songs, none struck me as outstanding enough to warrant attention in this book – which focuses on *great songs*. This is in no way a criticism of such artists or their accomplishments, which may be very significant. They deserve a book of their own.

Q: How did you choose these songs?

A: I did not use any kind of formal points system or other quantifiable means to rate songs. Instead, I chose the songs that have brought me the most enjoyment even after repeated listening, which in some cases spans decades of my life. I was mindful not to avoid songs that are hard to describe nor to choose songs just because they would be easy to write about.

Q: Why don't you cover reggae from outside of Jamaica?

A: This book does cover some reggae from expatriate Jamaican artists living in the UK (such as Linton Kwesi Johnson), and from UK reggae bands that consisted primarily of Jamaicans but included members from other backgrounds (such as Steel Pulse and Black Slate). As to reggae from outside of

Jamaica recorded by non-Jamaicans, there is no shortage from which to choose. But I would urge you to fully explore the songs in this book first. Non-Jamaican reggae never achieves crossover popularity in Jamaica, and not without good reason. Let's put it this way: If you were standing in the middle of a spectacular garden, would you have any desire to look at even a beautiful arrangement of artificial flowers?

The Jamaican Music Roadmap

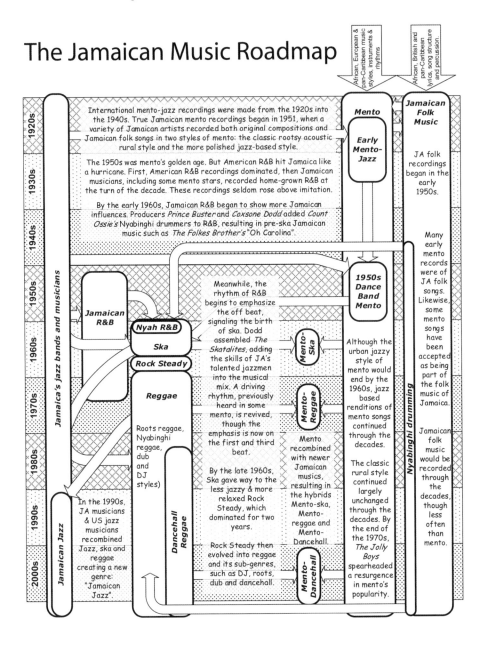

1 Jamaica's history of great records

"Sweet Jamaica, With A Population Of 2 Million People,
Plenty of Sunshine, Plenty of Beaches, Music is a Way of Life."
From the album cover of the 1972 Prince Buster LP, *The Message*

Jamaica, music isle

Though its population is less than three million people, since the start of the 1950s Jamaica has produced an astounding number of records. By this reckoning, Jamaica's per capita musical wealth is unmatched. The closest comparison requires broadening the subject to include the oil wealth of Kuwait, coincidentally a country with a similar population size. But if the artistic achievement of a nation's people is under consideration rather than what the earth holds under their feet, then the density of Jamaica's wealth is unique. How appropriate it is that one of reggae's most-loved record labels would be called Treasure Isle.

Being a people that loves music, and being blessed with a vast number of musically talented individuals, Jamaicans have made their home an island of music. Jamaican music consists of multiple genres and sub-styles. The earliest were its varied folk and religious vocal and percussion musical traditions. From them came mento, Jamaica's first recorded music, followed by the burning advent of ska that would cool into rock steady, only to explode into a variety of reggae styles that included roots, dub, DJ, dancehall and others. Not only did Jamaicans treat themselves well with their indigenous music, they embraced musical styles from other countries as well, producing fine home-grown jazz, R&B, gospel and calypso.

No matter how you define what makes music good, Jamaican music has it in abundance. It is rich in melody, rhythm and texture. There is great singing, lyrics, musicianship and sound production. Creativity and emotion emerge as hallmarks, with Jamaican heads and hearts equally enriching the music. Music is one of the island's greatest resources, one that is enjoyed by virtually all Jamaicans. And more than anything else it produces, music is Jamaica's greatest gift to the world. There's no other music like it.

Reggae conquers the world

So inspired and sustained was this flow of music that it was only a matter of time before it would be fully appreciated by the rest of the world. Today, Jamaican reggae artists, past and present, are popular on every continent, with the late Bob Marley counted amongst the biggest music stars in the world. This has led to reggae being recorded locally in numerous countries and languages around the world. Take, for example, the recent *reggaeton* phenomenon, where this Spanish-language derivative of dancehall reggae was simultaneously at the top of the charts in virtually every Latin country.

The love affair between reggae and the world outside of Jamaica was preceded by four decades of flirtation. From the 1920s into the 1940s, US record labels released singles by Trinidad-born bandleader Sam Manning and others that were jazz renditions of Jamaican folk/mento songs, such as 'Sly Mongoose'. These recordings occasionally featured Jamaican musicians and musical elements. In the 1950s, Harry Belafonte had a number of big hits performing Jamaican folk songs such as 'Day-O', though the music was not particularly Jamaican in style. Spurred by Belafonte's popularity, late in the 1950s US record companies included albums by Jamaican mento artists such as Lord Flea, The Silver Seas Calypso Band and Lord Foodoos in the flood of calypso LPs they released. But none of the Jamaican artists were successful by the financial standards of these labels. Around the same time, some Jamaican mento records were licensed for resale in the UK, such as the 10-inch LP, *Authentic Jamaican Calypsos*, released by the London label.

Flirtation moved to love in the middle of the 1960s. In 1964, Jamaica's Millie Small had transatlantic success when her cover of the US pop hit, 'My Boy Lollipop', reached number 2 in both the USA and UK. A ska-pop hybrid, it was recorded in the UK with a mix of Jamaican and non-Jamaican talent. But pure unadulterated ska would quickly follow. That same year, Prince Buster's 'Al Capone' entered the UK top 20 and Don Drummond & The Skatalites' 'Man in the Street' cracked the UK top 10. In 1966, Desmond Dekker & The Aces reached number 14 in the UK with the rock steady of 'Shanty Town'. In 1967, Don Drummond and The Skatalites charted well again when 'The Guns Of Navarone' broke into the UK top 10. In 1968, it was again Desmond Dekker & The Aces' turn, as 'Israelites' reached number 1 in the UK and number 9 in the USA. This was followed by the international success of the film and soundtrack LP, *The Harder They Come*, in 1972. When Bob Marley & The Wailers released their 1973 LP, *Catch A Fire*, the world's love affair with reggae would be cemented as a lifelong commitment.

Why did this happen? Why did music by Jamaicans for Jamaicans come to capture the planet? Why is Bob Marley an iconic figure, whose image is immediately recognized around the world? Why do vintage reggae records routinely sell for hundreds of dollars on eBay? Why do reggae roots bands of the 1970s continue to tour Europe today? Why are dreadlocks a badge of the counterculture around the globe? Why did 1960s ska enjoy a revival in the England of the1980s that reverberated around the globe and across decades with additional ska revivals? Why is there a resurgent interest in mento? Why did a succession of club music styles arise from dub reggae? Why do rock steady aficionados happily explain that this music is superior to all other reggae, not to mention Motown? Why are contemporary dancehall reggae stars popular in and outside of Jamaica, and why are singers from the USA, the UK and other countries recording in this style? Why are there reissue specialists on both sides of the Atlantic releasing CDs that gather vintage singles of the Studio One brand of reggae?

It is because of the creativity, passion and excellence of Jamaica's singers, songwriters, musicians and producers, which was crystalized in the form of great records. Great records by Jamaican superstars, familiar names and one-hit wonders; classic records released on a myriad of Jamaican labels, legendary, obscure, or, sometimes, completely blank; self-reviewed records, with the accolade "Scorcher" stamped on the label; fantastic records that set trends and spawned hundreds of variations, and others just as good that stand unique; brilliant records that appear on countless CD compilations, and others never released outside of a small pressing of singles, but screaming to be re-released.

Is there anything more powerful, more pleasurable, more giving, than a great record? A love affair, perhaps? Or finding a pile of money? Though I certainly don't deny the value of either of these, consider that a love affair is limited to two people, and money can be spent only once. But, by its nature, a great record can be enjoyed by millions, whether they are local folk or live on the other side of the planet, with each person able to enjoy the song again and again, perhaps through a large portion of their lives. A great record makes its positive impact felt across geography and time like nothing else. The particular circumstances of Jamaica's recording industry would create practices that ensured the island's musical talent would produce a constant flow of great records, exciting and varied, from the time that Jamaica began making mento records in the early 1950s through to the ragga of today.

Mento

Contrary to entirely too many popular accounts, neither recorded Jamaican music nor reggae began with ska in the early 1960s, nor with Jamaican R&B at the start of that decade. They began with the mento that was first recorded at the beginning of the 1950s. It was then that 78-rpm singles began to appear from Jamaica's first record producers on their self-referentially named record labels: Stanley Motta and his MRS (Motta's Recording Studio) label, Ken Khouri and his Kalypso (with a "K") label, and Ivan Chin and his Chin's label. The producers' purpose was straightforward. Two of the three owned retail stores where records could be sold to Jamaicans and tourists alike, while the third struck a deal with Jamaica's largest department store, Kingston's Time Store.

The talented mento acts they recorded were already established as live performers, with repertoires of witty, original compositions and traditional folk songs waiting to be tapped by the producer. It's no wonder then that so many of these mento singles were so good. From the producer's point of view, it was simply a matter of having the band perform in front of the island's newly acquired recording equipment (first brought in by Motta). And a short time later, he came away with yet another single to enhance the stores' record bins. From 1955 to 1957, producer Ivan Chin recorded more than 70 tracks by the seminal rural mento group, Chin's Calypso Sextet, primarily for sale in his Chin's Radio Services electronics stores. In 2007, Ivan recalled to me, "The group was very talented and cooperative. There was never any problem with any member of the band. The band was always ready on time and had rehearsed as many times as was necessary." A flop would mean that the initial pressing of 400 copies would not be repressed, but a hit could quickly sell 10,000 copies or more.

Because the music of Trinidad was more established, Jamaica's mento musicians readily accepted the more famous "calypso" label, and mento is often referred to as calypso in Jamaica even today. But mento was, in fact, separate and distinct from the music from across the Caribbean Sea. (However, it was not uncommon for mento acts to perform mento covers of calypso hits.) Two styles of mento were recorded in the 1950s. Some singles were in the rustic, most Jamaican, rural mento tradition that could sound much like an antediluvian acoustic ska or reggae. The chief difference was the pre-electric instrumentation. Acoustic rather than electric guitar, hand percussion rather than a drum kit, a rumba box (a crate-sized version of the African instrument, the *kalimba*, also known as a thumb piano) rather than a bass, and home-made saxophones and flutes constructed of bamboo rather than professionally manufactured instruments were used. The banjo, another instrument with an African heritage, played a prominent role as both a lead and rhythm instrument in rural mento, and helped to characterize its sound. It's a shame that this instrument did not carry forward in the Jamaican music that followed (though there was a handful of exceptions), considering how good it sounded in mento. And some mento bands used fiddle or harmonica as a featured instrument. Rural mento often featured a distinctive vocal style – a high-register, nasal, country sound that, too, carries an African heritage. Not all recorded rural mento singers used this sound, though Harold Richardson and Alerth Bedasse exemplified it, as did reggae star Stanley Beckford decades later. Backing vocals would be provided by the band members regardless of their level of vocal proficiency. This resulted in a rangy overlap of motley country voices for the most delightfully rough harmonies heard in any style of Jamaican music. Rural mento enjoyed a broad gene pool, drawing qualities from European and African musical traditions. This was a trait it shared with the other exciting new musics of the twentieth century, including blues, jazz, calypso and rock. Great names in rural mento at this time included Count Lasher, Chin's Calypso Sextet, Lord Lebby, Harold Richardson & The Ticklers, Lord Messam, Count Owen, Lord Tanamo, Arthur Knibbs, Count Sticky and others.

Other mento singles were in the very different, polished, jazz-based urban style. It was only natural for Jamaica's talented jazz bands to record traditional folk songs, as well as originals in the same vein. This music did not sound like the ska or reggae that followed, but its jazz (including some of its prominent musicians) came forward into ska and carried on into reggae. Though any and all jazz instruments were heard in urban mento, piano and clarinet were the most common lead instruments. The vocals were more polished than those heard in rural mento. Great names in urban mento at this time included Lord Fly & The Dan Williams Orchestra, Lord Flea, Hubert Porter, Baba Motta and others.

The division between rural and urban mento was not always strict, as the records of Arthur Knibbs best attest. But whether rural, urban or something with attributes of each, mento was consistently upbeat, bright and happy, utilizing major key melodies. (How this would change by the roots reggae of the 1970s!) Songwriters concentrated on storytelling. Some stories were impressive observations of some aspect of Jamaican life at that time, rich in detail. There were a lot of painfully funny stories about relationship difficulties. Some of these were risqué for the 1950s, typically employing elaborate double entendres. Though naughty for their time, they were miles away from the *slack* (explicitly dirty) lyrics that would later arise in reggae. Occasionally, mento acts mentioned themselves in their songs, starting the tradition of self-referential reggae lyrics, leading to uncountable examples of reggae singers and DJs singing about themselves or their music. There were also songs about visiting Jamaica, catering to the island's tourists, with records clearly targeted as souvenirs. Not surprisingly, this was typically the least satisfying type of mento song.

But for all the talent of these mento acts, by the end of the 1950s, these records stopped selling. It may have been due to the fact that mento didn't change very much throughout the decade. The singles from the end of the 1950s sometimes seemed a bit stale and repetitious compared to the excitement and vibrancy of tracks that came earlier in the decade. And there was a new sound being heard, exciting and worldly, that made mento sound provincial and passé by comparison.

Rhythm & Blues would take over as the hot new music in Jamaica. US radio broadcasts of R&B could be received in Jamaica. Records brought over from America dominated at the sound systems (more on this subject in a moment). Quickly, some mento stars and new Jamaican singers alike would find themselves recording home-grown R&B singles. The success of this music would filter out mento instrumentation from the Jamaican music that came after. Banjo, clarinet, rumba boxes, fiddle and bamboo wind instruments (though there were occasional exceptions to this rule) would not pass through the R&B filter to ska, rock steady and reggae. Hand drums were left behind, but the influence of the Rastafarian religion would later bring their return, though played in a different style. By the end of the 1950s, the original Jamaican record labels ceased to release new singles and, of the original three producers, only Ken Khouri remained in the music business. Although mento was pushed out of the spotlight by R&B, it by no means ended. Mento is part of the fabric of Jamaica and continues to be performed and recorded up to the present day.

As the golden age of mento singles was ending, a new breed of Jamaican producer emerged. The exigency of their need to produce great records, their intended use, the premium on innovation and the immediacy of the feedback they received were all very different from the traditional retail model that mento producers worked under. This would all result in a very different approach to developing and recording music, one that would ensure that Jamaican music would never stagnate to be supplanted by a non-Jamaican style again. And it would give the world a windfall of great new Jamaican records.

The new record producers and Jamaica's sound systems

The Jamaican music that followed mento in the early 1960s was far more of a studio-based music. (This is not to say that Jamaican acts did not perform or were somehow deficient live. As the many thousands of people around the world who witnessed a concert by Bob Marley & The Wailers or the early 1980s incarnation of Black Uhuru can tell you, live reggae could compete with any rock performance.) Unlike mento, where a song and its arrangement were established through live performance long before it was recorded, the songs of the new Jamaican music would be fleshed out in the recording studio. Producing a new single would still be the goal, though the format changed from the 10-inch 78-rpm single to the 7-inch 45-rpm one. But the single was not necessarily intended for retail purposes.

Exciting new records were essential to attract patrons to the highly competitive world of the sound system. Emerging in Jamaica in the 1950s, the sound system was where the majority of Jamaicans went to hear and dance to music, often until daylight. It was a space where the operator brought his portable set-up of turntables, powerful amplifiers and huge speakers with their legendary bass and, most importantly of all, his collection of records. Admission was paid. Food and drink were purchased. Dancers in the audience made names for themselves. Disc jockeys bantered and became stars. The record "selectors", who chose the play order, became known by name, ages before the emergence of the celebrity DJ overseas. A sound system's signature songs would definitely be heard, and new ones were tried out. Jamaican records were played, as well as R&B records from the USA. The sound system owner would go to great lengths to acquire a hot, new R&B disc, scratching the information off the label and giving the song a new name to keep competing sound systems from acquiring the same record. A successful sound system could have multiple set-ups in operation, working simultaneously across the island. Though a sound system enjoyed brand loyalty from its followers, if it could not keep the music selection fresh, patrons might choose a competing outfit. Today, there are sound systems in operation around the world, with the operators trotting out their collections of rare reggae vinyl to delight the patrons.

To assure a stream of novel records, beginning at the end of the 1950s, sound system operators Arthur "Duke" Reid (The Trojan sound system), Clement "Coxsone" Dodd (Downbeat sound system) and (later, after leaving Dodd's employ) Cecil Bustamente "Prince Buster" Campbell (Voice of The People sound system) became the new guard of record producers. For these men, pressing copies of records for sale to the public was a secondary concern. Instead, the immediate need was to produce records to attract people to their sound system. In this way, the sound system created a backdoor that allowed Jamaicans of African descent to enter into record production, as these sound system operators were black. Before this, record producers were predominately from Jamaica's merchant class, where there were few Jamaicans of African descent, even though nearly every musician they recorded was black. This was a positive development for black progress on the island. But these new producers, although of the people, did very little to improve the small flat fees per record customarily paid to the artists.

To assure more efficient record production and greater control over the product, both Dodd and Reid opened their own studios in Kingston. The studio's house band would back a succession of vocalists in a given session. The singer might have been a Kingston-born local or a hopeful from the country. He might have passed the open auditions at the studio's gate that very morning, impressing the producer or his talent scout with his song or voice, in an a cappella or acoustic guitar-backed audition. Or he could have been part of the stable of singers that the producer was currently working with, cranking out singles just as quickly as the musical ideas flowed. Or he could be a star stopping by to work with this outfit, with both the singer and producer hoping that the collaboration would be mutually beneficial. But whoever the singer, greenhorn or veteran, urban tough or country bumpkin, these house bands and producers were expert at quickly fleshing out their raw song ideas into finished products.

Efficiency was honored. A song might be reassigned to a different singer if things did not immediately click, maximizing successes and never wasting a good musical idea. Turnaround was fast. It was common for tracks to be recorded in just one or two takes. Sometimes a recording would be made, pressed to disc and then rushed to the sound system all in the same day. Gauging the success of the record was as simple as watching the reaction of the crowd. Would people stop dancing? Or might they demand that the record be replayed over and over again? A novel record would cause a sensation or, as disc jockey U-Roy famously put it on his groundbreaking hit, would 'Wake The Town'. A hot new record and word of mouth would guarantee the operator a bigger crowd and greater earnings the next time his sound was in operation.

The immediacy and competitiveness of the sound systems drove not only the quality of these singles, but a rapid pace of innovation, as the Jamaican music fans not only demanded excellence, but delighted in hearing inventiveness in their music. Mento had quality, but its retail model gave it no reason to progress, and the records eventually stopped selling. These new producers would explicitly experiment and develop, ensuring that the music that followed would excite the fans.

Revenue from selling records would come to exceed earnings at the sound systems. The producers opened their own record stores. Quickly, more producers entered the fray, more studios opened and more labels were launched, all of which led to more singles being produced, recording more singers and musicians in more styles. Competition was fierce and music fans benefited greatly, as the flow of new records was unbridled.

Before one style could run down, someone ushered in a new style or unanticipated innovation. Great records came at every turn, making the six-decade run of Jamaican singles from mento through dancehall one of the greatest stories in the history of recorded music. Consider that between 1962 and 1982, upwards of 45,000 songs were released on singles in Jamaica. For that span of more than two decades, about six new songs were released on the island every single day. This is by no means to say that every reggae record was a great one, but there were rich veins of greatness threaded throughout. Consider this book to be your prospector's pan, helping you to find every gold nugget as we discard the lesser material.

Jamaican R&B

By the start of the 1960s, Jamaican talent was handily addressing the local demand for R&B records with acts such as Jackie Edwards, Keith (Stuart) & Enid (Cumberland), (Joe) Higgs & (Roy) Wilson, The Blues Busters, The Jiving Juniors, Derrick Harriott, former mento stars Laurel Aitken and Lord Tanamo, and many others. R&B was the least creative and the least Jamaican chapter in the history of its music. Though there were exceptions, it was largely imitative of American sounds. And it seems that the entire body of Jamaican R&B consisted solely of love songs, squashing the lyrical inventiveness and diversity of the mento that preceded it. But R&B was crucial in laying a foundation for the musical advances that would quickly follow, as the R&B era proved to be short. The R&B line-up of guitar, bass, drums, brass and keyboards would be the basis for the Jamaican musical styles that followed until the time when music would be produced in the digital domain. American R&B also had a major impact on the vocal line-up in Jamaican music by opening the door for vocal groups. This was a change, as the recorded mento that came before was a solo singer's province. But vocal groups proved to suit Jamaican R&B singers and fans very well, and would continue to steadily gain popularity through ska and rock steady, peaking in roots reggae. As we will see, they even continued into ragga in the form of *dancehall crews*.

Not all the producers of Jamaica's R&B records were sound systems owners. For example, British-born Chris Blackwell of Island Records and future Prime Minister Edward Seaga of WIRL (West Indies Records Limited) both began production in the R&B era, keen to record and release local music. But like the mento producers before them, they would document the music rather than drive it forward. This was not the case for the R&B records produced by sound system operators such as Reid, Dodd, and Buster. These producers witnessed the previous decade's decline in mento singles, as these records were part of their sound systems' selections. Duke Reid was more directly impacted. His earliest productions were a handful of mento singles at the end of the 1950s, just as the golden-age mento boom was ending. He would quickly move to R&B. These producers did not want the Jamaican R&B they were producing to grow stale. And they were mindful of the fact that no matter how much Jamaicans loved R&B, and no matter how well Jamaicans imitated this American form, this phase of Jamaican music lacked the originality, creativity and *Jamaicaness* of what had come before and of what could be. Buster and Dodd would intervene.

Early Nyabinghi experiments

Buster and Dodd wasted little time in experimenting with the R&B form, infusing it with Jamaican musical elements in the hope of making it more interesting, looking for the next sound system sensation. In 1960 and 1961, they each released songs featuring Count Ossie's Rastafarian religion-based Nyabinghi hand-drum troupe supplementing R&B. A hand drum and/or other hand-held percussion instruments were often heard on golden-age mento singles, but this was different. Ossie's troupe typically had three or more drummers, and they played in the hypnotic Nyabinghi style. The result was a handful of unusual records by singers such as Bunny & Skitter, Lacelles Perkins, The Mellow Cats and, most famously, The Folkes Brothers and their hit, 'Oh Carolina'. These Ossie-fied songs signaled the moving away from just imitating American R&B to a new form of recorded Jamaican music. Yet the brief period of Nyabinghi/R&B fusion is often misinterpreted or completely forgotten, as it was quickly eclipsed by another Jamaican modification of R&B called ska.

Ska

The road to ska began a few years prior to the Nyabinghi/R&B fusion. In 1956, bassist Cluett Johnson, saxophonist Roland Alphonso, drummer Ian Pearson, guitarist Ken Richards, trombonist Rico Rodriguez and pianist and singer Theophilus Beckford were in session, working on a rough, shuffling boogie song, with a melody that owed something to the mento standard 'Rukumbine', called 'Easy Snappin'. Producer Coxsone Dodd wanted something that would make the sound more distinctive. Ernest Ranglin, the great guitarist and one of Dodd's arrangers, suggested altering the rhythm. (However, as tends to happen when looking back at key points of Jamaican music history, another musician remembers it differently. Drummer Lloyd Knibb claimed that Dodd challenged him to develop a different beat, and it was he who provided it. Others have been credited as well.)

Beckford's rhythm piano chords would fall on the off-beat, striking in between the conventional beats played by the other musicians. And the ska beat was born. Although a number of R&B records with an inverted beat have been cited as a possible inspiration, it should also be remembered that certain mento rhythms and Nyabinghi drumming, which peculiarly emphasized the first beat of four, were influences that were closer to home. The ska beat was a distinctive, quintessentially Jamaican sound. It would continue past ska, but would slow and mellow over time until it ultimately became the languid heartbeat pulse of roots reggae. 'Easy Snappin' proved to have been too revolutionary for the adventurous yet cautious Dodd. He would leave it on the shelf (as he was wont to do) until finally releasing it in 1959.

Where did the word "ska" come from? There are two schools of thought. One is that it's short for Cluett Johnson's favorite made-up expression, "skavoovie". The other holds that it is a pronunciation of the genre-defining chop, as in "the rhythm goes, 'ska, ska, ska' on the off-beat".

Beckford's song was just baby's unsteady first steps compared to the athletics of the ska to come. But they were influential steps. By 1961, numerous Jamaica R&B songs took one halting step or another towards the ska beat. Then, as had also happened with mento, Jamaica's talented jazz musicians (first and foremost the stellar group that would come to call themselves The Skatalites) became involved in ska, greatly enriching the music. Ska quickly came to encompass sounds ranging from what would be simple vocal R&B, if it were not for the characteristic ska beat, to miniature magnum opuses of accessible instrumental jazz, with all stops in between. The tempo became fast-paced and, borrowing from a beat heard on some rural mento singles, would throb insistently. This throb was most often sounded by an impossibly persistent, intensely honking sax in a sound that helped define the genre. (The demands of this were so intense, Skatalite Johnny Moore believes that it contributed to the premature death of his bandmate, saxophonist Dennis "Ska" Campbell. Just listening to Campbell's astonishing 136 honks-per-minute performance on the Don Drummond track called 'Down Beat Alley' may raise your blood pressure.) With the Nyabinghi-infused R&B and variety of ska records being produced, imagine the excitement at the sound systems in the early 1960s whenever the disc jockey announced that a new record was about to be played.

The sound of ska was newer, more Jamaican, and more exciting than R&B. Its instrumentation was that of R&B and jazz, with saxophone, trumpet, trombone, piano, electric guitar, harmonica, stand-up bass and drum kit. Each of these instruments contributed greatly to the success of the music. For example, The Skatalites had an embarrassment of riches on sax with Tommy McCook, Roland Alphonso and Lester Sterling all providing great solos while the aforementioned Campbell honked away. Great trumpet was heard from Baba Brooks and Skatalite Johnny Moore. But two other instruments in particular idiosyncratically helped define the ska sound. First was the frequent presence of trombone as a featured instrument. Perhaps no other genre of music celebrated this instrument more than ska, thanks to the island's talented jazz *trommies*, most notably Don Drummond of The Skatalites. Second was the multicultural creativity, energy and generosity of rim shots heard from ska drums. Credit Arkland "Drumbago" Parks and Skatalite Lloyd Knibb, whose playing still leaps off the records. The snare drum was typically played with the rattle disengaged, giving it a sharper sound, a practice that would continue into reggae. Though present, piano was not a major force in ska, as it was more of a rhythm than a lead instrument. This is surprising when considering the abundance of fine jazz pianists heard in the urban mento that came before. The role of keyboards would grow with the introduction of rock steady, through reggae, up to dancehall. The same can be said for guitar in ska, as its limited rhythm role would later grow. The abrupt ascent of ska displaced the hand drums of the R&B/Nyabinghi fusion. But Nyah percussion would return to reggae, where its contribution would be greater than ever.

Ska – and for that matter, all reggae that followed – has a most pleasing approach to horns. Rather than massing a big horn section that blares in unison, a Jamaican horn section most often consists of two horns playing in unison, but never at the maximum volume that the instrument is capable of. The effect was easy to listen to and musically informative, as the listener could easily hear the qualities of the individual instruments, how they were being played, and the harmonics of their overlap, rather than a single glazed sound.

Ska took the brief musical introductions that often preceded the body of a song in mento and built on them, sometimes resulting in an elaborate mini-song. Song introductions, simple or complex, would persist all the way into ragga.

There was not a ska vocal sound, per se, as there was in mento. Both country and city Jamaican voices were heard. Some singers had rougher voices than what would be typical in rock steady, the style that followed. Solo singers and vocal groups were heard, and duos were popular as well. If a female singer was heard, it was in a support role, the singing often pitched incredibly high. Ska lyrics covered a diverse range of topics, but none that would characterize the style. But ska did introduce the rude boy song. "Rude boys" were the young, violent ghetto criminals who plagued Kingston – music's true original gangstas. Because of these songs, reggae fans around the world recognize the term "ratchet" as a type of knife that swings open and locks (the Jamaican equivalent of a switchblade/flick-knife), even if they have never seen one. Rude boy exploits inspired an impressive number of songs by a variety of artists, peaking in the rock steady era and continuing in some form right through into ragga. The views expressed in the rude boy song ran the spectrum: many rude boy songs took a firm stance against their crimes; many others celebrated or defended the rude boy. Some songs were ambivalent, others were blatantly self-contradictory, decrying the bad behavior while identifying with the rude boy. The young Bunny Wailer wrote pro-rudie songs, but when he recut them later in his career, having become a Rastaman and *conscious artist*, he altered the lyrics, removing any celebration of rude boy behavior. In the Jamaican film, *The Harder They Come*, based on a true story, we see the rude boy elevated to the status of a folk hero. This is not surprising, as the rude boy was sometimes perceived not as a petty criminal, but as a revolutionary fighting against an impossible social system that guaranteed poverty and oppression for most Jamaicans.

In addition to Dodd, Reid and Buster, new producers began recording ska, competing while sharing the talents of The Skatalites and other musicians. These included the great newcomer Leslie Kong and his Beverly's label and the less-prolific Justin Yap, who nonetheless recorded several classic Skatalites tracks on his Top Deck label. Each of these producers had his share of great tracks, with Buster and Reid undeniably getting their licks, but Coxsone Dodd is the producer who is most associated with ska.

Ska captivated Jamaica and even had some cross-over success in the UK. It subsumed Jamaican R&B, which was only seldom heard again with its traditional rhythm. (But, as American R&B developed into forms such as funk, soul and gangsta rap, it would continue to influence reggae singers and musicians to the point where you'd be hard pressed to find a reggae song that wasn't in some way influenced by black American music.) Jamaican pride in their new music aligned nicely with the national pride of Jamaica gaining independence from the UK in 1962. Jamaica would send a contingent of ska performers to represent Jamaica at the 1964 World's Fair in New York City (a demonstration I witnessed and was impressed by at the age of five). When listened to today, great ska records sound as revolutionary and exciting as they did when they were recorded five decades ago.

With the commercial and artistic success of ska, the die was cast. Ska established that, in addition to musical excellence, taking chances and making changes were now hallmarks of Jamaican music. Ironically, in just a few short years, ska would be a casualty of this.

Rock steady

Though its reign was short (1966–68), rock steady would completely supplant ska as the dominant style of Jamaican music. Though mento continued to be performed and recorded after its golden age had ended, and reggae performers would intermittently revisit R&B sounds well after R&B had ceased to be the dominant Jamaican style, rock steady seems to have permanently slammed the door on ska, leaving it to other countries to rediscover. The UK, Japan and the USA would all have "ska revivals" in the decades that followed.

Rock steady was an abrupt shift from ska in a number of ways. The tempo was significantly slower (ska tipped its hand by beginning to slow down by 1965) and, even more importantly, the insistence of the beat relaxed from feverishly hot to sweetly warm, or, sometimes, breezy cool. Since a new style of Jamaican music was typically ushered in with a new dance, the folks at the sound systems got to slow it down, as they rocked steady, as opposed to sweating to the ska. The rock steady sound was smoother and more polished than the sometimes strident ska. It was also somewhat simplified and less jazzy than ska was at its best.

Electric bass replaced ska's stand-up acoustic bass, and suddenly, the instrument was not only more audible, but had a more prominent role. It contributed to the rhythm and a surprising amount to the melody of rock steady. This would have lasting importance, as electric bass playing would continue to evolve and move closer to the music's forefront, ultimately helping to define the sound of the reggae that followed. Rock steady also gave keyboards a greater role than they had in ska. Piano was most frequently heard, often featured as the principal instrument, giving so many rock steady songs their characteristic sweet sound. Organ was also heard, more so than in ska (where it was rare), though not as often or as prominently as it would later be in reggae. The trademark ska emphasis on the off-beat persisted, but its instrumentation changed. Instead of the honking brass of ska, the chop was now sounded by a more relaxed keyboard or electric guitar, further setting the stage for reggae. Rock steady drum playing, though fine, was more subdued than the aggressive virtuosity previously heard from Lloyd Knibb and Drumbago in ska.

More polished vocals were often heard in rock steady compared to the rough vocals often found in ska and in the mento that had gone before it. This point was overtly reinforced by producer Duke Reid, who, legend has it, would burst into the sound room of his studio and discharge his firearm if the singer's vocals were not to his refined liking. While mento's lyrics emphasized storytelling and folk songs, and ska's lyrics were diverse, rock steady, like R&B, specialized in love songs, especially those records from Duke Reid's studio. But not exclusively, as rock steady is sometimes best remembered for its classic rude boy songs.

Artists that are primarily associated with rock steady include Ken Boothe, Derrick Morgan, The Ethiopians, Desmond Dekker, The Paragons, The Techniques, The Melodians, Hopeton Lewis, The Heptones, Alton Ellis and others. The top backing band was The Dynamites. Guitarist Lyn Taitt, a member of the Dynamites who began his career in ska, went on to be perhaps the premier rock steady instrumentalist. Not only did his distinctive rhythm guitar (complete with idiosyncratic chirps and slashes) play an important part in many rock steady songs, he also innovated the new sound by slowing the rhythm down at a session for Hopeton Lewis's 'Take It Easy', perhaps the first rock steady song. (Another contender for the first is Alton Ellis's 'I Have Got A Date'. Another Ellis song, 'Rock Steady', was the first to use the new style's name.) Though other producers were responsible for their share of great rock steady songs, for this style Duke Reid was the innovator, and for many, the sound he obtained on his Treasure Isle label was the very sound of rock steady.

Festival

An important Jamaican musical institution came into being at the same time as rock steady. It was in 1966 that the Jamaica Cultural Development Commission Annual Festival of the Arts, or as it was more commonly called, Festival, added a song contest to its program. Each year, a song would be named the Festival winner, an unmatched badge of honor until decades later, when reggae became a Grammy category in 1984. Existing hit songs and songs created just for entry into Festival would vie for the prize. The first winner was 'Bam Bam' by Toots & The Maytals. Since Festival seemed to favor songs with a country feel and/or songs that mentioned Festival, a subgenre of Festival songs that fit these criteria arose.

Versions

Rock steady would soon give way to reggae proper. But first, let's turn our attention to a production innovation that created a landslide of exciting new music. Paradoxically, it did so by using what had already been recorded. Called "versioning", this practice would prove to have enormous impact on reggae, resulting in an explosion of new records, new subgenres, and new stars of Jamaican music.

The world of popular music was already familiar with "cover versions", where one artist recorded a rendition of another artist's song. But the uniquely Jamaican practice of versioning was different. It referred to reusing a record's "riddim" (the local pronunciation of "rhythm"), as the instrumental backing was called, to make a new record. For example, at producer Coxsone Dodd's Studio One, it would become common for a different performer to sing a new song with a different melody and lyrics over the riddim of an already established record. The instrumentation of the version may have been identical to the original, or have been altered, with a horn replacing a familiar organ track perhaps, or some additional percussion. However, the version would always retain the drum and bass – the heart of a riddim. Suddenly, the task of a singer became quite different. Rather than working with an arranger and band on developing a song he or she had written into a finished record, singers found themselves using their malleable vocal and songwriting skills to fit a new song to the demands of an existing riddim. This proved to be no hindrance to Jamaica's singers, and the new versions were often as good as the originals, or even better. And rather than perceiving them as second-rate products in any way, fans found them to be as enjoyable as if the song had been set to new music. This would not have been the case if not for the high quality of the carefully crafted riddims. Some of them proved to be endlessly renewable and, decades later, are still being versioned today. Top riddims have been versioned hundreds of times. On Johnny Osbourne's hit 'Murderer', itself a vocal version of a dub version of the Vin Gordon instrumental 'Heavenless', he digresses from the narrative long enough to make the observation that he is versioning a version. Since riddims are named, typically after the first version that used it, reggae fans could shop by riddim, as well as by favorite artist, label or style.

Soon, singers would begin to follow up their hits by re-voicing the riddim with a new song, though this form of versioning seemed to have a lower yield of great new records compared to other approaches. But versioning wouldn't be limited to singers. Instrumental versions first spiced up the sound systems' selections and would become a popular B-side staple. With the singer dubbed out of a familiar recording, the strength of the riddim was fully revealed, showing that a good one could easily stand unadorned on its own. The instrumental was frequently listed with the title "Version" on the single's B-side. This led to "Version" being the most-used song title in reggae, if not in all of recorded music, representing thousands of different Jamaican B-sides. There were no rules for crediting the version. It might bear the singer's credit as it appeared on the A-side, the singer with an added band name, just a band name, a band name with the producer's name worked in or just the producer's name. The instrumental version soon led to the instrumental cut, where a musician was brought in to add a lead horn, keyboard, guitar, harmonica, hand drum, vibraphone, or other track atop the instrumental version. This created a potential B-side for a single, or, if the instrumental cut was a follow-up version of a hit, an A-side of a new single.

Though tremendously popular in the reggae of the 1970s and beyond, versioning originated in the ska era at Studio One. But before that, a form of versioning was heard on 1950s mento singles where, occasionally, the instrumentation from one song was recreated for a different song by the same or a different artist. Perhaps this is all rooted in the wellspring of Jamaican songs and Jamaican folk music, where several songs would share the same melody. Perhaps this is also the root of why so many Jamaican songs shamelessly took their melody from non-Jamaican songs; as if reusing someone else's tune for a new song is the most natural of musical acts. As you will see throughout this book, a surprising number of Jamaican songs turn out to be drawn from other places, ranging from popular hits to the most obscure of songs. What is certain is that versioning is as popular today as it ever was. Most new dancehall reggae CDs consist of a host of artists each having their own way with a single riddim. For some reason, Leslie Kong did not version his riddims, choosing to ignore the commercial and artistic successes that his competitors enjoyed with the practice. This might have changed had it not been for his untimely passing in 1971.

Though hugely popular in Jamaica, versioning was an innovation that would not be adopted by popular music elsewhere. As naturally as versioning fit into an enriched reggae, it's somehow hard to imagine The Beatles singing a different song over the backing to The Rolling Stones' 'Satisfaction'. But other musical conventions would arise outside of Jamaica that resembled versioning and that were no doubt influenced by it. For example, hip-hop and rock (and eventually reggae) would come to adopt sampling, where a portion of an existing recording would be used in a new song. Club music would commonly release disposable tracks of an anonymous singer performing a familiar song to the beat-simplified instrumentation of a different familiar song. Similarly, there is the after-the-fact cut-and-paste genre called "mash ups" (a term that has a different meaning in Jamaica, where to *mash up* is to destroy). Here, the vocal from one familiar song is lifted and dropped into the instrumentation of another. But the effect was that of a home-made novelty rather than actual song craft. But even though the rest of the musical world did not adopt the practice of versioning, the two new forms of reggae that versioning spawned, DJ and dub, would be copied in other countries. Though they had their beginnings in rock steady, they became pervasive in reggae proper. We'll pick up these threads of the story later in this chapter.

Reggae proper

In 1968, Toots & The Maytals announced the new style that would succeed rock steady with their song, 'Let's Do The Reggay'. (Though this is widely accepted as fact, few significant events in reggae's history go uncontested. Producer Bunny Lee claims that a song he produced, sung by his brother, Don Tony Lee, beat Toots to the punch, with 'Regay Time' being released earlier the same year.) What was the meaning of this new word, whose spelling had not yet been standardized? One school of thought held that it was a play on "ragged". Another view was that it came from the slang term "streggae" – someone wearing alarmingly inadequate clothing. In the 1970s, it was widely put forth by roots performers that it was based on an African term that meant "king's music". But Toots claimed that he just made the word up. The same is likely also true of the sound-alike word heard in the title and the nonsense chorus of Laurel Aiken's 1959 mento song, 'Rege Dege Ding'.

Equally unsettled was the initial sound of reggae. Its first few records featured a fast-paced, keyboard-led, shuffling polyrhythm for a high-energy party music sound. But the sound of early reggae quickly fragmented, with creativity and competition causing different producers to take different approaches for different sounds. For example, Lee Perry's early reggae productions were faster in tempo than rock steady, but were leaner and exhibited an idiosyncratically taut phrasing. Perry dispensed with jazz more than rock steady had, as he did with the mid-song solos that had been ubiquitous in Jamaican music since mento. The overall effect was an unadorned, lean, tough and efficient sound. Studio One had it both ways. Some of its output from the end of the 1960s to the start of the 1970s was a continuation of its rock steady sound. In this, mid-song solos – sometimes jazzy – were still performed (often by a former Skatalite) and could be adorned to the point of being baroque. But during the same time, Dodd produced music that was leaner and even less adorned than Perry's early reggae. At the same time, producer Leslie Kong recorded amazing reggae that was expertly executed and featured a refined rural flavor that sounded entirely unlike the music coming from anywhere else. Other early reggae could be very much like rock steady, but a bit more creative and chance-taking, typically with a more aggressive rhythm and tempo to some degree.

This has created confusion. For example, sources today frequently categorize Beverly's early reggae as rock steady (debatable) or as ska (just plain wrong). It's no wonder why there is no consensus on what the first "true reggae record" is (though 'Do The Reggay' by Toots & The Maytals, 'Nanny Goat' by Larry Marshall and 'People Funny Boy' by Lee Perry are frequently proposed for different reasons). Nor is it clear exactly when the cut-over from rock steady to reggae occurred (this boundary is especially blurry at Studio One). Though reggae would soon explode into several subgenres, its sound would coalesce enough to have at least a few constants as it moved into roots reggae. It would feature the slowest, sometimes languid, rendition of the ska rhythm, with the chop typically played on electric guitar. Describing reggae as a *naturalistic* music, its musicians and fans would commonly liken this rhythm to a heartbeat. This was never truer than when rhythm guitar began to affect the double-stuck banjo beat of some golden-age mento. Guitar was typically a rhythm instrument in reggae, though blues-based leads were not uncommon. If rock music's signature instrument was the guitar, then bass is the instrument that most signifies reggae. A reggae bass line is strong, highly melodic and often hypnotic, displaying a simplicity born of rumba box and a sparseness informed by dub. No other bassist but a reggae bassist could do so much with so few notes. Reggae drums were also distinctive. With a heritage that included jazz, R&B and Jamaican folk percussion traditions, applied to the challenges and opportunities of a slower version of the inside-out ska beat, reggae drums are rich in unusual patterns and creative fills. A great portion of reggae songs open with a drum figure, enabling a reggae fan to name the drummer within the first moments of a song. A second percussionist, playing a hand drum and/or other instruments, was often heard, adding to the rhythmic richness of the music. Keyboards were almost always heard in both rhythmic and melodic roles, organ now being the most popular. It was often employed for the drama it could bring, or it was played in what is called the *bubble-up* shuffle style to provide a song with a bouncy rhythmic effervescence that was pure reggae. Piano was still also common, but not as prominent as it was in rock steady. Electric piano, clavichord and synthesizer would also make their way into reggae. Horns were very often part of the mix, with a saxophone and/or trumpet and/or trombone enriching the melodic content with fine supporting lines and mid-song solos.

The reggae fan benefited greatly from the diversity and expansion that reggae would bring. Great riddims continued to be recorded by new and established producers. New vocalists hit the scene. New reggae sub-rhythms appeared, and were popular enough to be named, such as Rockers, Steppers and the One Drop. New bands entered the fray, including two especially great bands defined by their gifted rhythm sections. The Barrett brothers (Carlton on drums and Aston "Family

Man" on bass) would go on to be the nucleus of Bob Marley's group. Their influence on reggae cannot be overstated. The prolific Sly & Robbie (Lowell Fillmore "Sly" Dunbar on drums and Robert "Robbie" Shakespeare on bass) would soon be backing and producing numerous artists on their label, Taxi, and would join as members of Black Uhuru. Their sound was so distinctive that they practically constituted a reggae subgenre of their own. With so much talent, reggae exploded in new trajectories, leaving contrails of great records.

Dub

It was at Treasure Isle where a talented sound engineer born with the name of Osbourne Ruddock, but professionally known as "King Tubby", was hired by Duke Reid to remove the vocals from some of his rock steady hits to create instrumental versions for his sound system. This seemingly mundane task would prove to be profound twice over, creating two new types of versioning.

First, let's follow King Tubby to the start of the 1970s, where he enjoyed good crowds at his own sound system, Tubby's Hometown Hi-Fi. People flocked there to hear his "dub plates" – one-of-a-kind records that could be heard nowhere else. Rather than simply removing the vocal track, Tubby had begun to use the mixing board as a musical instrument in an entirely new way. The instrumental and vocal tracks were rhythmically dubbed in and out over the course of the record, leaving a partially completed jigsaw puzzle of sound, with new pieces vanishing or appearing rhythmically as the song progressed. Tubby had created the *dub version*. (Or so the legend goes. But in the 2007 book, *Dub*, by Michael Veal, antecedents are documented.[1]) Dub made reggae more enjoyable by deconstructing it. This "drop-out" and "drop-in" rhythmically revealed the struts and beams of the song, making its architecture better appreciated. It gave the listener an entirely new way to enjoy the individual components of a recording and how they interacted. No one understood this better than the dub-master (as the producer/engineer was called in this role). Less could be more, and in dub, absence became one of reggae's most important musical instruments.

The effect of dub on a familiar recording was amazing, as it rhythmically stimulates two different thought processes. First, there is surprise when the familiar vocal or other aspect of the song abruptly vanishes, prompting the brain to fill in the missing pieces from memory. Second, another part of the brain is gratified as previously unheard details of the recording are revealed. Literally, this was heady stuff. And artistic as well. In dub's reduction of a song to a series of angular rhythmic representations, the dub-master gave reggae a form of cubism. When dub reduced the riddim to just drum and bass, as it usually did for some portion of

---

1.   Michael E. Veal, *Dub: Soundscapes and Shattered Songs in Jamaican Reggae* (Middletown, CT: Wesleyan University Press, 2007), p. 52.

the track, it also gave reggae its own form of minimalism. And the introduction of new dub techniques would soon give reggae its own forms of electronic and psychedelic music.

This was when the dub tool-kit expanded beyond the crafty application of drop-out/in. Reverberation (more commonly called reverb), echo (including digital delay) and (if the producer was Lee Perry in the later part of the 1970s) flange were used as they had never been before to become dub mainstays. With this battery of sound processors, the dub-master could paint from a palette of Day-Glo colors onto the earth tones of reggae. This increased the excitement and drama of a recording. Reverb added gravity and could highlight a single note or beat as more important than the others, instilling a single guitar strum with a flashing transcendence. Echo could double a beat, making the rhythm more interesting. It could take a single syllable of voice or a humble guitar chord and splay it into something fantastic. Drop-out/in not only could enhance the rhythm by working within it, it could add excitement by momentarily subverting it. The same is true of echo, which could launch parabolas of sound that resounded to their own beat. All of this resulted in a very spacey listen, the perfect complement to the ganja that so many reggae fans in Jamaica and abroad enjoyed. Unlike any other psychedelic music, dub was unique in its emphasis on rhythm. By this, it was a treat not just for the head, but the feet. Dub became a popular staple at the sound systems, and a popular dance was named after it. Called the "rub-a-dub", the name was a pun, as it consisted largely of rubbing bodies together to the music in a rhythmic dry hump. And, unlike any other electronic music, dub, still fully reggae, was rooted in the organic.

Reggae fans could not get enough of dub, or as Pablo Moses sang in his great song of the same name, "dubbing is a must". Singles with a dub version B-side became the norm. These dub versions quickly became as important to the record-buyer as the A-side. These B-sides were titled 'Version', 'Dub', 'Dub Version', or some variation of the A-side's title with either the word Dub or Version worked in. There were no effective rules to predict when a great dub version would be heard. There were times that a rather dull A-side resulted in a very exciting dub version on its flip, making the A-side superfluous. An equal number of times, a great A-side resulted in an uninteresting dub version on its flip. The best example of this is how few of Bob Marley's B-side dub versions would qualify as great dub (though admittedly some were good). Soon, 12-inch singles were being released that continuously joined a song with its dub version. These records, called *disco-mixes*, extended the song's length, often twice, and sometimes even more. Frequently, an even dubbier version of the disco-mix's A-side appeared on the B-side. Disco-mix singles became very popular, sometimes appending a DJ version rather than a straight dub version to the original vocal track, and sometimes concatenating all three. It was not uncommon for the singer's climactic line to be truncated when the second version was affixed, in a never-resolved cliffhanger. When this happened, neither the disco-mix nor the original single mix was truly complete, and neither was definitive.

Quickly, dub effects invaded the A-side of singles as well, with the producer applying even more effects to the dub version B-side, with the drop-out/in of the vocal track all but guaranteed. By this time, dub was no longer something done after the fact to an existing record, but was part of the process of producing a new recording. Dub albums would soon appear. Most were collections of a producer's dub tracks from a variety of sources. "Clash" LPs, which had two dub-masters providing alternating tracks, were also popular. So were "showcase-style" LPs, which presented a collection of a singer's singles, each one followed by its dub version B-side. A few were dub versions of a singer's LP, track by track. Dub became so ubiquitous in reggae that live performances would often include a live dub jam, with the musicians mimicking the production effects of the dub-master.

Besides Tubby, the innovator, and Lee Perry, who on his Black Ark label would take dub production further than anyone else, Augustus Pablo was also a giant of dub. His melodica playing over a dub backing has become synonymous with this music. There were many other fine dub-masters as well.

By the time dub, Jamaica's psychedelic music, came into full bloom in the mid-1970s, the psychedelic rock movement was over in the USA and UK, having mutated into new styles such as heavy metal, progressive rock and jam-band. But, as we have seen with versioning, reggae never throws away a good idea. Dub would continue to enliven each form of reggae that followed up to ragga. Dub has branched out beyond Jamaica. The UK recently established its own distinct style of modern dub reggae, influenced by club music. Likewise, dub influenced the club music scene, and helped create such styles as Drum And Bass. Dub versions and the disco-mix single also influenced the 1980s "12-inch remix" rock and dance music singles from the USA and UK. Some of these were labeled as being dub versions, though they seldom sounded much like dub at all.

Dubbing the timeline

With the always innovative Coxsone Dodd again leading the way, the release of reggae singles became nonlinear. As if the producers were dubbing the very timeline itself, singles dropped out and back in, echoed forward or reverberated from the past.

Based on criteria known only to himself, Dodd notoriously would put good recordings on the shelf for any number of years before finally deciding to release them. Limited-run singles that had been out of print for years could suddenly be re-pressed, sometimes creating the impression that this was a new record, since the label of a reggae single never carries a release date. Some hits were re-released after a time, freshened with minor overdubs. Others dropped out permanently, never to be re-released again. An old riddim could be dusted off by a producer for versioning, days, months or decades after it was originally recorded. Producers also had their bands re-record popular riddims of the past, often with changes to make them sound more contemporary. Sometimes this would be a welcome development, like having an old friend show up in a new suit of clothes of the latest style. At other times, the original outfit, classic and timeless, was preferable. It became common for a singer to return to a past hit, re-recording it to revised instrumentation, often more than once over the years. All of these practices make the simple question, "Is this a new record?" problematic for a reggae release.

DJs

We have seen how King Tubby's dropping out the vocals from Treasure Isle hits led to dub, a new genre of reggae. But that was only half the story. The reason why Duke Reid wanted these dub plates in the first place led to another type of versioning, one that equaled the originality, audacity and impact of dub.

Instrumental versions were needed by the disc jockeys who acted as masters of ceremonies at sound systems. Hot DJs were a sound system's star draw – innovators such as the Count Machuki and King Stitt were doing more than just introducing the next song. They were also augmenting the records they played with all manner of vocal sound effects, exclamations, catchphrases, jive talk and other banter. This DJing was developing into song-length performances, and the vocal tracks on the records were getting in the way. By the end of the 1960s, DJs like U-Roy (most famously) and the aforementioned Machuki and Stitt were recording their chanted, rhythmic repartee over Treasure Isle riddims, creating DJ versions of these songs. The novelty of this was tremendous, and highly influential. The practice would catch fire, spreading to other labels, producers and DJs.

DJing (or *toasting*, as UK fans would come to call it) was an entirely new approach to vocalizing a song. Its rhythmic chanting is less formal and more conversational than singing. The DJs told stories, aggrandized themselves, dismissed rival DJs, name-checked the records and the musicians they were DJing over. A DJ song could consist of a stream of consciousness, as the DJ let you know everything that came into his mind. Or it could concentrate on just one subject, or something in between.

Many of the top DJs, such as Big Youth, Trinity, Papa Tullo, Dennis Alcapone, The Lone Ranger and the aforementioned U-Roy, came across as very enthusiastic, highly likable characters. A DJ record was music by the people, for the people, as if to say, "I may be a regular person rather than a singer, but I still have plenty to say and should be heard." This was reinforced by the fact that DJs often chanted in "patois", as the heavily accented speech of the common people, rich in slang and alternative grammar, was called.

Soon, DJ records were as popular as those from singers, if not more so. In 1973, a vocal group as successful as The Ethiopians found it difficult to find a producer to work with them. Instead, the producers wanted to concentrate on the demand for DJs records. Substyles arose. If a DJ spoke very rapidly, he was said to be DJing in the *fast talk* style. A DJ whose chanting bordered on singing was referred to as *sing-jay*. An explicitly dirty DJ worked in the *slack* style. DJ pairings became popular, as duos recorded one-off singles or became more permanent teams. DJ versions could be found on many singles' B-sides or anchoring a single's A-side. Often, the DJ chanted over a dub version of a familiar riddim, with the opening of the original vocal track still intact: a stub that gave the DJ the option of a lyrical jumping off point. Other times, the vocal was the DJ's alone. Twelve-inch disco-mix singles were released with a riddim presented twice, a singer performing first and then handing the baton to a DJ to chant over a dub version. Sometimes, the DJ would comment on the very song he just took over. These records were influential on the contemporary American urban music, as it would become common for a guest rapper to add a section to a singer's track. And, on the topic of rap, without Jamaican DJs, there would not have been American rap music. If the similarities between early rap and DJ are not enough to convince you, consider that when rap started in the Bronx at the end of the 1970s, several key players were immigrants from Jamaica. DJing continues strong in Jamaica, with most of today's dancehall stars vocalizing in the sing-jay style.

Nyabinghi music, roots reggae and Nyabinghi-reggae

Another important way reggae expanded, keeping the music fresh and relevant to Jamaicans, was by accommodating the full expression of Jamaica's previously suppressed Rastafarian religion. With interpretations of the Bible that resulted in dreadlocks, the smoking of marijuana as a sacrament and referring to Africa as Zion, Rasta caused discomfort and fear for many both in Jamaica and abroad. But consider that it arose from the poorest, most downtrodden people in Jamaica. Preaching peace, love, racial pride and personal humility, righteous behavior, vegetarianism, self-respect, equality, community, standing up for your rights, the eventual triumph over oppression, love of music and love of God, the emergence of Rastafari should have been neither scorned nor feared. Instead, it should be applauded, if not marveled at, when considered against the radical and hateful ideologies which arose from similar circumstances around the globe.

There had been inklings of Rastafarianism in Jamaican music before the reggae era. As we will see, Rasta sentiments were first recorded in the 1950s on Lord Lebby's mento song, 'Etheopia', with its back-to-Africa theme. Though this was not a common theme for mento, Lebby's song was not unique. Later in the decade also saw Laurel Aitken's 'Mas Charley', a song using the melody from 'Day-O', but including the chorus "me seh Jah". And we have seen how Rastafarian Nyabinghi drums, played by Count Ossie and his group, enhanced a handful of R&B singles at the start of the 1960s, as Jamaican R&B began its journey to a more Jamaican sound. Some have pointed out that there are Rastafarian references in the names that The Skatalites gave to some of their instrumentals, such as 'Addis Ababa' (the capital of Ethiopia) and 'Beardsman Ska' (another name for Rasta-men). But The Skatalites used all kinds of names and topical subjects for titles, including 'Confucius', 'Fidel Castro', 'President Kennedy' and even comic-strip star 'Dick Tracy'. Two song titles do not make The Skatalites' music overtly Rastafarian. However, it is true that many of its members were, in fact, Rasta.

But in the reggae era, records of actual Nyabinghi music would become popular, as Count Ossie and his group stepped out from their support role. Nyabinghi music consisted of a group of hand drummers and chanted vocals. (This last element would have a big impact on recorded Jamaican music, influencing the delivery of the reggae DJ and carrying over into Nyabinghi-reggae and roots reggae.) Sometimes an acoustic guitar was added, or perhaps a guest jazz musician would sit in. The songs could run long by reggae standards, once LPs made long-form tracks possible. This was a reflection of how the music was performed live, when it was not uncommon for a Nyah jam to pass the half-hour mark. The lyrics were spiritual in the Rasta way, with praise of God and African repatriation being common themes. The drums, though African influenced, were played more introspectively and meditatively, and less aggressively than most African percussion. One could argue that Nyabinghi music was not strictly reggae, but a separate thread of Jamaican religious music. But by merging with reggae and enriching it, it has been subsumed by reggae.

One form of this was Nyabinghi-reggae, a fusion where reggae instrumentation joined the drum-based, chanted, spiritual sound of Nyabinghi. With a string of albums in the 1970s, Ras Michael became the most recorded artist of this music. The Wailers were early practitioners, starting with a few late-1960s tracks. In the 1970s, Bob Marley & The Wailers' 'Rastaman Chant', 'Time Will Tell' and 'Babylon System' would become the best-known Nyabinghi-reggae tracks of all.

More prevalent, the 1970s also saw the advent of roots reggae – reggae with a Rasta sensibility and a Jamaican earthiness. Often, a single percussionist dappled the music with the precise yet loose playing of a Nyabinghi hand drum, a sound that proved to be a natural fit with 1970s reggae. Lyrically, roots reggae was typically serious in tone, emphasizing Rastafarian religious beliefs and/or social issues, such as the oppression faced by the downtrodden that practice it. References to Haile Selassie I or Jah Rastafari (God) and Babylon (the oppressors of society, ranging from its large institutions to individual policemen) are ubiquitous in roots reggae. So are references to the sacramental marijuana and the ways it's enjoyed (spliff, when rolled up in paper, though much bigger than the joints rolled overseas, or chalice, chillum or kouchie when smoked in a water-cooled pipe). A common theme was Africa as the true cultural and spiritual home of Jamaica's blacks and their religious Zion. There were also frank discussions on a variety of social issues in *sufferas* songs, as poverty and anguish became a potent inspiration for great roots reggae. And there was a lot of roots reggae about roots reggae; how it's loved, how it's cultural, how it's *Jah music*. The 1960s counterculture in the USA and UK may have valued their music more than previous generations did. But only in reggae did popular music rise to the level of a shared religion. By leveraging the musical talent and the devotion to spirituality of Jamaica's people, Rastafarianism elicited a body of religious music that is impressive in its size and quality. Though specifically targeted at the poorest and most disenfranchised Jamaicans, it's a remarkable testament to roots reggae that it gained worldwide popularity.

The style of roots reggae singing was typically plaintive but dignified, wounded but positive, full of longing but *upful*. Just as some, but not all, mento singers shared an archetypical vocal sound, the same was true of roots reggae. The classic roots vocal was high-register, nasal, wispy and possessed a pleasingly strident edge. It's a vocal sound that harkens back to Africa, helping the style live up to its name. Minor-key melodies are often employed and add to the emotional gravity of the music. And when roots had a dark heaviness, it was given the accolade of *dread*. Vocal groups peaked in popularity in reggae during the roots era, with a sound that was often haunting. Roots reggae instrumental arrangements could be sparse, but more commonly, a larger band was utilized, complete with multiple horns, guitars, keyboards and percussionists. The latter included a variety of hand-held instruments such as hand drums, wood blocks, maracas, claves, etc., expanding on sounds heard on some golden-age rural mento records.

To many fans, roots is the very definition of reggae. Burning Spear and The Abyssinians helped pioneer roots reggae. With nearly all reggae performers being or becoming Rasta, roots was recorded by many other vocal groups (such as Bob Marley & The Wailers, The Gladiators, The Wailing Souls, Black Uhuru, Culture, Israel Vibration and Black Slate) and solo singers (such as Dennis Brown, Gregory Isaacs, Johnny Clark and Cornel Campbell). Though reggae is currently dominated by dancehall, a flame of roots reggae still burns today.

Other reggae

Nyabinghi-reggae and roots reggae were not the only new styles to arise in the 1970s. When a reggae singer sang a sweet love song, the music was designated as *lovers' rock*. These records were defined by their theme rather than by an instrumental sound. And by a demographic, as although these records were enjoyed by all reggae fans, they especially appealed to the female ones. It was natural for a singer to release both lovers' rock and the most serious of roots without anyone batting an eye. Dennis Brown, Gregory Isaacs and Bob Marley did this amongst many others. But Ken Boothe is perhaps the singer who was lovers' rock's greatest specialist, best remembered for his rock steady hits in this style. Lovers' rock also took off in the mid-1970s in the UK, resulting in an offshoot subgenre that typically had a pop feel and often featured female vocalists.

Slackness was a very different, lyrically defined subgenre of reggae from lovers' rock. Typically voiced by DJs, these reggae records featured shameless sexually explicit lyrics. Only a few established artists ventured down this path, including Yellowman and General Echo, although later a good number of modern dancehall artists would release slack records. The winkingly naughty songs that were sometimes heard in mento are considered to be the cradle of slackness, but there was quite a gulf between the two song styles.

DJ reggae would give birth to a genre called dub poetry. Like a DJ, a dub poet would rhythmically chant-recite his performance to reggae (or, sometimes, without accompaniment). But the content and delivery of these poems was more serious in approach and subject than the sometimes frivolous lyrics of the DJ, while the lyrics were more composed and less extemporaneous. The UK-based Linton Kwesi Johnson was a pioneer, with a series of album releases beginning in 1978. Mutabaruka, who currently hosts a radio show in Jamaica, is another important dub poet with an impressive string of releases.

International reggae is a term with several meanings. Primarily, it refers to Jamaican reggae marketed to a broad international audience by major US or UK record labels. The goal here was to release albums which could be better marketed to the world than the singles that were the preferred format in Jamaica. This reggae could be uncompromised, or could feature blues/rock guitar to help open the ears of rock fans abroad. Top acts of this type of international reggae include Bob Marley & The Wailers and Peter Tosh (both from 1973 on), as well as Steel Pulse and Black Uhuru. International reggae could also refer to reggae with the rough edges sanded off, making it smoother and easier for foreign ears to appreciate. Groups such as Third World and the later line-ups of Inner Circle meet this definition. International reggae has also been used to describe "foreign reggae" – reggae from people and countries that are not Jamaican, and may or may not be sung in English. (If a non-Jamaican group is playing a reggae song with either timbales or steel drums, feel free to shake your head at these inaccurate clichés.) This book has its hands too full cataloging and describing the greatest *authentic* Jamaican reggae songs (including some recorded in the UK) to have any time or inclination to guide you to reggae *a foreign*.

I mentioned earlier that mento never went away. Beginning around 1973, it also fused with reggae, resulting in a new sound. Mento-reggae featured a more rustic form of reggae, with a pre-ska-influenced rhythm, rural lyrics and sweet country singing. Piano is often featured. Though he did not perform exclusively in this style, the best known performer of mento-reggae was Stanley Beckford. There were also the Prince Brothers and others. Tangentially related, in the 1970s, bamboo sax player Sugar Belly recorded instrumental reggae (as well as mento and calypso) that anachronistically featured his mento instrument.

Another subgenre was born in the late 1990s, with the advent of Jamaica Jazz, from artists such as Ernest Ranglin, Monty Alexander, Dean Fraser and others. In this alchemical process, jazz was re-infused into ska and reggae, with wonderful results.

Dancehall reggae

For some reggae fans (younger ones in particular) dancehall reggae is the only reggae that matters. Though some consider the DJ reggae of the 1970s the start of the genre due to its popularity in the dancehall and lyrics about the dance, true dancehall reggae as a distinct musical style arose later than that. Dancehall went through three stages as it rose to exceed roots in popularity. The first began at the end of the 1970s, courtesy of such talents as producer Henry "Junjo" Lawes, singer Barrington Levy and backing band The Roots Radics. The deviation from roots reggae began subtly. The rhythm became a bit more simplified, syncopated and driving. A mechanized feel began to suggest itself. Horns and jazz elements were cut out. Lyrically, the heavy concerns of roots reggae were left behind. After all, this was reggae to dance to. Solo vocalists dominated in this early stage of dancehall, leaving vocal groups with their most reduced role since the golden-age mento era.

The sound of dancehall became more mechanized, which suited the style's driving syncopation. Though they were flirted with in the roots era, drum sequencers rather than live drummers came to the fore. The bass, which had already evolved from the rumba box of mento, to the acoustic bass of ska, to the electric bass of rock steady and reggae, would be replaced by a keyboard – first the black and white keys of a synthesizer and ultimately the alphanumeric keys of a computer.

Interestingly, around the same time, there were parallel developments in overseas popular music. Hip-hop records began to appear that used "beat box" drum machines and inexpensive sequencing synthesizers, such as the seminal 'Planet Rock' by Afrika Bambaataa & The Soulsonic Force. This mechanization was as revolutionary as the rap vocals it backed. And even disco music, never known for being innovative, spawned a huge hit with Donna Summers's 'I Feel Love', its backing completely sequenced on synthesizers by Giorgio Moroder. Devo began to mechanize rock music, but with an arch sense of irony, even moving like herky-jerky animatronic figures on stage. Their cover of The Rolling Stones' 'Satisfaction' caused a minor sensation, as punk rock's second act, new wave, continued to upset the rock status quo. But where mechanization helped define rap, and briefly added variety to disco and rock, only in dancehall reggae did it completely and permanently transform an existing genre of music.

But as dancehall began to pull away from some of the traditions of reggae, it revived a pre-reggae Jamaican sound. Pocomania (also called Pukumina) is a traditional Jamaican folk music that sounds like an African-influenced snare and fife martial band. It was a welcome development when its distinctive drum rhythm was adopted by many dancehall riddims.

The second stage of dancehall reggae burst forth in 1985, when producer Lloyd "Prince Jammy" James was experimenting with an inexpensive Casio synthesizer. When slowed down, one of its canned instrumentations proved to fit as a ready-made riddim for singer Wayne Smith's song, 'Under Me Sleng Teng'. Though this was a first in reggae, it was not the first time that a synthesizer replaced completely traditional musical instruments in popular music. (In the mid-1970s, the German synth-rock band Kraftwerk began to have hits that were composed of vocals with instrumentation that was entirely sequenced on synthesizers.) Similar songs occasionally followed. But the impact of Jammy's "Sleng Ten" on reggae was more profound. It was a gigantic hit that led to tidal waves of versioning, varying and more versioning. Reggae fans couldn't get enough of dancehall records in the new "digital" or "computer" style. Traditionalists cringed, envisioning a future where Jamaica's music no longer used musicians. Singers like Tenor Saw, Nitty Gritty, King Kong and others benefited, rising to fame on this new style. The producer gave himself a promotion from Prince Jammy to King Jammy.

But this was just the jumping-off point. By the early 1990s, digital dancehall became more complex, composed on far more sophisticated electronic equipment, with a broad sonic palette of sounds and rhythms. This led to the third stage of dancehall reggae, which is often called "ragga". The term is a shortened version of "raggamuffin", as many dancehall performers were then calling themselves. Today's biggest ragga stars included Beenie Man, Bounty Killer, Buju Banton, Sean Paul, Lady Saw, Mr Vegas, Shaggy and TOK. TOK is an example of a *dancehall crew*: a self-contained vocal group complete with singers and DJs, as the vocal group returned to reggae in modernized form. New producers such as Danny Browne, Dave Kelly, Jeremy Harding, Sting International and many others made their name in ragga with their creative riddims. Ragga proved to be influential on the UK club music scene, helping to birth such UK dance music styles as Drum And Bass, Jungle, and the styles that followed. It also influenced Bhangra, a popular dance music of North India and Pakistan with a centuries-old tradition, and it has combined with rap and Latin sounds as Puerto Rico gave birth to reggaeton.

The sound of ragga varied widely from one riddim to the next, ranging from the candy-colored to dark and sinister. And the rhythms were even more varied. Sometimes the traditional reggae beat, whose lineage ran from mento through earlier dancehall, was not utilized. (When it was, it came to be called a "one-drop" ragga riddim.) A Pocomania beat might be heard, though its popularity would wane in the 1990s. Mostly, the rhythms were purely ragga – a dub-informed, electronic dance music that takes an anything-goes creative approach to rhythm and arrangement, often featuring novel synthesized drum sounds.

New ragga riddims appeared regularly with a brace of artists trying their hand at each one, resulting in a steady stream of single-riddim multi-artist CD collections. Jamaicans and reggae fans around the world couldn't get enough ragga, and the quest for novelty found ragga performers voicing riddims as diverse as the latest cutting-edge Jamaican ragga sounds, dusted-off 1970s roots reggae riddims, mento-ragga hybrids, hip-hop-ragga hybrids, etc. Meanwhile, Trinidadian soca, contemporary rap, 1950s rock and roll, 1960 surf music, Bollywood music and more would be pressed into service as dancehall riddims, as ragga impresarios threw everything at the wall to see what would stick.

Certain lyrical themes came to the fore in ragga. Gangsta rap influenced the lyrics and sound of some ragga, opening the door for rude boy songs to become more explicitly violent, complete with gun-love lyrics. This was not a stretch. Crime and violence have always been an unfortunate part of Jamaican urban life, and were reflected in reggae lyrics. This was true to an unprecedented degree for the ragga generation of performers, who were often ready to demonstrate their own street cred. The influence of gangsta rap proved to be bidirectional, as the sound of ragga also influenced the beats of some rap tracks and ragga stars made cameo appearances on rapper's recordings. Slack lyrics also became popular in ragga, with artists like Lady Saw making names for themselves with sexually explicit songs. Providing an alternative to this roughness were acts like Beres Hammond, Morgan Heritage and Tarrus Riley. Performing in a style that could have been called "adult-oriented reggae", their lyrics and music were consistently well-mannered, if not too mannered. There were also ragga performers who declared themselves *conscious artists*, and turned their backs on sex and violence and made a lyrical return to the values of roots reggae. Rooted in reggae history, neither ragga's explicit violence nor slackness came as any surprise. However, another lyrical theme that came from nowhere was far more disturbing.

Hateful anti-homosexual songs with lyrics that advocated violence and murder rose as a popular theme for more than a few ragga stars. While these artists defended such lyrics on religious grounds and offered other excuses, it was a stunning turnaround for a music that was previously known for its themes of peace, love, righteousness, living together in harmony, and the rights and survival of the oppressed. These songs drew censure from around the world, as overseas tour plans for the associated artists were cancelled. It gave reggae an embarrassing setback on the world stage – the same stage that took decades of great Jamaican records to surmount. At the time of this writing, it appears that dancehall as a whole has moved past such songs, allowing reggae to resume its forward march. But by the 2010s, though still popular, dancehall had lost some of its daring creativity and distinctiveness, with influences from outside of Jamaica at least partially to blame. This echoes previous chapters of reggae history. When the golden age of mento dimmed, Jamaican R&B emerged. When imitating R&B quickly ran its course, Nyabinghi R&B and ska resulted. When the flames of ska burned too hot for too long, rock steady appeared, and so on. If we are indeed seeing another stylistic twilight, I can't wait to see – or imagine – what will come next.

* * *

A great record is like a finely cut gem. Vocals, arrangement, lyrics, innovation, rhythm, chorus, verse, production, instruments, melody and emotion are the expertly rendered facets. The effect of each is multiplied by every other, and the resulting song dazzles. The records described in this book are like a bag of gems. They are the standouts: the most engaging and endlessly rewarding songs to come from this musically rich country. Let's pour them out, and enjoy what makes each one precious. Let's give these great reggae songs their due.

2   Great songs from the golden age of mento singles

It's hard to believe how often mento is completely omitted in accounts of reggae's history. Even the otherwise excellent 1993 Island Records box-set *Tougher Than Tough: The Story Of Jamaican Music* completely omits mento, starting the story instead with R&B, running through ragga. Though the reasons for mento's omission are not hard to understand, it's truly a travesty. Not only for the historical inaccuracy, but for the great mento artists and records that are overlooked. Many of the 78-rpm singles of the 1950s, mento's golden age, are strikingly good. And they contain the first appearances of themes and musical elements familiar from the reggae that followed. Let's set the record straight: mento is clearly part of the continuum of reggae, and a very important part of its story – the beginning.

Why does mento get truncated from so many histories of reggae? One reason was that by the time reggae took off internationally in the mid-1970s, there was very little mento available for purchase and very little written about it. For non-Jamaicans, this seminal chapter of reggae's history was hidden. This held true for decades. Then, in the late 1990s, a pair of budget CDs of 1950s mento tracks was released, though they were not labeled as mento. It wasn't until 2001 that a proper mento CD collection, called *Boogu Yagga Gal*, complete with excellent liner notes and lyrics, was finally released. Other mento compilations would follow and it's now possible to hear well over one hundred 1950s mento tracks. We'll look at the best of them. Let's hope these releases continue, because, as you will see, there are still some crucial mento records awaiting their first release since they were pressed up on a small run of fragile 78s more than half a century ago. In the meantime, the only recourse available to fans is to trawl eBay and other used-record dealers, or search the internet for streamed or downloadable recordings. Another reason why mento is omitted from many reggae histories is that not all of the styles of 1950s mento were reggae-like, clouding its lineage. The polished urban mento by such artists as Lord Fly and & The Dan Williams Orchestra, Hubert Porter, Baba Motta and Mapletoft Poulle was an accomplished style of music, but has to be considered Jamaican popular jazz rather than part of the reggae canon. Instead, it's the rural style of mento that's the primordial soup from which reggae sprang, and that is the start of our story. I hope that someone will write a book on jazz in Jamaica that would include a good account of urban mento. I will keep a place for it on my bookshelf.

Separate chapters are devoted to the two most prolific golden-age rural mento stars, Count Lasher and Chin's Calypso Sextet. First, here are some great golden-age mento records by other artists.

Lord Lebby

Born Noel Williams, in 1930, in Saint Mary Parish, Lord Lebby recorded ten golden-age singles, several of which warrant discussion below. A versatile singer with a strong voice, he went on to record an album of lesser mento material in the 1960s and dabbled in R&B and pop vocals, releasing a single of each the same decade. His R&B song, 'Caldonia', was something of a hit in the UK at the start of the 1960s.

'Etheopia'; 'Doctor Kinsey Report'

These two songs comprise a classic mento single as produced by Ken Khouri on his Kalypso label in the mid-1950s. It's a fine example of how the rural form of mento could sound so much like an acoustic version of the reggae to come later. It's also a fine example of the lyrical diversity of golden-age mento. Though their sound is similar, each side deals with very different subject matter. 'Etheopia' is a serious song and a historically important one, while 'Dr. Kinsey' is a light-hearted pleasure, showing mento's naughty side. In 2001, these songs, never previously released on any other medium than a 78-rpm single, would see their release on CD as part of the mento collection *Boogu Yagga Gal*. They have since appeared on several other mento collections as well. Though it was long out of print, 'Etheopia' made enough of an impact that it was remembered and covered in the 1960s by ska bandleader Carlos Malcolm, and in the 1980s by roots group Culture (calling it 'Forward To Africa') and Bunny Wailer (calling it 'Here In Jamaica', a song described later in this book; page 519).

'Etheopia' is the first back-to-Africa song in Jamaican music. The notion of African repatriation as a way to better the lives of Jamaica's slave-descended black population was first put forth earlier in the twentieth century by Jamaican journalist, orator and activist, Marcus Garvey. The Rastafarians would adopt this belief, elevating Ethiopia to Zion – their religious holy land. Many other back-to-Africa reggae songs would follow in the decades to come, especially during the roots reggae era. Some outstanding examples discussed later in this book include the ska/rock steady 'Africa' by The Gaylads, the seminal roots reggae of 'Satta Amassa Ganna' by The Abyssinians, 'African Teacher' by Burning Spear, 'Africans To Africa' by Black Slate, 'Exodus' by Bob Marley & The Wailers and 'Dreamland' by Bunny Wailer, which he recorded five times between 1966 and 1980, with The Wailers and without.

Though the label does not credit him, the great mento lyricist and Chin's Calypso Sextet member Everard Williams stated in an interview that he wrote this influential song in 1950. There is no reason not to believe him, with his trademark attention to detail on full display. The lyrics first describe how repatriation is an idea that's catching on in Jamaica at the grassroots level. Then, setting a template for the back-to-Africa songs that followed, Ethiopia is idealized as a welcoming paradise of plenty. Repatriation is described as requiring hard work and righteous behavior. Williams concludes by explaining that, more than his land and possessions in Jamaica, he values being buried in Africa.

Also interesting is Lebby singing to "black man", a phrase emphasized by a burst of backing vocals. James Brown is famous for celebrating black identity with songs like 'Say It Loud – I'm Black And I'm Proud' in the 1960s, and such discourse would become commonplace in late 1960s soul music and the roots reggae of the 1970s. But it was revolutionary for any artist to sing this phrase in the 1950s. This adds credence to the notion that Lebby was reggae's first *conscious artist* – a Jamaican term for those who feature spiritually and socially enlightened lyrics.

Lebby's vocal is emotional, and the unusual, angular melody he finds for this song gives his performance weight befitting the subject. His crack band, credited as The Jamaican Calypsonians, featured the classic rural line-up of banjo, acoustic guitar, rumba box, hand drum and incidental hand-held percussion. A proto-reggae rhythm simmers effortlessly. Every instrument contributes equally, creating a polyrhythm that's a reminder of rural mento's African roots. Guitar plays a wonderful swaying double-struck rhythm that would persist in some form throughout all forms of reggae that followed. Banjo picks out lead lines. Rumba box provides pungent bass. Flurries of hand drum spray the song and an additional percussionist plays wood blocks, foreshadowing the common inclusion of a second percussionist in roots reggae to eventually come. One listen to this superb song obliterates any notion that reggae began with ska. Mento is the source of the river.

On 'Dr. Kinsey', 'Etheopia's flipside, the subject abruptly changes from nascent Rastafarian yearning to a humorous consideration of social researcher Dr. Alfred Kinsey's then notorious book, *Sexual Behavior in the Human Male* (1953). Though a bit naughty, the song is filled with clever musings rather than smut. For example, Lebby likens the study's statistical analysis to baseball stats, wondering if one man "is batting a thousand". The backing music features the delightful and very Jamaican sound of rangy mento backing vocals and the instrumentation sounds even more like reggae than on the A-side.

'Jingle Bells Calypso'

As reggae fans are aware, there is no shortage of reggae Christmas songs. But many fans believe that this practice started in the ska years with songs like 'Sound The Trumpet' and 'White Christmas' by Bob Marley & The Wailers. Well, Lord Lebby's 'Jingle Bells Calypso' (also produced by Ken Khouri) predates these songs by a decade. Nor is it the only golden-age Christmas mento song. There was also 'Christmas Time', a one-off collaboration by golden-age mento stars Count Lasher and Lord Tanamo.

With a faster beat and a wild intensity not heard in the previous two songs, the 'Jingle Bells Calypso' foreshadows ska rather than reggae. It's a wild ride, with the chorus borrowed from the original 'Jingle Bells', while the verses find Lebby singing about a Christmas party. He's barely able to contain his excitement. His voice rasping with eagerness, he punctuates the song with all kinds of exclamations, crazy scat singing and voice noises. One stanza focuses on liquor, specifically dictating that there be whiskey, brandy, champagne, and gin, sometimes specifying quantities, brands and mixers. The next stanza then directs "Have'n got your liquor, please contact your nearest butcher" for turkey, chicken, hamburgers, and sandwiches. Add Lebby and his band and you have the perfect party.

Neither this track nor its flipside, the R&B-infused 'One Little Lover', have been available since its release as a 78-rpm single in the mid-1950s. Surely, there is room on the next mento or reggae Christmas compilation CD for 'Jingle Bells Calypso'. You really haven't heard 'Jingle Bells' until you've heard it played on mento banjo!

'Love And Love Alone'
'Love And Love Alone' is another fine Lord Lebby track that is readily available, as it was included on the 1997 budget CD *Souvenir Of Jamaica* on the Valmark label. It's an adaptation of a 1930s calypso song called 'Edward The VIII' by Trinidad's The Caresser. It concerns an infamous chapter in British history when King Edward VIII abdicated his throne in order to marry the American divorcée Wallis Simpson. In spite of its calypso beginnings, it's performed in a purely rural mento style. It carries a sway so languid, it serves as another lesson from Lebby of how much mento could sound like an acoustic version of the reggae to follow in two decades' time. Relaxed banjo strumming, hand drums, rumba box and maracas are on equal footing and interlock to produce a polyrhythmic bounce. Banjo also provides fine solos. Lebby keeps the chorus of the original, but provides new lyrics for the verse. This includes Lebby wondering what Wallis "got in her bone, that cause a king to give up a throne." His vocals are powerful, turning on a gravelly roughness as needed to underscore the emotion of the lyrics in a natural ability he shares with Bob Marley. The backing singers are especially good here, and are well-mannered for rural mento backing vocals. The sound is so nice and the song so entertaining, it's like a three-minute vacation.

Other great Lord Lebby songs
There are other Lord Lebby songs that are well worth hearing, all with similar instrumentation to those we have already discussed and all produced by Ken Khouri. 'Sweet Jamaica' is a fine cover of a Lord Kitchener track. Though a calypsonian from Trinidad, Kitchener lived for a time in Jamaica and wrote several songs from a Jamaican perspective. In this one, he captures the upheaval and homesickness of Jamaicans who moved to the UK to find work. With the waves of Jamaican

emigration in the 1940s and 1950s, this was not the only mento song on this subject – Count Lasher's 'Trek To England' is another example, which is described in the chapter on that artist (page 59). The theme would carry over into reggae, with Nora Dean's 'Dry Up Your Tears' being an example described in the chapter on that artist (page 243). At one point, Lebby (but not Kitchener) describes London as "Babylon", marking the first recorded use of this term that would become ubiquitous in roots reggae decades later. This is another instance of Lebby being the first artist to have recorded Rastafarian sentiments, two decades before roots reggae made them commonplace. 'Sweet Jamaica' can be heard with its flipside, a mento rendition of 'Mama No Want No Rice No Peas' (a Caribbean folk song given fame by Count Bassie) on the Trojan Records mento compilation CD *Dip And Fall Back*. Like 'One Little Lover', this mento–R&B track displays how Lebby's voice was as well suited for R&B as it was for mento. Another fine Lord Lebby single is awaiting the attention of those who compile CDs. It pairs fine renditions of two Jamaican folk/mento standards, 'Bargie' and 'Hol' 'Im Joe'. 'Bargie' has its origin in the calypso song 'Bargee Pelauri', as recorded by The Lion in the 1930s. It explains how to prepare the difficult-to-cook dish of the title. 'Hol' 'Im Joe' is a simple folk song about a thirsty donkey that's difficult to control.

Count Owen

Owen Emanuel was born in Saint Mary Parish in 1933, but moved to Kingston as a baby. He recorded about thirteen golden-age tracks for Ken Khouri's Kalypso label and Stanley Motta's MRS label. He also recorded five LPs in the 1960s that moved away from the rural mento towards something less distinct, and he went on to dabble in reggae and pop, with a single of each for producer Coxsone Dodd in the early 1970s. He still performs occasionally. (He and the infirm Lord Tanamo are the only golden-age mento recording artists still with us at the time of this writing.)

His golden-age singles were Owen's best work. He possesses an affable voice and an easy-going approach to singing that makes him automatically likable. His band was usually billed as "And His Calypsonians". Often, his fine banjo player, Euton "Lord Gayle" Gayle was credited on the disc's label along with the singer and the song's author. Gayle and Eddie Brown, the banjo player for Boysie Grant's Reynolds Calypso Clippers, were the only instrumentalists to be afforded this level of recognition on a rural mento 78.

'Brown Skin Gal'; 'Limbo'; 'Take Her To Jamaica'
These renditions of three oft-recorded songs come from a Stanley Motta-produced LP called *Calypso Date* that was released at the end of mento's golden age. 'Brown Skin Gal' is a sad Jamaican folk song about a girl who must mind her baby while the father is off at sea. 'Limbo' (about the acrobatic dance of Trinidad) and 'Take Her To Jamaica' ("... where the rum comes from") represent the more

touristy side of the mento repertoire. Though frequently recorded in Jamaica, better renditions of these songs would be difficult to find. All three songs feature Owen's pleasing voice, Lord Gayle's excellent lead and rhythm banjo, rumba box, quiet hand drum, maracas and introspective shading and an occasional quiet lead from Owen's electric guitar. The electric instrument's presence in rural mento points to a release date in the later part of the 1950s. Singing and playing with care and a reflective feel, Owen and his band give these old songs surprising new depth. The first and third songs were re-released in 2013 on the double-CD collection *Mento Not Calypso*.

'Love In Sweet Jamaica'; 'Nana'
A fine Count Owen single paired two originals on the MRS label. Both songs share many of the same fine qualities as the *Calypso Date* songs. But the band, now billed as "And His Five Stars", trades electric guitar for acoustic guitar and bamboo flute. The love song, 'Love In Sweet Jamaica', is really quite enchanting. 'Nana' is as good, but salty rather than sweet. It's one of several golden-age mento songs poking fun at a randy oldster: "Go away from me, Nana. You're too old and rude when you find yourself in the mood." Regrettably, neither this, the story of reggae's original rude girl, nor any of Owen's fine MRS material has been released on CD.

'Bull Dog'
Neither has Owen's 'Bull Dog', a single on Ken Khouri's Kalypso label, and one of the most endearing songs of mento's golden age, ever appeared on CD. Lord Gayle's excellent banjo playing is a constant presence and sax is heard this time around rather than flute or electric guitar. Owen's vocal is full of feeling in this tale that's both humorous and tragic, as circumstances have Owen in a difficult situation. He and his wife are preparing to have a turkey for dinner. But a neighbor's bulldog appears with its own designs on the bird. Owen repeatedly pleads with his neighbor to retrieve the invader. When she doesn't respond, he warns, "I have a loaded gun, and I don't want to be hard." The dog makes its move, and a fatal bullet is shot. Only then does the neighbor hear and appear, but too late. In spite of Owen's repeated pleas, his neighbor does not help the situation, and things do not end well for the titular intruder. Some fifty years after its release, this delightful example of mento storytelling by an under-represented golden-age great continues to wait for re-release.

'Hool-A-Hoop Calypso'; 'Island In The Sun'
Happily, there are two Count Owen golden-age songs of note that can be heard on CD. The aforementioned *Souvenir Of Jamaica* includes both sides of the Ken Khouri-produced single, 'Hool-A-Hoop Calypso' (here called 'Hula-Hula-Calypso') and 'Island In The Sun'.

'Hool-A-Hoop Calypso' acknowledges the hula hoop craze of the 1950s. Though it's not the most important topic ever tackled in a mento song, Owen makes it more interesting by wondering about the sex lives of the talented hoopers. Pleasingly strident nasal mento backing vocals are heard on the chorus. The same instrumental line-up as in 'Bull Dog' is employed, but Lord Gayle cuts loose on banjo. Owen urges him on in his second solo with "Play that thing, man!" Gayle eagerly complies, and puts a period on the solo with a strum across the headstock. He adds other interesting flourishes later in the song in perhaps his single greatest performance.

The Harry Belafonte-popularized 'Island In The Sun' gets a lean rural mento arrangement sans wind and electric instruments. It features a relaxed rhythm and languid pace that foreshadow reggae. Gayle's banjo solos are picked in a rippling style more associated with a mandolin, adding to the song's already wistful sound.

Lord Tanamo

Born in 1934 in Kingston, Lord Tanamo (Joseph Gordon) is far better known to reggae fans than are his fellow golden-age mento stars. This is because, after a brief dalliance with R&B, Tanamo successfully moved from mento to ska and reggae. For a time, he was a featured vocalist for The Skatalites' live performances. He also recorded with them, including a hit in 1965 when he adapted a US song from the 1930s, 'I'm In The Mood For Love', as 'I'm In The Mood For Ska'. His career would extend into reggae, going on to the start of the 1980s. It included another hit, a 1970 cover of Ray Charles's 'Rainy Night In Georgia'. In fact, Lord Tanamo is the mento star who had the greatest success in the ska and reggae arenas, with many of his fans not even aware of his previous mento career. (Laurel Aitken would rate the silver medal. Bronze would be shared by Count Lasher, who recorded one ska and a handful of reggae singles, Count Sticky, who would reappear as a reggae DJ on about a dozen singles in the late 1960s and early 1970s, and Lord Power for three reggae singles. Others like Count Owen were runners up, recording just one side in ska or reggae, while some, like Chin's Calypso Sextet lead singer Alerth Bedasse, were non-participants in this arena.)

But Tanamo's roots were undoubtedly fixed in mento. It was seeing a rumba box player that first interested the four-year-old future Lord in music. By the time he was a teenager, he was spending his days performing mento for tourists on a Kingston street corner accompanied by the same box player, wearing a straw hat and torn trousers to create the image of a poor country boy. In reality, this city boy was making good money in his night job, when he dressed up to perform in Kingston's nightclubs.

Tanamo recorded more than a dozen rural golden-age singles and two 1960s mento LPs. He also served for a time as the lead singer of The Hiltonaires, the long-standing mento band-in-residence of Kingston's Hilton Hotel, appearing on a handful of tracks on one of the group's six LPs. Tanamo's voice was born of mento. It has a touch of country roughness and beams out in a way that is perfect for storytelling.

In 2009, Tanamo's golden-age mento made its better-late-than-never CD debut. It was then that Down Beat Records released *Sound Man Shots*, a compilation with six of his mento sides as originally released on the Caribou label and produced by Dada Tewari. It includes one of the four great Lord Tanamo mento songs described below.

'Wedding Bells'; 'Crinoline Incident'
Tanamo's first single consisted of two fine originals, produced by Stanley Motta in the mid-1950s. 'Wedding Bells' is pleasingly relaxed, but under the surface the banjo supplies a hypnotic throb that hints at the ska to come. A bamboo sax provides subtle melodic shading. Rumba box, claves and sparingly heard rural vocals fill out the backing. The banjo and sax exchange solos, the former wild and the latter subdued. The instrumentation is rich, and Tanamo matches it with a song about the folly of marriage. (This contrasts with the songs by Chin's Calypso Sextet, discussed later in the chapter on this group, which marveled over weddings.) Singing about a husband named Joe, Tanamo rhymes "take a wife" with "jeopardize his life". The criticisms flow both ways, as the wife complains, "When we go to bed, you only snore. I want a man that can do more."

Its flipside, 'Crinoline Incident', is quite different. It features a marvelously stripped-down but propulsive rural mento band, consisting of just harmonica, rumba box, claves and what sounds like it could be someone slapping a table top. There is also a banjo lurking in the mix, quietly playing rhythm until it makes itself apparent with a solo, only to submerge again. But it's the busy harmonica that provides most of the music, playing frenzied leads and solos. It makes the song irresistibly uplifting and countrified, Jamaican style. This is true to form, as whenever harmonica is heard in a golden-age mento song, it dominates the sound and guarantees a happy, high-energy romp. Tanamo tells of a woman who demands a fashionable new – and expensive – crinoline dress from her man. He takes extra work in the Blue Mountains to pay for the crinoline, but when he appears in the rum bar with the material in hand, a small riot breaks out. Tanamo's predicament is the listeners' gain.

'Little Fist'
'Little Fist', produced by Dada Tewari, is a wonderful record that was on the verge of being completely forgotten, rare even by the standards of Jamaican 78-rpm singles. Thankfully, in 2009, it was remembered, rescued and released on the aforementioned *Sound Man Shots* collection.

Taking off at a gallop, it's a delightfully raucous affair, filled with crazy chiming banjo and raucous bamboo sax solos. As if shot from a cannon, Tanamo engages in high-energy call-and-response vocals with his country backing singers. Though the instrumentation is the same as on the previous single, the pace and intensity of 'Little Fist' gives it a very different sound. If 'Wedding Bells' hinted at ska, this song's faster tempo and the insistence of the throbbing banjo playing clearly make 'Little Fist' proto-ska, with double-strummed banjo fulfilling the role that would later be made famous by ska's honking saxophone. The result is a beat that is as easy to resist as a steamroller. All this energy spills over to Tanamo's ribald lyrics, as he describes a date. She must be attractive, because "right now my little fist get bad. I love it to be hard …". She then gives him "nice food", probably a play on "night food", a coded term for oral sex that was notoriously coined by Chin's Calypso Sextet, as described in the chapter on this band. Though their love-making is described like a violent fight, the song appears to have a mostly happy ending, as challenges and compliments are exchanged.

'Sweet Jamaica'

'Sweet Jamaica' is a different song from both Lord Lebby's and Count Owens's songs of the same name, as well as from Tanamo's later song, 'My Sweet Jamaica'. Being as rare as 'Little Fist', and never having been compiled, the producer is uncertain, though Dada Tewari seems likely. Slightly less frantic and more orderly than 'Little Fist', 'Sweet Jamaica' is another crucial piece of throbbing proto-ska. It's a simple touristy song, but rousingly delivered as Tanamo celebrates the island and its music. He points out that his world travels, which have taken him from Japan to Hawaii, lead him to conclude that "Jamaica is the king of the calypso". Acoustic guitar and hand drum are added to the arrangement while clave and bamboo sax sit this one out. A satisfying mento performance with elements of ska on display a full decade before the term was coined; considering the strong following Tanamo's ska career enjoys, it's an understatement to say that this song is overdue for re-release.

Harold Richardson

Harold Richardson performed solo and as a member of The Ticklers. This trio, with Charles Sang on guitar and Daniel "Lord Danny Boy" Slue on rumba box, were a talented and agreeable unit. They had a long stint of working for the Jamaica Tourist Board, which employed them as traveling musical good-will ambassadors. Richardson's solo recordings could be backed by a jazzy urban combo with piano and lead clarinet, or a classic banjo-led rural line-up or a stripped-down acoustic guitar-based arrangement. But one thing remained constant: Harold Richardson has the distinction of owning the finest voice in mento. It's a classic high, nasal mento voice, sounding so country Richardson might well have ridden from the hills on a donkey directly into the recording studio. This is praise, and by no means implies a lack of skill or sophistication. On the contrary, Richardson displays masterful control over his unusually expressive voice. He sings in a scale of his own creation, bending it to suit his expressiveness. (Decades later, the same could be said for reggae singer Gregory Isaacs, though this is not to say that the results sounded alike.) He could instill even a simple line with great depth. This gave his singing enormous charm and made him sound wise. Both of these qualities were amplified by his frequent use of the talents of E. F. Williams, the great mento lyricist and Chin's Calypso Sextet member. Richardson recorded about eighteen sides of golden-age mento. His career reached into the 1960s, when he appeared on several LPs released by the Tower Isle Hotel, where The Ticklers were then the resident "calypso" band. (Jamaica's resort hotels have kept a mento group in residence to entertain the guests, beginning in the 1940s through to today.) Amongst a mix of styles on these LPs, there is one track of Richardson getting his feet wet with ska. But his 1960s career was cut short by his untimely death in his early thirties. Richardson influenced many singers in Jamaica, perhaps none as obviously as Stanley Beckford.

Two of the four great songs described below, 'Glamour Gal' and 'Healing In The Balm Yard', are available on CD. These tracks, along with 'Country Gal', the inferior sequel to 'Glamour Gal', were included on the 2004 compilation CD called *Mento Madness*, released on the V2 label. 'Don't Fence Her In' saw CD release in 2010 on the French CD called *Jamaica – Mento 1951–1958*. 'Four Days Of Love' has not been re-released since it was pressed as a 78-rpm single, while other lesser Harold Richardson/Ticklers tracks have appeared on various CD collections.

'Glamour Gal'; 'Don't Fence Her In'

Harold Richardson & The Ticklers' debut single was one of the first rural mento singles recorded, and one of the finest. 'Glamour Gal', backed with 'Don't Fence Her In', was produced by Stanley Motta in the early 1950s. Both feature great E. F. Williams lyrics and utilize a simple arrangement. There's just a strummed acoustic guitar, rumba box, hand percussion, and fine rural backing harmonies from The Ticklers on the choruses. There is no banjo or bamboo, nor are there any solos, leaving Richardson's voice as the sole lead instrument. All the better to enjoy his singing, and, in each song, there is more music in his first line than in many full songs by lesser singers.

'Glamour Gal' is an astutely observed slice of life from Williams – a specialty of his, and this is one of his best. He comments in detail on the city styles (and snooty attitude) that have made their way to country girls. This includes a list of hairdos of the day, along with other ways to beautify, including padded bras, skin-bleaching, etc. (This last issue would turn up as a topic in future reggae songs, including Nardo Rank's dancehall song, 'Them A Bleach', a song described later in this book; page 557.) Listen to how masterfully Richardson delivers the opening couplet and how effortlessly this excellence is sustained for the duration, as Williams's lyrics capture the minutiae of a subject, time and place.

'Glamour Gal' sets a very high standard that the flipside, 'Don't Fence Her In', meets. Richardson brings to vibrant life Williams's song of relationship guidance.

He advocates that a man not fence his girlfriend in, but instead provide her with money and freedom without jealousy. Ironically, he finds himself with a girl who takes advantage of these policies, running through his money. And his girl reacts strongly ("She jump up with a piece a stick") in a further irony, as she points out that the one thing he is asking for in return, a baby boy, would, in fact, fence her in.

'Healing In The Balm Yard'; 'Four Days Of Love'

Like many other Harold Richardson songs, this Stanley Motta-produced single includes prominent clarinet played by Jamaican jazz star Bertie King. Clarinet was part of both rural and jazzy urban mento until the R&B filter knocked the instrument out of subsequent genres of Jamaican music. On these recordings, King, in addition to Richardson and Williams, distinguishes himself, as clarinet weaves an old-fashioned quaintness through the song. The line-up features piano and stand-up bass rather than the acoustic guitar and rumba box heard on the previously described single. Hand drum and maracas carry over to provide some rural feel.

'Healing In The Balm Yard' is a well-remembered song. Though it may not have been as reggae-like as some golden-age mento tracks, it was admired enough for there to have been reggae renditions that spanned styles and decades. Prince Buster did it as ska, Stanley Beckford as countrified reggae, Clint Eastwood & General Saint in DJ style and Welton Irie in early ragga dancehall style. Richardson's singing is ace as he tells Williams's richly observed story about the tawdry goings on in the *balm yard* – a piece of land with supposed magical properties. Cures, good fortune and black magic spells can all be obtained there from the *balmer*, a shady character who is in the game for money and sex. But Williams faults the customers as much as the con man, with situations such as "Jackie want to give Laura swell feet, because she said the gal dressed too sweet."

The flipside, 'Four Days Of Love', finds Richardson singing adorably about love. Williams's lyrics (mento's most inexhaustible gold mine) portray it as such a potent force that it can change a devil of a woman into "a turtle dove". This and many terms of endearment are uttered to Laura. But after the titular span of time, all hell breaks loose. The wrong term of endearment is tried, and Laura explains, "me no like, me have fe lick him with a chair". Lesson learned? In spite of the best of intentions, never call your girl "Chewing Gum".

Lord Messam

Born in 1924 in Kingston, Charles Augustus "Lord" Messam came to singing by first establishing himself as a dancer and dance troupe leader in the Montego Bay tourist scene. He preferred live performance to recording, and so his body of work is limited to eight rural mento songs recorded in the 1950s. That's a shame, as four of these were very good and two were superb. This was due in no small part to his backing band, which was simply billed as "And His Calypsonians" – a generic designation that was applied to more than one mento group. They featured a backing line-up that used the same instruments as other rural mento bands, but produced a unique sound. Not only was a throbbing proto-reggae beat fully evident, the playing exhibited a precise and dreamy music-box quality. The banjo, rumba box, acoustic guitar and percussion interlocked into an industriously ticking whole – a piece of clockwork with its cogs and gears carved from wood. Even the backing vocals, still mento sounding, are more orderly than the norm for other rural mento bands.

Lord Messam, though not totally ignored, has not been well served by mento compilation CDs. A lesser performance, a tired-sounding rendition of 'Monkey' (a song later recorded by Lord Flea, and described later in this chapter) can be heard on the 2006 CD compilation, *Take Me To Jamaica*. A better track– a spirited rendition of the famous Jamaican folk song 'Linstead Market' that contains perhaps Messam's best vocal can be heard on two CD collections, *Mento Madness* and *Jamaica Mento*. But his best material waits to be plucked for the next mento compilation CD.

'Jamaican Mentos' (aka 'Mango Walk' / 'Gi Me Back Me Shilling' / 'Chichi Bud Oh' / 'Hog In A My Mint Tea'); 'Holiday No'

Like other singers of mento's golden age, Messam liked to record renditions of Jamaican folk songs, often in medleys. The medley approach suited these songs, as many consisted of just a few lyrics. Being an oral tradition, in many cases, these golden-age mento singles represent the first recording – if not the first documentation of any kind – of these traditional songs. One side of Messam's great debut single is a fine example of this. Each song is recorded for the first time here (with the possible exception of the last, as folk singer Louise Bennett recorded it at around the same time). The music-box proto-reggae sound is on full display, and the polyrhythmic pulse, source material and unabashedly Jamaican backing vocals combine to make the track sound magical and exotic. It starts strong with a memorable rendition of the beguiling 'Mango Walk' that maps out a place between chanted invocation and nursery rhyme. It can only be faulted for being too short. It involves a dispute over a purported walk to gather the variety of mango called "number eleven". 'Gi Me Back Me Shilling' may in fact be just more of 'Mango Walk', its few lyrics involving an argument about a coin with the memorable refrain, "Gal you must be take me for a fool!" 'Chichi Bud' is a well-known song that chants the names of various birds ("buds") whose songs ("chi chi") are heard in Jamaica. 'Hog In A My Mint Tea' is very engaging. The last two words of the title are a misspelling of "minty" – a type of sweet potato, into a patch of which a hog has intruded. Reggae covers of this song have made it clear that this can be an allegory for theft, or for intrusion by a romantic rival. The song quickly jumps in subject to food and then to romance, in a montage of images.

Add two short but fine banjo solos played with music-box precision, and 'Jamaican Mentos' is pure mento enchantment.

The flipside is an original song, the humorous 'Holiday Number' (or 'Holiday No.', as the label has it). Musically, it has all the virtues of the A-side, but with fewer lyrics has room for longer banjo solos. Messam struggles with the demands of his current lover, a big girl with many requirements. "Me gal she want a flat. That make me love her not." Additional wants include an expensive hat, a parasol, panties, bra and a corset, new shoes, money for a hair styling, an expensive bag, a gold chain and a matching ring. He comes to realize that she'd be better off with someone who deals on the black market than with him, and concludes, "I cannot stand and fund, so me 'ave to cut and run". Inspired by the precise rhythmic playing of his band, Messam rhythmically speak-sings the song's short lines. With this delivery, an everyman story and his everyman voice, he presages the rise of reggae's DJs two decades later.

'Poun' Paper'; 'Don't Tek It For A Joke' / 'Rukumbine'

Lord Messam's second single was a follow-up with many similarities to his first, and is nearly as good. 'Poun' Paper' is another humorous original. As in 'Holiday Number', he explores the financial issues, expectations and tribulations of dating. Here, every aspect of his date is a disappointment. Not only does she steal the titular banknote, "the gal start to snore as I reach touch me bed". The flip is a medley pairing another original with a folk song. 'Don't Tek It For A Joke' is a serious exploration of the importance of getting along with friends and neighbors, recorded long before this became a prevalent theme in the songwriting of Bob Marley and roots reggae in general. He uses two Jamaican expressions to better make his point. "What is joke to you is dead to me" is a much more dramatic saying than the overseas equivalent, "I don't think that's very funny". "If you don't mash hands, you don't find him cut" means, if you weren't rubbing your hands together, you wouldn't even be aware of your minor injury, or, don't make a problem by exasperating yourself. 'Rukumbine' is the famous story of Mother Kuba and the accusatory questioning about her expensive new clothes. Ethnomusicologist Daniel Neely[1] traced elements of this song all the way back to seventeenth-century Scotland.

Arthur Knibbs

Arthur Knibbs was born in 1929 in Saint Ann Parish. The six sides produced by Stanley Motta listed below constitute the sum of his recorded golden-age output. He continued to record mento into the 1960s, releasing at least one single and,

---

1.   Daniel Tannehill Neely, "Mento, Jamaica's Original Music: Development, Tourism and the Nationalist Frame". Ph.D. dissertation (New York University, 2007), p. 78. (Available through ProQuest, catalog number AAT 3310562.)

after adopting the name of King Arthur, releasing at least one LP. However, as was invariably the case for golden-age mento stars, it's his 1950s singles that are this artist's best work. All six of these tracks are of high quality and consistent in their distinctive sound. The glass is mostly empty but fractionally full, as one of the songs was compiled on the 2010 French CD *Jamaica – Mento 1951–1958* on the Fremeaux label, thus rescuing Arthur Knibbs from being the greatest totally forgotten golden-age mento star.

Knibbs has a distinctive voice and style. Not only does he sing in a lower register than most other mento singers of his time, but he does so from his throat, giving his voice a thicker sound compared to the nasal or round tones of his contemporaries. He has an appealing, easy-going approach to his vocals and an immediately identifiable Jamaican accent, which all contribute to his having the most breezy, relaxing voice in golden-age mento. His band was just as distinctive. Cecil Knott & The Joy Bell Orchestra co-mingled rural mento with the jazzy urban style in equal measure. Better known as Cecil Lloyd, the Juilliard-trained Cecil Lloyd Knott was one of the island's top jazz pianists. He went on to record LPs of jazz and music in the jazzy mento style. Here, his accomplished, accessible and surprisingly lush playing shares the spotlight with an excellent banjo player, as acoustic guitar, rumba box, maracas and occasional backing vocals complete the Joy Bell Orchestra. There is no sign of a clash between the two styles. In fact, they fuse together beautifully, making for some wonderfully fluid mento. Jazz could do no harm to Jamaican music. Just as it enriched urban mento, ska, reggae and Nyabinghi, these records show how wonderfully it could do the same for rural mento.

'Belly Lick' / 'Bargie'; 'Teacher Lick The Gal' / 'Ada'; 'Sammy Dead' / 'Get Up Adina' / 'Mr. Ramgoat, Oh'; 'Banana'; 'Soldier Man'; 'When You Come America'; 'Cowhead'
Spread across both sides of three singles, all but two of these are familiar Jamaican folk songs. Each of these renditions is fine. In fact, you just won't hear better versions of such great old songs as 'Belly Lick', 'Teacher Lick The Gal', 'Banana' and 'Soldier Man'. 'Belly Lick' is a ribald song about carrying on with a sexy woman, though Knibbs's rendition is less explicit than others. 'Teacher Lick The Gal' is a jaunty, galloping song that opens memorably with a description of a woman's unlucky garment and the consequence of wearing it to school. The shift is ratchewed and ripped, but repaired by her mother. Then it gets burned in the same spot, resulting in the titular punishment, with "lick" meaning "hit". 'Ada' is about a woman who resists all courting. Here, it's mixed together with another folk song, 'Time So Hard', in which Auntie Lulu hears complaints about working like a dog. 'Sammy Dead', an even grimmer folk song, features an instrumental opening that comes from the melody of 'Mattie Rag', yet another folk song. It tells how Sammy, just trying to subsist, "plant piece of corn down a gully". But jealousy, grudges and thievery result in his murder. An older song than Lord Messam's 'Don't Tek It For A Joke", it's another reminder that neighborly discord (here

elevated to murder) was a concern in Jamaican music well before Bob Marley called for the end of *fussing and fighting* in so many of his songs. 'Get Up Adina' is about a girl who won't do her chores or apply herself to her schoolwork, being either extremely lazy or perhaps clinically depressed. "Sleep in her bed and die a-want [if you want]", Knibbs exasperatedly concludes. 'Mr. Ram Goat' is a celebration of goat-shearing. (Perennial mento act, The Jolly Boys, recorded a great rendition of this song that is described later in this book; see page 309.) The high-spirited 'Banana' is a celebration of a favorite fruit across the island, complete with a double entendre about "young girls want ... all night long". 'Soldier Man' is a cover of Trinidadian calypso star Lord Invader's wartime song, 'The Soldiers Came And Broke Up My Life'. (Invader recorded it twice, first in 1945, backed by Lionel Belasco and his calypso band. The remake around 1956 was recorded in New York City and featured a surprisingly mento-sounding band, with prominent banjo, acoustic guitar, hand drum and fiddle solos.) Knibbs sings about having to share his wife's love with an American soldier. She's pleased with the arrangement, but poor Knibbs is not, especially when he is mocked by his friends. He considers beating her, but decides against it, instead tolerating the situation as best he can. 'When You Come America' is a touristy song. 'Cowhead' is a rendition of 'Ten Penny Nail', a song made famous by smooth urban mento vocalist Hubert Porter. Like 'Bargie', it's a song about cooking a difficult dish, but with a twist. The cow's head seems to be not quite dead, rearing up and making sounds, causing the cook to run off screaming. Only 'Banana' is currently available, released on the aforementioned CD *Jamaica – Mento 1951–1958*. Any and all of the other tracks should be targeted with laser focus for the next mento compilation CD.

Boysie Grant

Like Arthur Knibbs, Boysie Grant's entire golden-age output consisted of six fine singles produced by Stanley Motta in a consistent style provided by a distinctive backing band. His career also reached into the 1960s, but rather than continuing to record mento, Grant may be remembered by UK ska fans for four sides on two 45-rpm singles credited to Ezz Reco & The Launchers With Boysie Grant. They charted in the UK with a cover of Jimmy Cliff's 'King Of Kings' in 1964, just prior to Millie Small's ska-pop hit 'My Boy Lollipop'.

Grant is a good singer, with a sly and playful style. He often utilizes vibrato that is reminiscent of singers from decades past, giving his vocals an old-fashioned touch. His backing band is the accomplished, rollickingly rural Reynolds Calypso Clippers. The fluent banjo is so good that the singles' labels bear the extra credit, "Tenor banjo – Eddie Brown". The aggressive hand drummer probably deserved a credit of his own, as he is the most accomplished and out-front hand drummer heard on any rural mento recordings. Acoustic guitar, rumba box and maracas round out the Clippers' line-up. Their rhythms were not as prescient of ska and reggae as some of their peers, but their mento was no less for it.

Three of the six songs below can be heard on the CD compilation called *Mento Madness*. Another compilation, *Take Me To Jamaica*, as released on the Pressure Sounds label, includes 'The Naughty Little Flea'. This leaves 'Noisy Spring', perhaps his best song, and 'Linstead Market' as unreleased since the 1950s.

'Noisy Spring'; 'Linstead Market'; 'Solus Market'; 'The Naughty Little Flea'; 'Come We Go Down To Unity'/'Old Lady Oh'/'Linstead Market'; 'Sweet Charlie'/'Matty Rag'/'Nobody's Business'

The humorous 'Noisy Spring' is Grant's only original. It's about a "lying" bedspring that makes his mattress unaccountably loud, causing Grant embarrassment. He worries to his wife, " the neighbors, dem will hear, and think a murder goin' on in here". As is the case for each of these songs, 'Noisy Spring' features one or more great Eddie Brown banjo solos. More unusually, it also features a hand drum solo that is equally accomplished.

The other tracks are drawn from Jamaica's folk/mento repertoire and are all very good. 'Linstead Market' is a rendition of the well-known folk song whose beginnings can be traced back to quadrille. Quadrille was a form of dance music that originated in eighteenth-century France and made its way to colonial Jamaica, where it is still performed today. It was an important antecedent in the formation of mento, and many mento bands would perform and record a bit of quadrille. In the song, a vendor brings his ackee (a fruit that must be cooked before eating that is very popular in Jamaica) to the titular market, but does not earn so much as a quattie (an old-time coin worth a penny and a half). This leaves the singer to lament: "Lord what a night, not a bite, what a Saturday night!" 'Solas Market' is a less famous though less regretful market song. Its simple lyrics find Grant admiring and buying bananas, as another hand drum solo is heard. Grant's rendition of Lord Flea's signature song, 'The Naughty Little Flea' (a song described later in this chapter) is the least inspired performance here.

'Come We Go Down To Unity' starts a medley of three songs. Consisting of only two couplets, it may or may not be describing a municipal improvement project for the Clarendon town of Unity that is haunted: "Fe go see duppy [ghost] run white people". 'Old Lady Oh', the folk song also known as 'Fire Sticks'', is such a pleasure, packed with so much melody in its few lyrics. It describes a mean old woman whose bitterness is demonstrated when she throws firewood at a dog. She is cautioned, "Old lady, oh, your salt a go bun [burn] you!". Grant reprises 'Linstead Market' to complete the medley.

Another medley begins with Grant's rendition of 'Sweetie Charlie', a song that has gotten around. Here it's about Charlie "a go bust Matty head with a kukku makka [a stick used to strike people]". We never learn what business prompted this none-too-sweet reaction. Nor does Clyde Hoyte's golden-age rendition, called 'Charlie's Song', reveal any more. Harold Richardson & The Ticklers recorded it as 'Hard Time' around the same time, but the melody was given entirely new lyrics.

When Sam Manning recorded 'Sweetie Charlie' in the 1930s, the lyrics were again different except for the titular refrain, the song now describing how the 'Sweetie Charlie' earned his name by being irresistible to women. Then in the 1950s, Harry Belafonte recorded the song as 'Matilda', deciding to use entirely new lyrics; it yielded a hit, while the 'Sweetie Charlie' melody continued to amass songs. Such situations were neither uncommon nor surprising, considering the oral tradition of these folk songs.

'Matty Rag' is another example of a folk song whose lyrics never quite co-alesced into a standard version across its numerous recorded renditions. These ranged from the 1930s with Sam Manning's 'Susan Monkey Walk' to Peter Tosh's 'Whatcha Gonna Do' in the 1970s, each with completely different lyrics. Perhaps the best rendition was the late 1950s mento take by The Silver Seas – 'Island Champions', called 'Charlie's Cow' (a song described later in this book; page 305). 'Nobody's Business' defends personal liberty in love and marriage choices (ironic considering the intolerance shown by some ragga singers decades later). Peter Tosh recorded a rendition with somewhat updated lyrics at the start of the 1970s.

Lord Flea

Lord Flea was born Norman Thomas in Kingston, in 1932. Sadly forgotten today, before Bob Marley, Desmond Dekker, Jimmy Cliff or Millie, Lord Flea was on the verge of being Jamaica's first international star when Hodgkin's disease took him at the age of twenty-seven. Before he died, he had performance residencies in Miami, Las Vegas and New York. He appeared on American television, in a pair of Hollywood (albeit B) movies and in American magazines *Life*, *Look* (with his picture on the cover), *Jet*, *Ebony* and others. He had an LP and a follow-up single on Columbia Records that were released around the world.

Flea started recording in the 1950s with about twenty sides of urban mento, but at some point in that decade, he made the jump to the rural style. In 1957, he released an LP, *Swingin' Calypsos*, for Capital Records. By this point, his singing had developed star-power charisma. His voice was strong, melodic and articulate. He would enliven many of his songs with his own brand of scat singing. He could take hold of old folk or calypso songs (Flea wrote few songs, as was true for a number of his contemporaries) and made them his own. His band had a unique rural mento sound, and they were tight. It most prominently featured the rippling banjo played so well by the man billed only as Porkchops, though born Charles Lorenzo Harrison. Also on board were two percussionists, a home-made washtub bass, backing vocals and Flea's acoustic guitar. The album is consistently strong and well worth hearing. This was made easy when, in 2009, Capital gave it a belated CD release, called *The Early Years At Capitol Records*, complete with both sides of the follow-up single as bonus tracks, and packaged as a cheapie twofer with a Harry Belafonte album.

'Shake Shake Senora'; 'Naughty Little Flea'; 'Monkey'; 'Mister, Give Me De Rent'; 'Out De Fire'; 'Magic Composer'; 'Love'

Though there are no bad songs on *Swingin' Calypsos*, a number stand out. Percussion drives 'Shake Shake Senora' (aka 'Jump In The Line'), an irresistible call to dance that features (like all the songs on this LP) Flea's strong vocals and crackling banjo leads from Porkchops. Based on an earlier calypso song, Flea's song seems to have been the inspiration for Harry Belafonte's hit rendition. I like Harry Belafonte's recording, but it sounds tepid compared to Flea's mento scorcher. Belafonte would record two more songs heard on this LP, both humorous tracks. Flea's signature song (and perhaps his sole original composition) 'Naughty Little Flea' is a slower song, allowing the story to breathe. It's a mildly naughty tale of a flea that knows no boundaries. Funnier is 'Monkey', a song recorded earlier in the decade by Blind Blake & the Royal Victoria Hotel Calypso Orchestra of the Bahamas, In it, Flea is flummoxed when a monkey follows him and imitates everything that he does, as banjo ripples impressively. Though it's based on a song by Trinidadian calypso great Lord Kitchener, 'Mister Give Me De Rent' serves as an example of a mento rent song. Not only was this a popular theme in mento (Chin's Calypso Sextet's 'Rent Worries' is an example in this book), it would carry over into reggae too ('Rent Man' by Black Uhuru and Max Romeo and 'Straight To The Government' by Papa Tullo are three examples described later). Here, Flea complains that his landlady is intrusive and demanding. And even though the apartment has no furniture or hot water, "she have the audacity to say I am living in luxury". 'Out De Fire', originally recorded by Trinidadian calypso star Lord Invader, is clearly a calypso song rather than a mento one, but how often do you hear burning calypso (complete with fire siren) with red-hot banjo? 'Magic Composer' is a fine rendition of the often recorded mento song 'Bargie'. Flea sings about a recipe for cooking bargie, complete with extra lyrics, scat singing and some playful call-and-response vocals. 'Love' is a rendition of Lord Lebby's 'Love And Love Alone', a song described earlier in this chapter. But Flea's rendition is dramatic, allowing him to show off show-business pipes, while Porkchops proves that the banjo can be played for pathos.

Other golden-age artists

Lord Composer: *'Hill and Gully Ride'/'Mandeville Road'; 'Gal A Gully'/'Matilda'*
Mento singer Lord Composer was born Omri Mundle (a name that looks like a hastily constructed anagram) in 1924. He should not be confused with Lord Creator, a Trinidad-born singer who had a successful calypso and ska career in Jamaica. Composer recorded a handful of rural golden-age singles, an LP in the same period and a few more mento singles in the 1960s. His first single, produced by Stanley Motta, overshadows everything else he subsequently recorded. It's a classic mento record that sounds unlike any other. Both sides feature a two-song medley of Jamaican folk songs. Both sides share a nearly identical arrangement in an early example of versioning. Both sides are scorchers.

Singing in a high register, Lord Composer's keening vocal explodes with energy and a touch of the exotic. Motta and Composer must have caught lightning in a bottle that particular day, as the laid-back vocals subsequently heard from Composer might as well have come from a different singer. The backing band, The Silver Seas Hotel Orchestra, match Composer's energy level with acoustic guitar, prominent claves, rumba box, maracas and backing vocals. Held in reserve until a mid-song solo, and then returning at the song's end is fife. Fife, bamboo flute and penny whistle had long been part of mento and other Jamaican folk music forms. It's a rare pleasure to hear fife in the spotlight, especially coming from such an accomplished player. Evoking Jamaica's past, it makes the sound even more exciting and exotic. All four songs sound great in this treatment.

'Hill And Gully Ride' is a work song with few lyrics beyond the title. Regardless of the numerous other renditions recorded in mento and reggae, the song has never sounded as vibrant as it does here. Equally spirited is 'Mandeville Road', another work song, again with few lyrics, but with a better developed narrative. Hard labor is casually described with, "We go to Mandeville Road, galang [go on] boy, fe bruk rockstone". Then, the tedium of breaking rocks is memorably portrayed with the counting up from *one by one*. The flipside has two less-known folk songs. 'Gal A Gully' is a *ring song* – a folk song for children to sing and dance to standing in a ring. It includes the encouraging lyrics, "Show me your motion, your pretty pretty motion". [We Love] 'Matilda' has been traced as being part of the Anancy songs and stories brought over from West Africa. Anancy was the spider-god of mischief that was such an important part of the folklore of the Ashanti people. It does not have many more lyrics than its title, making Matilda's exact link to Anancy or why she is so loved unclear. Composer enlivens his rendition with some wild scat singing. A fine Nyabinghi rendition of this song by Count Ossie is described later in this book (page 326).

Either side of this single can be heard on a different CD. *Mento Madness* has the 'Hill And Gully Ride' side, while *Take Me To Jamaica* has the other. Another fine example of fife-led mento could be heard a decade later on the B-side of a popular reggae single. The B-side of Nora Dean's 'Barbwire' (a song described in the chapter on this artist; page 238) on the Baron's label is 'Calypso Mama' by Brons. It's a mento cover of the Cuban song 'Peanut Vendor', a song that was popular in Jamaica and beyond.

Sir Horace and His Merry Knights: *'Morgan's Mento'; 'Mambo Jamaica'*
Before resurfacing in the early 1970s to record a pair of Festival singles for producer Coxsone Dodd, Sir Horace (Horace Abrahams) and his well-named band, His Merry Knights, recorded just two Ken Khouri-produced golden-age singles. That's a shame, as they are a joy and feature a sound of their own.

The two tracks described here come from Horace's much-appreciated debut disc. It served to inspire a stage name for Sir Horace Gentleman, the bassist for the

1970s UK ska revival band, The Specials. Even producer Khouri seems to have fancied this single, adding the unique legend, "A Real Treasure", to its label on both sides. Along with rumba box, maracas and claves, three instruments are heavily featured on both songs for a particular mento sound: bamboo sax, a warm, tube-toned electric guitar (pointing to a latter part of the 1950s release) and harmonica. Although all three instruments contribute greatly, the harmonica, with its ecstatic level of energy, dominates the sound (as tends to be the case with mento harmonica). The result is hot mento party music, like a feverish Jamaican polka. Horace's singing gets carried along by the giddy happiness of this backing, and his lyrics are equally enthusiastic.

'Morgan's Mento' celebrates Captain Morgan's rum, which, at one time, was a Jamaican medicinal product that combined therapeutic botanicals in a rum base. Horace is certainly impressed by the product, describing its "pleasing effect" and how drinking it is "a wonderful thing."

'Mambo Jamaica' keeps the party going. And even if it's a bit less crazed (perhaps due to the lack of rum), it's just as enjoyable. The slower pace allows Horace's enthusiastic singing a little more room, and his affable nasal mento voice can be better appreciated. He marks the addition of the mambo to the rumba and the tango as popular dances in Jamaica at the time. A new dance music never escaped the notice of at least one mento band, so, in addition to 'Mambo Jamaica', there were golden-age mento songs called 'Calypso Tango', 'Jamaica Tango', 'Jamaican Rumba', 'Calypso Meringue', 'Hula Hula Calypso', 'Rock And Roll Calypso', 'Calypso Cha Cha', 'Mambo La La', and 'Mambo Mento'. Six decades after this great single was pressed on ten inches of shellac at the end of the 1950s, it appeared again on the aforementioned CD collection, *Mento Not Calypso*.

Robin Plunkett & The Shaw Park Calypso Band: *'Shaw Park Blues'*
Though Robin Plunkett appears to have recorded just one golden-age single, it warrants discussion. He would later record several albums in the 1960s as a member of The Happy Smilers.

It was common for the resident mento band of Jamaica's resorts to bear the hotel's name, such as The Hiltonaires, The Silver Seas Orchestra, The Tower Islanders and, here, The Shaw Park Calypso Band. In fact, by the 1960s, when mento LPs supplanted the 78-rpm single, it was also common for these albums' jackets and liner notes to promote the hotel more than the musicians, sometimes to a maddening degree. But 'Shaw Park Blues' by Robin Plunkett and the Shaw Park Calypso Band is a unique specimen where the situation goes to an unintentionally comical extreme. It was produced by Stanley Motta, and features the mento tourist song 'Take Her To Jamaica' as the flipside, making this the most touristy of all mento singles.

In another foreshadowing of the versioning to come, 'Shaw Park Blues' by Robin Plunkett & The Shaw Park Calypso Band shares its melody with Lord Lebby's classic mento hit, 'Etheopia'. It even shamelessly co-opts its opening line and the general theme of finding paradise. But here, paradise is found in a resort hotel rather than Zion, making Plunkett's song all the more comically outrageous, as he sings a 3:16-minute commercial for the Shaw Park resort. . He mentions such attributes as the relaxing atmosphere, high elevation, surrounding scenery, gardens, dining-room, and the high-quality food and bar drinks. He points out that the Royal Family has lodged there, and you can too without having to abdicate, in another golden-age mento reference to the marriage of King Edward VIII and Wallis Simpson. With all this going for it, it's no wonder that a visitor to Shaw Park will "want to live here, or die here".

But we wouldn't be talking about these unlikely lyrics if 'Shaw Park Blues' was not a great record. It is. Plunkett's vocals are emphatic and he describes the resort's many virtues while successfully navigating the unusual melody of 'Etheopia'. He is backed by a rural line-up of acoustic guitar, rumba box, claves, bongo and incredible banjo. With all due apologies to the Shaw Park Hotel, the banjo player is the real star of this show. Featuring an exotic trebly music-box sound, the instrument is a "ukulele banjo" – a much smaller instrument that some Jamaican banjo players were playing at that time. It provides three long solos, at the song's opening, closing and midpoint, and it elevates the song from a commercial to folk art. This unique nugget of golden-age mento has never been collected anywhere since it was pressed on shellac more than fifty years ago. Taking the optimistic view, there are great mento compilations still to come – one day.

3   Count Lasher

Born in 1926 in Saint Thomas Parish with the less-dramatic name of Terrence Parkins, Count Lasher was golden-age mento's greatest star. Self-taught on piano and guitar, he came to Kingston after finishing elementary school, and was soon performing for cruise ship tourists in Kingston harbour. He seemed to never stop performing, popping up everywhere (movie theaters, hotels, beach parties, nightclubs, balls, rallies, calypso competitions, fund-raisers, athletic meets, etc.) to provide musical entertainment, tirelessly, for decades. His recorded output consisted of a total of nearly fifty diverse tracks. In the 1950s, he recorded both rural and urban mento with a variety of different bands. Working with a number of producers, these 78s appeared on such famous mento labels as MRS, Kalypso, Chin's, Caribou, and in a show of star power, Jamaica's first vanity label, Lasher Disc. In the 1960s, he released a string of calypso-influenced tracks and a wonderful but forgotten ska single. In the 1970s, he recorded a handful of reggae singles produced by Coxsone Dodd.

Lasher's golden-age recordings included renditions of Jamaican folk songs as well as originals. His compositions included well-observed slices of life and his specialty was wicked double entendres that are extended for the duration of the song. Both distinguished him as one of mento's best lyricists. He was also one of mento's best singers, marrying a fine voice to a sly, playful delivery – a killer combination that made him difficult to resist. None of his contemporaries and very few since could match that combination of talent. The great Count Lasher passed away in 1977. Though a fair number of his best songs can be heard today on CD, Count Lasher, the greatest single star of the first era of recorded Jamaican music, is not nearly as well remembered or appreciated today as he should be.

'Sam Fi Man'
'Sam Fi Man' is credited to Count Lasher And His Calypso Quintet, produced by Stanley Motta. Its opening seconds may take a reggae fan's breath away. With all the precise and dreamy music-box quality of Lord Messam's Calypsonians, reggae issues forth more than a decade before Toots coined the term. But it sounds as if it's coming from a forgotten age, played by preternatural beings. This tantalizing channeling of the future fades as the first of several banjo solos launches the body of the song. But it makes several returns as the song continues.
In the previous chapter, Harold Richardson introduced us to a con man in 'Healing In The Balm Yard'. Here, Lasher introduces us to another – the *sam fi man.* This scammer promises, for a fee, to make just about any wish come true. He

can get you a job, make you win a sweepstake, bind a lover, cure an ailment, kill an adversary, and more. Lasher sings conversationally, warning his audience of the sam fi man's con, and that once you deal with him, you're in deep. As Lasher sings engagingly, banjo and bamboo saxophone alternate solos as acoustic proto-reggae pulsates. This is a fine rural mento track, and that's no con. After half a century of unavailability, it was compiled on the aforementioned mento compilation CD, *Take Me To Jamaica*.

'Mango Time'

'Mango Time' is credited to Count Lasher's Seven. Like 'Sam Fi Man', it's a great song that after five decades of unavailability, recently saw the light of day on CD. This was when it was included on the *Jamaica – Mento 1951–1958* compilation. And also like 'Sam Fi Man', it's a Stanley Motta production that features a brief but tantalizing introduction.

The overall sound and instrumentation of 'Mango Time' is different from that of 'Sam Fi Man'. The tempo is faster and the rhythm is not predictive of reggae. Banjo sits this one out, as bamboo sax and an aggressively played hand drum share the instrumental spotlight. The latter instrument announces the start of the song. Two acoustic guitars, rumba box and claves join in for a brief but alluring introduction that is more reminiscent of African music than reggae – an unusual sound for a mento record. The lyrics rejoice in the arrival of mango season, and its importance for the people, as a bounty of mangos makes shopping and cooking unnecessary.

In the type of detail that mento's songwriters often work in, the chorus describes the arrival of the mango vendors. Their call is remembered, as are the many different varieties of mangos that were available: Beefy, Black Mango, Bombay, Calcutta, East Indian, Harris, Hilltop, Joellen, Kidney, Number 11, Robin, and Turpentine. The mangos are so plentiful, the customers become choosy, avoiding bruised fruit. But it's mango time and whether buyer or seller, "everyone is wearing a smile".

The song concludes with Lasher scatting nicely. Such a detailed slice-of-life, sung appealingly over a fine rural backing all contribute to making this song as sweet and juicy as a ripe, well, you know ...

'Slide Mongoose'

'Slide Mongoose' by Count Lasher And His Calypso Quintet was released on the Caribou label by producer Dada Tewari. It's Lasher's rendition of the Jamaican folk song that was far more frequently (though not always) called 'Sly Mongoose'. As is often the case with Jamaican folk songs, the lyrics vary from one rendition to another, as the mischievous antics of the titular character are described. Many renditions contain a reference to Alexander Bedward, a controversial Jamaican preacher who died in 1930, but Lasher's does not. The chorus, "Sly mongoose, now your name gone abroad", proved to be prescient, as the song became one of the best-known Jamaican folk songs around the world.

For example, jazz-calypso pioneer Sam Manning recorded a fiddle-led rendition in the 1920s. Benny Goodman recorded it as an instrumental in the 1930s. Calypsonian Lord Invader recorded it, complete with wartime lyrics, in the 1940s. Louis Armstrong and Charlie Parker each released a rendition in the 1950s. That same decade saw smooth jazzy urban mento renditions by both Lord Fly and Bertie King. The Skatalites recorded an instrumental rendition called 'Coconut Ska' in the 1960s. The same decade, Jamaican bandleader Carlos Malcomb recorded a Latin-jazz instrumental rendition. There were a number of reggae renditions in the 1970s, including I-Roy's DJ performance. Harry Belafonte recorded it three times that decade. In 2006, Monty Alexander performed a mento-jazz rendition that was televised internationally on the BET network. Perhaps 'Day-O' and 'Linstead Market' are the only Jamaican folk songs that are better known. We have already seen fine renditions of the latter in this book. But there really has never been a great reggae version of 'Day-O', leaving Bellefonte's rendition as the best.

Count Lasher's is not the only rural mento rendition, but it is the best. Several of the mongoose's brushes with the police are described. In between, "mongoose jump up on telegram wire, mongoose trousers would catch on fire", he asks for a job at the Palace Theater, gets chased by a shark during a swim and finds time to have sex with Miss Nancy. Meanwhile, Lasher's band can hardly wait to attack the high-energy source song, charging forth with a rollicking rural mento backing. Wild bamboo saxophone and banjo dominate even when they are not soloing. There is also rhythm guitar and prominent pungent rumba box, the latter at times plucked in a way to give the song its only percussive sound. 'Slide Mongoose' is included on the aforementioned CD, *Boogu Yagga Gal*, along with another rural and four less rural Count Lasher golden-age mento songs.

'Natta Bay Road'

'Natta Bay Road', billed to Count Lasher And His Pepsters, was released on the Lasher Disc label. Like each of the handful of releases on this imprint, it has never been compiled on LP or CD. That's too bad, because the song is effectively a follow-up to 'Slide Mongoose'. It has the same instrumentation and rollicking energy, and it too is a rendition of a Jamaican folk song, albeit a less well-known one. Its opening is reminiscent of the African-sounding introduction of 'Mango Time'. The few lyrics describe going to Annatto Bay Road one night, as the moon shines down. And although the words are few, Lasher's melody and the band's rhythm are captivating. Every aspect of the song captures the anticipation of heading to a rendezvous. Unusually for a Lasher track, there are backing vocals, and, most unusual for golden-age mento, it sounds like there could be female voices present.

'Mo-Bay Chinaman' (aka 'Don't Fool Round Me Gal'); 'Robusta Banana' (aka 'Jamaica Banana')

These two songs comprise the only single Count Lasher recorded for producer Ivan Chin. Since Chin has recently made the entire output of his label available on CD and some digital music services, these songs can easily be heard today. But be forewarned that the sound quality of both tracks is rough, having been mastered from a surviving 78. That's a shame, since both songs are great. Credited to Count Lasher's Calypso Quintet, both feature a banjo-enlivened early version of the reggae rhythm with acoustic guitar, rumba box and hand drum. The single presents an example of each of Count Lasher's two lyrical specialties: the well-observed story rich in detail and the naughty extended double entendre.

The more overtly reggae-sounding of the two is the bouncy 'Mo-Bay Chinaman'. It's the story of John, the title's Chinese man from Montego Bay, who goes to Kingston to win the affections of an uptown girl named Lila. He sets her up financially with the condition that she "never skylark with a ligger man", the song mocking John's pronunciation as well as the entire situation, which does not go John's way. He buys Lila furniture and "a first-class Radiophone". But there's a commotion ensues after "someone made John to understand that Lila was playing with a nigger man".

Lasher finds engaging melodies for both verse and chorus. It's no wonder then that, in 1977, Stanley Beckford would have a hit with a somewhat altered rendition called 'Leave My Kisiloo'. Lord Tanamo would record a more faithful reggae rendition of the song a year later called 'China Man From Montego Bay'. In 2010, The Tallawah Mento Band recorded a big, loving rendition called 'Kysilo'.

'Robusta Banana' gives us the coming together of two Lasher-esque themes. First, it's a song about fruit. He had at least three others, singing about 'Mango Time' and on that single's flipside, 'Breadfruit Season', as well as 'Fish And Ackee'. Second, it's one of his extended double entendres. Other examples include 'The Ole Man's Drive', in which an elderly fellow promises a younger woman a good ride if he can just get behind the wheel and drive; 'Water The Garden', in which a young lady wastes no time instructing her newly hired gardener to "take out the hose, it's watering day"; 'Female Boxer', which equates making love to a three-round boxing match; 'Miss Constance', which equates the same to a road race; and 'Count Lasher Rides' and 'Lasher Rides Again', both of which equate making love to a horse race. Neither 'Shepherd Rod' nor 'Man With The Tool' require much of an explanation. And 'Perseverance' likens making love to digging for water through rocks with an enthusiasm that excuses the unromantic analogy.

Here, Lasher is a banana vendor whose offerings are rejected by a female customer who is quite demanding and apparently knows her bananas ("Chinese banana, that one is worst!). She's not satisfied by the size and believes "it gets soft long before the pot gets hot". At the same time, recalling 'Mango Time', a number of locally grown varieties are named. She compares the virtues and shortcomings of the Chinese banana, Lacatan, Gros Michelle, and Robusta. (For the record, a Chinese banana is another name for the Cavendish, the banana that is widely grown by numerous countries for export around the world.)

An acoustic guitar and/or banjo strums only the first three insistent beats of four, skipping the last, and giving the third emphasis. This gets us halfway to the innovation of the ska beat, where the second and fourth beats are skipped. Meanwhile, the banjo solos take off nicely from the engaging melody of Lasher's chorus.

'Trek To England'

Billed to Count Lasher's Calypso Quintet, 'Trek To England' is another fine Stanley Motta-produced rural mento by Lasher. It opens with a melodic, wistful acoustic guitar solo, promising perhaps a simple folk arrangement. But soon bamboo sax and banjo are taking turns with this melody as a second guitar fills out the sound. The first three beats are sounded with the fourth skipped, as in 'Robusta Banana'. But this time around, the rhythm creates a gentle sway instead of a ska or reggae sound. The arrangement carries more than a touch of melancholy, befitting Lasher's lyrics and singing. The song is Lasher's take on the social upheaval created by the massive wave of Jamaican emigration to England. He focuses on several women who are desperate to join the exodus. For example, the young girl with her man who Lasher mistakes for her grandfather. And the barmaid working on Water Lane who feigns illness to sneak away to the docks. And the man who returns from work to find his wife has flown to England without him. Lasher warns all men, complete with a bit of British slang, "Watch yourself, I tell you mate, no make dem call you England bait".

It's a bitter-sweet song that helps establish Lasher's range as broader than perennially merry. Happily, it saw re-release on the aforementioned CD called *Mento Not Calypso*.

4   Chin's Calypso Sextet

If Count Lasher was golden-age mento's greatest single star, then Chin's Calypso Sextet was its greatest group. They were the golden-age's most recorded act, ultimately releasing more than ninety tracks of strictly rural mento. Chin's Calypso Sextet was anchored by two men: Alerth Bedasse and Everard Franklyn Williams. Bedasse was born in 1928 in Clarendon Parish, moving to Kingston when he was twenty-one. He was the lead singer and wrote the melodies of the group's songs. He passed away in March 2007 at the age of seventy-nine. Williams was the lyricist and guitar player. An older man than Bedasse, he was probably born before 1920 and died around the time the millennium ended.

Bedasse's distinctively rural mento voice was so high and nasal that it was the hallmark of the group's sound. Coming from a musical family, he started in music at age five, playing on a home-made bamboo guitar. Williams, a former schoolteacher, was not only mento's greatest lyricist, but must be acknowledged as amongst the finest ever to come from Jamaica. In addition to writing for his own band, he also wrote hits for various other mento acts, including many songs for Harold Richardson & The Ticklers and memorable one-offs for many other artists. (Examples of the latter in this book include 'Cutting Wood', which, as we will see, was recorded by Rita Marley, and 'Etheopia', a song by Lord Lebby whose significance we have already discussed.) He even provided songs for Count Lasher, a fine lyricist in his own right.

In the early 1950s, the pair began performing live as a duo, reminiscent of Slim & Sam, the popular Kingston-based mento duo of the 1930s and 1940s. (Though they never recorded, Slim Beckford and Sam Blackwood made a name for themselves by traveling about to perform their original, often topical, compositions.) They would come to add other musicians to fill out their sound by the time they began making records in the middle of the decade. Most frequently, Chin's Calypso Sextet included Cheston Williams on banjo, Wilbert Stephenson on bamboo sax, Aaron Carr on guitar and Vivian Lord on rumba box. They were uncompromisingly rural, but never sloppy, like a woodcarving that is both rough-hewn, but meticulously finished. Almost every one of Chin's songs is enriched by short solos and quick and ready jams, the latter indicative of a group used to playing together. With the exception of one song described below, Chin's Calypso Sextet did not preface the ska/reggae rhythm to come as much as records from other golden-age stars. Not all great golden-age rural mento did.

One of the group's first recordings was the most notorious of mento's golden age. It arrived in the first half of the 1950s, on Ken Khouri's Kalypso label, when they were billed as the Calypso Quintet. As we will see, the risqué 'Night Food' caused a sensation and was a huge hit for its time. This combination brought negative attention from the Jamaican government but positive attention from Ivan Chin. Chin was the owner of Chin's Radio Service, a chain of electronics stores that also sold records. Keen to try his hand at production, Chin signed the group to a deal for his new Chin's label, rechristening them as Chin's Calypso Sextet. Working in his Kingston store after closing time, together they recorded about seventy-two tracks that were released on about half as many singles from 1955 through 1957, plus other material. There were the expected risqué (for the time) follow-ups to 'Night Food', but the group was equally adept with other types of song. Many were richly observed slices of Jamaican life – something that Williams was unsurpassed at – songs about relationships, songs for children, mento renditions of Jamaican folk songs and more. But among all this variety, Chin's avoided recording touristy songs. This gives credence to the notion that while most golden-age records courted the island's visitors to some degree or another, Chin's Calypso Sextet concentrated more on a local audience. As the records' brown-paper sleeves proclaimed, Chin's Calypso Sextet was "The band that produces the type of records liked by most Jamaicans. Played in homes and all Sound Systems and Juke Boxes throughout Jamaica."

Always the producer, in the 2000s Ivan Chin made these tracks available again on a series of home-made CDRs and then on digital music services, more than a half-century after he first recorded them. All but one lost single is available, as well as some earlier tracks that were released on Kalypso, and even some performances that he had never released anywhere before. Thanks to Ivan Chin, the largest catalog of vintage rural mento ever recorded has been made available – a bona fide mother lode. With the smaller catalogs of other golden-age mento artists only appearing in dribs and drabs, the availability of the Chin's catalog is astounding. Quite consistent in quality, it does not contain a bad song. Let us discuss the better songs of Chin's Calypso Sextet, and dwell on the best.

Double-entendre songs

'Night Food'
It was certainly the most notorious and probably the most popular record of mento's golden age, 'Night Food' delighted the masses, selling by some accounts over ten thousand copies, a huge number for that time in Jamaica. It launched the career of the band, but when the group recorded a sequel called 'Night Food Recipe', it brought down the fury of Jamaican government officials, who called for a ban on such ribald records, describing them as harmful to Jamaica's youth. Though no laws were passed, mento performers, and Williams in particular, felt the pressure. He would eventually take Ivan Chin's advice and left the ribald behind to concentrate on other types of songs. But, really, there was so much

angst over so little. Although the subject is indeed sexual, it's couched in the titular double entendre. Only an adult with full understanding of the subject would recognize the song's true meaning, so it was unlikely that any young people were affected and it's hard to imagine that harm came to any adult.

The song finds humor in the reactions when a fast woman offers a naive man "night food", her term for cunnilingus. The woman is frustrated when she realizes that he thinks he's about have dinner cooked for him. Then she's furious when she makes him understand, and he rejects her advances, equating her offer to the Bible tale of Sampson and Delilah. Williams wrote not so much a dirty song as a humorous song about a couple who are woefully mismatched sexually. He also perfectly illustrated the conflicting attitudes on this subject that were present in Jamaica in the 1950s and are still very much in effect today. (See, for example, the Mr. Vegas song 'Heads High', described later in this book; page 564.)

It's easy to see why the song was so popular, considering all it offers. First, it has sex, and sex sells. It has a controversial subject. It has humor. And it introduced the group to their audience, as their few previous recordings were not commercially successful. The listeners heard an accessible rural mento backing with well-mannered bamboo sax providing lead lines, a swaying strummed acoustic guitar at the fore, and rumba box and maracas completing the backing. (As was the way for the earliest recordings by the group, there is no banjo.) And they heard a distinctive mento-voiced singer, who works a suitably playful melody to convey the story so well. It's nothing short of a golden-age classic, and decades later, Nora Dean, Lord Tanamo (though credited to Duke Reid) and others recorded reggae renditions of 'Night Food'.

'The Juicy Oyster'

Originally billed to Bedasse And Band and produced by Ken Khouri, 'The Juicy Oyster' was perhaps the most outrageous of all mento double-entendre songs. Ivan remembers it as being the group's very first record. What's it about? Well, you see, there was an oyster with, ah, desirable female attributes that contained a pearl. Men really wanted to get their hands on the pearl, but all failed in their attempts. Then a man who apparently knew how to squeeze oysters properly, succeeded in gaining access to the pearl, which he exclusively enjoyed until the day he died. In spite of this happy ending, no oyster company or pearl industry group has adopted this song as their corporate theme.

'The Juicy Oyster' featured an arrangement similar to 'Night Food', but the acoustic guitar gives the song a sway as languid as a palm tree in the breeze. Because this song has few words, guitar and bamboo sax solos abound in between the stanzas. Similar to and every bit as good as the far better known 'Night Food', 'Juicy Oyster' is just one of many great tracks that were rescued from obscurity when Ivan Chin released them on CD.

'Big Boy And Teacher'

'Big Boy And Teacher' is another naughty and well-remembered Chin's hit. It was subsequently covered across the decades, including reggae renditions from both I-Roy and U-Roy in the 1970s (the former DJing and the latter singing) and a ragga rendition from Little John in the 1980s. Set in a classroom, "questions begin to fall like rain" from Big Boy, as he bombards his teacher with queries about "catty". (In the USA, we would substitute the word "pussy".) Is he just naive, like the protagonist in 'Night Food', unaware of the double meaning of his questions? The leering bamboo sax opening tells us otherwise. So do his questions, which become harder to explain as queries about a cat: "Is catty clean or surround by bush? To reach it, do I have to push?" No, he's not asking about a cat at all. It's the teacher who's the naive one, never reacting to Big Boy's veiled mockery. The song features another example of mento emphasis on the first three beats, ignoring the fourth, creating a rhythm that is not ska, but would help inform it. It chugs along, led by the spare bass of the rumba box. Banjo rides atop, plucking out a playful melody as bamboo sax, bamboo flute and maracas all contribute. (Acoustic guitar is present, but plays a tiny role this time around, and you have to search to hear it.) Ivan Chin's CD releases would also include three previously unreleased renditions of the song; a looser vocal performance and two rollicking instrumental takes.

Other double-entendre songs

Chin's Calypso Sextet recorded other fine double-entendre songs. Naiveté and sex again combine to humorous effect in 'Honeymoon'. Even while bragging about the coming of the big event, the naive Rufus proves to know nothing about his wedding night duties: "When it was time for romantic interlude, Rufus said, 'Dear, why are you nude?'" 'Night Food Recipe' is the follow-up to their big hit. Would you be surprised to learn that the recipe calls for combining fish and tongue? Or at directions that include, "Then with a stick you can stir the pot. Continue do dat until it gets hot." 'No Money No Music' is a double-entendre song that equates music to love-making, each requiring pay. 'My Red Tomato' is no more a song about a vegetable than 'Juicy Oyster' is a song about an oyster.

Slice-of-life songs

But there was more to Chin's Calypso Sextet lyrics than double-entendre wordplay. Williams had a fantastic eye for detail and was attuned to Jamaican life, both the routine and the unusual. Here are some of the best examples of the slice-of-life songs he wrote for Chin's Calypso Sextet.

'Big Sid'

'Big Sid' is a wonderful song, with a story rich in drama and detail, complete with surprise ending. (Unfortunately, it's mastered from a 78-rpm single with sound quality that leaves something to be desired.) Along with another Chin's song, 'Not Guilty', 'Big Sid' is the first reggae courtroom song. This is a theme that would become popular in the late 1960s with songs from Derrick Morgan, Prince Buster, Peter Tosh and others, and would carry over to the UK in the 1970s with a good song by the Two Tone ska revivalists, The Specials. ('Tougher Than Tough' by Derrick Morgan and 'Here Comes The Judge' by Peter Tosh are each discussed later in this book; pages 137 and 225.) Musically, 'Big Sid' is as languid as anything the band ever recorded, and its pace, rhythm and ensemble playing all foreshadow late-1970s reggae. Rumba box, banjo, and acoustic guitar each simultaneously provide melody and a proto-reggae rhythm. Bamboo sax and flute add layers of melody. As the music rocks and sways, Bedasse takes his time telling the story of 'Big Sid', making all but a few of Williams's words discernible through the rough mastering. But even with this, the story would be incomprehensible if not for the explanation in Ivan Chin's liner notes. He explains that "Big Sid" was a name given to any big, foul-tempered cow and that there was "a very big and fat woman that people called Pearl Harbor". The latter name apparently was acceptable, but she reacted strongly to being called 'Big Sid'. "She did not like that name at all. So one day she caught a woman who called her 'Big Sid' and gave her two buck [a Jamaican term for a strike/blow] in her head, she fell to the ground". She was arrested and the following courtroom drama unfolded.

> "Pearl Harbor, why you buck that gal?
> Look 'pon her mouth, lips all a split
> Yet you want she with such repel
> Was it because she said she quit?
> A why you mash up the gal eyebrow?
> Tell me nothing but the whole truth now."

> "Your honor, I am guilty sir
> But allow me now to explain, please
> Anywhere me go along the street
> It's a habit for she to laugh and flee
> But they say no sir, that blow me lid,
> as when dem bawl out, 'Hello, Big Sid'

> "It must [be?] because me big and fat
> Why this maga gal come call me that? ["maga" is a Jamaican term for skinny]
> Cause night and day me can't walk in peace
> So me buck her down fe make it cease
> For me rifling, Pearl Harbor read
> 'How do you do sir, it's a Big Sid'

> "Man, no tell no lie, me grab her, sir
> Then me buck her about once or twice
> Then me kick her down any cow

And she stretch out flat with her lips down
But when she come down, listen what she did:
She look at me good, and shout 'Big Sid!'"

The judge say, "I don't blame you child
You are admonished and discharged
Me no know how she foolish so
She the police she should have charged
But she was foolish as a young goat kid
When she call that woman 'cow by the name Big Sid'"

'I Visited A Wedding'; 'A Food Wedding'

The Toots & The Maytals song 'Sweet and Dandy' (a song described in the chapter on this artist; page 159), one of the greatest reggae songs ever recorded, is a richly detailed account of a wedding. More than a decade before, Chin's had released not one, but two different songs that covered the same ground.

"I visited a wedding, for the first time in my young life, and there I learned with pleasure how, a man should take a wife" begins 'I Visited A Wedding'. From there, an enthusiastic account of the mechanics of a wedding ceremony is presented as the mento swings. Paraphrasing, Bedasse is impressed that the parson does not falter at the altar, and he recounts all that is said in the vows. There are three renditions of the song to enjoy. Two were previously unreleased, and it's great that they got to see the light of day, even if they are quite similar. But the third rendition, the one originally released as a single, is very different. It's slower and Bedasse sings in a lower register than his trademark norm. And, in a further surprise, an electric guitar is featured, the only Chin's single where this instrument was heard. All of this portends the end of Chin's Calypso Sextet; this would be their last single, the band breaking up in the latter part of 1957.

"It was a genuine kind of food carnival", Bedasse sings in 'A Food Wedding'. The tempo of the music is slow, allowing the song to focus firmly on the food being served, giving us a litany of wedding fare in the Jamaica of the 1950s. There were broad beans, dumplings, breadfruit, coconut cake stuffed with roast mashed corn, curried goat, fried rice, rice and peas, fried fish, bammie (a flatbread made from cassava), salt fish and ackee, coconut water, Captain Morgan rum and more. The singer enthuses, "I am telling you because I was there. It was a real lovely affair."

Other slice-of-life songs

These are by no means the only slice-of-life Chin's songs worth hearing, as Williams's keen eye and way with words resulted in an endless supply of tales. 'Rent Worries' is one of several mento songs on the topic of rent or landlord problems, a theme that would continue well into reggae. It includes Bedasse's memorably pained refrain, "The rent worries mash up me life, *whai, whai, whai!*" 'Uniform Madness' explains that women love a man in a uniform, and reveals this as the secret reason why members of mento bands dress alike when performing. The relaxed 'Guzoo Doctor' describes a new herbalist healer in town. It contains a stanza that defends mento against the charge that it's responsible for young girls becoming pregnant: "A gal say calypso swell her child, but the bush doctor only gave a smile, and said something else should get the blame because Calypso wasn't her boyfriend name". 'Boogu Yagga Girl' is the tale of an ugly ("boogu yagga") woman whose relationship is ruined when (in a familiar theme) her man emigrates to England. 'Letter From Jamaica' is another song on the subject of emigration. 'Look Before You Leap' is the story of a know-it-all young woman who does not heed her mother's guidance and winds up in the family way. 'Black Market Beef' is based on a true story about a time of shortage in Jamaica when some items were only available on the black market. A woman smuggles ninety pounds of illicit meat by pretending to be pregnant, leaving the singer to explain that he will stick to bread. 'Peaka Pow' is about the illegal lottery game, peaka peow, that originated in China and became popular in Jamaica. In it, Mistress Morgan desperately tries to channel her dreams into picking the right numbers and goes from obsession to swearing off the game. 'Monkey's Opinion' is a piece of social commentary from Williams. A monkey explains to two of his peers that people could not have descended from the superior monkeys, citing several examples of poor behavior by people to make his case. 'Monkey's Opinion' seems to have been influenced by a similar-minded song released the same year called 'The Monkey Speaks Its Mind' by American R&B singer Dave Bartholomew. Adding to the confusion was another similarly themed monkey song released at the same time: the urban mento of 'Monkey Talk', by Herbert Porter & George Moxey & His Calypso Quintet. Not to mention 'Monkey' by Lord Flea (a song previously described in this book; page 51).

Sometimes the situations being detailed are risqué. 'Rough Rider' is the tale of Ida, "the roughest girl anywhere around, but rougher still when lying down". Rufus from Barbados wants to show up Jamaican men, but is taken from Ida in an ambulance. A preacher hears of Ida and wants to save her soul with his "saving rod". "So he went one night to Miss Ida's room, but there he nearly met his doom". 'Weekly Lover' is about a woman whose demands of her lover are so exhausting that a compromise is reached as union work rules are adopted.

Other times, Williams's observations were closer to home, as he also wrote autobiographical songs for Chin's Calypso Sextet. In Jamaica, a pepperpot is a stew made with any and every ingredient that happens to be available. 'Calypso Pepperpot' is a medley of three songs that uses a self-reference device to set up the selections. For example, Bedasse sings,

> I was walking by the Spanish Town Road, and when I reached by Darling Street,
> Me hear Alerth Bedasse singing a song that sound like this ...

and

> I continue a little further, and when I reach Lambert Street,
> Me hear Chin's Calypso Sextet play a song that sound like this ...

A subject already touched on in 'Guzoo Doctor' is more fully explored in two songs, the pleading 'Calypso Opinion' and the defiant, bracing 'Why Blame Calypso'. These songs dealt with the attacks on mento records, when they were being blamed for incidents of pregnancy in young teens. Two such stories are explored in 'Why Blame Calypso', which opens with the plea, "It seems to me, anything go wrong, calypso catch the blame. Such I don't think is fair at all. In fact it's a burning shame ... let us play an honest game". 'Calypso Opinion' points out that even though "the tourists say, 'Jamaica, it's calypso land' ", there are parties in Jamaica that would "feel so nice calypso dead". The group defends its position, but ultimately capitulates: "No more 'Night Food' or 'Recipe', on that the subject we agree", as the group was pressured into abandoning ribald songs.

Men and women

Another area that Williams excelled in was songs about the relationships between men and women. With titles like 'Woman's Style', 'Woman Tenderness', 'A Woman's Mind', 'Woman Walk', 'The Woman And The Man', and even 'Woman Ghost Fool Man', you might even say he was preoccupied with the opposite sex. Here are some recommended examples. 'Depression' finds Bedasse having relationship problems to the point of singing, "Depression going to kill me dead" as the band supports him with a backing chorus of woeful "Ai, ai!"s. 'Money Is King' describes money's role in relationships, and how "money can open the bedroom door". 'Walk And Talk' also focuses on the exchange of funds for sex in a relationship. 'Give Her Love' finds a heartbroken Alerth lamenting about his luck after, "I took a gal and married her and gave her all that's good, yet she leave me and take my son. She want more firewood." 'Look Out Fe You Tongue' is a warning about a then newsworthy UK incident that was disconcerting enough for Williams to recount as a public service. In it, after a boy makes up after a fight with his girlfriend, he asks her for a kiss, and she bites his tongue off. 'Woman's Ghost Fool A Man' describes a relationship that is marred by the fact that the man did not realize the woman was a ghost. 'A Victim Of Love', with a rare Williams lead vocal, is a sincere song about his deep sadness whenever his woman is gone.

Other songs

Jamaican folk songs

In addition to the songs written by Williams, Chin's Calypso Sextet also recorded a number of Jamaican folk songs. These tended to be serious in tone. 'Jamaica Folk Tune #1' is a medley of three folk songs, separated by short instrumental jams. The third, 'John Tom', is the most familiar of the three. The second song is called 'Mussu', while the name of the first is unclear. The impassioned performance, unfamiliarity of the material and the fact that many of the lyrics are difficult to follow, all serve to make these recordings sound quite exotic. They remind us that the waters of Jamaican folk music run much deeper than such popularized hits as 'Linstead Market', 'Sly Mongoose' and 'Day-O'. The latter two songs of the medley were re-recorded in two renditions of a song called 'Mussu And John Tom'.

Children's songs

What better way to avoid further attacks by Jamaican government officials, Ivan Chin realized, than to record children's music rather than ribald songs. Four traditional Jamaican ring-game songs were recorded with no less skill or care because the target audience was children. The title of each includes the prefix, 'Let's Play Ring'.

'Farm Yard Cha Cha' includes all the sounds the animals make, making it fun for children and less so for adults. 'Riddle Me This' is enjoyable for all. Bedasse recites a series of riddles and band members sing their incorrect answers. It's musical and sweet, and includes a spontaneous moment where Bedasse cracks up at a particularly bad guess.

Bible songs

Decades before biblical themes made frequent appearances in roots reggae, Chin's recorded two songs based on biblical pairs. 'Adam And Eve' (a different song from the Bob Marley & The Wailers track of the same name) gives Williams the opportunity to pass on the lessons of the Garden of Eden that his teachers and grandfather taught him. 'Sampson And Delilah' uses the famous tale to caution "men never trust a pretty face. It may bring you bitter disgrace". (These were not the only Bible-themed songs of mento's golden age. The 1957 'Nebuchadnezzar' by Laurel Aitkin is another example.)

And more

Chin's Calypso Sextet also recorded a quadrille single with a guest lead fiddle player. As previously mentioned, this dance music was born in nineteenth-century France and found its way to Jamaica via colonialism. Though rural mento instrumentation is used, its rhythm and structure are not related to reggae. Instead, it sounds not unlike American square-dance music. Quadrilles are instrumental compositions that consist of multiple *figures*, or variations on a theme. When recorded as a single, the figures cover both sides, as is the case for the fine example here, called 'Quadrille Figures 1 & 2' and 'Quadrille Figures 3 & 4'. The group also recorded a trio of waltzes (an Ivan Chin favorite) in 'Come Back My Darling', 'I Am In Love' and 'Our Beautiful Wedding Waltz', the latter featuring an unknown guest vocalist. In contrast, 'Honey Bee' has a definite R&B flavor, even if it does feature a banjo played like a mandolin.

5 Great Jamaican R&B

American R&B hit Jamaican music like a tsunami. It influenced the sound of some mento records before supplanting mento as Jamaica's favorite music, becoming its most recorded style by 1960 or 1961. Many R&B songs and R&B-influenced songs are discussed in the individual artist chapters in this book, but here are some more examples of great Jamaican R&B. Some sound very similar to American R&B, while others less so.

Derrick Harriott: *'Answer Me My Darling'*
Derrick Harriott was born in Kingston in 1939. He enjoyed a long and diverse career as a singer and a producer. He began in R&B as the lead singer of vocal group The Jiving Juniors, with backing singers Eugene Dwyer, Herman Sang and Maurice Winter. They came together in 1958, had hits by 1960, but after recording about two dozen songs, broke up in 1962, just prior to when R&B gave way to ska. Unlike Harriott, thereafter a solo singer, the other members did not have much post-Jiving Juniors success. Around the time of the break-up, Harriott entered the field of record production by self-producing some of his own releases. Thus reinvented, he recorded himself and others through the ska and rock steady eras. His singing career was dotted with hits throughout, while his production career took off at the start of the reggae era, as various artists enjoyed hits on "Harriott's chariot". He started his own label and opened a record shop, the two so often going hand in hand with record production in Jamaica. In 1974, he produced (with King Tubby employed as engineer) one of the first dub albums, *Derrick Harriott Presents Scrub-A-Dub Reggae*, adding to the argument that his accomplishments as a producer exceeded those of his long successful singing career. Harriott recorded into the 1980s, performed live in the 1990s and produced into the 2000s. He recorded six albums, about one hundred singles, and produced about four times that number for other artists.

'Answer Me My Darling' is one of two songs Harriott recorded for producer Coxsone Dodd in 1961, making it either his first or second solo recording. It appeared as a single and on the 1961 LP, *All Star Top Hits*, a collection of Jamaican R&B singles that was the first LP Coxsone Dodd released. It can be heard today, as that entire album was subsumed into the Heartbeat Records double-CD compilation called *Ska Bonanza* (even though this R&B collection is clearly pre-ska). It's a peppy break-up song that sits comfortably in the R&B idiom, well sung by Harriott in his affable, down-to-earth voice. In spite of the impressive Jamaican talent on this song, it's striking how un-Jamaican it sounds compared to the mento that came before and the ska soon to emerge. It could have been slipped into the soundtrack of *American Graffiti* (a collection of accessible American early rock and roll hits from the 1950s). There are two tip-offs that this was a Jamaican record. One is Harriott's Jamaican accent. The other is that the expected saxophone solo (provided by Roland Alphonso) is followed by a trombone solo – atypical for American music, but soon to be common in Jamaican music – provided by a rocking Don Drummond. 'Answer Me My Darling' is an example of how well Jamaica could imitate American R&B. But the presence of Drummond's solo reveals the restlessness of Jamaican potential.

Higgs & Wilson: *'Manny Oh'*

Higgs & Wilson's 'Manny Oh' helped launch producer (and future Jamaican prime minister) Edward Seaga's newly minted WIRL (West Indian Records Limited) label in 1960. Being the duo's first record, it also launched the recording careers of Joe Higgs and Roy Wilson, who had begun working together two years earlier. They would record together for another four years, releasing about thirty singles before Higgs went solo.

Joseph Benjamin Higgs was born in 1940 in Kingston, while Neville "Roy Wilson" Williams was born a year earlier in Spanish Town. Though Higgs would have the longer and more significant career, Wilson was established first. After success on Vere Johns's *Opportunity Hour* talent show, he was recruited by the island's top comedy act Bim & Bam for their stage show. Talent shows were an important launching pad for many reggae singers, and no talent show was more important than John's. This Jamaican musical institution was broadcast nationally on the radio, eventually moving to TV.

Late in the 1950s, Wilson formed a duo with Jackie Edwards, but they don't appear to have recorded together. Then at a 1958 talent show, he found himself performing with Higgs solely due to a logistical accident. The serendipitous pairing of Higgs's baritone with Wilson's higher voice pleased both singers enough that they became a team. Their audience validated the pairing. As we will see, their first single was a smash hit. Their second single, 'Gun Talk', a straight-up R&B number also from 1960, was the first Jamaican song to deal with a subject that would become so popular during the rude boy era and again decades later in the ragga era. They would score five number 1 hits by 1961, making the argument for Higgs & Wilson being the biggest stars of Jamaican R&B.

Though they made the move from R&B to ska, Wilson left music in 1965. He would return to reunite briefly with Higgs in 1969 before emigrating to America, ending his musical career. Higgs continued as a solo artist into the roots era, and would play an important role in reggae's greatest story. A newly minted star at the age of twenty, Higgs tutored his Trench Town neighbors, including the fledgling Bob Marley & The Wailers, in the art of harmony. He was also instrumental in securing the group an audition at Studio One. Once they were hired, he assisted them in song arrangement, sometimes adding his own vocals to the mix. He would pop up on the occasional Wailers track for years to come, and even filled in for Bunny Wailer when, becoming disillusioned with life on the road so far from home, Bunny quit a 1973 overseas Wailers tour. Higgs's solo career lasted to 1995, accounting for approximately fifty singles and three albums over that time. In spite of being an R&B star, and also recording ska and rock steady, he is most remembered for his roots reggae. Higgs was working on a new album when he died of cancer in 1999. Wilson passed away in 2012.

Not only was 'Manny Oh' Higgs & Wilson's biggest hit, it was probably the biggest hit of Jamaica's R&B era, and deservedly so. Another Jamaican R&B star, Wilfred "Jackie" Edwards penned the song and Ken Richards & The Comets provided the rollicking backing. It opens with bawdy barrelhouse piano and then launches into an R&B groove with a chord progression immediately familiar to anyone who has heard 1950s American boogie. Piano stays out front, with bass, drums and saxophone providing the rhythm. Higgs & Wilson deliver a song about being abandoned by Manny, even though there was a promise of "having babies just for you". Fine harmony and doo-wop flourishes abound. The result is a great Jamaican R&B sound, a little rough around the edges, and all the better for it.

But there is something else going on here. The drum playing, though very simple, arrives just after the beat. It's distinctly different from how an American would have played, hinting at other drum traditions and potential approaches to rhythm. It makes the sound fresher and more exciting. So too are the vocals that sound more Jamaican than most other songs of the era, as the island's singers had by then mastered the art of imitating American R&B. Both these ingredients are missing from the single's B-side, 'When You Tell Me', which sounds more conventionally American, rendering it (like many records of the Jamaican R&B era) totally forgettable. The biggest hit of Jamaica's pre-ska R&B era, 'Manny Oh', was the song that began to turn away from pure imitation and back towards something more Jamaican. At the end of 2011, it made its overdue CD debut on a collection called *The Story Of Blue Beat: The Best In Ska 1960*, released on the Sunrise Records label.

Folkes Brothers: *'Oh Carolina'*
Conceived and executed by producer Prince Buster in 1960, the Folkes Brothers' 'Oh Carolina' was a bold gamble with a rich pay-off. What 'Manny Oh' hinted at, 'Oh Carolina' delivered in abundance. It provided an important wake-up call, reminding Jamaicans that they had much more musically to offer than merely imitating American R&B. The emergence of ska shortly thereafter made this evident.

The Folkes comprised lead singer and songwriter John and his brothers Mico and Junior on backing vocals. 'Oh Carolina' was their first recording. At an audition, their doo-wop song impressed Buster enough that he brought them to Duke Reid's studio to record it. The accompaniment Buster provided featured prominent R&B piano played by Owen Gray. But instead of the expected bass, guitar, drums and sax, the backing was instead filled out with Count Ossie's Rastafarian drum troupe. Technically, this might not be the first recording of Nyabinghi drums. A single by King Joe & African Drums, produced by Vincent Chin, may have been recorded earlier, though it was not released until later. And Buster recorded another song with Ossie's troupe earlier in the session, with Bunny & Skitter handling vocals, called 'Chubby'. But 'Oh Carolina' was probably the first to be released. And it certainly was the first to show the commercial viability of this uniquely Jamaican sound. At the time, this was a daring gamble rather than the sure thing that hindsight might have us believe. Rasta was then reviled and even feared by many elements of Jamaican society. With 'Oh Carolina', their music would move from the underground to sharing the stage with the popular American R&B sounds that ruled the day.

The song thrusts together the African sound of Ossie's rough and rollicking percussion troupe with the unvarnished Jamaican R&B vocals and piano sounds. The result was a strange bird with two unmatched wings that flies nonetheless. Pure excitement scrolled into vinyl, it was a big hit.

It opens with R&B piano, but some of the percussion quickly joins in, signaling that a straight Jamaican R&B record, in fact, was not in the offing. Instead, something more exotic, rugged and creatively Jamaican was heard. As the vocals begin, so does the rest of the percussion. There is a wild hand drum that is as much of a lead instrument as the vocals. It is played aggressively compared to the meditative style that is usually associated with Nyah drumming. A bass drum, shakers and hand claps are also heard. This backing brings out the Jamaicanness inherent in the Folkes' voices, even though they are singing in the R&B idiom. John makes a spirited appeal for the return of his lost love Carolina, sounding tortured as his melody takes some interesting turns. His brothers sing a soothing doo-wop chorus of "bop-chu-wah" in support. It was a big, big hit at the dancehall. Other Nyabinghi/R&B tracks would follow, but none nearly as good or as popular. This includes the single's B-side, 'I Met A Man'. The arrangement is largely the same, the chief difference being that the Folkes provide a spiritual rather than a love song. But somehow, where 'Oh Carolina' catches fire, 'I Met A Man' sits inert. Soon, the advent of ska would end this short-lived genre.

The book *Bass Culture: When Reggae Was King* by Lloyd Bradley illuminates the challenges Buster encountered during the recording session, and is recommended reading.[1] A less-determined producer would have never emerged with a completed recording. 'Oh Carolina' was chosen to bookend *Tougher Than Tough: The Story Of Jamaican Music*, the four-CD premier reggae anthology box-set. It opens with the Folkes' song and closes with the dancehall cover version by Shaggy (a rendition described later in this book; page 554). The Folkes would follow 'Oh

1.   Lloyd Bradley, *Bass Culture: When Reggae Was King* (London: Viking, 2000), pp. 59–60.

Carolina' with a handful of songs for Buster, plus two self-produced sides, all in the early 1960s. A hiatus of exactly half a century would follow, ending in 2011 when the trio reunited and released their first album.

Hugh Godfrey: *'My Time'*

Having recorded only a handful of sides in the mid-1960s, then releasing one more in the mid-1970s, Hugh Godfrey remains something of an obscure figure. Never compiled on LP or CD, his fine 1965 R&B track, the Coxsone Dodd-produced 'My Time', could have been completely forgotten. But its profile was raised by its appearance as the B-side of The Wailers' hit ska single, 'Cry To Me', one of many singles that Studio One continued to press for decades after the record's original release.

Godfrey's vocal on 'My Time' is well sung and he builds nicely to a climax. Musically, it takes from 'Love Potion No. 9', the late 1950s hit by the American R&B band The Clovers, though Godfrey supplies new lyrics about gaining the upper hand in a relationship. It's clearly an R&B song right down to the opening sax lines, but rather than slavishly imitating the American sound, the ska beat has infiltrated the form. As such, the musicians are comfortable expressing themselves in ways that are now seen as quintessentially Jamaican. The sax relentlessly sounds on every off-beat. The drummer is restless with the foursquare R&B drumming and adds ska accents and flourishes at every juncture. The short piano solo consists of a clichéd oriental melody, a practice that is a familiar part of the Jamaican music vocabulary from ska through roots. The result is R&B with a backing that an American band would find rhythmically challenging and downright odd. 'My Time' works not only as a fine example of a Jamaican R&B song, but as an example of how ska spiced up this American genre of music and, in the process, changed it into a Jamaican music.

Higgs & Wilson: *'Don't Mind Me'*

In 1969, Higgs & Wilson reunited and recorded another notable R&B track. Its sound registers both as the reggae of the day and as Jamaican R&B. Produced by Clancy Eccles, 'Don't Mind Me' is a strong, sweaty Jamaican R&B duet, sung in unison except for a few mid-song bars of solo vocal where Joe Higgs cuts loose. They sing of the difficulties of feeding one's family while food costs are rising. The song does not have a lot of words, and the repetition of the lyrics just deepens the groove. The big, hard-working backing is provided by the versatile Dynamites (who also famously backed Desmond Dekker, Toots & The Maytals and The Wailers) in R&B vamp mode. Jackie Jackson's bass drives the track, and the single-note slashing rhythm guitar from Lyn Taitt is as close as the riddim comes to having a lead instrument. A complete success on its own terms, no other track in reggae sounds quite like 'Don't Mind Me'. It can be heard on the Clancy Eccles compilation CD on Heartbeat records.

Derrick Harriott: *'Slave'*

In 1971, Derrick Harriott released a fine prison song, the self-produced 'Slave'. Over a funky and soulful backing, Harriott breaks out an engaging soul falsetto. He sings in detail about the activity that dominates his life – sledgehammering rocks. He longs for freedom, pleading, "Free me from this ball and chain, somebody. Somebody open this cage." Other than, perhaps, its bass playing, the song gives little indication of being Jamaican, and could have passed for an American release. But in 1978, Harriott re-released it as a disco-mix single. Featuring a new mix throughout, it was more Jamaican-sounding, and a good song was made into a great one. Reverb enlivens the rhythm guitar and echo is applied to backing vocals to fine effect. Dub drop-out/in juices the riddim. The distracting lead guitar is dropped out altogether, its absence revealing it to have been clutter. Then, a dub version is appended to the end of the track. It's good rather than great dub, but where else can you hear dub successfully applied to soul music? The disco-mix of 'Slave' is included on a reggae collection CD called *Sounds And Pressure, Volume 4.*

6 The Skatalites

Though there were other great Jamaican bands, none were greater than The Skatalites. The name represents a stellar collection of talent that remains unmatched in Jamaican music history. They had an enormous impact on the genre of reggae they were named for. And they released more than a few songs that still stand as amongst the best recordings ever to have come from Jamaica.

The original Skatalites were bandleader Tommy McCook, Roland Alphonso, Lester "Ska" Sterling and Dennis "Ska" Campbell (whose job it was to pulse the insistent ska chop) on saxophone, Johnny "Dizzy" Moore on trumpet, Lloyd "Richard Ace" Richards early on, then Jackie Mittoo, on piano, Jerry "Jah Jerry" Haynes on guitar, second-generation professional bassist Lloyd Brevett, Lloyd Knibb on drums and Don Drummond on trombone. (Yes, with three of them, The Skatalites could have been called The Ska Lloyds.) At the time of this writing only Richards and Sterling are still with us. It should be noted that variations to this line-up were far from rare. For example, Baba Brooks is heard on some Skatalites tracks released by the Treasure Isle label, the trumpet player being a favorite musician of producer Duke Reid.

These musicians were established in Jamaica's jazz scene, playing in such dance bands as the renowned Eric Deans Orchestra. Credit producer Coxsone Dodd – a lover of jazz. It was his idea to inject the talents of these musicians into the ska framework that had started as a more modest mixture of R&B and Jamaican rhythms. Adding some of Jamaica's best jazz musicians at the peak of their creativity greatly elevated the new music, sometimes to stunning heights.

The Skatalites played on 45s not only from Dodd, Reid and Buster, but from new producers as well. They backed virtually every singer and vocal group of the era (most famously, the young Bob Marley & The Wailers), and recorded instrumentals as well. Soon, this prodigious ska machine needed a name, and, as the story goes, after considering "The Satellites", the play-on-words Skatalites was hit upon and adopted in 1964. However, in reggae, band names are loosely applied and fluid. Not only did the name come late in the game, but names other than The Skatalites were sometimes used, or credit was given to a key Skatalite, most frequently Don Drummond, Tommy McCook or Roland Alphonso. But regardless of what they were called, The Skatalites were responsible for the music on hundreds and hundreds of ska singles in the brief time they were together, from 1963 to the middle of 1965.

McCook, Drummond, Moore and Sterling all began their musical training at an extraordinary institution: Kingston's Alpha Cottage School for Boys, whose students were destitute, abandoned or orphaned. In addition to the regular curriculum (with an emphasis on discipline), the principal, Sister Mary Ignatius Davies, placed a high value on developing the musical abilities of her students. By doing so, she became one of the most important non-performing figures in the history of Jamaican music, and certainly the most saintly. Over the period that Sister Ignatius served – from 1939 into the start of the new millennium – the march of familiar names to emerge from Alpha into Jamaican music is astounding. In addition to the four Skatalites, jazz clarinet great Bertie King, vibraphone player and jazz bandleader Lennie Hibbert, jazz saxophonist Joe Harriott, singers Owen Gray, Johnny Osbourne and the great Desmond Dekker, DJs Trinity and Yellowman, drummer (and star of the movie *Rockers*) Leroy "Horsemouth" Wallace, reggae trumpet players Eddie "Tan Tan" Thorton and Bobby Ellis, reggae saxophone players Cedric "Im" Brooks, Karl "Cannonball" Bryan (both to become members of the re-formed Skatalites) and Headley "Deadly Headley" Bennett, as well as reggae trombonists Rico Rodriguez and Vin Gordon (the former tutored by Don Drummond, the latter coming as close as humanly possible to replacing Don D after his death), all began their musical journeys as Alpha Boys.

Though every Skatalite was a talented musician, each achieved a different degree of fame. Don Drummond is perhaps the most celebrated, his legend hijacked by tragedy after losing his battle with mental illness. He was born in 1932 in Kingston and by 1950 he had already secured a place in Eric Deans's band, a lofty achievement for an eighteen-year-old. On New Year's Day of 1965, Drummond murdered his girlfriend, dancer Anita "Margarita" Mahfood. He would commit suicide in Jamaica's Bellevue Asylum in 1969. These tragic events seem to have been presaged by his trombone playing. His solos were typically played very quietly and introspectively for that instrument, evincing a deep melancholy. No one before or since played the trombone like the rightly revered Don Drummond.

Just as famous and just as talented, if not as revolutionary, were saxmen Tommy McCook and Roland Alphonso. Both were born in Havana, Cuba, and came to Jamaica as children. (A number of other reggae artists, or one or both of their parents, were born in that neighboring island, as movement between Jamaica and Cuba was then very common.) McCook was born in 1927, came to Jamaica when he was six and became an Alpha Boy at age eleven. Alphonso was born in 1931 and came to Jamaica when he was two. Both achieved a position in Eric Deans's band in the 1950s. Alphonso joined even younger than Drummond, at seventeen years of age. Both participated in the 1980s reformation of The Skatalites. Both would be awarded the Order of Distinction by the Jamaican government.

Roland Alphonso's first recording sessions were for mento producer Stanley Motta in the early 1950s. A few years later, he began his association with Coxsone Dodd, where his duties would include sax sessions and work as an arranger. Beginning in 1960, he recorded about 160 singles and half a dozen albums bearing his name. He played on many more records by other artists. Tragically, near the end of 1998, Alphonso suffered a brain aneurism during a Skatalites performance at a show in California and passed away some days later.

Tommy McCook regularly participated in Rasta "grounations" with Count Ossie, as the Rasta jam sessions led by Nyabinghi drumming were called. In 1954, he left Jamaica for a good gig in Nassau, not returning until early in the 1960s. Upon his return, in 1962, he recorded a jazz LP with several other future Skatalites for Dodd. Dodd suggested that McCook record the ska music with him, but, ironically, he declined. (This was probably for the same reason that Ernest Ranglin asked Dodd to leave his name off the credits for ska releases. Ska was so new and so downtown, it threatened the uptown jazz credibility that these musicians had worked hard to establish.) Dodd persisted, repeating the offer in 1963, and this time McCook consented to give it a try. He soon found himself taking a leadership role with the group of great musicians in Dodd's ska stable. The man who first passed on ska would become the bandleader of The Skatalites, the greatest collection of musicians ever in reggae. Along the way, Jamaica's top sax man also developed a proficiency in flute, which he also enjoyed playing. From ska through the roots reggae era, McCook was prolific. He recorded over 200 singles and about fifteen albums under his own name. He arranged or provided sax and/or flute on countless other artists' records. His skills were always in great demand, his playing articulate, accessible and pleasing even by the high standards of The Skatalites. Through all these accomplishments, McCook remained humble and soft-spoken. In 1988, pneumonia and heart failure took the greatest of reggae's great sax players, one of its few flute players, and the leader of its greatest band. He's probably leading heaven's top reggae group right now.

Jackie Mittoo was the youngest Skatalite, joining the band at age sixteen. Although he had a limited role in the band, he would make his mark after the ska era and would become famous in his own right. Other Skatalites also did reggae sessions, but not to the same degree as Mittoo, Alphonso and McCook.

If there is an obscured star in this galaxy of talent, it's drummer Lloyd Knibb. His talent and contribution to the sound of The Skatalites should have made him as famous as any member of the group but, as is often the case, the band member with the sticks tends to get the short end. He was born in 1931 in Kingston. The 1950s were enormously important for the Knibb. It was then that he rose to become a member of the prestigious Eric Deans Orchestra while also finding the time to jam Nyabinghi with Count Ossie and his troupe at Ossie's camp. By the time he reached The Skatalites, he sported a fine jazz technique that was informed by Jamaica's drum traditions, various Caribbean and Latin styles, and even military drumming. The resulting multicultural synthesis gave The Skatalites a propulsive, dynamic armature upon which to build. Amazingly, he was self-taught. His drumming skills were fully intact into his late seventies, as anyone who had the opportunity to see him perform could attest. He passed away from liver cancer at the age of eighty in 2011, as this book was being written.

Whether they were backing a vocal act or performing an instrumental, the range of sounds The Skatalites provided varied greatly. Arrangements could be simple or complex. Songs could lean towards R&B, jazz, Latin, march and more. A familiar melody or an original one could be employed. Though their playing was exciting and creative when backing a singer or vocal group, typically including a solo from one or two of the horn players, it was the instrumentals that gave the group the greatest opportunity to shine. And shine they did on the examples described below. Regardless of the year or producer, these instrumentals followed a pattern:

1. an introduction of varying length and complexity
2. a theme, typically led by one or more horns and repeated twice
3. one or more mid-song solos by the hornsmen, typically with the other horns repeating a supporting phrase underneath
4. the theme briefly reprised

These tracks best demonstrated the thrilling results of fitting fine jazz playing to the rhythmic excitement of ska. The performances were unfailingly tight, never meandering from the point for even a moment, enforced by the approximately three-minute limits of the 45-rpm single. Each is melodic and hook-filled, accessible but sophisticated. These qualities explain why I have encountered more than a few people who insist they don't like jazz, but still love these tracks. Many feel that the music represented in the following clutch of singles is the highest pinnacle of reggae achievement, something I won't argue against. By all means, judge for yourself, as these tracks are readily available on numerous Skatalites CD collections.

Duke Reid productions

'Silver Dollar'
'Silver Dollar' is, like all the tracks described in this chapter, an accessible, jazzy piece of instrumental ska. Bold and tense, it shows The Skatalites to be articulate storytellers, even without words. In its initial release as a 45-rpm single, it was credited to Tommy McCook rather than The Skatalites, but it's Don Drummond's wailing trombone that dominates.

Announced by two drum strikes, the introduction is brief and edgy. It is led by an ominous five-note horn phrase repeated over typical (but endlessly enjoyable) rhythmic ska elements: fine drum fills, a striding bass line and a sax intensely honking a single note on every off-beat. Drummond quickly enters to play a bold theme that's a continuation of the intro's phrase. Rather than developing it, he simply repeats the theme a number of times, allowing anticipation to build like a question hanging in the air. The wordless question is answered with Roland Alphonso's sax solo. Long and rewarding, articulate and enthusiastic, his nimble playing ranges from trebly trilling to long moaning notes at the lower extremity of his instrument, with much in between. Underneath, Drummond reprises the intro's five-note phrase as support. A drum roll announces an exchange of roles, as other horns take over the supporting phrase, and Drummond returns to the forefront with a solo. It becomes apparent that whatever message Alphonso's solo conveyed, it gave Drummond little comfort. He starts in his slow, quiet, introspective style, occasionally rousing himself, only to quickly fall back into the musical equivalent of deep, dark thought. He ends with notes of mournful beauty in an elegy. This is one of a number of Don D solos in this chapter to be cherished. Simply put, trombone just doesn't sound like this outside of Drummond's purview. The big, bold theme returns to fade-out, but it's hard to shake the unresolved moodiness of Drummond's solo.

'Thoroughfare'; 'Don D Lion' (aka 'Don De Lion')
'Thoroughfare', originally credited to Don Drummond, opens with the immediacy of an urgent message. A red-hot ska riddim is heard, with several instruments playing the ska chop in unison as drums accent every other beat. A staccato horn phrase calls out expectantly, repeating as apprehension builds. Drummond answers by leading a rich theme. It is long, and played just once, supported by a sax that casually joins in harmony. It starts with rousing short notes, but, turning on a dime, gives way to longer bluesy trombone swoops and slurs, as the spikiness of the backing pokes through.

An adroit sax solo is heard. Suddenly, a solo from Drummond comes crashing in, stepping on the toes of the sax's conclusion, adding to the air of urgency. Virtually every Don Drummond solo is interesting, and this one is no exception. He weaves together loud and quiet playing, exuberant and introspective at the same time, in a nameless state that only Don Drummond could convey. Emotions conflict and are left unresolved, but Drummond never loses sight of the rhythmic and melodic demands of the song. The theme makes a brief return, and The Skatalites have concluded another excellent instrumental.

Though also produced by Duke Reid and originally credited to Don Drummond, 'Don D Lion' is very different from urgent 'Thoroughfare'. The whimsical name (think 'dandelion') is a tip-off, as Drummond and company serve up some breezy traveling music. Pound-for-pound, it's the most Don Drummond you will hear in a Skatalites song. He is out front playing continuously for the duration, as intro theme and solos all blend together in an unbroken virtuoso trombone performance. All this Drummond and the unusually light-hearted tone of his playing make 'Don D Lion' a special song even amongst the company of outstanding tracks that make up this chapter.

'Eastern Standard Time'
'Eastern Standard Time' is again credited to Don Drummond rather than The Skatalites in a practice that producer Duke Reid often, though not always, employed. It had the distinction of being the favorite song of Sister Ignatius of The Alpha Cottage Boys School. .

Of all the songs in this chapter, this one is furthest from the typical red-hot ska scorchers that The Skatalites are rightly famous for. Instead, 'Eastern Standard Time' is relaxed ska for a lazy Sunday afternoon in a reminder of The Skatalites' range. It features a comforting melodic theme led by Drummond's trombone while two other horns quietly follow along. Part of its melody is reminiscent of the Jamaican folk/mento song, 'Matty Rag'. Meanwhile, the ska chop has cooled down to a chord progression played on electric guitar that dances with the bass. Lloyd Knibb's fancy cymbal work, playing idiosyncratically on the bell of the instrument, signals the end of the theme and time for a solo. An aggressive supporting phrase is introduced and its faster tempo builds anticipation. Drummond answers with a solo, entering awkwardly to play an oddly disparate series of phrases separated by pregnant pauses. It is neither his greatest solo nor one of the overtly introspective ones for which he is famous. If anything, he sounds stoned. But it matches the feel of this relaxed, slightly loopy, Skatalites song.

Coxsone Dodd productions

'Addis Ababa'
Named for the capital of Ethiopia, a country with great religious significance for the Rasta, 'Addis Ababa' is a classic amongst classic Skatalites songs. It's a tonic that can improve any situation.

An introduction of no more than a single drum strike announces the song. Rushing in before the next full beat, horns in unison begin an incredibly rousing, brassy, bold and glorious theme. A piquant descending staccato trumpet riff caps the theme and calls it to start again. Alto sax and guitar sound the ska chop together. Knibb's highly textured playing throws hints of Cuban rumba, Jamaican Pocomania and military drumming. There's a lot going on, all of it good. Taken as a whole, 'Addis Ababa' amounts to a ska march. Considering that the Alpha Boys' diverse musical training included military band marches, hearing The Skatalites performing parade music is not a great surprise. What is surprising is just how great it sounds in a ska context.

A robust sax solo bursting with ideas by McCook is played as a pair of horns repeat a supporting phrase distilled from the theme to urge him on. The phrase becomes subdued as McCook passes the baton to Drummond. His solo has a sadness that he tries to rally from, only to give in to quiet despair by its end. Then the trumpet riff returns to again call the theme: a restorative strong enough to cure the song's bout of melancholy, returning it to high spirits.

Every time I hear this record, I imagine how great it would it be to see a parade band coming down the street, playing 'Addis Ababa'. What a great way it would be to enliven the standard parade band repertoire! Marching bands around the world are hereby advised to start practicing now.

'Christine Keeler'

'Christine Keeler', originally credited to Roland Alphonso, takes its name from the showgirl whose affair with the British Secretary of War John Profumo became a scandal throughout the UK in the early 1960s. (*Scandal*, the 1989 film about these events, continued the ska-scandal connection by including ska in its soundtrack.) It takes its melody from the 1962 Mel Tormé song, 'Comin' Home Baby', but sets it afire to create a ska barnburner. It gets right down to business – no time for an introduction – bursting with energy and talent that the song can barely contain.

You may feel the urge to storm the dance floor from the song's opening trio of notes. By the time you arrive, you'll be moving to a saucy theme carried by a horn section of saxophones and trumpet, and a combination of sax, piano and harmonica sounding the ska chop. Then a trio of solos, each providing a variation on the theme, is heard. First up is Roland Alphonso and his tenor sax, concluding memorably with some low honks, followed by Dizzy Moore's long trumpet solo and Lester Sterling's alto sax solo. The theme is reprised, and Alphonso, caught up in the song's ebullience, steps out to solo over the other horns, complete with a reprise of his low honking notes. A more upbeat, higher-energy ska instrumental would be hard to find.

'Ska La Parisienne'

'Ska La Parisienne' gives some bite to the soundtrack music of Henry Mancini & His Orchestra's 'Mambo Parisienne', yielding a sophisticated ska instrumental. It opens with a jazz-by-way-of-Jamaica drum solo from Lloyd Knibb. Then Jah Jerry holds down the ska chop on electric guitar, allowing all the brass instruments to concentrate on the theme. They lay down an easy-going groove, comprised of long notes played in soft harmony over a sculpted backbone from Knibb. Dizzy Moore enters, his trumpet providing a repeated call that gives the theme a sharp counterpoint. Lester Sterling plays a solo and hands off to Moore, who pretends to have trouble finding the melody and then nails it, blowing notes all over it. The theme is reprised, with Moore coming in again to add his counterpoint phrase. 'Ska La Parisienne' is another example of how The Skatalites were cranking out miniature jazz magnum opuses, while making it look easy.

'Man In The Street'

Credited to Don Drummond, 'Man In The Street' opens delightfully with the most elaborately developed introduction heard in any Skatalites song. For just shy of ten seconds, a melody is playfully handed off in rapid succession between a single, pair or trio of instruments. It opens with bass and trombone, handing off to electric guitar, to a trio of horns, to piano, and this sequence is then repeated. It uncannily invokes the mid-1960s pre-psychedelic London mod sound, and would have fit comfortably in the soundtrack of a British film of the period as animated opening credits rolled by. This delightful introduction may have contributed to

'Man In The Street' charting top ten in the UK, an early forerunner of the success reggae would eventually have outside of Jamaica. But there is a lot more to enjoy from the eleventh second on.

A second introduction is heard, brief but tasty, with guitar and bass jamming over the ska chop. It sounds neither like what preceded it nor like what is to follow in this unusually rich song. The breezy theme is then played by several horns in unison. Unlike most Skatalites songs with their arbitrarily assigned topical titles, the theme of 'Man In The Street' sounds like its name. Simple and accessible, humble and hummable, this fanfare for the common man is one of The Skatalites' most beloved themes. After the second time through, a portion of the theme continues as support for the solos. Dizzy Moore gives his trumpet a proper thrashing, playing at a well-chosen angle to the underlying music. Then Don Drummond solos in his immediately identifiable quiet style. But he's more extroverted and less brooding than usual. In fact, he sounds celebratory, relatively speaking. With the solos concluded, the full theme is reprised to the fade-out of another Skatalites classic.

'Coconut Rock' (aka 'Passing Through')
'Coconut Rock' was originally released as 'Passing Through', credited to Roland Alphonso And The Skatalites. However, it should not be confused with a different song called 'Passing Through' that a re-formed Skatalites line-up recorded in 1984 and performed on tour. Nor should it be confused with 'Coconut Ska', The Skatalites' instrumental rendition of 'Sly Mongoose'. When it was pressed as 'Coconut Rock', the label attributed the recording to The Skatalites.

But neither title is truly accurate, because the song is actually a cover of a 1962 instrumental by Cuban percussionist and bandleader Mongo Santamaria called 'Get The Money'. (Santamaria's music was apparently a favorite amongst ska musicians. His recordings provided melodies for other Skatalites instrumentals, such as 'President Kennedy', described later in this chapter and for several by Baba Brooks described later in this book; pages 111–12.) The Skatalites mined the fine original for all that it was worth and turned it into a sublime piece of ska jazz.

A brief, mysterious rhythm guitar-led intro builds anticipation for the song's theme. It comes in two parts. First,a fine jazz melody led by trumpet with sax in tow, as another sax and harmonica blow the ska chop. Elaborate and tuneful, this melody alone could have carried the song, but there is much more to come. The second part of the theme suddenly enters, as a triplet of horn swells are heard, sounding like three surges of utter joy. They are answered by a short sax solo, and the three surges are heard again, daring you not to throw your hands in the air at each one. A sax solo from Alphonso and one on trumpet from Moore are then heard. Both are long and heady – a shade more jazz abstract than the norm for a Skatalites song. But because this is The Skatalites, melody and rhythm are fully honored. The themes are reprised and played to fade-out. Though perhaps the most ecstatic of all great Skatalites instrumentals, 'Coconut Rock' is not compiled as often as most of their other classics. It can be found on Soul Jazz Records' CD compilation called *Studio One Scorcher*.

'Dick Tracy'

'Dick Tracy' packs a lot of music into its less-than-3-minute length. It opens with a brief piano-led introduction that might have passed as R&B were it not for the manically honking sax. Then, with horns in unison, an acrobatic theme, rapid and tumbling, is heard while the non-brass instruments play a complementary line. This theme is retired and gives way to a second one. Still in unison, a *wicked* melody of long notes filled with bluesy yearning is heard. Roland Alphonso's sax and Dizzy Moore's trumpet each solo, as Don Drummond plays a counter-phrase underneath. Drummond then supplies a solo of his own, more aggressive than his norm. The second theme is heard again, closing the composition. Whew! 'Dick Tracy' would prove to have staying power. It's the one classic track that the re-formed Skatalites always include in their live set. It was also covered in Jamaica Jazz-style by Dean Fraser on *Big Up!*, an album discussed later in this book (page 535).

'Dr. Ring Ding'

Perhaps owing to its odd billing to Roland Alphonso & The Soul Brothers (and sometimes being attributed to Jackie Mittoo and The Soul Brothers), 'Dr. Ring Ding' is an unsung Skatalites classic, not appearing on any of the many best-of compilations for the group. It's based on a non-Jamaican song, 'Twine Time', a horns and organ soul workout by Alvin Cash and The Crawlers that reached number 14 on the US charts in 1963. It was perfect fodder for a ripping ska scorcher.

It opens with an introduction that's hearty fare for a ska fan. A rippling drum-roll calls up a substantial syncopated horn riff, as a sax bleats the ska chop. The riff repeats, building anticipation, promising a great theme. But before the introduction can finish, the boundaries between it, the theme and the solos become blurred, courtesy of Dizzy Moore. His trumpet invades the intro, providing its melody with a conclusion. This gives way to his long lead, as Moore establishes an ever-evolving, always-appealing theme. His playing is emotional, filled with both longing and joy. Eventually, he hands off to the saxmen. Roland Alphonso and then Tommy McCook continue interpreting the theme with long solos. Dizzy then reprises the theme, providing the song with another solo right through the fade-out. The backing and all four solos are pure, solid ska gold.

Three mixes of the song have been released. The original version, released as a 45-rpm single, has never appeared on CD. But the other two versions are more easily obtained. Each gives us a glimpse of the birth of DJ reggae and for this reason, the story of Dr. Ring Ding is continued at the beginning of 'More great DJ songs' (Chapter 45).

'Fidel Castro'

The introduction of 'Fidel Castro' builds an air of excitement. It begins with rhyth-mic jam led by Lloyd Knibb working out his cymbals, a serious bass line and piano sounding the ska chop. As sax takes over the latter, a short edgy theme is then heard. Played by several horns in unison, it's repeated a number of times before its key changes, increasing the tension. The tension is maintained through the song's two solos. First up is Tommy McCook, his playing filled with intelligence and feel-ing. Then comes Don Drummond with all of the idiosyncrasies of his playing on full display. He's quiet and introspective, with passages of wailing anguish. At a minute and a half, this is one of the longest solos in a Skatalites song. Because of its length, rather than the expected reprise of the theme, Drummond plays on to fade-out, taking care to make a slight return to the theme on his own. Never let-ting up, 'Fidel Castro' is a pressure cooker of a ska song.

'President Kennedy'

'President Kennedy' is The Skatalites at their easy-going best. Harmonica holds down the ska chop, giving the song a merry mento sound – a rare touch of the rural in The Skatalites' otherwise urban sound.

The melody and horn arrangement are relaxed and accessible, taken from another Mongo Santamaria song, 'Yeh-Yeh!', from 1963. The mid-song break fea-tures just one solo, a relaxed sax performance from Roland Alphonso. 'President Kennedy' is the perfect Skatalites instrumental for a day in the park.

'Roll On Sweet Don' (aka 'Heaven And Earth' or 'Nanny's Corner')

'Roll On Sweet Don' demonstrates the familiarity derived from long association that, along with their individual talent, makes The Skatalites such a crack unit. Having played together for years before ska arose and working together non-stop since, every Skatalite knew in detail the others' nuances and how best to complement what they were playing. Listen to the sharp, ominous groove of an introduction that is constructed by the non-brass instruments. Listen to how the brass theme adds a layer of dark melody that builds on the song's foreboding underpinnings. Listen to how the trumpet begins to harmonize with the trom-bone, joining in tentatively at first, then more fully as the theme is repeated, and how Knibb shows approval with a flurry of cymbals. Listen to how, by the final time through, the sax has opportunistically jumped aboard, further enriching the theme.

Drummond changes to a new, enthusiastic riff, and uses it as a diving board into deep waters. He solos, leaving other horns to take over the riff. In the depths, Drummond produces a musical embodiment of the feeling that some-thing important has been irrevocably lost. Meanwhile, the underlying riff seems to be urging him to surface. A sax solo follows that splits the emotional differ-ence, arbitrating between the polar moods. The theme is reprised to fade-out, this time with all three horns in full unison, fanning out the harmonics pleasingly. By this point, The Skatalites have made it easy to take their mastery for granted.

Justin Yap as producer

Born in 1944 in Kingston, the teenaged Phillip "Justin" Yap worked in his family's ice-cream parlor/restaurant. It was there that he found himself being drawn into Jamaica's music industry, first by setting up a small sound system that he named Top Deck, to attract more business to the restaurant from fellow teens. From there, to impress a girl, he moved into songwriting and production, leading to his label of the same name. Uniquely among his peers, Yap took pride in paying his musicians well, in cash and on time. He paid The Skatalites twice the rate of his competitors, and supplied the studio with food, drink, and ganja, fine treatment compared to what they were accustomed to. All of this helped to stimulate great playing in the few sessions that yielded the songs discussed below. Yap would leave Jamaica and record production at the end of the ska era, emigrating to New York City. His experiences there included working as a taxi driver, in the computer industry, and serving in the Vietnam War. Justin Yap moved back to Jamaica in the 1990s, and passed away from liver cancer in 1999.

'Ringo Rides' (aka 'Ringo')

Sometimes credited to Johnny Moore & The Skatalites, 'Ringo Rides' may have been a response to another ska band's hit. 'Bonanza Ska' by Carlos Malcolm & His Afro-Jamaican Rhythms was a raucous ska rendition of the theme from the hit American TV Western. Hugely popular in 1964, it was said to have outsold every other record in Jamaica that year, giving Malcomb the biggest hit of his career. It inspired other records, like 'Beverly Hillbilly Ska' by The William Granville Orchestra (which may be the only ska song that includes banjo) and 'Ska-ing West' by Sir Lord Comic & His Cowboys. It also inspired The Skatalites to answer and outdo 'Bonanza Ska' the next year with a Western-themed cover of their own. The resulting record was the completely improbable 'Ringo Rides'.

'Ringo Rides' should not be confused with 'Ringo's Theme', The Skatalites' similarly named cover of The Beatles song, 'This Boy'. But 'Ringo Rides' is a cover, too, although its source is from further away than either the UK or the American West. It faithfully employs the melody of 'Ringo Oiwake', a beloved Japanese song first recorded in 1952 by singer Hibari Misora, a popular artist in her native country. What musical alchemists The Skatalites were! Working their magic on Misora's wistful, unmistakably Japanese melody, they achieved a completely successful transmutation, turning it into a rousing ska theme for a Western movie. Though not the hit that 'Bonanza Ska' was, 'Ringo Rides' has undeniably aged better than Malcomb's song, with artistry that makes 'Bonanza Ska' sound like a novelty record by comparison.

Yap adds a cinematic touch by opening the song with the sound of galloping horses. Someone shouts, "Here comes Ringo!", gunshots are fired, and the body of the song begins. The theme, played by sax and trumpet in unison, does not alter Misora's melody, but the Japanese inflections do not come over in this context. Instead, the theme has a tone and sweep that invoke horsemen galloping across an open plain. Lovely as it is, the theme is regrettably brief, as is the whole song. At 2:15 minutes, it is the shortest Skatalites song discussed here. There is still time for trumpet and sax to each provide snaking solos, and for the theme to be briefly reprised. Several more gunshots are fired as the short but remarkable 'Ringo Rides' rides off into the sunset. The re-formed Skatalites would remake it as 'Ringo' in Jamaica Jazz style on their 1997 *Ball Of Fire* CD.

'Ska-Ra-Van'

With 'Ska-Ra-Van', The Skatalites add to the huge canon of covers of Duke Ellington's 1937 jazz classic, 'Caravan', as well as to the list of great Skatalites tracks. The melody of 'Caravan' is fully honored while the rhythm is transformed into crackling ska. A mid-song sax solo that abruptly hands off mid-phrase to a trumpet solo further celebrates one of the best-known melodies in the history of jazz. Three takes are available, with take 1 recommended. Take 2 is nearly indistinguishable, except for the solos and the fact that it breaks down in its final seconds. Take 3 is more calm and composed compared to the rocking pace of the other two.

'Confucius'

The title 'Confucius' may have been to honor the fact that the producer Yap is a Chinese Jamaican, since the same sessions also resulted in instrumentals called 'Chinatown' and 'China Clipper'. But, unlike the other two tracks, 'Confucius' avoids the clichéd oriental melodies that were popular go-tos for reggae musicians from ska through roots. Ultimately, it's another example of the often arbitrary naming of Skatalites instrumentals, as the hard-hitting arrangement would lead you to believe that 'Confucius' was an action hero rather than a philosopher. This 'Confucius' is unrelentingly tough and aggressive.

A cool introduction, led by taut electric guitar from Jah Jerry and typically great Lloyd Knibb drums, sets the stage for the song's very physical theme. With sax and trumpet playing in lockstep, lots of notes fly by. This is the fastest, busiest theme of any Skatalites song discussed here, even outdoing the first part of the 'Dick Tracy' theme in this regard. After this has been played through twice, the song's only solo is heard. Even the supporting underphrase is tough and cutting, and Don Drummond provides perhaps his most aggressive trombone in any Skatalites song. After this treat from Don, the theme is reprised and this 'Confucius' *mash up de place* to its final note.

'Smiling'

'Smiling' is as aptly named as 'Confucius' is incongruously. First, the overall sound is a very happy one. That it's a Don Drummond composition is a reminder that this artist's range was broader than the introspective sounds for which he is most remembered. Second, listening to the arrangement and musicianship of this Skatalites masterpiece is unfailingly a smile-inducing experience.

Like 'Man In The Street', 'Smiling' opens with a well-developed, playful introduction. Trombone leads bass and drums in a syncopated eight-note phrase. It is answered by six simple strums from Jah Jerry Haynes on electric guitar, giving him a rare moment out front. The exchange is repeated and the fun builds as, the fourth time through, Lloyd Knibb breaks things open, pre-empting Haynes with a short solo. This concludes one of the best Skatalites introductions and launches one of their best themes.

But Knibbs is far from done. As if shot out of a cannon, he studs the theme with an abundance of tight rolls, Latin flair, and a mother lode of rim shots. This continues unabated through the solos and the theme's reprise, giving us not only the single best performance from the great Lloyd Knibb, but the premier virtuoso drum performance of the ska era. It's a joy to hear.

The theme has two parts, and is played through twice. First, an exceedingly upbeat, joyful march is played in unison on trombone and trumpet, expanding on the trombone's melody of the introduction. It slips into the more serious second part, with long yearning notes and majestic feel. Meanwhile, in turn, sax, electric guitar or both play the throbbing ska chop. Drummond provides the song's lone solo – a tremendous trombone performance. Rather than the quiet, downbeat playing he is justly famous for, it's energetic and bustling with life, in keeping with the song's title. He sounds like a man who is surprised to find himself happy, and is enjoying the experience. Don Drummond smiles, and the ska is glorious.

Dada Tewari as producer

'Bellevue Special'

Producer Dada Tewari is best remembered for the mento singles released on his Caribou label in the late 1950s. However, he also recorded enough ska singles in the following decade to fill a CD. Only one of these singles was by a Skatalite, a pair of Don Drummond sides made available in 2004 on the Trojan Records CD compilation called *Gaz Mayall Presents Top Ska Tunes*. Their musical power and emotional payload combine like a kick to the stomach.

Knowing that Don Drummond wrote 'Bellevue Special' just after his deteriorating mental health forced a stay at Kingston's Bellevue mental hospital makes you hear it with new ears. The theme is fine, but has an air of desperation. The insistence of the ska chop played on guitar by Jah Jerry seems overwhelming. Drummond has the only solo. It opens with him wailing and thrashing as if in distress. It then falls back to a sad longing before tapering off and finally vanishing, leaving just a portentous absence. Even the supporting phrase that Dizzy Moore repeats under Drummond's solo – a mournful segment of the theme – is emotionally charged. 'Bellevue Special' is a remarkable song. It shows The Skatalites able to convey the turmoil and sadness of the band's current situation without it impacting their impeccable playing.

Only the first half of the last statement is true for a second take of the song, the single's B-side, released with the telling title of 'No More'. Here, the unfailingly sharp Skatalites sound is harried and frayed. And Drummond's long, desolate solo sounds like it's being played by a truly forlorn soul. It is as if 'Bellevue Special' was a brave front that could not be maintained in this take; Drummond's deteriorating condition is now affecting not just the man, but the group. The longest Skatalites song here at over 3:30 minutes, it's a difficult ride. And an augury for the end of a Jamaican great, a suffering man who was beyond his friends' ability to help. A short time after this session, Don Drummond's career ended with the notorious murder of his girlfriend and his subsequent death in prison.

7 Bob Marley & The Wailers, Part 1: Ska and more at Studio One

The story of the music of Bob Marley & The Wailers includes a galaxy of reggae talent. Besides Bob Marley, there are singers Peter Tosh, Bunny Wailer, Junior Braithwaite and The I-Threes; backing musicians The Skatalites, Ernest Ranglin, The Upsetters and The Dynamites; producers Coxsone Dodd, Lee Perry, Leslie Kong, The Wailers and Chris Blackwell; and others in each category. It's a fascinating musical journey that resulted in approximately a thousand tracks, beginning with Marley's first solo recordings in 1962 and continuing with the posthumous releases and the occasional new release from a surviving member of the Wailers family such as Bunny Wailer, Rita Marley, Marcia Griffiths or Judy Mowatt.

The extent, stylistic breadth, and consistent high quality of Bob Marley & The Wailers' catalog make it indisputable that they are the greatest artists in the history of reggae. Calling them the greatest musical act to ever come from the Caribbean would stir little debate, and this would hold true even if the focus was expanded to all of the third world. In fact, the career accomplishments of Bob Marley & The Wailers put them in a pantheon with such international contemporaries as The Beatles, Bob Dylan, The Rolling Stones, Pink Floyd, and few, if any, others.

What made Bob Marley & The Wailers so great? The vocals? Well, the vocals were accomplished, emotional and varied, with great leads from several Wailers and equally impressive backing harmonies, but this alone is not the main reason for their success. For example, Bob Marley's favorite singer, Dennis Brown, was as good as or better than any Wailer, but he did not become a household name outside of reggae circles. The instrumentation? The Wailers were always backed by a star-studded array of the best musicians in Jamaica. But not to exclusivity, as other singers and vocal groups used the same backing musicians, yet did not achieve the same artistic heights or massive popularity. The same is true of producers, as the Wailers worked with most of the best, but, again, never exclusively. Charisma? The Wailers had it in abundance, but, again, did not have a reggae exclusive on the trait. The Wailers had all these things, but what distinguished them from the pack was the fact that they were great songwriters. Bob Marley was gifted in this regard, and Peter Tosh and Bunny Wailer, though not as prolific, each wrote a body of great songs. In song after song, Bob Marley & The Wailers created perfect vehicles for their vocal talents, their personal charisma, and the skills of their bands and their producers. This formula also allowed them to make the leap that took reggae from the era of recording singles to the era of recording an album's worth of material at a time.

This book makes no attempt to add to the sufficient number of Bob Marley biographies available. The focus here is on the records; as such, only the biographical detail that pertains to the creation of The Wailers' music is of interest. The quantity and consistent quality of the group's recordings give us a lot to talk about, occupying many chapters in this book. It is a body of work that demands special attention, so in addition to focusing on their many great songs together, we'll at least touch on each song The Wailers released as a group and on each song Marley released after they broke up, as well as selected solo tracks by Bunny Wailer and Pete Tosh, in order to tell the complete story of the music of Bob Marley & The Wailers.

By now, just about every Bob Marley & The Wailers track has found its way to CD. This is a fairly recent development. For years, hundreds of the group's best tracks were only available on Jamaican singles that were long out of print. Fans made do with incomplete collections on multigenerational cassette copies of scratchy 45s taped from radio broadcasts. This situation began to be rectified from the 1990s, when several labels began nearly comprehensive reissue campaigns. This was excellent news, but the pendulum never fell back, as posthumous Bob Marley remixes and after-the-fact duet albums would appear. "Come and see the Mona Lisa – now sporting a new smile as painted over by a popular new painter!" Not surprisingly, these failed to add to the musical enjoyment of the original recordings. But such releases are easy enough to ignore, and, on balance, it's far better for there to be too much Bob Marley & The Wailers material released than not enough.

Prelude – Bob Marley's solo career at Beverly's

Robert Nesta Marley was born in 1944 to a musical family in the rural town of Nine Mile in Jamaica's Saint Ann Parish. From his earliest days, he was exposed to live mento, quadrille, and Jamaican folk music. As a boy, he announced to his mother, Cedella Booker, that he was finished with school and was instead a singer, demonstrating with a performance of the calypso/mento song, 'Don't Touch Me Tomato'. Early in his teens, he and his mother moved from the country to the city, relocating in Kingston, as so many of the rural poor did. There, he was able to hear American R&B on the radio and on jukeboxes, and was enamored of these new sounds.

Marley began his recording career as a solo artist. Before the Wailers were formed, a friend of his, the newly recorded Jimmy Cliff, obtained for Marley an audition with a new producer on the scene, Leslie Kong.

Kong was born in Kingston in 1933. Like Justin Yap, another Jamaican producer who started work around the same time, Kong came from a Chinese-Jamaican background and was employed in his family's Kingston-based ice-cream parlor when he moved into production. Kong would prove to have a longer and more successful music career than his competitor, even though it had an abrupt and tragic end.

Kong ran the Beverly's ice-cream parlor and record shop with his older brothers. It was there that Jimmy Cliff took a chance and pitched 'Dearest Beverly', a song plugging the shop, in the hope that Kong would produce him. This cold call proved to be fortuitous for both men, launching the careers of one of the most famous of all reggae singers and, for too short a time, one of its greatest producers. Kong would die of a heart attack in 1971 at the age of thirty-eight.

Marley's audition with Kong was successful, and the producer would release four Bob Marley ska tracks on his new Beverly's label in 1962. Three of those tracks survived, and two can be heard on CD. The third is the province of collectors, sitting in some unexplained blind spot, eluding every Bob Marley and/or ska LP and CD compilation for no good reason whatsoever. The fourth, 'Terror', remains something of a legend, as sources are sure it exists, but no one has ever seen a copy or (outside of Bunny Wailer) can say they have heard the song.

'Judge Not'; 'Do You Still Love Me'

The first recording that any Wailer made was 'Judge Not' by a teenaged Bob Marley. His vocal is earnest, mannered, and competent. He saves a rise in intensity for the song's conclusion. Instrumentally, 'Judge Not' is a rather relaxed ska track with an equally at ease saxophone solo by Roland Alphonso. It's distinguished by the surprising presence of a penny whistle, an instrument far more at home in mento than in ska, giving the song something of a country feel. The session's drummer, Arkland "Drumbago" Parks, was known to play this instrument, but because Jamaican studios were single-track affairs at this point in time, he could not have played both instruments. 'Judge Not' is an original song, and Bob introduces themes that he would return to time and time again throughout his career: self-acceptance, intolerance of being unfairly judged by others, disgust at hypocrites, the rocky road of life, and warnings of divine retribution as he employs Bible quotes to make his case. From this fine acorn, the mighty oak.

'Do You Still Love Me', the flipside of 'Judge Not', is Bob's first love song. An uncomplicated sentiment over a happy bopping ska backing (featuring harmonica by the wonderfully named Charlie Organaire, who was born Charles Cameron) makes 'Do You Still Love Me' a simple pleasure. There is no accounting for why it remains one of the very few uncompiled Bob Marley songs, largely unheard since its release as a single five decades earlier.

'One Cup Of Coffee'

'One Cup Of Coffee' is a cover of a song by the American country singer Claude Gray. This comes as no surprise considering the lyrics. Marley would have had little experience with divorce lawyers and alimony at that time and place in his life.

The ska here is more sophisticated than on the previous single. It features piano, a striding chord progression, and a springy bounce from the ska chop played by electric guitar, saxophone and harmonica in different combinations. Roland Alphonso is again on hand to provide a sax solo that briefly riffs on the old American folk song, 'Turkey In The Straw,' perhaps in a salute to the song's country source. Marley's vocal remains as controlled as it was on the previous two songs. This would soon change.

Though there was nothing wrong with these sides, they did not catch on. Sales of Bob Marley's Beverly's singles disappointed and he was dumped by Kong. These early solo records would prove to be something of a false start to the most successful career in reggae. Two years later, his recording career would resume at Studio One as a member of the Wailers. And it would do so in memorable fashion, as their very first track was a hit, launching The Wailers permanently into stardom.

Big group ska at Studio One

Neville O'Riley Livingston, one day to be known as Bunny Wailer, was born in 1947, gifted with the voice of an angel. Also hailing from Nine Mile, he became a boyhood friend of Bob's. With Bunny playing his home-made guitar, they played mento together. Following a path that was similar to Marley's, Bunny and his father moved to Kingston when he was a boy. When Bob's mother and Bunny's father became live-in lovers, the boys were raised for a time as brothers. This was in Trench Town, an impoverished area of Kingston. The boys continued to make music together, now concentrating on recruiting members for a vocal group.

Winston Hubert McIntosh was born in 1944 in rural Westmoreland, moving to Kingston as a boy to live with an aunt. Soon to be known as Peter Tosh, he was the most accomplished musician of the original Wailers, playing both guitar and piano. The son of a preacher, he came to music by way of the church (as many other reggae performers did), which influenced his early repertoire of songs and singing style. As teens, Bob and Bunny encountered Tosh performing on the street. Recognizing his abilities and realizing how his lower-pitched voice would complement their higher ones, they brought him into the fold. This established the core three Wailers, who for the next ten years would produce a fantastic catalog of recordings and prove to be the greatest of all reggae vocal groups. But perhaps to match their outsized ambition, they continued to supplement the group with additional members.

Along with other aspiring singers, the fledgling Wailers had begun to meet in the Trench Town tenement yard of Joe Higgs, of Higgs & Wilson fame. Higgs was keen to help tutor these young people in singing and harmony. It was in Higgs's yard that another vocal group, The Wailing Souls, also came together. And it was there that The Wailers added two more members. Franklin Delano Alexander Braithwaite was born in 1949. Unlike the other Wailers, he was a native of Kingston. Known as Junior, he was the youngest Wailer, and was thought to have the best voice of the four. No other Wailer could match the strength and technical proficiency of his cutting soprano. He would sing lead on four Wailers songs before emigrating to the USA in 1964. He returned to Jamaica in the 1980s to resume work with Bunny Wailer for a short time. In 1999, Braithwaite was murdered in Kingston. Beverly Kelso was recruited for the very high female backing vocals that were so prized in Jamaican R&B and ska. After a year, she departed and her role was filled at intervals by Ermine "Cherry Green" Bramwell, and then by Rita Anderson (soon to be Rita Marley), amongst others. The Wailers had more voices and a bigger vocal sound than any other ska act. They were also the only ska group to mix male and female voices; all other Jamaican vocal groups were exclusively male. The next group to do so would be Black Uhuru, when, more than ten years later, they added Puma Jones to their instantly classic line-up. There hasn't been another since.

The Wailers had four members who could sing lead, and three of the four could write songs. The group would eventually break up, launching several successful solo careers. All of this, and the fact that their recording careers began at around the same time, begs comparison to The Beatles. Even the lifespans of the groups were similar: The Beatles recorded together for nine years, while the original Wailers lasted a year longer. And like The Beatles, Bob Marley & The Wailers produced a catalog of a quality and consistency unmatched in their musical genre.

Producer Coxsone Dodd certainly recognized and made the most of this glut of talent. From 1963 to 1966 Dodd would produce Wailers singles featuring each of the four taking turns as the lead vocalist, most frequently Marley, and most belatedly Livingston. It is interesting to note that, at this point in time, Bob Marley did not have one of the better voices in the group. R&B specialist Junior Braithwaite's voice was clearly technically superior to Bob's, though his early departure from the group and lack of songwriting contributions make him something of a sidebar in the crowded Wailers story. Bunny Wailer's voice was at least as good as Bob's and certainly was more consistent – Bob's lead vocals ranged from triumphant to out of his depth in these early days of the group. Additionally, Bunny was an infinitely better backing singer, perhaps too valuable in the latter role, so that it took him the longest to be given the spotlight. For that matter, Peter Tosh, though clearly a less charismatic singer than Bob in these early days, did not have the problem staying on key that Bob sometimes displayed at Studio One. And Tosh, too, was a better backing singer, whether in his natural baritone or in a higher register. But what Bob sometimes lacked in technical proficiency, he made up for with his exuberance and charisma. Jamaican audiences had a great appreciation of *youth singers*, so a cracking voice or a slip off key was not only accepted, it delighted. And perhaps they could hear the seeds of greatness in this nascent voice that would improve to reach its full maturity after The Wailers' tenure at Studio One. In time, Bob Marley would prove to have one of the best voices in all of reggae.

Dodd put The Wailers to work. He paired them with the top backing bands of the time, most frequently and famously The Skatalites. They recorded ska, R&B, gospel and a bit of rock steady at the end. In spite of The Wailers' songwriting prowess, Dodd also had them cover hit songs from calypso and mento, as well as American hits from R&B, folk, soul, pop, and gospel. (This brings us back to The Beatles comparison, as both groups would record a large number of covers alongside their original gems in the earliest phase of their careers, only to leave this practice behind later on.) Dodd even used them as backing vocalists for other Studio One singers. One of these was Lee Perry, beginning the long and varied collaboration between him and Bob Marley & The Wailers. In just over two years at Studio One, The Wailers released about eighty songs, plus half that amount again of alternative takes, remixes, demos, and collaborations with other artists. The size and quality of this catalog is unmatched in ska, making The Wailers indisputably ska's greatest vocal act, just as The Skatalites were its greatest instrumental act. Nearly all of these songs can be heard on a series of CDs on the Heartbeat label. Let's dive into this delightfully unmanicured catalog.

'Simmer Down'

'Simmer Down', the very first track recorded by The Wailers, was a departure from Bob's humble solo singles. It was big in every respect. The five Wailers amassed what can only be called a vocal assault. Bob's lead vocal is intense, with an emotional abandon barely hinted at on his Beverly's sides. His lyrics are bigger too, as he unleashes a bold social commentary that is urgent and confrontational. The instrumental backing comes from The Skatalites, then with a headcount of nine musicians, producing a big ska sound. (Imagine the session with a total of fourteen performers, all having to get things right on Dodd's one-track recording equipment. It's enough to give today's tool-rich producers the night terrors.) Not only was its sound bigger than Bob's solo recordings, so was its success. A huge hit, 'Simmer Down' sold by one account 70,000 copies in Jamaica upon its release.

It opens with The Skatalites sounding a victorious theme, led by horns in unison. Then, covering a wide spectrum of tone, the four backing vocalists sing the titular refrain; it sounds as if we are being addressed by the massed voices of Jamaica's young adults. Over this, Marley enters passionately to deliver his message. With it, he supplies his best vocal at Studio One, right out of the gate.

Though some have taken it to be a description of a relationship going bad, 'Simmer Down' is in fact a rude boy song, even though the term is not used. It warns of the consequences if the escalating violence of Kingston's young ghetto toughs is not controlled. (In this context, "getting dropped" means killed, not dumped by a lover. And "I'm-a leaving you today" is directed at bad company, not to a lover.) This makes 'Simmer Down', if not the first, one of the first rude boy songs, launching an impressive string of such songs by The Wailers and many other artists that enriched ska, peaked in rock steady and went on all the way into the ragga era. Two Jamaican folk sayings are employed by Bob to help make his argument, in a reggae practice by no means limited to him. "What sweet nanny goat run him belly" means that what tastes good to the goat may still upset its stomach, or indulging your desires will have consequences. (This saying made its first recorded appearance in Lord Power's golden-age mento single 'I'm Sorry For Myself'.) And a warning against being caught unaware is made by a simple reminder that chickens are merry even when a hawk is close by. Bob would return to the wellspring of Jamaican folk sayings many times again.

Always the consummate backing band, The Skatalites richly add to – without stepping on – the crowded vocal picture. The ska is glorious, complete with the classic squonking sax-based ska chop, Lloyd Knibb's idiosyncratic playing on the cup of the cymbal and the aforementioned horn theme. A saxophone solo seems to take heed of the song's title, as it plays a mellowed rendition of the melody heard in the lead vocal. A challenging message, laced with familiar folk sayings delivered by youthful voices and backed with cutting-edge ska, the song hit Kingston's youth like a guided missile.

Though he later remade numerous tracks from this era, Marley went easy on his career-launching hit. It appeared briefly in 'All In One', a medley of past hits The Wailers recorded in 1971. There is also a bootleg recording from 1975 of a reunited Marley, Tosh and Livingston, bolstered by The I-Threes, performing 'Simmer Down' live in Jamaica, slowed from ska to a roots reggae tempo, and losing much of its magic in the process. Bunny Wailer revived this song in 1982 and again in 1995, both times on tribute albums to his fallen brother.

More big-group Wailers ska
The Wailers and Skatalites would follow 'Simmer Down' with a parcel of other rousing, high-energy, big-group ska tracks. But no song was more similar to it than 'Maga Dog', which launched Peter Tosh into the spotlight with his first lead vocal and song authorship. Following the same recipe, Tosh crafts a fine follow-up to The Wailers' first hit. It has a similar instrumental sound, and it too has an impassioned lead vocal and lyrics that employ a Jamaican folk saying. He warns that feeling too sorry for a maga (skinny) dog may result in getting bitten. This somewhat ungenerous sentiment is not surprising, as Tosh would display a streak of disappointment in human nature throughout his career. So the die was cast early for the differences in temperament that would become most pronounced in the post-Wailers solo careers of Bob and Peter. Tosh sings 'Maga Dog' in his natural baritone, as opposed to the higher register he typically employed at this time when singing harmony. Though Marley never fully remade 'Simmer Down', 'Maga Dog' became a signature song for Tosh; he remade it several times through his career right up to his last album.

The big-group line-up recorded ska covers of several traditional spirituals. The first was Tosh's sonorous take on 'Amen'. Another was 'I Am Going Home', based on 'Swing Low, Sweet Chariot', featuring Marley back on lead vocal and a Don Drummond trombone solo. Later, we will see that other spirituals quickly followed, with and without a ska beat. At the opposite end of the spectrum, quite unspiritual is 'Mister Talkative'. It finds rude boy Marley threatening the titular big-mouth with a protracted beating, recommending that the police be called if it's ever to end. It would later be remade as 'Mister Chatterbox'. Bob would never be so gleefully violent again. The driving 'Destiny' features a sax solo that touches on 'Pop Goes The Weasel' of all things. It's an early example of one of Bob's keystone themes – that we should all get along: "Love one another as how you love your mother." 'Donna' is a love song with a touch of R&B to it. It has a fine Dizzy Moore trumpet solo that cannot resist the apparently powerful lure of another visit to 'Pop Goes The Weasel'. 'I Don't Need Your Love' finds Marley's youthful exuberance taking precedent over disciplined singing. The similarly named 'Your Love' is rousing and melodic, using the large vocal group to its full advantage. Marley shares the lead with Tosh, with the chorus of high voices also getting moments in the sun. It's a solid song that got somewhat lost amidst all the ska The Wailers recorded. Seek it out.

Other Wailers/Skatalites big-band ska songs were in a less boisterous style than the tracks above. 'Do You Remember', a song that would later be remade, features an R&B feel and a more relaxed tempo. The latter is also true of 'Sound The Trumpet', Christmas ska that takes its melody from ' 'Tis The Season To Be Jolly', while the sax solo visits 'Santa Claus Is Coming To Town', and Bob affects a show-business voice. 'Nobody Knows' is a cover of Louis Armstrong's 'Nobody Knows The Trouble I've Seen' and features a nice swing to its rhythm. 'Dance With Me' nicely adapts the melody from the Drifters' famous 'On Broadway'. 'Tell Them Lord' is about a tough life of no work and no food. It features a long trumpet solo from Dizzy Moore and instrumental similarities to 'Destiny'. 'Wings Of A Dove' is a traditional spiritual that was popular in Jamaica, now sprouting ska wings. 'Climb The Ladder' features the chorus, "The harder they come, the harder they fall", years before Jimmy Cliff's classic hit song. 'Hoot Nanny Hoot' is absurd fun, opening instrumentally with the incongruous melody of 'Alouette'. Tosh's lyrics are notably innocent and carefree compared to the more serious tone that typifies most of his writing. It is often said that this song was inspired by *Hootenanny*, an American folk-music TV show that was popular in Jamaica, but the lyrics don't especially bear this out. Unlike The Wailers' other big-group ska songs, the backing band for the cover of American singer and songwriter Brook Brenton's 'True Confession' is not The Skatalites; another band with a big sound is used. Two instruments dominate: Roy Richards successfully sells the ska beat on harmonica and provides a solo, while Ernest Ranglin plays a lively slashing rhythm guitar throughout and provides a rhythm guitar solo, atypical for him but very enjoyable. 'Straight And Narrow Way' features Junior Braithwaite's first lead vocal, sounding both youthful and strong, while 'Habits', his other ska lead vocal, finds him more mature. As we will see, Braithwaite would make a greater mark with the two R&B singles on which he sang lead than he did with ska. Meanwhile, Bunny would not get a lead vocal until after the big group thinned.

R&B

While at Studio One, The Wailers also recorded a variety of R&B songs that were completely lacking the ska rhythm. Even though The Wailers were not as naturally suited to this style as they were to ska, Dodd seems to have been determined for them to keep alive the music from the start of the decade. He would pair each song with one of several backing bands, seeking the right instrumental sound. Again, most frequently but not exclusively, Marley was featured on lead vocals. Unvaryingly, these R&B tracks were love songs.

The Skatalites were often used, though the line-up was sometimes different from those we have seen. Lyn Taitt often takes the place of Jah Jerry Hinds on guitar and Vin Gordon may be heard on trombone rather than Don Drummond, two more additions to the deep talent pool that is the Wailers' story. And often, there are fewer horns or even no horns at all. One of the effects of this was to allow keyboardist Jackie Mittoo a bigger role than he had previously enjoyed. There is the touching R&B ballad 'I'm Still Waiting', with two takes available. It would be remade by The Wailers, and Delroy Wilson would have a number 1 hit with a mid-1970s cover version. The gentle 'Wages Of Love' features an overwrought lead vocal by Marley, singing exaggeratedly from his throat, with backing vocals by Bunny Wailer and Rita Anderson. Three takes are available. One is a playful rehearsal tape that survived these sessions with just the singers backed by Bob's acoustic guitar. It may be more enjoyable than the two completed takes. 'I Made A Mistake', a cover of an Impressions song, is a bluesy soulful ballad with fine backing vocals from Tosh and Kelso. 'Love Won't Be Mine' finds Marley a bit out of his depth, but with strong vocal support and two takes to choose from. Bunny sang his sole R&B lead on 'I Need You So', a competent Temptations cover whose slow pace requires a bit of patience from a ska fan.

A slightly larger Skatalites line-up was heard on other Wailers R&B songs. 'The Vow', a duet by Bunny and Rita, is a cover of a 1957 song by US doo-wop duo Gene & Eunice. (In 1965, Jamaica saw not one, but two, renditions of this song. The other was recorded by Jackie Edwards & Millicent, as produced by Chris Blackwell.) 'Where's The Girl For Me' is a good, slow-tempo doo-wop, as Bob sings of the difficulties of finding love. 'Ten Commandments Of Love' is a faithful cover of The Moonglows' famous song, and is perhaps most notable for being The Wailers' only Studio One song to top 4 minutes in length. 'And I Love Her' is The Wailers' rendition of the Beatles song. It's cast in more of an R&B mold than rock & roll or ska. The two different takes are good, but all involved somehow fail to master the song. (This was the only time that The Wailers covered The Beatles, while

The Skatalites covered 'This Boy', calling it 'Ringo's Theme'. A less-appreciative ska reaction to The Beatles was heard on 'Got To Go' by Keith & Ken.)

The rocking R&B of 'Can't You See' features a Peter Tosh lead vocal backed by a guitar-bass-drum band led by Lyn Taitt. The same band backs Marley leading Livingston and Tosh for a doo-wop-infused, unlikely but enjoyable cover of Irving Berlin's 'White Christmas'.

The Ernest Ranglin-led band heard in 'True Confessions' (though sans harmonica) is heard on other Wailers R&B songs. 'Where Will I Find', like 'Love Won't Be Mine', is a doo-wop song about finding romance. But here the pace is livelier, the vocals stronger and the overall result better. 'Oh My Darling' is a tender R&B ballad sung as a duet between Marley and future I-Three Marcia Griffiths. 'Teenager In Love' is a faithful cover of the hit song by Dion and The Belmonts. Even better is the delightfully melodic and bluesy 'I Need You' (not to be confused with the similarly named 'I Need You So'). But the best Ranglin-led Wailers R&B tracks – and Junior Braithwaite's finest moments – are the two songs described below. Along with 'Ska Jerk', they are the three finest R&B tracks of The Wailers' Studio One era.

'Don't Ever Leave Me'; 'It Hurts To Be Alone'
Though Junior Braithwaite sang lead on a pair of ska songs in his brief tenure in The Wailers, it's on these two R&B melodramas where he found his forte. They feature a different overall sound from all other Wailers songs, as if they represent the launching of a separate product line under The Wailers brand name. And a successful line at that, albeit one with a brief run. Both songs were hits, but Braithwaite's departure from The Wailers and Jamaica prevented the continuation of songs with this winning formula.

Although they are similar, 'Don't Ever Leave Me' is more imploring, while 'Hurts To Be Alone' is more sorrowful. On each, Braithwaite unfurls his strong, keening, youthful voice and expressive delivery. He nails the R&B ballad form without sacrificing his Jamaican essence. Meanwhile, Ernest Ranglin's four-piece band more than masters the sound of this American form of music. The only tip-off that the musicians are not from the USA is the fact that Ranglin's guitar is just too good – far better than what was typically supplied in the music they are imitating. As powerful as Braithwaite's singing is, Ranglin nearly steals the show by applying his virtuoso jazz chops to stunning guitar solos in each song. Because multiple takes of each song are available, a bounty of solos can be heard. And there's even more to enjoy. The backing vocals are engaging on both songs; the male Wailers are playful on the chorus of 'Don't Ever Leave Me', while the male/female chorus on 'It Hurts To Be Alone' is big and impressive. Richard Ace's piano is an important ingredient on 'Don't Ever Leave Me', and his wandering trebly notes at the song's end are a treat.

The post-Braithwaite Wailers would twice remake 'It Hurts To Be Alone', one rendition leaving much to be desired and the other, part of a medley, being more competent. In 2007 Ranglin recorded a rendition called 'Hurts To Be Alone'. All parties decided to stand pat on 'Don't Ever Leave Me'.

'Ska Jerk'
Though the title and refrain are altered, 'Ska Jerk' is a cover of Junior Walker's funky 1965 soul hit, 'Shotgun'. It gives The Wailers a larger-than-life soul dance number to add to their résumé.

The Skatalites set up a great smoldering groove with piano and tons of sax. One honks the ska chop, allowing an otherwise R&B track to meet the demands of the title. Dodd's production creates layers of murky depth. A jive-talking Marley implores everyone to dance the jerk. He follows Walker's approach, singing with a funky abandon, an R&B style that suits him better than the sometimes staid demands of doo-wop. Meanwhile, Livingston and Tosh repeat the song's title in reverb-dipped falsetto. Roland Alphonso adds a fine mid-song sax solo, and to end the song Dizzy Moore plays an exciting trumpet solo that rates as one of his best. Both solos are backed by groovy "oo-ah"s from Tosh and Livingston, still dripping in reverb. Marley's best R&B track, 'Ska Jerk' sounds unlike anything else from their Studio One days. That is except for the fact that there are two takes of the song to enjoy. Each has its merits, but the choice is not difficult. The one found on the *One Love At Studio One* CD is the hotter take and keeps the party going for 13 seconds longer.

Gospel and spirituals

Just as they did for R&B, Jamaicans had an appetite for another American music form – gospel music and spirituals. We have already seen that The Wailers recorded ska versions of 'Amen' and 'Wings Of A Dove', and we will soon discuss their ska rendition of another spiritual in 'Sinner Man'. They would continue to record such songs into the early 1970s. After that, their music continued to be very spiritual, but in a Rasta way rather than in the traditional one. Dodd also had The Wailers record a number of gospel and spiritual songs that featured more traditional arrangements, rather than a ska backing. If most of The Wailers R&B songs for Coxsone Dodd were good or better by the rough-and-tumble standard of Jamaican R&B, with three standout songs among them, than it's fair to say that their non-ska gospel and spiritual songs were a less-successful body of work. There isn't one great song in the batch, and several are not especially enjoyable listens.

One of the better such songs is 'Have Faith In The Lord', billed to Bob Marley & Spiritual Sisters, from 1966. It bops along amiably in a fusion of late ska, early rock steady and gospel, as Bob musters a good, if sometimes tentative, vocal. Though the chorus is comprised of traditional spiritual sentiments, the verse has lyrics decrying rude boy violence, as well as including Rasta symbolism, as Bob sings about the lion. He's supported by female backing singers and an organ solo.

Frequently forgotten in print and on albums, the song is said to have been collected on a CD called *Rare Singles*.

Lyn Taitt's band backed The Wailers on a trio of gospel tracks. The slow 'Let The Lord Be Seen In Me' features Marley on lead with backing vocals from Beverly Kelso and Cherry Green. Marley gives it his best in a genre that he is not naturally suited to, as Jackie Mittoo sells it on piano. Marley is backed by Livingston and Tosh on 'I Left My Sins', a more energetic song that holds together, but Bob still sounds out of his element. On 'Just In Time', Marley is backed by The Soulettes (Rita Anderson, Marlene "Precious" Gifford and Constantine "Vision" Walker, who would soon play a bigger role in The Wailers story). But little good can be said of this very slow gospel that finds Marley again singing exaggeratedly from his throat. The Skatalites back a Livingston and Anderson competent, if not compelling, duet on 'Bless You'.

Better than any of these are two acoustic recordings that came from the same session that gave us the aforementioned demo of 'Wages Of Love'. One is the traditional spiritual, 'This Train', sung as a duet by Marley and Livingston to acoustic guitar accompaniment from the former. They exchange leads and harmonies in a genuine captured moment. Even with Bob putting on his singing-from-his-throat voice, the vibe is strong. Other than this demo/rehearsal, The Wailers would not record 'This Train' for Dodd, but they did record it twice after departing Studio One, in two different styles, and Bunny Wailer recorded a solo version in his post-Wailers career. 'Where Is My Mother' is also a demo/rehearsal recording with Bob and Bunny singing to an acoustic guitar backing. It features melodramatic lyrics about a boy's mother passing on, and, yes, more throaty Bob. But suddenly the song takes off to the stratosphere, when Livingston takes the lead. Portraying the mother, singing lyrics taken from 'Little Boy Blue' by The Impressions, his voice is so heavenly, it's stunning. Dodd would overdub a band onto this track for release as a single in 1975, though the original simple acoustic recording is preferable.

Bob, Bunny and Peter continue the ska

Braithwaite's departure did little to stem the flow of ska from The Wailers. In addition to The Skatalites, Dodd backed them with new bands, resulting in a wider variety of ska sounds than had been heard before. But the sound would never again be as outsized as it was with the big group.

For example, the eight-piece Mighty Vikings band, featuring guitarist Hux Brown, provides the instrumentation for two love songs, 'Lonesome Feelings' (not to be confused with 'Lonesome Track') and 'There She Goes'. Both have a chugging riddim and a sound falling somewhere between ska and R&B that is affable and energetic. It contrasts nicely with the sharp, almost strident, vocals The Wailers sport on these songs. Both songs would later be remade. The Sharks, a five-piece band featuring guitarist Dwight Pickney, was used on 'Put It On'. It's a good song that would be remade several times in the 1960s and in the early 1970s, slowed down from this breathless initial rendition. The lyrics are a list of positive affirmations.

But most of these songs featured backing from The Skatalites. Even so, they too showed that the sound of ska had diversified from The Wailers' earliest days. For example, there was the excellent 'One Love', a powerful and melodic ska song with a gospel leaning. Calling for righteous behavior and unity, it proved to be reusable for various parties. Dodd would release two remixed versions of the single. Bob would remake it in the following decade. And eventually it was pressed into service by Jamaica's Ministry of Tourism for television commercials overseas. 'Playboy' is an acceptable adaptation of 'Do You Love Me' by The Contours with two takes to choose from. 'Hooligans', aka 'Hooligan Ska', is a harsh reprimand to rude boys with a sound to match. The spirited 'Do It Right' features a fine trombone solo by Vin Gordon. 'Do You Feel The Same Way Too' features a good melody, a memorable sax solo from Lester Sterling and a fine bass line from Lloyd Brevett. 'Lonesome Track' has some nice close harmonies from Bob and Bunny, and is one of several Wailers Studio One tracks to include rhythmic vocal sounds by King Sporty. Guitarist Jah Jerry gets a leg in the spotlight in the song's final moments. 'Another Dance', a cover of a song by Wailers' favorite Curtis Mayfield & The Impressions, is a bit forced. 'Diamond Baby' is a confident, if unremarkable, cover of another Curtis Mayfield song, 'Talking About My Baby'. 'Somewhere To Lay My Head' has spiritual-leaning lyrics and good harmonies, with two takes to choose from. 'Shame and Scandal In The Family' adds a ska rendition to this often-covered Trinidadian calypso song. Originally recorded by Lord Melody in 1962 but based on an earlier song by Sir Lancelot, it swept the Caribbean and beyond. Peter Tosh sings lead here in just one of his dips into the mento/calypso well. 'The Jerk' is bursting with head-over-heels ska energy, though the outcome doesn't quite match the exuberance. Based on the many R&B jerk songs that came from the USA around this time, it should not be confused with The Wailers' far better 'Ska Jerk'. 'Love And Affection' is ska with doo-wop elements. The verse in particular has a good melody and a busy horn refrain juices the chorus. Two takes are available. 'What's New Pussycat' is a cover of the Tom Jones pop hit. It demonstrates two things. First, that Dodd cast a wide net for songs for The Wailers to cover. Second, that when good people have bad ideas, no amount of talent can change things. But it's a handful of other Skatalites-backed tracks that were the standouts as Bob, Bunny and Peter continued the ska.

'Jumbie Jamboree'
We've seen that Peter Tosh recorded a ska cover of the pan-Caribbean hit, 'Shame and Scandal In The Family'. Far more interesting was his adaptation of another. 'Jumbie Jamboree' was originally recorded by Lord Intruder of Tobago in 1953. It was so popular that in Jamaica it became an entrenched part of the mento rep-

ertoire. (It also influenced a later calypso song, 'Love In The Cemetery' by Lord Kitchener, that would result in mento renditions and a DJ reggae rendition by Clint Eastwood & General Saint that is described later in this book; page 441.) The song, which features the famous chorus of "back to back, belly to belly", concerns zombies coming to life and creating havoc "in a New York cemetery". But in Tosh's autobiographical adaptation, the setting is changed to "The Palace – misery!" He tells of a riot at a Wailers performance in Kingston's Palace Theatre. The jumbies of the original song are replaced by hooligans who create mayhem when a power failure causes a premature end to the group's performance. Tosh is clearly disgusted by their behavior, some of which is described when Bob Marley briefly takes lead with a tight rhythmic listing of the violence and injury that was witnessed. For the chorus, Tosh takes from the old Jamaican folk song, 'River Ben Come Down'. But instead of the "Why-o, me glad you come over" of the original, Tosh is just glad to have escaped from the theater. The Skatalites provide a horn-rich introduction as Lloyd Knibb plays standout drums, and fine mid-song solos on trumpet and sax are heard. All of this contributes to 'Jumbie Jamboree' standing distinctly tall from the pack of good ska tracks that The Wailers recorded as a three-member group.

'Cry To Me'
The three core Wailers had been working with The Skatalites for a year and a half by the time 'Cry To Me' was recorded at the end of 1965. This well-oiled super-machine fashioned an emotional song with a nimble arrangement that revealed the sound of ska to be changing. The Skatalites strike up a slower ska tempo, giving the song more breathing space, as music begins its first steps towards rock steady. Livingston and Tosh provide falsetto harmonies that are strong enough to carry the song. They give Marley the freedom to stretch out and roam around the beat, emoting at will about betrayal and heartbreak. After a time, a saxophone begins to wander in and out, like Bob's kindred spirit. It plays lines over Bob's vocal, and Bob sings over the sax, both too distraught to care about one another.

The Wailers' ska had emerged fully formed from their very first recording. With 'Cry To Me', it became instantly clear that ska would evolve over time rather than stagnate, and that with their boundless vocal and songwriting talent, The Wailers were certain to adapt to whatever came next. Two similar takes of 'Cry To Me' are available for comparison. Coxsone Dodd would later remix a dub version and credit it to Dub Specialist, a generic name he used for Studio One dub releases. Bob would remake 'Cry To Me' on his 1976 album, *Rastaman Vibration*.

'Rude Boy'
From the simple, syncopated two-chord piano and guitar opening, The Wailers and Skatalites are completely masterful in the unique ska track, 'Rude Boy'. By omitting some expected elements, 'Rude Boy' becomes stronger, and a special

member of The Wailers' Studio One catalog. The lean instrumentation has no brass other than a sax honking the ska chop. The backing is a continuous vamp without chord changes or a mid-song solo. But these things are not missed, as it provides a riddim that's like a ruled composition book on which The Wailers place blocks of words.

The lyrics are a continuous collection of lines that are each repeated several times to make a stanza, abandoning the verse-chorus-verse song structure. The subjects of these lines are varied. They are phrases from mento ('Wheel And Turn Me'), spiritual, and R&B songs. There's a Jamaican folk saying, a couplet about rude boys and a line of nonsense scat. It serves as a catalog of lyrical themes that would occupy Bob Marley's songwriting for his entire career, but here they are strung together, with no attempt at narrative. It's one of the last lines that may hold the key to this curious song, when "ska quadrille" is repeated. As we have seen, a quadrille consists of four or five "figures", or variations on an instrumental theme, all played in a row. The various stanzas of 'Rude Boy' serve as the figures of this "ska quadrille".

Though Marley or Livingston are occasionally out front, 'Rude Boy' is mostly sung in unison by Bob, Bunny and Peter. This is one of the few Wailers songs that features the big three singing in unison, and that particular sound is always a treat.

Whenever 'Rude Boy' ends, I'm sorry the ride is over. It is fortunate, then, that two equally good mixes are available. The original longer mix includes a run-out not heard on the shorter mix. The shorter mix has some rudimentary dub effects added and alters the number of times each line is repeated, making it a game to try to sing along. The Wailers would later remake this song as 'Rebel's Hop' and Bunny Wailer covered it as 'Walk The Proud Land' in his post-Wailers solo career.

'Rudie' (aka 'Ruddie or Jailhouse')
'Rudie' is the Wailers' most direct dealing with the rude boy phenomenon. Here, the rudie is a ghetto youth, at odds with the oppressive police (and with the local girls, or "peego"), rather than a gangster. It's clearly a pro-rude boy song, as Marley devotes the lyrics to praising the rudie as righteous, wise, growing stronger, and destined to triumph.

Relatively speaking for ska, the pace is slow and the sound introspective. Marley leads with call-and-response vocals, and Tosh and Livingston answer with sing-song responses that are memorably spacey and detached. The entire backing is something of a drone and very spacey for 1966 reggae. And this is before Vin Gordon makes a surprise appearance near the song's end to layer on a trippy jazz trombone solo that melts into place. (This was the Alpha Boy's first session, launching a fine career. Already a Jamaican trombone great, he was all of sixteen years old.) There are even some early dub effects to differing degrees on two of the three mixes that Dodd released. All of this makes 'Rudie' one of the best Wailers songs of its era. It also may be The Wailers' first ganja song, sonically if not lyrically. In addition to the three titles listed above, this song has also been released as 'Good Good Rudie', 'Ruddie Boy' and 'Rudie Rudie'. Bunny Wailer would remake this track as 'Rule This Land' in 1980. But wanting to distance himself from rude boy behavior, he changed the word "rudie" to "rootsy".

And then there were two: The Wailers without Bob Marley

After the recording session that yielded both 'Rudie' and 'Cry To Me', with The Wailers at a peak in their creativity, Bob departed the group, moving to the USA to join his mother, who had taken work in Delaware. This might have been seen as a killing blow to The Wailers, since Marley was both the primary lead vocalist and the songwriter. Instead, for the better part of the year that Marley was absent, Livingston and Tosh simply stepped up into the spotlight, and Wailers excellence and creativity continued apace. In fact, it could be said that the best thing that happened to The Wailers collectively was Bob's temporary absence, as it afforded a period of accelerated development and increased appreciation of the talent of its other two members.

The Wailers' first sans-Marley record was a ska take on 'Sinner Man', the traditional spiritual that was popularized by American jazz singer Nina Simone in 1965. The entire song is sung in unison by Tosh and Livingston, and at no point are other voices missed. The harmonies are wonderful, enriched by Tosh alternating between singing high and his natural baritone. The swooping electric bass line by Bryan "Bassie" Atkinson foreshadows reggae even as ska has just begun to change into rock steady. Tosh would later remake 'Sinner Man' several times, finally and most famously as 'Downpressor Man' in his post-Wailers career (a song described later in this book; page 523). But more immediately, 'Sinner Man' would give The Wailers the best spiritual song they recorded at Studio One.

Nor did variety suffer from their being a duo. Peter and Bunny recorded the aforementioned R&B of 'Can't You See' and the spiritual 'Bless You'. There was also 'Guajira Ska', completely misnamed, being neither Cuban guajira music nor ska. It finds Livingston and Tosh vamping minimal lyrics in unison over a rock steady backing that contains references to 'Put It On' and, especially, to 'Ska Jerk'. But they would soon make The Wailers a trio again by enlisting Vision Walker from The Soulettes (who was Rita Marley's cousin) as a harmony singer until Marley returned. Together they recorded a fine body of work in a variety of ska sounds as the style continued to slow down and open up in the transition to rock steady.

Livingston provided sweet lead vocals on a number of songs in addition to the aforementioned R&B of 'I Need You So'. 'Who Feels It Knows It' resides in a place between ska and rock steady. It's an affirmational song based on the Jamaican folk saying of the title, complete with the beloved run-out titular refrain. Occupying the same stylistic place is 'What Am I Supposed To Do', a soft song with a pleasing melody. The lilting 'Rock Sweet Rock', with a simplified piano-based rock steady backing, is pleasant, if a bit innocuous. The agreeable rock steady and velvet-glove vocals of 'Rolling Stone' is The Wailers' only cover of a Bob Dylan song. Wow, is that Dream sharing the lead with Bunny? Choose the overdub-free single mix. Bunny would later remake the song in his solo career, with new lyrics as 'Ball Room Floor'. Bunny's vocals help make 'Dancing Shoes' the mellowest of ska tracks. It's a happy song about going to a sound system for love and dancing, and he would remake it too in his solo career. On the other side of the dance coin is another jerk song, known as either 'Jerking Time' or 'Jerk In Time'. In it, Livingston laments about his aching feet (perhaps he forgot his dancing shoes this time). After a cool drum-led introduction, it features a catchy melody, and – in another step away from ska – has an organ solo from Richard Ace. With these songs and the standouts to be described below, Bunny, like Junior Braithwaite before him, belatedly established a distinct line of music under The Wailers' brand. It features softer melody and sound than the rest of The Wailers' output, an occasional touch of quirkiness, and, of course, Bunny's wonderful voice out front.

Tosh sang lead on an equal number of Marley-less Wailers tracks. The rock steady of 'When The Well Runs Dry' features a fine soul melody and strong support vocals from Livingston, Walker and Rita Anderson, as folk wisdom is offered: "You'll never miss the water until the well runs dry." Unfortunately, it suffers from muddy sound in a rare misstep from producer Dodd. Tosh would remake it in his post-Wailers solo career, as he did too his funky ska cover of The Temptations' 'Don't Look Back'. This is a very good rendition, if more modest than the international hit that he recorded with Mick Jagger more than a decade later. The rock steady 'Treat Me Good' is the only song in this group not backed by The Skatalites, as a Lyn Taitt-led band provides the instrumentation. Tosh sings in a high register about treating your neighbor as you would like to be treated, employing a sing-song melody. It shows that Bunny did not have a Wailers monopoly on quirkiness at this time. Also good is the intoxicating light-hearted rock steady of 'Making Love'. It features a strong lead vocal performance from Tosh and rich harmonies from all three Soulettes. Listen to how, in the chorus, one of the female vocalists delightfully pulls off the word "love" with a twang. 'Lemon Tree' is a piano-filled ska cover of an American folk song popularized by both The Kingston Trio and Peter, Paul & Mary. With Tosh sharing the lead vocal with Bunny, and Rita Marley, Marlene Gifford and Vision adding to the harmonies, the song is more enjoyable than one might expect.

Though these songs were consistently good, there were other Marley-less Wailers songs that stood out as amongst The Wailers' Studio One best.

'Sunday Morning'
'Sunday Morning', from 1966, was Livingston's belated first lead vocal on a Wailers track. It is an achingly sad and beautiful ballad of heartbreak. And it serves as an example of Bunny Wailer's octave-spanning vocal abilities, giving credence to

the many who feel that Livingston had the best voice of any Wailer. His gorgeous singing is complemented by shifting backing vocals from Peter Tosh and Constantine Walker, and by the gentle, piano-led instrumentation of a Skatalites line-up with no horns and no hint of the ska beat. Unusually for an early Wailers classic, neither Bunny nor any other Wailer revisited this song. But, in 1980, Gregory Isaacs would record a popular rendition of 'Sunday Morning' and make it part of his live set.

'The Toughest'

Supported by a cocky saxophone riff and strutting bass line, Peter Tosh's 'The Toughest' is a swaggering rock steady rude boy song. The melody is lifted from an unlikely source: the soft soul ballad, 'I'm Your Puppet', that was a hit in 1965 for US R&B act James & Bobby Purify. The Skatalites and The Wailers perform a major overhaul as they toughen up the music, and Tosh replaces the passive lyrics with a new aggressive set. He boasts that because he's tougher, he's better at everything than the rude boy. Having established his superiority in the pecking order, he uses this position to demand that the rude boy live better and be a man. By this, 'The Toughest' is more than the simple song of braggadocio many have taken it for. It was released as a single with a pretty good dub version that, for all the many Peter Tosh compilations, has evaded CD release. It reveals the hypnotic underpinnings that reside under the song's aggression. Tosh would later remake this song in his post-Wailers solo career, as would Bunny Wailer.

'Rasta Shook Them Up'; 'I Stand Predominant'

These two groundbreaking songs are from the middle part of 1966; the first written and sung by Tosh, the second by Livingston. They feature overt expressions of Rastafarianism several years before the songs considered to have launched the roots reggae explosion. They signal a new spiritualism for The Wailers (and reggae in general), as Rasta would become a major influence in reggae. Covers of traditional spirituals from The Wailers would soon cease, as would rude boy songs. Instead, the seeds of the Rasta message that were planted with these songs would soon bloom.

'Rasta Shook Them Up' may be the first reggae song to include the word "Rasta" or "Rastafari" in its title. Written just days after the event, it's Tosh's account of the first and only visit to Jamaica by Ethiopia's emperor, Haile Selassie I, whom the Rasta view as a god. A hornless Skatalites line-up is led by Jackie Mittoo, whose piano strikes a most majestic tone, and Lloyd Knibb, whose busy drums are a treat. The melody was repurposed from a recent Trinidadian calypso song, 'Archie [Buck Them Up]' by Prince Galloway. 'Archie' proved to be popular in Jamaica, as mento band The Hiltonaires also did a rendition around the same time as 'Rasta Shook Them Up', and shortly thereafter guitarist Ernest Ranglin recorded an instrumental version that's a showcase for his virtuosity.

Tosh enters by speaking a few lines in Amharic, the language of Ethiopia that all good Rastas know a few words of. He sings jubilantly and conveys a genuine sense of wonder at Selassie's visit, providing a detailed account. People were happy and dancing in the streets and the police were unusually restrained, the expected beating not materializing. Selassie wept upon seeing the living conditions of the poor, and Babylon must look upon this with fear. The wicked will be punished while the righteous will be free. All the while, backing vocals (by vocal group The Gaylads rather than other Wailers) contentedly chant the titular refrain. The scaled-down-from-ska rock steady backing lacks not only horns but also solos and a mid-song break. This proves to be the perfect backing, as any interruption or distraction from Tosh's heartfelt account would only have detracted from this great song.

Bunny's 'I Stand Predominant' is a more inward-looking account of Rastafarianism. Vocally and musically, the song is quietly triumphant, as he describes the great strength he gains from his faith. He sings of "I and I", a phrase that would become ubiquitous in roots reggae. The first "I" refers to Haile Selassie I, while the second refers to the self. So "I and I" means "Selassie and me together". Bunny's vocals are confident and serene. He is well supported by Tosh and Walker, and a hybrid ska/rock steady backing from various Skatalites. The horns echo the feel of Bunny's serene victory, with Vin Gordon providing notable trombone work throughout. It's a great song that vocally, lyrically and instrumentally could only come from one place in the world. Bunny would later remake this song in his post-Wailers solo career.

'Dreamland'
Bunny Wailer's 'Dreamland' is the most famous of reggae's many back-to-Africa anthems. Livingston would remake 'Dreamland' with The Wailers, and again after he left the group, making it, perhaps more than any other, his signature song. Yet, as he sings about a paradise of abundant food, natural beauty, love and even immortality, he never mentions a place name. This is because, as revealed in the book *Bob Marley & The Wailers: The Definitive Discography*,[1] 'Dreamland' is a cover. An otherwise forgotten early psychedelic nugget from 1961 called 'My Dream Island' by an obscure American group called El Tempos gave Livingston nearly all the lyrics and melody for his song. But in the hands of Livingston and his backing, a good song about running away with a lover to a secret place is transformed to become a great song about arriving in a religious paradise. Befitting this, Bunny's singing is particularly lush and emphatic, even for him. His handling of the melody is so masterful, even the uncredited El Tempos would have to be impressed. Soft falsetto backing vocals from Tosh and Walker, and a softened ska

1.   Roger Steffens and Jody Pierson, *Bob Marley & The Wailers: The Definitive Discography* (Cambridge, MA: Rounder Books, 2005), p. 25.

sound from a hornless, piano- and bass-led Skatalites line-up carefully add to the ethereal lushness of this timeless track.

'Let Him Go'

Livingston wrote and sings lead on this, the final new rude boy song the Wailers would record (though new renditions of older ones would occasionally still be remade). He gives the genre a nice send-off in this rousing song backed by The Skatalites that can be described as either slow ska or fast rock steady. Once again, a stripped-down, hornless, piano- and bass-led line-up is heard. Count Ossie adds a Nyabinghi hand drum as he did on a just few Wailers songs from this time. Though they were occasionally heard in rock steady, and would become almost ubiquitous by the roots reggae era, hand drums were very seldom heard in the ska. Their presence, along with the slowing and softening of the beat, is a sign of the music moving away from the ska sound that was so revolutionary just a few years ago and on to something newer. A wordless expression of The Wailers' Rastafarianism, it also serves as another paving-stone in the path towards roots reggae.

Bunny crafts a song brimming with unique sing-song melodies, fine harmonies and two choruses in 'Let Him Go'. This pro-rude boy song finds the rudie framed and jailed.The opening chorus is direct and confrontational, as the rude boy has been freed on bail. It's repeated by Livingston, Walker and Tosh in three-part harmony, with Tosh dropping down to his natural register, adding tonal richness. For the verse, Bunny uncharacteristically stresses his voice, and never does he sound more like Bob Marley than in those moments. The call and response of the second chorus is memorable. It works the titular plea into a demonstration of the interplay of rhythm, harmony and melody that The Wailers were capable of. It results in such an irresistible hook, it's no wonder that rudie gets bail.

Two different mixes of this great recording are available. And Bunny would record it in his post-Wailers solo career. By then, firmly anti-rude boy, Bunny substituted the word "natty" for "rudie". But the remake, though good, pales by comparison to this Wailers Studio One classic.

* * *

Marley returned from the USA to The Wailers at the end of 1966, signaling a number of big changes for the group beyond the return of its most prominent member. Temporary Wailer Dream Walker would be displaced. Less amicably, they parted with producer Coxsone Dodd, who they felt did not pay them fairly. (Although Dodd is far from the only Jamaican producer to be accused of this by the artists he recorded, he may have been leading the league.) The ill feelings would never subside, and no Wailer would ever work with him again. Instead, they entered a phase of their career where they would work with a variety of other producers and produce themselves as well. They left the practice of recording numerous and sometimes inappropriate covers, a Wailers staple under Dodd, at Studio One's door. They turned the page on ska, staying current by moving to the newer rock steady and other sounds. The errant youthfulness and singing from the throat heard in some of Marley's earlier records were never heard again. Although those sounds were acceptable in the wild world of ska, they would have been very out of place in the more manicured sounds of rock steady. That's a lot of change all at once. But talented, adaptable and driven, The Wailers would continue with new music that, although different, was just as good as any they had previously recorded. We will resume their story in later chapters of this book.

8   More great ska songs

Here are more great ska songs, vocal and instrumental, not one of which should be missed.

Baba Brooks

Baba Brooks is another legendary name that was launched by ska. Certainly the greatest trumpet player of that era, he may very well be the finest on that instrument ever to come from Jamaica. Equal in talent but opposite in aspect, Brooks is the yin to Don Drummond's yang. Whereas Drummond's playing was famously quiet, brooding and dark, Brooks's trademark sound was as outgoing, happy and sunny as music could be.

Although Brooks was as accomplished and nearly as famous as his jazz/ska contemporaries like Tommy McCook, Roland Alphonso and Drummond, surprisingly little is known of his life. He was born Oswald Brooks in Kingston; some accounts estimate his birth year to be around 1935, but the actual date may be earlier. He was already called Baba by the early 1960s (if not earlier), an honorific that is usually reserved for older men, and some accounts have him dying of old age in the 1970s. By the 1950s, he was a member of Eric Dean's jazz band, a badge of achievement he shared with several Skatalites. He would soon start his recording career as a session man. The first track credited to him was on 'Musical Communion', produced by Duke Reid in 1962. In short order, he became an occasional member of The Skatalites, an arranger for producer Duke Reid, and a favorite of Prince Buster. He would release about one hundred tracks that bore his name, working with all of the top producers of the day (most frequently Reid, and least frequently Coxsone Dodd). This continued through 1967, but the details of his fate from that time forward are something of a mystery. He may be the greatest lead instrumentalist in reggae to have never recorded an album.

The great Baba Brooks songs described below are the only ska instrumentals on a par with The Skatalites' best. They concentrate as much happiness as has ever been etched onto one side of a 45-rpm single. Adding further to their joyousness, these tracks are readily available on multiple ska compilation CDs. But lest you think that Baba Brooks was only capable of one mood, also available on CD for your consideration is his aptly named, ominous instrumental called 'Dreadnaught'.

'Independence Ska'
Produced by Duke Reid in 1965, 'Independence Ska' celebrates the third anniversary of Jamaica's independence from the United Kingdom, Baba Brooks-style. His

recipe? Take excellent ska musicianship, add a classic melody and keep immersed in laughing gas before serving.

Even before the horns join in to provide a theme, the riddim achieves a delirious gleefulness. There's start-and-stop bass, hi-hat cymbals, a one-finger piano line, a sax squonking the ska chop and an inside-out xylophone phrase. The piano vanishes as the theme begins, but the rest of this madcap assembly continues throughout the song. Trumpet and sax enter to play a rousing, happy theme in unison. Its melody is taken from the Jerry Leiber and Mike Stoller R&B hit, 'Kansas City'. This song was previously covered instrumentally by Cuban bandleader Mongo Santamaria, who retitled it 'El Pussycat'. It's that rendition that appears to have been the inspiration for Brooks. As we have seen in the chapter on The Skatalites, Santamaria's music was a big favorite of the ska crowd.

The song is swollen with three solos, each creative, melodic and concise in the ska way. A trombone solo, probably by Vin Gordon, enchants. Played in a higher register than the norm, it's very playful, expressive and unfailingly jolly. A sax solo, perhaps from Roland Alphonso, is more serious. Brooks's solo has it both ways. He works off an idea from the trombone solo, opening with a playful circle of notes before slowing down and jazzing out. With that, the theme is reprised, punctuated with a few stray slashing guitar chords from Lyn Taitt. When else has jazz been such a fun ride? 'Independence Ska' appears on several Treasure Isle compilation CDs, sometimes credited to Lyn Taitt and The Baba Brooks Band.

'Shenk I Sheck'

Produced in 1963 by King Edwards, 'Shenk I Sheck' is another Baba Brooks happy pill. This is by no means to trivialize the song – it's a tour de force of Baba Brooks's prowess as a composer and lead instrumentalist, and a downright ska classic. Once again, his band lays down a backing that is so happy, it borders on the giddy. It's built of a busy little repeated sax phrase that is agreeable, even if a bit crazed, creative busy drums, happy piano and Lyn Taitt's guitar (this being his first recording session) handling the ska chop, all at a breakneck pace even for ska.

As this runaway train of a riddim repeats its theme, anticipation builds as the listener wonders what is going to be laid down atop. What comes is a brilliant and unique performance, whose melody reggae fans would forever cherish. It is one of reggae's all-time horn performances. Brooks enters shrewdly, contrasting the backing with a theme made of long laconic notes. He proceeds to twist these into pretzels as he toys with the theme's melody, pace, rhythm and volume. He elaborates with a raspy vibrato effect and fast runs of staccato notes. Taitt takes a tentative but playfully exotic guitar solo. Brooks returns to improvise further variations on his theme, keeping it interesting right to the song's fade-out. And before you know it, Brooks has played 2 minutes of lead trumpet – a skillful performance that is as accessible and engaging as it is creative and masterful. More than any other solo I can think of, it conveys the very joy of being able to play an instrument so well.

Incidentally, the song title is a misspelling of Chiang Kai-shek, one of several national leaders (President Kennedy, Fidel Castro, etc.) then in the news who received the honor of having a ska instrumental named after them. As described later in this book (page 313), reggae trumpet player Bobbie Ellis covered Brooks's song in 1977 as 'Shenk I Sheck' in a relaxed roots style.

'Bank To Bank, Part 1'; 'Bank To Bank, Part 2'
The Baba Brooks 1963 scorcher 'Bank To Bank, Part 1' was produced by Duke Reid. Glorious ska breaks out as stand-up bass grooves, piano chords lay down the rhythm and Lloyd Knibb's drums rear up and propel the song. Knibb's playing is informed by Jamaican Pocomania drum patterns and Latin flair, made extra crunchy with rim shots. The body of the song begins with several horns and harmonica playing a celebratory theme in unison. It's so festive and splendid, it feels so much like a national holiday that, when you hear it, you may neglect to go to work and start searching for a parade. An accomplished sax solo hands off to Brooks, whose solo is long and full of life. Meanwhile, Knibb boosts the song's already considerable energy by adding in fancy rolls. The theme is reprised briefly, the song fades out and more fun in just over 2 minutes can't be found.

'Bank To Bank, Part 2' is not a continuation of Part 1. Instead, in an atypical move, Reid released a different, longer, take of 'Bank To Bank' as the single's B-side. The theme is unchanged from Part 1, and it too features solos from sax and trumpet. But, as the simpler introduction shows us, this is a more relaxed take, with slower solos and a more subdued Knibb. If it had been the only released rendition it would have been loved, but compared with the sharper Part 1, Part 2 is merely a welcome but alternative take.

Other great ska songs

Joe Higgs: *'Dinah'*
Joe Higgs's first solo track without partner Roy Wilson is a winner. 'Dinah', produced by Coxsone Dodd in 1963, is a fine ska song with some unusual touches. For one thing, the second solo comes from flute. Although flutes, fifes and penny whistles were part of mento and various Jamaican folk-music forms, and flute would later occasionally appear in reggae, it was very seldom heard in ska, let alone providing a solo. The lyrics come off as unusual too.

'Dinah' opens with a nice little duel between piano and slide guitar over a rock-solid ska rhythm. It creates a confrontational vibe that sets up an impressive vocal by Higgs. He uses the full extent of his strong voice to craft several interesting melodies that support his foreboding lyrics. He confronts Dinah on her growing laziness, apathy, poor food preparation, and sleeping throughout the day. He concludes that she's gotten old and that she has to go. That's unusually callous; remember, he's singing about his woman, not a draft horse. Well, everyone likes Joe Higgs, so let's see if we can't exonerate him, at least partially.

It turns out that he based this song on 'Call Dinah', a Jamaican folk song that was first documented in a recording by Edric Connor in 1951. Edric calls on Dinah, who, due to pain in her back, "kean limber" (can't hurry) to respond. Her shopping for food is similarly affected. There's not much more to the lyrics; her infirmity is observed without any expression of sympathy. And we have seen that Arthur Knibbs recorded a golden-age mento rendition, called 'Get Up Adina'. Here, the unresponsive woman is a schoolgirl and the singer's reaction is exasperation, not sympathy. Higgs built on this unsympathetic song and, in creating a fuller complement of lyrics for his rendition, took it to its natural, if harsh, conclusion.

Amazingly, 'Dinah' has somehow eluded the many ska and all the Studio One compilation CDs that have been released. This points to the need for a comprehensive compilation of early Joe Higgs and Higgs & Wilson sides. While we wish and wait, a version of 'Dinah' can be heard – albeit with an overlay of some early-style DJing – on the CD called *Dance Hall '63 Featuring King Stitt*.

Laurel Aitken: *'Bad Minded Woman'*

Lorenzo "Laurel" Aitken was born in 1927 in the neighboring island of Cuba to a Jamaican father and Cuban mother. The family relocated to Jamaica when he was eleven. In his teens, he began singing for tourists and competing in talent shows. Aitken began his recording career towards the end of the 1950s, establishing himself with mento, R&B and recordings that blended several styles that are best described as sounding just like Laurel Aitken. By the new decade, he began to produce himself (mostly) as well as others. He made his biggest mark in ska when he became a crossover star in the UK. He continued to record until 1980 in a variety of styles. But he always returned to ska, performing live ska shows in the UK, where he was given the name "the godfather of ska", right up until his death from a heart attack in 2005. Throughout his career, he never stopped recording, releasing over 250 singles and about twenty-six albums.

Perhaps the best song of Aitken's long and diverse career was the 1964 George Edwards-produced ska track, 'Bad Minded Woman'. It is available on the Laurel Aitken collection called *Original Cool Jamaican Ska*. (Be sure not to wind up with one of the three inferior remakes found on other releases.) It features one of his finest vocals, as Aitken finds a melody that is tuneful and well-suited to his enthusiastic singing and somewhat limited range. He addresses an unrighteous, meddlesome gossip: "Go home, leave my business alone. You've been talking all day, you never kneel and pray." Backed by The Skatalites, a suitably sharp arrangement is crafted, featuring a busy little horn riff that is full of scorn. Harmonica, piano and guitar in different combinations provide a well-tended ska chop that serves to offset the otherwise sharp sound. Baba Brooks plays a mid-song trumpet that is a treat. The titular woman should feel honored to have her bad behavior reprimanded in such fine style.

Eric "Monty" Morris: *'Penny Reel'*

Trench Town-born Eric "Monty" Morris began his career recording as a short-lived duo in 1960 with Derrick Morgan. His debut solo record, 'Humpty Dumpty', backed by The Drumbago All Stars and produced by Prince Buster the next year, was a hit. His career thus launched, Morris worked with several producers, recording steadily up to 1975 and releasing about 125 songs before leaving Jamaica. Though primarily a solo singer, he also recorded in the duo Monty & Roy with Roy Panton, as well as occasional collaborations with Millicent "Patsy" Todd, while continuing to team up with Derrick Morgan, as duos were quite popular in the ska era. Morris was selected to present Jamaica's exciting new ska music at the 1964 World's Fair in New York, along with singers Prince Buster and Jimmy Cliff, and backing band Byron Lee & The Dragonaires. (Since 1950, this long-lived Jamaican band has provided slick music in whatever was the style of the day, changing over to Trinidadian sounds by the 1980s.) Being chosen by the Jamaican government to represent the island on this international stage speaks equally to Morris's popularity and his well-mannered behavior. The latter is why The Skatalites, Rastas from poor backgrounds, were left at home in favor of the safer "uptown" conformity of Lee's less-deserving group.

Morris's finest hour was 'Penny Reel', recorded at Treasure Isle for Duke Reid in 1964. It's a superlative ska scorcher and is many ska fans' favorite ska song. The recording sports an impressive lineage. It's a cover of a golden-age mento side from the era's most unruly singer, Lord Power, one of Reid's first productions for his original Trojan label and his first success. And Power's song is itself based on a traditional Jamaican folk song sometimes called 'Penny Wheel'.

Over a classic ska rhythm, the song opens with a blast of bawdy horns, the perfect introduction for the story about to unfold. Though not quite a rude boy song, it does deal with retribution, and depending on your interpretation, the behavior described is either very rude or very, very rude. In the most expressive vocal performance of his career, Morris serves up an unsettling blend that is in equal parts joyous and threatening as he encounters a woman who owes him money. He sounds like the cat that ate the canary as he presents her with his terms. With every line answered by a backing vocalist intently singing, "Penny Reel, oh", Morris sings:

> Ah, Penny Reel, oh
> Long time me never see you
> And you owe me lickle [little] money
> And you no have it there fe gimme
> I beg you turn your belly, gimme
> Let me rub out the money

© Westbury Music Ltd

There is some dispute as to exactly how Morris is requesting restitution, as many people hear "rob all the money" instead of "rub out the money". But in the second of three recitations of this verse (the song has no chorus, the role being filled with two rollicking saxophone solos), the second-to-last line changes to "I beg you turn you, push you, give me". This and the bawdy horns of the introduction lend credence to the compensation by friction view. There was never any confusion in Lord Power's original rendition. He sings, "young gal, I beg you tu'n and cushu gimme", with "cushu" being local slang for vagina. But a folk rendition from 1958 by The Frats Quintet has an outcome for the victim that is neither sexual nor larcenous. Instead, threats of violence are explicitly detailed. So regardless of rendition or interpretation, one wouldn't want to be caught short by the singer, even with a musical romp this fine as a soundtrack.

'Penny Reel' is rightly included on numerous ska compilations, sometimes credited to Baba Brooks & Eric Morris, and sometimes titled 'Penny Reel O'. Morris's stylistically similar follow-up, 'Fast Mouth', produced by Duke Reid the next year, is very good as well. But it has never been collected on LP or CD and remains unfortunately obscure compared to the famous 'Penny Reel'.

Derrick Morgan: *'Don't Call Me Daddy'*

Derrick Morgan was born in 1940 in Clarendon Parish. In the 1950s, he was successful on Vere Johns's *Opportunity Knocks* talent show with his imitation of Little Richard singing 'Long Tall Sally', launching a long and interesting career. After winning, he was snatched up by the island's top comedy act, Bim & Bam (as they had done earlier with Roy Wilson of Higgs & Wilson), to add his Little Richard imitation to their stage show. His recording career began at the very end of the 1950s with a string of R&B sides. The first was 'Lover Boy' for producer Duke Reid. But, as was then the producer's prerogative, Reid decided against releasing it, keeping it instead as an exclusive for his sound system. This angered Morgan, who quit Reid to work with other producers. But the dispute was temporary, and the song was eventually released and Morgan later returned to work further with Reid.

Morgan recorded steadily from 1959 through to 1977, and sporadically in the 1980s, releasing well over 300 singles and ten albums over this span. But it was the 1960s that was his decade, hit-filled and storied. Massively popular, at one point he simultaneously held the top seven spots on the Jamaican record chart (an unmatched feat), including the song described below. Meanwhile, he had a hand in launching the careers of some of the biggest singers in reggae. Working for producer Leslie Kong, he arranged Jimmy Cliff's first records. As a talent scout, he not only brought Desmond Dekker to Kong, but also helped him develop his first record. The first-ever live Wailers performance was part of a big show that was honoring Morgan's pending move to England. He would give Bob Marley feedback on his stage work, advising him to dance less and concentrate on his singing. He was a participant in perhaps the most famous of reggae's many musical battles. Morgan's one-time producer, Prince Buster, felt betrayed that Morgan left him for Kong, and released a single accusing him of lacking racial loyalty, called 'Blackhead Chinaman'. Morgan gave a 7-inch response called 'Blazing Fire' that, adding insult to injury, repurposed the melody of Buster's hit, 'Madness'. Naturally, Buster fired back. In the end, the feud resulted in five records, big hits for both combatants, and no hard feelings.

Though a solo artist, Morgan also recorded a fair number of duets, either with established male ska stars or the female supporting vocalists of the era. In addition to the aforementioned Reid, Kong and Buster, Morgan worked with Coxsone Dodd and other producers. He would also produce some of his own recordings and those of other artists. He even brought his brother-in-law into the production field, the prolific Bunny "Striker" Lee. In spite of failing eyesight, Derrick Morgan still performs occasionally today.

'Don't Call Me Daddy', a humorous ska hit with Morgan backed by The Baba Brooks Band, was produced by Duke Reid in 1965. Morgan sings a tale of exasperated woe. He, like his woman, is black, but the woman's child is of obvious Asian descent. Yet she maintains that Morgan is the biological father. He makes the titular plea, pointing out the physical differences, concluding that his woman must be insane. It's hard not to sympathize with his predicament. Perhaps Morgan can take solace in the fact that he is apparently not the only black West Indian to find himself in this situation. The same subject was explored by Trinidadian calypso singer Terror in his 1950 song, 'Chinese Baby' (as covered by mento group The Hiltonaires in the 1960s, a version described later in this book; page 305), as well as in the golden-age mento song 'Maintenance' by Joseph "Cobra Man" Clemendore, which was later covered as a reggae track by Count Lasher. Meanwhile, a propulsive ska riddim is heard, with much adorning it. Baba Brooks provides a stream of trumpet phrases that answer Morgan sympathetically. There are fine mid-song sax and trumpet solos and as the song runs out, Lyn Taitt provides a guitar solo working off Morgan's melody. Never has someone's family problems sounded so well appointed. This, the funniest of all ska songs, can be heard on the Derrick Morgan CD collection called *Moon Hop*. This is the preferred rendition, rather than a later remake.

Clive & Naomi: *'Open The Door'*
The short-lived ska duo of Clive & Naomi recorded three sides together. Clive Wilson also recorded a few singles as a solo singer and a small number more in collaboration with other female singers. Naomi Campbell recorded a handful of duets with Derrick Morgan. (She should not be confused with the British supermodel of the same name.) One of their tracks stands out from the thousands of songs recorded during the ska era.

'Open The Door', an atypical love song, was recorded in 1964 for producer Duke Reid. It's funny and endearing in a pre-political-correctness way. We hear the betrothed couple engaged in a spat, with Naomi having locked Clive out of the house. In their cute, youthful Jamaican voices, they repeatedly threaten each other with murder. It opens happily enough with a cheerful breezy horn theme as the ska chop is played on electric guitar, while organ pumps away at half its time. The chorus finds Clive demanding entry and threatening to break down the door. Naomi refuses, warning that he'll find himself dead before he gets in. The exchange is repeated and varied, but no one budges. Later, Clive threatens that his fiancé won't make it to the wedding alive. But Naomi is unswayed, answering, "No, no, no!" Although the song does not include an outcome, the light-hearted backing and easy-going sax solo leave no doubt that all will end well. 'Open The Door' is available on several ska compilation CDs.

9   Prince Buster

The career accomplishments and interesting life of Cecil Eustace Bustamente Campbell, better known as Prince Buster, and later also known as Muhammed Yusef Ali, deserve a book of their own. He was born in 1938 in Kingston and started his musical career in the 1950s as a nightclub singer. Not being particularly successful, he moved to a different track. Buster's success as a boxer gave him an entrée into Coxsone Dodd's sound system. He was hired to provide security, as rival sound systems would sometimes employ "dance crashers" to disrupt a competing sound by beating people up, smashing the equipment and even attempting to steal the sound's crown jewels – its collection of rare records. But Buster was more than muscle, and eventually left Dodd's employ to start his own sound system, The Voice Of The People. (His departure from Dodd's camp would create an opening for another important protégé, later to turn rival, in Lee Perry.) Buster began recording in 1959, his first release the spirited if unschooled R&B romp, 'Little Honey'. And, as we have seen, he would soon orchestrate the innovative session where Count Ossie's Nyabinghi drums supplemented the R&B of The Folkes Brothers' 'Oh Carolina'.

Like all successful producers of the day, he started his first label (Buster Wild Bells) and opened a record store in Kingston (Buster's Record Shack). His work as a producer spanned R&B thru ska, rock steady, reggae, DJ and dub, and even included some mento. He worked with a varied collection of talent that included such stars as The Skatalites, Dennis Brown, Big Youth, Dennis Alcapone, Monty Morris, John Holt, Stranger Cole and Toots & The Maytals. He would produce nearly a thousand tracks.

But as successful as Prince Buster was as a producer, he was better remembered as a singer. Working as both, Buster was then unique, though others would follow through the double doors he opened. Buster's vocals brought a sly intelligence to all types of songs, especially those he graced with his own crafty lyrics. (These two traits taken together are better compared to golden-age mento star Count Lasher than to any of Buster's contemporaries.) His varied originals included a run of semi-explicit records that delighted audiences, particularly in the UK, making his overseas fans well educated to the fact that "pum pum" was Jamaican slang for vagina. He was undoubtedly a lover of traditional Jamaican songs. His 1965 LP, *Ska Lip Soul*, contains a few mento tracks, and he also recorded ska versions of more than a few folk/mento songs. He recorded rude boy songs, love songs, feud songs and more. In all, he voiced over three hundred vocal tracks, each one self-produced. He additionally orchestrated over one hundred instrumentals, using musicians from The Skatalites along with others (he has a particular fondness for the great ska drummer Arkland "Drumbago" Parks), often branding them as The

Prince Buster All Stars. The largely instrumental 'Al Capone', with Buster providing early DJ vocal sounds, became one of the first Jamaican singles to chart top 20 in the UK.

While nearly all of Jamaica's reggae community was moving towards Rastafarianism, Buster had instead found a path to the Muslim faith. A meeting with fellow Muslim, boxer Muhammad Ali, during his visit to Jamaica in 1964 impressed Buster into joining The Nation of Islam. When he left recording behind in 1973, some believed that it was because he felt outside of the Rasta-fueled roots explosion that was then dominating reggae. Others thought it was to concentrate on his business endeavors. Happily, he has returned to music occasionally since.

Love of Prince Buster's music proved to be a major raison d'être for the Two Tone bands that revived the ska rhythm and combined it with punk rock in the UK at the end of the 1970s. For example, top Two Tone band, Madness, took their name from one Buster song, named their premier album, *One Step Beyond*, after another, and covered several of his songs. Their first single, 'The Prince', was a tribute to Buster. The Specials and The Beat each recorded several Prince Buster songs as well. The success of these Two Tone bands made ska safe for rock bands, and other waves of ska-rock followed. In this way, amongst many other things, Prince Buster is a musical grandfather of one-time "third wave" ska revivalists Gwen Stefani and No Doubt.

The availability of Buster's back catalog is as cratered as the moon. For all that he recorded, the last time I checked, just two insignificant Prince Buster tracks were available on iTunes. Few of his singles or his twenty-seven LPs have made it over to CD. I hereby declare a moratorium on box-sets in all genres of music until one collecting Buster's best sees the light of day. While we wait, be sure to track down the great Prince Buster tracks described below.

'Old Lady'; 'Pum Pum A Go Kill You' (aka 'Tonight')
Perhaps Buster's best ska rendition of a folk/mento song was the 1964 'Old Lady', a song I have already discussed in the chapter on golden-age mento. The ska instrumentation is fine, with several nods to the past to complement the source song. Trumpet repeats a fancy phrase, making the song sound old-fashionedly ornate. A solo on alto sax is reminiscent of the clarinet and/or bamboo sax of mento's past. So is the happy harmonica that emerges from its minor supporting role to play a gleeful solo to fade-out in the song's last moments. Buster sings with enthusiasm, genuinely enjoying the song's timeless melody. Admirably, he takes care with the lyrics, unlike many ska or reggae covers of folk/mento songs where the words lose fidelity. I'm sorry to say that this is one of many fine Prince Buster songs that have never appeared on LP, let alone CD, making it for the time being the province of those willing to track down rare reggae 45-rpm singles or recordings thereof.

The melody of 'Old Lady' proved too good for Buster to leave behind. He returned to it in 1969, for 'Pum Pum A Go Kill You', providing new and very different lyrics. Incorrigible fun, for those who might be keeping score, it ranks as the best of the five Buster songs with "Pum Pum" in the title. Horns kick off the immediately recognizable melody over a pleasing reggae riddim with double-struck rhythm guitar and an animated bass line. In the one-millionth example of reggae creativity, crazed trebly organ runs are a prominent and engaging feature of the sound. Buster comes in with a comic spoken performance. Gravelly voiced, he declares he's drunk, randy and looking for action. A fine chorus of sexy female backing vocals, perhaps meant to be old ladies, picks up the melody from the horns and treats us to a mocking reply. They warn that sex with them will kill a young man like Buster, pointing to a dead boy as proof. Buster counters, "Not me!" He then sings the chorus of 'Old Lady' in his normal voice, still supported nicely by the backing singers. The pixy organ solos crazily. The song ends with the drunk returning to mutter various quarrels and boasts. So the moral of the story here is, of course, um ... er ... that even when his songs aren't making a lot of sense, they can be very creative and thoroughly enjoyable. 'Pum Pum A Go Kill You' can most easily be found on Buster's *Wreck A Pum Pum* CD. Or if you are "feeling rough tonight", track down his LP *Big 5*, for the album with indisputably more songs with "Pum Pum" in the title than any other.

'Girl Answer To Your Name'
Buster's 1966 track, 'Girl Answer To Your Name', is a late-period ska track, from a time when ska began to slow down prior to its change to rock steady. It's a song with a lot going on, and much of it seems to have been influenced by then current music from outside of Jamaica. It makes for a strange, overstuffed hybrid of Jamaican and US/UK pop-rock sounds. As such, it has a unique sound not just for a Prince Buster song, but for any song.

The song's mixed heritage is evident right from its opening, when electric guitar chords put a mid-1960s pop-rock feel atop a ska rhythm. Even beyond this fusion, there is many a creative touch. A trumpet trill follows each of Buster's lines like a typewriter's carriage return. Bass and drums are given elbow room to stretch out and take chances. The creative mid-song sax and trumpet solos are each visited by reverb midway. They're accessible but slightly skewed towards the strange. The sax returns to duel with Buster as the song nears its end.

The vocals point away from Jamaica. Buster employs pop-rock gymnastics and frequently breaks into an uncharacteristic falsetto, double-tracked at times so that he can harmonize with himself. This style of singing and his melody would not have been out of place on a song by The Monkees if not for the fact that Buster's enthusiasm puts him over the top. This holds double for his lyrics. He sings about being lied to by a girl, but decides that he still loves her – sentiments that would fit in the pop-rock idiom. That is, until he explains that the otherwise sweet girl is promiscuous, engaging in numerous one-night stands.

The overall result is the answer to the previously unasked question, "If The Monkees were temporarily transformed into wildly creative and expressive Jamaican musicians, and they recorded a raucous ska-pop-rock adult love song, what would it have sounded like?" It would have sounded exactly like 'Girl Answer To Your Name', and be unique, exciting and fun. It can be found on the CD called *Prince Buster Sings His Hit Song Ten Commandments*.

'Too Hot'
The 1967 'Too Hot' is the best of the several rude boy songs that Buster recorded. It stands as a notable member of the body of great rude boy songs that came out of ska and rock steady.

Unlike the previous songs in this chapter, 'Too Hot' is rock steady, pure and simple. Rather than any sign of ska's insistent heat, Buster and the backing instrumentation emanate easy-going cool. The unhurried, uncluttered riddim features occasional elaborations by piano or guitar, and a sharp-edged sax solo. Where else but reggae could you hear such a great solo be dispensed so casually? Buster gives a great talk-sing performance, with a slow and deliberate delivery, as if he is explaining something very important. What he needs you to understand is that the rudies have made the town "too hot", an expression for rude boy violence that was also used by The Wailers on 'Simmer Down', the first rude boy song. Buster's lyrics are incisive, even for him. He describes how the rudies are too tough for the police, for the army and, most certainly, for you. He wryly offers sarcastic advice if you choose to ignore his warning. As long as you make sure your life insurance is paid-up and your funeral arrangements are in good order, by all means fight the rudies. The male backing vocals sound fittingly mournful.

The UK Two Tone band The Specials covered 'Too Hot' quite faithfully twelve years later on their first album. The song is sometimes erroneously co-credited to Prince Buster and Lee Perry. Though they worked together on another rude boy-related song, 'Judge Dread', Perry does not appear to be involved with this one. 'Too Hot' can be heard on the Prince Buster album called *Fabulous Greatest Hits*, sometimes available on CD.

10 Great Treasure Isle rock steady songs

Duke Reid is one of reggae's most eminent (and most flamboyant) producers. As we have seen, he was a sound system operator who began in record production at the end of the golden age of mento. But he reached his creative peak with rock steady, a genre he created at his Treasure Isle studio, and whose sound was defined by the records released on his label of the same name.

Born Arthur Reid, in 1915 in Portland Parish, he moved to Kingston late in his teens. Uniquely for a Jamaican involved in the island's music industry, he was first employed as a police officer. He left law enforcement after ten years, when his wife needed his help in running the family business, the Treasure Isle grocery and liquor store. A huge fan of R&B, he would there find an outlet for his love of music. Just as future producers Leslie Kong and Justin Yap began to play records to attract more customers to their families' ice-cream shops, so too did Reid at the family store.

By the mid-1950s, not only had Treasure Isle grown to the point of moving into bigger quarters, so had Reid's involvement with music. He started a popular sound system, its name (and eventually that of his first record label) taken from the Trojan truck he used for transport. He also began to sponsor and host a radio show called *Treasure Isle Time*, enriched by the R&B 78-rpm singles he brought back from shopping trips to the USA. These same records also attracted patrons to his sound system, where Reid crafted his larger-than-life persona. Aggressively demanding, this tough ex-cop was already an intimidating figure. This image was magnified when he was carried into the dance wearing a cape and a variety of weapons. A loaded revolver or two with an ammunition belt were de rigueur, though he sometimes accessorized with a machete or hand grenade.

By the end of the 1950s, he began producing records, starting with some mento sides by Lord Power on his short-lived Trojan label. (A UK re-issuer would later revive the name, and Trojan Records continues in that form today.) On a variety of labels, he quickly moved to home-grown R&B with acts like The Jiving Juniors. Though he initially disliked ska, Reid's productions would come to account for a nice portion of classics from that genre. But his best was yet to come, when he'd put his stamp on Jamaican music.

The ska supernova was burning out, and by 1965 its breakneck tempo had begun to slow. The need for a new sound was in the air. Reid fulfilled it by altering ska's formula. His rock steady productions slowed the tempo further and, to a degree, de-emphasized the horns and simplified the drums. Defining the style, he featured sweet piano and put the bass out front. This last was made easier by the move to an electric instrument and the employment of a young, gifted, game-changing bassist by the name of Jackie Jackson. Not to take away from the fine bass work heard in ska and R&B (nor failing to mention reggae's first thunderers, mento's rumba box players), Jackson's impact on reggae was greater than that of any bassist that came before.

Clifton Courtney Jackson was born in Kingston around 1951, where he was raised by his mother. She nicknamed him "Jackie" because of The Jackson Five. Though poor, Jackson's mother and her family were piano players, and young Clifton was gifted. He played piano until, as a young teenager, he saw a live performance by The Skatalites. He was so impressed by Lloyd Brevett, he quit the piano and learned to play the bass. After he had made the scene in a number of bands, Tommy McCook brought him in for his first recording session in 1966. It was on Alton Ellis's seminal rock steady hit, 'I Have Got A Date', for Duke Reid. Jackson would become Treasure Isle's resident bassist, a future Dynamite and long-time bassist for Toots & The Maytals, both in the studio and for innumerable live shows that spanned the decades through to today. His electric instrument gave Jackson the center stage, where he impressed with his creative playing that was so rhythmic yet melodic at the same time. By so doing, he paved the way for the instrument's great prominence throughout the reggae that followed.

But there was more to the sound of Treasure Isle rock steady than an updated arrangement. Catering to his personal preferences, Reid banished ska's wildness and rough edges. His rock steady was calm and polished, sweet and warm. This was especially true of the vocals. The singing had to be top-notch, lest Reid explode and reprimand the offender, as previously mentioned, sometimes firing off a pistol shot for extra emphasis. Whistle- clean and highly accessible, Reid's rock steady can be compared to Detroit's world-famous Motown sound, but the sound was unmistakably Jamaican.

Reid employed both dub pioneer King Tubby and pioneering DJ star U-Roy at his sound system, and had a role in the creation and popularization of DJ and dub records. He did not approve of Rastafarianism and found himself sonically and thematically at odds with the roots reggae that was emerging in the early 1970s. This quandary was never resolved as Reid's career came to an abrupt end in 1974 when he became seriously ill with cancer. He never recovered, dying the next year, but not before producing over 800 singles and sixty albums. The legendary producer was posthumously honored by the Jamaican government, when he was awarded the Order of Distinction in 2007.

Below, I list the cream of the Treasure Isle rock steady crop, as available on numerous Treasure Isle compilation CDs. As you will see, 1967 was an especially magical year for Reid's rock steady productions.

Freddie McKay: *'Love Is A Treasure'*
Freddie McKay was born in 1947 in Saint Catherine Parish. His first records were made in 1967 for producer Prince Buster. He would jump around to other producers for a time before settling in for a successful stint with Coxsone Dodd in the early 1970s. He next worked with a variety of producers and did some self-production, amassing about 140 singles and a dozen albums. He worked right up to the time of his death in 1986 of a heart attack.

The same year as his first records for Buster, McKay recorded his first hit, 'Love Is A Treasure', for producer Duke Reid. There must have been a falling out as the two never worked together again, in spite of their only collaboration being completely irresistible. Perhaps the problem was because the song was credited to Treasure Boy rather than Freddie McKay, with the Treasure Isle cross-advertising machine running rampant. (Subsequent LP and CD releases have long since corrected the credit.) The backing music, filled with easy appeal, is archetypical Treasure Isle rock steady. The arrangement is so different from the ska of just months earlier: the pace is not as fast; the chop is still there, but now moved to electric guitar, smartly keeping time without ska's pounding insistence; the drums are more laidback. And the bass, as played by the great Jackie Jackson, is the most different of all. Here, he plays octave-jumping staccato clusters of notes that are a prominent feature of the song, providing the bass with a second melody to complement McKay's. A sunshine-bright repeated horn phrase and just a touch of piano this time fill out the riddim.

McKay's vocal brings an unforced sweetness to the song. As he often does, he sounds like someone valiantly battling a head cold, giving his voice a comfortable, homey feel. He muses on how "strange but true" is the title of the song. Though he does little to explain this further, he manages to draw the listener into his confidence as he sings multiple levels of how "I know" that "you know" that this is true. And the wordless choruses of '*ooo ooos*' give the song a hook that exemplifies its easy-going vibe. 'Love Is A Treasure' yielded a popular riddim of the same name. A notable version is the 1973 Duke Reid-produced DJ version by Lizzy, also called 'Love Is A Treasure'. Using portions of McKay's vocal as a springboard, Lizzy amplifies the fun inherent in the original. It's exactly that quality that is somehow lost in McKay's otherwise acceptable 1977 of remake the song for producer Coxsone Dodd.

The Jamaicans: *'Ba Ba Boom'*
The vocal group The Jamaicans were made up of lead singer Norris Weir with Tommy Cowan and Martin Williams. They recorded a few singles in 1965 and 1966 for Coxsone Dodd that are all but forgotten today. Not so 'Ba Ba Boom', one of a handful of singles they recorded in 1967 when they started working with Duke Reid. In all, they would record close to fifty singles though the end of the 1970s.

'Ba Ba Boom' was an enduring hit and the winning song in Jamaica's second Festival. It was The Jamaicans' finest hour. Written by Cowan and Weir, it's a unique blend of the impeccable sound of Treasure Isle rock steady and the out-doorsy country party sound of a Festival song. The few lyrics nod to both, with references to rock steady and to Festival.

The opening eases you in with velvet rock steady gloves: The Jamaicans harmonize wordlessly on a cycle of chords, softly accented by the rhythm instruments. This is accompanied by a guitar rapidly picking out a single note at a time. It's more like how a mandolin is played than a guitar typically is, or, closer to home, the way the banjo is sometimes played in mento. Though never part of the vocabulary of ska, this style of picking was a distinctive ingredient in many rock steady songs, as well as in the reggae that followed. A number of guitarists newly on the scene (most notably Hux Brown) played in this style; here, it's the versatile Jamaican music stalwart Ernest Ranglin who is heard. He stays in the forefront after the introduction, rippling along appealingly throughout. Combining with the rhythm instruments, the staccato bass clusters in particular, this gives the song a well-textured foundation.

The Jamaicans sound wonderful, rock ready smooth and, living up to their name, full of local flavor. Cowan's mid-range lead is in full control as harmonies roam from up high, down to bass. The titular refrain provides the song with a powerful hook. 'Ba Ba Boom' is already a complete pleasure, when, late in the song, we learn that Reid was holding back on us. It's then that The Jamaicans stop singing in order for the band to unleash one of the most glorious horn phrases in reggae history. Its melody is familiar from The Ethiopians' 1965 Studio One hit, 'Train To Skaville'. But here it's slowed down and opened up to become the sonic equivalent of a dip in a mountain stream. The phrase is repeated unhurriedly for a time until The Jamaicans return briefly, only to hand the spotlight back again, to the fade-out of this one-of-a-kind classic.

The Paragons: *'Wear You To The Ball'; 'The Tide Is High'*
The Paragons were formed in 1964 in Kingston, and made their recording debut the next year as a ska act for Studio One. This original line-up of Garth "Tyrone" Evans, Bob Andy, Junior Menz and Leroy Stamp was short-lived. The great John Holt replaced Stamp, Howard Barrett replaced Menz (who defected to The Techniques to be their lead singer), and Bob Andy would depart to launch a successful solo career. Though not unsuccessful as a ska band, this work would be overshadowed by their greater artistic and commercial accomplishments as a rock steady act at Treasure Isle. Money disputes would drive The Paragons to break up in the early 1970s, after releasing approximately three dozen singles and an album. But, as we will see, this launched John Holt as a bona fide solo star. Reunion album projects occasionally followed in the 1980s – they needn't have bothered. By then, a string of rock steady hits had already permanently engraved The Paragons' name in the history of Jamaican music.

In 1967, the definitive Paragons line-up, with lead singer John Holt backed by Tyrone Evans and Howard Barrett, recorded the utterly disarming 'Wear You To The Ball' for Reid. Perhaps the prettiest love song in all of reggae, it was a big hit. Its instrumental introduction sets a quaint, homey feel, complete with an orderly ringing of a bell, creating a feel that can only come from rock steady. The instrumentation then moves aside, careful to avoid anything that would hamper the vocals. And considering these vocals, that is a very good thing. The Paragons' melody and harmonies are gorgeous throughout. Listen to how they harmonize within a tight tonal span, only to have one voice dramatically provide an accent by sliding up an octave into falsetto. They fully realize Duke Reid's vision of Jamaican vocals that, like those heard in black American soul music, were of a polished quality. But they did so without sacrificing their Jamaican character or creativity.

The lyrics are just as sweet as the harmonies. Holt is excited to be taking his date to a ball. Even though she has been rejected and even insulted by other men, he is proud to be with her. He has no doubt that they will have a great time and that those other men will see her in a new light. There is a playfulness in the lyrics, exemplified by the title. He sees her as being so attractive, he is proudly wearing her to the ball, as if having her on his arm makes him look better. There are few songs anywhere with sentiments this tender, sung so lovingly.

'The Tide Is High' was another 1967 Paragons Treasure Isle hit. (It would also become an international hit in 1980, with a post-punk calypso-inflected cover by US rock group, Blondie.) Quite unsurprisingly, the instrumentation is immaculate and tasteful. But Reid has a surprise up his sleeve with the addition of a rustic country fiddle. Although it had a role in rural mento, fiddle was not heard in R&B or ska, and would very seldom be heard again in rock steady or reggae. Here, it is such a prominent feature of the sound, it makes 'The Tide Is High' a more exotic treat than the usual rock steady fare.

Just like 'Wear You To The Ball', 'The Tide Is High' is a beautifully sung love song with a memorable melody. And once again, The Paragons pay great attention to their vocal arrangement. They alternate between Holt singing solo, Holt singing lead with supporting vocals, and all The Paragons singing in a deliciously wide-open ensemble harmony. Though the lyrics are few, virtually every line is a hook baited with sweet sentiments of love. The memorable chorus is beautifully rendered, with Holt sounding totally sincere as he sings of holding on in spite of the titular challenge. Specifically, he won't quit until he wins her love. "*Oh no!*" he will not and anyone hearing this song is not likely to bet against him.

Alton Ellis & The Flames: *'Cry Tough'*
Alton Ellis was born in 1938 in Kingston to a musical family that also saw his younger sister, Hortense Ellis, become a successful recording artist in her own right. Growing up in Trench Town, Alton proved to be a talented boy, excelling not only in singing and piano, but in dancing and athletics as well. Like Lee Perry

and Lord Messam, he began his career as a dancer, gaining credibility by winning the dance competition in Vere Johns's talent show. A few years later, in 1959, he began his recording career at Studio One as part of the duo Alton & Eddy, with Eddy Perkins. They recorded more than half a dozen R&B songs for producers Coxsone Dodd and Vincent Chin. The first, 'Muriel', gave Ellis and Dodd the first of many hits to come for each of them. Perkins would leave Jamaica and music, and Ellis started his solo career with a single for Prince Buster in 1962 (though he would also record one-off duo singles with David Isaacs, Joey, Ed Nangle, Zoot Simms and John Holt, the latter just before he joined The Paragons). Many of his records were credited to Alton Ellis & The Flames, but the latter designation was used for whatever backing vocalists were at the session rather than a permanent vocal group. (Another sibling, brother Leslie, was sometimes a participant.) Ellis quit music for a time, working as a printer, and returning in 1965 with more sides for Chin and a new association with Duke Reid. The Reid-produced 'Dance Crasher' scored his first ska hit. A hit in a third style would quickly follow, when in 1966 he recorded 'Rock Steady' for Reid, the first song with that term in its title. Although he is best remembered for his Treasure Isle work, Ellis went on to success with a variety of producers, including himself. His technically sound, versatile voice and broad interests made his body of work diverse. He recorded love songs, a run of anti-rude boy songs, gospel, Rasta reggae and had a specialty in covers of US soul hits. Even with a move to England in 1973, he recorded steadily into the mid-1980s and more sporadically up to 1990, totaling over 200 singles and better than a dozen albums. In recognition of a long, diverse, hit-filled career that all on the island admired, the Jamaican government awarded Ellis the Order of Distinction in 1994. Fighting cancer, he collapsed after a 2008 performance in London and passed away the same year.

'Cry Tough', another Treasure Isle rock steady track from 1967, engages with creativity at every turn. It starts with a crafty introduction, as bass and piano exchange tight little phrases, with egalitarian drums in support. But when the body of the song kicks off, this straight rock steady instrumentation is surprisingly augmented with fiddle moans (an instrument that producer Reid apparently had a soft spot for) and a touch of rhythm harmonica. In spite of these rural touches, the overall effect of the song is tough and urban.

Though the term is not used, 'Cry Tough' is one of Ellis's anti-rude boy songs. The lyrics are few and repeated often, as if Ellis believes his message needs to be driven home rather than elaborated on. He casts doubt on the idea that an adult man can be a rude boy, especially once he starts getting older and slower. It's as if he has given up talking to rude youth about their bad behavior, and is instead now targeting aging rudies. Alton generously shares lead vocal duties, as one of The Flames takes lead on the chorus. In a soft bass voice, in a slightly camp, completely charming way, the Flame wonders about a rough man's place in the world. This proves to be the perfect foil for Ellis's cutting, mid-range voice, making the song richer than if he chose to keep the lead all to himself. Rather than repeat the song's four lines for its full length, towards the end, with a burst of echo, Reid drops the vocals. This allows you to sit back and enjoy how piano, fiddle, harmonica, guitar, bass and drum come together in an engaging rock steady riddim.

There are several alternative takes of the song available, though none of them are very different from the most commonly available version. For example, 'Cry Tough Take 6'sounds like the common take without the vocal drop-out, making it repetitious, even with the song's less than two and a half minute length. 'Cry Tough Take 5' is nearly identical to Take 6, but with a single momentary extra vocal outburst. A take called 'Cry Tough Original' is actually a disco-mix with an instrumental version appended to what sounds like Take 6, bringing the length to over 4 minutes. None of these improves on the described take, simply called 'Cry Tough', without a take number.

John Holt: *'Ali Baba'*

Born in Kingston in 1947, John Holt was another Jamaican singer who launched his career on Vere Johns's talent show. He made his first appearance there at age twelve and was popular enough to return many times. But this popularity did not transfer to his earliest records. Two sides of a 1962 R&B single for producer Leslie Kong and a subsequent collaboration with singer Alton Ellis were not successful. But this was Jamaica, where a good singer can't be kept down for long. In 1964, Holt was brought in to serve as The Paragons' new lead singer when Leroy Stamp left the group. This move not only made Holt a star, it also launched The Paragons to greater heights. His solo career would resume while he was still a member of the group, and it continued well past their break-up in the early 1970s, reaching into the 1990s. With a fine voice and an often romantic singing style, Holt's forte was ballads and lovers' rock. But he was a versatile singer who recorded all kinds of songs, with specialties in conservative reggae covers of non-reggae songs (the UK had a big appetite for such material) and roots reggae. In addition to Duke Reid, he worked with producers Coxsone Dodd, Prince Buster, Bunny Lee and many others in a prolific career that resulted in well over 200 singles and more than three dozen albums.

'Ali Baba' was a deservedly huge hit for Holt in 1969. It spawned versions and cover renditions, as well as remakes from Holt, but none of them captured the magic of the original. And there is a lot of magic here, as the song has an enchanting storybook air in both words and music. Holt recalls his previous night's dream, which was populated by fairy-tale characters such as Ali Baba and the Forty Thieves, Alice in Wonderland, Little Bo Peep and the three blind mice, along with nameless princesses, dukes and duchesses. In a unique vocal performance, he sings in a soft voice that is suitably dreamy and filled with wonder. Yet, at the same time, he is vividly expressive. Listen to the feeling he instills into "Tom, Tom, the piper's son", a hook that grabs every time. Holt absolutely delights throughout.

The backing instrumentation is on the same wavelength, setting the tone before Holt begins singing. The introduction includes a horn line that invokes storybook castles, answered by fanciful flute lines. The instrumentation is polished and clockwork-tight even beyond the Treasure Isle standard. All of this makes 'Ali Baba' a beloved reggae classic that just does not sound like any other song. Whether intentionally or not, the family-friendly lyrics and softer sound make 'Ali Baba' perhaps the best all-ages reggae song ever recorded.

The Techniques: *'You Don't Care' (aka 'You'll Want Me Back');'Queen Majesty'*
The vocal group The Techniques was put together by singer Winston Riley during the ska era. Though there would be frequent line-up changes, the other original members were Franklyn White, Frederick Waite and future solo star Slim Smith. They received early international attention in 1963 when Columbia Records released the group's first single in the UK. But their best and most popular work would come during the rock steady era, when the band began to record for producer Duke Reid. (By then, Smith had departed. Later he would form a spin-off vocal group called The Uniques that included original Technique Franklyn White and, for a time, future star Cornel Campbell.) After parting with Reid, Riley would become a successful producer in his own right, and the name Techniques was also used for his record label and his backing band. (This explains how the great instrumental 'Stalag 17', a song described later in this book [page 312], came to be attributed to a vocal group.) The Techniques recorded through the early 1980s, although that period included the inevitable personnel changes, break-ups and reunions. In all, they released about 90 singles and four albums. Winston Riley met a particularly violent end, even by Jamaican standards. He died at the start of 2012, having been shot months earlier. This followed another shooting some months before and a later incident of being stabbed five times.

'You Don't Care', released in 1967, is sometimes billed to Pat Kelly rather than to The Techniques. Kelly was newly installed as The Techniques' lead singer when this track was recorded. The man he replaced, Slim Smith, had recorded a rendition of this song a year earlier for Studio One. That rendition is nearly as good, but this sprightlier version wins out.

The riddim is a classic piece of rock steady instrumentation. It opens with rock steady piano, spring-water clear and refreshing, that carries most of the melody. The bass line is in equal parts melodic and rhythmic. It's the riddim's secret weapon. Resolute and nimble, it dances for the full length of the track, and Reid's production assures it a prominent place in the mix. Drums, rhythm guitar and maracas complete the riddim. Their playing is simple but intelligent – each musician is capable of playing something more complex, but that would have hurt rather than helped the overall sound. Instead, the instruments complement one another, and the riddim becomes more than the sum of their parts, yielding a perfect rock steady groove. Once The Techniques come in, the piano falls back to rhythm duties, allowing the vocals, supplemented by the bass, to become the melodic focal points. There is no solo in this song, just a mid-song break in the vocals, allowing the riddim to shine through for a few bars. The 'You Don't Care' riddim would be used again, the most notable version being Nora Dean's 'Barbwire', a song discussed in Chapter 23, which is on this singer. Though the riddims are identical, Dean's vocals come in earlier than the Techniques'. Reggae fans are conditioned to name that tune as 'You Don't Care' rather than 'Barbwire' if vocals are not heard by the second bar.

The Techniques' vocal performance and lyrics are both up to the high standard of the riddim, right from the song's opening. Kelly realizes that his girl really doesn't treat him properly. By the second half of the song, the lyrics turn from aggrieved to victorious, as he shows her the door. Kelly sings in a soulful falsetto that sounds a bit exotic. Not only is his voice liberally treated with reverb, but his singing features an idiosyncratic little quiver and a slightly tilted approach to the scale, giving him an interesting edge. The backing vocals by Bruce Ruffin and Winston Riley are also sung in a high register in this treble-fest. They alternate between harmonizing with and responding to the call of Kelly's lead. The call and response is especially strong at the song's conclusion, when the girl runs and cries, wanting to come back, but is told that she is "too late, bye bye". Along with The Cable's 'Baby Why' (a song described later in this book; page 140), 'You Don't Care' is the very best of soulful rock steady.

Later in 1967, The Techniques recorded 'Queen Majesty', a cover of a 1961 doo-wop-soul-R&B song by Curtis Mayfield and The Impressions, 'Minstrel And Queen'. The resulting heartfelt rock steady classic would give The Techniques their biggest hit, and spur covers from a variety of other reggae artists. (One fine example is the roots reggae disco-mix by vocal group The Jays and DJ Ranking Trevor, as featured in the soundtrack for the film *Rockers*.) The Techniques add a distinctive instrumental opening that is not found in The Impressions' original: a syncopated series of bright ringing guitar chords supported by a conversation between piano and flurries of staccato bass and drums. It's an evocative introduction, as majestic as the title promises. And it foreshadows the romantic nature of the song by sounding not unlike a highly condensed version of Mendelssohn's 'Wedding March'.

The rock steady that follows sounds creamy by comparison. A rhythm guitar sounds like a contented metronome, as a picked guitar, bass, drums and maracas create a blissful riddim. Over this, The Techniques enter with a block of ultra-lush wordless falsetto harmonies in the soul by way of Jamaica way. The lead singer is the former Paragon Junior Menz. He has a good voice and is more conventionally soulful and less quirky than Pat Kelly, whom he had recently replaced. Menz gives his all in portraying a lowly court minstrel who proclaims his love to the queen. He acknowledges the difference in their stations, but senses that she may secretly love him back. In voice, words and instruments, 'Queen Majesty' could not be more romantic. In Jamaica, a land of great class distinctions, this tale of a bold and unlikely proclamation of love that couldn't be bound by social status resonated all the more deeply.

Phyllis Dillon & Hopeton Lewis: *'Right Track' (aka 'Get On The Right Track')*
Hopeton Lewis was born in 1947 in Kingston, and discovered his musical ability in church. He started his recording career at the tail end of the ska era, but became better known for his rock steady work. This included a pair of big firsts: 'Take It Easy', in 1966, is one of the songs considered to be the first rock steady track; and 'Cool Cool Collie', in 1967, is reggae's first song about ganja. (In this way, reggae was ahead of rock, which up to this point had songs about getting stoned, but did not explicitly describe smoking pot. For example, in the same year as 'Cool Cool Collie', Pink Floyd's first single was planned to have 'Let's Roll Another One' as the B-side. But their label forced them to bowdlerize the song, and it was rewritten as 'Candy And A Currant Bun'.) In 1970, Lewis won Festival with 'Boom Shaka Lacka'. He would continue to record into the 1980s, and although not especially prolific compared to some of his peers, he amassed approximately 70 singles and an album. By the mid-1990s, Lewis's singing came full circle and he began to record gospel CDs, releasing twelve such albums to date.

Phyllis Dillon was born in 1948 in Linstead, Saint Catherine Parish. Like Lewis, she came to music through the church. As a singer for a local band called The Vulcans, she was discovered by Lyn Taitt when the act made it to Kingston's Glass Bucket Club. He recruited her to Treasure Isle, and her first record was made there in 1966. She continued to work with Reid, recording her own compositions and rock steady covers of overseas hits through the early 1970s. But, because she was making little money despite her popularity, she left music and Jamaica at the end of 1967 and moved to New York City. Dillon returned to recording in the 1990s, working again with Lyn Taitt, obviously her biggest booster. She died in 2004 after losing a battle with cancer.

The tuneful 'Right Track', from 1969, is one of three collaborations by Phyllis Dillon and Hopeton Lewis. It's a perfect summer day of a song, combining the sweet vocal skills of two talented rock steady singers with an oh-so-catchy Treasure Isle backing.

Though some have taken this song to be an invitation to love, 'Right Track' seems rather to be another church-born train to redemption reggae song, especially considering the backgrounds of the singers. No matter the meaning, Lewis and Dillon sound as if they were born to sing together. Although Lewis takes a few lines alone, most of the song is sung in unison. Their superb, easy-going harmonies are born of a natural chemistry.

The instrumentation is perfectly arranged in the Treasure Isle way – interesting in its own right, but careful never to get in the way of the vocals. It's anchored by shuffling drums that are busy for Treasure Isle rock steady, understated but energetic bass, a clockwork rhythm guitar chop and jabbing organ chords that add spice. But best of all, there's a big fat hook in the form of a merry see-sawing organ phrase that's answered by horns. It's heard at the song's opening, middle and fade-out. Its easy-going nature matches that of the vocals, but its madcap melody provides a nice contrast to the seriousness of the lyrics. A unique and beloved Treasure Isle song with so much going for it, if you want to be on the right track for rock steady, this is a song not to miss.

11 Great rock steady from other studios

As strongly associated as rock steady is with Duke Reid, as distinct the Treasure Isle sound, as loyal the following it still enjoys today and as wonderful as the music is, this producer did not have a monopoly on great rock steady. You will see some proof of this in the individual artist chapters that follow. In this chapter I describe more rock steady songs that are just as great as those from Reid, from other producers both famous and lesser known. Often using the same musicians that Reid employed, these songs could sound very similar to what came from Treasure Isle, somewhat similar, or very different.

Hopeton Lewis: *'Sounds And Pressure'*
Hopeton Lewis's beloved rock steady classic, 'Sounds And Pressure', was produced in 1966 by Sam Mitchell and Keith Scott, the house production team for the original Merritone label. Bankrolled by mento producer Ken Khouri and his sons, this label sprang into existence at the dawning of rock steady only to vanish just as the era ended (though others would later revive it).

Whereas most great rock steady has a warm, easy-going appeal, 'Sounds And Pressure' has an oh-so-cool vibe that is no less appealing. Half the credit goes to Lewis. His singing is urgent, but controlled and very hip. He's strikingly cool, telling us about a well-attended dance, with his very Jamaican wordless choruses of "ooo-ooo-ooowee" and his imploring us to "dig me straight". The other half goes to the equally cool instrumental groove. The sound is dominated by piano played by Leslie Butler, along with a barely noticeable rhythm guitar and ultra-laidback bass and drums. Though piano is a signature instrument in rock steady, it's played so lush and jazzy here – especially in the mid-song solo – that it's reminiscent of the great playing heard in some golden-age urban mento. *Dig me straight*, this great, unique rock steady song is one you'll want to hear. It is readily available on a number of CD compilations. Lewis remade the song in the late 1970s, but it cannot compare to the original rendition.

Alton Ellis, Peter Austin, Zoot Simms & The Freedom Singers: *'Rude Boy Prayer'*
Dating from 1966 and produced by Coxsone Dodd, 'Rude Boy Prayer' is perhaps the greatest forgotten song in all of reggae. It has never appeared on any of the many compilations of Studio One, rock steady, rude boy or Alton Ellis material, though it would have been a crown jewel in any such set. Instead, serious collectors have to wait for a copy to appear on eBay, preparing themselves to bid hundreds

of dollars for a used 45-rpm single with a blank label. This latter feature has led to great confusion about this record and has perhaps contributed to it being omitted from the aforementioned collections. Of the artists listed above, this single has been variously attributed to any one or more of them. We have already met Alton Ellis. Peter Austin recorded as a member of the vocal group The Clarendonians and as a soloist from the mid-1960s to the early 1970s. Noel "Zoot" Simms enjoyed a long and interesting career, beginning as an R&B singer in the 1950s and recording into the early 1970s. It was then that he started his second career as the prolific roots percussionist called Skully. The Freedom Singers is one of the group names used at Studio One for backing singers. Additionally, Bob Marley and Peter Tosh have been apocryphally credited, Marley, because Alton Ellis could sound similar to a young Bob, and Tosh, because the single is sometimes attributed to Alton, Peter & Zoot. But close listening rules out any Wailer involvement. Again owing to the blank labels, the song is sometimes called 'Rudy's Prayer' or 'Save Me'. The latter is the name of the Motown song by The Miracles from the same year that 'Rude Boy Prayer' uses as a template. The melody and the chorus of "save me", along with a few other phrases, are carried over. But the unvarnished Jamaican sound, with vocals filled with raw emotional turmoil and an instrumental arrangement to match, bears little resemblance to The Miracles' highly polished lightweight stuff about a departed lover. The sound is so rough and ready that, if this recording had been tried at Treasure Isle, Duke Reid would have surely drawn his gun.

'Rude Boy Prayer' is more than another great rude boy song; it's a rude boy opera. Different singers and choruses play the parts of the rude boy, his mother, his lover and more. Youth vocals and other errant notes are common, adding to the street-level realness of the song. A chorus of voices begins with the sharpest and most personal rude boy censure heard in any song: "Mama says to rude boy, 'So you reap, so you die. And if you don't come back, I hope you drown in a ditch', she cried." In gloriously raw harmony with the backing singers, the rude boy pleads to God to be saved, admitting that his soul is wicked. He then confesses his crimes as a gunman. A chorus (representing either a narrator or perhaps the voice of God) repeats, "Last chance rudie", and an odd repeated organ phrase provides a devolved mid-song solo. We then hear from the rudie's girlfriend. She is conflicted over being with the rudie and asks God for guidance. The song ends like a soulful gospel review, with everyone raising their voices to exchange reprised lines, as the rudie despairs and begs for a new soul." It's enough to give you the chills.

When this rare record is played, 'Rude Boy Prayer' stops reggae fans in their tracks. Though immediately recognizable as part of the reggae canon, it sounds like no other song. 'Rude Boy Prayer' has appeared on a Japanese CD collection that I will decline to describe other than to say that it is an unauthorized pirate collection and that the song is both incomplete and pitched too fast. Recently highlighted by Mutabaruka on his Jamaican radio show, it's only a matter of time until this song finally sees its re-release.

Winston & George: *'Denham Town'*
The Spanishtonians: *'Rudie Gets Plenty'*
The Valentines: *'Gun Fever' (aka 'Blam Blam Fever')*
Great rude boy songs in the rock steady era were not just the province of star singers like The Wailers and (as we will see in the next chapter) Desmond Dekker. Everybody had something to say on this subject. Here is a trio of fine rock steady rude boy songs recorded by lesser known artists. In all three cases, the acts are best remembered for these songs alone. All three are available as part of the Trojan Records CD collection called *The Trojan Rude Boy Box Set*.

First up, opening with pistol report drums, is the savvy 'Denham Town' by Winston & George, as produced in 1966 by Leslie Kong. George Canic Agard is Desmond Dekker's half-brother; he is also known as George Dekker or, less frequently, as Johnny Melody. He recorded a bit as a solo singer, in other duos, as backing singer for Desmond and as a member of The Pioneers. Winston Ware was George's childhood friend. This song is the only track by the duo. They sing in unison with one voice high-pitched and strident, the other lower and flatter, creating a sweet-and-sour harmony. They craft a winning melody, delivering their lines in a rhythmically fixed way. The result is a distinctly Jamaican vocal sound, delivered over a basic but appealing rock steady backing. The song describes the escalating violence of the rude boys in the rough Denham Town section of Kingston, as hatchets, knives and guns are in play. An anti-rude boy song, it predicts retreat and then jail for the rudies.

A year later, Kong produced 'Rudie Gets Plenty' by the pride of Spanish Town, The Spanishtonians. Originally known as The Spanish Town Skabeats, this vocal group recorded a handful of ska and rock steady tracks in the mid-1960s for Kong and Prince Buster. 'Rudie Gets Plenty' could be a sequel to the Winston & George song, as once again strident and smooth voices in unison deliver rhythmically fixed lines to pleasing effect. The rock steady backing is a bit jauntier this time around, and a Nyabinghi hand drum is heard, anticipating roots reggae to come. Though there is violence, theft is the featured rude boy crime here, as "Shantytown get scanty". And although the lyrics are a condemnation of rude-boy behavior, there is a touch of ambivalence. The jaunty tone and shows of concern keep the song from being totally anti-rude boy.

The same year, Sonia Pottinger produced 'Gun Fever' by vocal group The Valentines. Credited on just two songs, The Valentines turns out to have been a short-lived pseudonym used by The Silvertones. (They would later record under another pseudonym, The Musketeers, sometimes oddly spelled as The Muskyteers.) The Silvertones were comprised of Carl "Gilmore" Grant of Saint Mary Parish, Keith Coley of Saint Elizabeth and, soon after their debut for Duke Reid in 1966, Delroy Denton, who would be replaced early in the 1970s. Though far from prolific, their career ran through the early 1980s. Under all their monikers, they recorded a total of about 60 singles and two albums. Sonia Pottinger is reggae's most successful female record producer, crashing an otherwise all-boys club. She was born Sonia Eloise Durrant in Saint Thomas Parish in 1931, but was brought up in Kingston. Her husband, Lyndon Pottinger, began producing in 1961, but gave it up in 1964. The next year, Sonia continued the family legacy, just in time for the rock steady sound she seemed so suited for. Many hear a welcome feminine touch in the records she produced. She worked until 1980, producing more than 600 singles. She passed away in 2010 after suffering from Alzheimer's. (Patricia Chin, wife of producer Vincent Chin, was the only other woman to break into this fraternity.)

The Valentines are looser and sound more confident than the groups in the previous two songs, and the instrumentation is more open and creative. The focus this time is on gun violence, a growing problem then in Jamaica that would only worsen over time. Guns would become so common (and some would say necessary) in Jamaica that, by the turn of the millennium, they were called "tools" in street slang. The song begins with a wailing voice singing about the return of rude boys and their "gun fever". Then, using a creative device that has been imitated in other reggae songs, another voice takes over, simulating the deep flat tones of a newsreader. He details the impact of escalating gun violence on Jamaica, where "blam blam blam" is often seen as the simplest solution. With these two characters telling the story, never has such a serious social problem produced such a fun, jaunty song. Only in Jamaica could a serious issue, musical talent and an appetite for novel songs collide to yield a track like 'Gun Fever'.

Derrick Morgan: *'Tougher Than Tough' (aka 'Rudie's In Court')*
Produced by Leslie Kong in 1967, 'Tougher Than Tough' is a true example of grace under pressure. This classic and frequently imitated track was commissioned under threat from Derrick Morgan by a dangerous rude boy named Busby who wanted to be celebrated in song. According to Busby's requirements, the song had to be written, recorded and pressed for a dance that was just days away.

The resulting 'Tougher Than Tough' is a good reminder that Duke Reid did not own a monopoly on crystal-clear rock steady. With Gladstone Anderson's bright piano out front over Bryan Atkinson's bouncing melodic bass, rhythm guitar chirps from Lyn Taitt and drums from Joe Isaacs, Morgan is provided a rock steady backing as fresh as any. He rides the breeze right into a courtroom. A drama unfolds that has Morgan playing the judge in a spoken-sung role. Desmond Dekker and his half-brother George, in tow to provide harmony, play defiant rude boys on trial. And in rude boy fashion, they steal the show, harmonizing plaintively and getting much more mic time than headliner Morgan. The judge calls the court to order and reads a list of serious charges. In addition to using ratchet and gun, these rudies are charged with throwing bombs. They begin their defense, singing lines of fearless defiance. Their closing argument consists of "Yeah, boy, rudies are free". No doubt won over by a well-sung legal argument featuring the irresistible power of Jamaican harmony, the judge agrees and adjourns the court.

'Tougher Than Tough' was great music and great fun. A big hit, it delighted rock steady fans. It also had a lasting impact, resulting in many similar songs over the decades. Though not reggae's first courtroom drama (see 'Big Sid' by golden-age mento band Chin's Calypso Sextet, previously described in the chapter on this group; page 63), it provided a particular template that others quickly followed. In particular, Prince Buster responded with a number of court records ('Barrister Pardon', 'Judge Dread', 'Judge Dread Dance'), in which, instead of being freed, the rudies received comically severe jail sentences. Morgan got the last word in this musical feud with his 'Judge Dread In Court', where the judge declares Buster a fraud and gives him jail time! Peter Tosh's 'Here Comes the Judge' (a song described later in this book; page 225) puts historical figures of colonialism on trial. Even the 1970s UK ska revivalists The Specials got into the act, and quite nicely, as 'Stupid Marriage' found the singer in divorce court. 'People's Court' Parts 1 and 2, by dub poet Mutabaruka in 1991 and 1994, continued the form, now sporting a roots reggae sensibility.

But there was no bigger fan of the song than Busby himself. Ironically, the lifestyle that spurred the song would severely truncate his enjoyment of it. Celebrating wildly upon hearing it played at the dance, he spilled wine on a rival gang's girlfriends. Morgan well remembers the next night at the dance, when a youth of about twelve, hands shaking, shot Busby in the head in retribution, while Morgan stood dangerously close by.

'Tougher Than Tough' is readily available today on several Derrick Morgan CD collections. It was also featured on – and gave its name to – Island Records' biggest reggae compilation, the 1993 4-CD box-set called *Tougher Than Tough: The Story Of Jamaican Music*.

Ken Boothe: 'Artibella'; 'When I Fall In Love'

The man called "Mr. Rock Steady" was immersed in music well before that age of reggae dawned. Ken Boothe was born in 1948 in a musically rich home in the impoverished Kingston neighborhood of Denham Town. His mother and a sister both sang, and he grew up listening to American R&B and gospel. His own talent was obvious from an early age, winning a singing competition at age eight. When he was fifteen, he made his first recordings as a duo with the more established Stranger Cole. Billed as Stranger & Ken, they had a number of popular songs in the ska era for producers Duke Reid, Coxsone Dodd and others. In 1966, he formed a short-lived duo with Roy Shirley, billed as Roy & Ken. The same year he began work as a solo artist, initially for Coxsone Dodd at Studio One. He would soon work with Leslie Kong and other producers. After the rock steady era, Boothe collaborated with singer B. B. Seaton in the early 1970s, forming a vocal group called The Conscious Minds, then another group called The Messengers. He would enjoy popularity in the UK as well as Jamaica, touring and releasing a number of popular records there throughout the 1970s. Released by Trojan Records, these were often reggae cover versions of non-reggae hits. He recorded steadily into the late 1980s, and sporadically into the new millennium. In 2013, he recorded an album to celebrate his fiftieth year in music. In all, he recorded about 200 singles and 25 albums (including a gospel album), the last in 2013. That same year, the Jamaican government awarded him the Order of Distinction for his contribution to Jamaican music, just one of several honors he has received. But perhaps the greatest honor came in the form of his nickname, as it was given by the people and could be awarded only once. And although his success was broader than rock steady, the Ken Boothe classics described below make it clear why he isn't "Mr. Ska", "Mr. Vocal Group" or "Mr. Cover Version" instead.

Ken Boothe's 'When I Fall In Love', produced by Coxsone Dodd in 1968, is more than a great rock steady song. This unequivocal piece of lovers' rock may be the most romantic reggae song ever recorded. Though always a good singer, Boothe has never sounded better than he does here. With a heartfelt melody and tender delivery, he passionately proclaims the absolute permanence of his love. He manages to convey not only the love he feels towards his girl, but a reverence for the very concept of love, clearly taking the subject very seriously. He is well supported by handsome backing vocals and a well-considered rock steady riddim in this serious sentimental love song.

A signature song for Boothe, numerous remakes of 'When I Fall In Love' were recorded over the years, even as late as 2012. However, none matches the original. The 2014 CD compilation, *Studio One Rock Steady*, released by Soul Jazz Records, made it easy to acquire this fine Valentine of a song. Many artists have covered it, including a single riddim CD in which Boothe collaborated with dancehall stars. Covers by Sly & Robbie and Augustus Pablo are good enough to be discussed in the chapters on these artists (Chapters 42 and 27 respectively).

Along with Hopeton Lewis's 'Sounds And Pressure', Ken Boothe's 'Artibella' is another example of a rock steady song that's too cool rather than sunny warm. Produced by George "Phil Pratt" Phillips in 1970, it's a remake of a frantic ska track that Boothe recorded as a duo with Stranger Cole in 1965 for Coxsone Dodd. Boothe would subsequently remake the song in various reggae and dancehall styles, giving him a second signature song, but this rendition is the best, and is widely available on Ken Boothe CD collections.

Even as Boothe begs his titular girlfriend to return after she has robbed and left him, he is supremely cool and composed. (For example, compare his restraint to the unbridled emotion heard on a later rendition by Black Uhuru's Michael Rose, a song described in Chapter 41, on this group. It's as if Boothe can't be out-cooled, so Rose takes the opposite tack and goes over the top.) Helping Boothe keep his cool is the crisp, clear, mountain breeze of a riddim from Ernest Ranglin's 'Surfin'' (a song described later in this book; page 180). Here, Ranglin's sensational guitar work is completely absent, replaced by a fine lead and rhythm organ track to join the riddim's strong drums and killer melodic start-and-stop bass line.

Let's not take for granted how well Boothe's melody goes with the riddim, sounding as if they were created for one another. But, in fact, the song's melody and riddim existed separately before Boothe put them together here. In doing so, he succeeds at what should be impossible: completely supplanting Ranglin's guitar, which is never missed, as he makes the riddim his own. Reggae's practice of versioning has once again allowed a classic to beget a classic. If you put a Jamaican producer in charge of a gold mine, not only would each and every molecule of the precious metal be extracted, some nuggets would somehow be extracted again and again. (And the miners would not be compensated for this magic.)

Lloyd Robinson & Devon Russell: *'Red Bum Ball'*
Lloyd Robinson began his recording career early in the ska era. He previously performed in a duo with Glen Brown and was a member of The Tartans before recording a handful of songs with Devon Russell. Robinson died in 2013. Russell had sung in ska vocal group The Bellstars and rock steady vocal group The Tartans (both of which included Cedric Myton, who would later form The Congos) and he later recorded roots reggae for Lee Perry under the name Devon Irons. By the late 1970s, Russell had branched out as a producer. He died of cancer in 1997. Several fine songs by Robinson and Russell as partners and as solo singers are described throughout this book, but their most famous song as a team was 'Red Bum Ball'.

Produced in 1968 by Derrick Morgan, 'Red Bum Ball' is a much-adored rock steady track. It's a soft-hearted song of schoolday memories. Singing in unison throughout, with forays into falsetto, Robinson and Russell recall a schoolyard playmate who smiled and then cried when her ball was taken away from her. The vocals are so heartfelt, they more than make up for falling below technical perfection, and their melody is well remembered and beloved by reggae fans. Well matched to the vocals is the highly approachable rock steady backing. Bass is the lead instrument throughout, bouncing like the titular ball. It's accompanied by dashes of piano, reggae chop guitar and non-threatening drums to produce a sound that is amiable even by the standards of rock steady. 'Red Bum Ball' has been versioned, remade and covered (one rendition is briefly discussed in Chapter 42 on Sly & Robbie), but this is another case of the original never quite being matched. It can be found on the rock steady CD compilation of the same name.

The Cables: *'Baby Why'*
The Gladiators: *'Rearrange'*
In the vocal group The Cables were Keeble Drummond, Elbert Stewart and Vince Stoddard. Group leader Drummond had previously participated in an unrecorded group called The Sylastians that also included two future Heptones (Barry Llewellyn and Earl Morgan) and a future Ace (Clive Campbell). Though The Cables had come together some time before, their first record was in 1966 for producer

Sonia Pottinger. They then moved to work with Coxsone Dodd and other producers, recording over 30 singles before breaking up in 1972. Drummond carried on with a solo career, and the group occasionally reunited, most recently in 1994.

In 1968, The Cables released 'Baby Why', a piece of rock steady perfection produced by Coxsone Dodd. An immaculate rock steady backing is heard with a summer's breeze horn line, an athletic bass line, clever understated drum work and a rhythm guitar chop with a springy bounce. But the arrangement also includes a nascent reggae element: a bubbling shuffle organ provided by Jackie Mittoo, the likes of which would be so frequently heard once rock steady gave way to reggae proper. Atop of this, The Cables sing of a love leaving for another with soulful vocals that are outstanding. The descending melody Drummond composes is captivating, and his voice is ripe with tremulous emotion. It's a technically skilled voice, but thankfully, not an overly polished one. Listen to how his emotional peaks are underscored with stridency, making a fine performance all the richer. Meanwhile, the backing vocals sound similar to Drummond, only more restrained, making his emotion stand out in relief. 'Baby Why' is a great example of the soulful side of rock steady. If this material had been brought to Detroit, it could have buffed into a Motown hit. But the song is better for having come from Jamaica.

The riddim proved popular, yielding dub and DJ versions. A decade later, in 1976, as he was wont to do, Dodd blew off the dust and had roots vocal group The Gladiators re-voice it as 'Rearrange'. Albert Griffiths was born in Saint Elizabeth, but grew up in Trench Town. After testing the waters as a solo singer, he formed The Gladiators in 1968 with two childhood friends. The group broke up, but in the early 1970s, Griffiths re-formed The Gladiators with two students from the music school he was running, Clinton Fearon and Dallimore Sutherland. This gave the group its classic roots reggae line-up. Unusually for a vocal group, they often handled their own guitar and bass duties. (Unusual, but not unique. In The Wailers, Bob was proficient on guitar and Peter was better, and also played keyboards, while Bunny played some hand percussion and was a budding bass player. But, as we will see, with only a few exceptions, they would defer to the ace backing bands they worked with. And Heptone Leroy Sibbles played bass on the group's recordings and on those of others.) As a roots reggae group, they enjoyed local and international success with the approximately 90 singles and about 37 albums that they released up to 2009. The group is still in existence, but with several second-generation Gladiators taking the place of their fathers.

In 'Rearrange', The Gladiators respond to this pre-roots riddim by adjusting their normal approach to harmony. This resulted in not only a unique sound for the group, but a unique record. They sing in choral block harmonies that are quite unlike the looser roots style and more like Jamaican folk music than reggae. Yet they bring a roots edge to their heartfelt singing. Reeling from the reality of violence in Jamaica, the lyrics are clearly from the roots reggae rather than rock steady or folk camps. They suggest that if the people meditate on the causes, the violence can be quelled. With 'Rearrange', The Gladiators created an unusual, very enjoyable version, even if following in the large footprints of 'Baby Why'. If versioning could be expressed as a formula, here is the math that Coxsone Dodd wrought: 1 riddim + 2 vocal trios + 2 vocal sounds + 2 subjects / 2 decades = 2 great reggae songs. Both versions can be easily found on CD.

The Slickers: *'Johnny Too Bad'*
The Slickers recorded in one form or another from 1963 to the 1980s. Backing singer Derrick Crooks, also a founding member of The Pioneers, was the only continuous member throughout the group's varied life span. Even by Jamaican standards, The Slickers have a notoriously clouded history, hazed by the use of pseudonyms, frequent line-up changes, incomplete memories and conflicting claims. For example, the first Slickers single to appear is said to have actually been recorded by The Pioneers, which would push the group's true debut up to 1966. They also recorded as The Survivors and The Mighty Survivors. In total, nearly 60 singles and two LPs bear one of these three names, the last in the mid-1980s. One song beams through the haze: The Slickers' only hit, the internationally known rude boy classic, 'Johnny Too Bad'.

'Johnny Too Bad' was produced by Tommy Cowan and Byron Lee in 1970. Along with Desmond Dekker's '007' (a song described in the chapter on this singer; see page 147), it's one of two rude boy songs included on the fantastic soundtrack for *The Harder They Come*, the Jamaican movie about the rise and lead-filled fall of a rude boy. As such, it was the first rude boy song that most of the world ever heard. And the world had every reason to like what it was hearing.

It opens with a fine, high-energy rock steady riddim from backing band The Dynamites, featuring a swirling lead organ from Winston Wright that makes a welcome return as a mid-song solo. A hard, dry reggae guitar chop perfectly suits the song's matter-of-fact lyrics. The bass line gave many their first exposure to how the instrument was used in reggae to add another layer of melody that musically enriched a song. Wonderfully Jamaican vocals follow. The Slickers sound closer to the street than the stellar voices heard on many of the film's other tracks by such big-name singers as Desmond Dekker, Jimmy Cliff and Toots & The Maytals. This street-level feel suits the song's lyrics, too. Abraham Green provides the fine lead vocal while Crooks and another singer provide snatches of backing vocals that are alternately wailing and soothing. They waste no time in describing the rude boy's swagger and bad behavior (theft and looting; stabbing and gunplay). It's not clear whether The Slickers are celebrating or decrying this behavior, until the issue of divine retribution is introduced.

Though there are other rock steady songs that are as good as 'Johnny Too Bad', none are better. Yet, you'll have to look hard to find another Slickers song that is nearly as good. Though it's in a very different style from 'Johnny Too Bad', 'Nana' is quite good. But it's rumored to have actually been recorded by The Pioneers.

Desi Young: *'I Don't Know Why (I Love You)'*

Producer Harry Zephaniah Johnson, better known as "Harry J", was born in 1945 in Westmoreland Parish. He began in music as a member of the vocal group The Virtues, which got a toe in recording, but he switched to production in 1968. Leasing time from Coxsone Dodd, he worked his productions at Studio One, creating an adjunct to the already considerable legacy of great music to come from that studio. In 1969, he produced 'Liquidator', a Winston Wright-led organ instrumental that was a big hit in Jamaica and the UK. Not only was it heavily versioned, it swam against the tide of reggae's appropriations from overseas songs when its introductory hook became the basis for the 1972 US hit, 'I'll Take You There', by the popular soul act, The Staples Singers. Harry J produced over 300 singles through 1985. He died in 2013 from complications of diabetes.

Desmond "Desi" Young, later to be known as Desi Roots, was not a prolific singer, recording about fifteen singles and two albums over an eleven-year span beginning in the early 1970s. 'I Don't Know Why (I Love You)' is his faithful cover of a Stevie Wonder song. Wonder's tale of love that resists poor treatment had also been covered by such big-name artists as The Rolling Stones and The Jackson Five. Though obscure to the point of non-existence in comparison to these superstars, Young's cover, as produced by Harry J in 1972, stacks up well against any rendition, and is fondly regarded by reggae fans.

One reason why Young's song works so well is that Harry J smartly chose a rock steady-style arrangement, even though the sound was already passé by this time. By doing so, he leveraged the similarities between rock steady and the Motown sound of the original. Both styles of music share a restrained approach to instrumentation, honoring the needs of the song without flashy shows of technique. But in neither case does this hinder the music, as the talents of these crack musicians shine through, with playing that is precise, winning and filled with hooks. Harry J's approach allowed all that was good in the original to transfer over to Young's song, with its Jamaican characteristics adding to the enjoyment.

Take, for example, the irresistible trombone riff first heard in the song's opening. Unique to this rendition, it gives the song a hook that's 24-karat Jamaican gold even before the singer is heard. The body of the song begins and there is more rock steady goodness, as a relaxed riddim is expertly played. It features a bass line that happily bounces around the song's rhythmic melodic dimensions, as pretty piano playing comes and goes as needed, converting over to organ by the song's end. In lieu of a solo, mid-song, there's a gnarly descending riff played together by guitar and bass, giving the song another creative instrumental hook. Desi is perfectly suited for this accomplished backing, his strong technique making it a mystery why he didn't record more. His singing displays rock steady cool, even when he shows his emotions. He feels the song deeply and makes the most of all the opportunities the lyrics offer, acquitting himself extremely well, even in the company of giants. Though it's something of an anachronism, it's wonderful that

'I Don't Know Why (I Love You)' extends the history of great rock steady songs. It can be heard on the *Trojan Motor City Reggae* box-set.

The Heptones: *'Book of Rules'*

Leroy Sibbles, Earl Morgan and Barry Llewellyn of Trench Town combined their talents as the vocal group The Heptones. In an example of inspiration springing from unexpected places, they were first known as The Hep Ones, but they decided to change their name when Morgan spotted a bottle of Heptones Tonic in a garbage pile. They recorded from 1966 through the 1970s and sporadically thereafter, most recently in 1996. They are best remembered for the rock steady they recorded for producer Coxsone Dodd. They also recorded other styles of reggae working with other producers. But they never recorded for Duke Reid, Dodd having all but an exclusive with the group throughout the rock steady era. The Heptones' career was a successful one, producing an impressive body of work of over 200 singles and seventeen albums. They helped other artists in a variety of roles; they provided backing vocals for other singers, and at Studio One Sibbles worked as a sessions bassist. Among many other songs, he played on at least two stone-cold classics described later in this book (pages 172 and 318): Sound Dimension's 'Full Up' and The Abyssinians' 'Satta Amassa Ganna'. He also auditioned talent for Dodd and became one of his arrangers.

One has to wonder whether producer "Harry J" Johnson was going for a tribute to Duke Reid or was trying to beat him at his own game with the Heptones' 1973 song, 'Book of Rules'. This carefully outfitted song features exceptional orderliness and polish that is retro-Reid rock steady, and then some. It was released well after the rock steady era – the same year that the international roots reggae game-changer, 'Catch A Fire' by Bob Marley & The Wailers, was released. Yet only the prominent Nyabinghi hand drum that adds a surprising amount of depth to the song gives any indication that it was recorded in the roots reggae era.

There is much good here. Along with the Nyah drum, a distinctive ascending trebly piano line, simple and elegant, stands out. Both the lead vocal from Llewellyn and the backing vocals are absolutely impeccable – technically flawless and polished, readily accessible for any music fan. The lyrics are poetry, literally, as they come from 'A Bag Of Tools', a popular poem by R. L. Sharpe, published in the USA in the 1930s. Exceptionally handsome from every angle, 'Book Of Rules' provides us with an final great rock steady song.

'Book Of Rules' was judged worthy of inclusion in the fine soundtrack for the movie *Rockers*. It caught the attention of The Grateful Dead's Bob Weir, who covered it on his 1981 LP, *Bobby & The Midnites*. Though it loses the original's return-to-Treasure-Isle feel, Weir took care in his reggae rendition, even preserving the ascending piano phrase.

12 Desmond Dekker & The Aces with The Dynamites at Beverly's

Desmond Dekker kicked the floodgates open. Though some earlier tracks charted, Dekker was the first Jamaican recording artist to have hit records outside of Jamaica with unadulterated reggae music. This paved the way for Bob Marley & The Wailers, Jimmy Cliff, Toots & The Maytals and all the others that followed, making reggae performers international stars and reggae one of the few genres of music that's performed in virtually every country around the world. Dekker's pioneering feat was accomplished by no other means than the sheer excellence of a series of rock steady songs he released from 1966 to 1968. On the strength of these records, Dekker would break through where a considerable body of earlier fine Jamaican music had failed.

Dekker's success would also give birth to the first rock/reggae collaboration. For his 1972 debut solo LP, Paul Simon traveled to Jamaica to record 'Mother And Child Reunion', giving him a hit. He employed Dekker's backing band and a singing style that is noticeably influenced by Dekker. Additionally, Dekker is assumed to be an influence on The Beatles pop-reggae song, 'Ob-La-Di, Ob-La-Da', with its protagonist named Desmond. (Released in late 1968, the timing is right, but this story, though widely repeated, does not seem to have ever been substantiated in print by any Beatle.) Many sources have this song as being the first reggae-influenced recording by a rock band. Well, that's only if you ignore the ska influence on several earlier Beatles songs, such as 'It Won't Be Long' from 1963, 'She's A Woman' from 1964, and the overtly ska-influenced section of 'You Know My Name (Look Up The Number)', for which recording started in 1967 although it was not released in its complete form until later. And, as we will see, Dekker was also an inspiration for – and a participant in – the late 1970s UK punk-ska Two-Tone scene.

For all his groundbreaking success and all that he would influence, Dekker's beginnings were humble, as was the case for so many reggae musicians. He was born Desmond Adolphus Dacres in 1942, in Saint Andrew Parish, but as a child he moved to nearby Kingston. Indigent and with an ill mother who would soon pass away, he attended the Alpha Boys' School, adding to its already amazing roll call of musically successful alumni. Determined to have a career in music, in 1961 he auditioned for both Coxsone Dodd and Duke Reid, but neither chose to work with him. However, Leslie Kong recognized a diamond in the rough, so he hired Dekker, but held him back, waiting for his songwriting to mature. It had apparently done so by 1963, when Dekker's first song, 'Honour Your Father And Mother', was a ska hit. Other hits followed, and Dekker would record over 60 songs for Kong, of which twenty became number 1 hits in Jamaica.

Though many of his ska songs were good, outstanding music would follow in the later part of the decade. It was then that Kong's productions found their own unique sound, not necessarily strictly ska, rock steady or early reggae, often featuring a rural feel. Credit the talented house band that Kong employed. The Dynamites (earlier known as Lyn Taitt & The Jets) featured Linsford "Hux" Brown (the reggae picking specialist) on lead guitar, Lyn Taitt (rock steady's distinctive strummer) on rhythm guitar, Jackie Jackson (of Treasure Isle fame) on bass, Winston Wright on organ, Gladstone Anderson on piano, and Winston Grennan (or sometimes Joe Isaacs) on drums, occasionally supplemented by former mento singer Denzil Laing on percussion, Val Bennett and "Deadly" Headley Bennett on saxophones and Bobby Ellis on trumpet. Brown's contribution to The Dynamites' sound cannot be overstated. He is a master of the rippling mandolin-like reggae guitar-picking style that emerged in the rock steady era and the most versatile practitioner of this technique. His execution ranges from a simmer to ripping, from loose and funky to machine-precise.

Though not often discussed as such, The Dynamites were one of Jamaica's greatest bands, backing numerous vocal acts up to and including Bob Marley & The Wailers. Their recognition was hurt, in retrospect, by poor branding. Their name rarely appeared on their best work, unlike that of The Skatalites, The Roots Radics and Sly & Robbie, for example. Though not nearly as famous as these other great groups, The Dynamites are in their class.

Working for Kong, they featured a versatile sound that was consistently polished and creative. As was also true of rock steady, they always supported without ever overstepping the vocals they're backing. Able to play in a variety of styles ranging from urban to country (the group's specialty) to funky, they were distinct enough to be always recognizable. Some of their finest work was done in support of Dekker in the songs discussed below. They did equally great work with Toots & The Maytals, as is seen in the next chapter. As we will see, their work with Bob Marley & The Wailers, though something of a disappointment overall, did yield at least some great songs.

The final piece of the puzzle was Kong's assignment of harmony group The Four Aces (brothers Barry, Carl, Clive and Patrick Howard, though this line-up experienced changes) as Dekker's backing vocalists. Under the shortened name, The Aces, they complemented Dekker's lead vocals with excellence and an instinct for altering their approach to best suit a song. For all the line-up changes and varied approaches, they consistently added great value and a Jamaican flavor to a song with their harmonies.

But make no mistake, as great as the supporting cast was, Desmond Dekker was the star. He possessed one of the best voices ever in reggae: instantly recognizable and beloved. It's a strong, sweet soprano blessed with a natural quiver. Expressive, emotional and endearing, his singing bursts with life. It's capable of conveying great joy or great pain, or even both at the same time. Dekker also had a talent for creating strong melodies, as evident in each of the songs described below. Lyrically, he was diverse. His best songs typically involved a conflict of one sort or another, allowing him to put his gift for drama to use. Movies obviously had an influence on Dekker's lyrics, as four of the songs discussed below include the title of one or more films. But his lyrics were typically based in reality, often illustrating the suffering endured by the righteous poor, a reality that Dekker was all too familiar with.

No other artist was quite as impacted by Leslie Kong's sudden and untimely passing from a heart attack in 1971 as Desmond Dekker. Left in a state of arrested development, Dekker would henceforth primarily record remakes of his earlier hits and covers of other artists' songs, rather than write new ones. These remakes do not stand up to the original versions. Nor did the horn overdubs added in the UK to some of his Beverly's tracks improve them in any way. A perfectly executed recipe does not benefit from an outside chef adding his idea of sweetening after the dish is done.

Along with Prince Buster, Desmond Dekker was a major influence on British youth when in the late 1970s the Two-Tone ska revival took off there. He would record as part of this scene and moved to the UK, where he continued to record and perform right up to his passing in 2006, like Kong, of a heart attack. By then, many had followed across the well-traveled bridge to international success that Dekker built, paved by the exciting and inspired songs described below. All seven were recorded between 1966 and 1968. With six of them coming from 1968, it's safe to call that his peak year. And if Dekker would never top these records, neither would anyone else, with only the best work of a small number of other artists ever matching their quality and excitement. Each is readily available on any number of collections, but no one collection has them all. Coming close are two double-CD collections from Trojan Records, *Rudy Got Soul* and *You Can Get It If You Really Want*; the former omits 'Problems', while the latter omits 'It Is Not Easy'. Both have many other good songs, such as 'Rude Boy Train', to name just one.

'Shanty Town' (aka '007')
The 1966 'Shanty Town' is a delightful rude boy rock steady song. It teems with confidence and excitement from the opening strums of Lyn Taitt's guitar, with Kong applying pre-dub reverb to brighten select chords. Dekker's effortless vocals shine. He's melodic and plaintive, expertly so. Notice how he bends a syllable, applies a quiver or wails wordlessly to increase emotion. He opens by naming 007 and *Ocean's Eleven*, movies that feature outside-of-the-law exploits. He then brings the discussion home to rude boy crime (looting, shooting and bombing) and punishment (arrested, convicted, but out on probation) in Kingston's

notorious slum, the self-explanatory 'Shanty Town'. Though it concludes with the rude boys being defeated, it's not clear whether Dekker is criticizing or celebrating their bad behavior, or both.

Dekker is buoyed up by the backing music's sprightliness. It more than bounces – it prances. The Dynamites accomplish much with little, as a reduced line-up of just rhythm guitar, bass and drums gives the song an incredibly airy feel, as reggae first recognized how less can be more during the rock steady era. Taitt returns to the spotlight mid-song to provide a minimalist rhythm guitar solo, again treated with reverb. The Aces sound like an extension of Dekker, whether harmonizing with him or working their fine call-and-response chorus of "a shanty town". The urbane 'Shanty Town' sounds as vibrant today as it did on the day it was released, as can be said for the other songs described here.

'Shanty Town' was yet another number 1 Jamaican hit for Dekker. It also began his march into the international market, making a run at the UK top 10, peaking at number 14. It did not chart in the USA, always a tougher market for reggae to crack than the UK. In 1972, it made a second successful international campaign when it was included in the soundtrack of *The Harder They Come*. Yet for all the musical and international sales success of '007', before too long, Desmond Dekker would record a song that completely surpassed it on both counts.

'Poor Me Israelites' (aka 'Israelites')
If you had to count the most storied of reggae songs on the fingers of one hand, Dekker's 'Israelites', from 1968, might be the index finger. Not only is it historically important, but it's a stone-cold killer of a track, a souped-up bulldozer tricked out with hooks of every kind. Not just a number 1 hit in Jamaica (old hat for Dekker), 'Israelites' became the first record of Jamaican origin to reach number 1 in the UK, and the first ever to chart in the USA, even breaking into the top ten, no less, to reach the number 9 spot. If these accomplishments were not enough, in 1975, it entered the UK top ten a second time as an encore. To know how 'Israelites' accomplished this, all you have to do is give it a spin. Just be sure to put on your seatbelt.

From the first moment, there is carefully crafted excitement and surprise. A single bass, guitar and cymbal note arrives in unison with Dekker's first syllable. Otherwise unaccompanied, this opening line is freely delivered by Dekker, grabbing our attention. The same treatment is given to his second line. But this time the instrumental accent plays with us, arriving a beat before the vocal. And is that piano tip-toeing about? For the third line, the tempo dramatically slows and backing vocals are added. This time, not one, but a triplet of instrumental accents are heard, just guitar and cymbal now, with a melodic pay-off of its own. Then, from nowhere, Lyn Taitt's groovy strummed guitar chords rev things up, and the body of the song begins, galloping off at a near-ska tempo. All this pay-off, and we're just 20 seconds in.

Dekker relates his own suffering to that of the biblical Israelites. He must work like a slave to feed his family. In spite of this, his wife takes the children and leaves him. His shirt is torn, his pants are shot ("Shirt, dem a-tear up, trousers a go"), but he will not steal, wanting to avoid the fate of Bonnie and Clyde, thieves killed in a hail of police bullets, as graphically depicted in the popular movie of the year before. Instead, he winds up wandering, like the Israelites of the Old Testament, destitute and homeless, but righteous and not wanting to be looked down upon.

Dekker's singing is emotionally articulate, adroitly spiked with unexpected ascents and wailing wordless phrases. The backing features a fine example of Hux Brown's work, as guitar percolates ascending lines and fills over understated piano, rhythm guitar, bass and drums. And the final ingredient in this perfect stew is the backing vocals. Though The Aces are usually trebly, here they memorably reach down into the bass register.

Dekker's accent and patois resulted in a famous example of a mondegreen, a commonly misunderstood song lyric. When, in the attention-grabbing first line, he sings "slaving for breads, sir", *breads* being slang for money (similar to the American *dough*), many heard "slaving for breakfast", or (in the UK, where such a thing exists) "baked beans for breakfast". Not exactly what Dekker had in mind, but not as badly misconstrued as rock's most famous mondegreen – Jimi Hendrix's "Excuse me while I kiss the sky" being heard as "Excuse me while I kiss this guy".

It was a given that a song as carefully wrought and exciting as 'Israelites' would hit big in Jamaica. But consider the song from the point of view of non-Jamaicans in the USA and the UK, many of whom had never heard any reggae at all: it's a song about poverty, sung in a sometimes difficult to understand accent, that pairs references to the Israelites of the Old Testament with Bonnie and Clyde, that features cutting-edge reggae instrumentation. It is a testimony to the excellence of 'Israelites' that, in spite of all that was strange to their ears, it made non-Jamaicans go out to the record store and buy their first reggae record.

'It Mek' (aka 'A It Mek')

Released the same year, 'It Mek' was the follow-up to 'Israelites'. It gave Dekker another UK top ten, reaching the number 7 spot. But it didn't chart in the USA and it was the last of Dekker's international hits, even though he continued to release some truly great songs. Surprisingly and admirably, Dekker and The Dynamites did not try to imitate their previous international successes. The closest it comes to 'Israelites' is with a variation on its syncopated opening, but this time it's played for relaxation rather than excitement. 'It Mek' differs from 'Israelites' and '007' in that it's more rural in subject matter and sound, with the laid-back tempo and the inherent sweetness of rural Jamaican music on full display. The rural style proves to be well suited to Dekker's vocals, and the melody he constructs is just superb. Gone are Kingston's rude boys, crime movies and poverty. Instead, childhood play is recalled, told in language that invokes the country and days past, quoting two mento songs and a Jamaican folk saying.

Dekker opens by singing of a girl, perhaps his sister, who takes a spill after jumping over a wall. This is borrowed from a mento song, 'Green Guava', as recorded in the 1950s by Harold Richardson under the pseudonym of Lord Tickler. Then Dekker checks on her, and after determining that she is OK, he reprimands her. He throws the song's title at her, "it mek", meaning "you made it happen", or "it's your fault". In the same vein, he also hits her with a folk saying, "what sweet nanny goat run him belly". This adage of responsibility is familiar from The Wailers' first single, 'Simmer Down'. (It also made an earlier appearance in Lord Power's golden-age mento single 'I'm Sorry For Myself'.)

Dekker is typically great and every time he draws out a syllable, it's a thrill. The Aces sound like an expansion of Dekker's voice, as if a chorus of Dekkers were richly harmonizing in a broader range than one Dekker can produce. Led by a bopping bass line, a larger Dynamites line-up is a model of subtlety, never crowding the track, yet always actively keeping the music interesting by creating a quiet busyness. Notice, for instance, how guitar and piano alternate the reggae chop. Or how intermittently appearing horns add to the music. All of the cylinders are firing on this song like a hand-tooled engine.

'It Mek' establishes more than that Dekker might not have been the most compassionate brother that a little girl ever had. On a song so different from his earlier hits, yet so wonderful in its own right, Dekker impresses with his versatility.

'Hey Grandma'
The criminally ignored 'Hey Grandma' is something of a follow-up to 'It Mek'. Both were recorded in 1968, feature a country sound, contain references to mento songs and recall an earlier time in Dekker's life. It finds a younger Desmond pleading for leniency from his strict grandmother, who is furious that he has come home past his curfew. Embarrassed in front of his date, he pleads that he was only late by a minute and that all they were doing was singing the old mento song 'Sweetie Charlie' (a song discussed in "The Golden Age of Mento Singles" chapter). But Grandma is livid, yelling so hard that Dekker is sprayed by her saliva, as her face wrinkles and "screws", a Jamaican term for an angry facial contortion.

It's a smaller drama than the violence of '007', the poverty of 'Israelites', or even the scare and reprimand of 'It Mek', but a drama nonetheless. This makes it a perfect vehicle for Dekker's affecting singing, as he pleads his case, crafting interesting melodies for chorus and the verse. The Aces keep their harmonies tight to Dekker's lead on the verse, and soar on the chorus. Instrumentally, Gladstone Anderson's rock steady piano dominates this time around, complete with a leisurely solo. This superb record was not available on compact disc until fairly recently, making what could have been a nasty hole in a lot of reggae collections now easy to fill.

'It Is Not Easy'

Also from 1968, 'It Is Not Easy' features topics now familiar from 'Israelites'. But Kong's production gives it a different feel. The instrumentation is in the rock steady vein, but its denser, busier sound differentiates it from that of the previously described songs, as well as from the rock steady in general. In this song, Hux Brown creatively ripples away, drums are more elaborate than the norm, the backing vocals are richly plaintive and horns, held back until a mid-song solo, eventually return to stick around. And just about everything is sonically thickened in a reverb bath, giving the sound a nice touch of muddiness. Using reverb more creatively than his contemporaries, Kong may have helped to pave the way for its greater use in the dub reggae that, ironically, would begin to take form just as he died.

Just as in 'Israelites', Dekker works hard but is poor, feels financial pressure from his family and others, but wants to live his life right and avoid the fate of a movie outlaw (this time Al Capone). Only Dekker can make anguish sound so wonderful. Naturally, his singing is fine and his melodies memorable. His interaction with the backing vocals is so rich, you might gain a pound from each listening. Just one backing singer is heard, singing in a voice similar to Dekker's but pitched higher. It creates great Jamaican harmony on nearly every syllable, enhanced by reverb. Unlike the other songs described in this chapter, this track is billed to Desmond Dekker, rather than to Desmond Dekker & The Aces, so likely candidates are Dekker's half-brother George, or possibly even Dekker himself. Whoever it is, the double-Dekker harmony is an aural treat.

'Problems'

Dekker is still plagued by money worries in 'Problems'. It takes him in rapid succession through surprise (at how fast it goes), humility (asking for employment, willing to take on a dirty job), humor (keeping your hands in your pockets as a means of holding on to money), resignation (over the responsibility of feeding his family) and frustration (at having no means to get any).

And even though the theme is familiar and the year is again 1968, 'Problems' has a whole different sound from "Israelites" and "It Is Not Easy", as rock steady is replaced by the funky, high-energy sound of the first records of reggae proper. The tempo is faster, the musicians are more aggressive and the arrangement is denser than ever. Even various Aces are freed to take lead on an occasional line. An elaborate mid-song reggae-soul jam is heard, led by a duel between organ and wordless voice. The overall result is a wild early-reggae ride: a jaunty, shuffling, rowdy departure from the orderly calm of rock steady-based sounds. And although this is more of an ensemble effort, Dekker is too big a talent to get lost in the sauce. For example, if you weren't aware that the word "problems" has nine syllables, you had better give this fine example of early reggae a spin.

'Fu Manchu'

We have already seen how Dekker likes to reference movie outlaws in his songs. But he is completely immersed in a film for his 1968 song 'Fu Manchu'. The lyrics describe the despair of finding himself in the lair of Fu Manchu, Sax Rohmer's fictional villain of numerous movies and books. The story inspires Dekker to a tremendous song, graced by what might be his single finest vocal performance.

All of Dekker's vocal skills are fully exploited by the over-the-top emotion of this song. His "It make no sense at all ..." proclamations convey great pain and hopelessness each and every time they're repeated. And every time we hear Dekker's slow realization that he's in the villain's domain, there is drama of the highest order. An already great vocal is made better when Dekker provides an added treat. For the last half-minute of the song, he scat-sings in a wonderful performance that's melodic and playfully rhythmic, filled with rolling *r*'s. It gives a great song a fine finish that leaves you wanting more.

The Dynamites match Dekker's performance with one of their very best. The arrangement is well-appointed rock steady, the early reggae sounds of 'Problems' and the murk of 'It Is Not Easy' are nowhere to be found. It lurches to life with an organ solo as the rhythm guitar creates tension by striking just after the beat. Hux Brown's guitar picking simmers warmly, and the rhythm section is in a playful mood. But the instrumental star this time around is Winston Wright. Not only does his organ open the song, but it's out front for the duration, and provides a fine mid-song solo. Similar in register, it makes a fine foil for Dekker's vocal throughout the song. The Aces, as always, add to the proceedings. The drama of the song is heightened by their harmonies, which are often wordless, wailing and ominous. Everyone is superb, and 'Fu Manchu' is one of Desmond Dekker's very best records, and therefore, one of the finest records described in this book.

13 Toots & The Maytals

Toots Hibbert is a national treasure, or, judging by his tour itinerary for the past forty years, an international one. The man who coined the word "reggae" has been recording and touring pretty much without pause since the early 1960s, a period of live reggae that is unprecedented and uncontested.

Frederick Nathaniel Hibbert was born in 1945 in May Pen, Clarendon Parish. Living in this rural town for thirteen years before moving to Kingston helps explain the country sound heard in some of his best songs. As a child, Toots sang in church, giving his vocals a joyous gospel grounding (or, as they say in Jamaica, a *churchical* sound). But most of all, Toots was blessed with a natural gift of soul, his voice frequently drawing comparison to Otis Redding. All of these features combined to create a voice that is completely unique in reggae. It's one of the greatest and most joyous voices in the history of recorded Jamaican music.

In Kingston, as a young man, Toots became a barber. This may be why, when he became a Rasta, he atypically chose to keep his hair cropped short and neat rather than dreadlocked. His fame as a barber quickly grew, not because of his haircutting skills, but because of his singing while he cut hair. This attracted the attention of Henry "Raleigh" Gordon and Jerry Mathias, singers who featured more of a traditional rural Jamaica sound than Toots. The three formed a group, The Maytals, named after the lead singer's home town. Some of their earliest records were credited to The Vikings, the name of the more established instrumental backing band they were recording with. Others were attributed to The Flames. In time, the act became Toots & The Maytals, a name that would persist after the other Maytals had departed and retired in 1981. But Toots's greatest records were made with the original Maytals in place. Strictly backing singers (as their soon-forgotten Toots-less "solo album" showed), their fame would never compare to that of The Wailers' Peter Tosh and Bunny Wailer. Nevertheless, Gordon and Mathias provided some of the greatest – and most Jamaican-sounding – backing vocals ever put on vinyl.

Starting their recording career at Studio One in 1962, and continuing to the present day, Toots & The Maytals recorded in diverse styles, including gospel/ska, ska, R&B, mento, rock steady, rural reggae, roots reggae, funky reggae and various permutations and combinations thereof. (As a solo artist, Toots would add rock and American country and Western music to his résumé.) They worked with great producers such as Coxsone Dodd, Prince Buster and Leslie Kong. As he pushed into his sixth decade in music, Toots had long since amassed more number 1 singles than anyone else in Jamaican music. He won the first, fourth and seventh

Festivals with songs so great they didn't give the competition a chance. (All three are described below.) The Specials and The Clash covered him. He won a Grammy. He released hundreds of singles, dozens of albums of new material (with the flow continuing at the time of this writing) and an even greater number of hits collections. And even though he gave up doing the splits in his stage show a few decades ago, he's still going strong as a live performer. Toot's shows typically find the audience singing along with every hit, and he is wont to offer the mic to audience members to enthusiastically contribute a line to a song that they know and love so well. In 2012, the Jamaican government honored Toots by awarding him The Order of Jamaica.

For all of the Toots & The Maytals best-of collections available, Toots has not been well served by compilers. Too many of his early singles have never been released on CD. While several of the great songs described below have appeared on dozens of collections, one has never appeared at all on CD. How many other great Toots songs are in danger of being forgotten, unheard since they were pressed on a limited run of 45-rpm singles as much as fifty years ago? Hopefully, a collection of these singles will be put together with the care that Toots Hibbert, living legend and the longest-running show in the history of reggae, rightly deserves.

'Broadway Jungle' (aka 'Dog War')
The Maytals' standout ska song is the wild romp, 'Broadway Jungle', a gem of a record produced by Prince Buster in 1964. Bursting with uncontainable levels of joy, it's so ecstatic that The Maytals are literally barking at the moon. The fun starts right from the playful introduction, a clichéd oriental melody played on piano, punctuated by wordless vocal sounds. This abruptly gives over to propellant ska, with Toots joyously scat-singing for a few bars, while one of The Maytals begins an off-the-wall array of high-pitched barks, hoots and hollers that make this already exciting ska even wilder. The lyrics begin, and it becomes clear these sounds are intended to be jungle noises. Toots sings of being lost in the jungle and dying there at the hands of an unnamed adversary. Then he leaves the jungle and goes to Broadway, where things are good. His vocals are very celebratory, and he may be singing about leaving Studio One, where he had done most of his previous work, for his new producer, Prince Buster. (Dodd was well known for paying little and demanding a lot from his artists, and grudge songs about former producers are not uncommon in reggae. Lee Perry's 'People Funny Boy', a song described later in this book (page 256), is another fine example.) Whatever the inspiration, it puts The Maytals in an exceptionally good mood. They charge on with too much abandon to develop chorus and verse. Along the way, Toots breaks into the call to dance chorus from Lord Flea's golden-age mento song 'Shake Shake Senora' (a song described earlier in this book; page 51). A trumpet solo gives them a respite, but singing and animal sounds come crashing back in as soon as it ends.

The barking gives this record the most common of its three alternative names, 'Dog War'. It was released with this title on a competing label, owing to shady record industry dealings. It is unrelated to another song that features barking and a similar name: the old mento song 'Dog War (Inna Matthews Lane)'. Less often, 'Broadway Jungle' has also been released with the titles 'Jamaica Ska' or 'Ska War'. It's readily available on numerous CDs under one of these names. A strong cover by Bunny Wailer is discussed in Chapter 49.

'It's You'

Also from 1964, 'It's You' is an exciting love song in the R&B-ska style. Produced by Ronnie Nasralla, a member of Byron Lee & The Dragonaires, it's buoyant and winning as only The Maytals at their best can be.

Electric guitar figures are out front as sax honks the ska chop, creating a fine field for The Maytals' vocal athletics. They are utterly *alive* here, popping with energy. The interplay between the three is a joy, and Mathias and Gordon remind us why the group was then called The Maytals, not Toots & The Maytals. It opens with the titular refrain repeated in three-part harmony. From this launching pad, they open up and jam, with Toots singing a series of *iya*s while the backing vocalists sing a string of *hey*s. This gives the song an early rhythmic pay-off and a sound that is inimitably Jamaican. Even as Toots gets into the meat of his love song, the words continue to be peppered with rhythmic vocal interplay. Then, a descending guitar run announces a solo. Toots lets out a cry, and a joyful trumpet solo from Baba Brooks is heard. The vocals are reprised, but instead of coasting, Toots increases the intensity of his delivery. It's as if the girl didn't respond to Toots's happy proclamation of love the first time through, and now he's getting a bit anxious. But don't worry for Toots. I'm sure she couldn't resist this wonderful ska serenade. 'It's You' can be heard on the Toots & The Maytals collection called *Time Is Tough: The Anthology*. It should be sought out rather than the more commonly available but far less vibrant 1971 remake.

'Treating Me Bad'

The Maytals recorded 'Treating Me Bad' in 1965 for producer Prince Buster. This is an excellent soulful R&B workout, with no sign whatsoever of a ska beat. Yet the sound is still very Jamaican. With the great vocals from The Maytals and an equally impressive performance by drummer Arkland "Drumbago" Parks, 'Treating Me Bad' is a fine example of how Jamaicans could elevate R&B into something more exotic and exciting.

The Maytals are as impressive and energetic here as they were on 'It's You', but more soulful and bluesy this time around. The vocals begin with Toots wordlessly wailing and it takes him more than a few beats to coalesce into language. He roams freely where he wills, as Gordon and Mathias anchor the song with orderly harmonies. In their wonderful soul-by-way-of-rural-Jamaica vocals, they lay out the story for Toots to embellish upon. It seems that Toots is being dumped, but doesn't understand why. He conveys this in a liquid combination of words, emotional wordless singing and by working a single word like "baby" or a phrase like "you don't know", repeating it over and over again. Sometimes he sings over the other Maytals, at other times he leads them in call and response, as his wounded heart takes him. There is no break or mid-song solo, because the musical flow of Toots's pain cannot be staunched.

The backing music is soulful, with its grooving horn line, piano and chirping rhythm guitar copying American sounds with fidelity. But there is something more – the song's secret weapon. It's the playing of Drumbago, one of the two drum greats of the ska era (the other being Lloyd Knibb of The Skatalites). He creatively loads the song with rococo fills and rolls. These are informed by Jamaican folk rhythms of the Pocomania drum tradition that would later be tapped to play a large role in ragga. Whereas American soul drums would have been static, Drumbago's playing is dynamic and attention-getting. It gives the song a Jamaican spine that, like the Maytals' vocals, makes 'Treating Me Bad' so much more than mere mimicry of American R&B sounds.

Though there have been Toots & The Maytals best-of CD collections beyond counting, somehow none of them include this tour de force of Jamaican R&B. This leaves two options: tracking down the rare original 1965 single on the Wild Bells label or the obtusely named 1974 LP, *Prince Buster Record Shack Presents The Original Golden Oldies Vol. 3 Featuring The Maytals*. 'Treating Me Bad' should not be confused with the similarly named but different Toots & The Maytals song 'Treat Me Bad' (aka 'Treating Me So Bad') or, for that matter, with the one called 'Treat Me Good'. There is a live version of 'Treating Me Bad' on the 1980 album, *Toots Live*, retitled as 'I Love You So'. Though triple its length, it cannot compare to the original. The next person responsible for compiling a Toots & The Maytals best-of is now officially on notice.

'Bam Bam'
Produced by Ronnie Nasralla in 1966, 'Bam Bam' is a great record. Good enough for Toots & The Maytals to win the song contest at the first Jamaican Cultural Development Commission Festival of The Arts. Good enough to set the country-kissed tone for future Festival winners. Good enough to be frequently covered and for Toots to remake it several times. He recut it in a straightforward reggae style, a dubby reggae style, and as a roots rendition with new lyrics called 'Rasta Man', a dancehall rendition recorded with Shaggy and, most recently, an acoustic rendition, not to mention several live renditions. But as is many times (but certainly not always) the case in reggae, the original rendition of this song is the best.

Though never described elsewhere as such, it's hard to call Bam Bam anything other than a mento record. It opens with some adept bongo playing in a pre-Nyabinghi style that is often heard in rural mento. Other instruments enter, such as a second drummer, who plays in a sharp style reminiscent of some jazzy urban mento recordings of the 1960s. An acoustic guitar plays a gentle rhythm with a tropical sway also familiar from numerous golden-age rural mento records. A bass line simple enough to be played on a rumba box and organ chords fill out the sound. Completely absent is any trace of the characteristic reggae chop. The resulting music is a wonderful reminder of the pleasures of Jamaican music from a time well before Toots coined the term "reggay". In fact, more than anything else, it recalls the simple mento arrangements of the classic Harold Richardson & The Ticklers singles such as 'Glamour Gal' and 'Don't Fence Her In' (songs described earlier in this book; page 43).

The Maytals open with a chorus of the song's title, the expression being a Jamaican term for a beating. Toots enters famously with a long, octave-spanning, descending wordless syllable. It's a hook so big, it's suitable for whaling. At its conclusion, it resolves into the first word of his opening line, as Toots proclaims himself on the side of right. Sparring with a saxophone that briefly appears, he explains that he's not one to trouble other people, so if anyone gives him trouble, they'll catch a beating. With this warning, we see another side of Toots's otherwise *irie* (a term meaning "positive, good, happy") personality. After all, Jamaica is a tough place. The lyrics are good, but it's the long wordless hook that's the song's lynchpin. Listen to how the verses steadily ascend, building to its reappearances. Listen to how the second time through, Toots extends it with a flourish. It's so spirited, it's hard to listen to the song without trying it out yourself.

In 'Bam Bam', Toots created a modern Jamaican folk song. Two cover renditions are good enough to be described later in this book: a faithful cover by Pliers and a loose interpretation by Sister Nancy (pages 556 and 445). The original can be heard on such collections as the Toots & The Maytals CD called *Pressure Drop: The Definitive Collection* on Trojan Records.

'54-46 (Was My Number)'

'54-46 (Was My Number)' is an autobiographical song. The title refers to Toots's prisoner number when he served an eighteen-month sentence for ganja possession, causing the longest interruption in his tireless fifty-year career. Such arrests were not uncommon for reggae performers, although this was a stiff sentence, and Toots has always maintained his innocence. He explained that the police had planted the ganja in a suitcase he left behind at the police station after The Maytals were arrested for having an extra rider on a motorbike and he had to provide bail. Such a frame-up is not difficult to believe when one understands the clash between Jamaica's powerful, conservative police force and the poor, pot-smoking, authority-challenging Rastafarian reggae community.

Toots has released at least six scat-filled studio or live renditions of '54-46', and it's hard to choose one as best. The 1968 original, produced by Leslie Kong and recorded with The Dynamites, is just fine. It's a crackling rock steady performance that includes lyrics describing Toots's resistance to answering to a number, a theme that was dropped in subsequent renditions. But I prefer a remake produced by Warrick Lyn in 1971, backed by Byron Lee's Dragonaires. The lyrics shift to the issue of Toots's innocence and the absurdity of the charge – that he would have willingly left his bag behind with the police if it contained ganja. Rather than the rock steady of the previous decade, the sound here is soulful funky reggae, fully allowing Toots to exercise those particular muscles of his. For example, he pulls a stanza from the original and turns it into an exciting soul-style introduction, playing the role of one funky policeman. He introduces another soul music element into this rendition, with calls of, "Give it to me one time", varying the count as The Maytals answer with that number of *uh!*s with syncopated support from The Dragonaires. Singing with a rasp, emoting fully, Toots bridges soul and reggae as only he can.

The song would explode in live renditions, with neither the band nor the audience able to contain themselves. Listen to the ebullience and the sing-alongs on the Toots & The Maytals Live rendition that jammed on to triple the length of the studio versions. But, first, do check the studio versions. Both are available on a myriad of collections, and can be distinguished by their lengths: about 2:55 minutes for the Kong-produced rendition and about 3:10 minutes for the Lyn-produced one.

'Pressure Drop'

'Pressure Drop', produced by Leslie Kong in 1969, finds Toots & The Maytals jubilant as they sing of the consequences of bad karma. The vocal group and the backing band urge each other to higher heights.

The Dynamites open with a busy, funky, early-reggae riddim that, crisp and piano-filled, manages to keep a foot in rock steady. Jackie Johnson's bass is at the heart of the instrumentation, fully in the spotlight, especially with Hux Brown absent from the track. Strict followers of the law of sufficiency, The Dynamites must have realized that his lead guitar just wasn't needed in this already perfect riddim. Johnson's start-and-stop clusters of notes simultaneously bring the funk to reggae and vice versa. His melody complements that of the vocals, while his sparseness is in contrast.

The song ramps up nicely. First, The Dynamites establish their groove, distinctive and expert. The vocal group enters, teasing with a wordless three-part harmony for a few bars. Then Toots lets loose with a fervent "It hits you!", and The Maytals provide him with a glorious confirmation in the form of elongated wordless syllables. After just five words, the song is vocally rich, and 'Pressure Drop' soars.

Launching into the verse, Mathias and Gordon sing in an easy falsetto, contrasting with Toots's roughened baritone lead. In 'Bam Bam', Toots promised to deliver retribution to those who'd trouble him. Here he sings again of consequences catching up with wrongdoers, but this time, Toots keeps us in the dark. We don't know what the transgression is. And all we know of the retribution is its titular description, and that the wrongdoers will know when it hits, as they "gotta feel it!" One thing is certain. By the time Toots starts ecstatically repeating "pressure!", there is no doubt that justice is undoubtedly being served.

This combination of Toots, The Maytals, The Dynamites and Kong all at their peak is musical magic. Later remakes (live and studio) can't compare, even with such guest star collaborators as Willie Nelson, Keith Richards and Eric Clapton. Covers by UK artists The Clash, Robert Palmer, The Selector and The Specials do not amount to much more than a reminder of how special was the convergence of time and talent that produced the original. So stick to this rendition, as available on the soundtrack for the film *The Harder They Come* and countless other reggae collections and Toots & The Maytals compilations. Just be sure not to get cheated, as 'Pressure Drop' is sometimes edited down by as much as a minute from approximately 3:45 minutes. You'll want the full ride.

'Sweet And Dandy'
Produced by Leslie Kong in 1969, if there was a superlative as well-crafted and singular as 'Sweet And Dandy', it would have been inserted here. It won Festival that year, its entry into the competition an unfortunate development for all the other hopefuls.

A clumsy instrumental intro is heard, lumbering and stiff, but it's just a feint. A drum roll sounds, Toots cries out jubilantly, and streamers of joy shoot out in every direction as the body of the song is launched. The riddim is a lissome canter with an unusual make-up. Led by rhythm guitar, it's a dense mix of musical languages from the earliest reggae proper, mento and calypso. It gives the song great drive while instilling a homey, country feel.

Over this, The Maytals sing the entire song in unison. Covering a wide tonal range, their harmonies are earthy and beautiful, as they elevate one another to ecstatic heights. It's a sound as rich as foie gras wrapped in bacon dipped in butter. Non-Jamaicans, consider yourselves warned: it may forever spoil your enjoyment of harmonies from the USA and UK. Lyrically, the song is just as skilled. 'Sweet And Dandy' is a well-observed account of a wedding, and one of reggae's best slice-of-life tales. (In these ways, along with its country sound, the song recalls the Chin's Calypso Sextet mento songs on the same subject, as described in Chapter 6 on this group.) The families deal with Etty and Johnson, the young couple who are overwhelmed by the occasion. In one room, Ettie's mother is trying to get her to stop crying, while her father points out that she's too smart and educated to act this way. In another room, Johnson's uncle is trying to get the groom to pull himself together, while his aunt says that his wedding day is no time for foolishness. Meanwhile, the guests party on. Toots calls them perfect partners and blesses the couple, calling them sweet and dandy.

Even in his autobiographical '54-46 (That's My Number)', Toots's lyrics have never been so acute. In addition to the dual dramas, he details the wedding: everyone was wearing white for the occasion, there was dancing, the guests drank a lot of cola wine (a soft drink), and the cost of the wedding cake was one pound and ten shillings.

Extraordinarily fine in every way, of all the songs in this book, 'Sweet And Dandy' is the one I'm most compelled to play again as soon as it's over (or, *lift it up again*, in sound system parlance). It's so perfect a song, you can safely ignore the many covers (in styles that range from mento to dancehall and more), which can only pale by comparison. Toots remade the song and recorded live renditions, but all you need is the original. In the movie *The Harder They Come*, you can see a re-creation of the recording session for 'Sweet And Dandy', complete with assorted Dynamites and Leslie Kong at the mixing board. In spite of the lip-syncing, Toots & The Maytals and their song is such a force, the scene is very enjoyable indeed.

'Pomps And Pride'

The country-fresh 'Pomps And Pride', produced by Warrick Lyn, is a beloved record, winning Festival for a third time for Toots & The Maytals in 1972. It borrows from an earlier song, but it is upgraded by all involved. Toots improves it with enigmatic new lyrics and a better-developed melody. The Maytals give it an incomparable vocal arrangement. The Dynamites give it a memorable rural reggae backing that pitches and chugs. This results in a song of enormous appeal. In addition to the expected reggae covers, its rural feel made it a popular choice for mento bands as well, with The Jolly Boys recording it in 1977, for example. Even a polka rendition of 'Pomps and Pride' has been released.

The song is announced with seven drum strikes, followed by a joyous ascending guitar riff supported by horns. (The song is continuously see-sawing up and down, always in melodic ascent or descent.) The body of the song then begins, and fine rural reggae is heard in ensemble playing. Picked guitar, horns, bass, organ and rim shot-laden drums all interlock in a spiky, pulsing riddim. This is accentuated by the lurching organ stabs that give the song its distinctive start-and-stop halting grace. The Maytals are drawn in by this, and their falsetto backing vocals surge like the distinctive organ. And Toots's delivery is more tightly rhythmic than his norm. But this in no way inhibits his full-voiced delivery, as he heartily belts it out. He sounds jubilant, playfully singing the scale to add to the fun.

His lyrics are interesting, but vague enough to present a mystery. Understanding the song's history gives us a possible explanation. 'Pomps And Pride' is based on an earlier Jamaican song called 'Come Down'. Although its exact origin is uncertain, it probably was a traditional spiritual, warning against pomp and the sin of pride. For example, when Ras Michael & The Sons Of Negus recorded a Nyabinghi rendition in 1968, they sang of coming down off pomps and pride to hear the voice of Jah. When Lord Tanamo recorded a ska rendition in 1963, he made it more about social than religious issues, singing about unity and giving aid as coming down off pomps and pride. Even Bob Marley recorded an informal, rambling demo version of the song, not long before his death, which also was a call to righteous religious behaviour.

In this rendition, Toots observes a gathering of people revelling in pomp and pride. Then, in an oblique passage, he describes their great excitement in anticipation "to see the light". But when it is seen, the light is not as bright as expected, leaving the gathering confused. "Everybody was crying, sighing, dying to see the light. And when they see it, they see it's not bright. Can this be right?" Putting together the song's history together with the then current groundswell move to Rastafarianism in the reggae community, 'Pomps And Pride' may be seen as a veiled criticism of churchgoers who, for all their pomp and pride, find the service they've come for is a spiritual disappointment. Other interpretations are certainly possible.

'Pomps And Pride' can be found on numerous reggae collections and Toots & The Maytals compilations, though none include its largely instrumental dub version B-side, called 'Pomps And Pride Part 2'. Several live versions and remakes have been recorded by Toots, but once again, the original is the recommended rendition. Also again, beware of edited mixes and make sure you get the full 4:30-minute cut.

'Funky Kingston'
The album title track 'Funky Kingston' was produced by Warwick Lyn in 1973. Though it was only a year after 'Pomps And Pride', big changes were afoot. The great Raleigh Gordon and Jerry Mathias were gone, replaced by comparatively generic Jamaican female backing singers. (This may have influenced Bob Marley, who within a year would replace the departing Bunny Wailer and Peter Tosh with female vocalists. But perhaps not, since, unlike Toots, Marley already had a long history of recording with female backing singers.) Toots would retain The Maytals name, henceforth billing himself as Toots & The Maytals (just as Bob Marley would retain the Wailers name after Tosh and Livingston departed, henceforth billing himself as Bob Marley & The Wailers). And the rural sound that had proved to be such a superb showcase for his talents over the past seven years would be put aside for a new brand of reggae. An unabashedly soulful, sax-filled funky reggae is unveiled. It proves to be an excellent vehicle for Toots's considerable ability as a soul singer. A great groove is established and Toots, alternately smooth and raspy, tears it up. He's so excited, he can't help but verbally conduct the instruments. 'Funky Kingston' is a simple pleasure that shows Toots's range. And no one else on the island had a greater right to record a song called 'Funky Kingston' than Toots Hibbert. The rendition on the 1980 *Toots Live!* album is also quite good, as Toots's funky material came off much better live than did his more rural songs.

14 The Ethiopians

Many reggae fans are aware of The Ethiopians from the misnamed rock steady track, 'Train To Skaville' and its follow-up, 'Engine 54'. These are good songs but the ones described below are better. Together, they make a case for The Ethiopians being the most underrated of all reggae acts.

Born in 1942, lead singer and songwriter Leonard Dillon moved from Port Antonio to Kingston while in his teens. There he became acquainted with Wailer Peter Tosh, who was impressed with Dillon's skills. (They had in common a baritone voice and a church-based musical background.) In 1965, Tosh ushered Dillon to Studio One, where he would record several ska sides under the name of Jack Sparrow. One, 'Ice Water', featured The Wailers on backing vocals. A year later, Dillon formed a vocal trio including Stephen Taylor that would quickly downsize to a duo. They called themselves The Ethiopians, the name an early declaration of Rastafarianism in reggae, since the Rasta viewed Ethiopia as their religious Zion. As we will see, they were (largely unsung) early practitioners of roots reggae themes. Sadly, in 1975, Taylor was struck by a van and died, leaving Dillon too distraught to record for several years. He eventually resumed, now sometimes billed as The Ethiopian. This was good news, as Dillon's singing is a special pleasure for reggae fans. He has a voice of unusual depth and rural charm, coming off as wise and trustworthy. At the same time, it's a voice that has seen too much struggle not to sound a bit world-weary, but with too strong a spirit to give up. It's a unique voice, one perfectly suited for roots reggae and one that could only come from Jamaica. The Ethiopians recorded through 2009, releasing about 175 singles and a handful of albums, as well as a greater number of compilations. As this book was being written, towards the end of 2011, multiple cancers took Leonard Dillon, one of the most reggae of reggae voices. All the songs below can be easily acquired on various Ethiopian CDs, unless stated otherwise. They should be considered compulsory for any reggae fan.

'I'm Gonna Take Over Now'

'I'm Gonna Take Over Now', a straightforward ska produced by Coxsone Dodd in 1966, is as and sweet a song as you will ever hear in that genre. It opens with an outsized, descending jazzy bass line reminiscent of – and probably influenced by – the one featured in Nancy Sinatra's number 1 hit of the same year, 'These Boots Are Made For Walking'. Then, a single drum strike launches ska. It's uncluttered and agile, with drums and bass swinging nicely, the latter carrying most of the instrumental melody, while sax and piano concentrate on the ska chop. The sax later provides a fine mid-song solo. Smaller than most ska backings, this four-piece band is indicative of the changes happening at the end of the ska era, when the music was moving towards rock steady's simpler and more relaxed approach.

Four pieces proves to be the optimal number for this particular song, giving the music a breezy feel. All the better to support The Ethiopians' easy-going vocals in one of their best performances. Rootsy and sweet, it's easy to get caught up in. Listen to how they alternate phrases, with Dillon singing alone or in two-part harmony, always understated but uncannily musical. In the song's few lyrics, The Ethiopians launch the softest of coups d'état, as their patient waiting for Rasta-farianism's rise is now coming to pass. Who can resist a takeover that rolls in on a ska breeze like this?

A rare expression (albeit couched) of Rasta sentiments in a ska song, and a fine song at that, for decades 'I'm Gonna Take Over Now' had not been collected on LP or CD. It was rescued from obscurity in 2004 when Soul Jazz Records made it part of their CD compilation called Studio One Ska. Just be careful not to accidentally wind up with the lesser 1978 roots reggae remake called 'I'm Gonna Take It Over', as produced by Alvin Ranglin.

'Free Man' (aka 'Free')

The Coxsone Dodd-produced 'Free Man', from 1966, is another great Ethiopians track residing on the cusp of ska and rock steady. It has the pace, insistent honking sax and creative busy drums of ska, but also the lead piano, the uncluttered smaller group and immaculate air of rock steady. The piano and bass collaborate on the riddim's melody and the drummer takes advantage of the elbow room to stretch out and play creatively.

An instrumental opening led by bass repeats an ominous phrase for a few bars. (It's later reprised to serve as the track's mid-song break.) But when The Ethiopians come in, the heavy mood is lifted. Singing a rootsy two-part harmony in unison, they sound pleased and confident. They criticize an unrighteous indi-vidual (perhaps a woman, or perhaps a symbol of Babylon) and the company she keeps, and the group banishes them to hell! Strong words, but sung without rancor or other emotion, instead as a simple statement of fact. Dillon goes on to proclaim that he is a free man and is "ringing the bell for freedom", complete with sonic affirmation from the drummer. 'Free Man' is a perfect illustration of The Ethiopians' quiet power that is unmatched by any other vocal group.

'Reggae Hit The Town'

Produced by Harry Robinson in 1968, The Ethiopians' 'Reggae Hit The Town' observed the arrival of rock steady's replacement. As is typical for the handful of 1968 songs to use the word "reggae" (or "reggay", as it was known in its initial spelling) in their title, the sound was busy, fast-paced, funk-touched party music. The riddim is loaded, with a horn section, solo sax lines, tons of happy organ, piano and a guitar playing the reggae chop, all anchored by hard-working bass and drums. The result is a fast-moving reggae groove, cooking sweet and hot. Atop of this, The Ethiopians, usually the most composed of singers, get caught up in the excitement. In falsetto harmony, they sing a series of exclamations around and about the titular announcement. Then, where you might expect to hear a mid-song solo, The Ethiopians have a conversation. After Taylor ascertains that Dillon is feeling "nice, nice", several topics are then discussed, including a hound dog, complete with simulated barks, and praise for James Brown. By the time they reprise their falsetto harmony singing, the song is glowing with warmth. Reggae proper hits the town, and it's wild and woolly and irresistible.

'Everything Crash'
'Everything Crash', produced in 1969 by Carl "Sir J. J." Johnson, exploits an interesting spot between rock steady and emerging reggae sounds. The riddim's featured piano and upbeat horn phrase and general tidiness are pure rock steady. But the pace and level of intensity are ramped up from rock steady norms towards those of early reggae. Meanwhile, the discontented lyrics (and the presence of a stern Nyabinghi hand drum) preface the roots reggae to come, as 'Everything Crash' is a demonstration of an Ethiopians' specialty: making bad social news palatable through great records.

Belying the upbeat horn phrase that opens the song, Dillon sings about the strikes that were then plaguing Jamaica. Firemen, watermen, the telephone company and the police are all on strike, amounting to the assessment of the title.

Having made these observations, Dillon employs two Jamaican folk sayings to express his views on the matter. The more common of the two tells of the bucket that pulls up water from the well every day without fail, until the day that its bottom falls out. This quintessentially Jamaican expression of inevitability would become familiar the world round in the next decade, when Bob Marley used it in his hit, 'I Shot The Sheriff'. And "what gone bad a morning can't come good a evening" is Dillon's warning that a problem does not improve with time.

The Ethiopians chant-sing in unison, fitted to a clipped, rhythmic structure. They would use this style of delivery again, as would other vocal groups around this time, especially those working for producer Lee Perry. Dillon's lead vocal is matter-of-fact, his tone showing little in the way of an emotional reaction as he lists these difficult realities. Taylor's backing vocal shows more feeling, but Dillon has The Ethiopians grounded in resignation. It's as if he doesn't have to sugarcoat the facts when a fine reggae riddim ensures that the song will be agreeable. The Ethiopians' unflinching approach to social problems was a powerful (and undercredited) influence on roots reggae that was just emerging and would come to dominate Jamaican music.

This piece of social commentary became a hit in Jamaica and begat imitations, such as a cover by Prince Buster called 'Pharaoh House Crash'. The Ethiopians also recorded a rendition of 'Everything Crash' with producer Coxsone Dodd on a 1980 LP of the same name. It's difficult to find, but not to worry, as it's not nearly as good as the widely available Sir J. J.-produced classic.

'One'
'One' is also produced by Carl Johnson and from 1969, but is very different from 'Everything Crash'. It's an early example of Nyabinghi-reggae, and a rather unusual one. Rather than chanting or even conventionally singing, 'One' features the down-to-earth sound of Ethiopians chatting about their faith, building on a technique they used in 'Reggae Hit The Town'. After an exchange of Rasta greetings, The Ethiopians begin *reasoning* (conversing about their religion) and *giving praises* to Jah Rastafari. Dillon calls it "school time" when they must learn about themselves as Rastas, and the other two Ethiopians affirm and expand on his statements. Though speaking, there is music in their voices. And the contrast of Dillon's resonant baritone and the higher nasal voices of his bandmates is just as rewarding here as when they sing. It gives the impression that Nyabinghi sessions were no longer just for large gatherings at Rasta camps, but were also being conducted by smaller groups in *a yard* (at home). As we will see later in the book, this song had at least one descendant of note. This was when, a year later, The Abyssinians had a big hit with their re-voiced version of 'Satta Amassa Ganna' called 'Mabrak', similarly a conversation about their faith.

The Nyabinghi-reggae backing in 'One' is a melange of Jamaican sounds. There's a rock steady underpinning from bass, drums and piano. A prominently featured hand drum brings the Nyabinghi sound. So does the strong horn phrase heard at the song's opening, midpoint and conclusion. Played in unison by trumpet and sax, it's tarter and earthier than the rock steady norm. Rather than providing the song with any sign of the reggae chop, electric guitar instead plays an unusual phrase. Rootsy and droning, it invokes Rasta mysticism while managing a nod to 1960s soul. It first serves to comfortingly answer the horns and grows to be a distinctive feature of the song. When the horn phrase is heard for the final time, the hand drummer rallies and The Ethiopians conclude their session with laughter, bringing the song to an end. 'One' is common-man Nyabinghi-reggae and perhaps the only Nyabinghi-reggae song that can be called cozy.

'No Baptism'
'No Baptism', produced in 1970 by Derrick Harriott, is another Ethiopians classic. By now, the very busy, high-energy early reggae sound of 1968 had relaxed into something unhurried and more thoughtful. Most indicative of this is the creative organ riff that opens the song and returns mid-song. Sounding like an inebriated high-wire tightrope walk, it adds an extra measure of melody and a touch of giddiness to the stately riddim.

An archetypical Ethiopians performance finds the group calmly and confidently facing a social issue with an earthy Rasta sensibility. 'No Baptism' is a rejection of the colonial religion by a Rastaman, as symbolized by the title. But, rather than anger, the tone is quietly steadfast. The Ethiopians go on to *reason* on their beliefs, with each line sung twice for emphasis. Humming affirmations add to the song's grounded certainty, and give it a wordless vocal hook. Dillon leaves no stone unturned in making his case. There's a folk saying and a Bible quotation, followed by a line from left field: "Dem bless pork and call it Arnold". This can only be a reference to the American late-1960s television comedy *Green Acres*, which featured a pig named Arnold that was treated as a son by its owners, childless husband and wife farmers. The implication here is that Arnold's fine treatment makes little sense coming from a culture that, unlike Rasta, chooses to eat swine. 'No Baptism' is a perfect illustration of how The Ethiopians are reggae's masters of the bitter-sweet when taking on any issue.

In addition to the readily available original rendition, The Ethiopians later remade the song for Coxsone Dodd on the aforementioned *Everything Crash* LP. That rendition is as good, sacrificing some tasty piano and rhythm guitar work for Nyah hand drum, greater length and some modest dub effects. Either way, a reggae fan can't go wrong with The Ethiopians' 'No Baptism'.

'Bad To Worse'

In roots reggae's *sufferas* songs, just as in American blues, Jamaicans sing their way through life's pain, turning difficulties into heartfelt music. But not even the helplessness of 'Everything Crash' prepares you for the 1970 Carl Johnson-produced 'Bad To Worse', undoubtedly the most inconsolably pessimistic song in all of reggae. Although the line "We were all looking for a change, but no changes seems to be made" suggests that the impetus of the song may have been post-election disappointment, 'Bad To Worse' serves as a universal anthem for bad times.

The backing is softly upbeat, and the vocals are gently delivered, with Dillon singing in a higher register than his natural baritone, as he sometimes did. So, sonically, 'Bad To Worse' is the spoonful of sugar for the bitter medicine of the song's lyrics. A bongo roll announces its start, and an unsuspecting bouncy rock steady riddim begins. Rippling picked guitar that could only be Hux Brown makes it likely that The Dynamites are the backing band. Then, in impeccable minor-key two-part roots harmony, The Ethiopians begin their velvet-boxing-glove lament. These lovely vocals open with the unflinchingly negative chorus: "Things a-get from bad to worse every day." Then Dillon elaborates:

> You think you had it hard last year?
> Well, you better tighten up you belt
> and rest up in yourself
> For-a this-a here malo!
>
> 'Things A Get From Bad To Worse' by Leonard Dillon,
> © published by Music Like Dirt, administered by Kobalt
> Music Publishing Ltd

Yes, things are so bad – and about to get worse – that Dillon has to employ a second language, using the Spanish word "malo" for "bad", to emphasize just how bleak the situation is. All reggae fans should have this song as part of their music library. When things are going bad, you'll want to play it as a musical alternative to gallows humor.

'Empty Belly'

Another track on the aforementioned 1980 *Everything Crash* LP was The Ethiopians' take on the "Hot Milk" riddim, originally recorded as an organ instrumental of that name by Jackie Mittoo ten years earlier. (Another version, Tommy McCook's sax cut called 'Tunnel One', is described later in this book; page 181.) The new vocals and the old riddim prove to be a perfect match, as the resulting 'Empty Belly' is one of The Ethiopians' finest tracks.

The riddim is an example of Studio One understated excellence. Fine drum work stands out, especially now that it is enhanced by the addition of a Nyabinghi drummer. The track is further augmented by a restrained electric piano that pleasingly brings a touch of jazz flavor to the song. The grumbling organ that defines the riddim's opening is heard. But the Nyah drum tips off the listener that something other than Jackie Mittoo's lead organ or Tommy McCook's lead sax will soon follow. What is heard – Leonard Dillon's seasoned voice – is just as good. With his clear-eyed, histrionics-free approach, he exemplifies roots reggae's ability to turn *sufferation* into bitter-sweet reggae. He unleashes a classic *sufferas* song about slaving in Babylon, having to work for wicked people, and still not having *dunnie* (a variation of *dunza*, both meaning "money") for food. This leads to the song's key refrain, as even the staple dish of rice and peas can't be afforded, resulting in the hunger of the title.

Inexplicably, this song was missed by every best-of The Ethiopians collection. Thankfully, it was rescued by its inclusion on the CD collection called *Studio One Rub A Dub* on Soul Jazz Records.

15 Great Studio One rock steady and reggae instrumentals

Though others had innovations of their own, or a run matching him in impact for a time, Coxsone Dodd is acknowledged to be reggae's greatest producer. Starting in 1959, Dodd's career spanned six decades, over which time he released thousands of singles and hundreds of albums. They covered every genre and style of music that Jamaicans recorded, and encompassed at one point or another nearly every significant vocalist or musician in reggae. The sheer volume of his work is unmatched.

However, in its quantity, we should not lose sight of its qualities. A high percentage of his productions can be considered better than the norm, and a good number of these were great records. Ska was created at his request, which succeeded in steering Jamaican music away from its dalliance with imitating R&B, back to a more Jamaican sound. He was instrumental in the formation of The Skatalites. The practice of versioning was his innovation, prismatically multiplying the number of reggae records to come. He was the first to record Bob Marley & The Wailers, and made them stars. He presided over the first roots reggae sessions. Lee Perry and Prince Buster, both talented, high-impact producers in their own right, started their careers in his employ. He had several "signature sounds", whereas other producers would have given their right hand to have one. And so on.

The vagaries of health took the great Duke Reid and Leslie Kong out of contention for "greatest ever". Their accomplishments were significant, but fate truncated their careers well before they could even try to match Dodd's iron-man achievements. Likewise, economics would cause the quick retirement of Justin Yap and others. Perry was perhaps the island's second-greatest producer, on the basis of a varied career and taking the sonics of reggae production to their topmost heights. Reid or Kong could also be argued for. Maybe, instead, it's Buster, whose career was long and varied with an innovation or two of his own. Or golden-age mento producer Stanley Motta, who started Jamaica's recording industry. Or King Tubby and his dub. A battle royal could arise over who is number 2. But few would argue against Dodd holding the spot as the number 1 greatest reggae producer.

Born Clement Seymour Dodd, in 1932 in Kingston, the man called Coxsone owes his nickname to his teenage cricket skills. They won him comparisons to the famous Alec Coxon, then a top player for a British county team. Dodd's upbringing was not Kingston-bound; he spent time as a boy with relatives in Saint Thomas Parish and later worked in the USA as a cane-cutter. A big fan of American R&B

and jazz, he used some of his hard-earned dollars to travel to various cities in the USA in search of records to bring home to Jamaica. In a situation echoed by the Kingston ice-cream parlors of the Kong and Yap families, and Duke Reid's wife's grocery and liquor store, Dodd's parents had a liquor store, where he began to play his record collection to entertain the patrons. This proved to be a stepping stone to the launching of his "Sir Coxsone Downbeat" sound system. As previously described, this would lead into record production at his soon-to-be-famous hit factory, Studio One. Starting successfully enough with R&B, Dodd then created the ska explosion, and rode its shock wave through rock steady, reggae proper, roots, dub, and DJ, right up to early dancehall, while also releasing mento, jazz, gospel and calypso along the way. Dodd's contributions to music were well recognized in Jamaica. In addition to his being awarded the Order of Distinction in 1991, Brentford Road, the location of his studio, was renamed Studio One Boulevard in 2004. Just a few days after this ceremony, Dodd died of a heart attack, ending one of the greatest success stories in Jamaican music.

The rock steady from Duke Reid's Treasure Isle studio, the dub productions from Lee Perry's Black Ark studio, and, for that matter, Studio One ska are each justly celebrated for their high quality and distinctive sound. Exactly the same qualities describe the instrumentals that came from Coxsone Dodd's Studio One post-ska. Whether you call it rock steady or early reggae, the sound comprises a subgenre of reggae all its own. And one with a surprising number of truly great recordings that were hits when first released, and have never stopped being appreciated.

Sound Dimension

By 1967, ska had given way to rock steady, and The Skatalites, Dodd's house band during that era, had broken up. But without so much as a hiccup, Studio One would continue to release great music. Many of these songs featured great riddims provided by his new house band, Sound Dimension. Also sometimes randomly billed as the Soul Vendors or the Soul Brothers (the latter a generic name Dodd began using in the ska era), this band was led by former Skatalite Jackie Mittoo on keyboards with a large rotating cast of ska greats and newer talent. For example, Mittoo's former Skatalites bandmates Rolando Alphonso, Johnny Moore and Lester Sterling were on board, as were guitarist Hux Brown and percussionist Denzil Laing of The Dynamites. So too were a variety of other established players (such as trombonist Vin Gordon and saxophonist Headley Bennett) and soon-to-be-established players (such as bassist Brian Atkinson, drummers Joe Isaacs, Leroy "Horsemouth" Wallace and Fil Callender, horn players Bobby Ellis and David Madden and guitarist Eric Frater). Bassist Leroy Sibbles and guitarist Ernest Ranglin also participated on at least one Sound Dimension recording.

The most unsung member of the group – and therefore of Studio One's post-ska sound in general – was drummer Fil Callender. Born in Panama, teenager

Filberto Callender migrated to Jamaica in the mid-1960s. He was inspired by hearing The Skatalites and immersed himself in the music scene of the time, quickly learning to play drums. Studio One session guitarist Eric Frater, who played with Callender in a band, brought him into Dodd's employ when the scheduled drummer no-showed a session. Callender would continue to provide drums for Studio One recordings into the early 1970s. His playing is an absolute joy to hear, spicing the riddim by slinging eccentric fills, rolls, and trick shots, often nailing the beat at the last possible moment. This makes his drumming immediately identifiable and just plain more fun to hear than the work of his contemporaries. And no other drummer's work would prove to be better suited to dub than Callender's. All it took was a little reverb, and his playing popped into 3-D. Why isn't he better known? Well, for one thing, when he received printed credit (which was not very often, being a sessions drummer), his name appeared in every permutation and combination of Fil, F. and Phil with Callender, Callendar, Calendar and Calender. Nor could it have helped that his name sounded like a jokey placeholder name for a to-be-decided studio musician for a future session, as in the need to "fill calendar". His career path proved to be unique for a reggae drummer. Callender also played some lead guitar and once he left Studio One to work with other producers, he would transition to this instrument outright. His guitar can be heard on some songs described elsewhere in this book: Max Romeo's 'War Ina Babylon' (page 271), The Slickers' 'Johnny Too Bad' (page 142), and (it has been suggested) Bob Marley & The Wailers' 'Punky Reggae Party' (page 482). He would eventually form and lead a band called The In Crowd, where he provided vocals in addition to guitar and was the group's primary songwriter. In 2013, Filberto Callender was honored with Jamaica's Order of Distinction.

Where science failed, Sound Dimension succeeded in creating perpetual motion machines. The three instrumentals described below were insanely popular, having been versioned countless times across the decades, as hundreds of singers, DJs, instrumentalists and dub mixers each had a go (or two, or more) at these classic riddims. No riddims have been versioned more often; the total for the three of them may exceed a thousand, and (the motion being perpetual) they continue to be worked today. Yet, despite all the versions, there may be no better way to enjoy these songs than in their originally released instrumental form.

'Real Rock'

From 1968, 'Real Rock' is a title that should not be taken literally. It's neither rock music, authentic or otherwise, nor is it rockers, a reggae rhythm that would emerge in the 1970s. Instead, it's a fine example of the particular sound of Studio One post-ska instrumentals. And a remarkably popular one at that.

With over four hundred and counting, 'Real Rock' has the distinction of being the most versioned song in the history of reggae. This is a tribute to what a crafty and agreeable piece of work this instrumental is, with its many engaging elements all working in easy coexistence. It has a strong backbone of whip-smart rock steady bass and drums, while a guitar sounds a grounded reggae chop. Atop of this, Mittoo repeats an incisive three-note organ hook that snaps right into the bass. It's a marvel how just three notes in this particular setting can be so compelling. Then, after a stuttering drum roll, Vin Gordon's trombone joins in, playing a theme in his patented style, as catchy as it is woozy, mellowing the organ's sharpness. The pair give the listener a choice of hearing the riddim as relaxing or bracing. This same quality gave the many artists who recorded a version different avenues of approach. Mittoo soon begins to switch between the organ hook and melodic rock steady piano. Gordon expands his theme with a mid-song solo that manages to be both majestic and wobbly. Filled with so much creativity and *upful* reggae vibe, 'Real Rock' is the perfectly formed acorn from which a forest of oaks grew.

While a much fatter book than this would be required to describe all the versions that followed, two unusual ones appear later in this book: a Jamaica Jazz version in Chapter 50 and a spacey dub melodica cut in Chapter 27, on Augustus Pablo (pages 536 and 253). The malleable appeal of 'Real Rock' was demonstrated when singer Willi Williams's 1979 roots reggae vocal version, 'Armagideon Time', jumped genres and an ocean to be effectively covered by UK punk rock band The Clash the same year. But for all the hundreds of versions available, I recommend the original Sound Dimension instrumental straight up over any other. 'Real Rock' is available on several Studio One and Sound Dimension collections.

'*Drum Song*'
'Drum Song', originally credited to the Soul Vendors in 1967, is also misnamed. This instrumental is not a song about drums, nor is that instrument featured – trumpet and organ are the stars of the show. But there are reasons to forgive the misnomer. 'Drum Song' is an excellent and unique reggae classic with an unlikely source of inspiration that was popular enough to spawn numerous versions. It would come to be Jackie Mittoo's signature song, as he is featured on this original rendition and remade it several times under his name. Though the remakes maintain a high level of quality, the original Soul Vendors rendition can't be beat.

In 'Drum Song', reggae has its own answer to Ravel's *Bolero*. The opening section sets up a rhythmic drone in an odd time signature. It's dominated by a continuous haunting picked-guitar phrase floating in a nimbus of reverb. Interlocking bass, drums, rhythm guitar and hand drum complete the song's rhythmic underpinnings. The latter two have enough freedom to ensure that the drone is not too static, making it interesting as they roam. Atop this, long, mournful organ and trumpet notes join in to develop a dramatic snaking theme. It's not the theme from *Bolero*, but it sounds influenced by it. Mid-song, the trumpet breaks away and plays a muted solo, followed by a longer one from Mittoo on trebly organ, both honoring the drone. For the song's final minute, they renew their commitment to the theme, completing a unique classic utterly unlike any reggae that came before.

Sometimes credited to Mittoo, the original rendition of 'Drum Song' can be distinguished from his remakes by its running length of about 4:22. If you are tracking down his remakes, don't miss a fine, dubby rendition called 'Brain Mark'. A good version by the Hippy Boys called 'Capo' is described later in this book (page 313). Another unusual and effective use of this riddim was the popular 2005 vocal rendition called 'Africanize Dem' by German reggae singer Patrice. At the time this book was written, Monty Alexander began performing live reggae renditions of the song graced by his jazz piano that are too good not to be part of his next release.

'Full Up'

Sound Dimension's delightful instrumental 'Full Up' was released in 1969. Another massively versioned riddim, the secret of its popularity is how it weds contrasting sounds. For example, a vice-tight rhythm is paired with a loosey-goosey approach to melody. The riddim's rock steady bloodline is in full effect, as bass, drums, guitar, piano and metronomic reggae chop guitar maintain orderly control, even while exploring the more expansive creativity of nascent reggae, as the melodic lead is tossed around between instruments. In the process, the song bounces between emotional poles.

A piano provides an underlayer of cheerful melody that is present for most of the song. A guitar enters with a simple riff that builds on the piano's light-hearted mood, but is heard only briefly. It's replaced by stabbing organ from Robbie Lynn (filling in ably for Jackie Mittoo), providing the famous riddim-defining hook – a very long note abruptly terminated by three short ones, which steers the song from happy to ominous waters. After a few iterations, a reedy saxophone is layered atop. It steals the spotlight with simple two-note phrases, and suddenly the sound is relaxed and homey. A happy organ lead follows. A mid-song solo from Lynn splits the difference between R&B buoyancy and jazz introspection. Then the leads and their associated moods are each reprised and handed around again. The result is a riddim that offers singers, DJ and instrumentalists diverse angles of entry for their versions. It's no wonder that not only was the original cut of the riddim popular for versioning, but it was recut in contemporary style in the ensuing decades, each time serving as a platform for more versions to amass. Most famous was the great 1981 roots reggae hit, 'Pass The Kouchie', by vocal group The Mighty Diamonds (a song described later in this book; page 402) and the many versions it spurred, based on a roots recut of the riddim. Another version that is recommended is the nice DJ ride, 'Minister For Ganja', by the short-lived duo of Rapper Robert & Jim Brown, based on the original cut, as found on the *Studio One Kings* compilation CD on the Soul Jazz label.

Vin Gordon

Trombonist Vin Gordon has already been mentioned in this chapter and the one on The Wailers at Studio One (pages 90–110). Born in 1949 in the Jones Town section of Kingston, he was part of the extraordinary parade of talented musicians that emerged from Kingston's Alpha Cottage School for Boys. After school, he played in Montego Bay's Salvation Army Band, and in a number of bands thereafter, including some live gigs with The Skatalites around 1964. All this while he was still a young teenager. He was recruited to Studio One by Skatalite and fellow Alpha Boy Roland Alphonso. As we have seen, his first recording session was for no less than The Wailers in 1965, at the age of sixteen. Although Gordon's career started in ska and extended into the international reggae of the 1980s, it was in rock steady where he had his greatest impact. Given the honorific nickname Don D Junior or Don Drummond Junior, no one in reggae ever had bigger shoes to fill. Yet he filled them well. Undoubtedly influenced by Drummond, Gordon also played with great creativity and more quietly than the norm for his instrument. But whereas Drummond's playing was usually mournful, coming from a place of personal pain, Gordon's playing was happy and peaceful, wonderfully loopy and rather stoned. The sound of Vin Gordon's trumpet is one of the unsung instrumental treasures of reggae. In addition to appearing on numerous records by other artists, he recorded over 50 singles and three albums under his own name(s), the last in 2009.

'Heavenless'

The 1968 Studio One classic post-ska instrumental 'Heavenless' has been variously credited to Don D Junior or to Don D Junior & Sound Dimension (both acceptable), to The Skatalites (obviously wrong chronologically and stylistically), to Don Drummond himself (tragically impossible, considering that Drummond was by then incarcerated in an asylum) and only more recently (and most accurately) to Vin Gordon. Even though the riddim has much good going on, let's give Vin Gordon his due. He is the star of 'Heavenless', a song that serves as a perfect showcase for his unique trombone style that elevates the track to something special.

The riddim snaps to with a rhythm guitar dispensing a double-struck reggae chop, swaying with melody. In lockstep are a rollicking rumbling bass line, drums from the incomparable Fil Callender with his bag of tricks opened wide, a second guitar playing a muted picked pattern of notes and, if you listen hard, a touch of piano buried deep in the mix. Joining in unison, a sax and a trumpet add a brisk little phrase, repeating it unaltered, beckoning someone to join in. And mid-way through its fourth iteration, someone does, as Vin Gordon's trombone comes crashing in. He plays a woozy theme that sounds like the town drunk stumbling home. Long notes, lazy, loopy and bent, are juxtaposed against the short, tight precise notes that make up the backing. At mid-song, the drunk stops, pulls himself somewhat together, turns to you and dances as Gordon cuts loose with a solo.

Gordon and Callender are two of the era's most outlandishly distinctive musicians. And here they are given full rein, while the other ace musicians hold the fort. The result is amazing, combining the sound carefree intoxication with stone-cold-sober expertise. This makes 'Heavenless' a special treat, the like of which could only be found in the reggae of a particular time and place. It can be heard on the Soul Jazz Records compilation CD called *Studio One Scorcher*. There it is credited to Don Drummond and The Skatalites and appears in disco-mix format with an appended minimalist dub version that adds subdued lead guitar and organ. The 'Heavenless' riddim proved to be very popular, spawning many versions, but none as great as 'Murderer' by Johnny Osbourne, a song described in Chapter 52 (page 543).

'Joe Grazer'
Early in the 1970s, Burning Spear released a roots reggae song with a fine Studio One riddim by the name of "He Prayed". Soon, versions appeared that repurposed the riddim for a completely different subject. There was great excitement in Jamaica over its hosting of the 1973 Joe Frazier/George Forman boxing match, in which Forman would handily defeat the heavily favored champion. (Boxing is popular in Jamaica. There have been enough boxing-themed reggae songs to fill the CD collection called *Sucker Punch: Jamaican Boxing Tributes*, and enough for at least a second volume.) Two popular DJ versions of 'He Prayed ' captured the excitement. 'Joe Frazier' (also called 'Big Fight') was from Big Youth (who would re-voice a sequel called 'Round Two – Foreman Versus Frazier'). 'Joe Frazier Round Two' was from Dennis Alcapone. Dodd also released a dub version of 'He Prayed' that was titled 'Joe Frazier'.

But Vin Gordon's 1972 trombone cut called 'Joe Grazer' surpasses all other versions. Though the title may be a mash-up of "Joe Frazier" and "Gordon", when the song originally appeared on 45-rpm, it was credited to The New Establishment. This was another of the handful of band names that Dodd might arbitrarily apply to whatever collection of musicians from his impressive stable he happened to employ on a given session. But when it appeared on the Soul Jazz Records compilation CD, *Studio One Scorcher Vol. 2*, credit was belatedly bestowed to Gordon.

This version keeps all of the riddim's best features intact. The distinctive descending trumpet riff that opens the song, and the big gap-toothed bouncing bass line complemented by an undercurrent of piano are on board. When the trumpet riff tails off (for now, as it will be twice reprised), Gordon is there to immediately fill the breach where Spear would have been heard. It's prime Vin Gordon, playing inventively, musically conveying the sensation of being happily stoned (though not nearly as woozy as 'Heavenless'). He pauses and a ghost vocal is heard, as the vocal track from Spear's version bleeds through. (When heard in a version, this limitation of analog magnetic tape is not seen as a detriment so much as a naturally occurring dub effect.) He resumes with madcap slide work –

loopy and eccentric, without being frivolous or sloppy. He picks up on something that was subtly inherent in the riddim and expands on it. The song is another instrumental that sounds influenced by Ravel's *Bolero*, though not as overtly as was 'Drum Song'. This ganja *Bolero* may very well be the great Vin Gordon's single most accomplished performance.

Further versions of the "Joe Frazier" riddim would follow. They include a branching off by producer Lee Perry in a stylistically different recut called the "Dub Organizer" riddim, several versions of which are described in a chapter on this artist (page 260).

Jackie Mittoo

As a member of The Skatalites and Sound Dimension, the name Jackie Mittoo is by now a familiar one. He was born Donat Roy Mittoo, in 1948, in Saint Ann Parish. Learning from his grandmother, he began playing piano at the age of four and never stopped. While playing in a number of live bands, he was discovered by Dodd and ushered into Studio One while still in his early teens. There, he was made a member of The Skatalites – a teenager in the company of the older, far more established jazz players. It's no surprise, then, that Mittoo's contribution on many Skatalites records was reduced to a support role, playing rhythm piano. But Dodd's instincts were correct, and after this incubation period, Mittoo's impact bloomed. As ska approached rock steady, it began to slow down and utilized smaller, less horn-filled bands. Mittoo took full advantage of the additional room this afforded his piano. (Many examples of this were seen in the later songs discussed in Chapter 9, on the Wailers at Studio One.) Then, once rock steady dawned, he switched from piano to organ as his primary instrument and the one he is best remembered for.

From 1965 through 1971, Mittoo recorded almost exclusively for Dodd, even though he moved to Toronto in 1968, limiting his Studio One work to trips back to Jamaica. He would headline nearly 100 singles and six albums, while contributing keyboards to an uncountable number of Studio One tracks by other artists. He was also a talented arranger, and Dodd would use him in this capacity as well. All of this makes Jackie Mittoo the single most important keyboardist ever at Studio One and one of the most important musicians ever to work with Dodd.

From 1972 onward, Mittoo worked with a variety of producers in both Jamaica and Toronto (including some self-production), while still remaining involved with Dodd. In all, he recorded nearly 150 singles and thirteen albums. He was the music director for the Broadway musical, *Reggae*, which ran for twenty-one performances in 1980. He recorded right up to his death from cancer in 1990, even briefly rejoining the re-formed Skatalites the year before. Passing away at the age of forty-two, he undoubtedly still had much to give. Yet, in spite of his untimely death, and for all the great Jamaican jazz pianists who came before him and all the great reggae keyboardists who came after him, none can approach the accomplishments of Jackie Mittoo, reggae's greatest keyboardist.

'Jumping Jehosophat'; 'Choice of Music Part 2'

Two great Coxsone Dodd-produced Jackie Mittoo songs can be heard on the Soul Jazz Records 2006 Studio One compilation CD called *Studio One Soul 2*. They share a similar lineage as each is an organ cut of a riddim from a 1970 song by The Heptones and those songs themselves were covers of US soul hits.

'Jumping Jehosophat' is an organ cut of the riddim from The Heptones' cover of The Temptations' 'Message From A Black Man'. The liner notes explain that this track is previously unreleased, giving credence to the widespread but not fully substantiated belief that Studio One's tape vault is loaded with uncirculated gold. (For example, would Dodd and his estate really still be sitting on the long-rumored album's worth of unreleased Wailers Christmas songs said to have been recorded in the mid-1960s? I have to believe that if these tapes existed, the combined draw of their high earning potential and historical importance would have long since resulted in their release.)

A lively, funky introduction sets the tone, as the psychedelic guitar/keyboard riff from The Temptations' original translates to reggae keyboard/horn without losing any of its inherent drama. Mittoo answers this with a song-length trebly vibrato organ lead that putters along with ease. Bluesy and soulful, it's emotionally articulate in a way that belies his casual approach. It carries the track along and the listener along with it. Let's hope that there is more such material that Soul Jazz can extricate from the vault.

A modest dub version of this track called 'Message From A Dub' can be heard on the long-out-of-print 1974 Studio One LP, *Dub Store Special* by Dub Specialist. This version takes the tack of completely omitting Mittoo's organ track, allowing the riddim's other elements to take center stage. It's interesting, but there are many examples in this book of other songs on rare vinyl that are more worth your effort to track down.

The riddim for 'Choice of Music Part 2' comes from The Heptones' cover of The Impressions' 'Choice of Color'. The Heptones' track was good, but neither it nor a DJ version by King Sporty bearing the same name was especially interesting. Faring better was Jackie Mittoo's organ cut called 'Choice Of Music' that featured fine playing by Mittoo and reverb-enhanced rim shots. But the crafty application of effects on its dub version, alternately called 'Choice of Music Part 2' or 'Choice of Music Version', springboards it to greatness and makes it the preferred version of this riddim. A spree of well-executed drop-out/in, reverb and echo reshapes and retextures the riddim, illuminating its strengths and making the track crackle with excitement.

Propulsive rhythm guitar is the riddim's engine in a chassis of smart-sharp drums, bass and a rippling picked guitar. Riding this is Mittoo's organ. Out front for most of the song, he keeps us engaged with melody and drama. Dub is the gas that makes the riddim fly, and the octane is high. Early on, the rhythm guitar becomes unstuck in time, a wobbling signal that there's a dub ride to come. Suddenly, everything but the bass and reverbed drums drops out. The other instruments fade back in, but soon more drop-out reduces the band to a trio, with bass, dubbed drums and organ. But now the organ is reverbed and mixed to sound distant, and it wanders stereophonically between the left and right channels in a mixing-board effect that is more common in psychedelic rock than dub. Further drop-out/in slides different elements into the spotlight at rhythmically determined points. Echo is subtly applied. Mittoo temporarily switches to piano. This latter element pops with aural excitement in this dubby setting, while the moment is hardly noticed in Mittoo's non-dub version. By comparison, all other versions of the riddim are like reading a well-formatted, illustrated document that's been reduced to plain text. You'll get the idea, but the aesthetics are lost.

Jackie Mittoo: *'Sidewalk Doctor'*
Lennie Hibbert: *'From Creation'*
The original rendition of 'Sidewalk Doctor' was a 1970 Byron Lee-produced flute cut by Tommy McCook. In 1972, he would find himself recutting it for producer Rudolph "Ruddy" Redwood, this time putting his sax as well as his flute skills to work. Redwood also used the riddim for a popular DJ version by I-Roy called 'Sidewalk Killer'. The riddim gained its greatest fame as the backing for Phyllis Dillon's Duke Reid-produced 1972 hit, 'Woman Of The Ghetto', cover of a song originally recorded by New York soul singer Marlena Shaw.

As all this happened, in 1970 Coxsone Dodd commissioned an incisive recut of the riddim for his own use. The resulting Studio One versions were diverse: The New Establishment recorded a melodica cut called 'Poco Tempo', featuring Augustus Pablo disciple Pablove Black on the lead instrument; Vin Gordon recorded a trombone cut also called 'Sidewalk Doctor'; and there were two unremarkable DJ versions by two sons of sovereigns, Prince Francis and Prince Jazzbo. But it's a pair of outstanding Dodd-produced instrumental cuts that are the best versions. Both lead instruments provided a perfect counterbalance to the riddim's featured sound: a guitar that's down-and-dirty with distortion and compression. A vibraphone cut by Lennie Hibbert in 1971, called 'From Creation', showed the admixture of his instrument and riddim to be special. And in 1982, twelve years after Tommy McCook's initial version, Dodd released a Jackie Mittoo organ cut called 'Sidewalk Doctor'. As good as, if not better than, Hibbert's version, Mittoo's is a showcase for his ace organ playing.

Mittoo's lead soars on 'Sidewalk Doctor'. He banks melodically, throttles rhythmically and yaws texturally for a thrilling organ ride. Serious and intense, it's a performance that makes so many other reggae organ instrumentals seem trivial in comparison. It's available on the Soul Jazz Records compilation CD called *Studio One Scorchers*, in the disco-mix format just as it was originally released on a 10-inch 45-rpm single. The appended dub version opens with just dub-touched drums and bass, revealing the swinging groove that is the foundation for the riddim. From there it's an exercise in drop in and out, extending what may be Jackie Mittoo's greatest performance. In 1979, Sly & Robbie recorded a very good cover of 'Sidewalk Doctor'. It gets dubbier as it progresses, growing more introspective even as it dips into the melody of The Temptations' 'Get Ready'.

The man who would bring the great sound of the vibraphone to reggae was born in 1928 in Mavis Bank, a town situated between Kingston and the Blue Mountains. Lennie Hibbert entered the famous Alpha Cottage School for Boys when he was eight. Supplementing his studies with musical training in the Alpha way, he learned to play drums. After leaving school, he worked in a variety of bands including a military outfit, where he became a self-taught vibraphonist. By the 1960s, he was the island's resident vibraphonist, playing with various local jazz bands. Like many Jamaican jazz musicians, Hibbert was known to visit Count Ossie's camp and jam with the Nyabinghi drummers and chanters. His jazz credentials gave him an entrée into Studio One, where Coxsone Dodd used him as a performer and arranger in the late 1960s. Hibbert recorded with Dodd through 1975, cutting a few sides with other producers along the way. In all, he would record eight singles and three albums. Although his technique is not known to have turned Lionel Hampton into a chronic insomniac, Hibbert demonstrated an unfailing grasp on how jazzy vibes could complement reggae. He made a return to Alpha in the capacity of bandmaster, and could count trombonist Vin Gordon as one of the students who benefited from his attentions. His impact in this role was such that the school would name a hall after him. Hibbert was awarded the Order of Distinction by the Jamaican government for his contribution to music and his work with Jamaica's youth. He died *circa* 1984.

'From Creation' may very well be Lennie Hibbert's best track. The backing begins, and at the exact point you expect Mittoo to enter with an undulating blanket of vibrato organ, we instead hear pointillist vibes ruling the show. It's a musical surprise, the likes of which can only be delivered by versioning. Hibbert exhibits the strong respect for melody that was consistently demonstrated by the Jamaican jazz musicians who moved into ska and reggae. He creates a song-length solo that is introspective and creative while being accessible and engaging. Mid-song, he moves into a segment where he plays at a speed that is at the limit of his technique. He backs off this with a brief funky interval before returning to explore his opening melody, slowing it down to the point of trance minimalism. A complete pleasure, Lennie Hibbert's reggae vibraphone tour de force 'From Creation' can be heard on Soul Jazz Records' compilation CD called *Studio One Roots*.

Other Studio One instrumentals

Soul Brothers: *'Crawfish'*
Soul Brothers, like Sound Dimension, Soul Vendors, Brentford Road All Stars, etcetera, is one of a rotation of names that Coxsone Dodd used for his post-Skatalites

house band. In 1966, they released a cover of 'Crawfish', the playful instrumental from the 1962 debut album by Herb Alpert & The Tijuana Brass. They transmute Alpert's marimba-infused mariachi-pop-jazz brass into pure Studio One post-ska gold. And in the process, they created what can be considered the great lost rock steady instrumental. Every bit as good as the other classic songs in this chapter, unlike them it has never been compiled on LP or CD, and has never been versioned (other than as a 12-inch remix discussed in a moment). But it was never totally forgotten. For one thing, Wailers collectors found it as the flipside of Rita Marley's Studio One single, 'You Lied', a single that was also released in the UK on the Rio label, now with Jackie Mittoo's name added to the song's credits. Yet 'Crawfish' has somehow scuttled away from the attention of CD compilers to hide under a rock. That's really a shame because the song is an unadulterated joy, sounding like a self-celebration of rock steady. Only Baba Brooks's 'Independence Ska' and 'Shenk I Sheck' (both songs described elsewhere in this book; pages 111 and 112) sound comparably elated. Not coincidentally, it most probably is Baba Brooks's trumpet that leads the way.

A condensed drum roll kicks off the introduction. A simple foot-stomping cycle of bass notes is established and continues throughout the song. Atop of this, horns and other instruments get in on the chop that throbs with swollen syncopation. Everyone sounds like they're in a blissful trance, with only the drummer (who sounds likely to be former Skatalite Lloyd Knibb) adding complexity. In just ten seconds, before the lead instrument is even heard, 'Crawfish' has already established itself as droolingly happy.

Sunny sprightly piano bursts forth to play the theme that was handled by marimba in Alpert's original. It's answered by a happy horn phrase from trumpet and trombone in unison, playfully elongating the last note. The horns then take over the piano melody, and the jubilation grows as they take the theme through changes to a satisfying conclusion. A short masterful trumpet solo is heard. So good, it can only be faulted as too short, although if it ran for minutes, I might still have raised the same complaint. After the solo, the theme returns for a second airing, completing 2:30 minutes of sterling music. Hello? Record company people? Will someone please release this track? It would be like bottling pure sunshine.

Thirteen years later, in 1979, a 12-inch remix of 'Crawfish' appeared, this time credited to The Soul Vendors. This record is rarer than the original 7-inch 45, and a lot stranger. There was something in the original – perhaps its bass pattern – that must have reminded Dodd of American rural music. Here, he adds intermittent square-dance fiddle swoops (simulated on guitar) to the mix, along with some additional percussion. Then, where the original would end, a dub version of sorts is appended. The bass continues, the drums gain dub, and everything else drops out. A guitar track with a backwoods feel is added to provide a hillbilly-style reggae chop, and more fiddle swoops are heard. This and an array of dub effects scramble 'Crawfish' like a Rubik's Cube, making for a strange and unexpected hillbilly/rock steady/dub hoedown. This wonderfully weird variation is enjoyable in its own right, though nothing can improve on the original mix.

Ernest Ranglin: *'Surfin''*

He is universally admired and celebrated; few have contributed as long to Jamaican music and none as diversely as Ernest Ranglin. The self-taught guitar virtuoso was born in Manchester Parish in 1932. His first contact with a guitar was as a child, when he would wait for two guitar-playing uncles to leave for work. He began a more serious study at the age of fourteen, teaching himself from books. By the time he was in his teens, he was good enough to be in demand by Jamaica's jazz bands, including The Val Bennett Orchestra and, later, The Baba Motta Band. By the early 1950s, he was a member of Jamaica's top jazz band, The Eric Deans Orchestra, as he rose to become Jamaica's undisputed greatest guitarist. By the mid-1950s, he had played on jazz mento and Jamaican R&B singles. In 1958, he impressed a young Chris Blackwell sufficiently to be a featured artist on an LP that was the first-ever release on the Island label. As an arranger, he is one the musicians credited with the creation of ska while working for Coxsone Dodd. In the 1960s, he gave lessons to Skatalites guitarist Jerry "Jah Jerry" Haynes. He did innumerable reggae sessions as a guitar player and arranger. This included the first reggae crossover hit, 'My Boy Lollipop', by Millie Small. He also arranged and played on some of The Wailers' earliest hits, gracing several with memorable solos. He was voted the top guitarist in *Melody Maker*'s 1964 poll. He even played bass on several Prince Buster hits. Before the decade was over, he scored a reggae hit of his own, the instrumental classic 'Surfin'' that would become his signature song. In all, he recorded a dozen singles, 29 albums under his own name, plus eight more in collaboration with pianist Monty Alexander that encompassed jazz, calypso, reggae, African music and the new genre of "Jamaica Jazz" – the re-fusion of reggae and jazz that Ranglin helped create. To the delight of his fans, he still performs live, and usually plays 'Surfin''. At one New York show in 2004, he was introduced as "Jamaican guitar virtuoso Ernest Ranglin". He took the microphone and humbly said, "Not yet, but maybe soon", and then proceeded, in a 90-minute display of guitar technique, to show that the announcer had it right. Jamaica cannot be accused of ignoring Ranglin's accomplishments. The government honored him with the Order of Distinction in 1973 and the Musgrave Medal in 1992. In 2004, the University of the West Indies in Jamaica made him a Doctor of Letters, while the government raised his honor to Commander of the Order of Distinction. There's still time to make him king.

Apparently inspired by the guitar instrumental hits of American surf music earlier in the decade, Ranglin named his 1969 reggae guitar instrumental 'Surfin''. To date, reggae's indigenous surf music remains a subgenre consisting of just the one specimen. This is not to say that surf was otherwise ignored in Jamaica. In 1965, The Skatalites covered The Chantays' 'Pipeline', converting guitar to horns and giving it a tortured pun for a name: 'Miss Ska Culation'. In 2008, dancehall star Ce'cile covered The Ventures' 'Wipe Out', converting guitar to singing and DJing in 'Goody Goody'. In 2011, Jamaican guitarist Dwight Pinkney released a CD of reggae surf covers called *Plays The Ventures Jamaican Style*. But 'Surfin'' remains reggae's only surf original. This is probably because the song was too good. No other Jamaican guitarist could approach it, and even Ranglin would have a tough time matching its originality. Rather than try, he took the remake route, recording more than a few new renditions throughout the decades.

'Surfin'' uses a riddim familiar from a song already discussed in this book (page 139): 'Artibella' by singer Ken Boothe. Here, with the organ gone, the riddim is stripped down to its showcase bass line and smart drums with just a simple *chica-chica* guitar fleshing the rhythm out. It's a perfect stage for Ranglin's performance. He wastes no time jumping in, lighting up the riddim with a picked guitar that's dripping with reverb and kissed by echo, working off the distinctive bass. Then the song's theme is heard, built of notes bent by the hands of an expert. He goes on to give a master class on vibrato, slurring, harmonics, fast-picked runs and more. But it's done in the service of the riddim rather than showing off. For that reason, in spite of the outsized technique on display, the playing is more than accessible – it's irresistible. 'Surfin'' is reggae's undisputed greatest guitar instrumental as performed by its undisputed greatest guitarist.

'Surfin'' can be heard on the CD compilation *Studio One Rockers*, released on Soul Jazz Records. There is another mix of the song with a dubbier backing that includes spectral wordless backing vocals and extra percussion. This alternative mix is just as good and can be heard on the vinyl edition of *Version Dread: 18 Dub Hits From Studio One*, on Heartbeat Records.

Tommy McCook: 'Tunnel One'
'Tunnel One' is an excellent horn cut of the "Hot Milk" riddim, which was also the basis of The Ethiopians' song, 'Empty Belly', described in Chapter 16. Here, the riddim receives a spikier mix, with razor-sharp guitars, bass, drums and grumbling organ cooking up a crunchy reggae groove. McCook's lead is wonderful, changing things up frequently, packing a lot of music into the 2-minute riddim. With his sax in unison with a trumpet player, a lovely two-part theme is let loose. First, long notes flow, so cool and laid-back. It gives way to a more ornate mid-tempo theme. The theme gives McCook a jumping-off point to supply a winding sax solo, and a short, mellow trumpet solo follows. The second theme is reprised and the horns begin to jam, but just briefly, as the song's fade-out brings an unwelcome end to the track. By the time it was released in 1976, the sound of McCook's sax was something that reggae fans were well acquainted with and always happy to hear more of. In 'Tunnel One', McCook gave us a piece of reggae that's perfect for a lazy morning. It was chosen for inclusion in the 1978 film *Rockers* and can be heard on its excellent soundtrack.

16 More great Studio One rock steady and pre-roots reggae songs

Though the large number of great post-ska instrumentals might lead you to believe otherwise, make no mistake: vocal tracks dominated the Studio One post-ska era in number and popularity. In addition to the examples found in those chapters of this book devoted to individual artists, here is sundry more vocal gold, produced by Coxsone Dodd from the late 1960s through the 1970s. Most feature a sound that is recognizable as coming from Studio One sound, while the last three are in different styles.

Larry Marshall: *'Nanny Goat'*

Fitzroy "Larry" Marshall was born in 1941 in Lawrence Park, Saint Ann Parish. He is an older cousin of the Barrett brothers of Upsetters and Wailers fame. Marshall's voice is a distinctive one, throaty and constricted, yet this does not limit his range, strength or control of vibrato. He recorded his first single in 1962 for producer Philip Yap and his Top Deck label. Stingy remuneration would lead Marshall into a period of rattling around between Yap and other producers, including Coxsone Dodd and Prince Buster. In 1968, he recorded 'Nanny Goat' for Dodd, the song that put him on the map. Marshall continued to record steadily into the mid-1980s and sporadically to the present day, releasing about 95 singles and eight albums. In the 1970s he began a second musical career, when Dodd employed him as an engineer and arranger of other artists' records. Marshall is also known for ushering fellow Saint Ann resident Burning Spear to Studio One for his first recording sessions, and is said to have added his backing vocals to the proceedings.

The original 1967 rendition of 'Nanny Goat' was billed to Larry & Alvin, as Marshall recorded this track with his occasional partner at the time, Alvin Perkins, a backing singer with a less-impressive résumé. As previously mentioned, this is one of the songs frequently cited as being the first proper reggae song – that is, the first to fully break from rock steady conventions. But the lyrics would not be out of place in a Treasure Isle rock steady song. Marshall tells a fickle lover that he's not going to allow her to leave him. He quotes the folk saying about the nanny goat and her belly, which we are familiar with from our discussion of the Desmond Dekker song, 'It Mek' (page 149). By his use of this proverb, Marshall is telling his lover that if she were to move on, she would find that the new love interest is not good for her. Neither do the vocals represent any great departure from rock steady. Pleasant and tuneful, Marshall is well supported by Perkins's often wordless singing. But the instrumentation is another story. It's busier, faster and wilder than what was heard in rock steady. There's a rocked-out rhythm guitar from Eric Frater that drives the song. It's so like an electrified version of the old mento double-stuck banjo rhythm, and so unlike the mellow rhythm guitar heard in rock steady. It heralds a sound that would become very popular in reggae by the latter half of the 1970s. There's the excited organ playing of Jackie Mittoo in the form of a crazy-happy riff that gives the song a hook. Along with slightly strange drum accents and bells from Fil Callender, it gives the song a creative oddball charm. Larry & Alvin's 'Nanny Goat' can be heard on several Studio One compilation CDs.

Marshall went on to remake 'Nanny Goat' a number of times. One rendition may be even better than the original, just on the basis of Marshall's vocal. It's to be found on the CD called *The Sound Of Channel One: King Tubby Connection*, a compilation of various artists' tracks that Tubby produced from 1973 to 1981. Its dub-touched opening drum roll comes running head over heels to meet you like an excited puppy. But, overall, the arrangement is more relaxed, with the rhythm guitar toned down from the original, as was typical for reggae proper as it developed in the late 1960s. Marshall's delivery is exceptionally deliberate on this remake. So much so, he sounds stentorian, which suits the song in several ways. First, it contrasts nicely with the whimsical organ playing. Second, it matches his determined, confident lyrics. If 'Nanny Goat' was only noteworthy for its historical interest, it would not be described here. But it's a great song, with two great renditions waiting for you to choose your favorite.

Larry Marshall: *'Throw Me Corn'*
'Throw Me Corn' by Larry & Alvin, from 1970, is an example of how Studio One could casually slipstream a song that sounded so little like anything else that was then being released. It was inspired by a Winston Shand song of the same name from a year earlier that was in the shuffling, poly-rhythmic, high-energy style of the first records to be called reggae proper. Marshall's song is a deconstruction of that sound. The fast pace and energy level remain, but the instrumentation is boiled down to a hypnotic see-sawing pattern of staccato start-and-stop bass, accompanied by trebly piano, simple drums and reggae chop guitar. Peppy and melodic while being droningly minimalistic, the riddim is unusual and irresistible. Its popularity, particularly in dancehall remakes, is not surprising, as this riddim presaged the mechanistic playing of early dancehall.

The vocals are unusual and engaging as well. With Perkins again providing harmony, Marshall marches to the riddim's staccato beat. He works within a limited range of notes, crafting a melody whose constraint adds appeal. As was the case for 'Nanny Goat', 'Throw Me Corn' gets its title from a Jamaican folk saying.

Marshall sings of throwing corn (distributing feed) for his fowls, but then failing to call them to eat. (The expression is familiar to Bob Marley fans from its use in 'Who The Cap Fit', the original rendition of which was released around the same time. Coincidentally – or perhaps not – 'Throw Me Corn' also contains the folk saying that gives the title to that other song.) But it's not until he sings of a third party retrieving this feed that the reason why Larry is marshaling this folk wisdom begins to come into focus. By the time he sings of fussing and fighting, theft, murder and race, we see that the song is a call to treat one another better, whether a neighbor or any fellow Jamaican.

Fine, unusual vocals and instrumentation, and a message of living together that combines folk sayings and confrontation, all come together in a great song. And, as mentioned, a very popular one. There were all manner of remixes, remakes, versions and covers. The riddim was revived and updated later in the 1970s, then again in the 1980s, 1990s and 2000s. In 1990, Charlie Chaplin recorded a live-style DJ performance to a Pocomania-influenced dancehall remake of the riddim, called 'Throw Some Corn' that has a lot to like. Check this version on Chaplin's 1990 *Take Two* CD. The original Larry & Alvin song, credited to Larry Marshall, is available on the Heartbeat Records CD collection called *The Best Of Studio One*.

Devon Russell: *'Make Me Believe In You'*

Devon Russell's 'Make Me Believe In You' is another fine song that utilizes the 'You Don't Care' riddim. This riddim is responsible for at least two outright reggae classics, The Techniques song that gives the riddim its name and Nora Dean's 'Barbwire', each described elsewhere in this book (pages 130 and 238). Russell's version came after these in the latter half of the 1970s, and unlike the other two, it was produced by Coxsone Dodd rather than Duke Reid. This is just one example of how producers had no means of locking up their prized riddims. The culture of Jamaica's recording industry and the lack of copyright laws made re-creating another producer's riddim – or even pirating a recording of it outright – a common practice. On a given day, a producer could find himself the benefactor of this practice, the victim, or both. Only the fans consistently benefited.

Here, the riddim is retooled with additional percussion and the piano de-emphasized, sliding the sound from its rock steady origins towards the reggae of the day. To it, Russell brings a peculiar falsetto performance of a funky 1974 Curtis Mayfield song. The lyrics are largely faithful to the original, describing a girl who plays around, bats her eyes and tries to talk her way out of trouble. Even more than these lyrics, it's Russell's delivery that keeps the song interesting throughout. He rides the riddim by bringing odd pacing, shifts in emotion, pregnant pauses and an intermittent vibrato. It's a quirky and captivating performance, and one with the acumen to give the beloved instrumentation the opportunity not just to support his vocal but to shine through it. Far less famous than 'Barbwire' and 'You

Don't Care', Russell's version should also be heard. It's available on the CD compilation *Studio One Soul 2* on the Soul Jazz label.

Delroy Wilson: *'I Don't Know Why'*
Jennifer Lara: *'Consider Me'*
Singer Delroy Wilson was born in 1948 in Kingston's Trench Town slum. He began his career young, recording for Dodd at the age of thirteen in 1962. This helped pave the way for other *youth singers* such as Jamaican superstar Dennis Brown, who would begin recording for Dodd at age twelve. Perhaps this is part of the reason why Brown identified Wilson as the singer who most influenced him. And perhaps because their prolific careers began as youth singers, both were genuinely loved by the people of Jamaica. After a long and exclusive partnership with Dodd, Wilson would go on to work with a variety of producers. His career went on into the second half of the 1980s, encompassing ska, rock steady, reggae, roots, lovers' rock, an influential election song and dancehall, with an impressive number of hits throughout. In all, Wilson recorded about 350 singles and 25 albums. In 1994, he received a special award from Prime Minister P. J. Patterson in recognition of his contributions to Jamaican music. A year later, Delroy Wilson lost a long battle with various health problems, and died at the age of forty-six from liver failure. Though already long, it was a career that was cut tragically short.

In 1971, Delroy Wilson released 'I Don't Know Why', perhaps his greatest song. He is backed by a tart riddim that's pure Studio One magic. Taking its name from Wilson's lyrics, it would come to be known as the Movie Star riddim. Clocking in at just over 2 minutes, this is a little powerhouse of a Studio One riddim. Bass is the lynchpin, providing a smart foundation melody and setting the brooding tone that the rhythm guitar picks up. A piano builds on the melody while staying in lockstep with the rhythm, thereby strengthening it. The drums are understated and moody, but enlivened by Fil Callender's patented accents. It's a great example of ensemble playing with all of the instruments having an equal role as they play off one another in order to best contribute to the whole. This would have been enough to carry the song, but there is more. A repeated organ phrase, answered by clipped guitar chords, gives the riddim the sound of unresolved need. In addition to emotional heft, it gives the riddim a memorable hook. No wonder 'Movie Star' gave us not one but two emotional classics.

Wilson taps into this for an expressive love song. He sings that, although his girl does not have movie-star beauty or wealth, he loves her deeply. He goes on to defend her against the cruel criticisms of others. And when he breaks from the song's flow to exclaim the title, it's nothing less than emotional dynamite. Meanwhile, Dodd achieves a perfect balance by leavening Wilson's sharp voice and affecting delivery with male backing vocals that are lush and composed. This beloved, quintessentially Jamaican love song can be heard on the Delroy Wilson CD collection called *The Best Of: Original Eighteen Deluxe Edition*.

At the other end of the decade, Dodd blew the dust off the Movie Star riddim for singer Jennifer Lara's 'Consider Me' in 1979. Her version is every bit as good as Wilson's song. Lara, an underrated singer, is the sister of solo singer and Tamlins member Derrick Lara. She began her career in 1969 as a backing vocalist, appearing on an untold number of records by stars like Freddie McGregor, Dennis Brown, Johnny Osbourne and Delroy Wilson. Although she worked with other producers, most of her sessions were at Studio One. It was there that she made the jump to lead singer in 1979, with 'Consider Me' her first song. She had completed a tour as a backing vocalist for The Ethiopians and was back working with Dodd when she died of a stroke in 2005 at the age of fifty-two.

Dodd altered the riddim for Lara's song. He added new organ and sly rock guitar leads from Ernest Ranglin that fit as if they were always there. Assured, the guitar answers and resolves the longing of the riddim's defining organ phrase. This suits the trajectory of Lara's lyrics. And her singing has never sounded finer than here, strong and well complemented by female harmony singers. It's an emotional performance, but in contrast to Wilson's vocal in 'I Don't Know Why', she is very composed.

The song's title and much of its lyrics are an appeal for acceptance, making 'Consider Me' seem at first glance to be a love song. But one key line reveals it to be more. It references two Bob Marley & The Wailers songs, by now so deeply entrenched in Jamaica's consciousness that she might as well be quoting folk sayings. The chorus of 'Nice Time', a statement of good things being overdue, is combined with reference to '400 Years', a song whose title describes the duration of the African slave trade. In this context, the nice time Lara is longing for is not romance, but social justice. Lara ultimately asks Jah to respond to this injustice by letting the land be free rather than wiping it away with brimstone and fire. And by then, the notion that 'Consider Me' is a love song is completely forgotten. 'Consider Me' can be heard on two compilation CDs: *Feel Like Jumping – The Best Of Studio One Women* on the Heartbeat label in the USA and *Studio One Classics* on the Soul Jazz label in the UK.

The Minstrels: *'People Get Ready'*
The rock steady vocal group The Minstrels recorded just a few tracks. Their 1967 song, 'People Get Ready', gives us a fine example of Studio One gospel-reggae. Jamaica has long had an appetite for gospel and recorded it locally. This started as early as the 1950s, when golden-age mento singer (and co-author of Jamaica's national anthem) Clyde Hoyte, released a 78-rpm single for producer Stanley Motta with a mento song on one side and 'Plenty Road Lead To Heaven', the first Jamaican-recorded gospel song, on the flipside. Dodd was especially keen to provide home-grown gospel. In the mid-1960s, he began to produced gospel and gospel-reggae singles and LPs, often releasing them on his specialty label, Tabernacle. He even had his star ska act Bob Marley & The Wailers record a variety of gospel and spiritual songs (as we have seen, with decidedly mixed results).

The opening of 'People Get Ready' is pure gospel instrumentally, with slide guitar and humble bass and drums. But this soon gives way to a riddim that would be pure rock steady, were it not for the occasional revisits from the slide guitar. The Minstrels enter with lovely soulful gospel vocals and soaring harmonies. Rather than a traditional song, they've chosen The Impressions' popular gospel-influenced soul track. In all, it's a perfect fusion of US and Jamaican sounds and styles. Though this fine recording awaits inclusion on CD, it was re-released as a Studio One single in 2013.

The Viceroys: *'Fat Fish'; 'Ya Ho'*
Wesley Tinglin was born in Saint James Parish around 1947, moving to Trench Town when he was twelve years old to live with his sister. There, along with The Wailers and many others, he became one of Joe Higgs's students, learning to harmonize. He formed the vocal group The Viceroys with backing singers Daniel Bernard and Bunny Gayle. After passing an audition with Coxsone Dodd, they began recording at Studio One in 1967. Though not particularly prolific, they recorded steadily through 1984 (calling themselves for a time The Interns), spanning styles from rock steady through roots reggae and recording about 60 singles and five albums. Along the way, Bernard and Gayle would depart, leaving Tinglin in ownership of The Viceroys name.

'Fat Fish' is from The Viceroys' first recording session. It's a breezy, sweet song, and as uncomplicated as any in reggae. The instrumentation is basic rock steady, but with a leanness that foreshadows the reggae that's soon to come. Likewise, the strident edge of The Viceroys' harmonies are more of a roots reggae sound than the creamy vocals associated with rock steady. The Viceroys are joyful right from the song's opening wordless harmonies. Then, needing just a few lyrics, they excitedly tell their story. They are going to the beach to fish and cook out, and invite us along. We're then regaled with their wisdom, as they share favorite tips on catching and preparing fish. Even though it's a short song at less than 2 minutes, 'Fat Fish' is a big treat.

'Ya Ho', from a year later, finds Dodd again choosing a simple instrumental backing. But it's quite different from the rock steady-grounded sound of 'Fat Fish'. Restlessly creative drums, bubble-up organ and sinewy reverbed reggae chop guitar all presage the reggae of the next decade. The songs are otherwise similar, as 'Ya Ho', too, is short and its few lyrics are simple and fun. So much so that it could pass as reggae for children. 'Ya Ho' is a dead man's chest of pirate-tale clichés. It opens with some suitably pirate-sounding moaning harmonies. Then the story begins with, "Long ago and long ago", rather than the more common "long ago and far away". But remember, "far away" would not be accurate from the vantage point of Jamaica, where pirates were once given safe haven. They continue with various pirate clichés, both new and familiar. The expected "Yo ho ho and a bottle of rum" is changed to the titular refrain. Fortunately, The Viceroys'

melodies and vocals are infinitely better than their memory of pirate exclamations. So, whether with the kids or with some rum, be sure to hear 'Ya Ho'. And
don't be surprised if you find yourself singing along.

'Ya Ho' was a hit and is available on several CDs, including The Viceroys CD collection on the Heartbeat label that bears the song's name. The original version is
recommended over any remake or remix, including the one also included on the
CD that triples the length to 6 minutes and reminds us that, sometimes, more
is less. 'Fat Fish' was not a hit and was far less collected, but can be heard on the
same Heartbeat CD.

17 Bob Marley & The Wailers, Part 2: Self-produced singles in their middle period

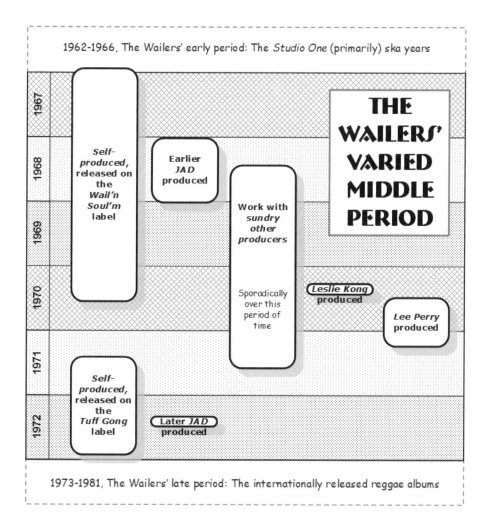

1962-1966, The Wailers' early period: The *Studio One* (primarily) ska years

1967

1968
Self-produced, released on the *Wail'n Soul'm* label

Earlier *JAD* produced

1969
Work with sundry other producers

THE WAILERS' VARIED MIDDLE PERIOD

1970
Sporadically over this period of time

Leslie Kong produced

Lee Perry produced

1971
Self-produced, released on the *Tuff Gong* label

1972
Later *JAD* produced

1973-1981, The Wailers' late period: The internationally released reggae albums

The Wailers' middle period

We have already discussed The Wailers' early period, when they were recording ska and other music at Studio One from 1962 to 1966. Later, we will discuss their late period; the decade-long run of internationally popular albums that began in 1973. This leaves a span of time from the end of 1967 into 1972 as the group's middle period. It yielded a significant body of work of over 250 tracks, including new songs, remakes, dub versions and alternative mixes. The middle period found The Wailers at their most varied, even more than they were at Studio One. With scant exceptions, they recorded their final rock steady, gospel, R&B and covers songs. They began playing early reggae proper, funky reggae, roots reggae, Nyabinghi-reggae and even internationalized pop-reggae. They did so working with a variety of producers: they recorded over 100 tracks for Lee Perry; they recorded an LP for Leslie Kong. Hoping to break overseas as performers or songwriters, they recorded a collection of demos and finished songs for the American JAD group. They began self-production, resulting in an impressive and varied collection of tracks, starting with their first single after leaving Studio One. Plus there were smaller bodies of work with other producers, as small as a single single. There were gems all along the way, as you will see in the next five chapters.

It's interesting to note how many sources label The Wailers' middle-period recordings with Lee Perry as the group's best work. Not to take anything away from this excellent body of music, but I find it difficult to say that it is significantly better than their self-produced work in the middle period or their early-period work with Coxsone Dodd, or, for that matter, their later period of internationally released albums. Meanwhile, their middle-period LP for Leslie Kong is sometimes derided, yet with two of the ten great songs and none that are bad, I don't find it so easy to dismiss. The Wailers were extremely talented singers and songwriters, and consistently collaborated with the best backing musicians in Jamaica. Regardless of the producer or the era, The Wailers recorded great songs at each juncture. This is even true of the JAD sessions, when they were working with non-Jamaican musicians, often with the goal of recording demos of songs other artists might consider for recordings of their own. This body of work resulted in many more enjoyable recordings than one would have reasonably expected. Although I respect those individual opinions, in my personal view, there is neither a bad nor a best era/producer of Wailers recordings.

With the few exceptions noted, all of The Wailers middle-period tracks are available on a series of box-set collections. The bulk can be found on three box-sets on the Universal label: *Man To Man*, *Grooving Kingston 12* and *Fy-Ah Fy-Ah*. "Dub versions" of many tracks are included, though these are typically better described as instrumental versions of the riddim. Some songs featuring Peter Tosh on lead are found instead on his box-set called *Honorary Citizen* on the Sony label.

Self-produced singles on Wail'n Soul'm

The Wailers' middle period began with a series of self-produced singles released on their new Wail'n Soul'm label, running from 1966 through 1970. They then took about a year off from self-production to concentrate exclusively on recording with other producers. When they resumed, they released singles on their new Tuff Gong label, leading up to the period of internationally released albums. For years, these singles were treasured possessions of Wailers fans. This is because The Wailers pressed and sold them locally, making them hard to find, yet they failed to release a strong LP (or two) culled from this material that could have been marketed both locally and overseas. Although these tracks represent the great lost Wailers LP, thankfully, some twenty-five years later, they did begin to appear on CDs.

The Wailers followed their 1966 self-produced debut single ('Freedom Time' and 'Bend Down Low', as detailed below) with a double-sided hit single in early 1967. They were backed by a band comprised of many of The Dynamites, though their great guitarist Hux Brown is not present. This same line-up appeared on the majority of the group's Wail'n Soul'm recordings. (Later, the full Dynamites line-up would back The Wailers on their 1970 LP for Leslie Kong.) This single paired the sharp, tart 'Hypocrites' with the soft, sweet 'Nice Time'. 'Hypocrites' takes on one of Bob's favorite targets. He decries those who undercut their fellow man even as they preach loving him. They do so, he explains, because they are "grava-licious", or greedy. The flipside, 'Nice Time', is a gentle love song. The chorus wor-ries about the long delay since their last "nice time", which other lyrics imply to be a love-making session. But the issue is approached as gently as possible, and the chorus provides the song with a harmonious hook. The polished and accessible sound of 'Nice Time', and a reference to rock steady, brings to mind Duke Reid. The Wailers would never work with rock steady's most celebrated producer – the only significant producer of the time that they did not. The conservative producer disliked working with Rasta or with anyone whom he couldn't fully control in the studio, both conditions making work with The Wailers unfeasible. But Reid would have had to approve of the fine, mannered, polished, Treasure Isle-like rock steady of 'Nice Time', the bigger hit of the two. The Wailers would remake 'Nice Time', and its lyrics made it an obvious choice for the famous Wailers reunion concert in 1975. The latter opens with Bob reciting the chorus, and the audience laughs as Bob, Peter and Bunny were reunited on stage for the last time. (There was also a lesser-known reunion show in 1974.)

'Don't Rock My Boat', from 1968, is the first rendition of a song that would be remade several times over the years. Bob sings gratefully of being in love and hopes that nothing changes. The original is terser than later versions, in the style of some post-rock steady early reggae. The sharp, uncharacteristically undisci-plined organ line from Winston Wright is an inescapable presence. The original rendition of 'Mellow Mood' from 1967 is also terser than the rendition that fol-lowed, sounding a bit stiff compared to the remake that sways. It finds Bob again contentedly in love, expressed in a series of simple double entendres. The year 1968 also saw the original rendition of 'I'm Hurting Inside', a dramatic song of childhood lost love, in which Rita and Peter back Bob with a riddim that has a foot each in the rock steady and reggae camps. It was popular enough to be remade and covered, plus Peter Tosh would take the melody of its chorus for his mid-1970s solo song, 'Jah Guide'.

'Comma Comma' is a simple love song from 1970 that features The Wailers providing guitars and keyboards with bass and drums from the Barrett brothers, drummer Carlton and bassist Aston. The result is a somewhat ramshackle arrangement with a surging beat. Not shockingly, The Wailers' never remade it, but Johnny Nash was able to sand off the rough edges for his cover version. The sluggish 'Chances Are', from 1968, is a not entirely successful return to the R&B ballad form. Better, but not great, is the 1970 R&B track, 'Black Progress'. Based on James Brown's 'Say It Loud – I'm Black And I'm Proud', Bob gets to emulate one of his biggest inspirations, while the Barrett brothers lead a band that can imitate the sound of Brown's. As we will see, much better James Brown-influenced sounds and a whole lot more would come from the long collaboration between Bob and the Barretts. The Wailers also released two upbeat spiritual/gospel songs on Wail'n Soul'm. Though these fared better than similar songs they recorded at Studio One, great spiritual music from The Wailers would have to wait for the inspiration of Jah. The original 1967 rendition of 'Thank You Lord' can be called rock steady with traditional spiritual lyrics, and is pleasant enough. Bob shares the lead with Bunny, but would handle it himself in the remake soon to come. 'The Lord Will Make A Way' features more of a gospel instrumental arrangement. Bob hangs in better than he did with most Studio One gospel, but by now it was clear that this would never be his forte.

The Wailers' first Nyabinghi recordings came in a 1967 session, with a rendition of 'This Train' and an instrumental called 'Lyrical Satirical I'. The instrumentation of each consists of Peter Tosh's acoustic guitar, doing impressive work in a style he is not typically associated with, and a trio of Nyabinghi drummers comprised of a Wailer from the past, the present and the future: former Wailer vocalist Vision Walker joins Bunny Wailer and percussionist Alvin "Seeco" Patterson, who would become an instrumental Wailer in the 1970s. Seeco was an older man, who previously worked with mento star Lord Flea, and is said to have had a role in tutoring The Wailers and bringing them to the attention of Coxsone Dodd. Here he makes his Wailers debut, beginning an association that would last through Bob Marley's last album. Thus, he enjoyed the longest musical relationship with Bob of anyone other than Rita Marley and Bob's on-and-off work with Lee Perry. 'This Train' features Bunny Wailer on lead, marking the first time a post-Coxsone release did not have Bob Marley as lead vocalist. Bunny's unhurried, emotional vocals and dramatic backing vocals from Peter and Bob marry well to the acoustic guitar and Nyabinghi drum backing. The rendition is good enough to render superfluous Bunny's subsequent remakes whether with or without The Wailers. 'Lyrical Satirical I' is a lovely instrumental, led by Tosh's acoustic guitar as the drummers play quietly along. A bright and peaceful awakening, it's the ideal reggae song for the dawn.

Bunny would make a partial return to the Nyabinghi style in 1969 with 'Tread Oh', an odd song from every angle. The line-up was atypical, consisting of Peter on organ and backing vocals, one Joe Starky on backing vocals, Ras Michael on hand drum, plus bass, piano and a guitar, and no participation from Bob Marley. The resulting sound is one-half Nyabinghi-reggae and one-half strange. Bunny makes little sense as he sings of food, sex, blackbirds, rituals, sex, love, vanity, bottles and sex, yet he has maintained that this is a spiritual song! Not a bad song, but certainly as eccentric a one as The Wailers ever recorded. In 1970, Bunny and Peter, again without Bob, recorded another track with Nyah hand drummer Ras Michael, an instrumental called 'Rhythm'. Bunny plays guitar, Peter plays piano, along with bass, drums and organ. It's a strange Nyabinghi-reggae jam, atypically led by piano, with a hint of vocals buried low in the mix.

Peter Tosh's first Wail'n Soul'm lead vocal belatedly arrives in 1968 on 'Funeral', a song that was later remade several times as 'Burial', including solo renditions by Bunny and Peter (each described in the respective chapters on their post-Wailers work; pages 514–28). Kicking off with Johnny Moore playing "Taps" on trumpet, the song is a rejection of common funeral practices and attitudes towards death in favor of Rastafarian beliefs that de-emphasize these things. A defiant vocal from Tosh on a serious topic is musically assuaged by soft backing vocals from Bob and Rita and Winston Wright's rock steady piano. Nyah drums from Seeco Patterson split the difference, as the balance boosts the song's appeal.

Also in 1968, Tosh sings lead on his original rendition of 'Stepping Razor', a song written by Joe Higgs. He warns bullies that treating him badly is done at the peril of their lives, because he's a "walking razor". The lyric, "don't watch my size", actually makes more sense coming from the shorter Higgs than from the six foot three Tosh, but this did not stop it from becoming a signature song for Peter after he left the Wailers. The backing, featuring Nyah drum from Seeco and vocals from Bob and Rita, plus sax from Ska Campbell, is suitably tough. Tosh's solo rendition is, too, described in the chapter on his best post-Wailers work (page 524).

'Dem A Fi Get A Beatin'', again from 1968, is the original and best rendition of an exciting song that Tosh would twice remake. It features the fast pace and aggressive, busy arrangement of early reggae proper. Peter, singing lead in unison with Bob for most of the song, describes reaching a breaking point over bad economic conditions and other injustices for Jamaica's slave-descended population. The oppressors will get a beating, though exactly who will give it or how is left unsaid. Tosh goes on to recommend acting sooner rather than later and his belief in God's support of these actions.

Complete with a spoken opening, Tosh supplies a fine lead vocal on 'Fire Fire', also from 1968 (as we can see, a break-out year for him). He nicely hands off lines to Bob at various points, as Rita provides close, sweet backing harmonies. The melody comes from a Jamaican folk song called 'Mamma Me Wan' Fe Work', but the lyrics are all new, describing standing up for righteousness and the fiery outcome for those who don't. A popular song, both Peter and Bunny remade it in their post-Wailers careers, as did various other artists.

'Oppressor Man', recorded without the other Wailers in 1970, is an inferior rendition of 'Sinner Man'/'Downpressor Man' from Tosh. Though he was the producer, it appeared as a single on the obscure Trans Am label rather than Wail'n Soul'm. It's totally superfluous, and only completists are advised to find it on the Peter CD collection called *Simpleton*.

Though originally credited to her group, The Soulettes, Rita Marley's 1968 song 'Play Play Play' can be considered part of The Wailers canon, as Bob and Peter provide her backing vocals. Rita admonishes those who play all day without understanding the importance of religion, yet manages to sound coquettish at the same time. Johnny Moore's trumpet is the featured instrument in a solid rock steady backing.

These self-produced Wail'n Soul'm sides add up to a consistently good collection of tracks. But we haven't even discussed the eight best songs from these sessions, as seen below.

'Freedom Time' (aka 'People Get Ready'); 'Bend Down Low'
The first Wail'n Soul'm release was a 1966 single with a pair of breezy rock steady songs. Both have Bob singing lead with Bunny and Peter backing. The instrumental arrangement is provided by three former Skatalites: pianist Jackie Mittoo and the Lloyds, Brevett and Knibb, on bass and drums. With a trio of that caliber, and The Wailers engaging in a wide variety of harmonies, no other musicians are necessary to achieve excellence. 'Freedom Time' (aka 'People Get Ready') is a declaration of freedom, with Bob receiving mandates from nature in the form of whispering trees and directly from God. Specifically, Bob is calling for freedom from the injustices suffered by Jamaica's poor black population, recalling the labor their ancestors did as slaves in a stanza that he would re-use in another song, 'Crazy Baldhead', ten years later. And it is meaningful that this was The Wailers' first post-Dodd recording. The song can be seen to have a second meaning, describing freedom from the financial exploitation at Studio One. (Songs attacking past producers are common in reggae.) Later, The Wailers would record 'Small Axe', commonly believed to be another such attack.

The flipside, 'Bend Down Low', was a popular song that was remade by The Wailers several times after this crackling initial rendition (including an exciting remake by Bunny Wailer described in the chapter on his post-Wailers work; page 518). A large part of its appeal is the intimacy Bob introduces when he makes the request of the title because he wants to "tell you what I know". He builds on this with subsequent lyrics as he gets personal about relationship issues. On both tracks of this single, Knibb shows an effortless transition from a great ska drummer to a better drummer than rock steady calls for. He swings and brings the track along with him.

'Bus Dem Shut' (aka 'Pyaka')

Expressed in a hash of local idioms and patois, The Wailers have much to say in 'Bus Dem Shut'. It inspires them to unusual harmony work that is outstanding even by Wailers standards, making this 1967 release a terrific song. It's a shame The Wailers didn't tackle it again at some point, though Rita Marley, Marcia Griffiths and Bunny Wailer each recorded solo renditions.

Led by jingling piano, the instrumentation is melodic, uncluttered rock steady. This leaves room for plenty of thoughtful reflection, or, as they put it, "Come-a, come-a come-a, we go reason now". They rebuff "pyaka-ism", a term for bad behavior that encompasses greed and dishonesty, and advocate the pursuit rather than the rejection of happiness, even in the face of pain. How does accepting this positive, Rasta-influenced mindset make Marley feel? So proud he can "bus dem shut" In other words, a joy so great that his chest swells to the point where he bursts his shirt. This pride is evident in the confidence and energy of the vocals, which shine with enlightenment. There's call and response, with Marley's enthusiastic lead answered by folky harmonies from Peter and Bunny. Full and in a lower tone than the norm, their harmonies have a different sound from those on any other Wailers song, and they are a delight. Then Bob joins with Bunny for a harmony sound not heard enough in the Wailers' body of work. Peter joins in, adding a counter-line, pushing his baritone to bass to best contrast with Bob and Bunny's high harmonies. Then they move into three-part harmony, reminding us of what a treat this is, and leaving us to wish they sang this way more often. A showcase for The Wailers' harmony skills, with socially conscious lyrics all riding on a breezy rock steady backing, 'Bus Dem Shut' perhaps the most underrated song The Wailers ever released.

'Pound Get A Blow'

Like 'Bus Dem Shut', 'Pound Get A Blow' is a title that requires explanation. This 1968 song is about the financial blow to Jamaica when, in 1967, the UK devalued the pound. The rock steady backing features a frilly trumpet refrain from Dizzy Moore that helps give the song something of a rural sound for the steadfastly urban Wailers. Once again, they vary lead and backing vocal roles throughout, creating fun and excitement. It begins with a dour Peter Tosh singing how the situation is causing destructive upheaval and even starvation, as Bob and Rita provide backing vocals. Then Bob sings lead for a stanza, with Peter and Rita providing backing. Adding to the ruralness of the sound, he's a bit off-key. Using a vocabulary of terms established in two previous Wail'n Soul'm songs, 'Bend Down Low' and 'Bus Dem Shut', he continues the already established dialog with his audience, as he brings us into his confidence to assure us that all pyakas will get their just deserts. Rita steps up with a brief lead of sorts, echoing two of Bob's lines. For all the backing vocals Rita provided The Wailers, it's very unusual for her to have even a brief turn out front on a Wailers record. After a few more lines from Bob, anchorman Tosh retakes the baton for the final lap. Though it creaks along with a touch of the rustic compared to the slicker 'Bus Dem Shut', 'Pound Get A Blow' is another topical song that's a vocal showcase for The Wailers, giving them another standout Wail'n Soul'm track.

'Stir It Up'

The rock steady original rendition of 'Stir It Up' is less famous than the remake on the *Catch A Fire* album. But it's clearly the better of the two, crackling with energy, making the later rendition sound lethargic by comparison. The piano-led instrumentation is sharper and cleaner. The vocals are better too. Like the remake, it starts with love-song lyrics and a double entendre, as Bob promises to push the wood into the fire. But where the remake adds more double entendres for its second half, in this rendition Bob cuts loose, playful and cooing, making his sentiments heartfelt in a way that the remake never rises to. It's a performance that makes 'Stir It Up' the best love song of the Wail'n Soul'm material and one of the most seductive performances of Bob's entire career.

'Give Me A Ticket'

Recorded in 1970, 'Give Me A Ticket' is a cover of the Box Tops' 1967 hit, 'The Letter', though the sound is jarringly different. Whereas the Box Tops' song was a model of crisp pacing and professional pop sensibilities, The Wailers' rendition features a slower, very deliberate pace and a sing-song delivery. And where the original had a full sound complete with sweetening from strings and horns, the cover has a precisely played but sparse rock steady-based arrangement, with funky, flinty rhythm guitar strumming that belongs to the reggae of the day. Understated and tidy, it's equally different from the hit cover by Joe Cocker and his very large Mad Dogs and Englishmen band.

The Wailers released two mixes of 'Give Me A Ticket'. In the original, Peter sings lead over backing harmonies from Bunny and Rita. Though it's an endearing performance, he sounds unpracticed. It's not Peter's best lead, and this is not the recommended version. In the other mix, Tosh is entirely dubbed out except for some ghostly tape leakage, and the song opens up. Bunny and Rita's backing vocals are effectively given battlefield promotion to lead. Their performance proves to be up to the challenge, with Rita sounding particularly good here. Sweet without ever being saccharine, they sing in unison falsetto voices, Bunny with vibrato, Rita without. They are unhurried, but there is an urgency to their halting delivery. They augment this with assorted wordless phrases that add drama and playfulness. It's a performance so unusual and so strong, Peter's lead is rendered utterly unnecessary, and this mix of 'Give Me A Ticket' becomes a delicacy for a Wailers fan.

'Trouble On The Road Again'; 'Trouble Dub'

'Trouble On The Road Again', from 1970, marks a stark departure from the bright, sunny rock steady sounds of previous Wail'n Soul'm releases. The sound here is reggae, dark and ominous, strange and wonderful. It's another early collaboration between The Wailers and the bass and drums of the Barrett brothers, with no other musicians participating. Multi-tracked guitars and keyboards from Bob and Peter complete the lurching, deliberately murky reggae riddim. High-pitched, rapidly strummed rhythm guitar and trebly piano combine into a sound that gives an unusual texture reminiscent of the metallic tang of mento banjo. The likes of it would not be heard in another Wailers song.

Bob's anguished lead vocal is mixed low, creating the impression of a distant cry for help. He sings about a troubled, rain-slicked road as a threat to the well-being of people, a metaphor he used in his very first recording, 'Judge Not', and would expand further in two future songs, 'Caution', and 'Wake Up And Live'. It's a generous Bob Marley vocal. At points, he punctuates it with James Brown shouts, calls and grunts. Then he affects us as he sings emotionally of the people's struggles. Meanwhile, Peter and Bunny provide mournful support with ghostly falsetto backing vocals, furthering the drama.

A remixed version of this song called 'Trouble Dub' is even better. The whole song is altered to sound slower and darker, building towards a nightmarish air. The bright banjo-like sound is gone, the bass is brought up and drop-out/in is applied to the backing vocals. It's a longer mix by half, with additional vocals that sound like Bob's wrestling with nightmares. The mix you choose may depend on how you feel that day – dark or darker. Bunny Wailer did a good rendition of this song in his post-Wailers solo career, managing to turn the song into a more *upfull* affair.

'Feel Alright'; 'Dub Feeling'

'Feel Alright' shares a number of qualities with 'Trouble On The Road Again'. It's also from 1970, reggae rather than rock steady, features a band with just the Wailers adding their instrumental skills to a rhythm section, a dark production sound, and has a dub remix that is longer by half and the better version. Called 'Dub Feeling', this dispenses with the cluttering bells heard on the original, adds reverb to the vocals and deepens the bass, creating a sound that is as murky as a room thick with ganja smoke. Bob's guitar and Hugh Malcolm's drums are all but lost in the fog. Peter plays an organ rhythm that churns like waves in a storm. Wandering in and out is a tinkling piano from Bunny that sounds like it's under water. Lloyd Brevett's bass stands out like a beacon in the fog.

The Wailers pair this dark, foreboding sound with vocals that burn with intensity. All of which is an unlikely feat, considering that the song is based on 'There Was A Time' – a happy-go-lucky James Brown party song. (Bob adapts Brown's line where he calls his home town "Augusta, G. A." by changing "G. A." to "J. A.".) The rasping, quivering, grunt-filled lead shows a James Brown influence. But the song is not otherwise sung like the original, as The Wailers make the lyrics sound far more dramatic than they read. This is especially true of the counting-based call-and-response that is the song's highlight. Each time Peter and Bunny are heard with the titular chorus, they add one, two, three or four exclamations of *ah!* Sometimes, Bob tips it off just before with interjections like *one time!* Other times, he echoes the count after the fact with the same number of grunts or groans of his own. But, mostly, it's impossible to guess how many *ah!*s are coming at the end of any given line; you're only sure that it will sound great. Pure ear candy, never has such a device brought so much playfulness and passion to a song. Another atypical but wonderful Wailers song, 'Feel Alright', and especially its dub remix, lives up to its name.

Self-produced singles on Tuff Gong

After taking a year off to work with producers Leslie Kong and Lee Perry, The Wailers resumed self-production in the latter part of 1971. Having retired their Wail'n Soul'm imprint, they released most of these songs on their new Tuff Gong label. Others by Peter and Bunny appeared on new labels of their own. These later self-productions ran through most of 1972. By then, rock steady was a distant memory and reggae ruled the roost. Though none are highlighted here as great, this was a fairly consistent body of work with many very good songs. Together, they represent a ramp up to 1973's *Catch A Fire*, the Tuff Gong/Island Records LP that launched their later period of massively popular internationally released albums.

The tough, unyielding original rendition 'Concrete Jungle' (and its similar alternative take) is good, if very different from the famous remake that would appear on *Catch A Fire*. Here, it's something of a dirge rather than a rocker, with organ, saxophone and trombone in the forefront, rather than guitar. Bob sings of the inescapable darkness of oppression and hard living, and wonders if he can find love or happiness. Peter and Bunny are good here, but nowhere near as revelatory as they would be on *Catch A Fire*.

The happy original 1971 version of 'Trench Town Rock' is a joy to hear and not just for featuring perhaps the greatest opening line in the history of song: "One good thing about music, when it hits you feel okay." Bob then slings Jamaican jive about his rough Kingston neighborhood, as early roots reggae backing is heard. Bunny and Peter are joined by Winston "Pipe" Matthews of vocal group The Wailing Souls, adding to the rootsiness, as do the Nyabinghi drums of Seeco Patterson. They would remake this song two more times, but first it was quickly followed by a version called 'Kingston 12 Shuffle' (named for Bob's Trench Town address), in which The Wailers and DJ U-Roy share the vocals.

The same year saw three different but largely similar takes of 'Screw Face', with The Wailers making a case with biblical language that Rastafarians need not fear the titular subject. "Screw face" is a term that literally means someone with an angry face. It's often used to describe someone who is openly hostile, or it can refer to the devil. Bob seems to be addressing both meanings. He states that he will intimidate any would-be intimidator, referring to himself as a screw face. This powerful pronouncement of fearlessness is sung self-assuredly by Bob, with falsetto backing from Bunny and Peter, and an upbeat reggae backing toughened with tart horns. The supernatural angle is expanded in two of the takes, as *duppies* (ghosts) are included as something Rastas need not fear. It's a theme that is also featured in a better-known Wailers song, 'Duppy Conqueror'.

'Redder Than Red' deals with a less-weighty piece of Rasta business, resulting in a simple pleasure of a song. A languid reggae backing featuring a hazy organ and early touches of dub sets the tone as The Wailers sing that they are "redder than red".In this context, "red" means very high on marijuana, from how bloodshot the smoker's eyes can become. Bob points out that red makes dread, and positive Rasta vibes ensue, as Bob sings of being true to loved ones and protecting people. He was probably too red to remember to remake this song for his *Kaya* album, where it would have fit famously.

Meanwhile, the merry 'Pour Down The Sunshine', recorded with many of The Dynamites, would have fit comfortably on the LP that The Wailers recorded with producer Leslie Kong and that band. 'Satisfy My Soul Jah Jah' and 'Satisfy My Soul Babe' are essentially different renditions of the same song (and a different song from the later, better-known but similarly named 'Satisfy My Soul'). It features a heavy dread vibe and a touch of dissonance that a neophyte fan of reggae would find challenging. In the 1971 'Music Lesson' (aka 'Music Gonna Teach'), Bob takes on the Jamaican school system's emphasis on the deeds of Marco Polo and Christopher Columbus while ignoring anything African. It's a theme that The Wailers, especially Peter Tosh, would return to. In 'Craven Choke Puppy', Bob warns against being greedy (craven) and envious. He concludes by quoting a folk saying that speaks to the futility of such emotions. "Wanty, wanty cyaan getty, getty, getty no wanty" means that people want what they can't get, while those who have don't want it. Tommy McCook on sax and Vin Gordon on trombone do fine work on the song's opening, closing and middle break. The indispensable reference book, *Bob Marley and The Wailers: The Definitive Discography*[1] explains the meaning of Lick Samba. It's patois for "lick some back" – an expression for making love. Bob sings about not being able to resist lick samba, even though he knows he will be hurt by his lover. It's a seductive song with a sway to the music and a lush chorus of backing singers as Rita and two of her Soulettes join Peter and Bunny. A sweet confection of a Wailers song, it is often forgotten and underappreciated.

'Guava Jelly' never struck me as an especially good Bob Marley & The Wailers song, cloying in sound and weak in arrangement. But the fact that artists as diverse as Stanley Beckford, Johnny Nash and Barbara Streisand all saw fit to cover

---

1.   Roger Steffens and Leroy Jodie Pierson, *Bob Marley and The Wailers: The Definitive Discography* (Cambridge, MA: Rounder Books, 2005), p. 60.

it leads me to believe that there may be more to the song than I hear. The original 1971 rendition of 'Lively Up Yourself' is good but compared to the playful swagger of its later remake and live renditions, comes off as a bit stiff.

Peter Tosh sang lead on several self-produced tracks in this period that were released on his own Intel Diplo and other labels rather than Tuff Gong; they feature Bunny but not Bob on backing vocals. For the tart and funky 1972 'You Can't Blame The Youth', Peter returns to the theme of 'Music Lesson', taking the Jamaican educational system to task for teaching nursery-rhyme nonsense and aggrandizing pirates and colonialists as great figures. It features Peter's clavinet, a defining feature of his solo career sound. The song would become a live staple for Tosh, first with The Wailers and then solo. 'Leave My Business Alone', from 1971, has a softer sound, aided by Tosh's joyful melodica playing. The liner notes of 'Honorary Citizen' and *Bob Marley and The Wailers* (p. 58) both erroneously assign authorship to blues singer Bessie Smith, confusing it with a similarly named song. This is actually a Jamaican folk song about minding one's own business that was often performed by mento acts. On the 1971 'Once Bitten', Tosh uses a familiar adage, "once bitten, twice shy", perhaps in an attempt to explain his often prickly personality. He supports this with folk wisdom, pointing out that the dog that bit you earlier in the day is likely to still want to bite you later in the day. (Between this and 'Maga Dog', Tosh apparently did not have a lot of positive canine experiences.) It's a pleasant, if unremarkable, listen. The same can be said for two previously difficult-to-find songs also from 1971: 'Here Comes The Sun' is Peter's cover of George Harrison's Beatles song, with some nice country strumming on acoustic guitar. 'Lion' rhymes *iron, lion* and *Zion* years before Bob's song of that name. Tosh warns of divine retribution for those who lie about leading a righteous Rasta life.

Bunny Wailer sang lead on several tracks from this period that were released on his own Solomonic label. Further mirroring Tosh's Intel Diplo songs, Peter is Bunny's sole source of backing vocals on these tracks. The 1972 original rendition of 'Pass It On' sounds quite different from the meditative, pastoral remake heard on The Wailers' 1973 LP, *Burnin'*. This rendition features a resolute air and strident saxophone lines. The song advocates helping others and sharing rather than selfishness, familiar Rasta themes. Bunny also had two songs from this time that are currently unavailable on CD. One was the original rendition of 'Bide Up', an unexceptional song that he would remake for his first solo LP, *Blackheart Man*. The other was much better, 'Arab Oil Weapon', a song that is described in the chapter on Bunny Wailer's best solo work (page 514).

18 Bob Marley & The Wailers, Part 3: The JAD productions in their middle period

While vacationing in Jamaica, American pop star Johnny Nash was introduced to Bob Marley, who impressed him with an impromptu demonstration of his song-writing prowess. This led to The Wailers recording several dozen tracks for the JAD production team of Johnny Nash, Arthur Jenkins and Danny Simms throughout 1968 and again in 1972. The intent of these sessions seems to have been two-fold. First, to break Bob Marley & The Wailers internationally. Second, to amass songs for consideration by other artists to record, such as Nash himself. He would record Bob's 'Guava Jelly', 'Stir It Up', 'Nice Time', 'Comma Comma', 'Reggae On Broadway', 'Mellow Mood', 'Rock It Baby', 'You Poured Sugar On Me' (which Bob wrote but never recorded) and the Peter Tosh-penned 'Love'. Many believe that Bob also wrote Nash's biggest hit, 'I Can See Clearly Now'. It was released in 1972, so the timing is right, and the lyrics are stylistically Bob-like, if in a more light-weight vein. But this assumption has never been substantiated, so it may have, in fact, been written by a Marley-influenced Nash.

The resulting body of recordings is a mixed bag. Just a few tracks were released at the time, resulting in two singles. The rest are demos, ranging from raw to polished. Some were later overdubbed to "finish" them for release (sometimes more than once over the years). But just because they are demos, they should not be dismissed. As rock fans can happily explain, demos by favorite artists can be of great interest and give special pleasure. Recording sessions occurred in Jamaica and in overseas studios, sometimes with Jamaican musicians, at other times backed by non-Jamaican sessions men. Backing arrangements ranged from non-reggae to reggae-lite, or no backing at all. There were remakes of songs The Wailers had previously recorded, some new songs and even songs that were written by outsiders for The Wailers to perform. In a bid for international commercial appeal, Rasta sentiments were put on hold in these sessions. Instead, love songs were emphasized, and an easy-going sound typically employed. Even the normally acerbic Peter Tosh showed his versatility by joining the pleasantness with aplomb. Bunny Wailer is barely involved in these sessions, as he was serving a jail sentence for ganja possession. But the Wailers' collective again proved its strength. Just as Peter and Bunny rose to the occasion when Bob was absent during the end of their Studio One years, Rita filled in ably for Bunny. And when Bunny is present,

Rita is still heard, making it difficult not to consider her anything less than a full-fledged Wailer in these sessions.

The JAD team was supposed to usher Bob Marley & The Wailers into international stardom. In this regard, they would fail. The two singles were flops, and the rest of the material might not ever have seen release, but it did eventually ride on the coat-tails of the highly successful run of Island albums. Artistically, although the JAD sessions did not live up to either the consistency or the uncompromising nature of most of the other portions of The Wailers' body of work, it produced some gems nonetheless. The best and the rest of the JAD recordings are described below.

'Mellow Mood'

A 1968 remake of 'Mellow Mood' features Bob on lead vocals backed by Peter and Rita, with The Dynamites providing instrumentation. The versatile band uses a light hand to keep with the JAD goal of an accessible sound. The terseness of the original rock steady rendition is replaced with a slower, softer arrangement. This serves to open up the vocals, making the rock steady rendition sound stiff by comparison. And it's a better fit with the song's easy-going lyrics that intermingle love, sex and music. You won't pine for a reggae beat with the swaying rhythm guitar-led arrangement that's so lush and sexy, as this rendition outdoes the Wail'n Soul'm original in every way.

'Mellow Mood' was released as a single in the UK and France, paired with a less-impressive remake of 'Bend Down Low' as the flipside. It was credited to Bob, Peter and Rita rather than to The Wailers. It flopped, but as we will see, JAD would try again one more time.

'Hammer'

'Hammer' is a song from 1968 about fighting unspecified oppression. Bob sings lead with backing from Rita and Peter. But Peter is the song's author, and he would later record a solo rendition of his own. As one would expect from the title, the few lyrics are simple and direct, calling for a hammer and a rammer (whatever that exactly is) to beat down adversaries. But the sound is so much softer than the words, with easy-going reggae-lite instrumentation from The Dynamites, a sweet melody and rich, exuberant backing vocals. The dichotomy between the sound and words makes this song a velvet hammer.

'What Goes Around Comes Around'

'What Goes Around Comes Around' is from the very first JAD session, an informal affair in Jamaica at the start of 1968. Written by Jimmy Norton, Joe Venneri and Al Pyfrom, no fewer than twelve remixes of 'What Goes Around' have been released over the years by JAD. Yet none of them approaches the simple pleasure of the original recording buried in the "Enhanced" CD portion of the 1996 JAD release called *Soul Almighty*. There, you can hear Bob, Peter and Rita joined by Johnny Nash and others singing in folk glory, with the barest minimum of instrumentation. The rich, full backing vocals are reminiscent of those heard on some of Harry Belafonte's best Caribbean songs – a pleasing sound, and a different one for The Wailers. All of JAD's attempts to better this performance by grafting on instrumentation simply spoil an already fine recording that sounds exactly like it is supposed to.

'Love'

'Love', from 1968, is one of Peter Tosh's two lead vocals heard on these sessions, and one of the two songs he wrote. He rewards his producers by keeping with the sunny JAD sound, putting aside the discontent that fuels so much of his songwriting. He creates a delicate love song, sounding more content than he ever has before. In fact, he sounds fulfilled to the point of being post-coital.

Lyrically, 'Love' is a trifle, but as Peter sings gently, and Rita Marley provides fine backing vocals, the effect is delectable. A group of US session pros provide a cloudbank-soft R&B instrumentation that is enhanced by a prominent contribution from South African trumpet great and third-world cross-over pioneer Hugh Masekela. He plays gentle trills throughout as well as a silky solo. Peter Tosh once explained to an interviewer that he does not make "smiling music". But in 'Love' he made a song that is The Wailers' foremost expression of grinning bliss. Johnny Nash was impressed enough to record a rendition of his own. Tosh's 'Love' is currently unavailable on any Wailers collection in print, but it can be tracked down on the 1998 JAD CD called *The Complete Wailers: 1967–1972, Part 1*.

'Stay With Me'

'Stay With Me' was recorded as part of the last JAD session, in 1972, at a studio in London. Bob is the only Jamaican involved, working with a backing band of session musicians from the USA and UK. As is the case on several JAD tracks, backing vocals are provided by Johnny Nash and Doris Troy, doing a decent job as faux Wailers. (Troy's résumé is impressive. She also recorded backing vocals for The Rolling Stones, George Harrison and other big names. She is best remembered for her 1963 hit, 'Just One Look', and for her wailing vocals on Pink Floyd's 'Great Gig In The Sky'.) Bob implores his lover not to leave him. This simple sentiment is enrobed in plush instrumentation. There's a simplified reggae beat, with vibraphone and guitar out front. It shuffles and bubbles, thanks to a collection of percussion – drum kit, Nyabinghi hand drum, timbales; and the sound of steel drums is evoked by the vibes for a pan-Caribbean sound. Every aspect of the song is sweet, and every note played on the vibes is like dropping candy onto an ice cream sundae. This pop-reggae confection stands on its own, and should be enjoyed without guilt, as there's nothing wrong in mixing an occasional sugary snack into a diet of more substantial meals.

'Reggae On Broadway'

'Reggae On Broadway' was recorded by Bob in the same 1972 session as 'Stay With Me'. It was released the same year as a CBS single in the UK, credited to Bob Marley. JAD pulled out all the stops with a rocked-out pop-R&B arrangement more Broadway than reggae, loaded with guitar power chords, horn lines, backing vocals, keyboards and percussion, though none of it Jamaican sounding. Bob unleashes a strong James-Brown-by-way-of-Kingston vocal for overseas consideration. And although it's enjoyable for what it is, Bob's voice, would have ultimately been better served by a straight reggae backing. A Jamaican producer and band would, at the very least, have avoided burying Bob's voice, as sometimes happens here. Like 'Mellow Mood', 'Reggae On Broadway' was a commercial flop and would end JAD's aspirations for The Wailers. Credit Island Records owner Chris Blackwell for both undauntedly picking up the torch and for finding the right formula to break The Wailers big overseas. As we will see, JAD was not too far off in its approach. The team just needed to have more faith in the sensibilities of The Wailers and reggae.

Other JAD tracks

The easy-going 'Rocking Steady' finds Bob backed by Peter, Rita and The Dynamites, but the arrangement continues to shy away from a full Jamaican beat. That's too bad, considering the song's heritage. Its verse is an updating of Count Lasher's 1950s cha-cha-charged mento song, 'Calypso Cha Cha'. In it, Lasher sings, "When first I heard the cha-cha, it thrilled me to the bone". Then it was updated in the 1960s when Delroy [Wilson] & Paulette, backed by The Skatalites, recorded 'Dance The Ska', with "ska" taking the place of "cha-cha". Now, at the end of the 1960s, with another change in the prevailing style, Bob repurposes Lasher's lyrics, substituting "rock steady" for "cha-cha". (This, a couplet heard in 'Rude Boy', and, less directly, as the chorus of 'Rat Race' – a song described later in this book (page 473) – is the extent of Bob Marley touching on mento in his recordings. Peter, Bunny and even Rita would each dip more frequently into the mento well.) Though it's well sung and musically pleasant, a true rock steady backing would have made more sense and a better song.

A vocally lush R&B remake of 'There She Goes' with The Dynamites is a simple pleasure and provides an interesting contrast to the loose and loopy original Studio One version. After that, there is a precipitous drop in quality in the remaining JAD recordings. Remakes of 'Nice Time' and 'Bend Down Low' with non-Jamaican musicians did not improve on the earlier renditions. The former smothers good vocals in bloated horns, strings and distracting piano noodling. Nor did the presence of The Dynamites help a messy remake of 'It Hurts To Be Alone' that only serves to make us miss Junior Braithwaite and Ernest Ranglin. The Dynamites-backed 'How Many Times' (a retitled remake of 'Do You Remember') fairs better with pleasing if unexciting doo-wop vocals. A remake of 'Put It

On', again with The Dynamites, is an orderly and pleasant enough rendition of a song that would be remade again. The same can be said for a stately remake of 'I'm Hurting Inside', recorded by Bob with US session talent. A half-reggae re-do of 'Lonesome Feeling' is innocuous at best.

Though The Wailers had no shortage of songwriting talent, as we saw with 'What Goes Around Comes Around', JAD provided a number of songs for the group to record. Time could have been saved by not recording 'Fallin' In And Out Of Love', 'Stranger On The Shore' or 'Splish For My Splash'. This goes double for 'Milk Shake And Potato Chips', a song so thoroughly unsuited for The Wailers, it makes one wonder what JAD was thinking. On the other hand, another song given to Bob to record, 'Gonna Get You', recorded at the same session as 'Stay With Me', resulted in an entertaining half-reggae song. Outside writers also provided Peter Tosh and Bunny Wailer with a good song each: 'The World Is Changing' and 'Treat You Right', respectively, both featuring backing vocals from the other three Wailers.

The balance of the new songs The Wailers brought to these sessions did not result in a strong batch of recordings for JAD. 'Dance Do The Reggae' is in the same hopeful cross-over vein as 'Reggae On Broadway', though it's a lesser track. It's a weak pop ballad with a half-hearted, inconsistent vocal from Bob and an arrangement all over the place. (It's ironic that these two pop songs are The Wailers' first to use the term "reggae" in their title.) The pop of 'Oh Lord, I've Got To Get There' is as immediately forgettable as anything from JAD. The original rendition of 'Soul Rebel' is mismatched with smothering non-Jamaican horns and an arrangement that seems to be off key to the vocal. To make matters worse, the non-Wailer backing vocals are immediately noticeable as inferior to the norm. A later remake for producer Lee Perry would greatly improve on this rendition. 'Rock To The Rock', from the same session as 'Love', has none of that other song's magic and would, no doubt, have been improved with a proper rock steady instrumental backing. Somewhat better is the competent, if draggingly paced, R&B of 'Chances Are'. Rita provides high backing vocals while Tosh provides low doo-wop. The soulful 'Touch Me' is a promising song that could have been made better with full Jamaican instrumentation, but since it was abandoned after the JAD sessions, this casual take will have to suffice. A reggaefied remake of the Studio One R&B ballad 'I'm Still Waiting' is innocuous enough, if you don't mind its rambling. 'Mellow Skank' is a backing track with no vocal and didn't really need to be exhumed from the vault. It sounds as if the non-Jamaican band is struggling in a concerted effort to put down an authentic reggae groove. (It should be pointed out that "skank" has a very different meaning in Jamaica than it does in the USA. In Jamaica, skanking means to dance, specifically to a low-down, gut-tight, reggae beat.) 'You Say I Have No Feelings' turns up on a reggae compilation called *Works Of Jah Reggae*. Demo vocals from Bob are clad in a ham-fisted bluesy soul arrangement, and seeking it out is not recommended. Also conspicuous in its unavailability is a song called 'Lonely Girl' that features Rita Marley in her only JAD lead vocal. You'll have to track down a French JAD LP or an American LP on the Jamaican label, each of uncertain title, to hear this track, and stand to be disappointed for your efforts. Recently, several informal acoustic performances of songs familiar and unfamiliar were needlessly released on JAD collections, probably only in order to have "contains previously unreleased tracks" appear on the packaging. 'Cry On, Down By The River' (not Neil Young's song) and 'One Love True Love' were both abandoned at an early point of song development for a reason. Acoustic takes of 'Soul Rebel' and 'Wisdom' sound a little better, but are much closer to superfluous than crucial.

19 Bob Marley & The Wailers, Part 4: An LP produced by Leslie Kong in their middle period

In May of 1970, Bob Marley reconnected with producer Leslie Kong, who had produced his pre-Wailer sides of the early 1960s. With JAD still trying (and ultimately failing) to break the group internationally, and their many self-produced singles and work with miscellaneous other producers more geared for their local fan base, The Wailers hoped that Kong might be their ticket to overseas success. After all, he had by then already broken through with cross-over hits for Desmond Dekker and Jimmy Cliff. The plan was ambitious. They would record an album of new Wailers material, rather than a collection of already released singles – a first for reggae. Remakes would largely be avoided, as all the songs but one were new. Even the title Kong chose was lofty: *The Best Of Bob Marley & The Wailers*. The backing group would be the versatile and excellent Dynamites, then Kong's house band, with whom The Wailers had worked before. All the pieces were in place, but the album failed to break The Wailers internationally. Why? Kong made a number of decisions that, although understandable at the time, are revealed as strategic mistakes from the vantage point of hindsight. What should have been a match made in heaven didn't even make it to the honeymoon.

Although the album contained two great songs, most were undistinguished. It could not have helped that the session was brief. Accounts vary, but generally it is thought just one month was allocated for this ambitious project. A further problem was the decision to concentrate on new songs. This was probably Kong's decision. Unlike other producers (and the antithesis of Coxsone Dodd), Kong seemed resistant to remakes and versions. By this, he ignored The Wailers' track record that belied the notion that remakes equated to second-rate material. By contrast, when The Wailers soon worked with producer Lee Perry, remakes would abound. Not only were these typically fine, the practice allowed them the opportunity to fully develop their new songs, strengthening that output. Kong also tied The Wailers' hands lyrically. Though the group's passion for Rastafarianism had proved to be an inspiration for many fine songs, as was the case for the JAD sessions, Rasta topics were put aside when courting the overseas market. It's no surprise then to find a number of songs with underdeveloped lyrics. It sounds as if The Wailers were champing at the bit to fully express themselves, but were thwarted. There was also a decision to use a funky reggae style, no doubt, to open doors overseas. The reggae chop rhythm guitar is not heard on a single song. Bob was unlikely to have complained, as infatuated with James Brown as he was. Nor is rural reggae tapped, something that The Dynamites excelled in when backing Desmond Dekker and Toots & The Maytals. In retrospect, the LP would have benefited from the stylistic variety that the vocal group and backing band were both capable of. The instrumental palette could have been a bit broader too. Each song is backed by guitar, bass drums, organ and some piano. Hux Brown's lead guitar is a joy throughout the LP. But a touch of horns or some additional percussion could have gone a long way to vary and expand the sound. And all but two songs are under 3 minutes. Some of these shorter songs could have benefited from more development. Even Kong's use of The Wailers themselves was less than optimal. Rita Marley is unheard, surprisingly considering how frequent and pleasing her participation in other Wailers middle-period material had been, especially in the JAD sessions. More surprisingly, Bunny has no lead vocals, even though Peter has four on the album's ten tracks. This may point to conflict between Bunny and Kong. Bunny was open in his displeasure with the album's title, feeling that calling it "best of" was premature. This grew into the legendary story of Bunny putting a curse on Kong's head for refusing to change the LP's title. Supernaturally or not, in the space of a week, the great Leslie Kong would die suddenly of a heart attack at the age of thirty-seven, making this his swansong production. It's sad that a perfect storm of large ambitions, limited time and well-intentioned but misguided decisions would ultimately make it a disappointment.

In the end, Bunny was correct; *The Best Of The Wailers* is a misnomer. But, although it is not a great LP, it does have a pair of great songs. And if the remainder are not very good, they are not bad either. The LP can be found on a CD that preserved the original cover art including a cool Wailers *W* logo; it also adds two instrumental versions. But beware that it shares its name with innumerable compilations, both legitimate and illicit.

'Caution'

'Caution' is a potent song. It shows The Wailers' mastery of mood through expert manipulation of melody, harmony and message lyrics. And the Dynamites are up to the challenge. It opens with Hux Brown's guitar out front, rippling forebodingly over dramatic organ as Bunny adds edgy cooing sounds. With a disquieting air fully established, Bob enters: "Here I am, walking down the street, and children, everything is so sweet". But things quickly turn. Using a favorite metaphor, he warns of a road bringing peril. The three Wailers harmonize with intensity and stirring key changes, and it's enough to make you shiver when they sing:

> When you wet, it's slippery, yeah
> When it damp, it crublin'
> If it's slidin', you will tumble down,
> Don't want you on the ground

Oh-oh-oh! Caution, the road is wet
Black soul is black as jet
Caution, the road is hot
Still you got to do better than that

Bob is speaking to his people, showing concern for their well-being. He sees their position as precarious in spite of their best efforts. He urges them to stay resolute. Because the album is geared for overseas acceptance, the oppression that endangers and how Jah Rastafari empowers his followers are not specified. For the same reason, somewhat incongruously, Bob releases his inner James Brown by interjecting a repeated line, "Hit me from the top, you crazy mother funky". Although it did not help to grab the attention of fans overseas, it did catch the record company's attention, and the second half of the phrase was excised from some pressings when 'Caution' was released as a single. Tight as a drum and overproof strong, 'Caution' is the best song from the Kong LP and as good as any from The Wailers' middle period.

'Soul Shakedown Party'
Though equally great, 'Soul Shakedown Party' couldn't be more different from 'Caution'. Instead of a heavy dramatic message song, it's a happy funky party song, with Bob singing carefree observations. What it does share with 'Caution' is more James Brown-influenced lead vocals from Bob and vocal harmonies that are excellent even by Wailers standards. Bunny and Peter's work is startlingly rich in texture, whether they are singing wordlessly, answering Bob or harmonizing with him. The Dynamites are spot on, featuring a warm organ theme from Winston Wright that adds to the inviting spirit of the song. 'Soul Shakedown Party' is a great song in its own right and an important precursor to the other, more famous, party songs that The Wailers would record, such as 'Lively Up Yourself', 'Jammin'' and 'Punky Reggae Party'.

Other tracks
'Back Out' is a high-spirited and mischievous song. Bob sings of Mistress Martin and her naughty behaviour. But the details are so veiled, it's a lyrical missed opportunity. Still, there is much to like here, such as lively playing by The Dynamites complete with an organ solo, cries of *yasso!* and a fun chorus of "sweet soul music!" 'Soul Captives' is pleasant enough, though it's more memorable for a rare Hux Brown guitar solo than for the vocals or the tepid message that does not live up to the promise of the dramatic title. 'Cheer Up' works in some Rasta themes (the end of slavery and freedom) without explicitly referencing Rasta. But in spite

of a good melody and positive message, the song seems underdeveloped. 'Do It Twice' is good, but is made superfluous in this set by the musically similar 'Soul Shakedown Party' and the thematically similar 'Back Out'.

Peter Tosh's leads include a remake of the Coxsone Dodd-produced 'Can't You See'. The new rendition is slower paced and less distinctive than the rocking original and does not compare especially well. (Neither would a later remake in Tosh's post-Wailers solo career.) Faring better is the original rendition of 'Soon Come', a song that Tosh would record in his post-Wailers solo career and that would be a staple of his live shows. Its title is a Jamaican expression that literally means "in a little while", but is used ironically to suggest anything but. Here, neither the backing vocals nor the instrumentation seem up to the task of matching the biting disapproval of Tosh's words and singing, and the remake is superior. Tosh sings lead on a competent gospel-reggae reading of the traditional spiritual 'Go Tell It on the Mountain', a song that was recorded numerous times by artists as great and diverse as Mahalia Jackson, Simon & Garfunkel, The Weavers, Bobby Darrin, Aaron Neville and Odetta, as well as many others – even Andy Griffith. In the same traditional vein is the original rendition of Tosh's 'Stop That Train'. Like The Wailers' 'This Train', it's a spiritual train song, but with some *sufferas* lyrics and a dose of self-pity thrown in for good measure. It's a more joyous and soulful rendition than the somber dignity of the gospel-reggae remake that would appear on *Catch A Fire*. The best rendition may be determined by the mood of the listener.

20 Bob Marley & The Wailers, Part 5: Produced by Lee Perry in their middle period

After the LP with Leslie Kong, The Wailers went on to work with producer Lee Perry. Rainford Hugh Perry was born in 1939, in rural Kendal in Hanover Parish. A storied career left him bedecked with nicknames, like medals pinned on a general. He was most commonly known as Lee Perry or Scratch (short for Chicken Scratch, the name of an early hit), secondarily as The Upsetter (a name he also applied to one of his labels as well as to his house bands), also as Little Perry (due to his short stature), and would eventually refer to himself as Pipecock Jackxon (later in his career, when his eccentricity sharply increased). Like golden-age mento star Lord Messam before him, his skills as a dancer put him on the scene and gave him an entrée into making music. Coming to Kingston with the goal of becoming a singer, Perry first worked with Duke Reid, but the association was short-lived. The producer gave away Perry's song to another singer rather than releasing Perry's recording, which did not live up to his high standards. Perry quit Reid and went to work for Coxsone Dodd, first as an errand boy and a record distributer, next as a songwriter, then as a singer (recording a few dozen sides at Studio One), and ultimately as an A&R man. It was Perry who urged Dodd to give Toots & The Maytals a try after other producers passed over them. The Wailers first met Perry and began their long-running association with him at Studio One by adding their backing vocals to a few of his tracks. But by the end of the ska era, feeling the sting of inadequate recognition and compensation, like The Wailers, Perry departed Dodd's camp. He worked briefly with other producers before striking out on his own. Success as a producer came quickly, and he was well established by the time he started producing The Wailers. (Neither Perry's work with Bob Marley, nor his personal accomplishment as a producer would end in The Wailers' middle period, as we will see in subsequent chapters.)

By this time, Perry had gathered an exciting new house band around him anchored by the rhythm section of the Barrett brothers. Aston ("Family Man") on bass (replaced by Lloyd Parks on a handful of tracks) and Carlton, on drums, had previously worked with The Wailers on various sessions. The Barretts had recorded for different producers under various names that included The Aggravators, The Reggae Boys and even The Hippy Boys. Perry rechristened them The Upsetters, a name already in use from his previous house band. He would use it again for his subsequent bands after The Wailers departed from these sessions, taking the Barrett-based band with them. But we are getting ahead of ourselves.

The Barrett-led Upsetters were a cutting-edge outfit, with a sound that, though versatile, was undoubtedly new. It was a battle-ready sound: strong, lean and accomplished. Sometimes they played reggae in an uncompromising early roots style, at other times it was as funky as any Wailers backing. The core instruments of bass, drums, guitar (typically two playing rhythm) and keyboards were occasionally supplemented by a horn or additional percussion.

Perry's aesthetic for these sessions was distinctive as well. As was his way for early reggae, mid-song solos were not called for, as reggae's jazz element was de-emphasized. He mixed the bass loud, helping to make this a defining feature of the music going forward. And you get the sense that he was fully aware that all involved were advancing the art. The sessions' overall sound seems to have been wrought from the monochrome palette of a serious black-and-white movie. This differs greatly from both the brightly colored palette The Wailers employed on their later international LPs and the shimmering Day-Glo hues of Lee Perry's later Black Ark dub productions.

This exciting new sound inspired The Wailers to excellent vocal performances and to write fine new songs. As usual, Bob took the lead for the lion's share, with Peter and Bunny getting a few songs each. Bob's vocals show continued maturation in these sessions even beyond his rock steady work of just a short time earlier, as his control grew with time, reaching full development in time for the start of The Wailers' international LP releases in 1973. Peter and Bunny continued to provide great backing vocals, as they couldn't help but do. Rita Marley and her fellow Soulette, Hortense Lewis, added their backing vocals to a pair of tracks. But Rita is otherwise unheard, continuing Leslie Kong's consolidation around the three core Wailers. She would return to Wailers prominence as a backing singer, but not until 1975 in response to Marley, Tosh and Livingston going their separate ways. Dave Barker, one of Perry's stable of singers, provides backing vocals for two tracks. The Wailers returned the favor during these sessions, providing backing vocals on several of Barker's tracks.

The Wailers recorded with Perry at the helm between August 1970 and March 1971 with almost no interruption by work with other producers. They would record about 45 different songs. More than a few were either remakes of songs they had previously recorded, or songs they would later remake, or both. If you include all the alternative takes and alternative mixes that Perry released, the count is closer to 60 tracks. If you include dub versions, the number of sides released nearly doubles. Sixty Lee Perry-produced dub versions of Wailers' music may sound more exciting than it actually is. Remember, this is the very start of the 1970s, so most of these are instrumental versions and just a few are a little more than that. They can be enjoyable in their own right, as long as one isn't expecting Perry's later dub wizardry.

Perry culled three LPs for Jamaica release, with one also released in the UK, licensed to Trojan Records. But the big international breakthrough sought by producers JAD and Leslie Kong proved equally elusive for Perry's casual attempt. In a situation both parties had found themselves in before, arguments about money and disputes over songwriting credit (there is evidence that Perry did participate) drove The Wailers to quit Perry. (Later in the decade, Bob would resume working with him, but Bunny and Peter never did so again.) The Wailers would next resume work with JAD and assorted other producers, as well as resume their self-productions, before signing with Island Records and finally breaking big overseas.

Many fans consider the Lee Perry productions The Wailers' finest work, and these recordings are indeed top-shelf. This large body of work kept the quality high and created a parcel of hits and standout tracks. Judged by this, the Perry sessions are clearly a greater accomplishment than their work for JAD, Leslie Kong or the miscellaneous other producers they worked with, though those sessions were not without their great songs. And it can be argued that this body of work is more consistent and better focused than their work at Studio One. But it's harder to say that the Perry sessions were simply better than those for Dodd. Did The Wailers ever burn more brightly than on their best ska tracks? Nor can one definitively say that the Perry material is on the whole better or more consistent than The Wailers' self-produced singles from Wail'n Soul'm or the international LPs that were to come. The Lee Perry productions are great, but the top shelf is crowded by more than one Wailers product in bottles big and small.

Almost every song described below is available on the aforementioned boxsets on Universal Records (see page 190). Many of these tracks appear on numerous other collections as well. Most of them are illicit, as The Wailers suffered more piracy than perhaps any other act in the history of recording.

Funk-reggae

The Wailers loved American R&B and soul music, with Bob particularly liking – and influenced by – James Brown. They found themselves a perfect match in The Upsetters, a Jamaican outfit that could play like Brown's funky backing band as readily as they played cutting-edge reggae. So it comes as no surprise that about one-third of the songs from the Lee Perry sessions are in a tough funky reggae style, even though these sessions are often inaccurately described as being purely reggae. In an impressive demonstration of quality control, every one of these songs is very good or better. But one stands out from the rest.

'Rebel's Hop'
'Rebel's Hop' is a retitled remake of The Wailers' great Studio One song, 'Rude Boy'. With remarkable improbability, this song is airlifted from ska and dropped onto a tight, crunchy funk vamp with no trace of ska or reggae whatsoever, and the resulting rendition is just as good as the classic original.

The Upsetters cook, as gritty rhythm guitar and organ grind it out in the front line. Drums, loud deep bass and cowbell support from behind. They jam this tough funky groove continuously, with no regard for chorus and verse, nor need for development. Atop of this The Wailers add a splendid vocal performance. The song starts with the familiar plaintive *Whai!*s, with all three Wailers singing in unison. But many of the lyrics are altered from the original rendition. The most Jamaican content (the mento quote, folk saying and references to rude boys, ska and quadrille) is replaced by quotes from The Temptations' 'Cloud Nine', with Bunny singing lead. At this point in time, singing American soul music was more exciting to The Wailers than repeating already expressed Jamaican topics. But when they performed the song live in 1973, the original lyrics were restored, as was the case when Bunny Wailer recorded a version in his post-Wailers solo career, retitling it 'Walk The Proud Land'.

A perfect groove, you'll wish it didn't have to end. But you can make it continue. The instrumental dub version gives you the opportunity to better hear The Upsetters play funk. The tape starts rolling early and you can hear someone calling for order, requesting a noisy musician to "arrest yourself, man". Perry also versioned the riddim for a soulful Dave Barker song, 'Run Away Child', itself another Temptations cover.

Other funky jams and soulful sounds
Credited to The Upsetters rather than The Wailers, 'In The Iwah' (aka 'In The Iaah') was a nearly forgotten Wailers track. It's a casual funky jam with Bob, Bunny, Peter and Lee Perry providing all manner of jive vocals that are woven into the jam rather than being out front. The James Brown-style funk is old hat for all involved, but not so the song's US psychedelic soul elements and UK mod vibe. Not present on Universal box-sets or most other Wailers compilations, it's worth seeking out on several Upsetters collections.

Having already quoted its titular refrain in 'Rude Boy'/'Rebel's Hop', The Wailers give the 1965 soul song from Curtis Mayfield and The Impressions, 'Keep On Moving', a proper cover. It features a reggae backing with a funky lilt and soulful vocals. All three Wailers sing in harmony for the chorus and each takes a turn at lead for a stanza of the verse. Any Wailers song with either of those vocal approaches is especially enjoyable, so 'Keep On Moving' doubles the pleasure. A story of being falsely accused of murder, the song may have been an influence on one of Bob's hits. A few years later, Bob would up the ante, with the homicide in self-defense of 'I Shot The Sherriff'. 'Keep On Moving' was a hit for The Wailers, breeding versions and remakes. Perry released two remixes and three dub versions, though none necessarily improved on the original. Bob would record a new version of the track late in the decade that spawned three dub versions of its own. Bunny Wailer would record it three times and Peter Tosh used it as the basis of his song 'Wanted Dread And Alive'.

'It's Alright' features a hard-working funk-reggae vamp riddim that is well suited to the lyrics. Bob plays with a double entendre about "working" all night. The Upsetters' hammering staccato beat suits either meaning. With some tightening of focus and additional lyrics, it would be remade into the less funky, headier 'Night Shift' on Bob's 1976 album, *Rastaman Vibration*. But not before Perry released an alternative take and a dub version with an inside-out organ melody.

The upbeat funk and fun party lyrics of 'Soul Almighty' make it a sequel of sorts to the Leslie Kong-produced 'Soul Shakedown Party'. It's good, but not as good as its sparkling inspiration. A wild, guitar-saturated later remake called 'Shocks Of Mighty' featured Lee Perry and Bob sharing lead vocals, with Peter and Bunny absent. 'Keep On Skankin'' also features Marley and Perry providing all the vocals. Bob provides a high-spirited double-tracked vocal while Perry kicks off the proceedings with spoken-word *reasoning* as only he can. It's built on an ebullient funky jam, complete with electronic cicada sounds, all to a bopping skanking beat. It wasn't until 1974 that Perry recorded Bob's vocal over a backing track that dated from these sessions. The world is a trifle better because they did.

'No Water', though a bit feverish, is fun, with lyrics all over the map and odd warbling-bird backing vocals. The primary theme, of a particular "thirst" that is unrelated to water, fits the funky backing well. And the desire for a nurse predates Gregory Isaacs's biggest hit, 'Night Nurse', by a dozen years.

Perhaps influenced by a James Brown song of the same name is the confident, tight-as-a-drum funk of 'Try Me'. Bob promises a woman comfort and satisfaction and, à la James Brown, he proclaims with pride that he is black. Waves of rippling picked guitar and the addition of Dave Barker on the fine, wordless backing vocals add to the song's appeal.

'Stand Alone' shows The Wailers' mastery of the R&B ballad, a form that sometimes eluded their greatness earlier in their career. This bitter-sweet song about a difficult break-up is expertly rendered and engaging throughout. Bob's skill is evident in the way he loads the lyrics with interesting phrases, filling the song with hooks. The backing vocals keep getting better as the song progresses. And the gentle staccato funk is unlike any other The Upsetters uncorked. Perhaps because it's a ballad, or perhaps because this (and its instrumental dub version) is the only rendition of this song, 'Stand Alone' is usually ignored in conversations about The Wailers' Lee Perry material. But a song this good should never be overlooked.

Reggae

Although a good portion of The Wailers' Lee Perry-produced tracks were funk, most were in the excitingly new, hard, early roots reggae style that Perry and his band brought to the table. The Wailers responded well to this sound. There may be a handful of substandard tracks, but their number is small compared the many strong ones that were recorded, including six standouts. Starting with the best, these are the tracks for which these sessions are so fondly remembered.

'Put It On'; 'Duppy Conqueror'; 'Mister Brown' (aka 'Who Is Mister Brown?')
Three of The Wailers' most memorable reggae songs from the Lee Perry sessions were related musically and thematically, describing Rastafari empowering the individual to overcome a variety of life's obstacles.

'Put It On' proves the versatility of a good song in The Wailers' hands. The original rendition was a strong surging ska recorded at Studio One. Next came a pleasantly easy-going remake for JAD that a later (and final) remake for their 1973 LP *Burnin'* owes something to. But this 1971 rendition with Perry at the helm is something else again. Along with the irresistible ska sprint original, this is the best rendition of 'Put It On'.

Here, the song is headier and stoned-sounding, with loopy instrumental creativity busting out all over. It's also heavier and bassier in the new reggae way. The riddim is built of a stop-and-go bass line, heaving organ and unusual rolls from fill-in drummer Hugh Malcolm, along with guitar and piano. Rare for these sessions, a trombone is heard, providing intervals of ghostly wailing. All of this contributes to a *dread* sound – a deep Rasta vibe rich in spirituality, social consciousness and ganja.

The vocals continue this feel. The Wailers open with wordless harmonies with a relaxed vibrato. Bunny and Peter continue their vocals, providing the first half of the song with an impressive dread duet. Bob makes his belated entrance, sometimes answering Bunny and Peter, other times harmonizing with them. On other material, he might have done so in the R&B jive style he was adept at, but here he sounds introspective. Instead of him rattling off funky throwaways, a list of positive Rasta affirmations are heard. The Wailers feel elated and thankful to God for their religion, and feel empowered by it, and we feel empowered just from listening. A Wailers CD collection called *Soul Adventurer* has a mix called 'Put It On (Full Length)' that restores half a minute of music to the end of the more common 3:30-minute mix. An instrumental dub version of 'Put It On' is also available.

Released a year earlier, in 1970, 'Duppy Conqueror' shares similarities with 'Put It On'. The riddims are essentially the same, though Carlton Barrett is back on drums, the trombone is gone and the arrangement that surges and pumps is tighter here. Bob sings lead throughout this time. He again sounds introspective, as Bunny and Peter provide vibrato harmonies, this time augmented with trilling bird coos. And once again, Rastafarian beliefs empower The Wailers. Bob tells a friend of being freed after being falsely accused and arrested. He was freed from prison bars and oppression by the "*most I*", the Rasta way of saying "most high" or God. On a roll of spiritually fueled empowerment, Bob describes how he can now overcome a variety of adversaries. He does so in a stanza that is such a dense mix of Jamaican expressions (*duppy*, meaning "ghost", *cold I up*, meaning "keep me down", and *bull-bucka*, meaning "a bully – literally, one who likes to butt heads with a bull") and Rasta symbolism, it would have never been allowed by JAD or Leslie Kong with their notions of what was suitable for the international market. Bullies and oppressors are thus on put notice. They are of no consequence for a Rasta who can conquer the supernatural. ('Screw Face' was another Wailers song that sounded the same theme.) This rendition contains a stanza missing from the generally inferior remake featured on the 1973 Wailers LP, *Burnin'*. In it, Bob warns against the mistake of choosing to bully him on a lark to impress their friends. Kingston is a tough place, even for the enlightened.

'Duppy Conqueror' was an impact hit in Jamaica, and Perry followed it with so many dub versions, he had to resort to numbering them. There was 'Duppy Conqueror Version', and 'Duppy Conqueror Version 4' and one called 'Zigzag'. 'Conqueror Version 3' (aka 'Upsetting Station') features DJing and singing by Dave Barker, sometimes reprising his aforementioned song, 'Run Away Child' (see page 214). In 1971, Perry recut an engaging horn-led instrumental version (unless you count the laugh machine sound effects as vocals) called 'Big Joke' that was credited to Lee "Scratch" Perry & The Upsetters. Also of interest is an instrumental by Jackie Mittoo called 'Peenie Wallie', produced by Coxsone Dodd. The riddim is very similar to that of 'Duppy Conqueror' though not as *dread.* Both songs were released in 1970, so clearly one is based on the other, but it's unclear which.

Though an alternative band, The Soul Syndicate, is used, anchored by Carlton "Santa" Davis on drums and George "Fully" Fullwood on bass, the riddim of 'Mister Brown' is very close to that of 'Put It On' and 'Duppy Conqueror'. In fact, it comes from the original and rejected session for the latter song. Though Perry did not think it good enough for 'Duppy Conqueror' and had The Upsetters re-record it, he deemed it suitable for the fine follow-up song, 'Mister Brown'.

The chief difference is a sonorous organ riff. Bassoon-like, it's macabre, giving the song a strong horror-movie vibe, complementing the ghost-story lyrics and the maniacal horror-movie laughter that opens the song. Marley describes the titular figure who shocks whenever he appears in various towns, riding in a coffin topped with laughing crows. The police are called in, but by the time they arrive Mister Brown has faded away. Midway, Bob's voice is made ghostly with some early dub effects and it spookily morphs into processed maracas, as Perry exercises his production skills. Though it was not their goal, in 'Mister Brown' The Wailers and Perry had created a perfect piece of Halloween reggae.

So fearsome is 'Mister Brown' that in one stanza Bob has no choice but to call in his persona from a previous song, asking the *duppy* conqueror (who by now is established as the big *bull-bucka*) to work his skills on the apparition, providing a fine climax to this excellent song trilogy.

'Sun Is Shining'
The ever-popular 'Sun Is Shining' was ahead of its time for early 1971. Its propulsive backbone of shuffle organ from Tyrone Downie, sparse bass, melodica lines and slowed rhythm all contribute to a heavy reggae sound that is more associated with the ganja-fueled dub reggae of the late1970s and early 1980s. Also presaging the future is the absence of Bunny's and Peter's voices in a Wailers song, as 'Sun Is Shining' features Bob with no backing vocals. His languid singing sounds, in keeping with the title, sun-baked, if not otherwise baked. The lyrics are an example of

stoned free-association writing, with Bob at one point proclaiming himself to be a rainbow. He opens with simple words that give us an anthem for the joys of good weather, as the sunshine makes Bob so happy, he wants to dance. Later, he builds to a surprising intensity on lyrics about connecting with others. It all amounts to a song that is sun-worshiping magic.

This great song would have a long and somewhat surprising life. First, not unexpectedly, Perry released two instrumental dub versions plus a recut DJ version (sometimes called 'Heathen's Rage') with Nyabinghi hand drums and Bob turning most of the vocals over to one Johnny Lover. Then Bob would recut this track for his 1978 LP, *Kaya*. (Though the original is great, the rendition on *Kaya* is a masterpiece.) A rare alternative dub mix that collectors cherish was also cut. More surprising was when, at end of the 1990s, Marley's vocal was dressed in new club music clothing, and 'Sun Is Shining' became an international dance hit. Numerous club remixes and covers resounded for years to come.

'Fussing And Fighting'

'Fussing And Fighting' advocates peace, love and harmony over the titular alternative. Rejecting fussing and fighting became a common sentiment, not only in Bob's songs, but throughout reggae, once a Rasta sensibility opened the door for lyrics that asked for all manner of social improvement. (But it didn't start there, as we have already seen examples of such sentiments in golden-age mento.) It's especially meaningful in often-violent Kingston, and at the time of its writing was also applicable to the USA and UK, where the end of the 1960s was a tumultuous time. One line, about cheating and back-biting, may or may not be a commentary on Coxsone Dodd, who worked with both The Wailers and Lee Perry until bitter money disputes ended these relationships.

Befitting a song that has an impassioned plea of *stop your fussin' and fightin'!* as its chorus, the music starts with a few moments of chaos. It then coalesces into a loaded, surging riddim. The bass and drums are both busier than the norm for the Barretts in these sessions. Pumping organ and tinkling piano meld rhythm and melody together. Lead sax lines from Headley Bennett make the arrangement even fuller. Though the lyrics are few and simple, they are delivered with a fervor that gives the song great weight. Bob is impassioned to the point of sounding desperate. Bunny and Peter's backing vocals anchor him with equal fervor but greater control. They put a powerful edge on the last syllable of "I want to *know!*" You are answering to The Wailers! Though Perry released an instrumental dub version of the song, 'Fussing And Fighting' may be the best of the few songs from these sessions that The Wailers neither previously recorded nor would record again later.

'Send Me That Love'

'Send Me That Love' upsets the norms of The Upsetters sessions, with great results. The atypical line-up seems to signal a self-produced Wail'n Soul'm single, while the lush vocals and love lyrics point to JAD. Its soft, loopy sound makes 'Send Me That Love' a unique entry in The Wailers' catalogue.

A chorus of Peter, Bunny and Soulettes Rita Marley and Hortense Lewis join to give a lush varied backing to Bob's lead. The lyrics are non-taxing, as Bob emotes in a somewhat wobbly way about looking for love. The instrumentation finds The Wailers giving The Upsetters the day off. Along with Hugh Malcolm on drums, Bunny handles bass, Bob guitar, and Peter finds his way on xylophone, opening the song by chiming like a doorbell. They create a lazy, tinkling, ragged-around-the-edges reggae that is sweet in its own loose-limbed way. It couldn't be more different from the hard, precise sound typical of the rest of these sessions.

In 1967, 'Send Me That Love' became the only song The Wailers would ever enter into Festival. They lost to the more archetypically Festival-sounding 'Ba Ba Boom' by The Jamaicans (a song described earlier in this book, page 125). Though too quirky for Festival, 'Send Me That Love' is still a standout track. And a singular one as well. It's the only song from the Lee Perry sessions that was neither a remake nor would be remade later, and was not versioned by the producer.

More strong reggae

There were many more strong reggae tracks from the Lee Perry sessions. A remake of the JAD soul ballad 'Soul Rebel' is the preferred rendition. Melancholy and laconic, it stands out from the pack of brisk Lee Perry productions. It features a haunting melody and emotional lead vocal from Bob. The lyrics are somewhat oblique, as Bob advises ignoring gossipers and proclaims himself to be a soul rebel, a soul adventurer and a living man. He also sings that if life isn't good, travel may become necessary, a message that must have resonated with Jamaica's many expatriates who had left the island for better employment opportunities. Several alternative versions and dub versions followed, including a re-voicing called 'Run For Cover' that is short on lyrics.

The tuneful 'Corner Stone' is based on Psalm 118:22: "The stone which the builders refused has become the head stone of the corner." Returned to in many other songs, it can be considered Bob's favorite Bible quote. Here, he uses it to ask a woman not to reject him. The song ends with all three Wailers harmonizing on the chorus in unison, until Bob pulls off and freestyles to the fade-out. In addition to a dub instrumental version, Perry had The Wailers re-voice it with new lyrics as 'Jah Is Mighty'; the new version surpasses the original. The delivery is more spry as Bob's Rastafarian outlook changes the focus from romantic rejection to being rejected by society. Bob finds this especially unjust when Jah "sit with the lowly". Meaning, if God sits with those low of station, it can't be acceptable for a better-off segment of society to be so rejecting. These powerful sentiments took on new meaning when the 2012 documentary film, *Marley*, revealed that Bob wrote 'Corner Stone' after being shunned upon going to his late father's business to ask for a job.

'Don't Rock My Boat' is a slower reggae remake of The Wailers' self-produced rock steady single of a few years earlier. Bob is excellent, embellishing it with many a flourish. The absence of the rangy lead organ of the original as well as any backing vocals makes it easy to enjoy every detail of Bob's singing. Perry and The Wailers released good alternative versions of 'Don't Rock My Boat', including one that adds Bunny and Peter, plus a hand drum, and another that was released under the name of 'I Like It Like This'. When Bob remade the track for his 1978 LP, *Kaya*, it gained a third title, appearing as 'Satisfy My Soul'. Though its title comes from the lyrics, the new name is confusing, especially since The Wailers had already recorded songs called 'Satisfy My Soul Jah Jah' and 'Satisfy My Soul Babe'.

'Memphis' is a rare Wailers instrumental song. Over a tight reggae backing, Peter Tosh provides playful lead melodica. As it was released in the same year (1971) that Augustus Pablo began to make this instrument popular in reggae with songs such as 'East Of The River Nile' and 'Java', many have incorrectly assumed that it is Pablo playing on 'Memphis'. The dub version drops the melodica, leaving the flinty rhythm guitar to carry the melody.

'Kaya' features simple lyrics celebrating the smoking of ganja, and is the first overtly pro-marijuana song The Wailers would record. Perhaps fearing retribution by the police, they used a then unfamiliar term for marijuana, rather than the many more popular names available. As a result, fans of Bob Marley & The Wailers around the world recognize "kaya" as one of the litany of names for marijuana. Regardless of what it's called, it sounds like all involved were practicing what they preached. The vocals sound stoned, a little off-kilter, often whispered and accented with the sound of drawing on a spliff. Unusual for these sessions, acoustic guitar is featured. This helps to give 'Kaya' a mellow, naturalistic feel and broadens the sound of the Lee Perry sessions. That the playing is undisciplined adds to the stoned feel, as does the hypnotic, melodic bass line from 'Family Man'. 'Kaya' was a hit, and a number of remakes and remixes were quickly released by Perry and The Wailers. In addition to the obligatory instrumental dub version, there was a similar take with stronger vocals and the stranger "scat version". Featuring wordless vocals and odd percussion additions (the latter a taste of things to come from the producer), it was not compiled in the Universal box-sets, but is available on several other collections. Likewise, a more adventurous dub version called either 'Sin Semilla Kaya Dub' or 'Kaya Skank', credited to Lee Perry rather than The Wailers, is available on his *Blackboard Jungle* album. In1974, with Perry producing, Marley would re-voice the riddim with new lyrics as 'Turn Me Loose', using portions of the scat version as backing vocals. A final remake of 'Kaya' served as the title track for Bob's 1978 album.

'African Herbsman' takes Richie Havens' down and dirty funky soul workout, 'Indian Rope Man', and converts it into introspective roots reggae. Haven's oblique lyrics about the Indian rope man are adapted into a slightly less oblique song about African identity and former slaves in Jamaica. Bunny and Peter steal the show from lead singer Bob with gorgeous harmonies and bits of lead in the chorus. A staccato plucked guitar contributes greatly to both melody and rhythm, and subtle flute lines add to the reflectiveness. Surprisingly for such a satisfying song, other than the instrumental dub version, The Wailers did not revisit 'African Herbsman'.

In 'Small Axe', a triplet of aggressively struck buzzing guitar strums signifies the arrival of the three Wailers to chant down oppression. In a verse that's rich in Bible language, Bob confronts the unrighteous behaviors of evil men. Believing in God's eternal goodness, he does so with the confident delivery of someone who sounds enlightened. Bunny and Peter give new meaning to the term "supporting vocals" as they back Bob with "if a-so, a-so", meaning, "if it's true, then it's true". Then, in the chorus, with all three Wailers singing together, they proclaim themselves to be an axe that may be small, but is sharp enough to cut down the big tree. This has broad appeal as metaphor for any underdog defeating a bigger, more entrenched foe. But a reference to "my master" later in the song makes racial oppression born of slavery a more specific interpretation. Another form of exploitation that both The Wailers and Lee Perry experienced has led to a different interpretation. In this, they are the small axe taking on the big three (pronounced *tree* in patois) Jamaican record producers who would rather not have their status quo disturbed by these upstarts. Though popularly repeated, this interpretation may be a bit of a stretch. However, the triplets of guitar strums lend sonic credence that the big three are the targets.

No matter what the interpretation, inspirational lyrics sung so well over a powerhouse reggae arrangement (with rock steady great Jackie Jackson of The Dynamites filling in on bass) ensured that 'Small Axe' was a hit. Evidence of this fact are the remixes and remakes that followed, including two mixes of a looser, electric-guitar-strewn take called 'More Axe', and two dub versions, one called 'Battle Axe' and the Nyabinghi drum-enhanced version called 'Axe Man'. The Wailers would again record 'Small Axe' on the 1973 LP, *Burnin'*. But an alternative take from the *Burnin'* sessions that appeared on the soundtrack album for the film *Countryman* and the original Perry-produced version are the sharpest small axes.

Medleys were popular in Jamaica. We have already seen golden-age mento singles where two, three or more folk songs would fill one side of a 78-rpm single. Continuing this practice was 'All In One' and 'All In One Part 2', a medley of Wailers hits, mostly from their Studio One days, that filled both sides of a 45-rpm single. The A-side opens with Perry announcing, " 'S all in one, and one in all. So sweet! Let's have a ball!" Then, with Bob on lead throughout, the following songs are heard: 'Bend Down Low', 'Nice Time', 'One Love', 'Simmer Down', 'It Hurts To Be Alone' and 'Lonesome Feeling'. The B-side also features a Lee Perry introduction: " 'S all in one and one in two. So sweet! 'S all for you!" A rewinding-tape sound effect is heard as 'Lonesome Feeling' is backed up a bit and concludes, followed by 'Love And Affection' and a blending of 'Put It On' and 'Duppy Conqueror'. Throughout, there's not a thing not to like.

'Man To Man' opens featuring soft organ paired with harsh rhythm guitar. The contrasts continue as The Wailers sing beautifully while describing injustices that people, even those who pose as friends, perpetrate on each another. The song features a fine melody, a good rootsy sound and an impassioned lead vocal from Bob, as Peter and Bunny take chances with their harmonies. Yet neither it nor 'Nicoteen', the name given to the requisite instrumental dub version, is the best rendition of the song. Bob would remake 'Man To Man', renaming it after another of the song's lyrics as 'Who The Cap Fit' on his 1976 LP, *Rastaman Vibration*. The remake includes an additional block of lyrics (employing the folk saying about throwing corn, but not calling fowl) that adds so much to the song, but does not appear in the original. But if you listen closely to 'Man To Man', you can hear Bob just begin to sing the start of this passage before it was for some reason excised from the mix by Perry, leaving an interval without vocals. This makes it easy to call the remake the superior rendition. Also better is the odd alternative mix of the original rendition called 'Man To Man Full Length Alternate Take' that appeared on a collection called *Soul Adventurer*. In addition to some added dub effects and forty-five seconds of additional music, it restores the missing vocals. At two points in the song, a rudimentary form of the "throw me corn" lyrics can be heard. These factors more than make up for the substandard sound quality.

The original rendition of Peter Tosh's '400 Years' has a more impassioned lead vocal and a more urgent instrumental arrangement than the more famous remake on the 1973 Wailers LP, *Catch A Fire*. Tosh condemns the Jamaican government's often violent oppression of its black youth, finding it to be born of the same beliefs that led to four hundred years of slavery of Africans. He intimates that African repatriation may be the solution. Another Peter Tosh song, 'No Sympathy', is a tale of shameless self-pity. It features a bone-dry, clipped delivery, a see-sawing melody and another fine lead vocal from Peter. Its breezy instrumental dub version, called 'My Sympathy', is worth a listen, as is the "Full Length" version that appears on the collection called *Soul Adventurer*, which adds an additional half-minute of music. Peter Tosh would remake 'No Sympathy' several more times throughout his career, including a fine rendition described in the chapter on his best solo work (page 522). Tosh's 'Brand New Second Hand', and its very similar alternative take, 'Second Hand', is an enjoyable reggae tale that opens with some doo-wop backing vocals from the three Wailers. Peter rejects a woman whose make-up cannot disguise her undesirable behavior. She is brand-new second-hand, or not as unused as she would suggest. In addition to two instrumental dub versions, some collections include a rather unnecessary track called 'Brand New Second Hand (False Start)'. It contains six unrevealing seconds of the song's opening in a take that breaks down before the vocal begins.

The spiky reggae that The Upsetters provide for a remake of 'Sinner Man', called 'Downpressor', gives us another fine rendition of this song. Here, it's a Peter Tosh vehicle with Bunny backing rather than the equal duet between the two, as heard on the original. Tosh would later record it as 'Oppressor Man', the one bad rendition in a series of remakes that were otherwise all very strong, and finally and most famously as the mighty 'Downpressor Man' during his post-Wailers career (a song described later in this book; page 523).

Bunny Wailer sings lead on his song, 'Brain Washing'. It opens with some unusual imagery, recalling Bunny's previous, incomprehensible composition, 'Tread Oh'. But as the lyrics coalesce to familiar nursery rhyme quotes, the song's meaning comes into focus. Like Peter Tosh's 'You Can't Blame The Youth' and 'You Can't Fool Me Again', or Bob Marley's 'Music Lesson', Bunny is faulting what Babylon chooses to teach to Jamaican youth, concluding, "I don't care for no more brain washing. It isn't good for my soul." Galloping rhythm guitar and strange high organ notes contribute to a hypnotically repeating backing. Bunny's strong vocal shows that Marley was not the only Wailer to come under the spell of James Brown. But somehow, the vocal and the backing seem at cross-purposes. Something of an odd duck, 'Brain Washing' would not be remade other than as an instrumental dub version.

'Dreamland' is a fair remake of Bunny's Studio One song. The performances are fine, but the harsh steely backing is not suited to the dreamy vocals or imagery of African paradise. Two other versions were released; one is a dub that retained portions of the vocals, while the other is an organ cut, supplanting the vocals entirely.

Under-the-bar reggae

With so many good and great songs, the bar is set high for The Wailers' mid-period work with Perry. There were a few tracks that did not reach this standard. One of the very first songs of these sessions, 'My Cup', was a cover of James Brown's 'I Guess I'll Have To Cry Cry Cry'. It suffers from a frantic pace and an overcrowded arrangement that don't fit the mood of the song. Not even the presence of the great Hux Brown on guitar can fix things, and the instrumental dub version might be the better listen. As the title hints, 'Long Long Winter' is not indigenous to Jamaica. It's another Impressions cover, but an unremarkable one from every angle. The latter judgment could be made of 'Love Light', whether the original mix, the alternative cut that features Soulettes Rita Marley and Hortense Lewis adding their backing vocal to that of Bunny and Peter, or the instrumental dub version. 'Reaction' sounds unfinished lyrically and everyone sounds a little lost. The instrumental dub version does not improve things, and another "Full Length" mix that adds a full minute of music only succeeds in prolonging the problems. Bunny's lead vocal on 'Riding High' somehow does not jell with The Upsetters, as they sound out of time with each other. This problem makes an otherwise interesting song a near-miss. In the early 1980s Bunny tried and failed to redeem it with an electro-funk remake with the shortened title, 'Riding'.

21 Bob Marley & The Wailers, Part 6: Work with sundry other producers in their middle period

We have already explored The Wailers' middle-period self-produced work and their sessions with JAD, Leslie Kong and Lee Perry. In addition to this, over a span of time running from mid-1968 through mid-1971, The Wailers did sporadic work for a variety of other producers and labels. This resulted in an assortment of songs with a variety of sounds. Other than a few notable clinkers, the quality here is quite high and quite consistent, with one song standing out as great.

Produced by Edward "Bunny" Lee, 'Mr. Chatterbox' is a remake of the violent ska song 'Mr. Talkative', done in the terse, clipped style of 1970 reggae. It opens with the producer and Bob talking up the session, and ironically, considering the title, Bob can scarcely get a word in. With Peter absent, Bob is backed by Bunny in close harmony for most of the song. Lee also produced a handful of instrumentals that are unremarkable except for the fact that they are credited to Peter Tosh for his lead organ work. One of these, 'The Crimson Pirate', features a deliberately awful lead from Tosh that gets my vote for the worst-ever song with a Wailers name attached. Gluttons for punishment are directed to the Peter Tosh compilation CD called *Arise Black Man*.

Surprisingly, yes, 1970's 'Sugar Sugar' is a cover of the bubblegum hit by the US cartoon band, The Archies. Propelled by a funky bass line from Jackie Jackson, Bob, with backing vocals from Rita, Bunny and Peter, manages to toughen up the song while giving it an infusion of real emotion. The result is a lean juicy cut of Jamaican R&B and an unexpectedly good cover of an unlikely source song. It was produced by Randy's: Clive Chin and family, now famous for their VP label. Four other songs were produced by Randy's. A faithful cover of Junior Walker and The Allstars' 'Hold On To This Feeling' is an exuberant doo-wop – perhaps the best that The Wailers ever recorded. It didn't hurt for Bob to be backed by Bunny, Peter, Rita and her fellow Soulettes, Hortense Lewis and Cecile Campbell. Peter's 'You Can't Fool Me Again' is a sequel of sorts to his 'You Can't Blame The Youth'. It contains one of his most direct attacks on the teachings of the schools and churches in Jamaica, equating acceptance of colonial religion to a return to slavery. It ends with a stanza of nursery-rhyme nonsense that Peter likens these teachings to. 'Field Marshall' is a Peter Tosh-led melodica instrumental. This currently out-of-print track is not bad, but no one should lose sleep over not having heard it. It's hard to find anything good to say about the vocal, instrumentation or choice of source material in Tosh's cover of O. C. Smith's pop hit, 'Little Green Apples', the rotten apple in the good run of work with Randy's. If you insist, it can be found on the Tosh collection, *Simpleton*. While we're on the subject of this CD, it also contains the track that gives the collection its name, a Peter Tosh song that is only notable for being the only work that a Wailer did with producer Prince Buster. Actually, that's being too kind. The song is notably bad.

The Wailers recorded four spiritual/gospel tracks at a session for Dutch producer Ted Powder in 1970, using the versatile Dynamites as the backing band. The material is consistently mediocre. 'Adam And Eve' is doo-wop gospel. 'This Train', a song The Wailers recorded a number of times, gets an overtly gospel arrangement on this rendition. A remake of 'Thank You Lord' gets a reggae arrangement that is looser and funkier than the rock steady original. 'Wisdom' combines a more elaborate arrangement, featuring multiple keyboard and percussion tracks, with spiritual lyrics. It was remade by Peter Tosh as 'Fools Die' in his post-Wailers solo career. Its Bible quote, "The lips of the righteous feed many, but fools die for want of wisdom", is also used in Bob's later song, 'Stiff Necked Fools'.

The 14-minute Bob Marley acoustic medley was an informal hotel room performance never intended for release, but it made a fine addition to his career-spanning *Songs Of Freedom* CD box-set. Bob, accompanied just by his own acoustic guitar, wanders through his songbook and even includes a never otherwise recorded 'Dewdrops'. Producer credit goes to JAD sessions keyboardist John "Rabbit" Bundrick for turning on the tape recorder. Included are 'Guava Jelly', 'This Train', 'Corner Stone', 'Comma Comma', 'Dewdrops', 'Stir It Up', 'I'm Hurting Inside' and 'Cry To Me'. Peter Tosh also was wont to give impromptu acoustic demonstrations of his songs, and a number of them were collected on the CD, *Talking Revolution.*

Peter Tosh recorded six songs for producer Joe Gibbs in 1971 that did not much involve the other Wailers. For that reason, they are typically omitted from Bob Marley & The Wailers compilations. Gibbs was not intimidated by Tosh's dealing directly with black identity or his sometimes provocative reactions to social injustice. For example, there is 'Here Comes the Judge'. In it, Tosh utilizes a popular American catchphrase of the time for its title, a more militant rendition of The Abyssinians' "Satta Amassa Ganna" riddim and the courtroom device heard in Derrick Morgan's 'Tougher Than Tough' (both songs are described elsewhere in this book; pages 318 and 137). In this drama, Peter plays the title role, rhythmically speaking rather than singing. Two members of the roots vocal group The Wailing Souls along with Vision Walker gravely sing the chorus, announcing that the court is in session, and have small speaking roles. Tosh addresses a roll-call of history's explorers and conquerors who are on trial for their crimes against black people. Early on, he promises that he is a judge who doesn't believe in mercy, and this is borne out when the song concludes with his verdict. The defendants will all be "hanged by the tongue", with no chance of appeal. Judge Peter has cleaned the historical house in a wish-fulfillment fantasy. He continues in a black-consciousness vein with the interesting 'Black Dignity'. This opens with Tosh addressing us in Amharic over stray organ chords. It moves into funky organ-driven Nyabinghi-reggae, as Tosh *reasons* on Rasta topics. He describes the fate of the wicked, how he will lead a righteous life, and praises the people, reminding them to hold their heads up to God. The self-explanatory 'Arise Black Man' also has a spoken introduction, but in English this time. The melody is strong and Bunny Wailer adds backing vocals and plays Nyabinghi drum. A remake of Tosh's debut song, 'Maga Dog', trades the frenzy of early ska for a more relaxed approach, sweetened by backing vocals from Soulettes Hortense Lewis and Cecile Campbell. Lewis and Campbell likewise sweeten a remake of 'Them A Fe Get A Beatin''. Meanwhile, reggae with dueling horn and organ lines replaces the rock steady of the original. It features the unusual rhythm section of Arkland Parks and "Family Man" Barrett on drums and bass and the result is as good as the original rendition. Tosh would record it again in his solo career. Finally, there is 'Rudie's Medley', with Tosh impressively imitating Desmond Dekker on '007' and 'Rude Boy Train' before closing by reprising his own 'I'm The Toughest'. These songs can be heard on the *Honorary Citizen* box-set or on the *Arise Black Man* CD.

'Selassie Is The Chapel'
Perhaps the best song of The Wailers' work with miscellaneous producers comes from someone who was not a producer by trade and produced just this one single. In 1968, Rastafarian elder Mortimo Planno produced 'Selassie Is The Chapel', pressing only a small number of copies, thus making it the rarest of all Bob Marley 45s outside of the legendary, lost 'Terror'. Thankfully, this wonderful Nyabinghi rendition of the gospel standard, 'Crying In The Chapel', is now readily available on CD. The song was written in 1953 by Artie Glenn for his son Darrell to sing, and it became a hit. But it's better remembered for the covers that followed by The Orioles, Rex Allen, Elvis Presley, Aaron Neville, Don McLean and others. It was most frequently performed in a dramatic doo-wop-influenced gospel style.

A Wailers line-up consisting of Bob on lead vocals backed by Peter, Rita and Vision Walker stays true to the original's melody and its dramatic spirituality. In fact, the three-part falsetto backing sounds like the gates of Rasta heaven opening wide. The lyrics, which had previously described crying from the joy of religious contentment at being in church, are altered to become an ode to the divinity Haile Selassie. The instrumentation consists solely of a Nyabinghi drum trio playing softly and reverently (as only a Nyah drum troupe can do) accompanied by Peter strumming an acoustic guitar. These elements coalesce into a lovely, heartfelt and electrifying Wailers song. The B-side of this single, 'A Little Prayer', features Planno speak-chanting over a Nyabinghi backing. The Wailers have a small supporting role but the song remains unreleased on CD.

22 More great early reggae

Although they come from artists and producers who do not have a chapter of their own in this book, the following early reggae songs are in no way, shape or form less great than those from more famous names. In fact, each is a classic of late 1960s or early 1970s reggae.

The Pioneers: *'Long Shot'; 'Long Shot Kick De Bucket'; 'Jack Pot'*
The vocal group The Pioneers first recorded in 1965, when they were comprised of brothers Sydney and Derrick Crooks and Winston Hewitt. After two years of struggle, they neither had the opportunity to work with the era's best producers nor did they find artistic or commercial success. Not surprisingly, they broke up. Derrick Crooks would go on to form and lead The Slickers, who sometimes included Sydney in their early recordings. Winston Hewitt decamped to Canada and remained active in music there. Sydney re-formed The Pioneers for Joe Gibbs in 1968 with lead singer Jackie Robinson, and then added Wayne Williams, who would leave after a time. Hits, like 'Long Shot', 'Jack Pot' and others quickly came. But by 1969 they had moved to producer Leslie Kong. George Agard, aka George Dekker, Derrick's half-brother, was recruited into the group. It was this combination of talent that is said to have given us the classic, 'Long Shot Kick The Bucket'. But closer examination indicates that a two-piece Pioneers line-up is at work, so it may have been recorded pre-Agard. The Pioneers worked for other producers as well, including Bunny Lee, and a one-off with Jimmy Cliff. And Sidney Crooks would come to produce The Pioneers and other artists as well. For some reason, The Pioneers also recorded as The Reggae Boys and under other names, resulting in about 140 singles and thirteen albums in all. Their popularity in the UK and Europe led to the group re-forming for European tours through 2005.

Although some of Leslie Kong's best production work has been described in the chapters on Desmond Dekker and Toots & The Maytals, his 1969 production of The Pioneers' 'Long Shot Kick De Bucket' is not only one of the best to come from his studio, but stands with the very best tracks in reggae. Few songs' storytelling can compare to this Greek tragedy, in which The Pioneers tempt fate by betting on a racehorse called "Long Shot". With singing that is the epitome of great Jamaican harmony and a jaunty up-to-the-minute early reggae backing, even after uncountable listens, I'm still rewarded every time I hear it.

The song has its origin in the shorter-titled 'Long Shot', a rendition from a year earlier produced by Joe Gibbs. Joel "Joe Gibbs" Gibson was born in Montego Bay, in 1942 or 1945, depending on the source. Like golden-age mento producer

Ivan Chin, he found his way into production through having an electronics shop that also sold records. Again like Chin, he set up a small studio in the back of his shop and began to record local talent. He received support from another producer in Bunny Lee, and he employed a more experienced man in Lee Perry, who had recently left producer Coxsone Dodd. Gibbs and Perry worked together closely for a time, but would split acrimoniously. (As we will see in the first chapter on Lee Perry (Chapter 26), their divorce was tried in public, their testimony taking the form of a series of grudge records.) Gibbs's first records were released in 1967, and he quickly found success. However, it is not for this rock steady work, but for the reggae productions that followed that Joe Gibbs is best remembered. He prolifically recorded roots, lovers rock, DJ and dub for numerous artists including such big names as Dennis Brown, Gregory Isaacs, Peter Tosh, Big Youth, The Ethiopians, Trinity and The Heptones. This continued into the first half of the 1980s, when legal battles over his productions are said to have ended his once-prolific work. Over this span, he released over 900 singles and twelve albums. He died in 2008 of a heart attack.

The Gibbs-produced original 'Long Shot' is a very enjoyable song in its own right. It's built on an unvarnished reggae vamp that unusually includes a steel drum, helping to make it a nicely ramshackle affair. After the song opens with the racetrack bugle theme, "The Call To The Post", The Pioneers sing in unison about their ill-advised wager being a bust, as the horse "couldn't bust de tape" of the finish line.

The remake under Kong finds The Pioneers once again betting on Long Shot. But this is a more fleshed-out tale, full of generous detail, and with an even more dramatic outcome. "The Call To The Post" again opens the song, but here it's played mournfully, presaging the unfortunate events to come. So does the new opening that describes a great upset at Kingston's Caymanas Park racetrack. As the title tips us off, not only does Long Shot again not bust the tape, he in fact dies during the race! We learn that this happened in the first race and it cast a pall over the track. A play-by-play report of the event is provided: Giblet was in the lead, followed by Combat, Carousel and then Long Shot. Suddenly, tragedy strikes, as Combat falls. And as a result, " Long Shot fell – all we money gone a hell!"

Musically, the band plays a grinding vamp, repeated unaltered for the duration of the song except for the jaunty piano that provides a hint of a solo at mid-song. The steel drum of the original is dispensed with, but Kong finds a different aural spice, as the rhythm guitar playing has a proto-dub feel. (Although Kong is well recognized for his impeccable arrangements, not enough has been said about his groundbreaking sonic experimentations. Here, and in Desmond Dekker's '007', for example, he was dabbling in dub effects before there really was such a thing.) Also sonically unusual for reggae is the extreme use of stereo, with the instrumentation in one channel while the vocals are in the other. Although this makes for rough headphone listening, it does have the advantage of allowing you to hear a cappella and instrumental versions by adjusting your player's balance, as if three versions were packed into one recording. The Pioneers sing the entire song in a harmony that is so musical, so expressive – so Jamaican – that it's an inexhaustible pleasure. The sincerity they convey and the details they share make it hard not to feel sympathy for their bad wager. At least they can't place any more ill-advised bets on the horse called 'Long Shot'.

Featuring soft Jamaican harmonies, 'Jack Pot' is a re-voiced version of 'Long Shot', also from 1968 and produced by Joe Gibbs. In this sequel, The Pioneers' fortunes have turned around, as they win a jackpot at the track. Opening with a "hip hip hooray", they are thrilled to "lick me finger" – to have to moisten their fingers to count their winnings. Instead of concentrating on the race, this joyous song describes their anticipated celebration. Once home, he plans to enjoy music and have a special meal of rice and chicken. And to drink? "Hot hops, like dirt a yard". *Hot hops* is warm beer, as it is enjoyed in the ghetto, and *like dirt a yard* is a folk saying meaning in endless quantity. And to top it all off, his woman is happy.

What better place to end than on the one song in The Pioneers' wonderful racetrack triptych that has a happy ending. All three songs can be heard on some of the better Pioneers collections. Just don't make the mistake of winding up with the plainly inferior (and thankfully less often compiled), much later synthesizer-laden remake. That would be as tragic as betting on the horse called 'Long Shot'.

Lloyd Robinson: *'Cuss Cuss'*
'Cuss Cuss', produced by Harry "Harry J" Johnson in 1969, finds Lloyd Robinson getting something off his chest over a powerhouse pre-roots reggae riddim. This riddim is an energetic conglomeration of chiming picked guitar, slurred slide guitar, a scrubbing rhythm guitar, reggae chop piano chords, creative Fil Callender drums, busy bass, a thick layer of reverb-treated bongos, great key changes, two guitar solos and an organ solo for good measure. It's a dense matrix of sound and by the time Robinson and the backing vocalists are added, the song is so propulsive, it's like a baroque missile.

Bolstered by this pressure-cooker backing, and sounding genuinely irritated, Robinson vents his spleen about people who use curse words everywhere – even in his home. The second time through, he broadens the song's focus from this pet peeve to the more common reggae complaint of fussing and fighting. Robinson uses the slide guitar solos heard mid-song and at the song's end as a cue to plead impassionedly to the lord for help in these matters. His melody is so gnarled and his delivery so intense, he has no problem standing up to the riddim's abundance of goings-on. Only in reggae can a singer bring his exasperation to a fine riddim and use both to launch a song that's so creative.

A popular track, 'Cuss Cuss' is available on several reggae compilations. It didn't sound quite like anything that came before, and the various cover versions and a remake that Robinson recorded with producers Sly & Robbie in 2001 in no way captured the excitement of the original. However, a saxophone cut of the riddim by Karl "Cannonball" Bryan called 'Soul Scorcher' did, and it is described later in this book (page 313).

The Melodians: *'Rivers Of Babylon'*

The vocal group The Melodians included lead singers Brent Dowe and Tony Brevett (brother of Skatalites bassist Lloyd Brevett), backing singer Trevor McNaughton and, unusually, a non-performing member in Renford Cogle, who supplied song-writing and arranging skills. They came together in Kingston, and began record-ing rock steady singles for Coxsone Dodd and Duke Reid in 1966. They would begin working with other producers, including Leslie Kong, around 1969. They were a successful act, but their 'Rivers Of Babylon' for Kong in 1971 was so great and so popular, it towers over their other accomplishments. Dowe would leave the group in 1973 for a successful solo career. Shortly thereafter, the group dis-banded, with Brevett too enjoying a measure of success as a solo artist. The Melo-dians would periodically reunite thereafter. They recorded nearly 100 singles and five albums into the mid-1980s, and toured into the new millennium. Dowe died of a heart attack in 2006 at the age of fifty-nine. The remaining Melodians con-tinued a heavy tour schedule and planned a new album for 2013, but this was impacted by Brevett's passing in the latter part of that year.

Not only is 'Rivers Of Babylon' by far the best song The Melodians ever recorded, it stands its ground as one of the best songs on the star-laden, rightfully revered soundtrack album for the film *The Harder They Come*. The instrumenta-tion is ruthlessly good: not only is Kong's impeccable house band, The Dynamites, in peak form, but the producer hired no less than Ernest Ranglin as the song's arranger. The resulting riddim is polished yet folksy. It perfectly supports the song by being every bit as smooth as rock steady, while capturing the more introspec-tive and earthy aesthetics of nascent roots reggae. The Melodians' performance is even more multifaceted than the riddim, with a combination of styles, moods and themes that require a song with two different choruses to contain them all. They are introspective one moment, solemn the next, only then to suddenly burst out with joyfulness. Their Duke Reid-forged rock steady refinement is fully evi-dent in their singing. But so too are the newer sounds of roots harmonies and the older sounds of soulful gospel. The lyrics are primarily roots reggae. Born of Rasta belief, they are thoughtful, spiritual and soothing. They make 'Rivers Of Babylon' the one roots reggae member on *The Harder They Come*.

The lyrics are mostly constructed of Bible passages. The song opens with an adaptation of Psalm 137:1, "By the rivers of Babylon, there we sat down, yea, we wept, when we remembered Zion." It's easy to see why this sad image of a people longing to return to their home country would resonate with the oppressed, slave-descended Rastas and their awakened African identity. Then, by bringing a focus to the musicians,it becomes even more meaningful for the reggae community, with one of the song's choruses based on Psalm 137:3–4: "For there they that carried us away captive required of us a song."

The song's emotional peak comes from an adaptation of Psalm 19:14, "Let the words of my mouth and the meditation of my heart be acceptable in thy sight, Oh Jehovah" (but with the last word changed to the Rasta "Fari"). Delivered as a soothing prayer, they have made their captive musical performance an offering to God.

These heavy sentiments are leavened by the song's other chorus, with the only lyrics not derived from the Bible. Injecting a soulful gospel element, Dowe drums up positivity and joyfulness. He further celebrates the power of music with a series of exhortations such as "Sing a song of freedom, brother!" The 'Rivers Of Babylon' does not contain a single word that isn't loaded with meaning and feeling.

Expert in its execution, introspective, soothing, spiritual, soulful and uplifting, no song can fully match 'Rivers Of Babylon'. Remakes and covers followed (though little in the way of versioning, this being a Leslie Kong production), but none improved it. It attracted a number of artists from outside of Jamaica, with Sinéad O'Connor, Sublime, Neville Brothers, Linda Ronstadt, Jorma Kaukonen and others covering the song, including the Germany-based disco act Boney M, who had a UK hit with their 1978 rendition. But nor did any of these improve on the impeccable original.

23 Jimmy Cliff

Jimmy Cliff is one of the very best singers to ever emerge from Jamaica. He brandishes a high-powered instrument – a soprano with great range and a plaintive lilt that is capable of a keening emotional intensity and soaring joy. It would make him a star at home and abroad, and garner him many honors. He was awarded Jamaica's Order of Distinction, then its Order of Merit, and was inducted into the Rock and Roll Hall of Fame in Cleveland, Ohio (the only reggae star other than Bob Marley to achieve this, even though neither of them recorded much that could be considered rock and roll).

He was born James Chambers, in Saint James Parish, in 1948. It was as a boy in church that he first became aware of his talent for singing. Hearing records by Prince Buster, Derrick Morgan and Monty Morris made him aware that a career as a recording artist might be available to him, and he made it his goal. Chambers began to write songs and compete in the talent shows that were then such an important outlet for vocal talent in Jamaica. At fourteen, he moved to Kingston, a change he welcomed as it would get him closer to his ambitions. But after a number of auditions, all the renamed Jimmy Cliff had to show was one unsuccessful side each with two minor producers of the day. This led to a previously described inspired/desperate move (see page 91). Cliff convinced ice-cream shop manager and music fan Leslie Kong to enter the field of record production by recording him. Cliff has claimed that he barged right into the shop at closing time, but other accounts have the established singing star Derrick Morgan brokering the meeting. Either way, the outcome was to launch two significant careers.

The second or third Kong-produced single (accounts again vary), the R&B-ska 'Hurricane Hattie', was a 1962 hit for the fourteen-year-old Cliff. Others would quickly follow, as he became a ska star. Like Desmond Dekker, Cliff would be instrumental in popularizing reggae outside of Jamaica. First, he was one of the contingent of ska stars (again, along with Dekker) to perform at the 1964 World's Fair in New York City. In 1969, a cover of Cat Stevens's 'Wonderful World, Beautiful People' became his first international hit. His 1970 song 'Vietnam' drew further international attention when Bob Dylan called it the best protest song he had ever heard. But Cliff's big break came when he landed the starring role in the 1972 Jamaican film, *The Harder They Come*. (Other movie roles and soundtrack work would follow later in his career.) The movie and its soundtrack album featured Cliff's anthemic title track – a showcase for his soaring vocals at their very best. With this movie and song, Cliff was catapulted into international reggae stardom.

Cliff was poised to wear the international reggae crown, but Bob Marley would soon step into that role. What went wrong for Cliff? First, with Kong's passing, the quality of his reggae with other producers did not always measure up to his voice. And too often, the reggae was compromised in an attempt to appeal outside of Jamaica. Second, as his other three songs on *The Harder They Come* soundtrack demonstrated, Cliff's ambitions extended beyond reggae. The mod horn-bolstered musical pep talk, 'You Can Get It If You Really Want', was mostly reggae, but 'Sitting In Limbo' is far less so, and 'Many Rivers To Cross' was a fine gospel song with little or no reggae aspect. Cliff would too often concentrate on non-reggae material, releasing albums with no reggae to be heard. In 1982, less than a year after Bob Marley's death, he made a timely return to pure reggae, with the album *Special* and a successful tour. But his commitment to reggae soon again withered. In all, he recorded about 110 singles and 28 albums. His last four albums covered a variety of non-reggae sounds as well as reggae, ska revival, Nyabinghi-reggae and dancehall. But his most recent, *Rebirth*, in 2012, was an outright return to the music that made him a star, earning him a further international honor in the form of a Grammy.

'The Harder They Come'

'The Harder They Come' is one of the most famous and most inspirational songs to come out of Jamaica. With its sunshine-bright instrumental sound, great Jamaican vocals and optimistic message, for many people, the world around, it is the very sound of reggae – the quintessential reggae song. Produced by Leslie Kong, it was released in 1972 after Kong had died, making its success a fitting send-off for the Cliff/Kong partnership that launched two great careers.

The year before, the original rendition, called 'The Bigger They Come, The Harder They Fall', was released as a single B-side. Suffering from a subdued vocal performance and a string-laden arrangement, the recording was summarily ignored. But it was a totally different story when the song was dusted off for remake. Though the lyrics are the same apart from a single word, 'The Harder They Come' was vastly superior in every way.

It provides a perfect vehicle for Cliff's instrument. His singing is nuanced, bringing pain, determination or triumph to every phrase. After opening with a few bars of wordless singing, he gets down to business. He sings about overcoming oppression, a staple subject in reggae, and the topic of hundreds of songs. But Cliff makes his story memorable, saying much without needing many words. For example, the defiance of his opening line, calling the promise of heaven "pie in the sky", immediately pulls you in. This promise, coming from those who would ignore his needs throughout his life, chalks no score with Cliff. And although the oppressors may believe they've defeated him, Cliff never gives up fighting for the things he wants. This may put his life at risk, but he'd rather be dead than lead the life of a puppet or a slave. He's fired up, and gives the righteous battle-cry of the song's title: "The harder they come, the harder they'll fall, one and all!" While his lyrics hook right from the start, his singing is more of a time-bomb. He holds back at first, riding the rhythm through the opening verses. But by the mid-song chorus that he ushers in with wordless cries, he allows his voice free rein and the song redoubles with emotion. There is not another singer who could approach this particular vocal performance, as borne out by the fact that there are so few reggae covers of a song this popular.

The Dynamites provide a lanky riddim that rings as bright as a bell (and is unencumbered by the strings of the original rendition). Each instrument is lively and the band sounds like they are having a ball – masters at play. Listen to the organ pumping out a variation of the reggae chop and how it combines with the bass and drums to give the song a solid rhythmic framework. Listen harder for subtle input from piano and an even more subtle contribution from guitar, both instruments discharging melody as they jitterbug around the rhythm. The result is a slightly funky bubbling polyrhythmic reggae that is so pleasing to the ear. With this backing and Cliff so strong, Kong saw that no backing vocals, strings or instrumental solos were needed. He wisely realized that all involved had achieved perfection and nothing could improve this pearl of a song.

'Originator'

Cliff's Nyabinghi-reggae song, 'Originator', is not the first such song he recorded. There was also the very good 'Bongo Man', which he recorded in 1971 with Ras Michael's drum troop backing. But with a surprising arrangement and an interesting message, 'Originator' stands as a unique entry in the genre. It appears on his 1982 album, *Special*, as produced by Cliff and Chris Kimsey. Its lyrics take a smart, thrilling turn, when a wailing Cliff proclaims himself "the originator" and "the creator", certainly not an imitator. It's a demand for respect from Cliff to the performers who came after him, not to mention his critics, now that he's chosen to return to reggae.

Befitting the Nyabinghi sounds, his voice never sounded rootsier than it does here. A backing of Nyabinghi drums, acoustic guitar, flute, kalimba, other percussion and a lush chorus of male and female voices makes for an unusually sumptuous Nyah sound and a one-of-a-kind track. 'Originator' was a memorable number for his tour that year, as the opening act for Peter Tosh. Cliff's proclamation stayed in the air as he put on an excellent show featuring tracks from *Special* and old favorites. It was as if he was moving to usurp Bob Marley's vacated crown from headlining contender Peter Tosh. If only he had been able to build on the momentum from this song, album and tour, but he was again drawn away from pure reggae sounds.

Special contained some other good songs, pairing fine melodies and strong vocals from Cliff with an international roots reggae backing. One was 'Peace Officer', a serious song with a fine skanking beat infused with restrained guitar from Rolling Stone Ron Wood. Two others are described below.

'Roots Radical' (and 'Roots Radical' 12" version); 'Treat The Youths Right' (and 'Treat The Youths Right' 12" version)

Two other good songs from *Special*, each featuring jubilant vocals and sparkling melodies from Cliff, were extended and improved when they were remixed for release as a 12-inch single. 'Roots Radical' is keyboard-filled reggae with a skanking beat. Cliff sings emphatically about his place in the world with a beaming chorus, proclaiming himself a "roots radical" and a true born Jamaican." The remix opens with an added harmonica and dub effects, which both continue throughout. Echo, reverb and dropout are all pleasingly applied, but not always in a traditional dub style, suggesting that a non-Jamaican remixer was employed. The flipside 'Treat The Youths Right' is a plea for better treatment and a life without violence for Jamaica's young people. It's a shining upbeat reggae song filled with horns (utilizing the horn section late of Bob Marley's band) and distinguished by its use of a cuíca as a rhythm instrument. Not part of reggae instrumentation, this Brazilian friction drum was also heard a year earlier on Bob Marley & The Wailers' 'Could You Be Loved'. A more traditionally Jamaican use of dub unpacks the song, highlighting different instruments at different points as it makes the track longer. There is also some scat singing from Cliff that is not on the album mix, as well as an added jazzy synthesizer solo and extra organ, all enlarging and improving the song. These 12-inch versions have never appeared on CD and are ripe for the picking as bonus tracks for *Special* or for inclusion on the next Jimmy Cliff best-of collection.

24 Nora Dean

More than any other singer in reggae, Nora Dean has a life story shaped by contradiction and irony. She possesses one of reggae's most beguiling voices. And she
has recorded one of reggae's most beloved songs, along with other memorable
tracks, including one that might be reggae's strangest. Yet most of her music is
currently unavailable, never having been released on LP or CD, and next to nothing has been written about her. She didn't write many songs, but her first attempt,
which was not even complete, resulted in a classic. A good portion of her songs
were about sex, but she would have preferred to have stuck to gospel, which she
began recording at age fifteen. Now a born-again Christian after a serious illness,
Nora Dean is a pious woman, who released a series of self-produced gospel CDs
(as did Hopeton Lewis) out of New York from the mid-1990s through the mid-
2000s. From that vantage point, she looks back at her reggae career with nothing
but regret. Yet these songs have brought so much joy to so many.

Nora was born in 1952 in Spanish Town, Saint Catherine Parish. She moved to
Kingston and began her recording career around 1966 as a member of The Soul
Sisters, a Jamaican gospel duo that recorded for Coxsone Dodd on his specialty
label, Tabernacle. One such song, 'Man From Galilee', was particularly appealing.
Nora soon found herself recording rock steady for Dodd as a solo singer. It's not
hard to see why. Her voice was very pleasing – which could be said for many other
Jamaican female vocalists. But Dean had something extra, something very singular.
Her voice has a certain edge that makes her different, giving her singing uncommon depths of emotion. Even her earliest records marked her as an "old soul", with
an expressiveness that belied her young age. It also gave her a personal approach
to the scale that increases her distinctiveness. (The same can be said for Gregory
Isaacs, but this is not to say they sound similar, as they certainly do not.) Distinguishing herself even further, Dean would introduce a wide array of idiosyncratic
vocal sounds and wordless cries that enlivened many of her songs. As you will see,
in her best songs (as described below), she could be sexy, scary, or both at the
same time. She could sound down to earth or like someone from another planet.
But each of these songs is emotionally rich and completely captivating. Whether in
Jamaica or elsewhere, there just isn't anyone else quite like Nora Dean.

By no means prolific by reggae standards, Nora would go on to record a variety of records with other producers after her rock steady tenure at Studio One.
She recorded *slack* reggae, R&B reggae, *sufferas* reggae, dancehall reggae and a
calypso single. She covered songs by Elvis, Shirley Bassey, Doris Day, and others,
not to mention two from the golden-age mento band Chin's Calypso Sextet, while

basing other tracks on traditional mento songs. Along the way, she also led a vocal group called The Ebony Sisters, had a short stint as a member of Rita Marley's re-formed Soulettes, and provided backing vocals on an album by Jimmy Cliff. In all, she recorded close to 50 singles and one album before a long hiatus and her second musical career of gospel CDs. At the time this book was written, Nora Dean was in poor health, and all prayers are with her.

It's hard to call the singer of 'Barbwire', one of the most beloved of all reggae songs, under-appreciated, and yet she is. Hopefully, the review of her best records below will help remedy this. With apologies to the others who achieved greater fame or had longer careers, I would argue that Nora Dean should be celebrated as the queen of reggae, if only she wanted the crown.

'Mojo Girl'

After a small number of gospel sides as a member of The Soul Sisters, Nora Dean's first solo track was 'Mojo Girl', recorded in 1967 for producer Coxsone Dodd. The rock steady backing is unusually tense for the form, giving Nora's song a perfect stage. Dodd does not appear to have versioned this riddim, which is exclusive to 'Mojo Girl', perhaps realizing it could fit no other song.

Nora's vocal is gripping. She's controlled, making difficult observations without ever coming close to losing her calm. Yet, at the same time, she's very emotionally articulate and expressive. In the mostly wordless opening, addressing her lover, her voice undulates between two notes, between pity and reproach. She goes on to reveal to him that she is the witch of the title, and because he didn't treat her right, he'll never be allowed to escape. As she brags of her supernatural abilities, her voice shimmers with pre-dub effects. There's little doubt that her lover is in trouble. She calmly tells him that she will "mash your corn", meaning ruin his endeavors (though another, more physically threating, interpretation is possible), and "I'm gonna tie you down so you never be free". With this atypically eerie and threatening rock steady song, reggae's most interesting female voice was introduced to Jamaica. 'Mojo Girl' can be found on the compilation CD, *Rare Reggae From The Vaults Of Studio One*, released on the Heartbeat label.

'Heartaches'

A year later, Studio One released Nora Dean's second record, 'Heartaches'. As was the case for 'Mojo Girl', its riddim was not versioned, nor was 'Heartaches' ever compiled on LP or CD. This makes it an all-but-forgotten song that deserves much better.

'Heartaches' features a more typical rock steady backing than the edgy 'Mojo Girl'. It's sharply rhythmic, but it breathes freely, led by sprightly piano with bass and guitar plucked in unison. Dean responds with a song that is also typically rock steady. Her vocal is disciplined and quite lovely as she sings about the heartaches that come with love that no one thought to warn her of. An island of innocence,

Nora shows none of the previous song's edginess or the strangeness of songs that would follow. Still, there's something beguiling about the angles of approach in her phrasing, as well as the melody she crafts. She's a pleasure to hear, right through to how she ebbs at the song's end.

A fine record in its own right and of interest to Studio One collectors, rock steady collectors and Nora Dean fans alike, one has to believe a reggae re-issuer will ultimately bring 'Heartaches' to CD. (Are you listening, Heartbeat, Soul Jazz, Trojan, 'Blood And Fire', et al.?) If you are like me and can't wait, be advised, as you hunt the single down, that this record is often confused with the ska song called 'Heartaches' by Norma Fraser that was also produced by Coxsone Dodd.

'Barbwire'

'Barbwire' is one of the most beloved reggae songs of all time, showing up on more best-of-reggae compilations than perhaps any other track. It's deserving of its adoration. Released in 1969, a time when straightforward rock steady love songs dominated, 'Barbwire' did have a rock steady riddim (and a classic one at that). But Dean's song was anything but a love song, and her eccentric emotional delivery sounded like nothing else. It stood out, baffling and delighting reggae fans *a yard* and around the world from the time of its release to the present day. But, to the great dismay of Dean, in addition to being one of reggae's most beloved songs, it's also reggae's single most misunderstood song.

The story begins one day at a Treasure Isle session, when Nora, then seventeen, stated to the musicians present that she would write a song. She decamped to the bathroom and emerged with 'Barbwire'. In its original form, the song was a description of an actual incident in which Nora was attacked by a madman with barbwire on his head as she was walking home through a rough part of Kingston where vagrants congregated. Session engineer Byron Smith matched the song to the fine 1967 Duke Reid-produced riddim from The Techniques' 'You Don't Care' (a song described earlier in this book, page 130). He also told Nora to change the phrase "barbwire on his head" to "barbwire in his underpants". This would change Dean's song of terror to one of titillation, eventually causing her great embarrassment. This misunderstanding was even greater for overseas listeners who didn't realize that in Jamaica "lick" means "strike". The voicing session lasted four hours, but in the end Smith went back to the first take.

> Oh, mama! Ma ma ma!
> I met a boy the other day, he got barbwire in his underpants.
>
> Oh, mama! Ma ma ma!
> I got a brick in my back, I lick him hard upon his head.
>
> Oh, mama! Ma ma ma!
> Ah ya ya ya ya ...

Oh, mama! *Ma ma ma!*
I didn't trouble that boy, that why I lick him hard.
Ah ya ya ya ya …

Oh, mama! *Ma ma ma!*
That boy is coming at me, that boy is coming at me.
Ah ya ya ya ya …

© Westbury Music Ltd (reprinted with permission)

Regardless of your interpretation, the lyrics grab you as Dean cries for solace from her mother. This goes double for the singing. Dean is quirky, starting with the way she bursts into the song on the last beat of the first bar, charging it with urgency. I don't think I've ever heard a vocal more full of life than when Nora moans and wails her upset. The last "ma" is elongated and bent like the bleating of a lamb. Working just two words, Nora manages to open the song with an irresistible hook.

The rest of her performance is just as compelling, with a double-tracked Dean sounding so fresh and new over the familiar riddim. This includes whole sections of verse with Dean singing blocks of *Ah ya ya ya ya*. This creates an air of mystery, as if there is more that is unmentionable to this sordid tale. But in reality, the new song-writer just didn't have enough lyrics to fill her first work. Treasure Isle house bassist Jackie Jackson remembered the session in an interview with Mark Gorney published in the fanzine, *Full Watts*.[1] Jackson thought all the *ah ya ya*s would doom the song to failure, and that it would not even be released. This established a high negative correlation between reggae bass skills and clairvoyance. It was such a huge hit that Duke Reid and Smith became locked in a battle for ownership. By 1998 'Barbwire' had sold a reported thirteen million copies worldwide. This does not even include an untold number of pirated copies, not to mention the copies sold since. As for Dean, she received only 30 pounds over a nine-month period for the song, since Jamaican record producers long employed a flat-fee, no-royalties payment plan for their artists. Especially in retrospect, it's easy to see why Jamaica's record producers, seen as heroes by the reggae-craving world, were villains to the artists they produced. It also explains why so many artists turned to self-production.

Dean would recut 'Barbwire' for producer Sonia Pottinger in the 1970s. The remake has not been compiled on LP or CD, but it's not really necessary to invest time and money in finding this single, released on the High Note label. Not because it's bad, but because there may never have been another reggae remake that sounds so close to the original. You might not even realize that it's a different rendition after a casual listen. The B-side is a dub version called 'Electric Wire'. Dean performed a more interesting remake for producer Bunny Lee in 1975, called 'Scorpion In Her Underpants'. In spite of a minor change to the title and lyrics, the song is the same, with Nora again uncannily recreating the unusual inflections of

1.   Mark Gorney, *Full Watts reggae zine* (self-published, 1999), page 22.

her original vocal. But the rock steady instrumentation is scrapped as 'Barbwire' is retrofitted with a mid-1970s dub reggae backing. Lee utilized Augustus Pablo and his band as well as King Tubby's mixing abilities and studio. The result was an exceptionally spongy dub riddim, bouncing in slow motion like a pogo stick on the moon. The dub version of this track, called 'The Sting', is better than 'Electric Wire'. It finds a dubbed Nora first sharing the spotlight with, and then supplanted by, Pablo's melodica. Both of these tracks can be heard on the Augustus Pablo CD called *Pablo And Friends*.

'The Same Thing You Gave To Daddy'

In 1969, Lee Perry produced a Nora Dean song, and the results have to be heard to be believed. Gone is the orderly instrumentation of rock steady. A manic drum roll announces a chugging, rip-roaring reggae riddim. Also gone is the immaculately clean sound of a rock steady production. Instead, this song shows the murkiness characteristic of many of Lee Perry's productions of this time. A sludge of bass, organ, piano and drums gushes out. Nora enters singing a cover of 'Mommy Out De Light', a jazz-calypso song originally recorded by US singer Marie Bryant in 1953. Though primarily a jazz singer, Bryant recorded a handful of calypso sides that were released in Jamaica on the Kalypso label and became very popular there. It was subsequently recorded by others, including the US duo Mickey & Sylvia, of 'Love Is Strange' fame, in the late 1950s. But in these renditions, 'Mommy Out De Light' is a sweet song, in which a little boy won't go to sleep until he gets a kiss, like the one he saw his father receive the night before. Apparently, the chorus, in which he demands "the same thing you gave to daddy last night", was taken differently by Perry and/or Dean.

In this rendition, Nora can't understand why her little boy won't go to sleep. She changes his diaper, offers him tea or breastfeeding, but to no avail. He makes the titular demand of his mother, followed by a lewd series of unsavory grunts that leave no doubt he observed more than a kiss. Nora's pained response of "No, no, no" is countered with another set of grunts. She is so distressed, she resumes singing verse in the middle of the chorus. This unusual turn works wonderfully as Dean makes her own shock disorienting for the listener too. In the hands of a different singer, 'The Same Thing You Gave To Daddy' would have been little more than a tawdry novelty song. But Nora elevates it to something more. Her emotional expressiveness makes the story more real, and you can't help but feel for her in this unpleasant but humorous predicament. Only the combined talents of Nora Dean and Lee Perry could take such an unsavory theme, present it in a misshapen song, and have it be such a musical delight.

'Wreck A Buddy'

In 1969, Prince Buster took a child's street song and recorded 'Wreck A Pum Pum'. This is a dirty song, with the American equivalent of the title being "pound a pussy". Yet it's incongruously set to the melody of 'The Little Drummer Boy'. Crazy? Awful? Sacrilegious? Maybe, but it proved to be quite popular. The same year, Buster orchestrated a follow-up (sometimes retitled 'Wreck A Buddy') with a quickly assembled female vocal group, called either The Sexy Girls or The Rude Girls, depending on the pressing. Also that year, Lord Creator and Nora Dean covered the song.

The best of these was Dean's rendition, also called 'Wreck A Buddy', produced by Joe Gibbs. Though the song is credited to The Soul Sisters, briefly reviving the name – but certainly not the music – of her gospel group, there's never any doubt as to who is singing. Nora is unusually *slack*, describing her need for a man to "wreck him buddy", or, how to put this, to *apply himself to her* to an extent that his, er, little buddy is wrecked.

> I need a man to wreck him buddy.
> A big strong man to wreck him buddy.
> And if he's ugly, I don't mind.
> He has a dick, and I want to grind.

And so on. With singing as expressive as Dean's supplemented by a moan or two, you believe every word. Meanwhile, if you think that such a vocal set to the melody of a Christmas song couldn't get seedier, well, you've underestimated the musicians involved. The backing is lurching reggae with a saxophone that absolutely leers and organ that bubbles lasciviously. Even the male backing vocalists sound a little disreputable. Merry Christmas, everyone! The Soul Sisters' 'Wreck A Buddy' is available on a number of reggae compilation CDs.

'Ay Ay Ay' (aka 'Angie La La')

In a 1970 recording session at Treasure Isle, producer Duke Reid, Nora Dean and his assembled musicians must have all agreed to try for something different. The resulting song bore little resemblance to any type of reggae, and was more reminiscent of non-Jamaican artists from Y to Z (Yma to Zappa). Dean's vocals are a masterpiece of eccentricity that recalled – and exceeded – the strangeness of 1950s Peruvian exotica singer Yma Sumac. The instrumentation was reminiscent of late-1960s West Coast psychedelic rock, most closely resembling Frank Zappa's psychedelic raga rock epic, 'Help I'm A Rock', from his aptly named debut album, *Freak Out!* 'Ay Ay Ay' is quite a thing.

A droning psychedelic groove, heady and intense, is set up. It features San Francisco guitar and an organ that pumps like breath being inhaled and exhaled. Nora is more than up to the challenge of this strange backing, responding by effortlessly producing an incredible free association of singing and vocal sounds. There are moans and groans of ecstasy, rhythmic gasping, reverbed mouth clicks, bird calls and animal cries, including some from species not previously cataloged. There are what might be foreign-language phrases or speaking in tongues, as unrecognized syllables flow. (The song's two titles, 'Ay Ay Ay' and 'Angie La La', are drawn from this.) It's surprising when a stray line of English emerges as comprehensible. This is not to say that Nora in any way provides narrative. Instead, the message of the song remains out of reach, and the mystery makes the song better. A crazy whirling dervish, 'Ay Ay Ay' is reggae's premier piece of exotica and its very strangest song. It can be heard, sticking out like a sore thumb, on the album called *Groundation: Indomitable Spirit Of Rastafari*.

'Let Me Tell You Boy'
From the same year as 'Ay Ay Ay', but far more grounded, is 'Let Me Tell You Boy', credited to The Ebony Sisters. Produced by Harry Mudie, it's a Jamaicanized R&B track with bold horns and a big soul-review sound. But the churning riddim driven by fat bass and chugging guitar supplemented by organ, and the surfeit of reverb muddying the production, brings reggae to the table. Likewise, Nora belts it out in soul-review style. But the planes and angles of her singing make her too different to be mistaken for an American soul singer. The same can be said of the nicely strident harmonies from her backing vocalists (including former Soulette Cecile Campbell). The lyrics are reminiscent of 'Mojo Girl', but more down to earth. Nora again wants to be treated well and does not want to be dumped for another girl. But there is no threat of supernatural retribution here.

'Let Me Tell You Boy' was a hit. It spawned a dub version (called 'African Home', billed to Mudie's Allstars), a popular DJ version by I-Roy and a remake by Nora in 1978 that lacks the powerhouse energy of the original. The original is best and can be heard on Trojan's *UK Reggae Sisters* double-CD compilation.

'Peace Begins Within'
Produced by Sid Bucknor in 1971, Nora's 'Peace Begins Within' is a departure from these previous tracks. There is nothing remotely sexual, whimsical or lighthearted here as Nora records an excellent *sufferas* song. It's a cover of a 1970 anti-war/anti-poverty song by US Christian rock pioneer Mylon Lefevre, who performed it in a halting funk style. Around the same time as Dean's cover, it was also covered in a more fluent funk by blind Louisiana gospel and R&B singer Bobby Powell. But Dean's voice fills her rendition with raw emotion in a performance that puts the other renditions to shame.

A harried and anxious reggae riddim is heard, made tenser by stabbing horn bleats. Female backing vocals sing the titular refrain, sounding beleaguered rather than pretty. Nora enters, her voice as clear and interesting as ever, but with an edge of desperation. Singing of a pressure-cooker life of despair, her pain is evident in every word. Even the long, handsome mid-song horn break fails to change the mood, sounding like it's trying to dig out from under an oppressive weight. In 'Peace Begins Within', Nora, band and producer have taken a forgettable song and turned it into a one that brims emotion and immediacy. And in the process,

Dean shows the extent of her range. From frivolous to fraught, she is capable of lighting up songs of any kind.

'Dry Up Your Tears'; 'No Time To Lose'; 'Play Me A Love Song'
These three songs are from Nora's only album, the 1979 *Play Me A Love Song*, produced by Clarence "C. S." Reid. (He also billed himself "Duke Reid Junior", but was not related.) Sadly, it's been out of print for decades and never released on CD, so hunting for a copy from used-record dealers is the only way to currently enjoy these tracks. This is especially unfortunate, as this is Nora's last reggae release, and a matured Nora Dean is evident. Her voice is as interesting and expressive as ever, but she sounds older and wiser. Taken together, these three songs seem to be telling an autobiographical story. It has a sad beginning, but a happy ending.

'Dry Up Your Tears' opens with a cutting organ riff over a tart reggae backing. The Sly & Robbie-backed band skillfully supports while staying out of the way of a powerful lead vocal, as Nora tells her story. Telling her not to cry, her man leaves, promising that he will return. Without her having to say it, Jamaican listeners would understand Nora to mean that her man is leaving to find work overseas. This economic reality is a common topic in reggae, as early as mento's golden age, with Count Lasher's 'Trek To England' and Lord Lebby's 'Sweet Jamaica' being two examples described earlier in this book (pages 59 and 37). But never has the story been told with so much emotion. A distraught Nora sounds raw (even more than on 'Peace Begins Within'). Her keening barely stays on key and her voice breaks at times. This builds as the song nears its end, and she recalls the passing of time. This and her account of waiting at the gate for the postman are heartbreaking, as is the fact that there is no resolution to the story, just waiting.

'No Time To Lose' features a classic Nora Dean vocal, sexy and filled with her idiosyncratic vocal frills. Far removed from the despair of 'Dry Up Your Tears', it opens with Nora cooing happily over light-hearted reggae dominated by keyboards, picked guitar and playful drums, all building an air of anticipation. She is looking forward to a date with her lover, and is anxious to get on the night train, an easy double entendre. Her singing is playful with pauses between lines that she later fills with her trademark *ay ay ay*s, *whoa*s and the like. By this point it's clear that the syllable *ay* was created by God for Nora to sing. She goes on to defend her needs against her mother's instruction to behave properly with "I'm a grown woman, and need love". She's certainly grown up since an earlier encounter with her mother, when she cried, barely articulate, with childish helplessness in 'Barbwire'.

'Play Me A Love Song' finds Dean having arrived at her date. The opening lines bring the previous two songs together. Nora asks the DJ to play a record that will help her celebrate her lover's return from far away.

Reunited with her love, Nora sounds joyous. So does the instrumentation, with its streamers of organ and guitar. The song has more than a touch of early dancehall, the only such example in a Nora Dean song. There's a Pocomania-influenced lanky drum rhythm and lyrics about the dance. And despite the rain, it will be a good party, as long as Dean continues to select for the DJ. She asks for a song that's both soft and nasty, with spicy words that "would send us reeling". Sounds like Nora is requesting a Nora Dean record!

25 Augustus Pablo

Mento has banjo and rumba box, ska has trombone, rock steady has piano and reggae has electric bass. Dub, too, has its signature instruments. First is the mixing board that made the music possible. Second is the melodica, due to the music of one man, Augustus Pablo. If you are not familiar with a melodica, it's a hand-held keyboard that is blown into, making it something of a cross between a harmonica and an accordion. Before Augustus, it was less known and less respected than either of these instruments, disparaged as a teaching keyboard and certainly not thought suitable for recording. But the instrument was common enough in Jamaica and reggae musicians were resourceful and open-minded enough to see no reason *not* to utilize the melodica. To be fair to Peter Tosh, he had begun to use the instrument on a few tracks by The Wailers beginning in 1971, the same year that Pablo first recorded with it. And Bobby Kalphat also recorded with the instrument around the same time. But whereas these other keyboardists could have used organ just the same, it was Pablo who gave the melodica a new voice.

If you are not familiar with the music of Augustus Pablo, you are in for a treat. The pastoral cover photo of his album *East Of The River Nile*, with its idyllic photo of dreadlocked Rastaman Pablo sitting by a stream, playing his melodica, visually reflects the sound. Pablo's playing brings an organic, *naturalistic* element to the otherwise electronic dub reggae.

Pablo was born Horace Swaby, in 1954, in the parish of Saint Andrew. As a youth, he was initially enamored of the guitar, fashioning a home-made instrument. But access to organ at school and a piano at home gave opportunities that he could not ignore, and instead he became a keyboardist. He dreamed of a life in music, playing in bands with other local young teens, including Tyrone Downie, who would go on to become The Wailers' primary keyboardist during their international album years.

The birth of Pablo's recording career is the reggae version of Lana Turner's Hollywood discovery at Schwab's Drug Store. One day in 1970, producer Herman Chin-Loy (a cousin of Leslie Kong) spotted a teenaged Horace Swaby holding his melodica in Chin-Loy's Aquarius record shop. The producer was frustrated with a singer's performance on his newest riddim and was looking for an alternative. He booked a session for Swaby and his instrument. The track was credited to Augustus Pablo, a made-up name with a mysterious air of gravity that Chin-Loy was already using for his instrumental releases. The resulting track, 'Iggy Iggy', was successful enough to result in a string of follow-ups for Swaby, including the 1971 career-establishing hits, 'Java' and 'East Of The River Nile', the latter for producer

Clive Chin. A badge of Swaby's success was his taking ownership of the Augustus Pablo name from Chin-Loy. These early hits not only established him commercially, they also established his trademark style that would come to be called his "Far East" sound. Characterized by exotic, wistful, longing, minor-key melodies, it transcended time and place, but could only have arisen in the 1970s from a Jamaican musician. Some credit these tracks as the birth of minor-key melodies that would come to take hold of much of roots reggae. Though many of his early 1970s singles were a bit rough around the edges (making them preferable to some reggae fans), more sophisticated and frequently sublime sounds would soon follow.

After working with a sequence of producers, in 1972 Pablo would begin to produce himself and others on his Hot Stuff, Message and, most famously, Rockers labels. He would soon be synonymous with rootsy melodica instrumentals, dub, and, naturally, dub versions of rootsy melodica instrumentals. Pablo released about 200 singles and approximately 31 albums (and another 20-plus compilations) including a classic dub album in 1980's *Rockers Meets King Tubbys In A Firehouse*. Myasthenia gravis, a neurological disorder, claimed Pablo in 1999, but not before he had released a significant body of work that legitimized the melodica and helped change the sound of reggae.

Rockers Meets King Tubbys In A Firehouse

The title of Pablo's 1980 album conveys a lot: *Rockers* [Augustus Pablo and his band] *Meets King Tubbys* [collaborates with dub-master King Tubby in his studio] *In A Firehouse* [which is located in Waterhouse, using the ironic nickname for the too-hot Kingston neighborhood]. It's good that the title credits everyone, as it's not only Augustus Pablo's best album, but King Tubby's as well, making it the best dub album ever by anyone. Yet many sources hold that an earlier album, *King Tubbys Meets Rockers Uptown*, is the best – even the unnamed author of *Firehouse*'s liner notes in its CD release. Let's set the record straight: Though *Uptown* has a few famously great tracks (which are described later in this chapter), *Uptown* cannot touch *Firehouse*'s consistency and flow. *Uptown* sounds like what it is: a collection of singles, brilliant and otherwise. *Firehouse* is uniformly great, and sounds like it was recorded to be enjoyed as a coherent whole. Yet the music originally came from a variety of sessions, as four bassists and three drummers are credited. And several of the riddims were originally vocal tracks that were released earlier. But a uniform approach to dub levels these differences. Surprisingly, there is relatively little of Pablo's trademark melodica, as on this set he concentrated instead on piano and organ. A four-piece band is most often heard, though some tracks include a horn or additional percussion. It's a purely instrumental album, without so much as a brief drop in of vocal, though someone exclaims *cho!* at the start of several tracks.

Firehouse features a particular style of dub. It's a product of a master craftsman's expertise rather than a showcase for experimentation. Its sound is crystal-clear rather than the hazy distortion of some other dub. It's sober rather than giddy; focused rather than loose. The edges are so sharp and the angles so precise, the effect is almost cubist. Augustus Pablo is listed as producer, while King Tubby, his protégé Prince Jammy (who would later so change reggae), and Pablo are credited as mixers. Too many cooks may spoil the broth, but apparently not this dub album.

'Rockers Meets King Tubbys In A Firehouse'
The title track opens the album, and the first thing heard is the drummer striking his sticks together. But even this incidental sound is dubbed, wet with reverb to the point of being aquatic, and the album is launched. Though he is not credited, the drum roll that follows is unmistakably from Carlton Barrett, whose tricky skanking playing is rich in the promise of more dub. Pablo keeps Barrett's promise. A textbook is presented on the drop-out and drop-in manipulation that gives dub its name. A strong and melodic bass line and drums anchor the track as guitar and keyboard (Pablo alternating between piano and organ) vanish and reappear at rhythmically optimal times. Echo is applied, but sparingly, like a treat. Without warning, selected strums of a scrubbing rhythm guitar are flash sky-bound with reverb. The instruments interact differently from normal, as dub rewrites the rules of fluid dynamics. Although there are just four musicians, it sounds like there are more. And, in fact, there are, as even when subtracting sound from sound, the dub-masters are an audible presence, leading the music.

'Short Man Dub'
Unlike the title track, 'Short Man Dub' does not telegraph the fact that it's a dub track. Once the introductory *Cho!* is exclaimed, it starts as a straight instrumental dominated by glorious wailing descending sax lines from "Deadly" Headley Bennett and busy drumming augmented with an additional percussionist. But echo sneaks in and touches the one-note rhythm keyboard. Emboldened, it grabs hold of the sax, and the final note of each phrase echoes away into the ether. On cue, everything other than the partner-in-dub sax and keyboard drops out, then back in, dub now fully launched. Reverb is dispensed from a fifty-five-gallon drum. Guitar is occasionally dropped in for belief intervals. A subdued bass anchors, but is not immune to drop-out/in. The irregular pattern played on the snare is indicative of how reggae drumming can give fits to non-Jamaican drummers, made harder to ken by an interlocking second percussionist playing wood blocks. 'Short Man Dub' is a fine ensemble dub piece. It demonstrates that dub is equally compelling applied to jazz-elaborate lines as it is to a one-note rhythm.

'Zion Is A Home'
'Zion Is A Home' is the exception. It does not sound like the other tracks on the album. Opening with a tumbling echoed drum roll, featuring the loosest version

of a reggae chop you will ever hear, a bass line that seems content to do little and Pablo's melodica meandering throughout, 'Zion Is A Home' is a stoned-sounding dub. Though no one would argue that it's the best track on the album, it serves well in breaking up the two razor-sharp dubs that precede it and the two that follow.

'Dub In A Matthews Lane Arena'
Decades earlier, a popular mento song called 'Dog War A Matthews Lane' warned against going to that mongrel-infested street. But now Pablo suggests a reason to reconsider. 'Dub In A Matthews Lane Arena' is a dense, kinetic piece of dub. A trombone plays a strident lead over a backing that shuffles forward. It's percussively rich, with drum kit, incidental percussion and a Nyah hand drum that pelts the riddim with the quasi-regularity of sleet. Everything is blessed with echo except for the marching bass line. (To do so would be anathema, as I don't think I've ever heard echo applied to bass on a single dub track.) Dub makes it all molten around the edges, without slowing the track's forward progress. Even the dogs would have stop fighting and listen.

'Jah Say Dub'; 'Son of Jah Dub'
'Jah Say Dub' is as fine a piece of dub music as you would expect with a title that indicates it was recorded at God's behest. A reverbed drum roll announces the song and Pablo's piano and a rhythm guitar launch interlocked. They make it a delightfully industrious theme. Somehow it manages to be uncomplicated yet heady. Allowed to continue unaltered for a few bars, it suddenly decays away in a storm of strobing echo and drop-out/in. At one point, only bass and residual echo are heard, like the aftermath of an explosion. The dub-masters then begin to layer the tracks back in/out, building/reducing to an eventual full complement of instruments. Reverb dubs the drums large and paints bodies in motion. Stripped-down intervals focus us on bass that's visited by brief flashes of rhythm guitar or stray organ. The industrious theme is heard again, whereupon it is deconstructed and reconstructed again, as Jah's will is done.

'Son of Jah Dub' is a different take of 'Jah Say Dub'. The drums and bass are not very different, but the tempo is slower and the arrangement is altered. The theme is now carried by slide and picked guitars (piano is not heard) and is sluggish rather than industrious. This gives the 'Son' a brooding feel compared to the extroverted 'Jah Say Dub'. The dub is different as well, with blunter applications of echo, reverb and drop-out/in. Though the son does not best the father, all alternate takes should be this good.

'Simeon Tradition'
'Simeon Tradition' is an unusually urgent piece of dub. Its riddim is fast-paced, with intensely chopped rhythm guitar, busy bass and drums and bubble-up organ. From this launching pad, the dub-masters execute drop-out/in, reverb and echo

with the sole purpose of driving up the urgency quotient. The result is the dub equivalent of a red alert.

'Selassie I Dub'

'Selassie I Dub' shimmers like it's bathing in the full glow of the Jamaican sun. It opens with Pablo's melodica and organ harmonizing on a theme that is pure Pablo. It's naturalistic, appealing and carries a touch of the wistfulness associated with his Far East sound. These instruments drop out, leaving bass and rhythm organ to carry a simplified version of the theme as the drums gain a dub dimension. Then the organ drops out, leaving only the bass and reverbed drums. They play host to a hypnotic parade of keyboards and guitars that artistically flicker in and out *dubwise*. Piano occasionally takes up the theme for short intervals, but relinquishes it as if it doesn't want us to notice. Easy to listen to, 'Selassie I Dub' is a generous and non-taxing dub sound collage.

'Jah Moulty Ital Sip'

Things slow down and relax in 'Jah Moulty Ital Sip'. It's a homey reggae instrumental made better with dub. The melodic bass line again is the anchor as organ, drums and guitar chop are given a relaxed dub treatment. Ultimately, so is the bass, as its harmonics are altered to sound fattened. A bell is repeatedly sounded in what may be a nod to another dub-master, as it is a familiar item from Lee Perry's oddball bag of tricks. 'Jah Moulty Ital Sip' is a perfect closer, letting you come down easy with a dub track that is as comfortable as an old pair of slippers.

'House Of Dub Version'; 'Son Of Man Dub'; 'Rasta To The Hills'; 'Twin Seal Dub'

The 2003 CD release of the album added four bonus tracks that do little to improve on the original LP's nine. 'House Of Dub Version' is another version of 'Zion Is A Home' that does not compare well to the original. 'Son Of Man Dub' is a version of 'Son Of Jah Dub' that includes some substandard vocals by an uncredited singer. 'Rasta To The Hills' is a new riddim of no special note that features the same singer. Another new riddim, 'Twin Seal Dub', is an instrumental dub track kicked off with melodica. It's the best of the four, but still not up to the quality of the original collection. The best that can be said for the bonus tracks is that they can be ignored, leaving the original album unaffected.

Other great Augustus Pablo tracks

In no particular order, the following great Augustus Pablo tracks were all self-produced and are readily available on CD except where noted.

'East Of The River Nile'

Whether you prefer your reggae redefined or raw, there's a rendition of 'East Of The River Nile' for you. The original 1971 rendition for producer Clive Chin was a rough-and-tumble affair, as if all parties involved were too excited by what they had hit upon to spend any time grooming it for presentation. What had they hit upon? Well, it starts with a funky James Brown-style vamp of a riddim, similar to some that Lee Perry and The Upsetters provided for Bob Marley & The Wailers at around the same time. The band here is less polished, a fact fully revealed by the melodica-free alternative mix on the *Skanking With Pablo* CD collection. But the appearance of Pablo's Far East melodica, other keyboards and touches of dub, though again a bit crude, elevates the song to something that was then very new, exotic and exciting. It can be heard on the aforementioned *Skanking With Pablo*, as well as on several other CD collections.

Pablo remade 'East Of The River Nile' as the title track of a 1977 album. This time he took care to nourish the song's potential as space-reggae. All the instruments and dub production are fully developed. The sound has a light touch but is still funky. Sublime and refined, this rendition sounds like reggae for the dancing of planets.

'Ethiopian Binghi Drums'

'Ethiopian Binghi Drums' is the confluence of heartbeat Nyabinghi-reggae and Pablo's introspective Far East melodica playing. Not surprisingly, these naturalistic sounds fit each other like two hands in a pair of gloves. A Nyah drum troupe is joined by acoustic guitar and deep bass (the only electric instrument here). To this, Pablo brings yearning lead melodica lines and occasional touches of other keyboard. Choosing to keep the sound grounded, Pablo foregoes dub effects, and they are not missed. The pastoral, meditative and very relaxing 'Ethiopian Binghi Drums' is a match made in heaven. It can be heard on Pablo's 1999 album *Valley Of Jehosaphat*.

'Jah Light' (aka 'Forever Love'); 'Forever Dub' (aka 'Jah Light Version')

For years, 'Forever Love' and its dub B-side 'Forever Dub' remained perhaps the best Augustus Pablo single not to have been collected on CD or LP. This was rectified when they were added as bonus tracks on a 2005 CD edition of Pablo's 1977 LP, *East Of The River Nile*, albeit with new titles. 'Forever Love' is an instrumental cover of Ken Boothe's über-romantic 'When I Fall In Love' (a song described previously; page 138). But where Boothe's delivery was reverently serious, Pablo's delivery bursts with unrestrained joy. Not every instrument executes perfectly or is necessarily in tune, which only serves to make the track more exciting. Pablo provides two energetic melodica tracks. One sounds a double-struck reggae chop, occasionally adding a brief flourish, complete with the clearly audible sound of fingers raking over the keys. The other provides a lead, translating Boothe's melody into a raucous demand for love. Appealing, short and dub-free, it leaves us wanting more, and the single's dub B-side delivers. Drop-out/in juices the riddim. Most of the melodica goes missing, and the piano, barely noticed in the

A-side, takes a prominent role. When it drops out, a bold and beautiful bass line finds itself in the spotlight, and acquits itself nicely. Reverb is liberally applied and each instance of sporadic echo seizes the attention. As bonus tracks go, these rate very high.

'Islington Rock'
'Islington Rock' is another excellent bonus track that was added to the *East Of The River Nile* CD. Though there is fine playing all around, Pablo's melodica is the highlight. He is in full Far East mode, taking a riddim that is already full of yearning and deepening it with a melancholy theme. Of all of Pablo's recordings that cover a broad emotional range, this might be the one that's best described as heartbreaking. 'Islington Rock' is a dub-free song, and rather than the expected dub version, Pablo seems to have consigned the riddim to Lee Perry to have his way with. Perry versioned it many times, including two described later in this book (pages 261–2): a fine vocal version called 'Words Of My Mouth' by The Gatherers and a dub masterwork called 'Words', attributed to Sangie Davis.

'Cassava Piece'
Jacob Miller: *'Baby I Love You So'; 'King Tubbys Meets Rockers Uptown'*
Sharing a riddim, 'Cassava Piece' and 'King Tubbys Meets Rockers Uptown' are two tremendous pieces of dub that were built up over time rather than emerging already formed. In 1972, Pablo recorded the original version of 'Cassava Piece'. It was an OK record, but sounded unpracticed and under-realized, and if Pablo had abandoned the riddim, it might have been quickly forgotten. Instead, he stuck with it, spinning off undistinguished versions such as 'Cassava Rock', a DJ version by Big Youth. He then recut the riddim, and his persistence was rewarded. Not only did this vastly superior rendition result in an immediate classic, its versions were better too.

The remade 'Cassava Piece' features an unusual opening, the likes of which can only be heard in reggae. It opens with a few seconds of dreamy melodica chords that sleepwalk about without adhering to any beat. Four ascending piano notes awaken the song, calling it to structure. It's accented by a reverb-fattened snare strike near, but not on, the third beat, pregnant with the promise of reggae and dub. On the cymbal-accented fourth note, the promise is kept, as a three-piece rhythm section takes off with the drive of a locomotive. Hot rhythm guitar plays a double-struck reggae chop. It has a classic mento rhythm at its heart, but its surface shimmers with modern dub production. The busy, hi-hat-dominated drums with their odd fills leave reggae fans arguing whether Carlton Barrett or the lesser known Lloyd "Tinleg" Adams (who gets my vote) should be credited for such a fine, idiosyncratic performance. The textbook-perfect start-and-stop bass line turbocharges the riddim's drive while giving Pablo a melodic springboard. It is similarly disputed as being either Aston Barrett or Robbie Shakespeare. (Check the album credits? Especially when an album is comprised of a collection of singles, as is the case here, musician credits on a Jamaican reggae album, if present at all, are more casual than definitive.) Atop of this, Augustus plays a longing melodica melody alternating nicely between faster rhythmic passages and slower, floating wistful lines, sometimes touched by dramatic vibrato. It's a performance that forever puts to bed the notion that the melodica is a toy rather than a musical instrument. And it establishes Augustus Pablo as the instrument's master – a position that no one has come close to since. 'Cassava Piece' is a dense track that sounds like there are more than four musicians playing. This is due to its busy play rather than any dub effects, which are few and subtle. Reverb thickens the rhythm guitar, a bit of restrained drop-out/in and some panning of tracks between the left and right stereo channels is the extent of these. But it's enough that the song is heard as a dub track. 'Cassava Piece' is as kick-ass a piece of dub as has ever been heard.

One of the many versions that the recut riddim yielded was the hit, 'Baby I Love You So' by singer Jacob Miller. Dueling with the version's new melodica track, Miller builds on the melodies inherent in the riddim, while riding its energy. It's a fine vocal performance that may lack his trademark stutter singing, but is spiced with some scat at the song's end, which he concludes with contented laughter.

As was the case for the *Rockers Meets King Tubbys In A Firehouse* LP, Pablo collaborated with King Tubby on the dub of Miller's version, 'King Tubbys Meets Rockers Uptown'. Once again, a synergy took hold, as 'Uptown' is a monster of a dub track. It's so great, it not only beats the remade 'Cassava Piece', it also has the unfortunate effect of making Miller's 'Baby I Love You So' superfluous, as if Miller's version only existed as an organ donor for the better track. It opens explosively. The dreamy introduction to 'Cassava Piece' is dispensed with, and without warning the first thing heard is a single snare strike, burbling with echo that melds it with the onset of bass. A wistful, Western-sounding melody theme is newly added. An acid-intense dub treatment transforms the locomotive drive of the riddim into a more exotic engine powered by strange energies, propelling us to unfamiliar places. Everything other than bass is liberally treated with reverb and echo, creating a snakes' nest of shifting polyrhythms as echoing snatches of vocals, melodica, drums and guitar fly by. Even as drop-out is employed, echo maintains a high level of density and motion. The exchange of melodica and guitar dub lines sounds like two aliens conversing, while the fine bass and drum work provides a conduit. Isolated fragments of Jacob Miller's vocal appear at random, his syntax shattered, and the less-is-more magic of dub makes it riveting. Further treated with reverb and echo, he sounds as if he was altered to serve as the intermediary between the familiar and new worlds. 'King Tubbys Meets Rockers Uptown' is quite the trip.

'Cassava Piece', 'Baby I Love You So' and 'King Tubbys Meets Rockers Uptown' are all readily available on numerous CD collections. The original rendition of 'Cassava Piece' can be found on the Augustus Pablo CD collection called *El Rocker's*. Augustus returned to this riddim frequently, and fans of it enjoy tracking the good (if lesser) alternative dub versions. There is the fine 'Cassava Dub' (not currently available on CD or LP), the heavy 'Sweet Cassava Dub', complete with a false start from the previous take (available on the Augustus Pablo CD collection *Dubbing With The Don*), '132 Version' (also included on *El Rocker's*), the satisfying 'Straight A Yard' (which can be found on the 1992 LP, *Rockers International 2*) and 'Jah Jah Dub' (a track on the very first dub LP, the 1975 Herman Chin-Loy-produced *Aquarius Dub*, now available on CD). I'm looking out for more.

'El Rockers Chapter 3'
'El Rockers Chapter 3' is one of four numbered versions of the same riddim found on the 1991 CD collection *Augustus Pablo Presents Rockers International*. It's the best of Pablo's total of seven goes at the classic Sound Dimension instrumental 'Real Rock' (a song described earlier in this book; page 170). It's also Pablo at his breezy, dubby best. His melodica playing, relaxed and trippy, and the dub treatment make this a floating soap bubble of a song.

'Mr. Bassie'
'Mr. Bassie' is a bitter-sweet melodica instrumental based on the Horace Andy song of the same name (a song described later in this book; page 388). It should not be confused with the similarly named but lesser song called 'Pablo Meets Mr. Bassie'. It's genuinely exciting when Pablo plays a dramatically wistful rendition of the Mr. Bassie melody over a simmering cauldron of dub. He goes on to improvise on the melody with a jazz-like flow. But the music does not sound like jazz. Pablo's idyllic dub reggae sounds like what it is and little else. 'Mr. Bassie' can be heard on Pablo's 1983 album, *King David's Melody*.

'Natural Way'; 'Nature Dub'
'Natural Way' is a fine melodica instrumental featuring an emotionally wrought minor-key melodica theme that's dramatic even for a Far East song. It's fine, but is outshone by its dub version, 'Nature Dub'. Here, melodica, a breathy synthesizer, dub guitar chords, piano and intervals of just bass and dubbed drums rotate on a dub carousel. The effect is that of a journey through a mystical dub landscape. Both songs are available on the Augustus Pablo CD, *East Of The River Nile*. The title 'Natural Way' invokes the cover photo of Pablo sitting on a rock in a stream as he plays his melodica. The photo alone is worth the price of the CD, but you'll want to put the disc in your player before you hang the CD on your wall.

'1 Ruthland Close'
Ranking Trevor: *'Whip Them Jah'*
His 1974 instrumental, '1 Ruthland Close' (sometimes called '1 Rutland Close'), is an unusual Augustus Pablo track. Unlike the peaceful ethereal instrumentals that he is famous for, this one is deliberately harsh and provocative. If rock has heavy metal, this is a rare example of dub reggae's equivalent: *hard dub.* This is wrought

by Pablo's production, as the riddim does not sound this way in other versions. For example, the melodica-heavy vocal cut that gives the riddim its name, 'Jacob Miller's False Rasta', sounds ordinary. And Ranking Trevor's DJ cut (produced by George "Niney the Observer" Boswell), 'Whip Them Jah', with its crazy popping-bubble and insect sounds and the thick-throated Trevor riding the riddim as if he's swimming through quicksand, makes the riddim sound dreamlike.

On '1 Ruthland Close', the riddim is made to sound completely different. The song's opening sets the abrasive tone. A stripped-down introduction gives way to an oddly shaped echoing snatch of melodica. But it's a tease, presented so you can feel its absence, as melodica is barely heard again. Instead, the bass comes booming into the forefront, mixed loud even for reggae. It plays a heavy stop-and-go descending line like a ton of bricks tumbling down on your head. Meanwhile, heavy-handed drop-out/in pummels the riddim like a storm. There are sparse reverbed rhythm guitar chords that flash harshly, and in-your-face cymbal strikes.

This unusually tough piece of dub is a tremendous track that stands unique. Even with Pablo returning to the riddim several more times, no other version is as bracing. '555 Crown Street' is a melodica cut with more dub smoothing out the sound. Its dub version, '555 Dub Street' is further softened with more echo. 'Hungry Town Skank', a dub version based on Jacob Miller's vocal cut, is spacy, not tough. '1 Ruthland Close' can be heard on the Augustus Pablo rarities collection CD, *El Rockers*. Also recommended is its aforementioned antithesis version, Ranking Trevor's 'Whip Them Jah'. This can be heard on the CD compilation called *Niney The Observer – Roots With Quality*.

26 Lee Perry before the Black Ark

Earlier in this book, we saw how mutually beneficial Lee Perry's production skills and The Wailers' music were to one another. And in the next chapter there is an examination of Perry's famous Black Ark period: the pinnacle of his (or perhaps anyone's) production prowess. But besides these bodies of work he also produced himself and other singers on a number of great tracks that should not be missed, especially when they are all readily available on any number of CD collections.

Lee Perry & The Sensations: *'Run For Cover'*
Perry serves as the lead singer and producer on the 1967 rock steady song, 'Run For Cover'. In spite of being loaded with pugilistic metaphors, this is the most charming song Perry ever recorded. His vocals are earnest and endearing, making the very most of his somewhat limited vocal range. Downright lovable here, you want to pick him up and carry him around in your pocket.

Producer Perry wisely supplements singer Perry with the backing vocals of The Sensations. The fine Jamaican falsetto harmony from this pair of male singers is downright succulent. By contrast, the rock steady instrumental backing is dry and austere. It's stripped down to bass, mixed up-front and loud, providing most of the melody, drums, rhythm guitar and rhythm piano. A rhythmically picked guitar embellishes the riddim for the mid-song break. This leaves little to distract from the vocals.

Perry opens by throwing down the gauntlet, but at whom? "Run for cover now; I'm taking over. So please step aside, because I ain't gonna sympathize." Then, with The Sensations qualifying each line with "Musically!", delightfully pronounced in four syllables, the nature of the conflict becomes clearer:

> Boy, I'm gonna lay it on (Musically!)
> From dusk till dawn (Musically!)
> With a right to the head and a left to the cheek (Musically!)
> Boy, I'm gonna knock you down (Musically!)

He is probably describing the sound system business with its "dusk till dawn" operation. By this, Perry is promising to knock out his competition, musically speaking, by laying on a barrage of choice records all night long. It's a singularly Jamaican topic wonderfully delivered by one of Jamaica's true characters at his best.

'Run For Cover' can be heard on several Lee Perry compilations, where it is often credited to Lee Scratch Perry or to Lee Perry and The Upsetters. Don't confuse it with the Perry-produced Bob Marley & The Wailers song by the same name (not that you don't want to hear that song too).

Lee Perry: *'People Funny Boy'*
In 1968, Perry again served as singer and producer for a great song in 'People Funny Boy'. But the mood couldn't be more different from the sweet 'Run For Cover'. He addresses the behavior of his former employer, producer Joe Gibbs, whom Perry worked with for a time after he left Studio One. With his voice strong with anger and contempt, he sings of Gibbs's success making him arrogant and ungrateful for Perry's role in that success. For example, he recalls helping a down-and-out Gibbs and can hardly believe that the other producer has no recollection of this, now that Perry himself is in need. At one point, he describes Gibbs's success as winning a jackpot. That word choice is a dig at the Gibbs-produced Pioneers hit of earlier that year, 'Jack Pot' (a song described earlier; page 229). And subsequent lyrics about coming into money and being able to afford good food are lifted right from that song, making the dig deeper. In fact, the riddim of 'People Funny Boy' is an aggressive, hurried rendition of the riddim of 'Jack Pot'. All of this makes Perry's attack more personal, and adds to the song's immediacy.

Fueled by anger and urgency, 'People Funny Boy' bristles with life. It's in the faster, busy, polyrhythmic style of the very first records to be called reggae, as a differentiated style from rock steady. In fact, 'People Funny Boy' is one of a handful of songs that have been tagged as the first reggae-proper song. A few elements stand out from the bigger-than-rock-steady band, making the sound raucous and new: a roughly scrubbing rhythm guitar, rollicking electric piano, a cowbell, a very un-rock steady-like dose of distortion and a crying baby. (To further mock Gibbs, Perry notoriously added a recording of a baby bawling into the mix's opening.) It is somehow rhythmically and melodically correct, adding to the music's riotousness without irritating. This was seen as a watershed moment in Perry's career, marking the beginning of his development from just another great Jamaican producer to a chance-taking master of sonic experimentation.

This record by no means escaped the attention of Joe Gibbs. He had The Pioneers record a single, each side a response to 'People Funny Boy'. In 'People Grudgeful', Gibbs pretty much throws 'People Funny Boy' back in Perry's face, concluding, "You're crummy, boy". In 'Pan Ya Machete', using a different riddim, Gibbs turns the mockery of the crying baby back on Perry, using a recording of a yapping dog. It brings further criticism on Perry's head, calling him out by his two most famous nicknames, "Scratch" and "Upsetter". But neither song holds a candle to 'People Funny Boy'. The same is true for Perry's two responses, 'People Funny Fi True' and 'You Crummy', as the great grudge-record battle royal of 1968 came to a close, with only 'People Funny Boy' still standing.

The Bleechers: '*Check Him Out*'
The Bleechers were a short-lived vocal group consisting of lead singer Leo Graham and backing singers Wesley Martin and Sammy, whose full name appears to have been lost. They recorded about a dozen tracks from 1969 to 1971, almost exclusively for Perry. However, this number may be inflated, as another vocal group, featuring a future Congo, Watty Burnett, may have also been recorded under The Bleechers name. Graham would continue on, recording sporadically as a solo singer into the late 1970s.

Their 1969 song, 'Check Him Out', is a matchless example of the terse, clipped style of reggae of that time which producer Perry sometimes specialized in. It stops me in my tracks every time I hear it, with its wonderful sound and its twist on self-referential reggae lyrics.

Opening with a brief tumble of drums, the backing music sounds like a rock steady band being told to play in the newly unveiled style of reggae proper. The riddim is tight, mannered and melodic, expert and appealing, like rock steady. But the pace is juiced and the arrangement more busy and takes more chances in the way of the new style. A two-piece Bleechers line-up sings the entire song in delectable Jamaican harmony. The backing singer's falsetto is the perfect enhancement to the lead singer's mid-range vocals, with reverb blurring the line between them. Their delivery consists of short, clipped lines uttered in a structured rhythm, one after another, like bricks forming a wall atop the instrumental foundation. There is no chorus or verse, just a block of lyrics, sung twice. A brief rhythm guitar solo, also structured and terse, provides a break halfway.

With vocals and instrumentation as good as this, the song can be enjoyed just on the basis of its aural merits, without listening to a single word. But once the lyrics come into focus, the song becomes doubly enjoyable. What is the subject that inspired The Bleechers and band to these heights? It's a list of directions to Perry's Upsetter record shop, "where music's sweet". That's a lyric that you would only hear in reggae, where the artists were fully cognizant of the incredible body of new music they were creating, and frequently commented on it. You would have to go back to the golden-age mento song 'Shaw Park Blues' by Robin Plunkett & The Shaw Park Calypso Band (a song described previously in this book, page 53), for such a helpfully detailed advertisement. But whereas Plunkett's song is an outrageously shameless commercial, 'Check Him Out' comes off as more sincerely helpful.

The alliteration of the lyrics, which repeat the words "stop", "shot", "spot", "street" and "sweet", mesmerizes (but, surprisingly, the word "shop" is never used). Though Perry the producer is most frequently remembered as being a master of sonic modern art, 'Check Him Out' reminds us that he was first of all a master craftsman of traditional production and arrangement techniques. Not to be missed, this track is available on several CD collections.

The Versatiles: *'The Thanks We Get'*
Kingstonian vocal group The Versatiles (Junior Byles, Louie Davis and Dudley Earl) recorded close to twenty sides for a number of producers from 1968 to 1971. It was Perry who discovered the group and brought them to producer Joe Gibbs to record for the first time. Kerrie "Junior" Byles was born in 1948 in Kingston and first learned music in church. His departure for a successful solo career effectively ended the group. He was a devoutly religious roots reggae artist, and in 1975, unable to accept Haile Selassie's death, he attempted suicide. Happily, he survived to record a total of over 50 solo sides, most frequently with Lee Perry producing, and three albums into the early 1980s.

In 1970, Perry produced The Versatiles (though the song is often credited to The Upsetters) singing a composition of his called 'The Thanks We Get'. It recalls both the grudge lyrics of 'People Funny Boy' and the terse, clipped vocal delivery of 'Check Him Out'. Though some time had passed, the song is presumably again directed at Joe Gibbs. Once again Perry complains of ungratefulness, recalling the times he would go as far as to refuse an offer of tea, not wanting to add even slightly to the other party's financial burden. He uses a folk saying to explain his need to air his grievance: "If you don't mash hands, you no find the cut."

The tight terse sound employed on 'Check Him Out' is taken to the extreme on 'The Thanks We Get'. In close unison and ripe harmony, their voices welded together with reverb, The Versatiles sing in a rhythmically clipped staccato. Nearly every syllable has equal emphasis and their melodic range is compressed to just a few notes. But for all these constraints, the resulting vocal has great appeal and is very catchy. It's well paired with a backing that clearly has put the sterling manners of rock steady squarely in the rear-view mirror, going down the rougher, wilder reggae road. In particular, a pungent organ, grimy with distortion, helps give the song its considerable grit, foreshadowing Perry's greater use of distortion in his later production work. So does the mix, which is deliberately murky, submerging the drums, piano, rhythm guitar and odd percussion touches beneath a layer of vocals, organ and bass. Reggae's subversive genius of production is sprouting up here on his way to full bloom.

Junior Byles remade the song for Perry in 1974. It includes a simultaneous vocal track from Perry's child Omar in a production gambit that did not pay off. This rendition should be avoided and the original one sought out on CD collections such as *Stay Red* by Lee Perry & Friends.

The Upsetters: *'Cloak And Dagger'*; *'Sharp Razor'*
Jah Lion: *'Bad Luck Natty'*
"Greetings, music lover" begins the dubby spoken introduction of Lee Perry's 1973 instrumental, 'Cloak And Dagger'. He goes on to muse over the power of music and concludes with the assertion, "music like shower". Well, only Lee Perry would equate music to a shower (and he would again with 'Bathroom Skank', the next

song in this chapter). But to his credit, 'Cloak And Dagger' is welcoming and revitalizing, with a horn line as life-affirming as the dawning of a new day. It would not be at all out of place in the soundtrack of your morning bathing.

The riddim is a second-generation one, derived from or at least greatly influenced by the classic Studio One riddim called "Joe Frazier" (a riddim described previously in this book; page 174). Perry's update, often referred to as 'Dub Organizer', is as good in its own right as the original. It achieves a perfect reggae groove by equally balancing the instruments in an ensemble piece. Reggae's one-millionth great stop-and-go bass line and keyboards equally give the song its melody while also contributing to its rhythm. There is no dub to be heard nor is any needed. The groove is good enough not to need a lead instrument, but Perry layers on a wonderful horn line. Sax and trumpet in unison play an engaging two-part theme that occupies the length of the song. As the song is sometimes credited to The Upsetters & Tommy McCook, we know who the sax player is. The trumpet player is likely to be Bobby Ellis. Their theme is full of life, accomplished but accessible, in the reggae horns way. Before you can even consider being bored, the key changes and the register drops lower for the theme's second half, as we are given two great lines for the price of one. The theme starts up again, and rather than play the second half, first the trumpet breaks loose with a solo, and then the sax. The theme is then reprised to fade-out.

With horns providing a splendid theme and solos, the structure of 'Cloak And Dagger' is reminiscent of the previously described great Skatalites instrumentals of a decade earlier, even as fiery ska is translated to languid reggae. That 'Cloak And Dagger' compares favorably with these great ska classics is high praise indeed.

'Sharp Razor' is a dub version of 'Cloak And Dagger'. Most of the horns, keyboards and guitar are strategically dropped out to be dropped back in *dubwise*. Perhaps deliberately, perhaps due to the limitations of analog tape, the horns quietly bleed through, allowing you to choose between ignoring and hearing them. This leaves the bass to take the spotlight, giving us the opportunity to appreciate how each note (especially the absent ones when beats are skipped) is well chosen. Drums gain a nimbus of reverb. This is a simple dub compared to what Perry would soon unleash, but it is a highly enjoyable treatment of a fine riddim nonetheless. Both songs appear on the Lee Scratch Perry and The Upsetters album, *Cloak And Dagger*.

'Scratch The Dub Organizer' is another dub version of this riddim, but is inferior to 'Sharp Razor'. It serves as a basis of a DJ version with the shortened title 'Dub Organizer'. Though they are the riddim's namesake versions, both can be safely ignored. Recommended instead is a far better version: 'Bad Luck Natty Dread' by sing-jay Jah Lion, on his 1976 album *Colombia Colly*. Jah Lion recorded and produced throughout the 1970s either as Pat Francis (his birth name), Jah Lloyd (a Rastafarian take on his middle name), or less frequently as Jah Ali or Junior Dread, before Perry gave him his most dramatic moniker of all. Over the decade, he released a total of about 80 singles and nine albums. Two different but equally tragic accounts have him either being gunned down or dying destitute in 1999 at the age of fifty-two.

He is captivating on 'Bad Luck Natty' as he emphatically tells his story with a sing-chant-talk delivery enlivened with whistling. Closer examination reveals that he is singing and expanding on the old folk/mento song 'Teacher Lick The Gal' (a song discussed previously in this book; see page 47), although the melody and pace are altered, and the titular line is omitted. Signs of the time: (1) his voice is drenched in the echoing effect of digital delay; and (2) he resonantly roughens his voice to highlight certain phrases, showing the influence of Big Youth. The riddim is dub-juiced and rearranged. The horns are largely suppressed, percussion is added, as is electric piano with a condensed sound that Perry sometimes favored. The resulting version is as good as any using this riddim. Especially when the great horn theme comes out like the sun in the song's final seconds, making sure you don't miss it too much.

Lee Perry: *'Bathroom Skank'*

Another spoken introduction from Perry, and we learn that this track was recorded at King Tubby's studio. And, more importantly, that the water has been turned on. We're now ready for this 1973 track where Perry instructs us how to take a shower. The Upsetters lay down a bouncy, funky vamp for Perry to chant over, as someone adds bubbling mouth sounds. Perry tells us step by step how to wash your body – in case you were in the shower and happened to forget. 'Bathroom Skank' is an unserious song with a seriously good groove that could only have sprung from Lee Perry the singer and Lee Perry the producer.

Lee Perry: *'Blackboard Jungle Dub (Version 1)'*

From the 1973 LP of the same name, 'Blackboard Jungle Dub (Version 1)' shows the continued development of Lee Perry's production creativity. It's a serious track with a sound that is meditative, but with a nocturnal sound and a spooky vibe. Having already given us reggae for activities as diverse as grudges, record shopping and showers, here Perry gives us the perfect reggae song for a séance. It begins with another spoken welcome from him. Treated with dub, it sounds like an invocation. An eerie audio montage follows, with a stray snatch of flute, creaking sounds, vocal whooshes and a loose bass and drum jam that previews the riddim to come. A drum roll calls the song to order, and the elements coalesce into a track dominated by a double-tracked flute, repeating a melody reminiscent of Jackie Mittoo's 'Drum Song' (a song described earlier in this book; page 171). In place of a traditional solo, the flutes pause for an odd interlude of processed moans and creaks, as if they have succeeded in contacting the spirit world. Rather than damaging the musicality of the song, these strange proceedings only add to it.

The LP also contains 'Blackboard Jungle Dub (Version 2)', a shorter and more straightforward take, with trombone taking up the phrase played by flute on Version 1 and providing a solo.

The Mighty Diamonds: *'Talk About It'*

The Trench Town-born vocal trio The Mighty Diamonds are Donald "Tabby" Shaw, Fitzroy "Bunny" Simpson, and Lloyd "Judge" Ferguson. Formed in 1969, they are still together at the time of this writing, 150 singles, 29 studio albums, 5 live albums and forty-plus years later. Though their earliest singles were pre-roots reggae with vocals in the soul vein, as devout Rastas they quickly grew into (and almost exclusively stayed with) the roots reggae style that they are so much associated with.

In 1974, Perry produced The Mighty Diamonds' love song, 'Talk About It'. Compared to their hit 'Pass The Kouchie' (a song described later in this book; page 402) and the rest of their catalog, 'Talk About It' sports a different sound. It marries a lean, mean riddim to urgent vocals, making for a very tough piece of reggae. The pace is brisk. There are no horns adorning the tight four-piece band, with just a flinty rhythm guitar and muted rhythm electric piano embellishing the bass and drums. Perry's single use of dub is to add reverb on the backing vocals, giving the song its only soft sound. If you are craving a nice crispy, crunchy reggae song, bite into this.

This backing elicits a more intense vocal performance than The Diamonds' norm. Lead singer Shaw sings of seeing a couple in love, and proclaims his devotion to his own lover. But things are not that simple, as the song includes an incongruous but memorable refrain bewailing the fact that nothing is going right, justifying such an edgy sound for a song primarily about love. Shaw sings in a high register, and most of the backing vocals are sung even higher, nicely glowing with reverb. It foreshadows the reggae heavenly-choir sound that Lee Perry's Black Ark production would later bestow on The Congos, as described in the chapter on that group. The song also contains an example of one of Perry's unsuccessful eccentric production gambits. The long, repetitious, unmusical coda of processed voices appended to the end of the song can easily be skipped, however, with no damage done. 'Talk About It' can be found on several CD compilations.

The Gatherers: *'Words Of My Mouth'*

Sangie Davis: *'Words'*

Some great reggae songs emerge fully formed, while others are built up over time. Perry's production of 'Words' by Sangie Davis is simultaneously an example of both scenarios. It starts with Augustus Pablo's wonderfully haunting 1972 melodica instrumental 'Islington Rock' (a song described in the chapter on this artist; page 251). In 1973, Perry took this recording and had The Gatherers voice it as 'Words Of My Mouth'. Led by Anthony "Sangie" Davis, this group recorded only a few sides, and this song is clearly an unmatched achievement for them. Vocals replace almost all of Pablo's melodica, and it's a testimony to The Gatherers that Pablo is not missed. Backed by a single harmony singer, Davis sings a fine rootsy lead, his voice breaking with emotion. He sings Rasta-*conscious* lyrics, finding inspiration in Psalm 19:14, just as The Melodians had done previously for 'Rivers Of Babylon'. A Nyah hand drum adds further to its roots reggae credentials.

But, as was his way, Perry was not done. Never one to rest on his laurels, he viewed any successful recording as a launching pad for other versions. He would release a number of dubs of this Gatherers' song. In 1977, a dub version appeared, with a revised title, revised billing and a new sound. Retitled 'Words' and attributed to Sangie Davis, it's amazing what Perry has wrought. There is absolutely no air in this version. Instead, you breathe thick dub protoplasm that has everything from The Gatherers' version floating in a suspension of dub sound, surrounded by odd percussion organelles at every turn. This dense, cluttered and genuinely strange sound is unique. It makes what was already a fine piece of roots reggae into something special. Though not in the mold of his Black Ark sound, 'Words' is no less an achievement of the dub-master's art.

For maximum impact, I recommend playing Augustus Pablo's 'Islington Rock' and 'Words' back to back. As the fine but dub-free sound of 'Islington Rock' ends, the reverbed single drum strike that opens 'Words' ushers in the strange aural landscape as the riddim continues. Together, they make for the best disco-mix single that never existed. 'Words' makes Perry's other versions of the "Words Of My Mouth" riddim superfluous, as it did to the 2005 remake by Davis on his album of the same name.

27 Lee Perry and the Black Ark sound

By the midpoint of the1970s, Lee Perry's accomplishments as a producer had already eclipsed his work as a singer. Yet, new heights were just around the corner. It was then that the music coming from his studio, Black Ark, began to exhibit its amazing namesake sound.

Black Ark may be the most legendary of the great Jamaican recording studios, even considering the venerable Treasure Isle and Studio One. Extraordinary music came from all three, but Perry's notorious struggles with mental health at one point compelled him to cover each and every surface with handwritten text, and ultimately led him to burn the studio down. But before this, from 1976 through 1979, Black Ark was a factory for amazing reggae with a unique dub sound. No reggae producer – and for that matter, few people in any capacity – could harness chaos the way Lee Perry did with the Black Ark sound.

Perry created the most immediately recognizable production sound since Phil Spector's "wall of sound". In the same way, his mixing and arranging became more important than the artist he was recording. But whereas Spector's sound could be readily mimicked by any motivated producer, the Black Ark sound proved to be inimitable, even for Lee Perry later in his career.

Reggae had possessed polyrhythmic simmer and bubble since the days of rural mento, and this effect was often increased by dub. But only the Black Ark sound could make reggae *shimmer* with extra vitality. It was as if a palette of Day-glo earth-tone colors that couldn't otherwise be seen by the human eye was suddenly made visible, Perry's sliders and knobs shining like black light. Rather than accenting the music with effects as most other dub-masters did, Perry inundated the music with persistent processing. As with most dub, reverb was heavily utilized, as well as drop-out/drop-in. Perry also used echo, but not the way other dub-masters did. Instead of making skyrockets of echo a lead effect, Perry used digital delay to give instruments a continual, more subtle, form of echo. He dabbled with distortion in a way no other dub-master did, and probably made the immaculate King Tubby cringe.

His processing reinvented some instruments with idiosyncratic new sounds. Most commonly, he used oversaturation to distort the hi-hat cymbal, making it sound like the rhythmic tapping of a blacksmith hammering at something steely atop an anvil. This was a signature of the Black Ark sound. Brass could be altered in a way that made you picture horns of previously unseen exotic shapes, or a swarm of insects. Perry used flange frequently, while his peers used it seldom, if ever at all. It made rhythm guitar swirl incredibly or orbit like a flying saucer for another

Black Ark signature sound. When he pushed it to its extremes, Perry could make individual instruments resemble plastic objects recovered after a fire – charred, melted into interesting new shapes, but still recognizable. Or he could alter the sound of several instruments until they were completely melded into a thick psychedelic swirl.

Numerous artists, big and small, would be graced by Perry's Black Ark sound. This included new artists, obscure names, Perry's stable of vocalists and the island's biggest stars. Bob Marley & The Wailers recorded there, though the resulting "fast version" of 'Smile Jamaica' was not outstanding by Black Ark standards. Junior Murvin, whose pre-Black Ark career had stalled, relaunched himself at the Ark, recording one of the greatest reggae albums of all time, which is the focus of another chapter (Chapter 28). The newly formed vocal group, The Congos, recorded their debut music there, creating several stunningly great tracks that are discussed in a later chapter (Chapter 29). Non-Jamaican talent also sought out the Black Ark sound. The Clash, Robert Palmer, Linda McCartney, a pair of musicians from Zaire, all made the pilgrimage to Jamaica to record with Perry at his studio.

Video footage exists of Perry dubbing at Black Ark – altering sound by working the mixing board and other studio controls. His hands move purposefully as he grimaces, dances and leaps in response to the music he shapes. Thus, sonic art unintentionally becomes performance art as well. No wonder his label's alternative name was Black Art.

All the great Black Ark songs described below are readily available on CD. As is the case throughout this book, dub versions are only discussed if the version is notable.

Lee Perry: 'Dreadlocks In Moonlight'

Let's start with 'Dreadlocks In Moonlight'. This 1976 song pairs a good example of the basic Black Ark sound with a vocal from Perry that is one of his best from any stage of his career. Listen to how the hi-hat cymbal is front and center in the mix and the oversaturation Perry applies to it. Hear how the rest of the drums are processed with reverb, compression, etc. The opening drum roll is made to sound fuzzy and pliant compared to the way drums normally sound. Listen to how effects give a pumping organ a more organic nature. And the guitar chop that is so processed with effects, it sizzles. Only the bass is unaltered, the music shimmering all around it, giving it added authority, even without placing it forward in the mix. This is the Black Ark sound. As good as it is, other songs would build on this sound, taking it further.

Perry the singer strikes a pleasing melody, singing confidently in his amiable way. A subtle echo effect softly ghosts his voice. The song is *Rasta business*, such as triumphing over police oppression, hypocrites and parasites, and he reinforces his message with various Bible quotes throughout. At this stage of his career, Perry's lyrics are just beginning to become more oblique, a trend that would later accelerate along with a decline in his mental health. His voice never sounded more like Bob Marley than in this song. Therefore, it comes as no surprise to learn that Perry recorded it as a demo for Marley, but released it himself. Of course, Perry's voice has a more limited tonal range and lacks Marley's power. But he makes up for this with his earnestness and vulnerability, and in the end it's hard to imagine anyone else but him singing 'Dreadlocks In Moonlight'.

'Dreadlocks In Moonlight' is available on several compilations. But no one has yet compiled the 12-inch disco-mix version that nicely lengthens the ride with an understated dub version, originally called 'Cut Throat' when it appeared as the 7-inch single's B-side. Also available on some CD collections is a remixed version of the song cluttered with many overdubs, called 'Big Neck Police'.

Eric Donaldson: *'Stand Up'*

Eric Donaldson was born in 1947, in Kent Village, Saint Catherine Parish. He began recording in 1964 for Coxsone Dodd, but although his music was pressed for use at the sound system, it was never released. Donaldson then formed a vocal group called The West Indians with Leslie Burke and Hector Brooks. They enjoyed modest success, releasing a handful of singles for producers Carl "J. J." Johnson and Lee Perry in 1968 and 1969. But the group split up, leaving Donaldson again a solo act. His fortunes changed when he submitted a song and won the sixth Festival Song Competition in 1971 with 'Cherry Oh Baby' (a song described later in this book; see page 302). His light songwriting touch and appealing country voice would lead to an unmatched seven Festival wins (though, to be honest, the later Festival songs could not compare to the glory of the earliest winners). He would enjoy a career comprised of more than 60 singles, 14 albums and as many compilations, recording into the new millennium.

Eric Donaldson had previously recorded a rendition of 'Stand Up' with a similar melody and vocal performance, but as a soulful reggae song with a slow-burning groove. It's a good rendition, but it's unfair to compare it to the Black Ark remake, where Perry's production skills had evolved to the full extent of his genius for sound.

Perry opens (and closes) Eric Donaldson's 'Stand Up' with an echoing random syllable of his voice, as if to alert the listener not to expect the countrified Festival sounds he is most famous for. The music begins, and it's bathed in a pulse of warm percussive waves of Black Ark roil. A heavily processed drum (or something) throbs throughout, like the beat of a perpetual motion machine. A shaken tambourine fills space with emanations of reverb and other processing. More instruments and effects come and go in a dense throbbing mix. The sound shimmers like the sun beating down on a brook filled with silver and gold pieces. For a brief interval, all unprocessed instruments and vocals drop out, leaving only the denizens of the Black Ark sonic realm in the spotlight. Later, in an inspired move, the opposite is true, as with a flourish of echo, Perry briefly drops out all the Black Ark elements. Suddenly an unaltered piano, bass, drum and a processed guitar are heard, free of the pulsating froth that is so prominent in the song. It's like a brief peek back to the monochrome denizens of Kansas from Technicolor Oz. But after giving you a look, the gauzy veil is drawn closed again as Perry's mixing board slides the Black Ark sound back in.

Donaldson is by no means a passive rider in this splendid vehicle. His "stand up for your rights" lyrics don't break new ground. But he sings with great strength and passion, fashions a fine melody and, double-tracked, his strident country harmony is rewarding. Midway, however, he delivers a surprise. The melody changes as Donaldson makes an impassioned plea that we shouldn't cry for him. He does not explain why he's raising this issue, merely reassuring us that all is well. This unexpected change, to what is practically a different song, adds to an already loaded track, giving the impression that it's much more than its 3:30-minute length. And that's a very good thing considering how enjoyable a song 'Stand Up' is.

The Upsetters: *'Bird In Hand'*
Originally appearing on Perry's 1977 Upsetters LP, *The Return Of The Super Ape*, 'Bird In Hand' has since been found worthy of inclusion in a large number of Lee Perry collections. No wonder, as this track is exotic even by Black Ark standards. It features an unusual vocal melody that is sung phonetically in Hindi. (This tricky challenge is well met by an uncreated singer: Sam Carty. Born in Clarendonian, Carty is known as a solo singer as well as the lead singer of The Astronauts.) It's a cover of a love song called 'Milte Hi Aankhein', which appeared in a 1950 Indian film called *Babul*. How it came to Perry's attention is unexplained, but it was for-tuitous for reggae fans.

Though there have been roots reggae songs with sentiments fortified with a line or two of Ethiopian Amharic, and DJ songs showing off a few phrases of Span-ish or French, an entire Jamaican reggae record in a foreign tongue –Hindi, no less – is unusual, to say the least. But 'Milte Hi Aankhein' with its haunting melody turns out to be an inspired choice. The phonetic delivery has the effect of making English-speaking listeners feel like they should be comprehending the lyrics, even as the words remain strangely out of reach.

More than the song's source is exotic. 'Bird In Hand' opens with a decon-struction of the typical drum introduction heard in so many roots reggae songs. Perry reduces and refines it into miniature sound sculpture. First, a single echo-ing drum strike is launched with a mallet strike and warble of dub. After a preg-nant pause, it arcs back to earth to impact with the thud of a deeper drum strike, the sound reverberant with an echoing guitar chord. This aural story takes only the song's first second to tell. The body of the song begins, and the vocals exhibit Black Ark touches of transgressional, disorienting experimentation. A double-tracked Carty carries a burr of buzzing distortion. The second voice joins, in a noticeable moment late, and takes a few lines to sync up with the first voice. He sings like a storyteller who's trying to overcome the language barrier with a surfeit of expressiveness. But before the song reaches the halfway point, the vocals unaccountably drop out for the remainder of the song, leaving drums and an assortment of percussion to take center stage. The song ends with Perry supplying some wild screams, processed to the point of sounding like they are coming from out of the ether. Three-times exotic, 'Bird In Hand' is a unique and excellent reggae track,

Mystic I: *'Forward With Jah Orthodox'*
The Upsetters: *'Orthodox Dub'*
Mystic I, the roots reggae vocal group led by Lesburn Clarke, might have become better known if they had stuck to one name. Over their dozen or so sides from the late 1970s into the early 1980s, Mystic I also recorded as Mystic Eyes, Mystic M, Mistie I, *just* Mystic, Roots And Soul, or as Lesburn Clarke. But inconsistent branding does not stand in the way of 'Forward With Jah Orthodox' being a great song. It's a fiery Nyabinghi-reggae protest song, whose chorus sounds a pro-religion theme and an anti-income tax stance, centered on the chant of, "Let's forward with Jah orthodox, and get rid of the income tax". The latter point is a bit unusual, as Rastas normally prefer to turn their backs on the specifics of political policy. Along with chanted singing, hand drums are clearly the lead instrument, but other hand percussion, guitar, bass and drum kit are also heard. Black Ark processing is kept down to a minimum, with only the guitar and drums subtly psychedelicized. Perry's restraint suits the rough and rootsy sound of the song.

Paradoxically, so do the excesses he applies to the dub version, called 'Orthodox Dub', credited to The Upsetters. The extra effects start with the vocals, which are so oversaturated they become grained with distortion, taking on a strident edge. Things get even more interesting when they are dropped out. Perry does this for the first verse, like a farmer clearing a field for future use. In subsequent vocal-deprived verses, quivering stalks of Chinna Smith's Black Ark-processed guitar strums spring up like triffids to sway weirdly to the rhythm. The song grows wilder, with bold applications of drop-out/in and reverb. By the song's conclusion, the strums are further mutated to grow monstrous. Processed with distortion, each strum sounds like railroad locomotives being clashed together by a giant, throwing sparks, debris and distortion everywhere. You've heard all manner of guitar processing from Les Paul to Jimi Hendrix on forward, but you'll never hear guitar sound quite like this, as Perry takes Black Ark processing to its extreme.

Ras Michael: *'Hear River Jordan'*
Ras Michael, also sometimes called Dadawah, was born Michael George Henry in Kingston, in 1943. He was raised in a Rastafarian community in Saint Mary

Parish, where he began to play hand drums as a young boy, and became quite proficient. By the 1960s, Coxsone Dodd was using him as a sessions player. By 1967, he was releasing self-produced singles of his Nyabinghi drum troupe, Ras Michael & Sons of Negus. The death of the legendary Count Ossie in 1976 left Ras Michael the undisputed top Nyabinghi recording star. He would record more than 25 singles, but found the LP format more amenable for long-form Nyabinghi jams and released 19 of them. Michael is currently living in California and is still musically active.

'Hear River Jordan' is a different song from Michael's similarly named 'Roll River Jordan' and from the traditional spiritual, 'River Jordan'. It's not the only collaboration between Perry and Ras Michael, but it's the only one that produced magic. Like 'Orthodox Dub', it's a Black Ark treatment of Nyabinghi-reggae. But where 'Orthodox Dub' was made strange by Black Ark production, here it only serves to deepen the rhythmic and meditative qualities of Ras Michael's song. It's built around a chanted refrain that, supported by Nyah drumming, is more than a little hypnotic. "I've got to be on ya [there], walking Jerusalem just like Jah". Already satisfying, Michael charges the refrain with vocal turns that surprise and delight, such as "Oh-la, my father!".The uncredited rootsy falsetto backing vocal that adds greatly to the song sounds suspiciously like The Congos, who were also recording for Perry at this time. They win the prize for "Best Supporting Vocalists In A Guest Appearance".

It's a song that would have made a fine record in the hands of any producer. But in the hands of Lee Perry in his prime, the production doubles the goodness of 'Hear River Jordan'. Perry does not allow dub effects to alter Michael's vocals or his Nyah drums (though there are moments when the Black Ark froth splashes onto the vocals, briefly enlivening them with dub). Instead he throws the reggae instruments that supplement the drum troupe into the Black Ark cauldron. There, they are candy-coated with a pulsating psychedelic swirl that serves as a lead instrument. Semi-solid objects briefly rise up, only to fall back quickly to dissolve in the chaos; sometimes the instrument is recognizable, at other times not. Thus, 'Hear River Jordan' is an "opposites attract" marriage, as peaceful acoustic Nyabinghi music and the electronic chaos of the Black Ark sound are joined blissfully. It can be heard on the Ras Michael album, *Love Thy Neighbor*.

The Upsetters: *'Underground Root' (aka 'Underground')*
There is something primal about Perry's 'Underground Root'. There are just four instruments – vocals, guitar, bass and drums – but each is altered from the norm. It's as if Perry had re-cast air, water, earth and fire with four new elements for this song. First is the unusual-for-Black-Ark out-front bass line, set at a level to stun. Played by Boris Gardiner, Perry's regular bassist of this time, it's a model of efficiency, sparse even by dub reggae standards. Though the notes are few and spaced

out Gardiner has no problem conveying a melody and a groove that carry the track. It's musical magic; a picket fence with most of its pickets missing that does a better job than a complete fence. Second are the Black Ark drums that stumble in to open the song, possessing both a haze of digital delay on the skins and a corona of oversaturation on the hi-hat. Third is Chinna Smith's rapidly strummed guitar, again processed to sound like the alien quiverings of triffids, unable to resist jerking to the bass. Fourth is the occasionally heard uncredited female vocalist who harmonizes with herself digitally as she provides choruses of *da da da dum*s and the titular refrain. Appealing but slightly detached, there's something of a 1960s mod Carnaby Street sound to the wordless vocals. But totally Jamaican is how what essentially should be a backing vocal track is promoted to lead by the utter dubbing out of a non-existing lead vocal track. These four elements are more than alchemist Perry needs for a strange and wonderful Black Ark dub. The arrangement very spare, all four are seldom heard at once, and there are intervals of just bass and drums. More than any other track, 'Underground' simultaneously triumphs in two arenas that are not naturally complementary: a creative Black Ark production and minimalistic dub.

'Underground Root' can be heard on the Lee Perry album called *Super Ape*. For the curious, four other versions of this riddim can be heard on the awkwardly titled Lee Perry double-CD collection called *Ape-ology Presents Super Ape Versus Return Of The Super Ape*. 'From Creation' features an entirely different vocal performance, keyboards, and a few effects and lacks the magic of 'Underground'. 'Creation Dub 1', 'Creation Dub 2' and 'Creation Dub 3' spotlight Smith's treated guitar and provide the missing links between 'Creation' and 'Underground'.

Augustus Pablo: *'Vibrate On'*
In 1977 two of dub's most distinctive sounds came together: Augustus Pablo's melodica and Lee Perry's Black Ark production. Though not their only collaboration, this is the one that fully lives up to sky-high expectations with an exciting dub-overload.

The song opens oddly with some Black Ark splatter and a strange dubbed spoken piece from Perry with a jazz sax accompaniment, none of it related to the song that follows. The body of the song begins and a dense arrangement with no white space whatsoever is heard. Out front, Pablo provides his far-east melodica, setting a spirited theme and then improvising on it. Lyrics are reduced to the essentials. An uncredited singer urges Pablo on, chanting, "I beg you vibrate on" with regular interjections of *hey!* Unprocessed, Pablo, the singer and the bass stand out in relief from the storm that Perry brings.

A mix of Black Ark techniques, some very familiar and some less so, are heard, as waves of sound whirl and eddy as if Perry was channeling King Neptune. There are busy drums with the hi-hat overmodulated, prominent flange, fuzzy-buzzy guitar riffs, springy sounds of uncertain origin and a random voice so processed it sounds like a buzzing insect. Already roiling and dense, Black Ark-fashioned sound effects appear after the 2-minute mark. If they were created by musical instruments, there's no telling which ones. Dub galloping horses come and go. Something like bullets fly by. Something like a dub horse neighs. The electric-cow-foghorn sound that Perry favored more and more as the Black Ark's time drew near makes an appearance. A sound that could be a creaking hinge or an animal in distress ends the sound montage. For reasons unknown, Perry has apparently mashed a dub Western into the track, and it's richer for it.

This dub treat can be heard on several Lee Perry and Augustus Pablo CD collections, but be mindful of the different mixes. The preferred one is on the Augustus Pablo CD, *Skanking With Pablo*. But the mix on the box-sets *The Rockers Story: The Mystic World of Augustus Pablo* and Lee Scratch Perry's *Arkology* is too clean, lacking the introduction and the sound-effects montage. There is also a superfluous dub version (called either 'Vibrator' or 'Vibrate On Dub Version') that adds nothing to the A-side.

Max Romeo

Briefly recording under the even more provocative names of Johnny Stud and Ben Rude Dick, the reggae artist better known as Max Romeo came into the world with a far less exciting name. Maxwell Livingston Smith was born in 1947 in Alexandria, Saint James Parish, and would enjoy a long and diverse career as a reggae singer. He moved to Kingston at age nine and soon was a runaway, living on the streets and doing menial labor as a teen. Winning a local talent show gave him the hope of a singing career. He secured a job doing various tasks for Ken Lack, the producer and owner of the Caltone record label. One day, Lack heard Smith singing while he worked and gave him a shot. This is not surprising, as Smith had a fine singing voice that would prove to be very versatile. It may be the most underrated voice in reggae.

Romeo's first recordings were as a member of a vocal group, The Emotions, that also included Lloyd Shakespeare (brother of reggae bass great Robbie Shakespeare, who would die young from a work accident just a few years later) and Kenneth Knight. They recorded a handful of successful Romeo-penned rock steady love songs, giving him the confidence to depart for a solo career. (The Emotions would continue, but in name only, with a new line-up.) Around this time, he took his stage name. It was suggested by his friend and producer-to-be Bunny Lee, based on Smith's way with women, though another story attributes it to a wisecrack from a passer-by as Max waited under a window.

Romeo's solo work began with Lee in 1968. This quickly yielded a big hit with the *slack* 'Wet Dream'. Not only did the lyrics cause a sensation, but it featured an extended organ opening, the like of which the UK was then devouring. (Lee Perry fed that appetite by producing a string of reggae organ instrumentals around that time that were popular there.) So it's not surprising that as well as being a hit in Jamaica, it was popular enough in the UK to earn a spot in the top ten and a BBC ban. This led Romeo to a string of ribald follow-up songs that are less well remembered. But he was too diverse to limit himself to that style. For example, he also recorded more than a few mento songs, covered hits by The Wailers, Bob Dylan and Buffalo Springfield, recorded love songs, Nyabinghi-reggae and roots reggae. It's as a roots reggae artist, who just happened to also record 'Wet Dream', that Romeo is best remembered.

By the late 1960s, Romeo found himself the lead singer of The Hippy Boys, then predominately a live gig. Anchored by the Barrett brothers, this band was about to be adopted by Lee Perry as his new Upsetters (only to be stolen away a few years later by Bob Marley as the basis of his instrumental Wailers). So it's not surprising that by 1970 Romeo had begun an on-and-off relationship with Perry. This paid off richly starting in 1975, when Romeo became a prominent beneficiary of Lee Perry's Black Ark production. The singer had written some fine new roots reggae songs and they would recorded enough material together for two albums, from which the *War Ina Babylon* LP was culled. The album made Romeo an international success for the second time in his career. As was the case for most artists who recorded with Perry during his studio's heyday, though good material followed, it rarely compared to the glories of the Black Ark. Romeo moved to New York City for a time in 1978, where he branched out. He realized Bob Marley's 1972 promise of 'Reggae On Broadway' by co-writing (with Jackie Mittoo) and starring in a Broadway musical called *Reggae*. The show was not a commercial success, closing after only 21 performances. That same year, Romeo was heard as a backing vocalist on The Rolling Stones song, 'Dance'. From there, it was back to Jamaica, where he was one of a handful of Jamaican acts keeping the flame of roots reggae alive in the face of dancehall's popularity. At the end of 2009, after five decades in the business, having released about 175 singles and 18 albums, he announced he was retiring from music, passing the torch to his sons Romario and Ronaldo Romeo.

'War Ina Babylon'

The title track is one of three standout songs discussed here from Romeo's internationally successful 1976 album, *War Ina Babylon*. This is a roots reggae song that balances an abundance of good vocals, instrumentation and Black Ark effects.

It opens with an introduction that is a mini-montage of what is to follow. The vocalists sing a piece of the chorus in unison. A tremulous winking two-note keyboard hook develops. A textured rhythm guitar (the missing link between rock fuzz-tone and Black Ark froth) is unveiled. And there's a taste of odd Black Ark percussion. The body of the song begins, and these seeds bloom.

Romeo's strong vocal, expressive and edgy, draws you in. He is backed by a vocal chorus that sound in turn like different combinations of male falsetto, female, and youth vocalists. He sings of the "tribal war ina Babylon", as there is animosity in Jamaica between the Rasta and the established society:

> De barber man no like de dreadlocks man.
> De dreadlocks man no like de barber man, no.
> De policeman no like de dreadlocks man.
> De dreadlocks man no like de policeman, no.
>
> © Westbury Music Ltd

He goes on to cite Marcus Garvey and the Bible to validate his point of view. Fatalistically, Romeo concludes, "It sipple [slippery] out there. So what fe do? Make we slide out there" and "I-man sat-a at the mountain top. Watching Babylon burning red hot". Meanwhile, both surprise notches of drop-out/in and a varying amount of haze from the hi-hat keep the backing interesting to the end. But Perry honors Romeo's fine song, taking care not to overwhelm it.

The *War Ina Babylon* CD collects an alternate version whose chief differences are the absence of the keyboard hook and its greater length. Far better is 'Sipple Dub', credited to Lee Perry and available on the collection called *The Upsetter Shop, Volume 1: Upsetter in Dub*. Either is better than Romeo's re-voiced version of the riddim, called "Fire Fe The Vatican". Thoroughly unpleasant, it takes the use of the Pope as a symbol of Babylon to an ugly place. A lesser vocal from Romeo, lesser backing vocals and a lesser production from Perry suitably join this lesser message.

'One Step Forward'

'One Step Forward', also from the *War Ina Babylon* album, is a superb reggae song. So much so that Perry throttles back the effects and concentrates on crafting the perfect arrangement. As a result, only the lightly overmodulated hi-hat makes it immediately apparent that this is a Black Ark production.

A solemn tone is set as guitars lay down bluesy minor-key chords and somber picking over martial drums and bass. A touch of piano and reverb on the drums complete the sparse arrangement. Finding it a fitting description of living the Rasta way in a society that oppresses it, Romeo presses the old adage "one step forward, two steps back" into use as his chorus. But there's nothing offhand about his delivery. Sounding grave, the melody dwells on a single note, while the backing singers provide pungent harmony. At one point, he scats to portray someone who is emotionally overwhelmed by this oppression, struggling back to form. The verses chide those who abandon their faith as well as those who pretend to be Rasta for commercial benefit. The latter is probably referring to reggae singers and industry types who suddenly grew dreadlocks, but were not true Rastas. (This was the only time and profession where the adoption of Rastafarianism could be financially beneficial, as the popularity of roots reggae exploded in the 1970s.) In the roots reggae way, the difficulties described are counteracted by a message of hope and perseverance, as the chorus changes to "Onward, forward, don't step backwards".

Even a subdued Perry can't help but keep the arrangement interesting. Late in the song he applies an attention-grabbing single notch of drop-out/in that sets up the scat. There is also the errant syllable from the backing singers. Perry was known to slave over a production for hours until it was exactly to his liking. Apparently, he liked the sound of this mistake and chose to leave it in. 'One Step Forward' is a great song and a great demonstration of how judicious Perry could be with his ever-deepening Black Ark bag of tricks.

Max Romeo: *'I Chase The Devil'*
Lee Perry: *'Disco Devil'*
'I Chase The Devil' is the third great track from Romeo's *War Ina Babylon* album. It features a production that's loaded with incidental percussion rather than the typical array of Black Ark processing effects. This allows the listener to enjoy Romeo's fine reggae voice as he audaciously brags of his intention to chase Satan off the planet. He stands bravely alone, unadorned by backing vocalists or double-tracking. His only accompaniment is the alternation of a moon-bounce reggae picked guitar and a Black Ark-inflected guitar chop. Perry again demonstrates his instinct for applying the right degree of his unique production techniques, nurturing 'Chase The Devil' to its fullest with the right amount of air.

Released a year later, Lee Perry's 'Disco Devil' is a weird invasion of Max Romeo's 'I Chase The Devil'. It's as if Perry tried to devour Romeo's song, but parts of it are escaping out his ribcage. The song begins with a wild, dubbier mix of 'I Chase The Devil', with Romeo's voice heavily phased, while the drums and reggae chop guitar are dub altered. A bubbling sound effect is added, as are cooing female backing vocals that repeat the song's new title. They usher in Perry, who proceeds to co-opt the song. In an endearing croak he decries the titular figure (whoever exactly that is) and then busts some anti-cocaine lyrics. Mid-song, and again at its end, Perry begins to borrow some of the lyrics from Romeo's song. He also dubs in the first syllable from each of Romeo's lines. This supplements his vocal, as he creates a new alloy from both voices.

It's a tough call to say which is better, the straight Romeo song or Perry's madcap version, the stately or the strange. You can decide for yourself, as 'Disco Devil' is available on several CD compilations. It's often in disco-mix form with an uninspired dub version and a late appearance by an even less inspired DJ appended to the song.

28 Junior Murvin at the Black Ark

Singer Murvin Junior Smith was born in 1949 in Swift River, Portland Parish. (He should not be confused with the similarly named guitarist with Bob Marley & The Wailers, Junior Marvin.) A month after he was born, his family moved to Port Antonio, where he grew up. As a child, Smith showed a proficiency for singing popular ballads, a talent he shared with his father, who died when Murvin was a baby. When he was in his teens, the Smiths moved to Montego Bay, where Murvin began to sing in stage shows. At this time he was influenced by soul singers, especially the falsetto singing of Curtis Mayfield that captivated so many on the island. Murvin then moved to Kingston to live with his aunt in Trench Town, where he got to know the many reggae stars who lived there, such as The Wailers. Impressed by Murvin's voice, Alton Ellis was especially encouraging, as was Ken Boothe. Eric "Monty" Morris and Derrick Harriott taught him harmony, he learned to play guitar and he adopted a stage name suggested by Morris: Junior Soul.

An audition at Studio One did not pan out, though he did make the acquaintance of Lee Perry there, and that would pay off later. Depending on the source, in 1966, 1967 or 1968, he recorded his first record, 'Miss Cushie', for producer Sonia Pottinger, launching his recording career. His voice on his early records was fine, but unremarkable, giving little indication of the stunning reggae falsetto he would later unveil. He continued to work live, singing on the hotel circuit and specializing in soul music. Murvin next began recording for singer/producer Derrick Harriott. In 1972, Harriott covered one of Murvin's songs, 'Solomon', giving himself a big hit. A New York-based singer named Junior Soul had emerged, causing Murvin to seek a new stage name. With both Derrick Harriott and Lee Perry independently suggesting Junior Murvin, the new name seemed inevitable. But the newly rechristened singer was not satisfied with his career to this point. He retreated home to Port Antonio to further develop his songwriting and guitar playing. Jamaica's worsening social conditions caused a shift in Murvin's outlook and he began writing songs in a harder roots style than he had previously used. He returned to Kingston, but failed to achieve commercial success with any of the producers he worked with, even after launching what would prove to be reggae's greatest falsetto on the original 1974 rendition of 'Rescue The Children', produced by Harriott.

Using a tape recorder, he created a demo of a newly written song. He then describes having received a vision that he should bring the tape to Lee Perry. The vision would serve singer, producer and reggae fans well. The resulting song,

'Police And Thieves', was an international hit that still resounds today. The session led to an album of the same name, Murvin's first. It too was an international hit, and one of the greatest albums in reggae history.

A proposed second album for Perry did not come off as the Black Ark's demise truncated the project. Murvin subsequently recorded seven albums for other producers, the last in 2007, and amassed a total of approximately 50 singles throughout his career. His non-Black Ark work could not reach the high pinnacle achieved with the *Police And Thieves* album. Little reggae could. But that is not to say that there weren't other strong songs. 'Cool Out Son', a track that owes to his first song, 'Miss Cushie', produced in 1978 by Joe Gibbs and set to the "Real Rock" riddim is very good, with Murvin in fine voice. 'Jack Slick', produced by Prince Jammy in 1986, is also rewarding. But, rightly, Junior Murvin will forever be remembered for 'Police And Thieves'. Struggles with diabetes and hypertension ultimately took reggae's greatest falsetto from us at the end of 2013.

Police And Thieves

Junior Murvin's 1977 LP, *Police And Thieves*, is the most consistently excellent of any Black Ark-produced album, and one of the very best of all reggae albums. Its ten songs are varied but sound like a cohesive whole. And not one of the songs resembles a second-tier track, let alone a weak one.

Murvin brought to the table a spate of newly written socially conscious songs with a Rastafarian sensibility, along with his great sense of melody, expressive singing and a mighty falsetto. Sounding not quite like anyone else, soaring high and pure, his falsetto rolls across these songs like beads of mercury. Perry brought his Upsetters band and the production and arranging skills of reggae's most creative producer at their peak. He applies Black Ark effects both familiar and surprising. Horns are frequently heard, but they are altered. Compression and other effects give their sound a fuzzy burr. It's as if Perry had re-sculpted the bell of the instruments to his own unique specifications. And many songs sound as if a redshift has occurred, as Perry has the backing vocals and all the instruments (even, to a degree, the bass) join Murvin in the high-frequency range rather than at their norm. Traditional dub effects, most commonly in the form of notches of dropout/in, are also employed. *Police And Thieves* is a reggae sonic treasure. Below, I discuss the original ten tracks along with a look at the bonus track added to various expanded CD editions, as well as sundry other versions of these great songs.

'Roots Train'
The album's opener is the joyous and rousing 'Roots Train'. Songs in which trains conduct their worthy passengers to God's glory were originally a staple of American spirituals. They resonated especially well for the religious of Jamaica, where railroads once played a greater role than today, and these songs crossed over from gospel into reggae. (The Wailers' 'This Train' is perhaps the best-known example.)

Then train songs began to serve a second purpose: as a way in to celebrate the day's hottest topics. (This gave us such songs as The Ethiopians' 'Train To Skaville' and Desmond Dekker's 'Rude Boy Train'.) Murvin's train song fulfills both purposes, as he sings about boarding a train to Rastafarianism. ('Zion Train' by Bob Marley & The Wailers is similarly themed, an equally great train song.)

As is typical in such songs, Murvin explains that you have to be righteous of spirit and in behavior to board this train. Mid-song, he achieves religious ecstasy when he sings of the train's destination being a paradise where "everything is great!" The last word of each line gains even more emphasis when the backing singers jump in.

Though the song's theme is a traditional one, the Black Ark production is innovative. The song opens with an oddball production touch, as the introductory horns fade in with the beginning of the first note missing, further altering their already unusual sound. Nyah hand drums, ghostly sounds and various squiggling effects provide an undertone like nocturnal creatures scurrying on the floor of a cave. Introducing an effect that would be used on several songs on the album, processing comes to the bass, the instrument most typically left alone in a dub production. Toggled on and off rhythmically throughout the track, it becomes oddly squeezed with compression and trebly, adding to an already exotic-sounding song. Though seemingly strange bedfellows, Murvin's song, with a lineage from back in time and overseas, and Perry's state-of-the-art Black Ark Jamaican production could not be more mutually beneficial.

In addition to the dub version included on the deluxe edition that is described later in this chapter, another version, called 'Roots Train Number Two', made a surprising appearance in 2010. The standout track on the CD *Sound System Scratch*, released on the Pressure Sounds label, this energetic version is completely different from and just as good as the more commonly known dub. Horns and lead vocal receive most of Perry's attention in the form of processing and drop-out/in respectively, as the backing vocals are allowed to shine through.

'Police And Thieves'

It's safe to say that most record buyers in the USA and the UK had never heard anything quite like the title track of the *Police And Thieves* album. Grounded in earthy roots reggae, the sound would have been exotic enough for the uninitiated, but at the same time everything is so processed, it's psychedelically plush. The singer has an angelic falsetto, while he's singing about violence in the streets. How did foreign audiences react? The same way as they did in Jamaica – by making 'Police And Thieves' an enduring hit.

Perry doesn't equivocate, opening the song with a soft onslaught of Black Ark elements. An introductory drum roll is flanged. The hi-hat cymbals are oversaturated. A weirdly bobbing guitar chord resounds. The bass line and a pumping rootsy organ anchor the sound as Black Ark froth swirls all around them. Backing vocalists enter first, humming peacefully. Then Murvin enters gently with "Mmm, yes", and begins his song. With a chorus describing the gun-fueled conflict of the title, Murvin inadvertently created a universal soundtrack for any incident of civil unrest met head on by the authorities. Yet he delivers this strong subject so softly. His falsetto is languid with an effortless vibrato. The backing vocals often match him in register, making the song rich in treble. They're provided by Barry Llewellyn and Earl Morgan of The Heptones, who were on hand to record their own Black Ark album. (Somehow, there was little chemistry on that LP, *Party Time*, leaving The Heptones to criticize Perry's Black Ark sound.) The liner notes also state that superstars Sly Dunbar and Ernest Ranglin perform on the track, but it sounds more like Perry's house musicians than these recognizable players.

About midway through, Perry, hands on faders, applies notches of drop-out/ in that tug at the listener's attention, keeping the instrumentation dynamic and interesting as the song progresses. Murvin does the same with his vocals, introducing his wonderful idiosyncratic scat singing. With so much delivered in such an easy-to-listen-to song, 'Police And Thieves' is as intoxicating as a Jamaican cocktail where fresh fruit juice hides a dose of overproof rum. Audiences everywhere couldn't get enough of it, as borne out by the number of covers from the USA and UK that have appeared over the decades. With the best of intentions and a predictable outcome, the UK punk band The Clash covered the song in 1977. Though a spirited performance, one couldn't help but miss the sonics of the original that were flattened out punk style. It was successful from the band's point of view, but from a reggae perspective, it's not difficult to see why Lee Perry openly derided it. In 1998, former Culture Club lead singer Boy George recorded 'Police And Thieves' in a reggae style that nodded to the Black Ark sound. In 2007, former Nirvana member and Foo Fighter leader Dave Grohl also recorded the song in a style that was more of a cover of The Clash's cover. Perry frequently versioned the riddim, but perhaps too often too soon, stretching himself thin. Still, two of these versions are well worth hearing and are discussed later in this chapter.

'Solomon'

'Solomon' is a remake of a song Murvin recorded in his rock steady days. Though the 1967 original was not a popular record, his producer, Derrick Harriott, quickly covered it and had a hit. It was covered several times after that. The lyrics are clearly from a time before Murvin's mid-1970s enlightenment that brought him to Lee Perry with a parcel of new *conscious* songs. He brags about his knowledge of women being greater than Solomon's and how it protects him from gold-diggers. In the remake, rather than equivocate by introducing roots lyrics, Murvin happily embraces 'Solomon' and unfurls another incredible falsetto lead.

The earlier renditions of 'Solomon' by Murvin and Harriott were fine songs, but rock steady just didn't shimmer and throb like this. The Black Ark remake is preternaturally vivid, with a rotating kaleidoscope of stop-and-go bass, come-

and-go guitar, buzzy horns and intermittent rich harmony vocals. There is a twitchy chirping rhythm instrument that might have been a guitar in a past life. There are also big blunted notes that could be coming from either a heavily processed guitar, or a horn, or something else. Thanks to Perry's brilliant fader work, these notes are missing their heads, maneuvering into place just a moment before being too late. No, rock steady did not sound like this.

'Rescue Jah Children'

'Rescue Jah Children' is another superior remake of a song that Murvin previously recorded for his erstwhile producer Derrick Harriott. He trades the funky sound of the 1976 original for a dirge-like roots sound. The opening is so downbeat, it sounds like a funeral march. Why so down? Because Murvin is reading a newspaper that's filled with stories about starvation, pollution, abortion, poverty, false Rastas, black-on-black violence, financial corruption and wars in Rhodesia and Mozambique. Murvin laments this onslaught of bad news and wonders who will save the children from the state of the world.

This heavy message is delivered atop a lurching Black Ark riddim, built around a big, slow, flanging rhythm guitar, circling in lazy orbit. The horns are so processed that one can only imagine what these instruments from another planet look like, and a piano dares you to find it in the mix. Yet the sound is rootsy, with a Nyabinghi drummer and a rumbling bass line that heavily emphasizes the first beat. The vocals, as is consistently the case on this album, are excellent, with lead falsetto answered by a falsetto backing. As the song ends, all involved shake things up. Murvin delivers one of his distinctive scats and the backing vocals drop octaves lower to take on the chorus, as Perry drops out all the instruments except those which are most Black Ark-processed: the flanged guitar and buzzy horns. What other lament sounds so arresting?

'Tedious'

'Tedious' opens with a bravura performance of Black Ark production creativity. An introductory drum roll is so flanged and phased, it's made to play melody. From it, dramatic reggae springs forth, but suddenly gives way to a single processed sustained note of Murvin's falsetto. Perry makes it bounce in with an echoing effect – so strange, as echo typically makes sound bounce out instead. This gives way to a return of the swirling drums that reintroduce the reggae. It spins and buzzes with otherworldly horns and heavily processed vocal murmurs. Such attention to sound and mastery of production elevate the music to a new artistic level. Comparisons are few, but consider how the attention to sonics by Pink Floyd helped take their blues-based rock to something artistically grander.

Murvin eases himself into this sonic sculpture. With Black Ark emanations all around while the bass line steps up strong, he enters quietly by plaintively mentioning Moses, and Joshua, and then launches himself into the song. He begins with a story drawn from the Bible: Exodus 17:9, in which Moses gives Joshua a rod to lead with. He then takes this religious theme in a political direction: "Selassie gave Michael the rod to lead" the backing vocalists exclaim excitedly. Michael is Michael Manley, who adopted this Bible passage during his successful run for Jamaican Prime Minister in the early 1970s. During the campaign, he would brandish a walking cane that was a gift from Haile Selassie, calling it his "rod of correction" and he adopted the nickname Joshua. Murvin and the reggae community of Jamaica – the singers and musicians, the poor, the Rasta – were overwhelmingly pro-Manley, with his pro-poor message, promise of socialism and the apparent approval of God. Singing with great joy, Murvin explains that Manley will bring the faithful closer to Zion. He implores, "Let's get together" to build a new Jamaica, his beseeching pronunciation of "let's" requiring two syllables ("leh-hets").

Mid-song, where another producer might have added a sax solo, a long dub segment is inserted. Vocals are dropped out except for hints of murmurs and echoing stray utterances floating on a sea of Black Ark reggae. It makes 'Tedious' the longest track on the album, topping 5 minutes. By the time it fades out, you are struck by how this tremendous song is anything but what its name suggests.

'False Teachin''

'False Teachin'' is one of the best of this collection of fine songs. (Though my favorite changes each time I listen to the album, this one often bubbles to the top.) In optimal balance, Murvin's songwriting and singing, the instrumental arrangement, traditional dub and Black Ark effects all shine brightly.

Opening with a wailing cry, 'False Teachin'' is vehemently anti-alcohol (which Rastas reject as unhealthy and unholy) and pro-ganja (which they revere as healthful and sacramental). It's an indictment of the hypocrisy that makes one legal and the other not. Murvin takes Jamaica's institutions to task over this issue, calling the teacher a liar, the winemaker anti-child, and the preacher duplicitous, who "button his collar behind his back! Hiding his face from the pack". Humorously lampooning the authority of the parson was a theme in mento back long before Jamaican music was recorded. Here, the practice persists, but little humor is found. Murvin's vocals are mournful but emphatic, as if he takes no joy in singing so wonderfully about this travesty. Yet it's a joy to hear him. He adds an interval of great Junior Murvin scat to the song. And one of his interjections *It's true!* sustains the last syllable to soar as only Junior Murvin can.

For his part, Perry tinkers with the ingredients for this bowl of Black Ark sound, building an aural platform that elevates Murvin's song even further. The blacksmith-tapping-away cymbals and other familiar Black Ark sounds are heard. But the rhythm guitar is relatively unprocessed and stands out like bald granite on a green hillside. Organ and bluesy guitar licks appear only at moments deemed optimal by Perry and quickly evaporate. As is common on the album, short intervals of drop-out/in are heard intermittently, each giving the song a charge. Horns are processed, but not as much as on some of the album's other tracks. On the other hand, the swollen, strangled bass sound is perhaps the most processed reggae bass ever recorded, and adds even more sonic punch to the song. An oddball production touch emerges midway and grows to dominate the end of the track. At the end of each line of vocals, a single syllable from a second track of Murvin abruptly appears, only to be quickly choked off. By the end of the song, this builds into a strange, plaintive chorus of *ah!... ey!*, the likes of which can only be heard in a Black Ark production.

A dub version/melodica cut of 'False Teachin'', called 'Strong Drink', can be heard on the 2011 CD called *The Return Of Sound System Scratch* on the Pressure Sounds label. A largely instrumental version re-voiced by Murvin called 'Emotional Dub' can be heard on the Lee Perry 2013 release entitled *Roaring Lion*, where it is credited to The Upsetters.

'Easy Task'

'Easy Task' is a bluesy *sufferas* song, replete with bluesy guitar and a sad horn line. It opens with Murvin getting to the heart of the *sufferas'* dilemma. He muses that living is anything but easy, yet it's better than the alternative, while backing vocals trill and coo. But, as per the positive Rasta outlook, perseverance overcomes despair. On this song, Black Ark effects flow rather than roil, but Perry still brings some odd and inspired touches. A strange fluttering sound of indeterminate origin comes and goes throughout the song. And on a whim, Perry has the backing vocalists answer Murvin on the word "coffee" more emphatically than the song can otherwise explain. More of a solid member of the album than a cutting-edge track, 'Easy Task' is nonetheless a great song.

'Lucifer'
Devon Irons: *'Vampire'*

Sounding appropriately sinister, 'Lucifer' opens dramatically. The backing singers chant about the followers of 'Lucifer' with emphasis on the word "death", intoning in a much lower register than the norm for this album, as Black Ark production surges threateningly. Murvin cries out as if from the depths of the abyss. He condemns 'Lucifer' and his followers: the slavers of Jamaica's past. Murvin's outrage is incontrovertible as he lists their crimes. He sings of light conquering darkness in a voice that is the very beacon that cuts through the night.

Unlike the other songs on this album, the riddim for 'Lucifer' had a life prior to Murvin's version. It appeared a year earlier as 'Vampire' (aka 'Ketch Vampire' or 'Catch Vampire') by Devon Irons. There, the riddim was longer, had more dub and featured a relentlessly rhythmic organ/guitar combo where 'Lucifer' featured horns. Irons's version is just as good as Murvin's. It can be found on the Black Ark CD box-set collection called *Arkology*. (Choose this mix over the 12-inch disco-mix with DJ Dr. Alimantado that is found elsewhere.) The modest dub version, 'Ketch A Dub', can found on a CD called *The Upsetter Shop Volume 1 – Upsetter In Dub*.

'Workin' In The Cornfield'

Black Ark production gives 'Workin' In The Cornfield' a slow-motion spin. It's a dreamlike cyclone that inextricably pulls you in, driven by a slowly strummed rhythm guitar that's heavily flanged and echoed. It whirs in a strange elliptical orbit around the big, thick bass line. Murvin responds to this backing with a languid, bluesy vocal as he takes the larger social issues of this album and brings them down to a very personal level.

'Workin' In The Cornfield' is about the strength of the family unit. Poor laborer Murvin's lot in life is long days of fieldwork, sweating in the heat, unable to take a break for water or the toilet. But at home he has an unspoiled wife and son, Mary and Jerry. Although they're hungry, they're content in having one another and Jah, a point Murvin celebrates with a scat. Affectingly told, the production brings tremendous sonic weight to the notion that a good family and God are all one really needs.

This late in the LP, one might expect to have already reached the extent of Perry's production creativity. But in addition to the extreme flanging and familiar Black Ark buzzing horns, wordless backing vocals and come-and-go instruments, he continues to unveil new sounds. For example, there are picked blues guitar notes processed to the point of sounding like the mewing of a cat that is emoting along with the song. And there are two instances of a squelching sound that accent the song strangely but effectively. 'Workin' In The Cornfield' pumps very strange blood through its very human heart.

'I Was Appointed'

An introduction of buzzing horn(et)s kicks off the album's rocking closer, 'I Was Appointed'. It's an urgent song with a harder drum sound and a loping pace. Featured elements include the return of the strangled bass sound, a single beat of drop-out/in, the appearance of lead guitar at the song's end and, most surprisingly, rhythm piano that's completely unprocessed. They contribute to a perfect platform for Murvin to lay down some proclamations.

With great authority, Murvin makes the titular declaration that God has made him his messenger. As such, he sings again about issues already heard on the preceding songs on the album, such as the duplicity of the parson, abortion, pollution, financial corruption, thanking God and the need to do more for Jamaica's youth. Though it's not a concept album, 'I Was Appointed' still serves as a fine thematic summary, musical conclusion and explanation for the *Police And Thieves* album.

2009 Deluxe Edition

2003 saw an expanded edition of the *Police And Thieves* CD that added five bonus tracks to the original ten. Then, in 2009, Island Records expanded the album again, this time as a two-CD Deluxe Edition that includes the fifteen previous tracks and added another eighteen more, the focus of the following discussion. Surprisingly, especially since it is not mentioned on the case or in the liner notes, several of the original album cuts are presented here with significantly different mixes from any released before. The good news is that these alternative mixes are more often than not better than the familiar album mixes, and the fidelity is slightly better across the entire set.

The title track has a dubbier, spikier mix. Though the softer sound of the original mix is tough to beat, this wilder alternative is also great to have. 'Solomon's mix is the same, but here it gains a little curlicue of a jazz horn introduction and an ending that is extended by one minute. Though nothing revelatory happens at the far end, the groove was too sweet to have been truncated all these years. Likewise, the otherwise unchanged 'Rescue Jah Children' gains a minute on its end. It makes for a clearly better mix as Murvin continues to spar with the backing vocalists. 'Tedious' omits the long dub section with the dropped-out vocals and adds an extended ending. Tamer and coming in at half a minute shorter, the album mix is clearly preferable in this case, but this alternative is plenty good enough to merit its release.

The 23 bonus tracks include versions and alternative takes of the album tracks, as well as other songs from the Junior Murvin/Lee Perry collaboration, along with two short radio adverts. Understandably, after more than tripling the number of songs, few of the bonus tracks measure up to the original set. Having said that, there are some fine additions.

Of the many versions of the title track and its riddim, there are two standouts. 'Bad Weed' is a re-voicing of the riddim by Murvin. Rather than being about substandard marijuana, he sings about weeding out wolves in sheep's clothing – someone who appears to be a Rasta, but instead preys on the community. Here, the riddim is mixed for a softer sound and features oddball incidental percussion. It's a long track at more than 8 minutes, but it's not a disco-mix. Instead, it's a continuous vocal performance from Murvin. (A shorter version of 'Bad Weed' is also included.) Also worth hearing is the dub version of 'Police And Thieves' called 'Grumblin' Dub'. The riddim is made bouncier with echo effects and Perry applies maximum creativity in dropping Murvin's vocal track out and in. By mid-song, Murvin's vocals are masked and echoed to become clustered jumbles of Murvin sound, Black Ark style.

The dub versions of 'Tedious' ('Tedious Dub'), 'Roots Train' ('Version Train') and 'False Teachin'' ('Teachers Dub') are all very good, especially the last. It allows you to better appreciate the brilliant bass line that ranges unusually high. Perry again allows only select syllables and phrases from Murvin to come through. There is also a disco-mix of 'Roots Train'. It features added saxophone, an appended dub version and a DJ version by Dillinger.

Two alternative takes of album tracks are included. 'False Teachin'' features slightly different lyrics and a less-developed production, sounding like a stepping stone to the rendition released on the album. The alternative take of 'I Was Appointed' is more different from its album rendition than is 'False Teachin'', with its skankin' riddim. Though they are less revelatory than the correctly chosen album takes, fans of the album will certainly want to give these alternatives a listen.

'Cross Over'

There is a rendition of Junior Murvin's Lee Perry-produced 'Cross Over' that was only released on a 12-inch single; it is far superior to the mixes that have appeared on LP and CD, including the two versions on the Deluxe Edition of *Police And Thieves*. My copy is a US pressing on the Orchid Records label. Isha Morrison, Perry's then wife, has co-production credits bestowed on her. It's as brilliant as anything on *Police And Thieves*, but in a completely different way. Whereas 'Police And Thieves' is precisely rendered, 'Cross Over' is loose and spontaneous. It pairs an amazing, very stoned-sounding vocal by Junior Murvin with a spare, odd by its own standards, Black Ark backing. This loopy wonder sounds like it came from a celebration after wrapping up the *Police And Thieves* album.

An unchallenging reverb-soaked drum roll announces the song, as reggae's most astounding falsetto cuts loose with a heraldic wordless cry. The body of the song begins, and it's unusually relaxed for a Black Ark production. A two-note Hawaiian-sounding slide guitar phrase is featured along with assorted informal synthesizer burbles and brief touches of piano and picked guitar. The bass is subdued, and, really, it's the drums that are the lead instrument. Loose and creative, they are well treated with dub and, apparently equally well, so is the drummer with ganja.

As Murvin implores everyone to cross over to Rastafarianism, he sounds exceptionally content, or stoned, or likely both. If 'Cross Over' continued to meander in this way to its conclusion, it would still be a great song, but there are two more treats in store for us in this 6-minute epic, each introduced by another heraldic cry. The first is a section that features a brief scat, and then anti-gun lyrics, as the drums step out to play an audaciously loose dubby solo. Second, for the song's conclusion, Murvin unfurls a long laid-back scat, as more synthesizer sounds are heard. To hear Murvin wordlessly exercise his falsetto over such a loopy backing is reggae caviar to be savored. Only Bob Marley's famously epic scat in 'Punky Reggae Party' and Desmond Dekker's scat in 'Fu Manchu' can rival it. You'll want to sing along, though you'll probably have to settle for a lower octave. Perry concludes the song with a creative production flourish that only he would hit upon. He turns the reverb on the drums to full, and then fades the cacophony out. With the uncountable number of Lee Perry compilations available, it's astounding this slippery prize has eluded all nets. Let's hope the next compilation reels it in.

29 The Congos at the Black Ark and elsewhere

There are many great roots reggae vocal groups, each with its own sound and strengths. But no other group sounded quite like The Congos, and none could surpass the stunning heights they reached. Cedric Myton and "Congo Ashanti Roy" Roydel Johnson were both born in 1947, in Saint Catherine Parish and Hanover respectively. Myton was influenced by the singing of Nat King Cole, as well as that of his mother. Johnson received guitar instruction from Ernest Ranglin and counted Lee Perry as a childhood friend. Both began their musical careers once they moved to Kingston. Myton was a member of rock steady vocal group The Tartans, with Prince Lincoln Thompson, Devon Russell and Lindburgh Lewis. Johnson made a brief run at a solo career with a solitary single produced by Perry. He next became a guitarist and backing singer for Ras Michael & The Sons of Negus, and then for The Righteous Brothers, a vocal group that also included Yabby You and Albert Griffiths of The Gladiators.

When Perry had his Black Ark studio and internationally popular albums by Junior Murvin and Max Romeo under his belt, he invited Johnson to try again. Johnson brought Myton and a song called 'Fisherman' to the session, to which Perry brought Watty Burnett, sometimes billed as King Burnett. Younger than the other two by four or five years, the Port Antonio-born Burnett had more than a handful of recordings on his résumé, including a few for Perry. The recording of 'Fisherman' was an obvious success and led to an album. And so The Congos were formed and their *The Heart Of The Congos* album recorded.

With Cedric Myton's supremely wispy falsetto, Johnson's homey tenor and Watty Burnett's deep bass, The Congos' vocals were impressive. The only other group to approach this tonal range was The Wailers when Livingston sang high, Marley mapped out the middle ground and Tosh pushed his baritone down to bass for a line or two. The spectral, plaintive roots voice of Cedric Myton was one of Jah's gifts to roots reggae. Just as Harold Richardson had the quintessential rural mento voice, Myton was the quintessential roots reggae voice. The earthy and likable, Johnson is always a pleasure to hear. Though essentially a harmony singer rather than lead, when Burnett's voice was added (he was only heard as needed), it completed a vocal group that wanted for nothing.

The Heart Of The Congos

The Congos' 1977 debut album, *The Heart Of The Congos*, was underappreciated upon its release. Island Records, who released other Black Ark albums internationally, inexplicably declined to release this one. But it is now recognized as a roots reggae masterwork, and the last great album from the Black Ark. The album includes four long tracks (each topping 6 minutes) that are so sonically rich, strikingly sung and deeply spiritual that enjoying them is an immersive experience. So good are these tracks that they can be argued to be the pinnacle of both Black Ark production and roots vocal groups – no faint praise on either count. (What about the production of Junior Murvin's *Police And Thieves* album? Though it's a more consistently great album than *Heart Of The Congos*, these four tracks reach peaks even higher than those on Murvin's album. What about The Wailers' vocals? Although more versatile, consistent and prolific, even the mighty Wailers could not match the audacious harmonies that The Congos unleashed on these songs.) The other songs are all good, especially 'At The Feast', but cannot help but pale by comparison to these four supernovas. In 1996, the LP was expanded by the Blood And Fire label into a two-CD edition that includes full-length versions of the songs along with alternate mixes and dub versions, all taken from the master tapes. Other mixes have been released on other LP and CD editions, both commonly found and rare, but the Blood And Fire release must be considered the definitive edition.

'Fisherman'

'Fisherman' is a big catch of a reggae song. If this book of great songs had to be edited down to a handful of pages, 'Fisherman' would undoubtedly be included. To its every dimension – the singing, lyrics, melodies, spirituality, production and arrangement – the participants bring their very best. And that adds up to a tremendous song.

'Fisherman' is based on a traditional song, though The Congos expand it with new lyrics. At first glance, it appears to be a tale of fishermen working to feed their families, particularly the many "hungry belly pickney [children]". The lyrics first reveal their spiritual meaning when the chorus mentions reaching a higher ground, something that does not apply to the physical world of a fisherman. Then fishermen Simon, Peter, James and John feed the hungry. These names are familiar from two passages of the New Testament (Matthew 4:18–22 and Mark 1:16–19) that involve Jesus calling fishermen to his service as apostles to "become fishers of men". So the song works literally and symbolically, as the hungry children also represent the spiritually hungry.

With these lyrics and the lovely melody of 'Fisherman', The Congos could have made a captivating recording with just an acoustic guitar accompaniment. Instead, Perry would bring all his forces to bear to make 'Fisherman' a magnum opus. He sets up the song with an extended introduction. Two simultaneous drum/cymbal strikes lead into a drum roll, announcing the song like a gong. A free jam filled with percussion provides a stage for introducing The Congos. Even when limiting themselves to a repeated wordless syllable, their harmony is attention-grabbing. Another drum roll launches the body of the song, opening a sonic floodgate. The full complement of Black Ark processing pours in, making the music effervescent. The idiosyncratic cymbal sound, flanged rhythm guitar, squiggling undercurrent of oddball percussion flourishes are in full effect. There's no lead guitar, keyboards or horns, as the dense stew of a riddim and vocals does not leave any room for these instruments. The snare drum pops, mixed very high and dub-processed. In fact, with the exception of the bass, everything is processed to some extent. And the voices are no exception.

There is the reverb and digital delay on lead singer Myton's quivery vibrato, enhancing its ethereal nature. Johnson's voice is lightly treated in his few lines of lead, as he answers Myton's question about the types of fish in the catch (there's wenchman, sprat and mackaback, or shad). And Perry has each Congo multi-tracked. Sometimes they back themselves. At other times, their voices amass a roots reggae heavenly choir unlike any heard outside of this album.

The active mind of Lee Perry keeps listeners engaged by surprising them throughout the song's 6-minute length. Once things are well under way, rattling percussion and quivering scrap-metal noises are sprinkled in, as sound fills every cubic foot of air. Then, just at the point where you expect the song to wrap up comes a big surprise. Burnett enters with an unexpected rare stanza of lead vocals, as the other voices drop out. His bass voice introduces a new topic, singing about the *collie man*, the ganja seller, and his fine product. For Rastas, some marijuana would be useful, whether the fishing is for food or for wayward souls. Towards the song's end, Perry introduces drop-out/in, and a previously unheard saxophone appears in the final seconds of the song. This leaves the only question whether to *lift it up again* and replay this masterpiece, or to play the dub version.

A dub version called 'Bring The Mackaback' is included on the Blood And Fire edition of the *Heart Of The Congos*. It is not the only dub version of 'Fisherman' available, but it is the best. The effects quotient is raised, including a bouncing echo that doubles the rhythm guitar to exciting effect. The vocals are soon dropped out and banks of sound are shifted out and back in as the guitar returns to its normal pace, only to be later doubled again. These shifts are pure dub pleasure delivered by a true dub-master.

'Can't Come In'
Like 'Fisherman', 'Can't Come In' combines great roots reggae vocals, biblically informed spirituality and unparalleled sonics from Perry into a 6-minute reggae tour de force. But whereas the overall sound of 'Fisherman' is folky and grounded (or "docked", in better keeping with the title), 'Can't Come In' takes wing and glides right up to heaven's gate, which just happens to be the subject of the song. It gets right down to business, opening with reverbed drums and a flanged rhythm guitar providing a backdrop for a brief solo of rippling Nyah hand drum. (The Nyabinghi drummer is heard throughout the song, while Watty Burnett is nowhere to be found.) A bass joins, providing a melody as Myton emotes word-

lessly. The body of the song takes off, propelled by bass and drums and a flanged guitar spinning like rotor blades.

Myton and Johnson sing in loose unison, with Johnson coming in early on some lines and Myton singing others alone. But every note they sing together, their different but complementary roots voices harmonizing, results in a beautiful sound, filled with emotion, simultaneously earthy and heaven-sent. They could sing a grocery list, and we'd still have a great song. "Can't Come In" warns that only the righteous will be admitted through the gates of heaven. The Congos want to be sure that everyone understands this, singing how they will repeat this again and again to make sure of it. Subsequent stanzas are adapted from the Bible to better make this point. They draw from Matthew 25 (The Parable of the Ten Virgins), describing the need to be spiritually prepared and not frivolous. They change this to ten brothers, half who were wise and half who were foolish. This can be read as a description of those Jamaicans who have adopted a righteous Rasta lifestyle and those who have not, respectively. Later, The Congos add a common proverb to the weight of their argument: "a rolling stone gather no moss". Here it's used to warn against waiting until it's too late.

As with 'Fisherman', Perry introduces surprises where most songs would settle for repetition. Something percussive is processed into a sizzling sound (perhaps it's a Black Ark rattlesnake) that comes out of nowhere and quickly returns there. And just as the song seems to be heading for a fade-out, there is an unexpected key change. The vocals digress, erupting in a funky wordless riff that would be more expected on an Earth Wind & Fire track than here. The song quickly returns to normal, but with new lyrics as explicit references to Rastafarianism make a belated appearance, though it was understood from the start. In the last minute of the song, Perry alters the sound by introducing drop-out/in, charging the by now familiar chorus, keeping the song riveting to the last. And when the song is over, it's easy to imagine The Congos, and Lee Perry with his band and mixing board inside the gates of heaven, providing a musical accompaniment as others ascend. Regrettably, there does not appear to have ever been a dub version of 'Can't Come In' for no ascertainable reason.

'Ark Of The Covenant'
If 'Fisherman' was grounded and 'Can't Come In' soars, 'Ark Of The Covenant' burns with fervor. It opens with a brief sonic tableau, as two Black Ark-processed sounds are paired. First comes the strange groaning sound effect familiar to Black Ark fans as "the cow sound". Here it may represent an animal in pain, a dub shofar, a creak from the ark, all of the above, none of the above, or nothing at all. It's followed by Black Ark reverberant drums complemented with the sizzling sound also heard in 'Can't Come In'. The body of the song begins, and immediately a sense of wonder is conveyed. Bass and drums find a middle ground between marching and dancing. Snatches of lead keyboard and lead guitar are briefly heard until the

flanged rhythm guitar swells to displace them. Myton and Johnson sound awed as they sing with urgency about the ark, alternating the lead or harmonizing on various lines. (Once again, Burnett is unheard.) In the Bible, the Ark of the Covenant is described as a wood-and-gold chest that held the tablets bearing the Ten Commandments. But in this song's few lyrics, the Ark of the Covenant, Noah's ark, and some less familiar ideas are blended together, as two of everything, including animals, princes, priests and warriors were preserved in the Ark of the Covenant.

Instead of a chorus, a blazing wordless vocal interlude is heard twice. Courtesy of Lee Perry and his mixing board, we are treated to the sound of rootsy falsetto scat singing from multiple Mytons. Multiple Johnsons provide a solemn backing of wordless long low notes, chants of "the ark" and lines revived from the verse. It's all redoubled again via murky digital delay echo. Stunningly dramatic and uniquely beautiful, it's so evocative one can imagine the ark in response opening with a blinding brightness. Then, without warning, all vocals drop out, and a dub version of the song begins, disco-mix style. Drop-out/in is fully utilized, and strata of the arrangement are removed as others are revealed. One long interlude allows us to hear just the flanged guitar, spinning alone in space until it is joined by selected isolated drum strikes. Is that lead guitar just at the edge of audibility? More echo is employed than is usually heard in a Black Ark track and it is particularly effective when applied to the few vocal syllables that Perry has isolated. The end of the track is strewn with various rattles, clangs and the return of the cow sound. In any other context, this would be considered weird, but for Black Ark fans, it's a familiar part of the vocabulary. The Blood And Fire release includes a dub version 'Noah Sugar Pan'.

'Congoman'

'Congoman' is the fourth epic song from *Heart Of The Congos*. Although the expanded *Heart Of The Congos* CD contains three versions, another mix, released on the Lee Perry box-set called *Arkology*, improves on these and so it is described here. 'Congoman' is a Nyabinghi-reggae track, but an odd one. Along with a reggae drum kit, a drum machine is heard, rather than the expected Nyabinghi drum troupe, In a lesser producer's hands this would have been a fiasco bordering on sacrilege, but in Perry's it's a risk that pays off well.

The song features a strong rhythmic drive, with a cymbal emphasizing the third beat while a guitar chop answers on the fourth. Meanwhile, deep loud bass plays staccato clusters (surprisingly, it's played by the great organist Winston Wright). A gently flanging sound cycles softly, devouring any silence. Various keyboards, guitars and percussion come and go, as if wandering in to check out the proceedings. The overall result is a groove that's deep, dark and dense, like a black hole. There's no escape from it.

The singing (once again, from Myton and Johnson, sans Burnett) is soft and lightly processed, like murmurs drawn in from the spirit world. They wail wordlessly, and then coalesce into words, to sing a spacey, distant Nyabinghi chant. It opens with The Congos singing in unison of the titular character emerging from Africa. A barely audible Myton takes over and seems to be musing about soul, songs, drums and voices. Johnson takes over and implores Jah, and the two continue to exchange chanted lines, quietly *reasoning* on Rasta concerns as the riddim continues its unassailable groove. This version of 'Congoman' sounds like nothing so much as Nyabinghi-reggae originating from another planet.

The Congos after Scratch

After *Heart Of The Congos*, the group continued their career, but without Lee Perry as their producer, most often producing themselves. This began with two LPs in 1979. One of these included the two songs below that established the fact that, although Lee Perry undeniably enhanced their sound and helped develop their material, The Congos were capable of recording great songs without his involvement. But their post-Scratch career was not helped by departures (auxiliary member Burnett would leave), split-ups (Myton and Johnson would record separately) and substitutes (at one point, Myton's former Tartan bandmate, Lindburgh Lewis, was brought in) and different degrees of reunion. This makes counting true Congos albums difficult, but the number is about a dozen. The number of singles they recorded is no greater, since they were an album-oriented group right from their inception. All three Congos reunited with Perry in 2009 to record an album speciously called *Back In The Black Ark* that reads better than it sounds. The album disappoints, inevitably, as it is hard not to use *Heart Of The Congos* as a yardstick. They reunited again for the 2011 album *We Nah Give Up*.

'Youth Man'; 'Yoyo'
'Youth Man' and 'Yoyo' both come from the self-produced 1979 album, *Congo Ashanti*. The sound is pure roots with no flash, Black Ark or otherwise. The album includes an unusual participant in bassist Philippe Quilichini of Corsica, the extent of his documented reggae work. His other claim to fame was to produce a solo album by The Velvet Underground's Nico.

'Youth Man' opens with an introduction featuring a macabre organ lead over the fine reggae drums of Santa Davis. The hand drum-filled roots reggae backing is austere other than the inclusion of a bird whistle, and the matter-of-fact production is dub free until the song's final seconds. After the intense trips on the Black Ark, this no-place-like-home roots sound is no less of a pleasure, if a simpler one. Johnson sings most of the lead, sounding more soulful than he did on *Heart Of The Congos*. He frequently hands off to the tandem of a delicate Myton and the solid Burnett. The contrast between the three is a roots vocal delight. They sing of common roots reggae issues: the celebration of their African heritage and standing up for one's rights. The Congos learned a lesson from Lee Perry, and introduce new elements to the song's second half, rather than merely repeating the arrangement. By the time we hear a mid-song Tommy McCook sax solo, the arrangement begins to fill out, with the addition of horn riffs and the Rasta drummer gaining prominence in the mix. Johnson's singing reaches an emotional peak and the vocals conclude, leaving just the instrumentation to take over with a touch of traditional dub that takes the song to fade-out. In 'Youth Man', The Congos ignore any temptation to replicate Black Ark production and play to traditional roots reggae strengths. In the process, they create a great song without needing Lee Perry's involvement.

The same is true of 'Yoyo'. It features a fine roots backing that is humbly quiet, allowing plenty of room for the vocals. And what vocals they are. Myton provides a fine lead and a number of fine melodies that keep the song spellbinding throughout. He sings of a Rastaman whoshould not be judged negatively by his appearance, even though he's dressed in "sackcloth and ashes" and is idly playing with a yo-yo. Instead, he should be admired, as he is spiritually fulfilled: "He's a highest esteem, he's a man of his own." The harmonies on 'Yoyo' are absolutely thrilling. Accompanying Myton's lead are Burnett's bass and a second track of Myton, singing falsetto haloed with reverb. The resulting harmony is audacious, beautiful and dramatic enough to give you the chills.

'Wheel'

'Wheel' is The Congos' contribution to the 1997 multi-artist tribute collection called *Fire On The Mountain Volume 2 – Reggae Celebrates The Grateful Dead*. The Congos prove to have an unexpected affinity with the source material and provide the CD with its standout track. A drum roll introduces a funky free-jazz opening and a second roll launches the body of the song. It finds The Congos (most likely a Myton/Burnett/Lindburgh line-up) in fine form, singing over a competent if unremarkable roots reggae backing. Starting with wordless wailing, they then take on Robert Hunter's lyrics, and it's a revelation how suited to roots reggae his words prove to be. The Congos wear them like a glove. In various lines, they move from thoughtful to wary, to imploring, depending on the demands of the lyrics. It's an impressive performance, especially considering that it was recorded a full two decades past the group's prime and almost as long after the peak of roots reggae.

30 More great dub

In no particular order, here are some more assorted great dub tracks. As you will see, great dub can come from famous dub-masters, other familiar names or from those who are neither.

King Tubby and Soul Syndicate: *'Dub Of Righteousness'*
We have already seen King Tubby's role in the creation of dub music. He was born Osbourne Ruddock, in 1941, in Kingston. His musical career had its genesis in his teen years as a radio repairman, where his affinity for the electronics of sound began. A natural, he would soon open his own electrical-goods repair shop. It is said that a particularly nasty period of dance-crashing *mash ups* of speakers by rival sound systems made Tubby a fixture on the dancehall scene. He then began to build powerful amps to meet the sound systems' special need for loud volume and deep bass. At the start of the 1960s, he built himself a radio transmitter and ran his own illegal radio station for a short time. In 1968, he combined all these skills and interests by launching his own sound system, called Tubby's Hometown Hi-Fi. Unsurprisingly, it was distinguished by its high sound quality and by Tubby's tinkering with the sonics, employing echo and reverb effects. When he was hired by Duke Reid to scrub the vocals from some of his rock steady hits to create instrumental versions, he did something more than that, creatively leaving in parts of the vocal, but dropping out the rest. Echo and reverb would quickly follow and these versions created a sensation at the dance. The dub version was born and was here to stay. In 1971, Tubby opened his own studio in his home, which he upgraded in 1973. Unsurprisingly, it was known for its immaculate sound. (Tubby was even known for keeping his equipment spotless.) Many producers worked with him there, often utilizing his dub skills. Kindred spirit Prince Jammy came to work there as an apprentice, and he too would come to change the sound of reggae. In 1989, outside of his home that was situated in Kingston's rough Waterhouse neighborhood, Tubby was shot and killed. It was assumed to be a botched robbery, and the gunman remains unknown today.

'Dub Of Righteousness' is just one example of how a dub-master like King Tubby could take a good song and make it a great one. The good song is 'Righteous Works' by Brent Dowe, formerly of The Melodians, from 1979, a song already tinged with dub. Dub paradoxes are rife in Tubby's version: it simultaneously sounds sparser and lusher than the original version. And the song's message is more powerful here, even as much of the vocal track is discarded. Dowe's song contained some incredibly strong lines, each of which is maintained here. But not all his vocals met this standard, and those which did not Tubby pruned away. When the vocals unexpectedly vanish, it actually increases the focus on what was just heard, emphasizing the message and making less into more. As in the original version, the dub version opens with Dowe wailing about the wicked getting their just deserts in the afterlife. But mid-sentence, the vocal suddenly echoes away, leaving the last thought unresolved for contemplation as we listen to sinewy instrumental dub. Processed drums and a see-saw bass line that hypnotizes lay down a groove. A rhythm guitar treated with reverb and echo joins in. The vocals drop back in abruptly and dramatically to deliver an emotionally charged couplet and echo away again. Later, reverb paints selected slats of rhythm guitar with incandescence until one chord suddenly springs off screen in a bouncing arc of echo. Heard in uncountable dub versions, this classic move is performed here by the man who made it a classic. 'Dub Of Righteousness' can be heard on the King Tubby's album *Freedom Sounds In Dub*.

Scientist: *'Round 7'*

Scientist was born Hopeton (though some call him Overton) Brown, in 1960, in Kingston. He learned about electronics from his father who, like King Tubby, was a repair technician. By the 1970s, he too was building powerful amplifiers for sound system operators. Brown was fascinated by the fact that, at the sound systems, the demands of King Tubby's dub versions would cause the amps he built to run red-hot. This inspired him to meet Tubby. He then became a frequent customer of his, buying electronics parts. Brown impressed Tubby enough to parlay the relationship into a job at his studio. At first he did electronics work, but later would become involved in mixing. He was given his moniker by another producer on the scene, Bunny Lee. Scientist's first production was Barrington Levy's 1977 'Collie Weed', and the two careers would cross paths many times thereafter. A popular and prolific dub-master, since 1980 Scientist has recorded about 40 albums, either alone or "clash style" (a term explained below). He is still active and is currently offering classes in dub mixing.

A great dub track can be found on the 1980 LP with the taxonomical name of *Scientist Versus Prince Jammy – Big Show Down At King Tubby's*. The meaning of this title is immediately clear to reggae fans: dub-masters Scientist and Prince Jammy are *clashing* at King Tubby's studio. In addition to the previously described *showcase* album format, the *clash* album is another uniquely Jamaican configuration. In it, two artists, whether singers, DJs or dub-masters, alternate tracks, competing for your favor. Scientist's track, 'Round 7', may be his single best production. It's a dub version of Barrington Levy's 'Bounty Hunter', a good song, but one with a bone-dry sound that cries out for dub. Its cries answered, 'Bounty Hunter' becomes one among no small number of songs that were all but rendered superfluous by a vastly superior dub version.

'Round 7' opens with a count up and informal drum roll that were omitted from 'Bounty Hunter', but left on here like the rind. The opening stanza of the original's vocal is intact, though the drums subtly drop out, tipping you off that there's more dub to come. So it's very satisfying when the expected first occurrence of echo hits, as a sharp guitar chop tightly echoes off to oblivion. But Scientist is just getting started, as he turns the song into a three-ring circus with Levi, the bass and drums each under a spotlight, while dub guitar and organ provides support. Levi's ring is empty often more than the others, as early on his voice echoes away. Late in the song, it makes a return, drenched in reverb and echo, seemingly back from a long journey to an unknown place. The hypnotic bass line is almost always present, but when it is not, its absence is just as mesmerizing. The drums receive more effects than is typical in dub. Not only are reverb and drop-out/in employed, so is echo, creating an exciting asymmetrical polyrhythm. Even an odd squelching effect is applied, as mixing-board sliders and knobs are worked. This makes 'Round 7' one of the most memorable examples of drum dub ever recorded. As for the album's clash, the winner is Scientist with a knockout in round seven.

Inner Circle and The Fat Man Riddim Section: *'Fidel At The Control'*
'Fidel At The Control' was produced in 1978 by Lancelot "Maxie" McKenzie, who was active from the late 1970s through the early 1980s. It's a dub version of the previous year's 'Peace Treaty Special' by Jacob Miller, a song whose melody was based on the popular American Civil War song, 'When Johnny Comes Marching Home Again'. Miller's original is a good song, even an important song. This was especially true when it was performed at the One Love Peace Concert, where headliner Bob Marley tried to end a near-civil war in Jamaica by bringing together the heads of warring political factions on stage.

But with the vocal completely dubbed out, and all the classic dub effects brought into play, the dense riddim is unpacked and allowed to fully spread its wingspan. Sly Dunbar's tom-toms, soaked in reverb, star. The bass anchors and brings the melody from Miller's version. All the other instruments flit in and out *dubwise*. They are rhythmically interlocked expertly, and are painted with reverb or echo, as the moment demands. In this, Maxie orchestrates a high-energy dub narrative that is as engrossing as a lead vocal. And as much as I love to hear Jacob Miller sing, this dub is so strong, he is not missed here at all. 'Fidel At The Control' can be heard on the CD with the ungainly title of *Inner Circle And Fatman Riddim Section – Heavyweight Dub + Killer Dub*.

Big Youth: *'Big Youth Special'; 'Black Man Message'; 'Dread Organ'*
It's 1975, and a session arranged by producer Tony Robinson for an LP by top DJ Big Youth is under way. There's just one problem: for whatever the reason, Big Youth's performance is turning out to be a substandard one for him. But all is

not lost. There's a more than capable backing band in Skin, Flesh & Bones, featuring the talents of Sly Dunbar on drums, Lloyd Parks on bass, Ansel Collins and Errol "Tarzan" Nelson on keyboards and Bertram "Ranchie" McClean on guitar, as well as a seasoned recording engineer in Errol "E. T." Thompson. And proving to be most important of all, there is an unidentified white American harmonica player present. (He is often assumed to be Lee Jaffe, who famously played with Bob Marley & The Wailers around this time. But it does not sound like Jaffe. It's more likely Jimmy Becker, who played with Skin Flesh and Bones on more than one occasion, as well as with Black Uhuru.) He plays red-hot leads over three of the session's riddims. Rhythmic and creative, his playing inspires Robinson and Thompson to salvage the session with three outstanding harmonica-based dub versions. Their inclusion on Big Youth's *Dreadlocks Dread* album makes this release essential for dub fans, if not for DJ fans.

'Big Youth Special' opens with a too-cool reggae groove, from a lean, muscular riddim of just bass, drums and rhythm guitar. The harmonica enters to jam hard and expressive. It evokes a Western-sounding bluesiness that becomes spacey when echo hits. It takes a break, and the trio recharges the groove, now tougher than ever. The harmonica remounts to ride the riddim to its end like a champion. 'Black Man Message' is a version of the riddim from the great Dennis Brown song, 'Some Like It Hot' (a track described later in this book; page 335). The trio kicks it off, and harmonica joins to revive Brown's melody. This lead is so articulate and inventive, dub can't improve on it. So the dub-master leaves the harmonica alone, turning his attention instead to the other instruments. All involved do Dennis Brown's great song proud. 'Dread Organ' is a more oblique track than the other two. Bass and drum set the stage as the dub casually cycles our attention between snatches of guitar, harmonica and saxophone, making this track more of an ensemble piece than a harmonica showcase. But by this point there is no doubt that, just as it did in mento, ska and other forms of reggae, harmonica had ensured its place in dub music.

Linton Kwesi Johnson: *'Peach Dub'; 'Victorious Dub'; 'Brain Smashing Dub'; 'Iron Bar Dub'; 'Shocking Dub'; 'Funny Dub'*
These vivid dub versions of Linton Kwesi Johnson songs (as described later in this book; pages 529–31) are the best from the 1980 album, *LKJ In Dub*. (Two other volumes of *LKJ In Dub* would follow.) Almost purely instrumental, full credit must be given to LKJ's MVP, Dennis "Blackbeard" Bovell, who serves as Johnson's multi-instrumentalist, bandleader, producer, and dub-master, as well as to his aptly named backing outfit, The Dub Band. Immediately recognizable by its distinctive sound, this is highly competent dub drawn in bold lines. Strong riddims from the big brassy Dub Band are treated with moderate amounts of drop-out/in, reverb and echo by Bovell's sure hand. With all involved being UK-based, this may be the best dub album to arise from outside of Jamaica.

Sly & Robbie and Groucho Smykle: *'Skull And Crossbones'; 'Back To Base'*
The two final tracks (joined together by a wild burst of effects) of Sly & Robbie's 1984 dub album, known alternatively as *Reggae Greats* or *A Dub Experience*, are a showcase for dub-master Paul "Groucho" Smykle. Groucho was born and bred in the UK. He started his career cutting dub plates for the UK's Shaka sound system. This work caught the attention of Virgin Records, which hired Groucho to mix dub versions. When Island did the same, and Groucho found himself versioning the label's superstar roster, dubbing Bob Marley & The Wailers, Black Uhuru (his work on their *Dub Factor* album is described in the chapter on the band; pages 363–4) and Sly & Robbie amongst others. Groucho has also worked with such non-reggae acts as Grace Jones, David Bowie, PiL, Miami Sound Machine, Big Audio Dynamite and others. Although he utilizes traditional dub techniques, he additionally employs others that are alien to dub from Jamaica. But his immediately recognizable sound still honors the spirit of Jamaican dub. Subsequent UK-based dub artists would deviate from this spirit to a greater degree.

'Skull And Crossbones', a dub version of Errol Holt's 'My Heart Is In Danger', opens with a flourish. Instead of settling for the introductory drum roll of the riddim, Groucho ups the ante by grafting a brief sound montage to the track's beginning. First heard is the sound of footsteps wandering across the stereo soundstage, which are abruptly replaced with two snippets of processed samples of Dunbar's electronic drums. These sonic fireworks serve to signal that the song we are about to hear is a Groucho dub. Holt's opening chorus of "My eyes told me that my heart is in danger" is left intact, until it echoes away. But not before it sets up the urgency of the track. Though traditional dub echo, reverb and drop-out/in are heard, everything sounds unusually juiced, with each instrument processed to sound extra punchy and percussive. Spacey sound effects, strangely altered voice samples, horns and the return of the vocal track are trotted in and out of dub spotlight. It's such ear candy, you'd better let the dentist check your hearing at your next examination. Midway, Groucho introduces an idiosyncratic twist. He makes it sound like the tape the song is being mixed on briefly breaks down, requiring a moment of rewind, as a couple of errant echoing syllables of vocal somehow escape the mixing board. All without missing a beat. It's reminiscent of – though more sophisticated than – a device used by Lee Perry on his production of The Wailers' 'All In One Part 2'.

'Back To Base' continues in this vein but this very introspective piece of dub is more exotic. It lacks any vocals and utilizes a riddim that is unfamiliar from any other version. All instruments get the dub treatment. This includes a strummed guitar playing a contemplative droning pattern that's atypical for reggae, majestic, heraldic horn lines, a bouncing, echoing keyboard and, of course, excellent bass and drums courtesy of Sly Dunbar and Robbie Shakespeare. To this, Groucho adds chirps, squeaks and what sounds like a percussion ratchet instrument squeezed through some heavy processing to become a scrunchy presence in the soundscape. With the latter, and in other ways, he recalls Lee Perry's Black Ark sound, great praise for a dub-master. But Groucho's sound is his own, rather than being Black Ark-like. His sharp, immaculate processing sounds digital, while Perry was analog in all its glory.

At one point, the horns return to usher in one of those complex rolls that only Sly Dunbar plays. Groucho drops everything except the drums and bass, allowing full attention to be turned to one of the greatest batteries in Jamaican history. Thus inspired, he really goes to work. With the bass playing on, he then drops out the drums, only to allow strategically chosen, carefully processed, shattered pieces to rhythmically drop back in/out. This is reminiscent of Lee Perry again, but of the way he sliced and diced vocals rather than drums. Groucho then restores the drums entirely, but with added clouds of processing around each strike, as the other instruments find their way back onto the field. An evocative, introspective and strange piece of dub, it's the perfect soundtrack for a march into inner space.

Burning Spear: 'The Ghost'; 'Black Wa-Da-Da'
In 1976, Burning Spear – or, more accurately, producer Jack Ruby – released Garvey's *Ghost*, a dub version of Spear's *Marcus Garvey* album from a year before. From it comes 'The Ghost', a justifiably celebrated dub version of the original album's title track.

'The Ghost' simply outdoes the respected vocal version, as on this day, dub was a more dynamic front man than the singer. Ruby's use of dub is singular. Echo is not employed at all nor is it missed. Instead, 'The Ghost' is an exploration of drop-out/in, perfectly suited for the dense arrangement of its source material. The vocal track is dropped outright, while the bass and drums are left intact for the entire track. On this scaffold, the surface area of the song is increased as doors rhythmically open and close on the remaining instruments, creating a baffle that reveals (and creates) musical details that would not otherwise be heard.

An opening drum roll from Leroy "Horsemouth" Wallace guarantees excitement. It's followed by a brief conversation between slurred roots lead guitar from Earl "Chinna" Smith and organ. They vanish, to be replaced by Nyabinghi drums sounding more aggressive than the norm, which vanish to reveal a striding reggae rhythm guitar, which in turn vanishes to introduce a repeated muted piano chord, distant and spacey with reverb, which vanishes to reveal Bernard "Touter" Harvey's clavichord appending an unexpected melodic tail to the piano. Fantastic! The various instruments begin to reappear and re-disappear, combining and recombining. A piece of a phrase from a horn section is belatedly introduced as the arrangement becomes more fleshed out as the song progresses. But never do we come close to hearing all the instruments at once. Drop-out/in this masterfully applied may make you wonder whether you will want to hear all the tracks of a reggae song simultaneously ever again.

Another fine track on Garvey's *Ghost* is 'Black Wa-Da-Da', the dub version of 'The Invasion'. Like Augustus Pablo's '1 Ruthland Close', this is a fine example of *hard dub*, as instruments drop in and out in a delightfully rough manner. This is softened by the song's creamy center, where Spear's vocal is dropped in with an emotional plea, for Jamaica's love. In this hard dub sonic context, Spear's appeal carries more power than it does in the original version.

Lone Ranger: *'Dentist Dub'*
'Dentist Dub' is a dub version of Lone Ranger's 1977 DJ track, 'Apprentice Dentist'. Though it's credited to Ranger, he is not heard at all. The riddim came from an earlier recording from the start of the decade; a Sound Dimension instrumental led by Jackie Mittoo's organ called 'The Thing'. All three versions were produced by Coxsone Dodd.

'Dentist Dub' is the version to hear. It's a shining example of the classic Studio One dub sound. The formula is to take a riddim from the cusp of the 1960s and 1970s that has an already electrifying rococo arrangement and apply just enough reverb and drop-out/in (but not echo). It creates a vivid new sound dimension, as if gilding the song's edges. Especially the drums.

There's an insistently chugging rhythm guitar, a brilliant and busy bass line and a frenzied organ riff that is answered by a calming two-note refrain from a horn section. Without the DJ or lead organ from the other versions, dub manipulation is the lead instrument. The deck is expertly shuffled as instruments drop in and out, while reverb makes key moments pop. Throughout the track, you can hear a singer (not the Lone Ranger) bleeding through, showing the limitations of mixing on magnetic tape. In other music, this would be seen as a major technological problem. But here, it's just another dub effect; the visitation of the ghost vocal from another (unfamiliar and perhaps never released) version that makes the sound more interesting. But for all this, the stars of the track are the drums of Fil Callender. 'Dentist Dub' is an especially good example of two things: how Callender's slinging, swinging drum-playing was such a precious and distinctive element of Studio One reggae of a particular time; and how the right application of reverb made his playing sound preternatural. Like a painting suddenly revealed to be a bas-relief, dub makes his playing equally enjoyable as art and as artifice. 'Dentist Dub' is available as a bonus track on the expanded edition of the Lone Ranger CD called *On The Other Side of Dub*.

The Revolutionaries: *'Kunta Kinte (Version One)'*
Specializing in roots and dub, backing band The Revolutionaries were prolific in the latter half of the 1970s. Also known as The Revolutionaires, their history includes the first coming together of the rhythm section of Sly & Robbie. The group started as the house band for producer Joseph Hoo Kim (also known as Jo Jo Hookim) at his Channel One studio, but they worked with other producers

as well, such as Sonia Pottinger. In just five years from their formation in 1975, counting co-billings, the group recorded about 45 albums and 60 singles.

Their instrumental 'Kunta Kinte' was produced by Jo Jo Hookim in the late 1970s. A number of mixes are available on different albums and singles, but the clearly superior mix became available in 2007 on the CD compilation called *Drum Sound – More Gems From The Channel One Dub Room 1974 To 1980*. It is said to have been rescued from a *dub plate* – a single-copy pressing of a custom mix for exclusive use by a particular sound system. It's good that it was. This is an exceptional piece of dub, tougher than tough and surprising throughout.

Take the opening, for example. It begins with a painfully loud bleeping note of feedback, like an urgent communiqué from a satellite. Over this, a dreamy organ riff is repeated, sounding like it wandered in from a Pink Floyd concert, circa 1974. A low fog-horn sound joins arrhythmically, adding to this experimental, spacey sonic collage that at the 30-second mark still has no hint of reggae.

But that changes in an off-the-beat instant, as bass, drums and guitar crash in. Sly Dunbar creates an absolutely *wicked* elaborate shuffling drum beat as only he can. Its kinetics sweep the introduction away. Robbie Shakespeare matches his partner's drive with a muscular bass line that gives the track its melody. A rhythm guitar enhanced with a bouncing echo effect and reverb adds to the song's energy, rhythmic complexity and melody. With just three instruments, The Revolutionaries established a complex and authoritative dub groove. Then comes the next surprise. The guitar drops out and a second drum track fades in, as Dunbar works out his tom-toms, giving the song a polyrhythmic charge. It ends in time for another surprise: an interval of syncopated rhythmic simplification of the type that was an early differentiator as dancehall began to split off from roots. Dunbar returns to the shuffle beat, only to elaborate on it, as odd ratcheting sounds join, and piano makes a belated appearance and then a quick disappearance. Each of these elements comes around again before the song's abrupt end, making for a most bracing and engaging dub.

31 Great mento-reggae by Stanley Beckford and others

The 1970s saw the advent of mento-reggae, reggae with mento musical elements and/or a strong mento feel. Though there were not a great number of songs in this style, and they were not totally uniform in their arrangement, the body of work was large enough for a classic mento-reggae sound to emerge. This was sunny reggae with happy piano and an exaggeratedly springy guitar chop that alluded to banjo. The rhythm is a simplified interpretation of a mento rhythm remembered from the past. The singer often had a country voice. Songs were frequently renditions or adaptations of old mento standards. And when they were not, they were lyrically mento-like, often a detailed observation of one of life's ribald predicaments. Woefully neglected by the CD format (with one exception), these songs are worth the effort to track down.

Stanley Beckford

Possessing a classic rural mento voice, high, nasal and expressive, Stanley Beckford did more to bring a country sound to reggae than any other singer, and he is mento-reggae's premier artist. He was born in 1942 in the parish of Portland. Both of his parents died when he was young, and he moved to Kingston to be raised by his grandparents. The early high point of his musical career came at the start of the 1960s, when, in his teens, he was successful on Vere Johns's Opportunity Hour. But this did not translate to immediate success as a recording artist. Instead, Stanley found himself occasionally performing live on the Kingston hotel circuit, but mostly working as a night watchman. It was his experiences in this latter job that led to his penning 'You Are A Wanted Man'. The song impressed producer Alvin "GG" Ranglin and opened the door to a recording career in 1973. Under his own name, briefly as Bellfied, with The Starlites and, later, as Stanley & The Turbines, Beckford recorded original reggae, reggae renditions of mento songs, and mento-reggae. (The latter includes a singular example of a mento-reggae waltz, the delightful 'Domestic Affair', recorded as a duet with a female singer and credited to Stanley & Clover.) He released close to 50 singles and four albums, primarily with Ranglin producing. After getting his feet wet with dancehall remakes of his songs, he belatedly began a mento career, a story we'll pick up in the next chapter.

With an impressive string of hits, and after winning Festival's songwriting competition no less than four times, Stanley Beckford was an extremely popular musician in Jamaica. He was also popular in South America, where there's a strong appreciation for rural reggae. (This seems especially true for Brazil, and for Panama, where they recorded their own rural mento, thanks to the influx of Jamaicans who worked in construction on the Panama Canal.) He is best known for his biggest hit, the double-entendre song, 'Soldering'. Described below, it's a great song, but certainly not his only one. Stanley Beckford passed away in 2007 after a battle with throat cancer, but not before winning fans around the globe and reminding reggae fans of the music's mento roots. Below are discussed Stanley Beckford's greatest mento-reggae tracks.

'Soldering'
'Soldering', produced by Alvin Ranglin in 1975, was Beckford's biggest hit and his signature song. Like many of his songs, it was adapted from a mento source, but in this case the lineage was more circuitous. In 1965 Desmond Dekker recorded a ska that is most likely the first recording to bear the title 'Soldering'. It was an adaptation of the old ribald folk/mento song 'Rukumbine'. Dekker increases the randiness quotient by adding a new stanza with a slightly varied melody about young girls wanting the unromantic titular expression for sex. He may have been influenced by an earlier, much milder song, a Chin's Calypso Sextet golden-age single called "Woman's Tenderness". Its chorus evinces the same melody and cadence, but here, women instead want tenderness, not soldering. A few years after Dekker's song, a hot fife-led instrumental mento version of 'Soldering' appeared on Sugar Belly's album, *Linstead Market*. It preserved the melodies from 'Rukumbine' as well as from Dekker's addition.

Beckford's reggae rendition features an outsized spongy bounce, the instrumentation's only mento-reggae element. It jettisons 'Rukumbine' altogether, and Beckford expands on Dekker's content, with lyrics showing that while the young girl wants soldering, she is quite selective:

> She said she don't want no young man, 'cause young man drink too much white rum.
> She said she don't want no soul man, 'cause soul man fast asleep in bed.
> She said she don't want no dreadlock, 'cause dreadlock smoke too much collie.
>
> © Westbury Music Ltd

Regardless of its origin, Beckford's new lyrics, spirited singing and country voice made 'Soldering' his own. It immediately spawned a spate of covers and answer records from a variety of artists. Even golden-age mento great Count Owen paid tribute, recording a rendition that was faithful to Beckford's in every way, as one of only two singles he recorded in the 1970s.

'Dada Beg Your Pardon'
Produced by Barrington Jeffrey in the late 1970s, the irresistible 'Dada Beg Your Pardon' is a mento-reggae song that combines the strengths of both genres. Fur-

ther demonstrating their versatility, the great rhythm section of Sly & Robbie, along with a rhythm guitarist, play a simplified mento-reggae beat. Reggae creativity is heard in the dueling guitar and bass sounds, processed to sound strangled. The hand drum enjoys its dual citizenship in the roots reggae and rural mento camps, while Beckford's voice is pure mento, as is his song. It's a lively, sweet, slightly naughty tale of what he assures his father was an accident. A double-tracked Stanley, harmonizing with himself, opens with the titular apology for destroying his father's garden. He then explains how this came about. He brought a girl, Madeline, into the garden. But when his father turned the lights off, a brawl ensued. The situation takes its toll on both Stanley and his father's garden, as the tussle moves from the dandelion bed, to the rose bed, onto the pumpkin patch.

Though his is an original composition, Stanley may have been influenced by an earlier song, but not an old Jamaican one. There are similarities in the refrains of Stanley's song and '[I Beg Your Pardon] I Never Promised You A Rose Garden', a massive US pop hit by country singer Lynn Anderson of the same year. 'Dada Beg Your Pardon' is available on the Stanley & The Turbines album called *Africa* in its LP release and *Brown Gal* in its CD release on the Tuff Gong label. It also contains two other fine mento-reggae songs in 'Broom Weed' and 'Brown Gal'. It can be recommended as the best Stanley Beckford album as well as the best album for mento-reggae (albeit there are only a few of these, and this is the only one to have been released on CD).

Great mento reggae by others

Prince Brothers: *'Ram Jam'*
The vocal team of Neil and Rupert Prince released a string of mento-reggae singles in the mid- to late 1970s including a hit in 'Ram Jam'. They also released an album collection with the same name, one of very few mento-reggae albums, though it also touches on R&B and calypso. The album's credits show that, in addition to singing, Neil was the songwriter when mento songs were not being covered, while Rupert handled the role of producer.

The popularity of 'Ram Jam' can be seen by examining the forensic evidence. It was released on five different imprints in Jamaica and the UK, with twice that number of labels printing variations, i.e. there were repeated pressings over time. It is not hard to see why this was the case, as it is a very likable song. It possesses all the requisites of the classic 1970s mento-reggae sound: sweet piano, a bouncy rhythm guitar beat and mento singing. The brothers Prince delight with their melodic, nasal, rural-style voices and country harmony. And they tell a richly detailed story.

The song is an expansion of the folk standard 'Hog Ina Me Minty', first recorded by golden-age mento artist Lord Messam (a song described earlier in this book; page 45) and by many others since. That song complains about the animal getting into the singer's sweet potato (aka "minty" or "coco") patch. In 'Ram Jam', the song's second meaning is built upon, as another man is getting into Neil's romantic territory. It opens with an introduction that finds the Princes sounding exhausted. They bemoan their failure to make their girlfriend both happy and faithful. The body of the song begins with music every bit as merry and sprightly as mento-reggae can be, and we learn more. Neil confronts his woman about running around while pretending to visit her mother. He calls her "Easy Girl" and threatens that, if she does it again, he will "tear out your ram-jam"! This threat turns out to be as ineffective as it is outrageous, as Neil recalls a galling incident at a dance. He remembers the date well: Saturday, July 8. One minute, Easy Girl was just sitting there. Neil turns around, and suddenly, "me see man ina me jam-a". This leaves the Princes to sing 'Hog Ina Me Minty', though it does not seem to give them much solace. Its popularity was so great, The Prince Brothers would return to the riddim, melody and subject matter of 'Ram Jam' for a sequel in 'Open The Door'.

Naaman Lee: *'Sweeter Than Sugar'*
Throughout the 1970s, producer and singer Naaman Lee was responsible for about a dozen singles. As a lead singer, he recorded mento-reggae and reggae. He also produced some rustic mento and even quadrille by The Old Timers, The Harmonizer, and others. The best record he was involved with was his late-1970s mento-reggae single, 'Sweeter Than Sugar'. As the title hints, it's a happy, appealing song. Lee muses about love, singing in his non-virtuoso but endearing mento voice. The backing features sharp, creative drum work, upbeat bass, touches of sweet piano and a springy mento-reggae guitar bouncing equally on all four beats. But it's the mad riffing on electric banjo that steals the spotlight every time it's heard. It gives the song an additional mento-reggae dimension and a distinctive sound. Unfortunately, like all Lee's singles, the deserving 'Sweeter Than Sugar' has never been compiled on LP or CD.

Eric Donaldson: *'Cherry Oh Baby '*
Eric Donaldson's 'Cherry Oh Baby', produced by Byron Lee and Tommy Cowan, won the sixth Festival in 1971. This put Donaldson in fine company, as reggae greats Toots & The Maytals and Desmond Dekker were among the previous winners. Like many Festival entries, 'Cherry Oh Baby' is a countrified reggae song, but at the reggae end of the mento-reggae spectrum. Appealing and accessible, it's a song that never fails to please. Not only were there the expected versions and covers made in Jamaica, but it is the only reggae cover that The Rolling Stones recorded in a career that has produced enough reggae to fill a CD. It was also recorded by UK reggae group UB40. Further proof of its popularity is seen by its inclusion in numerous best-of-reggae collections.

The song has a simplified stop-and-go chugging rhythm, in an impression of rustic pre-ska reggae. Organ is the featured instrument, alternating between prominent rhythm work and distinctive descending lines. Donaldson's country vocals ride the choppy rhythm to fine effect as he sings a simple, heartfelt declaration of love. He sings alone without backing vocalists or double tracking, adding to the unvarnished feel. He joyously accompanies the descending organ lines with wordless singing. These long keening *yeahs* electrify every time.

The more commonly heard rendition of 'Cherry Oh Baby', available on numerous mixed-artists collections and on Eric Donaldson anthology CDs, is actually a remake of the Festival-winning rendition. Anyone wishing to hear the very similar, slightly faster original can do so, as it's available on the Trojan CD compilation called *Baba Boom! Musically Intensified Festival Songs*. This collection also contains Donaldson's 1973 re-voicing of the riddim, called 'What A Festival', in which he decries the decline of Festival. It's a novelty to hear what is essentially 'Cherry Oh Baby' with such surprisingly sour lyrics. Donaldson also remade 'Cherry Oh Baby' at least two more times, including a 1977 release with Lee Perry producing. But these renditions did not improve on the earlier ones.

Other great mento-reggae songs
If your liking of mento-reggae is not satisfied by the above songs and artists, there are a few more singles by obscure names you may wish to track down. 'Country Girl' by Danny D, produced by DC Anderson and released on the Jericho label in 1974, features an archetypical sweet mento-reggae sound. 'Cookie Want Wood' by The Profits, produced by A. DeLisser and released on the Miracle label in 1975, might be best described as mento-roots-reggae. And, yes, 'Screw The Cock Tight', by the strangely named Mix Flower & Water (aka Shirley "Calypso" Williams), produced by Alvin Ranglin and released on the GG's label in 1978, is on the *slack* end of mento-reggae lyrics, outdoing the outrageousness of The Prince Brothers' 'Ram Jam'.

32 Great mento after the golden age

The golden age of mento singles came to a close at the end of the 1950s. Never again would Jamaica see such an abundance of creative, excellent mento recordings. But in no way did mento stop being recorded, nor did it completely change into the mento-reggae style. Though more sporadically, rural mento recording continued to be released in the 1960s and enjoyed a resurgence in the late 1970s that continued to gain steam up to the present day. These are some standout examples of great rural mento from the 1960s and later.

King Barou: *'Calypso Cha Cha'*
Not a great deal is known about King Barou. He was active in the late 1950s, but he did not make his recording debut until the early 1970s, when he and his band, The Mighty Swingers, released four songs on two Coxsone Dodd-produced 45-rpm singles. He was living and performing in Ocho Rios around that time. Three of the four songs were common to the mento repertoire; the fourth, an original of sorts, was special.

'Calypso Cha Cha' is not the most original of original songs. It takes its title (though nothing else) from that of a golden-age Count Lasher hit. Part of the verse has Barou counting up from "calypso one, calypso two...", as heard in another golden-age mento song, 'Calypso Ten', by Count Sticky. But King Barou's 'Calypso Cha Cha' is a great record, better than either of the recordings it borrowed from. Barou's rough-and-ready voice proves to be better suited for this spirited track than it was to his other three recordings. And there is some terrific playing that is unique to this song.

With an excited Barou and a rumbling rumba box pumping out deep, loud bass, this is a boisterous affair. But the virtuoso banjo steals the show. (The player may be named Cornel, as Barou calls this out before one of the instrumental breaks.) On the verse, he plays a rhythm-lead of fast triplets that frequently slips into expert bursts of rippling double-time strumming, precisely on beat and so pleasing to the ear. An accompanying acoustic guitarist strums to support and accentuate this superb playing. There is also the well-mannered instrumental break heard several times that serves as the song's chorus. It's led by a picked banjo playing a charming quadrille-influenced figure at a cantering pace. This is an accomplished rural mento sound unlike that heard on any other record. It gives credence to the lyric, "you like, I like".

Though it has never been compiled on LP or CD, the single of 'Calypso Cha Cha' is occasionally re-pressed on the Port-O-Jam label, and can often be found at reggae specialty stores. With labels on each side of the Atlantic releasing collections of Studio One singles, perhaps it will not be long before this track sees the laser light of day and is released on CD.

Silver Seas Calypso Band: *'Daphne's Be-Bop Walking'; 'Charlie's Cow'*
Ocho Rios' Silver Seas Hotel had a history of recordings from its eponymously named resident bands. For example, we have already discussed (page 51) a classic golden-age mento single by Lord Composer, backed by the Silver Seas Hotel Orchestra. Around 1960, the Silver Seas Calypso Band released an LP called *Island Champions;* with it, mento saw its first super-group. Hubert Porter, the popular golden-age star of smooth urban mento is on vocals and maracas. The great mento banjo player Eddie Brown proves to be a great mento acoustic guitar player and also provides vocals. (Lord) Jellicoe Barker, who recorded mento and calypso under his own name, contributes the same. Monty Reynolds provides rumba box and vocals. He is the only member not to be given a lead vocal, surprisingly considering he was lead singer on four Silver Seas-backed golden-age tracks. Levi Burke completes the group by providing impressive bongo-playing and vocals. Their massed talent resulted in an expertly polished and accessible form of rural mento. Banjo and bamboo are nowhere to be found, the arrangements being firmly focused on the vocals. Hopes were high for this super group. The LP was released on the New York-based Ritmo label and they appeared on *The Steve Allen Show* and other US television programs. But *Island Champions* does not seem to have made any significant commercial impact.

The LP's two best songs are 'Daphne's Be-Bop Walking' and 'Charlie's Cow'. The former is a cover of Clyde Hoyte's golden-age mento single 'Daphne Walkin''. Banjo player Eddie Brown provides a surprisingly fine lead vocal as he sings about a woman whose "potent" walk is provocative to distraction. The other Silver Seas provide backing vocals that are richly Jamaican, as acoustic guitars, rumba box, wood blocks and bongo create a soft rural bed. Similar in arrangement, but even better is 'Charlie's Cow', which is a renaming of the popular mento song, 'Mattie Rag'. There may be no better rendition. The accomplished Hubert Porter sings lead, about commotion in the family when Papa gets arrested for stealing a neighbor's cow. The backing vocals have even more Jamaican character than on 'Daphne Walking' '. This is especially true when the missing cow is discovered behind a coffee tree, and they sing, "Oh – oh, now I know!" The happy ending is celebrated with lyrics calling for someone to play guitar. On cue, Eddie Brown complies and a lovely acoustic solo concludes this fine song.

The Hiltonaires: *'Chinese Baby'*
Working out of Kingston's Hilton Hotel, The Hiltonaires released a series of six LPs of rough-hewn rural mento in the 1960s. Lord Tanamo, who provided the group with lead vocals for a time, appears on a handful of tracks. Their most

popular LP and the only one to see limited release on CD was *Big Bamboo*. It contains perhaps their best song, 'Chinese Baby', a cover of Trinidadian calypso singer Terror's 1950 song, 'Chinese Children Calling Me Daddy'. In it, the singer laments the "false children" his woman has given to him. He elaborates, recalling that in 1940 he met Imelda who, after three months, had a baby of obvious Chinese descent. They're both black, yet she insists that he is the biological father, regardless of timescale and genetic impossibilities. He laments his predicament with a series of exasperated, colorful statements. Meanwhile, the band, playing the role of his false children, provides a happy chorus of high-pitched, strident, backing vocals that mock him. Though the song is politically incorrect at points by today's standards, you can't help but feel for the poor guy. Perhaps he can form a support group with Derrick Morgan and with golden-age mento artist Cobra Man. Morgan's ska song, 'Don't Call Me Daddy' (as described previously in this book; page 116), and Cobra's calypso-y 'Maintenance' both deal with the identical theme.

Girl Wonder: *'Cutting Wood'*
'Cutting Wood', produced by Coxsone Dodd, is a 1965 cover of a golden-age mento song by Louise Lamb. The Kingston-born Lamb was the only Jamaican woman to have recorded mento in the 1950s, releasing at least four sides in the jazzy urban style. This makes her, along with Louise Bennett, Jamaica's first female recording artist, a significant fact that seems lost to time. 'Cutting Wood' is a double-entendre song, written by the great mento lyricist and Chin's Calypso Sextet member, Everart Williams, set to the melody of the old folk/mento standard 'Rukumbine'.

In Girl Wonder's rendition, the jazzy backing of the original is replaced by a stripped-down rural one. It's built of just strummed guitars that sway hypnotically and seductively in the way of some mento, accompanied by bass and with no percussion at all. Recording just two sides of a single, Girl Wonder could have remained just as obscure a figure as Lamb. But in an interview with Coxsone Dodd, ethnomusicologist Daniel Neely prised out the fact that Girl Wonder was none other than Rita Marley. She is very engaging here, managing to come off as innocent while sounding the sexiest that she has ever been. In fact, 'Cutting Wood' may be her best lead vocal, right up to the closing flourish of *ay yay yays*. The story is that, not feeling well, Wonder goes to the doctor. He prescribes the titular exercise, and Wonder seeks out trees to "bring them down to size". She chooses a neighbor for his fine specimen. It being her first tree, it was difficult going at the start, and so on, in the Williams's mento double-entendre way.

Unfortunately, this single remains one of the few recordings by the extended Wailers family that has never been available on LP or CD, not helped by Marley's use of a pseudonym. Let's hope this changes soon.

Percy Dixon & His Merry Boys: *'Bendwood Dick'*
Trinidadian star Mighty Sparrow's 1960 song, 'Bendwood Dick', is an example of a calypso hit that was popular enough in Jamaica to be adopted into the mento repertoire. It's easy to see why. Sparrow's song, about a most audacious visitor who is looking for the singer's sister, is an engaging, adult tale.

There may be no finer rendition of this song than the one by Percy Dixon & His Merry Boys from their 1964 LP, *Scandal In Montego Bay*. Sometimes billed as King Dixon and His Merry Boys, this Montego Bay-based rural mento band enjoyed a residency at the Half Moon Hotel but was unrecorded before the New York-based Sue Records label commissioned this, their only LP.

The cover lists the song as 'Ben-O-Dict', one of several songs to be sloppily mistitled by Sue. But there is nothing sloppy about the music, which is so precise and vibrant, it sparkles. This is razor-sharp rural mento with flawless rippling banjo, supported by acoustic guitar, rumba box and maracas. Dixon has a smooth, appealing vocal delivery, as do the backing vocalists, and they mine Sparrow's song for all their worth. Even the stereo recording is top-notch. Likable and accessible from every angle, it's a song I have used to introduce rural mento to those who have had little exposure to Jamaican music. Though long out of print, the LP's US origin makes it easier to find than a Jamaican LP from the same time. This song alone justifies hitting a few used-record stores or services.

Slim Henry: *'Mama Look A Boo-Boo'*
Slim Henry's 'Mama Look A Boo-Boo' has a lot in common with Percy Dixon's 'Bendwood Dick'. It too is a razor-sharp rural mento cover of a calypso hit, this time a 1955 song by Lord Melody that was popularized by Harry Belafonte later that decade. Like Dixon, Slim Henry (Henry Dudley Brown) was Mobay-based, enjoying a residence at the Montego Bay Hotel from 1954 into the 1960s, when he recorded his only LP.

Henry's rendition outdoes the original and renders Belafonte's cover completely forgettable. It's a sterling rural mento, with precisely sharp and polished musicianship. And Henry's band has a secret weapon wielded by an expert marksman. In addition to the usual line-up of banjo, rumba box and maracas, acoustic guitar is replaced by lead mandolin played by Lord Flea's talented banjo player, Pork Chops. With mandolin leads glittering like gold petals as banjo throbs a proto-ska rhythm, this track proves that rural mento does not have to be roughedged to be gratifying. Over this backing, the high-voiced Henry amiably sings Lord Melody's unfortunate but humorous tale. It is the story of a very ugly man whose problem is exacerbated by his children's reaction when he returns to his family after being away for a long time. Not only do they not know him, they immediately focus on his appearance and refer to him as a boo-boo. Their mother tries to end the embarrassing scene, telling them to stop because he is their father. This fails, as the precocious kids respond with a cry of outrage and "Oh, no! My daddy can't be ugly so!" Further family discord follows, as do delicious mandolin riffs and solos, making for a special mento delight. This track can be heard on the Ken Khouri-produced mento and calypso CD compilation called Rookumbine on the K&K Records label.

Stanley Beckford: *'Broom Weed'*
After a substantial break from recording reggae and mento-reggae, Stanley Beckford returned in 2002. In an inspired move, he was backed not by a reggae band, but by the venerable Blue Glaze Mento Band. With Rohan Dwyer and Sylvain Taillet producing, they released a CD called *Stanley Beckford Plays Mento*. This self-explanatory collection found Beckford remaking a bunch of his past hits along with a few each of mento repertoire classics and Bob Marley covers, all in rural mento style. Undoubtedly, this band had one of the highest average ages of any Jamaican band. In fact, sadly, over the time it took to write this book, Beckford, at sixty-five years of age, Blue Glaze bandleader and clarinetist Vincent Pryce, at seventy, and Blue Glaze banjo player Nelson Chambers, at sixty-six, would all pass away. But not before they had given several successful international performances and released a follow-up album, 'Reggaemento', in 2004.

'Broom Weed', a track from *Stanley Beckford Plays Mento*, stands out from both previously mentioned CDs. It's a remake of Beckford's 1978 single that was credited to Stanley & The Turbines. The original rendition was a very good mento-reggae track. But, from all indications, the full mento treatment is the way 'Broom Weed' was intended to be heard.

The stately Blue Glaze sounds splendid. They open the song with Pryce's lead clarinet previewing Beckford's melody. Strummed acoustic guitar, rumba box and tambourine run rhythm. And Chamber's banjo bridges the two. Beckford enters and his nasal, keening mento voice never sounded more at home, especially when he is joined by sweet backing vocals. The lyrics are an enigma. They are apparently about a man called 'Broom Weed', whose name may be Herman Nord, who could be likened to a herring bone and a mackerel bone by women, and has apparently gone east. Broom weed is a plant known in Jamaica for its medicinal properties and even for its use in the occult, but is most commonly used to make rough-and-ready brooms, not that this greatly adds to our understanding of this song. Mid-song, Beckford surprises by chanting like a DJ about the King of Babylon. He reprises this as the song nears its end, the chant giving way to a stylized percussive scat to fade-out. These breaks give an already rich song an extra measure of goodness, as the sexagenarian Beckford belatedly uncorks the single greatest performance of his career.

The entire *Stanley Beckford Plays Mento* CD is quite good. A remake of another of his songs, 'Rich Man', is lovely fun. Another remake, 'Brown Gal', is nearly as good. The follow-up CD, *Reggaemento*, is not bad, but nothing on it reaches these heights.

The Jolly Boys

With a lineage that is traceable back to the end of the 1940s, no group in Jamai-can music has been active longer than the Port Antonio-based rural mento group, The Jolly Boys. Although all the original members have died, some incarnation of the band has performed continuously until the present time, when they are more popular than they have ever been before.

The Jolly Boys first came to fame by providing music at Errol Flynn's parties at his Port Antonio estate in the 1950s. This original line-up did not record. By the time the first Jolly Boys singles appeared in the early 1970s, the line-up was already quite different. Two LPs followed later in that decade, with some songs showing Rasta sentiments and a roots-mento sound. The Jolly Boys next brought mento into the CD age with a run of four CDs (three studio-made, followed by a live set) released between 1989 and 1997, comprised predominately of familiar songs from the mento repertoire. They also appeared briefly in the 1989 Denzel Washington film, *The Mighty Quinn*. This line-up had by then changed again. It featured original Jolly Boy Moses Dean on banjo and vocals, Allan Swymmer (who would later leave the main group and lead a splinter edition of The Jolly Boys for a time) on lead vocals and hand drum and Joseph "Powda" Bennett on rumba box, vocals and, though lost on CD, dancing. (In his seventies, he would take over as lead singer of the band as the millennium turned over.) Their sound continued to be classic rural mento, with banjo, acoustic guitar, rumba box and maracas. (Wind instruments were never part of the Jolly Boys' sound.) This line-up was so consistent, it can be hard to recommend specific tracks from these CDs, but two do stand out for different reasons.

'Take Me Back To Jamaica'
'Take Me Back To Jamaica' is a song from *Sunshine 'n' Water*, The Jolly Boys' second CD, released in 1991 on the RYKO label. This Allan Swymmer-penned song is the only original Jolly Boys composition found on these CDs. It is a superior remake of their first single from two decades earlier. As always, the playing is fine from all The Boys, creating a comfortable groove that crackles with acoustic electricity. The high-energy double-struck rhythm that was an antecedent to the ska beat is in evidence. Dean provides his umpteenth fine, fun mento banjo solo, and then adds two more. With great spirit, in his strong tenor, Swymmer sings of missing the simple pleasures of the island "where I were born", creating an anthem for any homesick Jamaican abroad.

'Ba Ba Di Ya (Miss A Ram Goat)'
The old folk/mento song, 'Miss A Ram Goat', makes for an exceptionally good Jolly Boys track. The band is in consistently fine form with Swymmer's drum and Dean's banjo out front, as usual. But this song has something extra, as Swymmer shares lead vocal duties with the more traditionally mento-voiced Bennett. His

high nasal country voice heightens the rural feel of this song. This, plus the fact that it is the longest song on the three studio CDs and that it employs a looser approach than their norm, all contribute to a country jam feel. It can be found on their third CD, *Beer Joint + Tailoring*, released in 1991 on the First Warning label.

'Rehab'

The Jolly Boys were back in 2010 with some big changes and big results. In an attempt to reintroduce mento to a worldwide audience, producer Jon Baker and musical director Daniel Neely steered The Jolly Boys away from the folk/mento repertoire of their previous releases, as well as from the Marley/reggae repertoires that other recent mento albums were drawing from. Instead, the new CD, *Great Expectation*, would be a diverse collection of rock covers with source songs spanning the 1960s to today. The other leg of their "modern mento" approach was for the traditional banjo (provided by Neely), rumba box, hand drum, acoustic guitar and maracas to join the modern sounds of sequenced drums and sampling. The changes did not end there, as a new lead singer, Albert Minott, was featured. But perhaps "new" isn't the right word for him, as he had served as a fill-in Jolly Boy in the 1960s, with his apprenticeship now coming to an end at age seventy-one. Minott's career as a resort entertainer also included dancing and fire breathing. The kerosene used in the latter not only cost him many of his teeth, but etched even more character into a voice that was already shaped by all that life can throw at a man.

Although the CD retains the melody, tempo and spirit of the source songs, they couldn't sound more different from the originals. Blondie's 'Hanging on The Telephone' is a lot of fun, as is The Doors' 'Riders On The Storm', with guest sax from Cedric Brooks. Johnny Cash's 'Ring Of Fire', a song that had inspired The Skatalites' 'Occupation' four decades earlier, sounds like nuevo-mento party music, with the song's famous mariachi hook picked out on banjo rather than played by horns. Sonny Curtis's much-covered 'I Fought The Law' includes a banjo solo that visits the melody of 'Cherry Oh Baby' and Cedric Brooks takes it up on sax. At one point, all other instruments stop except voice and rumba box, introducing a touch of mento-dub. The song also reveals how much the fat, rangy synthesized bass sound of Sleng Teng-style digital dancehall sounded like a rumba box.

But the best song on the album is the cover of Amy Winehouse's 'Rehab'. A thurming rumba box, strummed guitar, hand drum and exuberant sequenced drums create a riddim with a smile and a nod to 'Money Generator' (a song described later in this book; page 328) in an effective modernization of a classic riddim. With impressive strength and range for a septuagenarian, Minott takes ownership of the song. His soulful Jamaican voice and his maturity both suit the story of someone resistant to the idea of going to drug and/or alcohol rehab, right down to the chorus of *no, no, no*. A handsome video adds to the enjoyment, fully revealing Minott's charisma (and dance moves), without neglecting Bennett (who would pass away in 2014), Swymmer or the other Jolly Boys. Even before the CD's release, the video became something of a viral sensation. With live appearances in Jamaica, the UK, USA, Europe and even China, *Great Expectations* would quickly become the most commercially successful release, not only by The Jolly Boys, but in the entire history of recorded mento.

Tallawah Mento Band: *'Stylish Girls'*
In 2010, as The Jolly Boys unveiled their modern mento sound, Tallawah Mento Band released *Ribba To De Bank*, an equally entertaining CD that instead reaches into the past. Tallawah is a big band with fine banjo and acoustic guitar, an abundance of flute trills, the expected rumba box and hand percussion, an unexpected accordion, and on 'Stylish Girls', guest trombone. (Though countless Jamaican songs feature banjo or trombone, this may be the only one to feature both.) The vocals are in the nicely old-fashioned folk choral style, as also heard on the 1950s and 1960s albums by folk groups The Frats Quintet and The Jamaica Folk Singers. In fact, banjo player Colin Smith was the band director of the latter. With a sound this big and satisfying, the group is well named, as *tallawah* means "substantial".

'Stylish Girls' is the song more commonly known as 'Salt Lane Gal' or 'Swine Lane Gal', whose origin can be traced back to the seminal mento duo, Slim & Sam. There have been many notable renditions of this beloved Jamaican song recorded over the decades. It was first recorded in the 1940s by Trinidadian jazz artist Sam Manning, the first individual to record Jamaican songs. Lord Fly, the Jamaican urban mento singer who was the first to record on MRS, Jamaica's original record label, recorded an equally jazzy rendition of it in the 1950s. The Skatalites recorded it as a ska instrumental in the 1960s. Cedric Brooks recorded a Nyabinghi-mento instrumental rendition in the 1970s. And although many others have been committed to wax, the Tallawah Mento Band's rendition stands with any other.

The song describes a meal of rice and peas cooked by a well-to-do gal that goes horribly wrong, detailed with deadpan humor. Everything in the pot is raw except for the burnt bottom, and the gravy tastes awful. The singer claims that the meal brought on a near-fatal dose of colic. What comes off much better is what's bubbling in the instrumental cook-pot. The song jams on, complete with a flute solo and several by the banjo, as the accordion pumps merrily and moaning slides from trombone denote the woeful outcome of the meal. The album's other highlights include similarly fine renditions of the old classic tune 'Iron Bar', a cover of Chin's Calypso Sextet's 'Uniform Madness' retitled 'Rebecca', and 'Kysilo' – the Count Lasher song 'Mo Bay China Man' that was a hit for Stanley Beckford when he later covered it as 'Leave My Kisiloo'.

33 More great reggae instrumentals

Varied in sound and style, here are half a dozen post-rock steady, pre-roots reggae instrumentals from producers other than Coxsone Dodd. They're guaranteed to make you forget about singers, DJs, other styles of reggae and Studio One for a little while.

Technique All Stars/Ansel Collins: *'Stalag 17'*
Winston Riley, leader of the rock steady vocal group The Techniques, moved into production as the rock steady era ended in the late 1960s. In 1973, he released an instrumental called 'Stalag 17' on his Techniques label, crediting the song to his band, The Techniques All Stars (or sometimes to featured keyboardist, Ansel Collins). The distinctive Stalag riddim became one of the most beloved in reggae history. It's been sung to, DJ'ed over and dubbed upon. It's been recut/modernized several times, each resulting in fresh rounds of versioning. A version subsequently described in the "Big Youth" chapter (page 415) and the three versions in the "More great DJ songs" chapter are especially good examples (see pages 444–7).

What makes 'Stalag 17' so enduring? As Peter Tosh would sometimes chant during his band introduction at live shows, "the bass, the bass, the bass is the heart of the reggae". 'Stalag 17' features an impossibly ripe, *wicked* little dance of a bass line from George "Fully" Fullwood. On one hand, it's a model of simplicity, with seven easy notes repeating for the entire track, gaining power as a drone. On the other hand, it features a jazz-informed melody and a rhythm that contains one of the greatest pregnant pauses in reggae history. It allows and inspires Fully's childhood friend, drummer Santa Davis, to exercise his skills, and a great, distinctly reggae drum performance is heard. Tricky quicksilver snare work keeps you guessing on which beat the next strike will arrive. Double-struck tom-tom accents help propel the rhythm and give it one of its defining features.

There is probably very little that would not sound good sitting atop this foundation, but the fine, creative musicianship continues. Horns provide an introduction with a simple, appealing theme. Guitar and a honking sax take turns sounding the reggae chop. Ansel Collins's organ appears, and alternates between sustained chords and fast runs. The guitarist takes a solo, slurring the notes in a sound reminiscent of James Brown's band in such songs as the instrumental called 'The Popcorn'. Then Collins plays a solo: trebly and red-hot. When I listen to 'Stalag 17', I cannot imagine the riddim without these fine solos. But – reggae magic – when I hear a version without (the organ solo is often dubbed out; the guitar solo virtually always), I never miss them. Collins's solo is reprised at the song's end, taking us to the fade-out, and to a procession of versions that spanned decades.

Bobby Ellis & The Revolutionaries: *'Shenk I Sheck'*
'Shenk I Sheck' is trumpeter Bobby Ellis's excellent 1977 remake of the Baba Brooks classic, 'Shenk I Sheck' (a song described earlier in this book; page 112). Produced by Sonia Pottinger, it brings the burning ska of the original into the aquamarine world of languid reggae. Brooks's performance comes over whole, but the intense joy of the original is replaced by a contented happiness. Ellis is relaxed excellence as he unhurriedly plays Brooks's composition over a laid-back reggae riddim, his trumpet kissed by digital delay echo. It's a tribute to both trumpet players that the ska song works just as well in this very different milieu. Unfortunately, Ellis's fitting celebration of a great ska song and a great ska musician has never been compiled on LP or CD. This leaves only the single, as released in Jamaica on the High Note label and in the UK on Treasure Isle. Well known to collectors, and not especially rare, it's worth looking for.

The Hippy Boys: *'Capo'*
'Capo' is a rendition of the Sound Dimension/Jackie Mittoo track, 'Drum Song' (a song described previously in this book; page 171), performed by The Hippy Boys and produced in 1969 by Sonia Pottinger. The Hippy Boys were the first group to include the famed rhythm section of the Barrett brothers, who would in a short time become the house drummer and bassist for Lee Perry, then the long-standing rhythm section for Bob Marley & The Wailers. But it's another Hippy Boy who's in the spotlight here: organ player Glen Adams. He handles the horn/organ theme of the original with chords made melodramatic by an abundance of vibrato. He also provides haunting trebly leads. There's something rural about the song's insistent, chunky, syncopated beat that borders on mento-reggae, transporting you to a harvest barn dance. Respectful without being overly imitative, 'Capo' is a fitting salute to the original 'Drum Song' and a fine track in its own right. It can be heard on the *Trojan Instrumentals Box Set*. It is also available on a Hippy Boys collection called *Reggae With The Hippy Boys*, but there it's called 'Mad Movie', and another of the album's songs is listed as 'Capo' in an apparent error.

Karl "Cannonball" Bryan: *'Soul Scorcher'*
Carl Bryan, more dramatically known as Karl "Cannonball" Bryan, or even King Cannon, learned his sax skills at the famous Alpha Cottage School for Boys. He began his professional career playing in Jamaica's jazzy dance bands of the 1940s and 1950s. A sideman who appeared on numerous records, he also recorded one ska song under his own name and about 45 more tracks during his heyday of 1968 through 1972, working with such producers as Coxsone Dodd, Duke Reid, Bunny Lee and Joe Gibbs. In 2004 he became a member of the reconstituted Skatalites, working with them until around 2007.

'Soul Scorcher' is a saxophone cut of singer Lloyd Robinson's popular song, 'Cuss Cuss' (a song described earlier in this book; page 229). Both versions were produced by Harry "Harry J" Johnson and released in 1969. Here, even with the emotional vocal and the wild reverbed bongo track purged, the riddim is no less compelling. And, without these tracks, details are revealed. A thriller of a bass line is built upon with chiming picked guitar, hard-working double-struck rhythm guitar, piano accenting each beat and a lanky, slightly eccentric drum performance (probably from Fil Callender).

At the same point that Robinson enters in his vocal version, Bryan's tenor sax blows into his, showing why he's called Cannonball. He unveils a monstrously busy, highly rhythmic riff that's topped off with what sounds like the cry of an animal. It's as if some huge bird-beast runs onto the stage to perform a startling herky-jerky dance, and then throws its head back to emit an avian cry of triumph, as reggae chugs underneath. Then, startlingly, he plays the riff again, but this time with twice the number of notes. He hands off to brief but tasty slide guitar and organ solos, each melodically simple and rhythmically exciting, locking right into the riddim. Cannonball returns, playing variations of his theme, as insistent rhythm piano surfaces. The song ramps down with another dose of slide guitar. It fades out to the sound of a sustained screeching sax note, as Cannonball's strange beast takes its bow. 'Soul Scorcher' is available on the *Trojan Instrumentals Box Set*.

Jackie Mittoo: *'Disco Jack'*

Jackie Mittoo's 'Disco Jack' was produced by Bunny Lee in 1973. Lee's name keeps popping up in this book, not only for all the many artists he recorded, but also for the producers he gave some form of support to. Just as singer Joe Higgs gave selflessly of his time and expertise by providing vocal lessons to Trench Town youth, Bunny Lee altruistically helped up-and-coming producers with encouragement, ideas and aid. This made him a unique figure in the usually cut-throat world of reggae record production.

Edward O'Sullivan Lee was born in 1941 in Kingston. As an infant he was called "Bunny", and the name stuck for ever after. A second nickname, "The Striker", was a shortened version of *The Hitch-Hiker* (1953), a film Lee saw and couldn't stop talking about to his friends. Meanwhile, a television show gave Lee another trademark, when he adopted the yacht captain's hat he saw worn by Buster Crabbe in *Seahawk*.

Having singer Derrick Morgan as a brother-in-law gave Striker an entrée into the music business. In 1962, he began working as a plugger, taking records to radio stations and trying to persuade them to play them. This was for Duke Reid initially, then for Coxsone Dodd and Leslie Kong. Plugging led to in-studio work with another producer, Blondel Keith "Ken Lack" Calnek at his Caltone label. Lee produced his first single there in 1966. This led to a prolific career that spanned rock steady into dancehall with all styles of reggae in between. He produced a documented 1400 singles (the actual count is likely to be much higher) and an album to boot, with a steady stream of releases from 1967 through the first half of the 1980s, then more sporadically up to 1991. At the time of this writing, Bunny Lee is still with us, perhaps the greatest living reggae producer.

Lee and Mittoo give 'Disco Jack' a surprising introduction. It opens sounding uncannily like Deep Purple's heavy metal guitarist, Richie Blackmore, and organist, Jon Lord, ominously building towards a jam circa 1972. This wormhole snaps shut as the introduction ends. And as the body of the song begins, one wonders why it wasn't called 'Skankin' Jack'. Instead of disco, it's an exceedingly skankin' jam with a midnight-dark skankin' riddim, as Mittoo provides a supremely skankin' song-length Hammond organ solo, and a skankin' sax inserts itself most skankingly ... well, you get the idea. Mittoo gives a great performance, even for reggae's master of the organ. A dub version also exists that drops out most of the organ and plays up the underlying riddim with accents of reverb. Both versions can be heard on the Pressure Sounds Records compilation CD called *Sounds And Pressure, Volume 3*. If you should come across the 12-inch disco-mix that seamlessly welds the best parts of both versions into one longer one, grab it.

Keith Hudson: *'Melody Maker'*

Keith Hudson was born in 1946 in Kingston. He had a respectable singing career, recording 60 singles and 12 albums from the end of the 1960s through 1982. Yet his career as a singer was outshone by that as a producer. He is said to have produced his first record, a one-shot, in 1960. If this is true, that would make him the youngest-ever producer in Jamaica. He resumed producing in 1968, and went on to work with such big names as Gregory Isaacs, Augustus Pablo, Dennis Brown, Big Youth, Dennis Alcapone, Alton Ellis, Ken Boothe, U-Roy, John Holt, Delroy Wilson and many others, including himself. He also was active in dub production; in 1974, he released *Pick A Dub*, considered to be the first-ever dub album. That same year, he decamped to the UK for a time before moving to New York in 1976. He died there in 1984 of lung cancer

His 1973 pseudo-instrumental 'Melody Maker' is undeniably a great reggae song. And it is one that (barring its versions) does not sound quite like any other. It's an ensemble piece with each instrument contributing distinctively and equally. Opening with a rhythm guitar phrase that creaks like boot leather, like 'Ringo Rides' by The Skatalites (a song described earlier in this book; page 86), 'Melody Maker' evokes the American Westerns that were so popular in Kingston's movie houses. This comes primarily from bluesy cowboy harmonica and the omnipresent dirgelike, wordless, long-rider backing vocals. But this is only part of the reggae creativity to be heard. There are thunderous flurries of bass notes that interlock with phased rhythm guitar phrases that might have been equally at home in soul music. There are drums with the occasional tumbling roll, supplemented by a hand drum, additional rhythm and lead guitar, and ecstatic interjections of *melody!*, all contributing to the song's deep, dense, unique reggae-Western groove.

Though short, at just over 2 minutes, this is the little riddim that could. Not only does it stand alone as a unique piece of great reggae, it also provided a riddim for a number of good tracks, including two others that warrant description later in this book (pages 580 and 412): 'Don't Think About Me' by singer Horace Andy and 'Can You Keep A Secret' by DJ Big Youth. 'Melody Maker' is widely available on Keith Hudson CD collections.

34 The Abyssinians

Calling themselves after an earlier name for Ethiopia, vocal group The Abyssinians consisted of singer Bernard Collins and brothers Donald and Linford Manning. Collins was raised in Saint Catherine Parish and was such a fan of American music, particularly Elvis, that he was called "Presley" by his friends. Not only did his recorded work not sound like his American idols, but he would help launch a new quintessentially Jamaican sound. He moved to Kingston and hooked up with the Mannings in Trench Town, forming The Abyssinians. Along with Burning Spear and Bob Marley & The Wailers, they would give birth to roots reggae. And they did so with their very first record.

The much-loved and revered 'Satta Amassa Ganna', produced by Coxsone Dodd in 1969, was that record. In addition to being a big hit, spawning the to-be-expected versions and covers, it has been accepted as the de facto "national anthem" of the Rastafarian people. And it had a strong influence on the sound of the roots reggae vocal groups that followed (The Congos come immediately to mind). So revolutionary was the sound of 'Satta Amassa Ganna' that producer Coxsone Dodd could not believe that anyone would want to hear it; rather than releasing it, he sold the master back to the group, who started their own label and released it themselves. The vagaries of reggae were such that even its savants could be fooled. But Dodd did not repeat his mistake, and he did release The Abyssinians' second record: the nearly as beloved and even more aurally arresting 'Declaration of Rights'. No one else in reggae, and very few recording acts in history, have ever opened with such a potent one-two punch.

Unfortunately, there was no place to go from there but down. The Abyssinians released about 40 singles and three albums, some good, some not, through the 1970s, when they broke up. This led to two competing outfits of Abyssinians, one led by Collins, the other an all-Manning line-up with eldest brother Carlton, who had previously successfully led the rock steady group Carlton & The Shoes, joining as lead vocalist. Then Donald Manning went solo. (Reminiscent of when former Congos member "Ashanti" Roy Johnson went solo under the name "Congo Ashanti Roy", Manning recorded under the name "Donald Abyssinian".) Inevitably, a reunion of Collins and the Mannings did occur, but not until 1998. And it was short-lived, as the group splintered once again. But all this churn hardly mattered. The Abyssinians were like a child prodigy whose gift fades at an early age. But nothing can detract from the legacy of their early accomplishments.

'Satta Amassa Ganna'; 'Mabrak'

In 1968, Carlton & The Shoes, the rock steady vocal group led by the eldest Manning brother, Carlton, which also included brother Linford as a member for a time, recorded a song called 'Happy Land'. Without mentioning any specific place, it's a back-to-Africa song, promising the righteous access to a faraway mystical land of paradise, where they can "Have peace and love deep in your soul. And you will never, never grow old". This Rasta theme can be traced in reggae all the way back to Lord Lebby's early 1950s mento classic, 'Etheopia' (a song previously discussed in this book; page 35). And, as in Bunny Wailer's similarly themed 'Dreamland', Africa did not have to be mentioned by name for the Rasta to know the location of their promised land.

This song gives 'Satta Amassa Ganna' most of its opening stanza, while the remainder of the song was written by Donald Manning and Bernard Collins. The role of 'Happy Land' in 'Satta Amassa Ganna' is often overstated. Playing them back to back makes it clear that 'Satta Amassa Ganna' is not a cover of 'Happy Land'. The revolutionary roots sound of 'Satta Amassa Ganna' makes the rock steady of the Carlton & The Shoes song sound tired and passé, even though they were recorded just one year apart. The reggae community was ready to give full voice to the Rasta themes that The Wailers were famously exploring, but a new style of reggae was needed to appropriately back this message. 'Satta Amassa Ganna' was that sound.

The riddim was taut, crackling with righteous energy and a fresh new roots sound. Leroy Sibbles's start-and-stop rumbling bass clusters helped define the genre from that moment forward. Flashing rhythm guitar chords from Eric Frater strike like revelations. Richard Ace's piano is more serious in sound than what was typically heard in rock steady or the newly emergent reggae proper of the previous year. Even Fil Callender's drums, excellent as always, dispense with the oddball touches that defined his style for a tauter, more sober sound. Atop of this, in a beautiful horn line saxophonist Headley Bennett and trombonist Vin Gordon instinctively harmonize on a prototypical roots reggae melody: a regal but mournful descending minor-key theme with a trilling finish. It adds even more emotional gravity to the majestic, solemn riddim. This melody too was borrowed from another song, but one from further afield than 'Happy Land'. It's drawn from 'Mafista', by Neil Hefti, from the score of the 1966 television show, *Bat Man*, in a most unlikely repurposing.

The horn theme ends with four drum strikes, announcing the entrance of The Abyssinians. They are electrifying, as Collins leads a tight minor-key harmony. It's ragged and refined, wispy and strong, earthy but spiritual, mournful but hopeful – contradictions that are resolved by the new sound of roots reggae. Their vocals alone create an incredible sense of longing that further increases the emotional pull of the song. And that's before even considering the words. They open with a stanza largely borrowed from 'Happy Land', establishing the existence of a faraway land of paradise. But instead of describing the wonders of this magical utopia, as done in 'Happy Land', The Abyssinians *give thanks and praises* for it (the translation of the title from Amharic to English), making clear that this Zion comes from God. It's interesting that in this Rasta anthem, Rastafari is never named. But, who was "the king of kings" is understood (or should I say *overstood*, the preferred Rasta usage, suppressing the negative implications of "under"). The song concludes with a stanza sung in Amharic – another indication that the Ethiopian King, Haile Selassie, Jah Rastafari, was the subject of the song and the inspiration for the new sound.

The Abyssinians recut 'Satta Amassa Ganna' a number of times throughout the years. Additionally, with Bernard Collins producing, they would record a re-voiced version of 'Satta Amassa Ganna', called 'Mabrak', in 1971. It was influenced by The Ethiopians' song, 'One' (a song described previously in this book; page 165). A stripped-down, bass-heavy, reverb-rich, dub mix of the riddim is heard. Then, instead of singing, a conversation begins. It memorably opens with a discussion of 'Satta Amassa Ganna', with one man asking the other if he believes that the song is true. "Mmm. I know so" is the answer. Further *reasoning* on the record's message is heard, complete with Amharic phrases and Bible quotes. Bernard Collins remembers it as "version business", but this record was a big hit. In 1975, the group recorded a remake of 'Satta Amassa Ganna', produced by The Abyssinians and Clive Hunt, that was nearly as good as the original, though later versions were not. Also of note is the opening of the 1978 movie, *Rockers*, in which The Abyssinians perform 'Satta Amassa Ganna' Nyabinghi-style with the backing of a drum troupe and acoustic guitar.

Many other artists covered 'Satta Amassa Ganna', including an overrated version by Third World, and an uncountable number of versions based on the Satta riddim have been released over the years. We have already seen a good example in Peter Tosh's 'Here Comes The Judge' in 1973 (see page 225). Another is the 1977 disco-mix produced by George "Niney" Boswell: 'Jah Is My Light'/'Wicked Eat Dirt' by Leroy Smart/I-Roy. This utilized an intensely surging, dub-flashing recut of the riddim that was popularly versioned.

In 2004, a CD collection called *Tree Of Satta* was released. It contains both the original versions of 'Satta Amassa Ganna' and 'Mabrak', plus eighteen other artists performing over the Satta riddim. Dean Fraser's sax cut, 'Dahina Dimps', is a standout. Fraser has never sounded sweeter, especially when his double-tracked saxophones harmonize, creating a feminine beauty that marries to the masculine rootsiness of the riddim. In 2009, forty years from the Satta's release, Queen Ifrica had a hit with 'Coconut Shell'. Its riddim is a modernization of the Niney recut, making it a third-generation Satta riddim.

'Declaration of Rights'

The Abyssinians' follow-up to 'Satta' was recorded in 1971 for Coxsone Dodd. 'Declaration of Rights' is another seminal roots reggae performance and unqualified reggae classic. It was written by Collins, who uses the backing vocals of Leroy Sibbles and George Henry on this session rather than the Mannings. The riddim is less expansive than that of 'Satta Amassa Ganna', lacking horns and flashing rhythm guitar. Instead, it sounds more self-contained, tick-tocking like a time piece, an urgent double-struck rhythm guitar serving as its mainspring. This leaves greater room for the vocals, and The Abyssinians make the most of the situation with a fine lead and beautiful, achingly poignant, harmonies.

The song opens with a melancholy roots melody played on organ. This sets up the entrance of The Abyssinians, who deliver an extended block of beautiful, wordless singing, wailing like mournful spirits. It's a sound that can give you the chills. To what is already a stunning piece of reggae, only now does Collins add his lead. Having previously sung about Jah and Zion on 'Satta Amassa Ganna', here he turns to other Rasta themes: the legacy of slavery and standing up for one's rights. Collins sounds wounded but righteous as he recounts how people were dragged "from civilization" to become slaves in Jamaica. The legacy this created for the slaves' descendants is a life worse than hell. The Abyssinians conclude the song with a soaring inspirational mantra in three-part roots harmony, repeating a rousing call to get up and fight for human rights. (Bob Marley and Peter Tosh were no doubt influenced by this song when they released The Wailers' 'Get Up Stand Up' two years later.) Musically compelling and with strong expressions of roots reggae themes, 'Declaration of Rights' hit with an impact that gave credence to the notion that righteous music can overcome social adversity.

As is the case for 'Satta Amassa Ganna', The Abyssinians recut 'Declaration of Rights' several times, but the original rendition is the best. Abyssinians CDs seem to favor the remakes, so pick Studio One collections, such as the eighteen-song edition of *The Best Of Studio One* on Heartbeat Records, to hear the original. There were also many versions of the riddim. One that is recommended is the simpatico DJ version called 'Version Of Rights' by Big Joe, as found on the CD collection on Soul Jazz Records called *Studio One DJs*.

35 Burning Spear

No one has more tirelessly brought the message of roots reggae to the world than Burning Spear. No one has even come close. Along with Bob Marley & The Wailers and The Abyssinians, he helped create the form. And he would stay strictly with the music and message of roots reggae right through to the present day. He is still recording and performing live around the world, more than forty years later. In fact, no Jamaican recording artist has had a longer duration of recording in just one style. (The Jolly Boys' run of rural mento records that started in 1973 is second. But remember, in this case there was a complete turnover of band membership.) Burning Spear's first record, 'Door Peeper', in 1969, was pure roots right from the get-go, sounding little like any other reggae of that year. Even his name was a nod towards the Rasta belief in black self-determination. Jomo Kenyatta was a freedom fighter who went on to become the first post-colonial ruler of Kenya. The English translation of his first name is "burning spear".

Though initially a duo for a short time, with bass singer Rupert Willington, and then a trio for a number of years, with the addition of backing vocalist Delroy Hinds (Justin Hinds's brother), for all intents and purposes Burning Spear is its lead singer and songwriter Winston Rodney. Depending on the account, he was born in 1945 or 1948 in Saint Ann Parish. He began writing songs and was interested in recording them. One day around 1968, he bumped into fellow Saint Ann resident Bob Marley, and asked how he could get started in music. Marley advised him to seek out Coxsone Dodd. Singer Larry Marshall, also from Saint Ann, claims that it was he who gave Rodney this advice. He certainly could have, without excluding Marley's having done the same. Whoever gave it, the advice was followed and proved to be good. Burning Spear's initial single was made at Studio One, where they recorded exclusively for a number of years.

Nothing else sounded anything like 'Door Peeper', not even the other nascent roots reggae from The Wailers and The Abyssinians. Nor did it sound like Nyabinghi or Nyah-reggae. It opens self-referentially, as only a reggae record can. Spear gives his record an explanatory spoken introduction. He explains that they are Rastafarians and issues some positive Rasta vibes. He then introduces the record with "Sounds from The Burning Spear". Roots reggae follows, featuring lead vocals that are deeply plaintive even for roots reggae, dread harmonies, lyrics praising Jah and chanting down Babylon, tart horns, a Nyah hand drum and rootsy bass, drums, guitar and organ. The overall effect was a fully realized roots reggae sound, with a thick, murky, dark dread sound. If The Abyssinians brought a specific spiritual sound to roots reggae, and The Wailers introduced roots lyrical themes, Spear brought to roots reggae a specific Jamaican earthiness, giving it a distinctive terroir.

After a long but not especially prolific stint with Dodd, they moved on to producer Jack Ruby in 1975. Lawrence "Jack Ruby" Lindo previously operated the Jack Ruby Hi Fi sound system before going into production. He worked steadily from 1973 through the end of the decade, then sporadically in the 1980s, slowed by the health problems that would eventually take his life in 1989. Though he worked with a variety of artists over this time, he is best remembered for his work with Burning Spear. His legacy includes a role as himself in the movie *Rockers* (1978), and his grandson, the up-and-coming pop-reggae hit-maker, Sean Kingston. Spear would record with Ruby for several years before moving more and more to self-production. At this juncture, the trio would break up, leaving just Rodney as Burning Spear.

To date, Spear has recorded 37 albums and more than 65 singles. Since the reggae category was initiated in 1985, he became a perennial Grammy nominee, picking up twelve nominations and winning twice. Closer to home, Jamaica awarded Spear the Order of Distinction in 2007. They should also name him roots reggae ambassador to the world.

In addition to the songs discussed below, notable versions of Burning Spear songs appear elsewhere in this book. These include 'The Ghost', the dub version of 'Marcus Garvey' (page 296); 'Joe Grazer', Vin Gordon's trombone cut of 'He Prayed' (page 174); 'Morning Ride', Yellowman's DJ version of 'Black Disciples' (page 443); and Ernest Ranglin's Jamaica Jazz cover of 'Black Disciples' (page 535).

'Jah No Dead'
The most memorable scene in the 1978 movie *Rockers* (and there are a number to choose from) is when Burning Spear walks drummer Leroy "Horsemouth" Wallace to sit down by the shore in the darkness of night. Sharing a spliff, Spear sings 'Jah No Dead' accompanied by nothing more than the roar of the surf. This a cappella rendition of his 'Marcus Say Jah No Dead' is so intimate and powerful, it renders the good original rendition unnecessary. (This is reminiscent of Bob Marley's backed and bandless recordings of 'Redemption Song'.) With no band, Spear's emotion and expressiveness grow to fill the night. Like Marley's 'Jah Live', it's a response to the news that Haile Selassie has died, but its lyrics are more personal. It's poetic and disarming when Spear ends the song by inviting travelers to the riverbank for further talk with him about this. 'Jah No Dead' is a unique and special performance in the annals of reggae. It can be heard on the *Rockers* soundtrack album and witnessed in the film.

'Social Living'
'Social Living' was self-produced by Spear in 1978, and backed by a large band led by Sly & Robbie. It's a structurally strange roots reggae sound sculpture, inside-

out and folded back on itself like a Möbius strip. Drop-out repurposes the planes of its surface. Surprising key changes bend the melody at unlikely angles. Swollen horn phrases protrude at acute angles. Arranged atop this are sections of guitars, organ, trombone, assorted hand percussion, disembodied backing vocals, bird whistles and a verse that is effectively intoned out of key. Most of the lyrics consist of a chorus in which Spear repeatedly asks whether we accept the titular refrain – a lifestyle of unity and treating one another well – as the best solution to many of the day's problems. Taken as a whole, 'Social Living' amounts to a unique, somewhat abstract but totally accessible roots reggae mediation on the importance of living right within a community.

'Social Living' can be found on nearly every one of the many Burning Spear best-of collections. Spear's album of that name also includes a disco-mix of this song with a pleasing dub version seamlessly appended. A better, razor-sharp dub version that nicely extends the abstract spirit of the original, called 'Pit Of Snakes', appears on the 1989 Sly & Robbie LP called *Raiders Of The Lost Dub*. Never released on CD, this album can be acquired on iTunes.

'African Teacher'

The Rastas take great pride in their African heritage, reclaiming a culture that had been suppressed in Jamaica by colonialism. Numerous roots reggae songs explore this theme, but none with greater conviction than Spear's 1980 self-produced 'African Teacher'. His contemplative vocal is handsomely backed by an exceptionally thoughtful roots reggae riddim provided by most of the instrumental Wailers, though drummer Nelson Miller is on hand rather than Carlton Barrett.

Spear's deep belief in Garveyism and its back-to-Africa imperative is seen as he explains that his cultural education can only be completed in Africa. Promising never to be absent, late or a difficult student, Spear humbly asks the titular figure to teach him. He sings this expertly chanting outside of the beat, giving emphasis to the strength of his convictions. By the end of the track, the singer and the band sound completely fulfilled, as Spear triumphantly chants of the pleasure of being taught Amharic and the joy of learning. 'African Teacher' is a wondrous song. It's a beautiful illustration of the thirst for cultural rediscovery that Rastafarianism awakened in its followers. You will be hard pressed to find another song as passionate about learning, no matter what subject, let alone one that sounds so good. 'African Teacher' is available on several Burning Spear CDs.

36 More great Nyabinghi and Nyabinghi-reggae songs

Well before they began to record, Count Ossie and his Nyabinghi drum troupe were born of – and would become central to – Rasta identity. Oswald Williams was born in 1926 in Saint Thomas Parish. Mentored in Rastafarianism and Nyabinghi drumming by a Rasta elder by the name of Brother Job, the young Williams would soon move to live in a Rasta community. By the late 1950s, Jamaica's best jazz musicians, as well as others visiting from abroad, would routinely come to Ossie's Rasta camp. There they would sit in with him and his drum troupe, the Mystic Revelation of Rastafari, on a *grounation*, as these jam sessions were called. With this musical openness, it's no wonder that Nyabinghi music frequently included a guest jazz instrument, not to mention welcoming collaboration with an entire R&B or reggae band.

No other style of drumming, not even the antecedent styles from West Africa and the Maroon people of Jamaica, sounded quite like Nyabinghi. Rather than the aggressive sound of so many drum traditions that had made "drums of war" a common idiom, Nyabinghi drums were quiet and introspective, meditative and spiritual – the drums of peace. Rather than being pounded, they simmered and bubbled.

Nyabinghi was the music of the Rastas, once Jamaican society's most feared and reviled outcasts. Yet it grew to prominence. By 1960, Ossie's drums would be employed to enliven R&B songs like The Folkes Brothers' hit, 'Oh Carolina' (a song described previously in this book; page 72). They succeeded to such thrilling effect that Ossie's drums were the death knell for Jamaican music's period of R&B imitation, ushering in a return to originality and a more authentically Jamaican sound. This paved the way for ska, but ironically this new form found little use for Nyabinghi drums. They would return to be occasionally heard in the rock steady era. It was during this time that Ossie's cultural prominence was recognized by the Jamaican government, which arranged for Ossie and his group to perform at a reception for Haile Selassie in 1966 during his only visit to Jamaica. By the reggae era, Count Ossie's legacy was established, and Nyabinghi drumming was a familiar sound around the island. He recorded albums and singles, and similar music troupes, such as Ras Michael & The Sons of Negus, also began to record. The Nyabinghi-reggae fusion subgenre arose. Even more popular was the roots reggae that often included a single Nyah drummer in a reggae band, making familiar names of Seeco Patterson (of Bob Marley & The Wailers), Isaiah "Sticky"

Thompson, Skully (formerly known as Zoot Simms, and as a singer) and Bongo Herman (Herman Davis). Count Ossie died in 1976, but not before establishing Nyabinghi music as a vital strand in the weave of reggae, and himself as one of the most important figures in Rasta identity.

Although Nyabinghi jams could sprawl to great lengths (the 30-minute title track on the Count Ossie & The Mystic Revelation Of Rastafari album, *Grounation*, is a recorded reminder of this), Nyabinghi could be just as effectively crafted into or grafted onto shorter-form songs that were more easily recorded. Here are some great Nyabinghi and Nyabinghi-reggae songs from Count Ossie and others.

Great Count Ossie Nyabinghi and Nyabinghi-reggae songs

Roland Downer & Count Ossie: *'A Ju Ju Wah'*
In 1968, Sonia Pottinger produced 'A Ju Ju Wah' by vibe player Roland Downer and Count Ossie. Downer remains a complete mystery, playing beautifully here, providing the single with a less-impressive B-side in 'Ethiopian Kingdom', and then never being heard from again. Most probably, he was a musician visiting from another country, sitting in at a session with Ossie. What is certain is that this is a sublime Nyabinghi track.

Just in case Nyah drum music at its most introspective is not exotic enough for you, this song adds three unusual elements. First is Downer's jazzy vibraphone that melts right into the music of Ossie and his troupe. His playing is very fluid, differentiating him from Jamaica's resident vibraphonist, Lennie Hibbert. He gives the track an element of intrigue with a captivating and exotic jazz melody while adding to the polyrhythm. Second is the strummed electric guitar that's the song's only non-percussion instrument. It minimalistically stays with hypnotic two-chord patterns, adding to the song's air of mystery. Third are the foreign-language vocals, sounding vaguely Middle Eastern, perhaps Amharic. Some phrases are recognizable, when Haile Selassie and the song's title are mentioned. (Though a different song entirely, there is a Jamaican folk song that has been spelled either 'Ay-Zuzuma' or 'Zuh Zuh Wah'.) With just one of these elements, 'A Ju Ju Wah' would have been a great Nyabinghi song. All three make it a stunner.

'A Ju Ju Wah' can be heard on the *Trojan Nyahbinghi Box Set*. Apparently, Trojan was so impressed by Roland Downer, they bestowed the title "Prince" to his billing, a designation that was nowhere to be seen on the song's original single release.

Count Ossie & The Mystic Revelation Of Rastafari: *'Martilda'; 'Bam O Say'/'Take Us Back To Ethiopia'*
From The Grassroots Of Jamaica is a 1969 LP presenting a variety of Jamaican folk-music styles. Recorded in the field, and with most of the uncredited performers amateurs, the LP gives you a sense of the diversity and pervasiveness of the music in Jamaican life. It was produced by Edward Seaga, then Jamaica's Minister of Finance and Planning, and later the Prime Minister.

Though the album sadly lacks liner notes, the jacket lists Rastafarian as one of the music styles. This refers to the two Nyabinghi tracks that, although uncredited, are unmistakably Count Ossie and his drum troupe performing live to a small, respectful audience. Both tracks are pure Nyah – just drums and voices. 'Martilda' is the old folk song often called '[We Love] Matilda', whose origin can be traced back to Africa. The lead and backing vocals are upbeat and melodic. The dynamic drums jam expertly in the Nyabinghi way as the song proceeds.

The second track is a medley of 'Bam O Say' and 'Take Us Back To Ethiopia'. The first is a rendition of the first Nyabinghi song ever recorded, 'Bam Mo She', by King Joe Francis & The African Drums, said to have been recorded by producer Vincent Chin in 1959, though not released until 1961. (Sometimes he is called Job rather than Joe, which raises the question whether this was the same person as Count Ossie's drum teacher, Brother Job. King Joe Francis would leave The African Drums behind to record a few ska singles in 1965, which does little to support this being anything more than a coincidence.) The track has the lead singer front and center with playful choruses of "ay ay ay" and a reference to The Folkes Brothers' 'Oh Carolina', while the backing vocalists chant the titular refrain. 'Take Us Back To Ethiopia' is more solemn in subject and sound: the troupe sings in unison while the drums pulse and boil.

Though it has never been released on CD, *From The Grassroots Of Jamaica* has been in and out of print often enough that it can be found without too much difficulty from specialty reggae music retailers. Another reason why a reggae fan might want to hear this LP is the track called 'Drum And Fife'. This fine example of Pocomania music will let you hear the folk rhythm that would have such a big impact on dancehall reggae in the years to come.

Count Ossie & The Mystic Revelation Of Rastafari: *'Marbat (Passin' Thru)'*
'Marbat (Passin' Thru)' comes from the 1973 album *Grounation* by Count Ossie & The Mystic Revelation Of Rastafari, as produced by Arnold Wedderbum. *Marbat* is Amharic for "light", "lamp" or "electricity", but since this is an acoustic performance, perhaps "light" best applies. The song's second title comes from the fact that it's a cover of jazz drummer/bandleader Chico Hamilton's 1962 song, 'Passin' Thru'.

Over Nyabinghi drums that are more martial than usual, a horn section repeats a riff. Atop of this, saxophonist Cedric "Im" Brooks plays a delightful solo, pauses and resumes. Born in 1943 in Kingston, Brooks was an Alpha Boy who had learned to play flute, clarinet and percussion at the school in addition to sax. Upon graduating, he began a long career in music, starting in the Jamaica Military Band. Though under-documented, this was not a unique career path for Alpha graduates on their way to Jamaica's jazz bands. In fact, at the end of the 1950s, MRS released an LP by The Jamaica Military Band, one side of which showed strong mento-jazz leanings. By the 1960s, Brooks had worked in a number of the jazz bands that were popular in Jamaica at that time, though the scene would soon wane. At the start of the 1970s, he began to record at Studio One, sometimes partnered by trumpet player David Madden. Later in that decade, he began a professional association with Count Ossie, serving as his sax player and musical director, while still continuing his solo career that included at least 25 singles and five albums. He was fond of performing 'Marbat' live until 2010, when multiple health problems put him in a coma. Sadly, he never fully recovered, dying three years later at the age of seventy.

Though the drums are unmistakably Jamaican and the horn melodies are faithful to Hamilton's jazz original, the arrangement of the horns recalls a third style of music. They sound as if they were pulled straight out of a New Orleans street band. 'Marbat' would make wonderful Mardi Gras parade music. Until this happens, we can enjoy this very cool multicultural groove on CD over and over again.

Count Ossie & The Mystic Revelation Of Rastafari: *'So Long'*
Also appearing on Ossie's *Grounation* album, 'So Long' is a classic member of the Nyabinghi repertoire. Ossie had previously recorded it as 'So Long The Negus Call You' at the start of the 1960s in the Nyah-R&B style. Dennis Brown would record a reggae rendition called 'So Long Rastafari' in 1972. The Jolly Boys recorded a mento rendition called 'So Long Babylon' in 1991. But none of these can compare to this recording. It's performed in pure Nyabinghi style, just drums and chanted vocals, similar in its sound to the two tracks discussed above. Any additional instrumentation could only have spoiled this performance.

'So Long' is a reminder of how Nyah drums are not only rhythmically engaging, but are more heady, meditative and relaxing than other drum traditions. Here, this is combined with chanted singing and a lovely melody that is far better than one might expect from a drum troupe. It's not clear who the group's lead singer is, as several singers are equally credited, including Ossie himself, but his vocals are joyous and warm. The lyrics are a simple, comforting statement that once you finally accept the long-standing call of Rastafari, you will be protected. Both the vocals and percussion take flight towards the song's end before tapering away. 'So Long' is an unparalleled example of naturalistic musical enjoyment that pure Nyabinghi music affords.

Great Nyabinghi and Nyabinghi-reggae songs by other artists

Max Romeo: *'Words Of Wisdom'*
Max Romeo's self-produced 'Words Of Wisdom', from 1971, is a gratifyingly strange Nyabinghi-reggae song. It's a re-voiced, rearranged version of 'Macabee Version', a song Romeo released the previous year. Start-and-stop bass, *chika-chika* guitar, drums and rhythm piano come together in a tough, flinty rhythm. It is a backing that would not have been out of place on one of the tough Lee

Perry-produced Bob Marley & The Wailers sides from that same time. But with the surprising procession of musical elements that Romeo trots out, it winds up sounding like nothing of the kind. That each of these unlikely elements proves to work individually and as a crazy whole is a credit to Romeo and his musicians.

The song opens with an organ playing the melody of the popular Christmas carol, 'Good King Wenceslas', an oddness carried over from 'Macabee Version'. Newly added is the accompanying spacey slide guitar that could have come from a Pink Floyd recording of the same time. Shakers are next heard, prefacing the Nyabinghi sounds yet to come. Then, of all things, someone starts strumming an autoharp. This may be the only evidence of this instrument across sixty-plus years of recorded Jamaican music. It plays a crazy inside-out theme, with a retrograde melody and overripe harmonics. Fitting the song while still sounding so *outside*, it raises the question whether there is any musical element that is not soluble in reggae if placed in the hands of the right producer. Then, simultaneously, a Nyah hand drum joins in as Romeo starts *reasoning*. He bestows his words of wisdom in an oratorical recital, far closer to lecture than singing. There prove to be many such words of wisdom, but they are frequently revisited by autoharp and slide guitar, brightening the sound and keeping the song strange rather than stern. This genuinely eccentric Nyabinghi-reggae track can be heard on the *Trojan Nyahbinghi Box Set*.

Karl Bryan and The Afrocats: *'Money Generator'*

Karl "Cannonball" Bryan's hopefully named 'Money Generator' was produced by Coxsone Dodd in 1972. Yet another classic Studio One instrumental, it is different from all others. It falls somewhere between Nyabinghi with a guest instrumentalist and full-blown Nyabinghi-reggae. Rhythm organ and guitar, along with Bryan's lead sax, all join a Nyah trio. But the line-up falls short of true Nyah-reggae, because drum kit and bass are not heard. And the rhythm is far more Nyabinghi than reggae; the bass drum thundering on the first beat of each measure is as close as we get to a reggae chop.

Working together, the two trios set up a midnight-dark groove. A skanking organ and a strummed guitar (reminiscent of 'A Ju Ju Wah') each stick to two chords, giving the song an underlying hypnotic drone. Atop of this, Bryan adds a saxophone skank, slow-burning and melodic, sly and smoky – as in billows of ganja smoke so thick you could dance on them. Bryan pauses for a time, giving the spotlight to a pulsating riddim. He then launches a fine mid-song solo with jazzy flights that are reminiscent of Tommy McCook at his best. This concluded, he returns to his skanking theme, only to briefly solo again at the song's end. 'Money Generator' is an inky groove so deep that you couldn't climb out of it, and so savory, you wouldn't want to anyway. Find it on the Soul Jazz compilation CD called *Studio One Scorcher*. If things worked solely on merit, it would have generated a ton of money for Cannonball.

Ras Michael & The Sons of Negus: *'Seventy Two Nations'; 'Zion Land'*
Ras Michael's second LP, *Peace & Love*, was produced by Lloyd Charmers in 1975. Credited to Dadawah rather than Ras Michael, the album consisted of four long songs. Two of these sprawling Nyah-reggae jams, 'Seventy Two Nations' and 'Zion Land', are especially good. This is reggae that is well suited for fans of rock jam-bands.

The subject of 'Seventy Two Nations' is introduced in the song's echoing spoken opening, as Michael exalts Jah. Funky soul bass and electric guitar from Lloyd Parks and Willie Lindo respectively begin to jam and the Nyabinghi drums soon join in. Dubby electric piano and drum kit (Lloyd Charmers and Paul Williams) bring the reggae. We have already seen how jazz and Nyabinghi proved to be a natural fit, and how Nyah could complement R&B and reggae. But here we see how jazz, funk, soul and reggae elements can simultaneously combine with Nyabinghi for a hearty musical stew. Michael sings alone, sprinkling in Amharic words and phrases. As the song progresses, he adds back-to-Africa lyrics to his praises of Jah. Just when you think the song is fading out, he brings in a 3-minute jamming, droning coda. Where else can you hear reggae that is in equal parts funky, soulful, spiritual and meditative?

Whereas 'Seventy Two Nations' was a soul, funk, reggae, Nyah jam, 'Zion Land' is straight Nyabinghi-reggae. It's actually a cover of 'Africa', a song by The Gaylads that is described later in this book (page 577). Although the title and lyrics are altered, the original's back-to-Africa theme is retained. But where The Gaylads' song is brisk and rousing, Michael's rendition is long, slow, hypnotic and mystical. It opens with carefully chosen trios of chords, played simultaneously on electric piano and guitar, supported by brushwork on cymbals. Glowing warm with reverb, this opening conveys the spiritual longing for the faraway Zion that the lyrics will soon describe. Keyboard and guitar jam, as introspective Nyabinghi drums enter gently. Michael begins to sing, filled with yearning, answered by soft bluesy electric guitar riffs, or by occasional backing vocals. A deep meditative groove is achieved and allowed to play out as per Michael's heart. Eventually, piano and a quick snatch of wordless soprano vocals join in, just as the song begins its long wind-down. Michael would remake 'Zion Land' on his 1978 *Kibir Am Lak* album, but that shorter, faster rendition lacks the magic of this one.

The *Peace & Love* album was combined with Michael's first LP, *Nyahbinghi*, for CD release, but that CD is now out of print. However, the entire content of both albums was subsumed into the three-CD Trojan Records collection called *Trojan Nyahbinghi Box Set*, where these two songs can now be heard.

37 Dennis Brown

Born in 1957 in Kingston, Dennis Emmanuel Brown loved music from childhood. The young fan who then favored American popular singers, especially the smooth tones of Nat King Cole, could not have known that one day he would own an impressive list of reggae credentials. He began performing as a child, at one point promoted by bandleader Byron Lee as "The Boy Wonder". In 1969, aged twelve, he began his recording career as a *youth singer* at Studio One. He had hits with his first singles, 'Lips Of Wine' and 'No Man Is An Island'. Many, many more would follow, and Brown would grow to become one of reggae's biggest stars, gaining the moniker "The Crown Prince of Reggae". He was prolific, releasing over 60 albums and well over 200 singles, with numerous hits throughout each phase of his career. He was one of the most beloved singers ever in Jamaica, his popularity rivaling Bob Marley. Speaking of Marley, he and Brown were good friends, and he consistently named Brown as his favorite singer. That wasn't nepotism, because Dennis Brown was gifted with a fabulous singing voice.

That voice. It certainly ranks with the technically best singing voices in Jamaica, along with Jimmy Cliff, Desmond Dekker and Bunny Wailer. Yet Brown sounded less idiosyncratically Jamaican than these other singers, with diction that never makes a Dennis Brown lyric difficult to understand by non-Jamaican ears. With a voice like his, he could have easily left reggae behind and enjoyed a career in international contemporary urban or even broader categories of popular music, as Jimmy Cliff attempted. But unlike Cliff, Brown never left reggae (only flirting with R&B-reggae sounds in the early 1980s for the USA-based A&M records). Both reggae and his career were better for it. And Jamaica loved him for it.

Beginning his career in 1969, and missing out on the earlier mento, R&B, ska and rock steady (except for a bit) styles, Dennis Brown can be called a pure reggae singer. So much so, he may be the only reggae singer who has never recorded as much as a couplet from a mento song. He performed early reggae, a lot of roots reggae, a good deal of lovers' rock, the aforementioned R&B-reggae, dub as a producer and dancehall. But by the time he was engaged with the newer sounds of that lattermost style, his voice had lost some of its beauty, roughening its sound, allegedly due to lifestyle choices. None of this stopped him from continuing to produce hits, since a sub-peak Dennis Brown vocal was still quite good and just as adored by reggae fans.

Dennis Brown died in 1999 at the age of forty-two of pneumonia, though by all accounts cocaine played a big role in the decline of his health. But this fact did nothing to diminish the love Jamaicans had for him. He was buried in Jamaica's

National Heroes Park cemetery, the first and only entertainer to receive this honor. It is a fitting tribute for the man with a voice that could have made him anything, who chose to stay reggae to the core. His best songs, discussed below, are all available on Dennis Brown CDs.

Words Of Wisdom

Dennis Brown may have released over 60 albums, but it's not difficult to choose the best one. His 1979 *Words Of Wisdom* (one of at least four LPs he released that year) stands out. The Mighty Two (Joe Gibbs and Errol "E. T." Thompson) produced it and a host of musicians contributed. Drummers Sly Dunbar, Neville Grant, Boo Richards and Leroy "Horsemouth" Wallace, bassists Robbie Shakespeare and Lloyd Parks, sax-man (and uncredited flautist) Dean Fraser, *trommie* (a Jamaican term of endearment for a trombonist) Nambo Robinson, trumpet player Willie Breakridge, guitarists Willie Lindo and Bo-Pee Bowen, keyboardists Franklin "Bubbler" Waul and Winston Wright, percussionists Ruddy Thomas and Bubbler are all credited. The backing singers are not.

The producers and musicians bring a consistent and distinctive sound to the album: ensemble playing by big line-ups, with each musician playing at his refined best. Meanwhile, Brown brings to the album a collection of fine new songs (*conscious lyrics* and lover's rock), his great voice at its peak and a sophisticated performance. *Words Of Wisdom* achieves a reggae fabric of a finer weave. It is unusual reggae – totally lacking any burr, yet completely uncompromised and thrillingly good. All this makes it an ideal album with which to introduce the less-than-musically-adventurous to reggae.

'So Jah Say'
'So Jah Say', the album's superb opener, establishes the sound of *Words Of Wisdom*. The arrangement is a finely balanced assembly of bass and drums, a horn section, refined male and female backing vocals, Nyah hand drum, organ, synthesizer, piano, Syndrums and a brief sax solo that breaks out at the song's end. All contribute equally without ever stepping on each other or intruding into the spotlight that is rightfully fixed on Brown. With great passion that is literally inspired by the fear of God, Brown sings about his faith. He does not want to disappoint God, and is aware that there will be consequences if he does. He sings with a virtuoso control of his voice. For example, listen to how he ends his lines, alternating between vibrato and holding the pitch steady. Listen to how he turns up the heat mid-song, as he discusses righteous and unrighteous behavior. And how he raises it even further at the song's conclusion, cutting loose to add cries to a stanza based on Psalms 37:25: "I [have] not seen the righteous forsaken, nor his seed begging bread". (Interestingly, the adaptation from Psalms and the song's title were shared with a previously released song, 'So Jah S'eh', on *Natty Dread*, a 1974 album by Brown's friend Bob Marley that obviously made an impact on him.)

With singing that's expert and passionate, heavy themes and fine music, 'So Jah Say' is a fulfilling listen. And it's just the first song of the album.

'Don't Feel No Way'

'Don't Feel No Way' is a relaxed, slightly funky song that takes its title from the Jamaican way of saying "don't feel bad". A song about music, everything about it is soothing. As the album's second song, it's well positioned after the pressure-cooker opener.

A jam between clavichord and trombone over a guitar, drum and bass backing serves as an introduction. It gives way to the body of the song, opening with blues guitar licks and Brown's funky wordless panting. "Don't feel no way, let Jah music play", he sings in this exploration of how important reggae music is to the people who love it.

> Oh Mister DJ, music is the love of my life.
> If the day should ever come, when music stop playing,
> I don't want to be around ...
> When I'm feeling down and out, music is my only relief ...
> Oh loving music, without you in my life, life wouldn't worth a dime...
> © Keep On Kicking Music Inc c/o Pigfactory USA LLC

It's sung with conviction that leaves little doubt that he means every word. Meanwhile, the backing vocalists repeat key phrases, as the horn section echoes key pieces of his melody. Synthesizer and electric piano are also heard this go-round. There are a lot of reggae songs about reggae, but few as heartfelt or as finely wrought as this one.

'Should I'

'Should I' finds Brown breaking up with an unfaithful girlfriend, but doing so with compassion rather than anger or hate. This makes for an appealing and rather noble piece of lovers' rock. He laments her inability to feel loved, and, without rancor, essentially wishes her the personal growth she will need for better relationships. Female fans across Jamaica swoon. Rather than using backing singers, Brown is double-tracked, harmonizing with himself to dramatic effect. He is supported by a riddim that features a rousing piano phrase, guitar chords quivering aquatically, Syndrums, reggae chop guitar and quiet haunting horn lines. The result is an exceptionally handsome lovers' rock riddim that befits Brown's sentiments.

'Cassandra'

'Cassandra' is a remake of a 1974 song Brown recorded for producer Niney The Observer. The original rendition was popular enough to spawn an equally popular re-voiced version a year later called 'Westbound Train'. But the more polished remake on *Words Of Wisdom* handily surpasses both of these fine earlier recordings.

Its opening borrows from two different Al Green songs. The famous introductory guitar riff from his 'Love And Happiness' is heard, though Green never thought to accent it with Syndrums. The opening lines from 'Here I Am Baby' are employed as well. And with all respect to Al Green, here possession proves to be ten-tenths of the law, as Brown and his song are so good, there is no aspect of 'Cassandra' that isn't heard as one hundred percent reggae and one hundred percent Dennis Brown.

One of several hits from *Words Of Wisdom*, 'Cassandra' is another lovers' rock song, but one that's more saucy than the selfless 'Should I'. And whereas the other song was a stately stroll, 'Cassandra' gallops. It finds Brown in a much better romantic situation than before, as he joyfully sings of his woman's faithfulness and how good she makes him feel. To the latter point, eradicating any feelings of loneliness and sadness he may have had, she gives him love around the clock. He salutes this by asking Cassandra to "ride on".

Brown's joy is nicely matched by an evocative riddim: a light-hearted skank that's tightly funky. Prominent bubbling organs (one holding down the rhythm, one dancing atop) are the featured instrument, while a muted wah-wah guitar track keeps an aspect of Al Green's guitar riff alive throughout the song. A busy bass line, rim-shots, Syndrums and other percussion accents complete the detailed, refined arrangement, in line with the rest of the album. 'Cassandra' is a delight.

'Black Liberation'

'Black Liberation' is Brown's *upfull* prediction of black unity and triumph over oppression. He does not explicitly identify the oppressors as Babylon or tie the story directly to Jamaica, broadening the message to other places on the globe where its themes apply. His performance brings such authority and passion to these words, the impact of his positive message is multiplied many times. The dignified backing music opens with an unusual synthesized mandolin-like sound and features a Nyah hand drum. It's further fitted with an extreme wah-wah guitar solo mid-song. Quiet backing vocals, guitar leads, reggae chop guitar, elaborate drum work, organ, piano and even a gong also contribute. 'Black Liberation', like several songs on *Words Of Wisdom*, is the very sound of triumph.

'Drifter'

'Drifter' is a cover of a fine bluesy song from 1969 by reggae singer Dennis Walks, about a man who can't be tied down. Producer Harry Mudie gave it a great riddim with a distinctive bass line and a memorable horn refrain. It is almost unfair to Walks that another Dennis with an unparalleled voice and with an inspired band and producers would cover his song. Brown's rendition is a classic, relegating Walks's original to footnote status.

The song provides a perfect showcase for Brown's gift. He unleashes a vocal performance rich with both blues and joy, as he makes the most of his vibrato. It opens with a big, simple reggae drum roll that pans across the stereo soundstage. Brown wails, "Oh girl!", the drum roll returns, and the body of the song comes in. The original's mighty bass line is intact as is the horn phrase, though handled here by organ. The riddim is rounded out by rim-shot-rich drums, blues guitar noodling, piano and reggae chop guitar. Though it keeps with its sound, it uses a smaller ensemble than is typical of the album. This suits both the song and Brown. His voice, without backing vocalists or double-tracking, fills the song, right up to the joyous closing refrain of "turn me on".

'Money In My Pocket'

'Money In My Pocket' is as close to a signature song that the prolific Dennis Brown had. It's a remake of the hit he previously recorded for Gibbs in 1972. It opens with Brown complaining that even though he has money to spend, he can't seem to land a girlfriend. It's fun to hear one of the most popular Jamaicans to ever walk on the island portraying himself as an Everyman unable to find love. He bemoans being so alone, and, whether you take him seriously or not, he sounds great.

Probably coming from another session, this track has a more typical reggae arrangement for its time than the rest of *Words Of Wisdom*. A smaller band with a more direct approach and drums out front is heard, rather than the fine-grained ensemble playing of the rest of the album. Although this remake is good, as is every rendition of 'Money In My Pocket', I prefer the original for its more detailed riddim. However, others may see the more restrained vocals of the original a reason to prefer this remake. The original is identifiable by its length of just over 2:30 minutes compared to the 3-plus minutes of the remake. Both are better than another rendition, a remake that was released a year after Brown's death that clocks in at about 4 minutes.

Other Words Of Wisdom songs

Rounding out the set are five more songs, all nearly as good, if not as distinct, as the songs above. 'Ain't That Loving You' is a rendition of the love song originally recorded by US soul singer Luther Ingram that has been frequently covered in Jamaica and the USA. The introspective title track, 'Words Of Wisdom', features synthesized flute and biblical lyrics befitting its name. 'Rasta Children' is an urgent roots reggae song where Brown longs for Zion while enduring Babylon. 'A True' is a devotional song that's more assertive than introspective, featuring lovely flute from Dean Fraser. 'Love Jah' is another devotional song. It features impassioned vocals, a fine melody, and yet another example of a big, detailed *Words Of Wisdom* instrumental arrangement.

Other great Dennis Brown songs

'Let Love In'
Produced by Phil Pratt in 1972, 'Let Love In' is a glorious piece of lovers' rock. Soft lead organ, romantic piano, idiosyncratic cymbal taps and rippling guitar picked halfway to mandolin territory, all give the arrangement a sound that is appealingly gentle. Rather than singing about a particular love interest of his, Brown plays Cupid for his legion of fans. He opens by reminding us how important love is and proceeds to dispense relationship advice. One gem is for the man to keep in mind a woman's remembrance of the love her father showed her. He is in fine voice throughout, singing unaided by – and in no way needing –backing vocals or double-tracking. And as so many of his songs do, this one ends with him cutting loose, his voice effortlessly soaring in a way that lesser singers can only envy. Though not as famous as many of his songs, 'Let Love In' is available on several Dennis Brown CD collections and should not be missed. Just be sure to get the original rendition (2-plus minutes) rather than the longer (4-plus minutes) 1984 Joe Gibbs-produced remake that appeared on his *Emmanuel* album. Though not bad, this rendition loses the gentle magic of the original.

'Some Like It Hot'
Quoting a nursery rhyme, Brown sings "some like it hot, some like it cold".This ensures that everyone will like this 1975 Sidney Crooks production, as it pairs a red-hot reggae groove with a stone-cold great vocal performance. It opens with three big, swollen syncopated beats. They tumble into a high-powered skanking groove, led by two instruments. A springy rhythm guitar adds a spongy bounce to every beat, while it gives the song a cycle of melody. It's complemented by bass playing double-time clusters with a melody that supports Brown's. Getting in on this are drums, piano that is buried in the mix and incidental percussion. Together they create a riddim sizzling with energy.

As hot as the riddim is, Brown plays it cool. He holds court, broadly musing on Rasta concerns. His vocal is vintage Dennis Brown, crooning as only he can, with articulation, tone control, phrasing and vibrato that are expert and effortless. He deems to raise his intensity just a bit, explaining that good behavior will be rewarded by God, and follows it with a brief wordless outburst. The double-tracking that subtly entered the song at an earlier point blooms, as a second Dennis Brown assists in bringing this terrific song to conclusion.

'Some Like It Hot' can be heard on a number of Dennis Brown collections. Its riddim that bears the same name was popular for versioning and enjoyed a revival in 2004. An impressive dub harmonica cut of the riddim, also from 1975, called 'Black Man Message', was described previously in this book (page 294).

'On The Rocks'
In 1981, Brown began a three-album run for the USA-based A&M label. Produced by the label's head Clive Hunt and Joe Gibbs, the musicians were mostly Jamaican

with a few US sessions aces thrown in. The body of work was uneven, with regular reggae, internationalized reggae and diluted reggae casting a wide net to catch overseas ears. 'On The Rocks' came from the first A&M album, *Foul Play*. It is in an international reggae style that sounds not unlike Brown backed by Third World at their best. It's anchored by a simplified drum rhythm and a funk-influenced reggae bass line, complete with thumb-popping. There's piano, sax and blues guitar wailing in the background, all of which would fit into any Dennis Brown song. But there are also jazz chords, fast syncopated runs, oversized sax solos and a squashed-funky synthesizer solo – sounds not typical of reggae. Not that this is a bad thing in this case. It's a good enough vehicle to have provided Brown with a potential international hit.

Brown's melodies are strong, and his singing is spirited, but the lyrics are eyebrow-raising. Another song on the album *If I Had The World* shows something of his state of mind, as he compares the good feeling he gets from a lover to the effects of cocaine. 'On The Rocks' is a thinly veiled song about addiction to freebase cocaine, the crack of its day. Brown explains that "livin' hard on the rock" is a bleak existence of insanity that is hard on the body as well. But lest he admit that this is an autobiographical song, he externalizes the problem to the story of a woman. He reproaches her, asking how she can choose to be a user. Other lyrics have a paranoid streak, with references to Glocks and plots, and the song ends off-puttingly with the female backing vocalists singing about using Brown. Although Brown and his backing vocalists give a great performance, close examination reveals that all was not well with the singer.

Gregory Isaacs and Dennis Brown: *'Let Off Supm'*
'Let Off Supm', produced in 1985 by Gussie Clarke, is not the only meeting of the era's two biggest solo stars. But it's the only one to live up to its billing. However, it cannot be said to be the meeting of two of reggae's best voices. By this point in his career, Dennis Brown's singing was affected by his smoking of substances stronger and less healthy than the ganja usually associated with reggae singers. Though his perfect voice was a thing of the past, he could still sing well enough that his popularity in Jamaica would continue unabated. And his hoarse voice suits the song's lyrics. Gregory Isaacs, by contrast, is in fine voice, supremely in control of his distinctive vocals as he always is.

They tell the story of a chance encounter between friends. Isaacs sings an intro and then Brown tells the story, with Isaacs interjecting in the role of Brown's friend. Brown is surprised to have bumped into his friend, especially when he asks for help, describing hard times, hunger and homelessness. The friend sings the song's title, meaning "please give me something". They then trade roles, with Gregory taking the lead, and go on to switch twice more. Brown's round tone and hoarse voice and Isaacs's nasal tone and angular delivery contrast brilliantly. In particular, every time the song is handed off to Isaacs, it's electrifying.

It features an austere backing, courtesy of Sly & Robbie, that suits the lyrics and gives the two stars the room they require. Sly by then had moved to electronic Simmons drums, and their sound gives this biting song even more of a chill. Adding to this, the bass, guitar and piano all sound mechanized to different degrees. Only a Nyah hand drum adds any warmth, a lone candle in the window of a dark house.

The preferred "original mix" is found as the B-side of the 12-inch single released on the Greensleeves label. The more commonly available mix effectively wrecks the song by adding smothering, persistent keyboards and superfluous backing vocals, cluttering things up beyond belief. It's a duet between Gregory Isaacs and Dennis Brown, backed by Sly & Robbie! Why crowd in more vocalists? Why are those ugly synthesizers playing over everything? A solo version of the song with Isaacs handling all the vocals also uses this unfortunate mix. Hopefully the original mix of 'Let Off Supm' will make its CD debut sometime soon. It's too important a track not to. In the meantime, having been released in the USA and UK, the Greensleeves single is not very hard to track down.

38 Gregory Isaacs

He recorded for a short time under the outrageous pseudonym William Shake-speare, and is sometimes called "Jah Toot' ", in recognition of a broken tooth received in an encounter with a policeman. But the adored reggae superstar Gregory Isaacs is known to his legion of fans by the accolade The Cool Ruler, or simply by his first name, without there being any doubt of the Gregory in question. Born in 1950 in Kingston, Gregory Anthony Isaacs lived a hardscrabble life that was brightened by a love of music. He began singing in his teens and by the end of the 1960s, boosted by an appearance on the popular *Vere Johns Opportunity Hour* radio show, he endeavored to go pro. Brought into recording by bandleader Byron Lee, he recorded short stints as half of a duo and then as a member of a trio. But success eluded him. Rather than trying a quartet next, he wisely went solo. A handful of singles recorded in 1970 for several producers included his first hit, 'All I Have Is Love', for Rupie Edwards. There was no turning back. He became one of the greatest solo stars ever in reggae, his popularity in Jamaica only surpassed by Dennis Brown and Bob Marley

His stardom was assured by his voice. Gregory Isaacs had perhaps the most distinctive singing voice in reggae. His approach to melody was unique, working exclusively within a personalized African-influenced scale. This suited his nasal intonation, idiosyncratic approach to phrasing and crooning delivery. The result is a singer who was immediately recognizable, one of a kind and iconic, just as Johnny Cash was in American country and Western music. It's hard to imagine that with a voice so individual he ever tried to blend in with a vocal group.

Gregory was a double threat, applying his talent with equal success to *sufferas* roots reggae and to lovers' rock. The men especially revered him for the former. The ladies especially loved him for the latter. With a career that began in the reggae-proper era, after rock steady and all the styles that came before it, Isaacs, like Dennis Brown, can be called a pure reggae singer. He released numerous singles, with a steady stream of hits for various producers (including himself, starting in 1974). In 1982, 'Night Nurse' crossed over to become a worldwide hit, giving people outside of Jamaica their first taste of this unique talent. Although the featured synthesizers make the riddim sound dated, the vocal performance is timeless, especially the pain/ecstasy of the chorus, "My night nurse, oh, the pain is getting worse". Isaacs was arrested and incarcerated on a gun charge a year later – a development that could not have helped any plans for further global success, especially since he had by then begun a long battle with crack cocaine. In 1990, another hit, 'Rumours', added to his résumé. It showed that the distinctive voice of Gregory Isaacs riding the hard synthesized dancehall sounds of early ragga could be a potent combination. In all, he would record over 200 singles and over 50 albums.

Gregory Isaacs's recording career came to an end with an album in 2008. Though he continued to perform live, he died in 2010 at the age of fifty-nine, a year after being diagnosed with the lung cancer that took away one of reggae's most distinctive voices. Much beloved, he was given a state funeral and was celebrated twice by his peers. First, at the funeral, with performances from Ken Boothe, The Tamlins, Judy Mowatt, Freddie McGregor and others. Then at a tribute concert with Bunny Wailer, Shaggy, Freddie McGregor, Junior Reid, Leroy Sibbles and Tony Rebel amongst others who wanted to commemorate the career of reggae's late, great Cool Ruler.

'All I Have Is Love'
Produced by Rupie Edwards in 1970, Gregory Isaacs's first hit, 'All I Have Is Love' shows him bringing his unique approach to melody and his other special vocal qualities fully formed. It fires a warning shot, announcing that there is a unique and talented new singer on the scene. He's singing about looking for love, and wears his vulnerability on his sleeve. You'd better keep an eye on your woman.

'All I Have Is Love' is a *loving pauper* song, a hallmark theme of lovers' rock. Songs where the singer offers true love in place of material wealth are popular in Jamaica. Dobby Dobson's 'I'm A Loving Pauper' was a rock steady hit that was covered by many including Isaacs in 1973. The Techniques' 'Queen Majesty' (a song described earlier in this book; page 131) is another popular example. Here, though the lyrics are few, the song is potent. The reggae riddim supports Isaacs perfectly. The see-sawing guitar and bass operate along the parameters of Isaacs's scale, assisting in his wooing. The outcome of his pleading remains unresolved. But with Isaacs's unique instrument so expert and new, there can be little doubt that his love prevails.

'Babylon Too Rough'
'Babylon Too Rough', produced by Joe Gibbs in 1976, is a cover of 'Easy Take It Easy', a Dennis Brown Studio One track from 1972. Brown's original and his subsequent remakes are very good, but Isaacs steals the song and tops any of Brown's renditions.

The dubby guitar strums that take the place of an opening drum roll tip us off about the stylistic change from the original. This is dub-infused, languid reggae, compared to the rock steady snappiness of Brown's song. In fact, if the rhythm section was any more relaxed, they would have put down their instruments. Spare piano, a rhythm guitar and touches of dub complete a riddim that sways in the air. Gregory enters with wordless singing somewhere between crooning and wailing – a place that only he can occupy. Like Brown he counsels the listener to take it easy but by the second line he alters the meaning of Brown's song, which was deliberately vague and could have been about anything. Isaacs brings the focus squarely on the oppression of Jamaica's Rastas by Babylon. Singing of Babylon's brutish behavior, his bluesy delivery sounds like he came to this knowledge by a hard path. He alternates between repeating the song's few lines and wounded wordless singing. It's as if the violence of Babylon is putting a bridle on his energies, keeping him at a low simmer. And, as less is often more in reggae, the understated 'Babylon Too Rough' is a song of great power.

'Extra Classic'

'Extra Classic', self-produced in 1976, is a standout lovers' rock song from a man who recorded many. The skillful instrumentation flawlessly supports Gregory's love song. The percussion is approachable, warm with rim shots and sweetened by tambourine. The organ and rhythm/lead guitar are accessible and create a romantic air. The bass line is affable, but no fool. It provides a countermelody to Isaacs's, while its staccato clusters are a contrast to his long notes.

As is typical, Isaacs is in total command of his voice. Notice how he leisurely bends notes at his own idiosyncratic angles for maximum dramatic effect. He proclaims his love, even though his woman doesn't have a movie star's looks. A popular lovers' rock theme, this exact notion was previously voiced by Delroy Wilson in 'I Don't Know Why' and is similar in sentiment to The Paragons' 'Wear You To The Ball' (songs described previously in this book; pages 185 and 126). But Isaacs's heart-melting performance makes this notion sound brand-new. He opens with affirmations that are accepting and soothing. He then croons to "Sister Love", pitching woo. And in the chorus, though she isn't a movie star, he finds her to be "extra classic". Coming from Gregory Isaacs, and considering the particularly twisty melody he brings to the sentiment, this accolade is special. By the time he makes a hook out of repeating "Sister Love", the song is awash in tenderness. But while the song is comfort food for the heart, make no mistake, the music is in no way insubstantial. The song fully lives up to its name.

'Extra Classic' can be heard on any number of Gregory Isaacs collections. But only the expanded CD edition of the *Extra Classic* album also includes its very good dub version, called 'Classy Dub'. Without losing its comforting nature, 'Extra Classic' gets shot through with spaciness in what was originally released as the single's B-side.

'Mr. Know It All'

Produced by Lloyd Campbell in 1976, 'Mr. Know It All' appears on various Gregory Isaacs collections in sub-3-minute and 4-minute edits. The recommended mix discussed here is the full-glory, 5-plus-minute version as found on the album called *Mr. Isaacs*. Don't accidentally wind up with the 1995 remake on the *Private Lesson* album that is also 5-plus minutes, as it has few of the strengths of the original rendition.

A vexing adversary and a well-appointed backing give Gregory a double spring-board from which to dispense cool. There is also an added attraction provided by the great reggae drummer, Sly Dunbar. He hints at what's to come by opening the song with a brief relaxed roll on tuned tom-toms. Then reggae comes forth, anchored by busy bass and deliciously sharp organ riffs that sound the censure of Isaac's lyrics. Touches of piano and bubble-up organ are also present. Dub is applied as selected guitar chops flash with reverb or take flight with echo, whir-ring like a cicada. Backing singers intone a chorus of "Yes, Mister Know It All". Hand percussion adds spice.

Gregory wears these elements like a tailored suit. He criticizes the titular figure who thinks he knows everything and talks a lot, but is pathologically evasive. If Isaacs asks about the hills, Mr. Know It All talks about the valley instead. If he brings up *The Gleaner*, Mr. Know It All talks about *The Star* (these being two of Jamaica's top newspapers). It's time for a dressing-down, but being The Cool Ruler, even though his annoyance is plain, Gregory is still calm and composed. He tells Mr. Know It All that people will soon realize that he actually knows nothing and he will then be ignored.

As the story winds up, dub plays a greater role in the mix, and Gregory soon echoes right out of the track's second half. But this is not a disco-mix, where a dub version of the riddim would now be heard. Instead, the riddim continues as Sly Dunbar enjoys a loose-limbed workout. Sometimes he is working hard, and other times he just seems to be enjoying the sounds his drums make. Meanwhile Robbie Shakespeare's bass holds together what grows into an odd jam. When a drummer of Sly Dunbar's caliber and accomplishments wants to free-associate, it's a good thing, especially when it's enriching and elongating an already fine song. And if this longer mix doesn't satisfy your appetite, a fine, surprisingly unrecognizable dub version called 'Know It All Dub' can be heard on the CD collection called *Gregory In Dub*.

'Mr. Cop'

'Mr. Cop' was produced by Lee Perry in 1977. It finds Isaacs confronting another adversarial mister, an honorific he apparently liked to use ironically. Though it's not their only collaboration, it's the best coming together of two great, distinctly reggae sounds: the voice of Gregory Isaacs and the sonics of a Black Ark produc-tion. Perry goes light for this song, using his Black Ark prowess to conjure a riddim that bounds unhurriedly across a cloudscape. The sound is further softened by lush backing vocals that offset Isaacs's nasal, incisive voice. For his part, Isaacs seems to be enjoying his time up in the clouds. He lives up to his Cool Ruler mon-iker, sounding relaxed and unbothered, even as he addresses an angry, intrusive policeman and suggests that he calm down. Isaacs rambles and repeats as the music floats by. Then he audaciously explains to the policeman that they were just "licking a cup" – lighting a water-pipe to smoke herb, as if that should be no big deal to a policeman. Finally, no doubt feeling good, he tries reasoning with the cop by presenting him with a nursery rhyme and asking him to mind his own business. He then delivers a rather fanciful version of the "ganja is part of nature" argument. The unlikely possibility that the policeman was in any way swayed by these stoned-sounding musings remains unresolved by the song. Rather than on one of the many Black Ark compilations, 'Mr. Cop' can be heard on several Gregory Isaacs CDs. Choose the one called *Extra Classic*, as it includes the even billowier dub called 'Mr. Cop (Version)'.

'Rock On' (aka 'Rock Away')

Produced by Niney The Observer in 1978, 'Rock On' combines a sad lovers' rock performance from Gregory with a bluesy riddim that draws you in. It's led by a bass line with a see-sawing melody that, unaltered for the duration, grows hypnotic. It's adorned at key points by slurred guitar leads that are cheerlessly bluesy. A touch of sad piano and rhythm guitar support, and the result is a low-key riddim in a down-low mood.

Matching this, Gregory sounds subdued and vulnerable, as he wonders whether his patched-up relationship will last. Opening by lavishing praise on his woman, he makes her importance to him clear. He is then moved by her to ecstatically sing a wordless stanza. But Gregory is unsettled by past events, recalling that she once left him. He begs her not to go again, lavishing more praise. And female reggae fans around the world gasp at the woman who would leave Gregory and, after gaining a second chance, could leave him again. 'Rock On' is available on the Gregory Isaacs album of the same name, as well as on several other collections. A compilation called *Niney The Observer – Roots With Quality* contains a dubbier mix of the song, which is good, though the original uncluttered version is most recommended.

'Rumours'

As digitally created ragga supplanted lovers' rock, roots and even earlier dancehall sounds, some may have worried about the future of Gregory Isaacs, a singer with such an organic voice. Not to mention a cocaine problem and a recent arrest and incarceration. That's why the 1998 Gussie Clark-produced 'Rumours' was nothing less than a triumph for Isaacs. Though the riddim was recognizably reggae, every instrument is replaced by a blustering digital equivalent. The most radically altered are the horns, replaced by a synthesizer set to whole-orchestra-at-once, bringing an ominous edginess to the riddim. Though a different sound for him, 'Rumours' was a big hit for Gregory.

In it, he addresses the top Gregory Isaacs issues of the day. He is aware of the rumors of his alleged move into drug-dealing. He dismisses them by wishing them "a gwaan" (be gone). He alludes to the rumor that he would retreat from the new sounds of ragga. Instead, he calls himself the Don (top dog or boss, as in Don

Corleone of *The Godfather*) of dancehall. He also points out that he is doing well enough financially to be generous to others while keeping himself well dressed. He had cause to brag, as 'Rumours' would not be a one-shot ragga hit. He continued to record successfully in that style, first with Gussie Clark and then with other producers. In another Gussie Clark-produced song, 'Rough Neck', Gregory continued to address his rumor-spreaders and detractors. He explains that, although he does not claim to be perfect, his critics need not bother because he will admit to anything he does wrong.

'Rumours' can be found on numerous reggae compilations and Gregory Isaacs collections. The namesake riddim was popular, spawning other versions, including a song that was as popular if not more so than 'Rumours' – Telephone Love' by singer J. C. Lodge and DJ Shabba Ranks.

39 Black Uhuru and Michael Rose

Starting out as an undistinguished roots vocal group, after a number of personnel changes Black Uhuru found a magic combination of talent and became one of the greatest of all reggae groups. In the early 1980s their acclaimed albums and live shows would vault them to the top of popularity in the international reggae arena. But the revolving door that made them great also proved to be their undoing, when this once-respected name became diminished.

Founded in 1972, Black Uhuru began recording around 1975 with a line-up of Euvin "Don Carlos" Spencer on lead vocals, along with backing vocalists Rudolph "Garth" Dennis and Derrick "Duckie" Simpson. By 1977, all of them but the perennial member Simpson had been replaced, most significantly with Michael Rose joining as lead singer. Born in 1957, Rose was discovered by producer Niney The Observer at a talent show. He recorded half a dozen singles before taking Carlos's place in the group. Rose was a Waterhouse singer. A rough Kingston neighborhood even by Kingston standards, Waterhouse is special place to reggae fans. That's because more than a few singers who hail from there feature an idiosyncratic style of vocalization, a wordless wailing that has been compared to sounds as diverse as yodeling, Native American chanting and Middle Eastern prayer. That's a lot of territory for one tough Kingston neighborhood to have taken in. To a reggae fan, Waterhouse singing is simply and unmistakably roots reggae, a product of nowhere but Jamaica. And no one was better at it than Michael Rose.

With Rose, Black Uhuru recorded their first LP, *Love Crisis*, in 1977 for producer Prince Jammy. Though it only hinted at the greatness to come, it was good enough to spawn a remixed LP (*Black Sounds Of Freedom*) and a dub LP (*Uhuru In Dub*, credited to Prince Jammy). For this session, Black Uhuru was backed as the rhythm section/bandleaders by drummer Sly Dunbar (who also hailed from Waterhouse and knew Rose) and bassist Robbie Shakespeare, though their best work with the group was still to come. Sly & Robbie had recorded with Michael Rose before, as we will see. And in time, they would join the group as members, making Black Uhuru, like The Wailers and Third World, not just a vocal group, but a completely contained musical outfit (with Sly & Robbie serving as Black Uhuru's producers to boot).

It was 1979 when the group first started to strike gold with a number of great singles for various producers and backing bands. That same year, further line-up changes cemented Black Uhuru's greatness. The third vocal spot changed for a second time, as Puma Jones, an African-American woman who had moved to Jamaica to find an artistic outlet, and had previously sung with Ras Michael, was recruited by Simpson to join the group. A woman joining a roots harmony group was unusual; the various female singers The Wailers used over time offer the only other examples. For an American to become a member of a Jamaican vocal group was absolutely unheard of. But there was good reason. Jones's bell-clear, haunting vocals were feminine and beautiful, the perfect foil for Simpson's dry, restrained and gritty roots singing. Together, their harmonies were dramatic and unlike anyone else's. And Jones also brought an element of dance to Uhuru's live performances. By then, Sly & Robbie were beginning to provide Black Uhuru records with some of their best playing (and that is saying a lot), as well as fine, dub-filled production. For his part, Michael Rose would prove to be the undisputed best Black Uhuru lead vocalist. The combination of these talents, all just beginning to peak, resulted in not only the best Black Uhuru line-up, but one of the greatest amalgamations of reggae talent, on a par with such great names as the Skatalites and Bob Marley & The Wailers.

This line-up released a fantastic string of singles in 1979 and 1980 that were collected with their dub version B-sides on an LP called *Showcase*. The group followed with two internationally released albums of excellent new material. *Sinsemilla* (1980) and *Red* (1981) were reggae dynamite. Only Bob Marley had a longer run of such solid reggae albums. The sound on these sets ran from roots reggae, to dub-soaked reggae, into progressive roots, a style that Black Uhuru exclusively owned. Horns were only rarely heard in Black Uhuru's music. In fact, not one of the songs chosen as their best and described below has horns.

Between 1982 and 1984, the same line-up released a pretty good live album (*Tear It Up*), two pretty good studio LPs (*Chill Out* and *Anthem*), and a pretty good dub album (*Dub Factor*). But the quality of what had come before just couldn't be maintained. Then Michael Rose departed the group, to be replaced by Junior Reid, yet another Waterhouse singer, only eighteen years old. The result was *Brutal*, an album with one great track, one good track and a spate of weak ones, as the once-formidable Black Uhuru was officially sputtering. By 1990, Puma had passed away, far too young, of breast cancer at the age of thirty-six. She was replaced by another female singer for the album *Positive*, a set that had only one strong track. After that, Sly & Robbie departed, original lead singer Don Carlos returned, re-departed, and so on. This left Duckie Simpson as the only constant member and owner of the Black Uhuru name. There have been attempts to put Rose, Simpson, Sly & Robbie back together, but sadly these efforts have fizzled.

Michael Rose: 'Artibella'

The first great Black Uhuru single was not actually by Black Uhuru. It was 'Artibella', a 1975 single by Michael Rose that featured two other future Black Uhuru members, the newly formed rhythm section and production team of Sly & Robbie. Starting in 1973, Michael Rose had previously recorded a few undistinguished sides for a number of producers. This, his first work with Sly & Robbie, showed a natural synergy that would soon be more fully exploited.

'Artibella' is a cover of one of Ken Boothe's signature songs (as previously described in this book; page 139). But the riddim Sly & Robbie provide is brand-new. An introduction featuring swirling organ and low piano notes sets a dramatic tone for Rose. And he takes a different approach from Ken Boothe's rock steady cool. Instead, Rose's raspy emotive vocal is full of pain in a melodramatic reading of the song. His Waterhouse inflections add even more to the drama, especially the brief outpouring at the song's end, a signpost of great Waterhouse singing to come. Amidst Rose's despair, the band drops the heavy drama of the song's introduction and shifts into a more playful mode. High piano notes, small organ phrases, and tambourine dance atop of a tricky, bouncing Sly & Robbie riddim. Whether you take it as high drama or as camp, this rendition of 'Artibella' is tremendously enjoyable. It's hard not to be thoroughly entertained by an idio-syncratically great singer and band, both emerging into greatness and giving their all to lyrics like, "Artibella, she took all my money and told me that she loves me."

Though there are numerous, repetitious Black Uhuru anthologies, 'Artibella' has not appeared on any of them. So for the time being, the only way to hear this track is to find the original single, as released on the Taxi label. It features a nice dub on the B-side, where Robbie's bass line becomes the centerpiece, and echo-ing vocal and guitar skyrockets decorate the dub canvas. Nor are you likely to hear Michael Rose perform this song live. In the early 1980s, before a Black Uhuru show in New York City, I had the opportunity to ask Michael Rose if he would be singing 'Artibella' that night. He smiled, covered his face with his hand in mock embarrassment, and answered emphatically, "No man, nooo."

Michael Rose: *'Clap The Barber' (aka 'Clap The Ba Ba'); 'Guess Who's Coming To Dinner'*
'Clap The Barber' is another great Michael Rose song from 1975, produced by George Boswell, who is better known as Niney The Observer. Sly & Robbie are not part of this recording. The song describes the barber as a symbolic oppressor of Rastafarianism, who comes to Mount Zion to cut off the Rastas' dreadlocks. Rose introduces the song with the stray line, "Ba ba, move ya," meaning "barber, begone". This is a clever play on a much earlier Jamaican song called 'Miss A Ram Goat'. This folk/mento song about goat-shearing time opened with "Ba Ba Di Ya".

The song is practically a duet for voice and bass, with minimal distraction from subdued guitar and drums, and piano faint in the mix. Different from 'Artibella', Rose's vocal is restrained this time around, which precludes any Waterhouse sing-ing. But midway, he cries out to other dreadlocks, "Do you hear that deadlock!?" with strong vibrato and sustain on the last syllable, sounding like the missing link between Jacob Miller and Dennis Brown. Sharing the spotlight with Rose, equally loud in the mix, is an incredibly fat, sparse, deliberate bass line that sounds like it could easily be translated to stand-up bass. It gives 'Clap The Barber' a distinc-tive sound.

Rose would re-voice the riddim for Niney, keeping the same melody but writing new lyrics. This was the first (though certainly not the best) rendition of 'Guess Who's Coming To Dinner'. As we will see, this song would be remade often even by reggae standards, and would provide both Black Uhuru and Michael Rose with their signature songs. 'Clap The Barber' and the original rendition of 'Guess Who's Coming To Dinner' are both available on the CD collection called *Blood And Fire: Hit Sounds From The Observer Station*.

Michael Rose: *'Born Free'*
Michael Rose's 'Born Free', from 1979, is sometimes credited to Black Uhuru, perhaps because the backing vocals sound like the group's pre-Jones line-up. Produced by Prince Jammy, who would later produce Black Uhuru's first album, it employs a non-Sly & Robbie backing band.

Though not as intense as some of the other Black Uhuru tracks described here, the song succeeds in meeting its own particular goals. It opens with a tumble of drums and a long, loping organ line over an exaggeratedly spongy, bouncing reggae beat. In simple lyrics, Rose sings a common Rasta theme: the pain of being in a country where he is oppressed rather than free. He's at a low boil, again free of Waterhouse flourishes. But his secret weapon is the dramatic twists and turns his melody navigates as the riddim bounces. Though the least striking of the Michael Rose/Black Uhuru songs described here, 'Born Free' still offers much and it would be a shame to miss it. It's available on a number of collections, more often than not in the format I recommend: as a 7-minute disco-mix with an appended dub version that nicely keeps the groove going.

Black Uhuru and Jah Grundy: *'Rent Man' / 'Resident Area'*
'Rent Man', also from 1979, finds Michael Rose as the lead singer of Black Uhuru, but it was recorded just before Puma Jones or Sly & Robbie had joined the group. It's a record so good that both Dennis Brown and Joe Gibbs claimed production credit. Let's get situated, as there are different mixes and renditions available on various collections. You will want the disco-mix with an appended DJ version from Jah Grundy called 'Resident Area'. You should avoid the original single mix, the disco-mix with DJ Jah Thomas and Mykal (one of several alternative spellings he would eventually adopt) Rose's 2008 remake. Now you're set to enjoy a tremendous slab of disco-mix roots reggae.

As we have seen, reggae has a tradition of rent songs dating back to mento, but Black Uhuru's 'Rent Man' takes this subject to a new level of intensity. These songs typically used humor to bemoan problems with the rental or the landlord. But this is roots reggae, where social problems are not laughed away as in mento, but confronted head-on. Black Uhuru is dead serious, showing the rent man resentment, advocating resistance, and provocatively mocking him (offering a single Jamaican dollar as suitable rent for the tenement).

Producer and band provide a highly competent roots backing that's subtly enlivened with touches of dub. The drummer emphasizes the third beat of every four and a typically fine roots reggae bass line is heard. The anchoring reggae guitar chop is alive with come-and-go reverb. A Nyah hand drummer creates a bubbling undercurrent of protest. Trebly organ and guitar runs adorn. The unobtrusive backing vocals sound like they are trying to calm the fiery Rose. They do not.

Rose is unleashed and his vocal is powerful throughout. He conveys desperation, sarcasm, resistance and pain in an expressive performance. It's rich with Waterhouse flourishes, such as his trademark *whoh-ho*. At the end of the song, with the backing vocalists chanting the titular refrain, Rose unleashes a series of wails that cumulate in an extraordinary Waterhouse yowl that has to be heard to be believed. The song is already dynamite, but it's not over yet.

The very moment Rose's wail ends, the DJ version abruptly crashes in, with Jah Grundy chanting about his experience with tenement living, being penniless, and the rent man. (In a production move you will only hear in reggae, no effort is given to matching up the beats of the two versions. This visible seam between the versions adds to the urgency of the disco-mix.) The otherwise unknown DJ rides the riddim as if he was born to record this song and retire. By taking up Rose's theme and serious approach, Jah Grundy helps validate Rose's views, strengthening an already strong record. The DJ version is longer than the vocal, and has additional dub at its end, making this mix of 'Rent Man' a 7-minute-plus epic.

But in case 7 minutes is not enough, the disco-mix single included an OK dub version on its B-side. But a better dub version – and one that's far easier to obtain – is the instrumental called 'Cayamanas Park Dub', which can be found on producer Roderick "Blackbeard" Sinclair's CD compilation called *A Blackbeard Production – Too Much Iron In The Fire*.

Black Uhuru: *'Wood For My Fire'*
'Wood For My Fire' shares with 'Rent Man' its year of release, its Black Uhuru line-up and a contested production credit. But the sound is different from 'Rent Man' and the other songs here. It's rootsy to the point of being able to smell the soil; rough and ready, with several instruments imperfectly in tune. For a roots reggae fan, finding a song this real is like uncovering a rare truffle in the woods.

Its introduction features two unusual sounds that immediately set a haunting tone. One is a synthesizer that plays a rapid cycle of organ notes, sounding like an impossibly fast double-picked mandolin. The other is Rose's Waterhouse singing unbound. He sounds earthy and exotic as he chants nonsense syllables and Waterhouse flourishes. Filling out the song are decidedly unflashy rootsy drums and bass, a reggae guitar chop, an undercurrent of grimy guitar leads and a shaker that adds a prominent rasping sound. Rose sings of familiar roots reggae concerns, such as how he's thwarted by poverty and oppression. The unobtrusive backing vocals are cool and dread, but overpowered by Rose's lead that manages to be stoical, yet fiery. With an imminent personnel change, the backing vocals would soon be too striking to ignore. 'Wood For My Fire' can be heard on *Ranking Joe's Zion High* CD, along with his DJ version. The single's dub B-side remains unreleased on CD.

Black Uhuru: *Showcase* (aka *Guess Who's Coming To Dinner*; aka *Black Uhuru*)

Once their best line-up came together (Rose, Simpson and Jones backed by Sly & Robbie), Black Uhuru hit the ground running. From 1979 to 1980, they released seven great singles, each with a dub B-side. These fourteen sides were collected as seven disco-mix tracks, presented showcase-style on an LP with *Showcase* as its title. With more than a few classics and lacking anything resembling a weak song, Black Uhuru's *Showcase* is one of the best reggae albums ever recorded and undisputedly the greatest of all showcase LPs. But this title was shelved when the album was released on CD overseas. In the USA it's called *Guess Who's Coming To Dinner*, released on the Heartbeat label, and in the UK it's eponymously titled *Black Uhuru*, released on the Virgin label. Each has a mix different from the LP.

Whatever it's called, it's a must-have reggae album. It unveils the exciting Rose, Simpson and Jones vocal group. They're backed by expert playing led by Sly & Robbie, fine organ from Keith Sterling and Winston Wright, blues guitar leads bleeding all over the tracks from Rad Bryan and hand drum. The sound is a thick bubbling stew of roots reggae, emotional lead vocals, Waterhouse singing, celestial harmonies, minor-key melodies, oblique roots lyrics, acoustic and electric drums, and a surfeit of dub. This is killer reggae.

(There were two other singles from this timespan by the same line-up that were not included on *Showcase*. Both were covers and neither was in the dubby dread style of the *Showcase* singles. 'No No No' was an ungraceful cover of Dawn Penn's 'You Don't Love Me Anymore'. Better, though not of the caliber of the *Showcase* material, was a cover of The Wailers' 'Let Him Go'.)

For several years in the 1960s, The Beatles and other groups released stereo and mono mixes of their recordings that could differ either slightly or more significantly. This led some hardcore fans – Beatles fans in particular – to seek out variant mixes, with foreign releases often targeted. I wonder what these collectors would make of this situation: when a DJ announces one of these seven *Showcase* songs, you still can't be sure what you are going to hear. It could be a familiar mix of the song, an entirely different mix you haven't heard in a long time, or one that you've never heard before. That's because the various 7- and 12-inch releases and re-releases of these singles carried a surprising number of significantly different mixes. Every time I think I've heard them all, another mix on an obscure pressing turns up. In that way, these songs have an organic quality, seemingly alive and always changing. A whole book could be devoted to documenting all the variations of these seven tracks. Nor did collecting them as an album create reference mixes. *Showcase* was released on at least three different labels with differing mixes. Sometimes, one track, 'Shine Eye Girl', was completely omitted. When it was later released on differently titled CDs on either side of the Atlantic, not surprisingly, the mixes varied yet again. Rather than hurt its identity , the album's multiple faces make the already strong collection even more enjoyable. And *Showcase* would give Black Uhuru a stepping stone to international prominence. Their next album was internationally released on Island Records, and world tours would follow.

Let's look at each song, with a mind to picking the best mix of those available, using the Heartbeat CD mixes as our starting point.

'Guess Who's Coming To Dinner'
This Black Uhuru remake of Michael Rose's 'Guess Who's Coming To Dinner' is the most famous song to come from either the singer or the group. It's one of *Showcase*'s upbeat numbers and, rare for the set (and, for that matter, the group), it features a touch of wry humor. The song's title is taken from a 1967 film about the social clash between white and black America when a young white woman brings a black boyfriend home to dinner with her parents. But here, there is happiness rather than angst, as Rose answers the titular question with an excited "natty dreadlock", as Simpson and Jones jump in to harmonize. There's much cause for excitement, as there is herb, reasoning and the giving of thanks and praises, all courtesy of this welcome dinner guest. The song begs for a sequel to the film, where the daughter dumps the well-groomed, educated, mannered boyfriend and brings a Rasta herbsman to the next family dinner.

The song opens with Dunbar's acoustic drums supplemented by his Syndrums. These electronic synthesizer drums caught Dunbar's fancy, and he would exploit their potential as no other percussionist did. Just in this song he uses them several ways: as a novel accent, for a siren effect that juices the excitement level, as a replacement for cymbal strikes and, in a trademark sound, as a thick mat of dense rumbling, flapping texture. This effect would be used by Dunbar in numerous recordings, though this is the only song on this set that features it. In the hands of a good rock drummer, such an effect probably would have resulted in an industrial sound. But inspired by Nyabinghi drumming, Dunbar keeps the sound organic and grounded in roots, even while using the latest technology. This percussion-filled arrangement didn't leave room for much else than melodic bass, bright rhythm piano and, if you listen very hard, a bit of guitar faintly in the mix. Rose is in an introspective mood, and throughout the backing vocals lend a glow to his reasoning. Dub is held until the appended version, where Sly & Robbie have fun slicing and dicing the vocals as the piano bounces to dub life.

This is the one song in the set that does not vary greatly between the two CD releases. However, on the Virgin mix, the song is half a minute shorter, owing to a shorter, different dub section, taking it out of contention as the preferred version.

There are even more mixes available. For example, the album *Raiders Of The Lost Dub* includes a different dub version entitled 'Who's in the Tomb?' And as released on a 12-inch single on the UK-based D-Roy label (and perhaps nowhere else) is a radically different mix. Though it utilizes the same vocal tracks, the backing is so different it can be considered a different performance. The Syndrums are different and fewer, allowing room for the new piano and guitar that create a more easy-going, if pensive, sound. It's every bit as good as, if not better than, any of the more commonly known mixes.

Rose recorded remakes and live renditions of this track, with and without Black Uhuru, before, during and after he was a member of the group, just as Black Uhuru would record live renditions post-Rose. The 1989 film *Mighty Quinn* included a high-spirited if musically simplified Michael Rose rendition. With all of these renditions, it became no challenge at all for a reggae fan to guess who was coming to dinner.

'General Penitentiary'

After the introspective but upbeat opener, 'General Penitentiary' establishes that the songs on *Showcase* will be varied in mood, as is the case for most strong albums. A lonely Syndrum strike, a brief martial drum roll, and the song is off and running. Though running may not be the best word, as the song more mopes along. A fine but unusually downhearted bass line is heard from Shakespeare. Dunbar's busy acoustic drums are supplemented by a regularly struck, dour Syndrum groan. Bluesy guitar leads befit the song's story, while the trebly one-finger tinkling piano phrases are like flickers of hope in dire circumstances.

'General Penitentiary' describes incarceration in Kingston's notorious prison. Full of despair and regret, Rose is at his most subdued. He describes the bad conditions of his cell: the heat, the dampness, and the smell. And he sings of a hard lesson learned. If you're stealing food to save your life, being sent to General Penitentiary is akin to losing your life anyway. The backing vocals have a greater role compared to the album's opener. Though they mostly support Rose in a three-part harmony, they occasionally continue without his lead in a dramatic, ghostly sound. And this song is dubby compared to the opener, with reverb and instruments coming and going. Though sonically pleasing, rarely has a reggae song been so thoroughly bleak.

The mix on the Virgin CD is quite different. It lacks dub reverb, causing the backing vocals to flatten and the rhythm guitar chop to fall back into the mix. There's no drop-out/in, making the instrumentation sound less dynamic. The bass is mixed louder and the drums sharper. Though this mix is 40 seconds shorter, it's taken from the dub version. The vocal version is actually longer, and it includes an instrumental run-out that is truncated from the other mixes. This makes the dub version quite short, which is a shame as it is more pleasing, with a softer sound than in the Heartbeat mix. So while the Heartbeat mix is preferred, you'll certainly want to keep the Virgin mix on hand.

'Abortion'

'Abortion' is an unapologetically direct anti-abortion protest song, born of Rastafarian belief. A sorrowful Michael Rose is far more emotional here than in the previous two songs, never so wrenchingly as he sings of a potential sister "going down the drain". Rastafarianism is also more broadly against birth control, the song condemning "boots" (condoms) and "pearls" (birth-control pills). Waterhouse singing adds to the mournful air he builds.

The instrumentation is big and creative. Blues guitar runs are again abundant and appropriate to the subject matter. Shakespeare provides a start-and-stop grumbling bass line. Dunbar provides idiosyncratic big, fat rolls, laced with Syndrums, dramatically delaying the concluding strike. There are two rhythm piano tracks, one handling the reggae chop, the other less frequently sounding a single bright chord. At the conclusion of the song, Jones, backed by Simpson, briefly takes a rare lead, to address all women listeners. Rose comes in to respond, equating women to stars, and after a Waterhouse warble, the dub version grabs the spotlight away. Unusually for the album, the dub version is longer than the vocal version. In spite of addressing a difficult, often controversial, subject – or perhaps because of it – 'Abortion' is a popular Black Uhuru track.

Though shorter, the mix on the Virgin CD is in many ways superior. It opens with an introduction that's missing from the other mixes, though present in their dub versions, in which Rose calls abortion first-degree murder. He echoes off into space, and the riddim restarts. The mix is more alive, with lots of reverb and some echo as well, both missing from the Heartbeat mix. Maracas, barely heard in the original, are mixed up front and reverbed to the point that you can track the path of each seed. But there's a negative. The dub version comes in too early, cutting Rose off right in the middle of his response to Jones's lead, requiring that you keep the Heartbeat mix around as well to enjoy them in equal measure.

'Natural Reggae Beat'

'Natural Reggae Beat' is a break from the Rastafarian roots of the rest of the album (though Rose does find the time to thank God for guidance in the face of oppression). Black Uhuru lightens up to celebrate the pleasures of the titular subject, which both makes you dance and makes you smarter. Rose offers a unique explanation of the physiology of reggae enjoyment: it sends an electric charge through the body that "come out through your mind".

As promised, this reggae will indeed make you dance. There's a romping bass line, prominent hi-hat cymbal work, double-struck Rototom drum, occasional Syndrum accents, reggae chop guitar, occasional piano, lead guitar low in the mix, maracas and a touch of dub that softens the sound. Organ is out front, as it adds a countermelody to that of the vocals and of the bass. Light-hearted and rollicking, it might be described by Americans of a certain age as skating-rink organ. As often is the case on this album, and in reggae in general, bass is the star attraction as much as the lead vocal.

The vocals are mostly sung in an easy-going harmony and the backing vocals are pillow-soft. At the conclusion of the track, there's a vocal surprise, as Simpson takes a brief, rare lead, singing some nonsense words. Then someone yells "version!" and the very nice instrumental dub abruptly takes over the disco-mix.

On the Virgin CD, once again, the rhythm guitar, lacking reverb, is flattened out while the maracas, barely heard on the other version, spring forth in an even trade. Though the bass is louder – automatically a positive for a reggae fan – the hi-hat is mixed too loud, making for a harsh sound. Worse, the dub version is introduced early, truncating Duckie Simpson's brief moment in the spotlight. I've got to have my Duckie. The Heartbeat mix makes the Virgin mix superfluous.

'Leaving To Zion'

Not to be confused with 'Going To Zion', an early recording by Black Uhuru's first line-up, 'Leaving To Zion' is a different and better song. After opening with Waterhouse chanting from the greatest of all Waterhouse singers, Rose dreams of leaving the violence of Jamaica for Zion (the holy land of Ethiopia in Rastafarian belief). His voice full of emotion, he crafts a powerful minor-key melody, as Rasta reggae's popular back-to-Africa theme inspires him to his best vocal performance of the set. Meanwhile, the plaintive backing vocals, sometimes wailing wordlessly, give the impression that the spirits are dramatically in accord with Rose.

The instrumentation sees the welcome return of elements by now familiar for the album, such as fine bass. Out front, it plays staccato clusters that add so much to the song's rhythm, while providing enough melody for two songs. Dub enriches the song with reverb on the rim shots and rhythm guitar, and echo on the rhythm guitar and vocals. It also contributes greatly to the song's climax.

The song steadily builds in intensity, with emotional Waterhouse singing and increasing levels of dub. It climaxes with Rose singing with intensity about the flag of Africa in a way that's distinct from the song's chorus and verse. As he does, everything but drum and bass drops out and the last syllable echoes ad infinitum. When it finally does die out, a skyrocket of echo guitar is cultivated and launched. It dies out too and we're left with just drums and bass. Then the drums drop out for a segment of the bass all alone. The drums return for a short time and the riddim restarts, *dubwise*. This is the boldest and most impressive use of dub on a dub-filled album.

The dub is different on the Virgin CD, substituting more drop-out/in for less echo, but falling short of a fair trade. Especially with the echo omitted from Rose's climactic lines, where it was so dramatically used on the Heartbeat CD. Making matters worse, the section of bass and drum that follows is truncated by the too-early appearance of a dub version that is lesser as well. So the Heartbeat mix is clearly preferable to the inferior and shorter mix found on the Virgin CD.

'Plastic Smile'

In 'Plastic Smile', Rose rejects the misplaced values of a woman whose mother is not Rasta, not from Jamaica and has the ways of Babylon. It's unclear whether her smile is "plastic" because it's used disingenuously or because it's made unnaturally perfect through dental work, or both. Whatever the case, Rose admonishes her to keep her smile to herself, turning it into a frown. He then instructs her, in his typically oblique way, about the Rasta values. He sounds very comfortable as he instructs, adorning his vocal with Waterhouse scats and his idiosyncratic mouth-trumpet sounds. (Something of an offshoot of his Waterhouse singing, this wordless, mournful sound is unique to Rose and never fails to enrich any song it appears in.) Simpson and Jones quietly harmonize on key phrases.

Taking a cue from Rose, the band gives a comfortable performance of its own. Shakespeare anchors the track with another bass line that could be a lead instrument for its catchy melody. Sweet guitar leads and piano dance around the bass. No dub effects are used, perhaps in deference to the lyrics that advocate staying natural.

The mix on the Virgin CD has a number of differences. The bass is louder, the vocals are lower, and the guitar and piano are nearly buried. It's mastered at a slightly slower speed. Dub is heard, with reverb and a touch of echo that appears mid-song. Most days I prefer the Heartbeat mix, but the Virgin mix has a superior dub version. The recommendation? Alternate, enjoying the Heartbeat mix on 31-day months. (You asked!)

'Shine Eye Gal'

Some roots reggae is described as having the desirable characteristic of *dread*: a certain heaviness of sound and seriousness of content. 'Shine Eye Gal' is intensely dread, right from its opening. An organ plays a mournful minor-key theme. Rose joins with wailing Waterhouse chanting and mouth trumpet. Bass confines itself to clusters of a single note. An edgy rhythm guitar is strummed. (It's provided by reggae fan Keith Richards of The Rolling Stones. This was not the end of their relationship, as Black Uhuru would tour as an opening act for The Stones in the early 1980s.) All this, and the best is yet to come.

Shakespeare unleashes a monster bass line. Throughout this album, he has impressed with bass that was, in any combination, stop-and-go, rumbling or busy. But here, he surprises with a repeated swooping three-note line. Deep in tone, descending in melody, dread in mood, it provides a continuous bath of satisfying low-frequency sound. Additional instruments join in, including piano, Nyah hand drum and a tapping sound perhaps played on Syndrums. There's so much to like, and we still haven't gotten to the song or its singers.

'Shine Eye Gal' is based on an old Jamaican folk song of the same name. They share a chorus and a central concern, that the titular figure "is a trouble to her man". But the melody, most of the lyrics and the heavy Rasta vibe are new here.

Rose sings of a woman who is un-giving, demanding and unappreciative. At one point, he takes a Jamaican folk saying,"wanty wanty, no getty, getty getty no wanty" (previously discussed in Chapter 17; page 199), and alters it to better describe her greed. That she brings these behaviors to bed is implied. All of this is disturbing to Rose, spurring him to another great vocal performance. He sounds exasperated, roughening his voice and utilizing his versatile but always emotional Waterhouse singing to show his vexation. Even the backing vocals sound tart. This is because the ethereal Jones and the rootsy Simpson are on an equal footing. Elsewhere on the album, it was almost as if Simpson was backing Jones, making for a three-tiered vocal approach. With so many good qualities woven together, it's no surprise that 'Shine Eye Gal' amounts to the longest track on the album at over 7:30 minutes.

The Heartbeat mix is dub-free, but the Virgin mix uses dub throughout, tinting some stands while making others wink in and out of existence. Plus, the appended dub version is better on the Virgin mix. In these ways, dub makes the Virgin mix the better of the two, even if it is shorter by nearly 2 minutes. There is also a significantly different mix on some of the pressings of the *Showcase* LP. The dubbiest of the three, it's immediately identified by additional Syndrums throughout the track. Their presence is usually pleasing, though a repeated Syndrum whooping sound is not. Fans of the song may want to track it down, as it has long been in print and available from reggae specialty dealers.

Sinsemilla

In 1980, Black Uhuru followed *Showcase* with *Sinsemilla*, an excellent album of new material released internationally on Island Records. Taken with the many fine singles they recorded in 1979 and 1980, *Sinsemilla* caps an astonishingly good two years for Black Uhuru.

Least changed on this album is the vocal group. Michael Rose still sings emotional, dread lead vocals, turbocharged with his ever-versatile Waterhouse singing and mouth trumpet sounds. He is still writing Rasta reggae songs with lyrics that are often oblique. Jones and Simpson continue to ply their unique brand of haunting backing vocals. In other words, Black Uhuru continues to be one of the most compelling of all roots reggae vocal groups.

And although Sly & Robbie again serve as the album's rhythm section, bandleaders and producers, the band, arrangement and sound of *Sinsemilla* have undergone different degrees of change from the *Showcase* material. Radcliffe "Duggie" Bryan is back on lead guitar, and his understated blues leads are still in full effect. Sessions veteran Ansel Collins is the new keyboard player, providing piano more often than organ, and supplying the clichéd oriental melodies that have been popular in reggae since ska. Rounding out the group but used sparingly are Ranchie McLean on rhythm guitar and Sticky Thompson on incidental percussion. Dub, such an important part of *Showcase*, is not heard at all on *Sinse-*

milla (though 'Push Push' arguably has a touch of drop-out/in). To their credit, instead of trying to reproduce the glories of the recent past, or imitate the sound of contemporary internationally successful albums by Bob Marley & The Wailers and Peter Tosh, Sly & Robbie instead choose to follow their own ever-developing talent and create a new sound. The overall tone of the album is dark, serious and rootsy but at the same time innovative and high-tech. The sound might be best described as *progressive roots*, a style that would develop further over subsequent Black Uhuru albums.

In this album, Dunbar and Shakespeare push the boundaries of roots reggae drum and bass creativity to new heights. Shakespeare challenges himself and furthers his bass vocabulary. He proves himself to be a natural at fashioning the line that best suits a song, while Dunbar consolidates his talent for augmenting his drum kit with Syndrums for the greatest rhythmic impact. Typically, two drum tracks are recorded, one acoustic, one electric. About half the songs use Syndrums to accent, while the others feature the dense mat of Syndrum sound as previously heard on *Guess Who's Coming To Dinner*'s title track. Only one song has no Syndrums at all. The doubled Dunbar makes the album dense with expertly played reggae drums, perhaps the reason why so little incidental percussion is heard. This density created great opportunities for dub, so its absence was a clearly conscious decision. Was it a fear that the international audiences the album would reach might not appreciate dub? Considering how groundbreaking and uncompromising its sound is, the decision to forgo dub on *Sinsemilla* must be considered an artistically rather than commercially driven decision.

Like *Showcase*, *Sinsemilla* not only includes some of Black Uhuru's very best work, but also some of Sly & Robbie's best playing, and not a single weak song – three reasons why *Sinsemilla* is one of reggae's most solid albums.

'Happiness'
'Happiness' kicks off the album in strong fashion. A cascading double-tracked roll of drums and Syndrums that is immediately doubly identifiable as Dunbar's work serves as an introduction. And then, a veil of dread is dropped. Drums, guitar and piano (has reggae piano ever sounded so serious?) lay down a head-swimmingly heavy rhythm over a wicked see-sawing bass line. Odd Syndrums effects bridge the piano and acoustic drums with a variety of sounds. But the lead instrument, of all things, is Dunbar's bass drum. Mixed up front, it brings more dread to the song than the work of a foot should make possible. Dynamic and crafty, just try to guess what beat it will fall on next. There may be more music in Sly Dunbar's right foot than in the populations of entire towns.

Rose's vocals smolder, but belying the song's title, his melody is plaintive and his singing is filled with angst. He opens by putting it out there that he is longing for some happiness. This universal theme immediately draws the listener in. Rose is specific on what would make him happy. Though his lyrics are typically oblique, it boils down to giving praises to Jah and sharing his love. Atypically, on this and on the album's second track, 'World Is Africa', Rose sings alone, without Simpson and Jones. But they are heard on all the subsequent tracks. It's as if the album did not want to roll out its many assets all at once.

Instead of a solo, mid-song, Dunbar elaborates his playing. Towards the end of the song, he snaps off a series of his patented one-handed snare rolls that cue the band for a rhythmic jam. Rose responds by chanting like a DJ. The instrumentation thins out in the song's final seconds, leaving just drums and bass to carry the music alone. Though everyone is excellent on 'Happiness', it's Dunbar who spearheads the new, fully realized sound of progressive roots reggae.

Unhappily, there does not appear to be a dub version of 'Happiness'. However, in an unusual move for a Black Uhuru track, Sly & Robbie would take this riddim and re-voice it themselves. This version, 'Coon Can', is described in the next chapter (page 369). Also, Michael Rose recorded a good dubwise remake of the song in his post-Black Uhuru solo career, calling it 'Dub Well Happy'. It can be found on his 1997 CD, *Dub Wicked*.

'Push Push'

As creative and dread as 'Happiness' is, 'Push Push' goes even further, right from its introduction. It's led by idiosyncratic stutter-step drumming, simple but heavy piano that's answered by quiet slurred guitar, and Michael Rose unveiling a stuttering consonant-filled variation of his Waterhouse singing. The body of the song begins, with a mighty bass line that pays equal tribute to the gods of rhythm, melody and dread. Rose sings of familiar Rasta topics such as marijuana ("I and I smoke a chalice twenty-four hours round the clock") and the oppression that gives the song its name. Not all of the lyrics are easily understood, but Rose more than makes up for this with an emotionally charged performance, enriched by soulful Waterhouse singing. The backing vocals, making their welcome debut on the set, raise the intensity level as they enrich the sonics.

You wouldn't think that a song could get more dread, but then it does. Never big on the mid-song solos that were so popular elsewhere in reggae, it's surprising when a mid-song break is heard from Black Uhuru ... and exciting, as it takes the form of a different song ... and delightful in just how captivating it is. The guitars and piano stop playing, and the hand-held friction percussion that had earlier snuck onto the track moves to the fore. The percussion-only accompaniment makes the great bass line stand out in relief. Over this, Rose, singing alone, reminisces about his mother. Valuing education, she made him attend school, which he remembers without complaint. But when he recalls being sent to church, he bristles at the memory of his mother, a poor woman, being forced to give money to the collection. The original song, along with guitar, piano and backing vocals, returns. But Rose is still bursting with creativity. He supplies a new throat-sound Waterhouse variation. As the song ends, he performs a wordless mockery of an authoritative voice that represents the "push push" of the oppressor, responding with a groan of pain at the conclusion. The instrumentation of 'Push Push' is so powerful that it empowers Rose to follow his muse wherever it takes him. The result is a stirring dread inner journey.

'Sinsemilla'

Though it keeps with the overall sound, the album's title track and featured single is the only light-hearted song on *Sinsemilla*. What is the source of this cheer? The titular plant Rose is growing in his backyard. Not only that, but a nearby house (not surprisingly described as *red*) is filled with ganja. In this paean to a favored variety of marijuana, the many virtues of *Sinsemilla* are explored. These include its health benefits, its potential to economically benefit the poor, a means to avoid wickedness and a way to elevate society. The song climaxes, as Rose wails an appeal to free marijuana – to make it legal.

In a show of reggae virtuosity, a totally inside-out bass line is held in place by interlocking acoustic and electric drums, blues guitar runs, tart piano and a countermelody from Rose. This is best appreciated on a dub version called 'The Monkey Is A Spy', found on Sly & Robbie's 1991 LP, *Raiders of The Lost Dub*. With most of the other tracks dropped out, the joyfully subverted bass line is fully revealed. This version was used as the second half of a disco-mix version of the song, appended to a remixed vocal version that adds additional lead guitar and dub emphasis on rhythm guitar and drums. This worthy disco-mix is included as a bonus track on later CD editions of *Sinsemilla*.

'Endurance'

'Endurance' opens dramatically and obliquely, even by Michael Rose standards. A swirling organ and off-the-beat drumming dominate, as an incomprehensible spoken piece is heard, sounding like a displaced carnival barker. The body of the song is launched with all three Black Uhuru members singing in unison that Rastas must endure "the fullness of the earth". This phrase refers to the hardships imposed by man rather than nature. Aptly supporting the lyrics, the instrumentation conjures up a sense of striving. Bass and drums are well supported by mechanistic rhythm-led guitar phrases, organ and Syndrums that map out the missing link between disco drums and early Devo. Though the sound is progressive, the song is infused with the sadness and hope that often inform roots reggae, where the two emotions, rather than conflict, combine into something strong and bitter-sweet.

'Vampire'

Introduced to Jamaica by American movies and television, vampires were fully entrenched in the island's consciousness by the roots era.

They provided a ready-made symbol for the class oppression and exploitation felt by poor Jamaicans, especially the socially conscious Rastas. As a result, vampire metaphors are common in roots reggae (for example, in 'Babylon System' by Bob Marley & The Wailers, a song described later in this book, page 494), as are songs about vampires (such as 'Vampire', by Peter Tosh, a fine example that is also described later; page 527).

Black Uhuru's 'Vampire', the album's closer, is more literal than metaphoric. So much so that Rose sings in amazement at seeing "a goddamn vampire". But just as Jah empowered Bob Marley to defeat the devil and ghosts in 'Screw Face', here he empowers Rose to prevail over vampires. He sounds *red* as he sings of putting a wooden stake through the vampire's heart, with God's help. Meanwhile, Simpson and Jones respond to the situation with a titular chorus that's mournful and spooky.

The supernatural theme spills over to the music's macabre air. Vampire is the only track on the album without Syndrums, perhaps not wanting to clutter Sly's great rim-shot-filled snare work and the skeletal vibe it creates. Robbie adds a second bass track with a Leslie-like effect to make it flutter like a ghost. These elements take the spotlight in the instrumental run-out, as the virtuoso reggae rhythm section closes the album with a progressive roots jam.

Other tracks from Sinsemilla

Sinsemilla is rounded out by three more tracks that are great, if not outstanding by the standard of the above songs. 'World Is Africa' is a galloping song about global black solidarity, reminiscent of the sentiment of the Peter Tosh song, 'African'. Dunbar's Syndrums fulfill the role of Nyabinghi drums, a piano solo from Ansel Collins builds off a familiar oriental cliché, Shakespeare's bass line is adventurous even by his standards, and Rose sings without backing vocalists. 'No Loafing (Sit And Wonder)' opens with Michael Rose's mouth trumpet over more oriental cliché piano. Bass, drums, a mat of Syndrums, rhythm guitar and skittering guitar leads join in. Rose is introspective as he sings, "I'm going to sit around and wonder what to do" about South African apartheid and oppression at home in Jamaica. 'There Is Fire' is bluesy dread reggae, featuring guest harmonica from Jimmy Becker.

Red

Black Uhuru continued their run of consistently excellent material with their 1981 album, *Red*. It's a continuation and expansion of the sound heard on *Sinsemilla*, though not without adjustments. There are changes to the guitar and keyboard ranks. Syndrums play a smaller role, opening up more opportunities for Sticky Thompson's percussion. But the sound continues to be progressive roots. This includes more of the mechanized guitar riffs, the likes of which were first heard on the *Sinsemilla* track, 'Endurance'. (This parallels similar sounds developing in dancehall around the same time.) Rhythmic and modern, this guitar fills a role previously held by Syndrums. But the practical advantage of this shift became clear when the group performed this material live. Adding another guitarist to play these riffs was easy. But there was no way to have a Dunbar each for full exploitation of acoustic and electric drums. Another change was the welcome return of dub after the dub-free *Sinsemilla*. Though there would be other good Black Uhuru albums and great Black Uhuru songs, *Red* would be their last great album.

'Youth Of Eglington'

'Youth Of Eglington' gives us a lot to like from the album's opening moments. Rose shouts as Dunbar recreates the bongo opening from The Yardbirds' 'For Your Love', while someone starts voicing rhythm guitar *chika chika* sounds, just as we saw King Sporty do decades earlier on ska songs such as 'Lonesome Track' by The Wailers. Piano, taking its lead from the bass, is out front, bravely making the song upbeat in spite of its lyrics. Meanwhile, guitars play a recurring mechanistic riff and other restrained fills.

The song is a detailed denouncement of gun love and criminal acts, targeting youth in Eglington (Toronto), Utica Avenue (Brooklyn), Brixton (England) and Kingston (Jamaica). It's affecting when Rose laments the innocent bystander named Jill who's shot and the impact is echoed by Jones and Simpson. Rose recommends Rastafarianism as an alternative. Dunbar provides mid-song and end-of-song jams with his idiosyncratic drum work looser than anything on the last two albums. And although his instrument offers a smaller palette by nature, Shakespeare never fails to match his partner in creativity. The result is reggae that's simultaneously progressive and rootsy; music like nowhere else on earth. A dub version, called 'Youth', is available on Black Uhuru's *Dub Factor* album.

'Sponji Reggae'

With a chorus that's a gleeful celebration of dancing to reggae, and an overall happy feel, 'Sponji Reggae' is something of a follow-up to *Showcase*'s 'Natural Reggae Beat'. The verses contain interesting and colorful autobiographical comments from Rose. One line seems to describe the critics of Black Uhuru's move from the traditional towards a more progressive sound. The critics want the music to stay unchanged, questioning Rose's sanity. But Rose defends Black Uhuru's new sound as being right for the time.

You can dance to the bubbly 'Sponji Reggae', that's for sure, but it's not constructed at all like any other dance music. First and foremost, there is Dunbar's heavy individualistic drum playing (listen to the bass drum work at the start of the song and how it interacts with the snare). Atop of this, of all things, he adds a glockenspiel that brightens an already upbeat sound. A mechanized repeated guitar riff, touches of dub reverb and, eventually, a layer of Syndrums add to the rhythmic imperative. And as per the song's title, there's a spongy, danceable reggae bass line. The song ends with an instrumental jam, enhanced with mouth trumpet and dub for your dancing pleasure.

Released as a single, 'Sponji Reggae' was perhaps Black Uhuru's biggest international hit. Not surprisingly, then, a dub version, called 'Convoy Hijack', was included on the Island Records dub compilation, *Raiders Of The Lost Dub*. And if you really want to "bum right here and bounce over there", a 12-inch remix of 'Sponji Reggae' is an included bonus track on later editions of the *Red* CD. At 10:30 minutes, it more than doubles the length of the original and includes some extra rhythm piano and a short piece of previously unheard vocals.

'Journey'; 'Trodding'

"Trodding the other day, on journey, so far away", begins 'Journey'. Though the lyrics quickly become increasingly opaque, it concerns emigrating to find employment, a subject in reggae since mento ('Trek To England' by Count Lasher and 'Dry Up Your Tears' by Nora Dean are two such examples previously described in this book; pages 59 and 243). But here, the story is conveyed with the ganja-fueled, heavy-dread perspective of a Rasta in a foreign Babylon. Unlike other reggae emigration songs, 'Journey' sounds like a missive from the furthest reaches of a foreboding mystical quest.

Dub, biblical language, intense lead vocals, wailing Waterhouse singing, eerie backing vocals and a knotty instrumental backing create a sense of total alienation from unrighteous society. Rose proclaims that Jah has empowered Black Uhuru to bring a righteous cleansing fire to Babylon. This fire is music. The instrumentation is just as dread. Syndrums and progressive elements are put aside, as great acoustic drumming is enhanced by a busy assortment of percussion from Sticky Thompson. Coming as little surprise, the wickedly twisty bass line at the core of the song is great. It manages to encapsulate the entire feel of the song on its own. 'Journey' is so evocative, every time I hear it I picture a wandering Rose emerging from the haze to look down over a strange city.

'Journey' is a song that begged for a dub version, and it received two. 'Trodding' is conveniently included as a bonus track on the *Red* CD. It's modest dub; basically an instrumental version with some drop-out. Nonetheless, it's a pleasing version that allows you to easily hear and enjoy the bass line that seems intent on leading the journey. The *Raiders Of The Lost Dub* album includes a dub 'Fire And Brimstone', a more adventurous version with echo and other effects. Your mood rather than their quality will determine which is best on any given day.

'Utterance'

'Utterance' is an unusually contented song for Black Uhuru. It features a loose and jaunty riddim and the simplest arrangement on the album. Rose takes stock of how the public impression of Rasta has improved over the years, largely due to the popularity of roots reggae. He recounts how mainstream Jamaica once viewed the Rasta as boogeymen who stole children. (This one-time belief is further explored in Bunny Wailer's song, 'Blackheart Man'.) But now Rose finds himself a Rastaman who's an international celebrity, whose utterances are widely appreciated. This leads to the titular chorus with Puma Jones's harmonies shining especially bright.

Other tracks from Red

'Sistren' is a song praising religious Rasta woman, though in terms that make it one of the most oblique of all Black Uhuru songs. It's distinguished by Shakespeare bringing thumb popping from funk to reggae, the odd, intermittently pounded, piano chords and the unusual vocal jam that closes the song, where Rose moves from Waterhouse wailing to wordless falsetto singing. 'Puff She Puff' obliquely describes a *suffera* woman as she faces hunger, poverty, and the choice between a life of crime and a Rasta lifestyle. Great drums again lead an uncomplicated but melodic arrangement. 'Rockstone' finds Rose lamenting his previous employment as a laborer on a construction site. He incurs the disrespect of his supervisors and equates the experience to slavery. The backing music appropriately opens in a bluesy style, and continues dry, sharp and unforgiving. The uninspired 'Carbine' returns to the themes of 'Youth of Eglington'. Traditional dub techniques might have served this song better than the effects utilized here. The closing track on *Red*, it's the weakest track on the last three Black Uhuru albums. It's hard not to look at it as a signal of the decline to come.

Live in 1981

In 1982, Island Records released *Tear It Up*, a live eight-track set from a 1981 show at London's Rainbow Theatre. It's a good performance (I don't think that the classic line-up of Black Uhuru ever gave a bad one) with less than great sound quality. But it pales on all counts compared to the two live tracks from the same year that appeared on the 1982 album, *Reggae Sunsplash '81: A Tribute to Bob Marley*.

The song listed as 'Plastic Smile' is actually a medley of 'Shine Eye Girl' and 'Plastic Smile'. It opens with a jam in which Rose chants an improvised band introduction, while the music crackles with creative energy. The band segues into a brief 'Shine Eye Girl', then into a full 'Plastic Smile'. The second track, 'Guess Who's Coming To Dinner', is long and jammed-out. The band so crisp and the vocals so strong, there is a mastery of the material afoot. Initially a double album in its LP incarnation, *Reggae Sunsplash '81* shed a few songs for its single CD release. Hopefully, one day a double-CD edition will be considered with other songs from Black Uhuru's set.

Great Black Uhuru tracks from *Chill Out* and *Dub Factor*

Though the quality of their live shows would continue unabated, 1982's *Chill Out* marked the beginning of the decline of Black Uhuru as one of reggae's greatest recording bands. Not that anything on *Chill Out* is bad, but there are only a few great songs amongst the otherwise fair material. On this album, Dunbar began his switch-over to the electronic Simmons drums that would soon supplant the tandem of acoustic drums and Syndrums. This, along with further emphasis on mechanistic guitar riffs, the favoring of synthesizers over piano or organ and even some vocoder-processed backing vocals gave the material a colder sound, making the album's title apropos. In 1983 a dub album followed that reworked tracks from *Chill Out* and *Red*. *Dub Factor* featured Paul "Groucho" Smykle's radical dub style that worked brilliantly on a few tracks and was forgettable on others.

'Mondays'

'Mondays' features deviously hooky robot guitar riffs, a synthesizer hook, electronic drums, a fat bass line and a touch of dub. Together they provide an irresistible polyrhythmic roil, combining sequenced electronic music, funk and reggae. This all makes it an archetypical *Chill Out* track, and a great one.

Rose agonizes over his dislike for the start of the work week that he equates to slavery. Jones and Simpson wail in support. Like Bob Marley & The Wailers' work, it's an anthem for anyone who hates the five-day grind, especially Mondays. A disco-mix of 'Mondays' taken from a 10-inch single can also be heard on some Black Uhuru collections. And *Dub Factor* includes a version entitled 'Android Rebellion'.

Other good Chill Out *tracks*

'Emotional Slaughter' is heartbreaking and beautiful. After a mournful instrumental opening and a stanza describing how Babylon stifles the potential of people, it goes on to consider the prevalence of murder in the ghetto. It does so poetically, commemorating each death as the rise and the fall of a star. Naturally, Rose is highly emotional here, and the backing vocals from Simpson and Jones have never been more haunting. The heavy use of synthesizer suits the song rather than sounding out of place, as the instrument can do on other reggae tracks from this era. The version on *Dub Factor*, called 'Slaughter', adds little to this strong recording.

'Right Stuff' is a good *Chill Out* song, but its single B-side dub version is much more interesting. It packs a polyrhythmic, hard dub punch as dub doubles the beat. Although a disco-mix of 'Right Stuff' is available on some Black Uhuru collections, and a version entitled 'Big Spliff' appears on *Dub Factor*, this better version has yet to appear on CD.

Great Dub Factor *tracks*

Dub Factor opens with 'Ion Storm', a spectacular dub version of *Chill Out*'s unspectacular 'Fleety Foot'. Dub-master Smykle gives it a spacey tone right from the opening with something distant clanging ominously in the ether. He uses an advanced application of traditional dub effects to de-/reconstruct the song for much the better.

Yet 'Ion Storm' sounds conservative compared to 'Boof N Baff N Biff', the dub version of 'Eye Market'. Again, the song was good on *Chill Out*, but the dub B-side of its single release showed that the riddim had more potential. (It and the previously mentioned dub version of 'Right Stuff' are natural bonus tracks in waiting for a future edition of *Chill Out*.) Best of all is Groucho's version, which sounds like a marriage of traditional dub reggae and David Byrne and Brian Eno's 1981 found-vocal multi-culti-electro-remix masterpiece, *My Life In The Bush Of Ghosts*. It opens with a science-fiction landscape populated by traditional dub elements. Suddenly, a monster arises from the ooze and mightily thrashes about, as Smykle twists sound into alien shapes. It's banished back to the ooze by the power of Ducky Simpson's exclamation of "*boof n baff n biff*".

The remainder of the song alternates between Jamaican dub and Smykle's bag of tricks, such as a vague crowd-like noise, similar to one heard on Byrne and Eno's album.

'Sodom' is especially intriguing because it's a dub version of a good Black Uhuru song that was never otherwise released. From what can be told from this dub, there was absolutely nothing wrong with the original, but perhaps its explicit lyrics, demonstrating Rasta views against sodomy (describing the touching and sucking as filthy), may have relegated it to remain unfinished or unreleased. Either way, it was fine fodder for Groucho, who finds the right approach to turn it into an exciting track. It leads with guitar that gives way to preternaturally bouncing keyboard that gives way to Groucho dub strewn over a devious Sly Dunbar drum shuffle pattern, as pieces of the vocal drop in unexpectedly.

Great Black Uhuru tracks after Michael Rose

Released in 1984, *Anthem* was the last album before the classic Black Uhuru line-up began to disintegrate. It features the mechanized sound of *Chill Out*, but with a more streamlined arrangement. Incongruously for the group, horns are utilized. While there is nothing bad on it, nothing stands out as especially good, at least not by the standards of the exceptional reggae that had come from them before. Releasing it overseas first in the UK, Island Records then tried to heat the set-up by remixing it (for the worse) in its US release. An exceptionally handsome box-set (though such treatment is largely undeserved), released by the Hippo Select label collects four of what by my count is now five mixes of *Anthem*. Following *Anthem*'s release, Rose would depart for a successful solo career. He was replaced by Junior Reid, better known up to this point as a dancehall singer. Island Records would drop the group, though a USA-based reggae label, RAS Records, picked them up.

'Fit You Haffe Fit'; 'Positive'
'Fit You Haffe Fit' and 'Positive', appearing on 1986's *Brutal* album and 1990's *Positive*, respectively, are the last great Black Uhuru songs. These tracks find Black Uhuru, previously known for roots, dub-roots and progressive roots reggae, now playing a unique dancehall-roots hybrid, as Reid combines roots reggae singing and dancehall DJing. 'Fit You Haffe Fit' is a celebration of healthy living, born of

exercise, the Rasta *ital* vegetarian diet and eschewing drug use. The delivery is staccato with Dunbar's fast bass drum leading the way. In a nod to dancehall, there are moments when the rhythm is simplified and syncopated. Reid gives it his all, adding Waterhouse cries and DJ chanting to his singing as the backing singers handle the changes in stride. With the subject and a riddim that's so propulsive and regimented, of all reggae songs 'Fit You Haffe Fit' is ideal to work out to.

'Positive' is similar to 'Fit You Haffe Fit', with Robbie's kinetic bass line setting the pace this time. A heavy metal guitar opening reminds us that Black Uhuru was still catering to an international audience. The song implores Jamaica's youths to remain positive in order to achieve their goals, rather than turning to crime. The lyrics take an unexpected turn to the self-referential in a way that would only be heard in a reggae song. Junior Reid successfully brings the fast-talk DJ style into the Black Uhuru fold (and gives the song a big hook in the process), by rapidly chanting a list of his family members who have told him they love "Positive", the very release we are listening to. And with that, we end the story of Black Uhuru on a positive note.

40 More great Sly & Robbie songs

When Sly Dunbar and Robbie Shakespeare, new drummer and bassist on the scene, began to work as a team around 1974, no one, not even they, could have imagined the incredible success they would have. They would become the biggest backing band in reggae history, playing on thousands of records by a myriad of artists. They would become bandleaders, producers, dub-masters and label owners. They would help launch Peter Tosh's international solo career. They would push the boundaries of reggae as members of Black Uhuru, recording cutting-edge reggae, touring and performing for fans around the world. Amassing an unprecedented résumé for reggae musicians, they would work with such non-reggae stars as The Rolling Stones, Bob Dylan, Ian Dury, Grace Jones, Joan Armatrading, Gilberto Gil, Herbie Hancock, Sting, Cindy Lauper, Ben Harper, Joe Cocker, Simply Red, Carly Simon, Tricky, Doug E. Fresh, Michael Franti, No Doubt, Carlos Santana, Sinéad O'Connor and others. No major talent in reggae goes without the accolade of a nickname, and they would be called "the riddim twins" or "Drumbar and Basspeare". They would enjoy the additional accolade of being the only reggae rhythm section ever to be sung about in a chart-topping American single. In an unusual tribute, 'Genius Of Love', a 1981 single by the Talking Heads spin-off group Tom Tom Club, contained a couplet that not only name-checks Bob Marley, but credits Sly & Robbie with expanding the sound of reggae. It's even followed by an imitation of Sly's one-handed snare rolls. All in all, not bad for a couple of kids from Kingston.

Lowell Fillmore Dunbar was born in Kingston in 1952. He picked up his nickname from his love of Sly & The Family Stone. He was inspired to become a drummer when, around age twelve, he saw The Skatalites on television and was fascinated by the work of Lloyd Knibb. He began playing in bands at Kingston's nightclubs, gaining his first recording session in 1969, when he was brought in by keyboard player Ansel Collins. The second recording he played on, 'Double Barrel' by Dave [Barker] & Ansel Collins, was a hit that also enjoyed cross-over popularity in the UK. Robert Shakespeare (no, that's not a stage name) was born in Kingston in 1953. His inspiration and mentoring were pedigreed. His inspiration was The Dynamites' great bassist, Jackie Jackson, and he took lessons from The Wailers' bassist, Aston Barrett, but the skill was his own. Like Sly, Robbie also played in bands on the Kingston nightclub circuit. He and Dunbar became aware of one another in 1972, each liking what he heard . They began to work together in recording sessions in 1974 or 1975 and established their own label, Taxi, in 1975, making them the producers of numerous artists. By 1976, they were the rhythm section on Peter

Tosh's album, *Legalize It*, and toured overseas with him. By then, the immortal bard of the bass and the sly fox of the drums were already stars.

In a perfect yin-yang relationship, the two seemed to feed each other's creativity. Sly greatly increased the vocabulary of reggae drumming in a way that was peerless. Robbie's accomplishments on bass were no less impressive. Their only competition came from the Barrett brothers, whose skills helped make Bob Marley a household name. Who is the better roots rhythm section is an impossible argument. But Sly & Robbie's recordings were more numerous, their range of styles broader and their contribution to reggae lasted longer.

Great songs that Sly & Robbie play on are found throughout this book (see the chapters on Black Uhuru, Peter Tosh, Dub, Roots and others). Here I discuss some additional great Sly & Robbie records, all self-produced, both vocal tracks and instrumentals, and in a variety of styles. All are currently available on CD and/ or digital music services.

Sly, Wicked And Slick

The CD edition of the 1979 album *Sly, Wicked And Slick* includes all the tracks from another Sly & Robbie album, 1978's *Simple Sly Man*. The resulting CD has a clutch of great Sly & Robbie songs in an assortment of reggae styles.

'A Who Say'; 'Mister Bassie'; 'Nigger Whitie'; 'Cocaine Cocaine'; 'Mr. Music'; 'Dirty Harry'
These songs comprised most of the 1978 *Simple Sly Man* album. The best way to describe the set is to say that it's all that is good in the literal meaning of "easy listening" without any of the bad, muzak connotations. The songs are in a relaxed, light-jazz reggae style, featuring laid-back horns and keys along with non-taxing, repeated chanted vocals. (A variety of singers was used, most frequently the female DJ duo of Althea & Donna, who had a hit with 'Uptown Top Rankin' for producer Joe Gibbs the same year.) It doesn't sound quite like anything else Sly & Robbie ever recorded – or anyone else for that matter. It's the perfect early-morning reggae.

'A Who Say' applies this approach to the "I Know Myself" riddim, best known from the Ernest Wilson song of the same name (as described later in this book; page 386). The riddim is intact, but substantially expanded by electric piano, guitar and sax (from either "Deadly" Headley Bennett or Tommy McCook, depending on who you listen to) and by Althea & Donna softly repeating the song's title. These overdubs transform the riddim into a laid-back jazzy groove that couldn't be more relaxing. The famous Mister Bassie riddim is similarly transformed with Althea & Donna again chanting the song's title. Sax, flute, harmonica, organ and Nyah hand drum join in a cool jam. 'Nigger Whitie' allows Dunbar to cover a song by his beloved Sly & The Family Stone. The only reminders of the stridency of the original in this smoothed-out cover is a driving reggae rhythm guitar and a tart harmonica. Vocals are credited to the otherwise unheard-of Bobby Annet Stennet, most probably a pseudonym for Dunbar. 'Cocaine Cocaine' is based on a DJ hit by Dillinger of two years earlier. With Bobby Thomas and Errol Francis providing vocal, this track adds funk to the formula. If it's an anti-coke song, it's not doing a very good job. The lush 'Mr. Music' owes something to The Brothers Johnson's US funk hit of a year earlier, 'Strawberry Letter 23' (vocals are uncredited). Leaving the easy-listening sound of the rest of the set behind is a rendition of the popular instrumental, 'Dirty Harry'. It keeps the famously gritty organ and sax parts intact, and the tasty reggae guitar heard at the beginning of the track is supplied by Rolling Stone Keith Richards. (For a fine – and dramatically sung – vocal version of the "Dirty Harry" riddim, try 'Realize' by Richie McDonald & Glen Brown. For a fine DJ version, 'Lost Mi Lover Ride' by Yellowman is recommended.)

'Oriental Taxi'; 'Senegalese Market Place'; 'Rasta Fiesta'; 'Bluesy Baby II'
A portion of *Sly, Wicked And Slick* was devoted to instrumentals that expanded the scope of reggae with other musical elements, while still staying in the easy-listening (connotations all still positive) style. The result sounds like good reggae of uncertain cultural origin.

'Oriental Taxi' is reggae mixed with soft, lush jazz that adds to the cultural displacement when, mid-song, it borrows the funky guitar riff from the Bee Gee's 'Staying Alive'. 'Senegalese Market Place' is Africanized reggae that includes marimba and a funky rendition of the bass line from Jackie Mittoo's 'Drum Song' (a song described earlier in this book; page 171). 'Rasta Fiesta' mixes reggae, jazz, funk and easy listening. Robbie's versatility impresses when he plays a funky slap-style bass during a mid-song jam. 'Bluesy Baby II' is a haunting funky jazz-reggae song with marimba, synthesized organ lines, bluesy sax wailing and acoustic guitar all contributing to the sound.

Other great Sly & Robbie songs

'Bum Ball'; 'When I Fall In Love'; 'You Don't Care'
The year 1981 saw the release of the awkwardly named LP, *The Sixties + Seventies + Eighties = Taxi = Sly & Robbie*. (The label has it as *60s + 70s Into The 80s*.) It was Sly & Robbie's love letter to some of their favorite Jamaican songs from the 1960s and 1970s, bringing them into the new decade with recut riddims in contemporary style. Some of the covers were instrumentals, but when vocals were heard, they were handled by Sly & Robbie, assisted by bandmates Tyrone Downie and Mikey Chung. Taking on some of Jamaica's greatest singers, they do not topple any giants, but I am happy to report that they owe few apologies for their singing. The standout tracks are these three rock steady classics, each performed lovingly. The original renditions 'Red Rum Ball' by Lloyd Robinson & Devon Russell, 'When I Fall In Love' by Ken Boothe, and 'You Don't Care' by Pat Kelly/The Techniques are each described earlier in this book (pages 140, 138, 130).

'Coon Can'

Having already proved his ability to sing, on 'Coon Can' it was time for Sly to try his hand at DJing. Although the results are surprisingly enjoyable, no DJ of the era reported sudden sleep difficulties. Not being a total fool, Sly chose one of his own great riddims for inspiration – the one he and Robbie created for Black Uhuru's 'Happiness' (a song described earlier in this book; page 356). This is as surprising as Sly turning DJ. Riddims from Black Uhuru's internationally released albums were not made available to other singers, DJs, or instrumentalists for versioning. But this is a welcome exception, as it gives us another way to enjoy the excellent riddim. And here, it's presented without the abundance of Syndrums in 'Happiness', allowing you to better appreciate Sly's playing on his acoustic kit.

Sly jumps right in and rides his rhythm, giving it his all, perhaps speaking to Robbie when he announces, "Come on, baby, let's put on a show". He chants about his desirability in love, but is not the master word machine that a professional DJ is. So one has to smile on hearing the great drummer, playing out of position, but earning an A for effort, with lines that are recalled from schoolroom arithmetic lessons. The highlight comes mid-song, as Dunbar chants about meeting Little Miss Muffet, concluding with a *yow yow*, as he breaks out his always impressive one-handed drum roll, somehow adding weight to this unserious and unlikely (yet thoroughly enjoyable) DJ performance.

'Coon Can' appeared on the otherwise instrumental 1980 Sly & Robbie LP, *Gamblers Choice*. Though it has never been released on CD, it is available on electronic music services, the perfect way to acquire it, as it's the standout track on the album.

'White Rum'

After a spoken opening, an exceptionally bouncy reggae riddim is laid down by Robbie and a reverb-enhanced Sly. A clavinet drops in and bounces up and down like it's riding a trampoline. Played by Ansel Collins, it expertly works the melodic and rhythmic nooks and crannies presented by the bass and drums. Later, the keyboard rests as Robbie steps out, elaborating his bass line rather than departing from it, for a solo. And that's the entire formula for this, a rare but wonderful three-piece reggae instrumental. Credited to Sly & The Revolutionaries, it can be found on the *Trojan Dub Box Set*.

41 Black Slate

Black Slate is a London-based roots reggae group comprised of Jamaican expatriates and members from other backgrounds. They initially came together in 1974 as a backing outfit for visiting star Jamaican singers performing in the UK. They recorded their first single in 1976 and would release about ten more, plus a run of seven self-produced albums through 1985. This included two UK hits, 'Amigo' and 'Sticksman'. But, rather than these songs, it's the ones below that represent Black Slate's best. Along with Steel Pulse and Linton Kwesi Johnson, Black Slate is one of the greatest reggae acts to come out of the UK's sizable reggae scene. By this reckoning, the tracks below are amongst the best reggae songs to come from a country other than Jamaica. Or, thinking with my ears instead of my brain, these are great reggae songs, period.

Though UK-based, Black Slate's sound is unadulterated roots reggae, serious and dramatic. If they have something in their sound that distinguishes them from Jamaican reggae bands, it's the guitar playing of rhythm guitarist Cledwyn Rogers, originally from Anguilla, and lead guitarist Chris Hanson, from Jamaica. Rogers sometimes took a tougher, dub-influenced approach to reggae rhythm guitar. Hanson's bright, slurred leads were an extension of a sound common to reggae, but developed further. If he had not emigrated to the UK, one wonders how many hundreds of Jamaican reggae records would have been graced by his playing. The group is completed by lead singer Keith Drummond and drummer Desmond Mahoney, both also originally from Jamaica, and keyboardist George Brightly and bassist Elroy Bailey, both born in London.

At the time of this writing, these Black Slate LPs are inexcusably out of print and have never been released on CD or digital music services. Instead, a 2007 CD called *Get Up And Dance*, by a splinter group called KE Black Slate that remakes many of the group's most popular songs, was available. But this album is not recommended. Then, in 2013, a Black Slate best-of LP called *Amigo* was expanded and released on CD by Cherry Red Records. It rescues three of the ten songs discussed below: 'Mind Your Motion', 'Legalize Collie Herb' and 'Boom Boom'. (Although there are two mixes of the latter, neither is the preferred dub-kissed mix from the LP.) For the rest, you'll have to troll used-record stores and web sites for the not terribly hard to find originals. In 2013 recordings by a new Black Slate line-up were released. Although these are good, since the only original members present were drummer Mahoney, keyboardist Brightly and bassist Bailey, the distinctive Black Slate sound was not recaptured.

'Africans To Africa'; 'Bondage And Slavery'; 'Mind Your Motion'
These three songs, from their eponymous 1978 debut LP, are archetypical great Black Slate. They're pure roots reggae lyrically and musically. Keith Drummond supplies fine vocals without the support or need of backing singers. His plaintive voice is well suited to roots, employing a quiver of vibrato to dramatically end his lines. The core band of bass, drum, keyboard and guitars is sometimes supplemented with horns or additional percussion. Idiosyncratic touches may come from the rhythm or lead guitar, or sometimes both.

Opening with emotional wailing from Drummond, 'Africans To Africa' is a stately roots reggae song describing African repatriation as a means for freedom. It's a gripping song that, in the roots reggae way, is mournful and hopeful at the same time. Guitar picking, Nyabinghi hand drum and dub drop-out are each dramatically employed. 'Bondage And Slavery' is a more urgent, fast-paced and busy track than 'Africans To Africa'. But it deals with similar subject matter: the way social oppression thwarts freedom. A horn section and off-the-beat drum strikes add to the excitement. A good dub version of this track, called 'Bondage Dub', was released on a 1981 Black Slate dub LP called *Ogima*. 'Mind Your Motion' is a mournful song, as Drummond directs the titular warning to black people who are in danger. He advocates a righteous religious life as a solution. The song features a deliberate rhythm, horns, subtle echo and the distinctive guitar playing of Hanson and Rogers.

'Boom Boom'; 'Legalize Collie Herb'
Two great tracks came from Black Slate's 1980 LP, *Amigo*. Though the sound and style are generally similar to those of the previous LP, there are some differences. Both songs have backing vocals, while the first shows a certain broadening of scope by the group.

'Boom Boom' finds Black Slate adapting their roots reggae sound to pay tribute to the easy-going Festival songs that enlivened the reggae of the previous two decades. In particular, it's influenced by The Jamaicans' 'Ba Ba Boom' (a song previously described in this book; page 125). Syndrums, electric piano and backing vocals lighten up the band's heavy roots sound, as does Drummond's vocal that is cheery (relative for him, as his is a voice more naturally suited to the serious). He sings Festival lyrics, with lots of references to dancing and singing, but describes it as a "Rasta Festival", where Rastas can let their locks down, enjoy the Festival vibes and rock steady. But Rastas also like dub, and the song ends with an instrumental dub section that concludes excitingly with a rhythmic guitar solo, agreeably treated with echo.

'Legalize Collie Herb' finds Black Slate back in pure roots territory. It features a lovely introduction with slurred guitar soloing over a pointillistic rhythm led by drums and bass. Drummond sings about the pain of being too poor to buy any herb, even as he sings a litany of its benefits. He pleads for its legalization in a particularly personal and heartfelt legalize-marijuana anthem. This is a strong song that stands with Peter Tosh's more famous songs on this subject.

'King David'; 'King Dub'; 'Rasta Reggae'; 'Rasta Dub'; 'Thanksgiving Dub'
In 1982, Black Slate released two LPs: *Six Plus One* and *Six Plus One Dub*, sometimes packaged as a double-disc set. They included several superb Black Slate tracks.

'King David' is soaring roots reggae, heightened by the use of dub and made doubly irresistible by the continued development of the band's idiosyncrasies. Rogers's rhythm guitar plays off-the-beat and chunky, with a dub sound that brings a strange time-shift feel to the track. Hanson's bright leads color outside of the lines, as slurred notes blur the beat. Their playing is so different, but they suit one another to a T, making an already strong song special. Mid-song, the riddim is dub reduced to barebones drum and bass. Then the other instruments are dropped back in to best maximize dub pleasure. This takes us to the song's climax, with Drummond dramatically invoking the names of biblical kings, his vibrato in full bloom. This triggers a guitar note to take off and echo like a dub satellite launch. The dub version, 'King Dub', plays on the riddim's strengths, altering the guitars with echo and reverb, and applying further drop-out/in. As heard on the *Amigo* CD, the riddim was re-voiced as the not-quite-as-good 'Black Slate Rock'.

'Rasta Reggae' surprises by integrating a string section into roots reggae. It is not used as sweetener, as one typically thinks of strings in popular music. (Reggae was not immune to this, as some UK record labels were known to add such strings to records they licensed from Jamaica.) Instead, they are playing in *dread* fashion, adding to the heaviness of the music. For example, when Drummond twice sings the titular refrain, it's separated by a furiously sawed two-note descending phrase that adds weight and excitement to the song. (That strings fit so well into reggae should not come as a complete shock. Fiddle was long part of mento and would occasionally stray into reggae, as on The Paragons' hit, 'The Tide Is High'. And the cello playing of Stephan "Cat" Coore was a highlight of live performances by Third World.) The sound of Anthony Brightly's electric piano provides an aural foil for the strings, and elaborate drum work supported with hand percussion gives the song a textured armature. The dub version, 'Rasta Dub', is a longer track by more than half. This allows all the elements of the original to be fully decanted dub-style, for an even better version of the song.

'Thanksgiving Dub' is an especially mystical-sounding piece of dub music that turns into a religious invocation by its end. Drum, bass, rhythm guitar and percussion build an urgent riddim. Dub permeates every aspect of the riddim and gives you a sense of being on a journey. A reedy saxophone joins, made sonorous and buzzy through dub. With simple phrases it manages to convey a story of struggle and perseverance. A trombone briefly replaces the saxophone and then takes its leave. Sax and bass and dub bring us to the song's climax, where Drummond makes a belated entrance with a dramatic spoken piece about the gates of thanksgiving and praising Jah. 'Thanksgiving Dub' is an example of how reggae was responsible for some of the most dramatic and sonically arresting religious music ever recorded.

42 Steel Pulse

Along with Black Slate and LKJ as backed by Dennis Bovell & The Dub Band, Steel Pulse is one of the most important reggae bands to come from the UK, and the most commercially successful of the three. Like the other two bands, Steel Pulse was comprised of expatriates from Jamaica and from elsewhere in the Caribbean and British-born members. Like them, they made roots reggae with a slightly expanded, worldlier sound that was nonetheless genuine reggae. Steel Pulse was very much part of the live reggae boom of the early 1980s. It was then that they, Bob Marley (playing what would be his final shows), Peter Tosh, Toots & The Maytals, Black Uhuru, Dennis Brown, Gregory Isaacs, Bunny Wailer, Third World, a reconstituted Skatalites and others criss-crossed the globe, performing reggae for ecstatic audiences all over the world.

The Steel Pulse story begins with David Hinds. Born in 1956 in Birmingham, England, of Jamaican immigrant parents, Hinds is the band's lead vocalist, songwriter and rhythm guitarist. And, for a time, he was reggae's (if not all of popular music's) most eye-catching bandleader. Even Jamaicans and reggae fans who were accustomed to the sight of *gorgons* (an honorific given to those with the most imposing dreadlocks) couldn't help but be impressed by the massive, strikingly vertical, ever-growing, "congo dread" that towered up from the top of Hind's head, parting the surrounding dreadlocks in its wake. In time, it would break down, a victim of gravity. Other Steel Pulse core members (the band had its share of personnel changes) include Selwyn "Bumbo" Brown, also born in Britain, on keyboards and backing vocals and Steve "Grizzly" Nesbitt, born in the Caribbean island of Nevis, on drums. Nesbitt would leave the band by their last CD in 2004. Steel Pulse is a fine name for a reggae band, but its inspiration is surprising: it was taken from the name of a famous race horse. But this is not the only time the track has influenced reggae naming. Singer Eek-A-Mouse acquired his strange name in the same way. And, as we have seen, The Pioneers recorded several classic songs named after a racehorse (see pages 227–9).

The group plays sinewy, urgent roots reggae, typically forgoing mid-song breaks. It's also an international reggae sound, emphasizing guitar and lacking horns. The backing vocals are non-virtuoso, but effective. They came to popularity in the late 1970s, as part of the British punk rock scene. Punk fans (and musicians) were very open to reggae, finding both musics to be more immediate and honest than the mainstream rock they rejected. Though Steel Pulse never played any music that resembled punk rock, there is something in Hinds's detached vocal quiver that's reminiscent of New Wave singers.

Their 1978 debut album, *Handsworth Revolution*, had some good songs that suggested future greatness. The title track was fine roots reggae, with Hinds talking directly to his community and calling for solidarity against injustice. 'Ku Klux Klan' finds Hinds imagining being attacked by this group, and calls for resistance. It was chosen for release as a single. 'Prediction' is a successful fusion of reggae and Spanish guitar. 'Macka Splaff' is a pro-ganja dub jam. The 1979 follow-up, *Tribute To The Martyrs*, contained a good song in 'Sound System', a celebration of the reggae heard at such gatherings. It too was released as a single. In 1980 came *Caught You* (retitled *Reggae Fever* for US release), an LP with two great songs as produced by Godwin Logie and Geoffrey Chung.

'Reggae Fever'; 'Reggae Fever Dub Version'

'Reggae Fever' is a glorious example of a popular subject for reggae songs: the love of reggae music. And making its case for itself, it packs in a lot to love. There's a deviously simple six-note skankin' bass line that gives the song a melodic and rhythmic foundation. There are guitars everywhere. One makes the bass line more interesting by mirroring it, taking over when the bass drops out for a note or two. Another provides clusters of a picked note that sounds like a dubby cooing bird. Another gives the song an undercurrent of growling leads. Another supplies long bent notes, informed by rock and tipped with feedback, that come to full bloom at the song's end. There are also drums dubbed with reverbed rim shots and occasional echo, washes of organ, incidental percussion and a *boing*ing keyboard sound effect. And that's just the riddim.

Hinds is great as he describes the ways his powerful love for reggae impacts his body. Not only does it give him a fever, it raises his blood pressure and makes his "liver quiver". Sounds serious, but it's a fever with unparalleled benefits. Dancing to reggae banishes troubles and replaces them with feelings of paradise and love. His intense-but-controlled quivering delivery and melodramatic exchanges of *oho* with the backing singers (led by him) suit this blissful fever-dream of a song. 'Reggae Fever' is a fitting tribute to the music it celebrates.

Also liver-quiveringly good is the excellent dub version of 'Reggae Fever' that was only available as the B-side of the 12-inch single release of 'Don't Give In'. One of its dubby pleasures is a better view of the fine drum work. Another is the inclusion of even more guitars, one providing a double-struck rhythm and another providing a brief, treated lead run that stands out and glitters. This version would make a tremendous bonus cut for an expanded edition of *Caught You*, or would improve any future Steel Pulse compilation.

'Drug Squad'

Opening with a police siren, 'Drug Squad' is reggae's thematic equivalent of Arlo Guthrie's 'Coming Into Los Angeles', as both songs involve getting searched by customs while in possession of ganja. 'Drug Squad' starts out as a song of social protest, but then reveals itself instead to be a cautionary tale, maximizing its entertainment value. Hinds is singled out for special attention at customs. He asks why, but this is sarcasm coming from Hinds, considering his unique mass of dreadlocks. He objects, explaining to the officials that with his appearance, he's the last person who would try to smuggle ganja. His indignation grows, complaining that they are wasting his time. But he is strip-searched, complete with an inspection from a sniffer dog. It turns out that Hinds was lying, as a stash of ganja is found hidden in his boots! The song ends with Hinds bewailing his arrest. This well-told tale is impeccably supported with a tough, rocked-out riddim leavened by fine electric piano that's a welcome prominent presence throughout.

True Democracy

Steel Pulse would next release two notable albums that were filled with great reggae: *True Democracy*, their best, and *Earth Crisis*, the less consistent. But after these releases, the quality quickly fell off, as changes in personnel and sound took their toll.

True Democracy, produced by Karl Pitterson in 1982, is a great reggae album. The sound is largely unchanged from *Caught You*, but there is a new maturity. Complex song structures with more than one chorus and the occasional jazz-inflected chord change are idiosyncratically featured. And every song demonstrates a mastery of melody that was only sporadically heard on their previous albums. This last element in particular helps make nearly every one of its songs great. Perhaps as a result of coming up through the punk ranks, this album has an unusually high energy level. But make no mistake, this is not punk, two-tone or any other blend or derivate – this is a reggae album. Though it is consistently strong, three songs stand out.

'Chant A Psalm'
'Chant A Psalm' opens with the lone strike of a triangle, leading to a gnarled rhythmic introduction. A second strike, dubbed to emanate a triangle sound in waves, calls the body of the song. What arrives is a riddim so crisp and crackling with energy, it can barely contain itself. There's a dancing bass line, clever drums, bubble-up organ, prominent rhythm guitar and assorted hand percussion, including more triangle accents that stand out like points of light on a night shoreline. Meanwhile, long synthesized organ chords shade some bars with a subtle dose of extra melody. With no lead instrument, or anything standing out, this backing is an ensemble piece. Hinds enters and welcomes us with a beaming message of unbridled positivity, happiness and acceptance. No other reggae album has ever opened so strong.

The positive vibes continue, as Hinds explains how religion is the remedy for feeling downcast and the temptation of dangerous behavior. His guidance is populated with Bible figures and quotes at every turn. With no room or need (the Rasta's *overstand*), Jah is not explicitly mentioned nor is any other Rasta terminology used. This gives the song a traditional spiritual vibe, especially when the old-timey expression "Get behind me Satan" is heard. But when it is heard, there's nothing old-fashioned about the sound, touched with dub and launching a surprising key change in an already melodically rich song. 'Chant A Psalm' is an impressive opening to a great album.

'Ravers'

Opening with a wicked guitar riff, 'Ravers' is, indeed, a high-energy rave-up. A reggae song celebrating reggae, it looks at the subject from several angles. Hinds sings about his girl who is looking for love and dancing. He can satisfy both interests by calling for some rub-a-dub. That's because "rub-a-dub" has two somewhat related meanings in Jamaica. One is dub music. The other is an intimate dance that involves sexually rubbing together to the beat of reggae music, especially dub. He continues excitedly, adopting the staccato rolling nonsense syllables of a reggae DJ. Hinds has a lot of fun with this in concert performances of "Ravers", leading audiences in a DJ sing-along, depending on the city, with varying levels of success. But the elaborate drum-shuffle response from Grizzly Nesbitt never fails. Having already advocated dub and chanted DJ, Hinds gets more specific by introducing self-referential lyrics. He explains that the very song we are listening to will only increase our appetite for more reggae. Then he moves to the global state of reggae, commenting on how everyone is jumping on the reggae bandwagon. Just as Hinds's tour of the state of reggae approaches it from a variety of angles, Grizzly Nesbitt's drums enrich the song with a variety of shuffles and fills in one of his finest performances.

'Worth His Weight In Gold (Rally Round)'

In 'Worth His Weight In Gold', Hinds condemns the crimes of the slave trade, and celebrates Garveyism. This belief, put forth by Marcus Garvey and adopted by the Rastas, holds that the descendants of slaves will find redemption by repatriating to Africa. As heard in The Melodians' classic "Rivers Of Babylon" (a song described earlier in this book; pages 230–1) and other roots reggae songs, Psalm 137 is quoted to poignantly illustrate this need. As a Rasta, Hinds sees African repatriation as being a return to biblical Zion that promises respect, liberation and, giving the album its title, true democracy.

Though these familiar roots reggae topics can sometimes result in a somber track, "Worth His Weight In Gold" is a live wire of a reggae song, right from its introduction – an unabashedly playful exercise in rhythm. The riddim's energy never flags and the song is further embellished with elaborate vocal harmonies. Propulsive and sleek, 'Worth His Weight In Gold' is an unstoppable roots reggae torpedo.

Other great True Democracy *songs*

'Find It ... Quick!' is a bracing song with an exciting, snaking melody. It concerns the need for love in society, and includes an especially poetic line adapted from Levi H. Dowling's 1908 spiritual book, the *Aquarian Gospel of Jesus the Christ*, about love being a golden cord that binds us to God's commandments. 'Blues Dance Raid' is set up by a police whistle. Brooding and rocking, it's about the brutality and destruction of property at the hands of the police when a London dance is raided. An exasperated Hinds advocates fighting back. 'Leggo Beast' is perhaps the fiercest anti-adultery song ever recorded, in which Hinds must deal with the aggressive advances of a married woman. Nyah hand drum makes an appearance, and the backing vocals are strong. 'Your House' slows the pace with an introspective love song. 'Who Responsible' would have been improved with a horn replacing the lead synthesizer. It and 'Man No Sober', an anti-alcohol song, fall below the high bar set by the rest of the album.

Dub bonus tracks

The CD release of *True Democracy* is expanded with several dub versions. Rather than a bonus track, 'Dub Marcus Say' is a dub version of 'Worth His Weight In Gold' that has been part of *True Democracy* since its original LP release. Starting with a song this exciting it's hard to go wrong, but this version might have benefited by being mixed in Jamaica. The same could be said for the dub portion of the 12-inch versions of 'Ravers' and 'Leggo Beast', as well as the dub version of 'A Who Responsible'. Faring better is the dub version of 'Your House'. It strips away most of the vocals, revealing surprising textures and an introspective bass line that has the entire song's DNA in miniature.

Earth Crisis

True Democracy's follow-up was the 1984 *Earth Crisis*, produced by Jimmy Haynes and Steel Pulse. Its best songs are more ambitious and as good as, if not better, than anything on *True Democracy*. But as a whole, *Earth Crisis* is a less consistent album. Though largely unchanged, the sound is expanded a bit with the addition of horns. Below are the last great Steel Pulse songs, as changes in personnel and direction would follow.

'Steppin' Out'

Thank goodness for CD bonus tracks. The version of 'Steppin' Out' as included on the *Earth Crisis* LP was just damaged goods compared to the "extended version" on the 12-inch single that Elektra Records would release. (This single included four versions of the song: the album version, the so-called extended version, a dub version of the extended version and an a cappella version of the same.) As the title promises, the extended version is a little longer, but more importantly, it's a vastly superior remix; decluttered, pulsating with dub, and spatially alive.

By comparison, the album mix, smothered with extra synthesizers and horns and without dub, is suffocatingly flat. With the inclusion of the extended version on the album's CD release, we need never talk about the original album mix again.

The dub-soaked riddim features spacey whooshes and an echo-doubled rhythm guitar reminiscent of that heard on 'The Sun Is Shining' from Bob Marley & The Wailers' *Kaya* album. (And anything reminiscent of that song is a good thing.) Snatches of keyboards, horns and Nyabinghi drum drop out/in optimally, as per the needs of the moment. Hinds leaps into this dub landscape flamboyantly, opening with a Marley-esque grunt. He portrays himself as a fantastical force for good and for the appreciation of reggae. He brings magic to bear with a cry of "Abracadabra" and claims to be a genie, who can grant wishes. And if magic isn't enough, he brings science fiction to bear as well, asking to be beamed up and revealing the existence of "the planet dread" where "it rains dub".

This storytelling is made even more colorful by the interplay between Hinds and the backing vocalists. Most lines are split, with the backing vocalists taking over for a phrase. When they sing along with Hinds, sometimes it's in perfect unison, while at other times they are a beat ahead of him. It further enlivens what is already a very lively song.

The dub version bonus track sounds like the work of a non-Jamaican remixer, but is enjoyable if not crucial. This leaves only the a cappella version from the 12-inch single unavailable on CD. But the dub version has an a cappella section that gives the same experience. It shows how the vocal interplay was entertaining enough to carry the song alone.

'Roller Skates'
'Roller Skates' opens and closes with the unexpected. The syncopated introduction is surprisingly elaborate, with a playful, bright jazzy chord progression that bobs and weaves. Buoyant reggae follows, distinguished by a synthesized steel drum sound and horn sounds played on a keyboard. Hinds tells the story of being out one night, roller skating, playing music on his radio, enjoying himself and the company of some ladies. A fat cat pulls up in an expensive car and asks for directions. Hinds tries to help, but is roughed up and relieved of his radio. Hinds laments that he can't live without music (apparently not even for a little while) and vows to catch the thief and beat him bruised and bloody. Hinds and company head out on their skates and locate the crook, who has taken not only the radio, but Hinds's whole scene. He's parked and out on the sidewalk, dancing to Hinds's radio, drawing a crowd. Exactly what happens to the thief is left unsaid and completely up to the listener's imagination.

Just as you would expect the song to end, there comes another surprise. 'Roller Skates' essentially becomes a disco-mix, as Hinds does something unusual for a reggae singer. Though he flirted with the form on *Ravers*, it's still a surprise when he busts a DJ version of the riddim. And he's not bad, creating perhaps the only disco-mix where the singer and the DJ are the same person. He chants of the outrage of having someone steal his music, and expands on its symbolic political meaning. Giving us the unexpected upon the unexpected, he is briefly accompanied by an accordion in this constantly entertaining song.

A "remix version" of 'Roller Skates', taken from a 12-inch single, is another bonus track on the *True Democracy* CD. But unlike 'Steppin' Out', there is nothing broken with the original for the remix to fix. Nor does it deliver any degree of dub satisfaction, making the remix completely superfluous. A dub version from the same source is not bad, but a Jamaican remixer could have made a much better version.

'Bodyguard'

The introduction of 'Bodyguard' carries a smooth R&B sound, but this feint is jettisoned when the body of the song begins. Heavy, bitter-sweet reggae is heard, anchored by a moody bass line processed to be oversized and strong horn lines. Atypically for Steel Pulse, a guitar solo provides a rare mid-song break. Hinds unspools another of his engaging complex melodies as he deplores those who have to protect corrupt politicians. He finds their job difficult and objectionable, and feels no pity towards anyone in the profession, effectively guaranteeing that the song would not be used in the soundtrack for the Kevin Costner/Whitney Houston movie of the same name that was released a few years later. Rhythm and melody come together impressively on the chorus. The strong backing vocals are led by Hinds.

Other Earth Crisis songs

The title track 'Earth Crisis' uses vocoder on some vocals to produce a science-fiction sound well suited to the lyrics about mankind bringing about the world's end, as horns help build an apocalyptic vibe. 'Tightrope' is embellished with jazz touches and Earth Wind and Fire-style soul horns. 'Grab Education' is unequivocally pro-education, in contrast to several songs by The Wailers that assailed Jamaica's education system. It's a subject that deserves better, since a weak melody drags the song down. The same problems impact the rather depressing anti-science song, 'Wild Goose Chase', and a love song, 'Throne Of Gold', recalling a time when Steel Pulse found good melodies harder to come by, and foreshadowing the decline that followed.

43 More great roots reggae

For many reggae fans, especially those outside of Jamaica, roots is the only reggae that matters. From the early 1970s through the first half of the 1980s, roots reggae dominated in Jamaica until dancehall rose up to knock it from the hill. Here's a variety of great roots reggae songs, presented chronologically and representing the full spectrum of the style's sounds and concerns, from artists who do not have their own chapters in this book. Singers and vocal groups – the famous and the not; those who recorded roots exclusively and those who had broader résumés; those who aimed at international audiences or strictly *a yard* – are all represented. Each of these fine songs is readily available on CD unless otherwise noted.

Max Romeo: *'Rent Man' (aka 'Rent Crisis', or 'Landlord And Tenant')*
'Rent Man', produced by Bunny Lee in 1971, is another great reggae rent song. Rent woes have long been fertile ground for Jamaica's songwriters. (We have already seen several great examples in this book dating back to golden-age mento, and there is a great DJ example yet to come.) Here, the subject is explored from the perspective of social protest born of roots sensibilities.

Romeo is so expressive and his song is so tuneful, it begs you to sing along. Part of the melody is adapted from the old mento song, 'Hold 'Im Joe', though a brooding Romeo makes it sound new. He is supported by an athletic backing singer (possibly Romeo double-tracked) working in a higher register, for a pleasing Jamaican harmony. Meanwhile, a tough, lean, early roots reggae backing is heard. It shows both its lineage from and contrast to the sweet rock steady of a few years earlier.

At just over 2 minutes, it's as exactly as long as Romeo needs to describe his untenable rent situation. It opens with someone knocking on the door and waking Max up, who turns out to be the rent man. "Whoi! What a pressure!" is his wailing response. He describes his already high, ever-rising rent, and the landlord's many restrictions. The rent man has an armed bodyguard, and if payment isn't made, he will return with a court official and the police for immediate eviction. *Whoi, what a pressure*, indeed. And fine fodder for a great early roots song. Under one of its three titles, the song is available on various Max Romeo best-of CD collections, but there was also a vastly inferior remake produced by Mafia & Fluxie. But there is little danger of accidently acquiring it, as it is not included on any of these collections.

Barry Biggs: *'Work All Day'*
Barry Biggs was educated overseas, and favored highly polished reggae covers of American pop-soul hits by The Jackson Five, The Temptations, The Spinners and

Stevie Wonder. He sang in a show-biz style, wore show-biz outfits and his Afro was groomed against any chance of becoming dreadlocks. Barry Biggs was the antithesis of a roots reggae artist, a fact that he made no bones about. He considered himself a Jamaican singer who recorded reggae amongst other styles, rather than a reggae singer per se. Yet something happened in 1972 while he was recording for producer Byron Lee (the leader of the versatile Jamaican band The Dragonaires, in which Biggs was lead singer for a time). Whether accidentally or deliberately, he created a gem of a *sufferas* song that stands with any in roots reggae. Apparently, the producer didn't know what to make of this roots gem, as it was not released until four years later. In spite of a career that many reggae fans understandably deride, this song stands up to similarly themed songs from some of roots reggae's biggest names.

'Work All Day' is a work song: a popular theme in reggae. Other examples in this book include Bob Marley & The Wailers' 'Work' and 'It's Alright/Night Shift', Black Uhuru's 'Mondays', Desmond Dekker's 'Israelites' and Junior Murvin's 'Workin' In The Cornfield'. As is typical for such songs, Biggs describes his work woes dramatically. He is anguished that having to work all day precludes spending any time with his woman and family, or having any enjoyment at all. Any reggae fans who work too hard at a job they dislike will love this song.

It opens dreamily with just Biggs, a somnolent organ and a distant foghorn sound. Singing in a reggae falsetto, he sleepily previews some of the lyrics, about laboring hard all day and longing for the evening when he can be with his woman and rest. Suddenly, he rouses himself, singing of being homeward bound, setting up the rhythm for the instrumentation that quickly joins. Fine bass, drum, guitar and keyboards and somber backing vocals come in. As is common in reggae, but especially noticeable here, is how the bass provides a stripped-down melody that other instruments (organ, piano and synthesizer in this case) ride upon. The backing vocals are impressive. But they are smart enough to stay out of Biggs's way, as he gives an impassioned performance. His falsetto is strong but vulnerable. He's bluesy as the song begins, but this burns off as it builds in intensity. He peaks mid-song, when his desperation causes him to wail an appeal to God, his falsetto reaching stunning heights. Then, with tight interaction from the backing singers, he recounts his lot in life, having to wake up every morning, only to work all day. As the song reaches its end, sorrowful backing vocals ground the song even as Biggs's anguish soars. I've just decided I'm calling in sick tomorrow.

Cornel Campbell: *'Jah Jah Me No Born Yah'*
You know Cornel Campbell has to be quite the roots singer, having earned the double-superlative nickname of Don Gorgon. As we have seen, Don means "boss", while a gorgon typically is an honorific reserved for a Rasta with notably impressive dreadlocks. But with his not-unusual dreads, in Campbell's case the label

instead describes a state of mind, as he recorded a spate of popular Gorgon-titled songs in 1975.

Though his high, strong, sweet voice was well suited for roots reggae, he started singing well before that era. The Kingston-born Campbell first learned to sing in church and recorded an R&B side that was released in 1961 prior to the dawn of ska. (Cornel remembers that the recording was made in 1956, when he was just eleven – young even for a *youth singer* – with producer Coxsone Dodd holding the record back for years, as he was wont to do.) Campbell moved through ska, rock steady and early reggae, sometimes as a member of a vocal group, working with a variety of producers including Dodd, with whom he continued to record throughout the 1960s. But greater success as a roots singer and his elevation to Don Gorgon lay ahead of him, in a fruitful collaboration with producer Bunny Lee. He has over 200 singles and more than 30 albums under his belt, the last made in 2013. Though known as a singer, Campbell is also a versatile musician, providing uncredited guitar, bass and piano for Lee on sessions by Derrick Morgan, Johnny Clarke and others. His sister, Cecille Campbell, was a member of ska group The Soulettes, along with Rita Marley and Rita's cousin and fill-in Wailer, Constantine "Dream" Walker.

Produced by Bunny Lee in 1973, 'Jah Jah Me No Born Yah' is a concise *sufferas* song, clocking in at just 2 minutes. Accomplished and smolderingly dramatic, it sounds much longer. It deals with the subject of starvation. The seriousness of this topic is echoed by its sound, filled with majestic, eastern-influenced descending minor-key melodies that invoke Old Testament drama as roots reggae sometimes does. This is especially true of Campbell's emotional wordless falsetto wailing that graces the song's opening and closing sections. 'Jah Jah Me No Born Yah' is a small, perfect roots reggae jewel. Sometimes mistitled as 'Jah Jah Me No Horn Yah', the song is available on several CD collections. Campbell would record a fairly good (but not nearly as great) remake in 1977, re-titling it as 'Free Meal Ticket'.

The Gladiators: *'The Race'*

Produced by Pat Chin in the earlier part of the mid-1970s, vocal group The Gladiators' 'The Race' is encouragement in a bottle. A knotty drum roll introduces a likable riddim that's full of music. It pits flinty rhythm instruments against sweet piano and quiet bluesy guitar riffing. Meanwhile, a trombone affably wanders around the track like a baby elephant. Lead singer Albert Griffiths sounds helpful and wise, supported by restrained harmony from the other Glads. He uses a race as a symbol for life, advocating perseverance and patience. He points out the value of intelligence over speed. He continues earnestly dispensing positive vibes, promising God's help and good outcomes for those who try. And as a music-loving Jamaican, he also reminds us to always keep "a song on your tongue". Having made its points as one of the most positive of all reggae songs, 'The Race' ends by setting a reverbed Griffiths free to wordlessly jam with the trombone. The Gladiators have belatedly provided a soundtrack for Aesop's fable of *The Tortoise and the Hare*, and it is superb.

It's nearly impossible to feel down after giving this track a spin. A remake in 1982 is good, but you will want to find the original rendition as included on several CD compilations of Randy's material.

African Brothers: *'Hold Tight'*

The short-lived vocal group The African Brothers was formed in 1969 when Kingston teens Winston "Tony Tuff" Morris, Lincoln "Sugar" Minott and Derrick "Bubbles" Howard came together at a soccer game that gave way to music making. As a group, they made their biggest mark in roots reggae, though their break-up at the end of the 1970s had a greater impact. Sugar Minott became a star, Tony Tuff enjoyed a successful career and Bubbles recorded some solo records as well, sometimes as Eric Bubble.

'Hold Tight' was produced by Clive Chin in 1974. From the opening drum roll and the introductory hot jam between slurred reggae guitar and piano that follows, this song is an unusually taut piece of roots reggae. Every aspect of the song is peppered with urgency, right down to how the reggae chop rhythm guitar is sounded. Lead singer Tony Tuff's rootsy nasal voice enters with the intensity of an imperative message, as he counsels against allowing anyone to keep you from a righteous, God-obeying life. The rootsy, strident backing vocals repeatedly impel the listener to "hold tight" to this advice. Short as a warning, the song hits, delivers its message and is done in just over 2 minutes. It too can be heard on several Randy's CD compilations.

Cornel Campbell: *'Natty Dread In A Greenwich Farm'*

Produced by Bunny Lee in 1975, 'Natty Dread In A Greenwich Farm' opens with a teasing introduction designed to keep you guessing what will follow. What does is a most enjoyable reggae song, equally notable for Campbell's fine singing, the story he tells and the backing music.

The latter is a picture-perfect combination of springy, dub-bouncing rhythm guitar, sweet piano, rumbling bass and lively drums that frames embellishments from organ and slurred guitar. It's uniquely reggae: so bouncy, pliant and alive. Incredibly upbeat, it provides a fitting vehicle for Campbell's voice but an unlikely one for his story.

Keying his phrasing to the bouncing rhythm, Campbell chooses a sing-song chanted approach. It gives his sweet, melodic, high-register singing a particular lightness here. But all of this belies the events of the song.

While visiting his friend Bongo [Black] Tom in the Greenwich Farms section of Kingston, he finds that the police are unable to tolerate a large Rasta presence. Campbell and his friend are accosted, physically restrained and beaten by the police. By the end of the song, Campbell sees the need for separation between Rastas and Babylon. These are weighty matters, but they are sung about with the breezy nonchalance of someone describing a walk in the park. Consider how much angrier is Linton Kwesi Johnson's similarly themed 'Sonny's Lettah' (a song described later in this book; page 530). One can only conclude that this event was so common an occurrence for Campbell and his Rasta bredren at that time that retelling it didn't work him up at all. 'Natty Dread In A Greenwich Farm' is included on several Cornel Campbell CD collections.

Al Campbell: *'Going The Wrong Way'*

Al Campbell was born in 1954, in Kingston, and like so many reggae singers, began singing in church as a child. (His father, a commanding presence, was not only the preacher there, but a former policeman.) Though he broke into recording in 1968 as a member of a short-lived vocal group called The Thrillers, and had cups of coffee in other groups (Royal Rasses, Mighty Cloud Band and The Heptones) and duos (with Freddie McGregor, Junior Menz and Ernest Wilson), Campbell is far better known as a roots reggae singer whose solo recording career began around 1973. It's as if his voice – fine, emotional and weathered – was waiting for roots to take off. He recorded about 125 singles and 20 albums into the mid-1980s.

'Going The Wrong Way', produced by Phil Pratt in 1975, is a terse, exciting, emotional song sporting excellent melodies and a distinctive riddim. After opening with some Waterhouse-style wailing, Campbell sings of his concern for Jamaica's youth. He sounds genuinely worried that the children may be following a path of wickedness rather than the righteous path of Rastafari. The song reaches a powerful emotional peak when he asks us how we'll react when God "stretch forth his hands" to lead the people to Zion. The riddim reminds us how reggae issued great bass lines like a mint prints money. Supported nicely by piano, it provides a countermelody to Campbell's melodically sophisticated singing. At the same time, it gives the song its drive and a touch of swing. The riddim has some idiosyncratic touches. Impossible to miss is the timekeeping on the bell of a cymbal that gives the song urgency. More subtle is how reverb enhances the rim shots. So too is the maracas' moment in the spotlight.

'Going The Wrong Way' can be heard on the *Trojan Rastafari Box Set*. Big Youth and dub transformed 'Going The Wrong Way' into the deep dread chant called 'Love Jah Jah Children', a song described in the chapter on this artist (page 413).

The Mellodies: *'Dread Oppression'*

The Mellodies is an obscure roots vocal group that recorded two songs at Studio One in 1975 for its only single. 'Dread Oppression' is sung in unison by three disparate voices, for a multigrain roots reggae harmony. The backing band provides austere roots instrumentation with few pretensions. A relaxed organ riff is answered by bent guitar notes that reappear mid-song and at its conclusion. A flinty rhythm guitar anchors with the reggae chop. 'Dread Oppression' repurposes the melody of the old mento song, 'Fire Stick', with new *sufferas* lyrics, as The Melodies and their backing band effectively transform a great mento song into a great roots reggae song. Somehow this humble but great track has yet to find its way to either a roots reggae or a Studio One LP or CD compilation.

Ernest Wilson: *'I Know Myself'*

Clarendon-born Fitzroy "Ernest" Wilson began his recording career in 1965 as part of the successful vocal duo The Clarendonians, having joined up with Peter Austin two years earlier. In 1967, Wilson began his career as a solo artist, though he would also have stints in a duo with Freddy McGregor and as a member of the vocal group The Techniques. Additionally, the versatile Wilson was in demand as a backing singer, appearing on records by reggae performers as diverse as Johnny Osbourne, Inner Circle and Beres Hammond, and as a studio musician, providing guitar on several sessions, piano on a Dennis Brown dub project and bass for Gregory Isaacs's *Cool Ruler* album. A modestly prolific reggae singer, Wilson recorded about 60 solo singles from 1967 through 1983 and a few albums, the last in 2007.

Produced by Jo Jo Hookim in 1975, Wilson's 'I Know Myself' is a song with much to speak for it. It features one of Wilson's most effective and soulful vocals, validating his nickname, "Soul" Wilson. It features the effortlessly excellent and endlessly creative rhythm section of Sly & Robbie in fine style. Even by reggae standards, it's impressive how well Shakespeare's bass line adds to Wilson's song. And no other reggae drummer could have fleshed out the rhythm quite like Dunbar does here, using his tom-toms as a go-to. There's so much music in the rhythm, the song doesn't really need a lead instrument. But it has one in the organ that repeats a wistful phrase that plays off the bass line. It gives the song a hook that could land a whale.

On top of all this is Wilson with a strong, *upfull* song. In so many words, it's about how his self-actualization allows him to overcome problems and criticism, and enables him to love his girlfriend better. There is urgency in his singing, as he badly wants to share what he has learned. So powerful is self-knowledge that it can replace violence and hostility with an inner peace. Though it's easy enough to read it into the lyrics, Wilson does not mention Rastafari or make any reference to religion. So if the American Psychiatric Association is searching for a reggae anthem, they need look no further. With an excellent riddim, fine heartfelt singing and therapeutic message, 'I Know Myself' is a winner.

'I Know Myself' is available on several reggae compilation CDs. Two excellent versions are described elsewhere in this book (pages 367 and 423). One is a 1978 Sly & Robbie track called 'A Who Say' that manages to transform the riddim into easy-listening jazz-reggae. Around the same time, the riddim would also serve for Trinity's wonderfully chaotic DJ romp, 'No Galfriend'. That makes three versions of the same riddim, each excellent, that couldn't be more different from one another. Less impressive is the 2007 remake on Wilson's CD, 'Still Love You', though it does find him in fine voice.

Horace Andy: *'Skylarking'*
Singer Horace Andy was born Horace Hinds, in 1951 in Kingston. He wanted a career like his elder cousin, ska and reggae singer Justin Hinds. But he didn't sound like Justin, nor much like anyone else for that matter. He possessed a high quivering voice that was unusual, but suited for reggae, especially the roots reggae that began to catch on just as Andy found recording success. As a teenager, he recorded a single side for producer Phil Pratt in 1968, but with no impact. Things would change when Andy came to work at Studio One in 1970, where he recorded almost exclusively for about two years, enjoying several hits over that time. Andy then went on to work with various other producers, and the hits continued. He has released more than 35 albums and 200 singles. He is still recording today, working out of the UK.

The 1975 Bunny Lee-produced 'Skylarking' is a superior remake of an already good song that Andy recorded a few years earlier at Studio One. Lead saxophone and a rhythm section of bass, drums, guitar and organ interlock into an impenetrably dense riddim that moves to its own chugging, stutter-step beat. Andy rides the riddim by drawing out his syllables in the song's few lyrics, showcasing his peculiar vibrato. He is double-tracked to harmonize with himself, intensifying his performance. He laments how the youth of Jamaica have taken to "skylarking" – begging for change on the streets – and he pleads that they find some form of honest work instead, as they are setting down a path that will lead to jail.

Though this Bunny Lee-produced version is the best, and the Studio One version is fine, there's yet another worthy rendition of 'Skylarking' by Andy. It's actually titled 'Skylarking – A Better Version'. Though it has a handsome harpsichord and a disco-mix with dub version to recommend it, the superior vocal on the Bunny Lee version prevents me from completely endorsing the song's name. And Lee Perry's 'Rude Walking' is a fine instrumental version (better than the one of the same name produced by Perry but credited to The Upsetters & Tommy McCook).

Horace Andy: *'Zion Gate'*
A year later, another fruitful collaboration between singer Andy and producer Bunny Lee followed. This was 'Zion Gate', a powerful, moving piece of roots reggae. It opens with a minimalistic drum roll that calls a regal descending horn line that spirals down from heaven. So rich in feeling and so full of gravitas, horns like this are the sole province of roots. Guitar and piano quietly respond, dusting the riddim with melody. In his idiosyncratic quivering vibrato, but sounding

humbled by the subject, Andy reverently sings about wanting to be on the right side when the gate to Zion swings closed. Outside the gate, he sees too much bad behavior, and agonizes how people have forgotten about Jah. Throughout, the song casts a subtle dub glow, courtesy of Lee's engineer, King Tubby. It's a song that is equally impressive for its sound and for its heartfelt faith. There are several mixes of 'Zion Gate' and some are recorded at different pitches, not to mention at least one inferior remake available on various albums. To be assured of the best mix, I recommend the disco-mix version recorded with DJ Jah Stitch, as found on Stitch's album called *Original Ragga Muffin*.

Horace Andy: 'Mr. Bassie'

Launching a classic riddim of the same name, 'Mr. Bassie' was recorded in 1976 at Studio One, where Horace Andy began his career in earnest a decade earlier. Andy's distinctive vocals are brought to bear on a tribute to someone of great importance: not a single individual, but the collective players of reggae bass. Andy salutes them by asking the titular figure to "play your song for me". In this, Andy celebrates the importance of bass in reggae by attributing the songs to the bassists.

'Mr. Bassie's' few lyrics form stanzas that are regularly placed, which suits the riddim. It lurches forward beat by beat, a machine built of overlapping slabs of rhythm guitar, organ, stiff hi-hat-dominated drums, a classic sax refrain, grunts, *oohs*, shouts and, yes, a great reggae bass line of the start-and-stop variety. These chunky components remarkably mash together to function as a coherent whole. It calls to mind one of the theories of the origin of the word "reggae" – that it comes from raggy or ragged. The riddim gracefully lumbers forward in a way that's unique to reggae, and is perhaps best exemplified by this track. It makes 'Mr. Bassie' a rhythmic and textural treat, even as the vocal and sax give the song an abundance of melody and hooks. Nothing less would be fitting for a song that pays tribute to reggae's bassies.

Make sure you get the Studio One original, not one of the inferior remakes. Recommended is the disco-mix version on the CD compilation called *Nice Up The Dance – Studio One Disco-mixes*. Other fine versions of the 'Mr. Bassie' riddim by Augustus Pablo, Trinity and Sly & Robbie are described elsewhere in this book (pages 253, 422, 367).

Jacob Miller: 'Tenement Yard'

In persona, and even in his appearance, Jacob Miller stood out from the crowd of his contemporaries. He was always laughing and smiling. The fact that he was chubby only served to magnify his jolly image. This all made him unique amongst reggae singers, who tended to come off as more serious, and were typically thin as rails. His singing style stood out too. He was gifted with a strong emotive voice, and he often affected a playful staccato stutter that became his trademark. A man of natural charisma and talent, there is no telling what he could have achieved if not for his untimely death at age twenty-seven.

Miller was born in 1952 in Mandeville, Manchester Parish, and moved to Kingston when he was eight. Beginning in 1968, he recorded a handful of sides showing a strong Dennis Brown influence, but commercial success eluded him. One of these songs was 'Love Is A Message', a Coxsone Dodd-produced *youth singer* reworking of Freddie McKay's 'Love Is A Treasure' (a song described previously in this book; page 125). Garth Swaby took a liking to it and played it frequently at his Rockers sound system. And Garth's helper and brother, Horace, aka Augustus Pablo, would soon play a role in Miller's career. By the mid-1970s, Miller would be recording hits for Pablo's newly launched Rockers label, although he did have success working for other producers as well. He joined the band Inner Circle, and immediately enjoyed a big hit with them in 'Tenement Yard' in 1975. In 1979, they would hit again with 'We Are Rockers'.

His charisma is on display in two films. First is his live set at the Bob Marley & The Wailers-headlined One Love Peace concert of 1978, as captured in the film *Heartland Reggae*. A fine performance is made even more memorable when the shirtless, rotund Miller, holding a spliff, dons a hat borrowed off the head of a policeman. This while he's singing 'Big Stripe', his song about how police get promoted for arresting Rastas. Second, in the film *Rockers*, where he acted against type, playing a humorless, dangerously ill-tempered character who was quick with a knife when a friend interrupted his meal and dared make a joke. Jamaican musical talent has had far more than its share of untimely deaths. But the highly likable Miller's fatal Kingston car crash in 1990 at age twenty seven at the peak of his popularity was particularly tragic – perhaps the most tragic early reggae death since that of golden-age mento Lord Flea at same age. Miller recorded about 65 singles and eight albums.

'Tenement Yard' was produced by Inner Circle band members Ian Monteith Lewis (bass) and Roger Lewis (guitar) in 1975, and its popularity makes it available on numerous CD compilations. Miller's idiosyncratic singing is in full bloom here. He stutters mightily and playfully affects exaggerated wails of woe as he complains about the lack of privacy in crowded tenement yard living. He bemoans how Rastas and their ganja are poorly suited for such government housing, with too much gossip ("su-su") and too many informers in close quarters. As a result, lighting up will bring a visit from a "beast", as he refers to the police.

'Tenement Yard's instrumentation features a grumbling picked guitar, bright piano accents, and a drum that nicely strikes just after the beat. But the bigger-than-life Miller is undoubtedly the star of the song. A year later, Miller re-voiced this track as 'Too Much Imitator'. This time, he bemoans the fact that every time he records a song, fifty imitations appear – an issue that is purely reggae. This version was only released as a single, making it tough to find. But don't despair. The easy-to-find 'Tenement Yard' is a better track vocally, lyrically and sonically.

Johnny Clarke: *'Cold I Up' (aka 'The Ruler')*
Roots singer Johnny Clarke was born in 1955 in Kingston. A talent-show win led to a debut single with producer Clancy Eccles in 1971. But it sank without a ripple, and Clarke would have to wait until 1973 before recording again, resuming his career with producer Rupie Edwards. That same year, he would also begin to work with producer Bunny Lee and his house band, The Aggravators. Though this band had a large rotating cast, a line-up led by drummer Santa Davis provided Clarke with a high-energy roots reggae rhythm called "flying cymbals", for his 'None Shall Escape The Judgment'. Characterized by relentless rhythm guitar and hi-hat cymbal, the ghost of ska was raised by this insistent, driving beat. Clarke is best remembered for a series of tough roots songs that featured this rhythm. He would record about 200 singles and 20 albums in all, the last coming in 2003.

Produced in 1975 by Bunny Lee, 'Cold I Up' is Johnny Clarke's decree that he will avoid dealing with anyone who might try to "cold I up", or keep him down. He sounds confident and suitably chilly as he lays down the law, describing his efforts to *live up*. Politics ("politricktion") is to be shunned, as are "two-faced" hypocrites and double-crossers. He will keep his head high in spite of those who tell lies about him. As he describes overcoming these challenges, he impresses with the composed dignity of his vocal. Though he does not have a virtuoso instrument, it's a pleasing voice, and he marshals a carefully modulated vibrato at the end of his lines. Backing vocals are not present – or missed. The tough roots reggae instrumentation is all the backing he needs. It's a cool, no-nonsense riddim, built of drums, bass, guitar, an undertone of piano, and enlivened by cutting organ and lead guitar phrases that are scattered throughout. It conveys the same attitude as Clarke's voice and words, making every aspect of 'Cold I Up' part of a singular proclamation. It is available on the CD collection, *Rougher Version: Johnny Clarke At King Tubby's*.

The Maytones: *'Money Trouble'*
'Money Trouble' by The Maytones is a delicious piece of 1977 reggae cooked up from a Studio One oldie, a dub-rich production from Alvin Ranglin and the richest performance of The Maytones' career.

Sometimes called The Mighty Maytones, Vernon Buckley and Gladstone Grant named their vocal group after their May Pen home, just as The Maytals had. They began recording in the rock steady era continuing through roots reggae, releasing over 100 singles from 1968 through 1984. They also recorded eight albums, one the result of a mid-1990s reunion.

There is no better example of how elastic late-1970s reggae could sound than this Maytones song. With so much play in its structure, it sounds built of living material. This is especially pronounced when it is compared to the original rendition of the song, Ernest Wilson's 'Money Worries', a Studio One rock steady track from the previous decade. Wilson's song, with its unusually stiff arrangement, sounds rigid and brittle next to the remake.

From the opening tumble of a drum roll, the sound is exceptionally pliant and full of life. There are playful drums and bass, buoyant bubble-up organ, a guitar chop that arrives just after the beat and a surfeit of incidental percussion (with tambourine, wood blocks, vibraslap, jingle stick, bicycle bell, bird whistle, *et al.*). Subtle dub, well applied, pumps even more life into the sound. The vocals are no less vibrant. Lead singer Vernon Buckley hooks us immediately with his opening titular lament by spicing it with some uniquely Jamaican wailing, of *Ah ya ya ya ya ya* and *Oi, yoi yoi yoi yoi yoh*. That sound is pure gold to the ears of a reggae fan. He couldn't sound more alive, or more Jamaican. The lead vocal that follows lives up to this opening, and the harmonies are lovely and equally heartfelt. With 'Money Trouble' a complete joy, The Maytones stand with any of reggae's more famous roots vocal groups.

'Money Trouble' is featured in the movie *Rockers* and can be enjoyed on its soundtrack CD in 12-inch disco-mix format, seamlessly giving way to a DJ version by I-Roy over a dubbier version of the riddim.

Doctor Alimantado: *'Born For A Purpose'*
DJ Doctor Alimantado's 'Born For A Purpose' was recorded in 1977, produced by Jo Jo Hookim and W. Thompson. The latter partially reveals Alimantado's real name. James Winston Thompson was born in 1952 in Kingston. After coming up the sound system ranks, he recorded his first DJ sides at the start of the 1970s. He would record about 70 singles and three albums. Strangely enough, one of his best songs, 'Born For A Purpose', was sung rather than DJed. And the result is a minor classic that is widely revered.

Alimantado tells an incredible biographical story. After nearly drowning during a swim in the ocean, he emerged from the beach, only to be immediately run down by a bus driver who, he believes, deliberately targeted him because of his dreadlocks. He wrote this song while recovering in the hospital. While *sufferas* songs are common in roots reggae, this is a step further. It's a survivor's song, with Alimantado confronting the individual who tried to take his life.

Punk rocker and big reggae fan Johnny Rotten of The Sex Pistols, while being interviewed on London's Capital Radio, played this song. He explained how he related to it, since he was attacked and badly beaten for his punk appearance. This greatly increased the sales of the song in the UK. The other seminal punk rock act (and equally big reggae fans) The Clash were impressed enough by this song to reference it in one of theirs; 'Rudie Can't Fail' mentions "the doctor who's born for a purpose".

'Born For A Purpose' opens with a horn melody that foreshadows the song's bitter-sweet emotional content. Alimantado joins this melody by chanting to Jah. The guitar goes dub, floating lightly and soothingly, contrasting with the industrious playing of the bass, drums, organ and Nyah hand drum. As Alimantado begins to sing, drop out/in and echo bubble like a healing hot spring. Alimantado proves to have a surprisingly good singing voice for a DJ, and his emotional delivery is born of reality. The result is a song that soothes even as it hits like a ton of bricks. A disco-mix of 'Born With A Purpose' that seamlessly appends a dub version can be heard on the *Doctor Alimantado* CD of the same name.

The Wailing Souls: *'Bredda Gravalicious'*
Like The Wailers, The Wailing Souls had their beginnings in the early 1960s at the yard of Joe Higgs. Like Bob, Bunny, Peter and others, Winston "Pipe" Matthews would learn singing and harmony from Trench Town's resident star, who generously gave his time to musically interested ghetto youths (who were in fact just a few years younger than he was). Pipe and his vocal group The Schoolboys would record more than a handful of ska sides for Prince Buster in 1963 and 1964. Pipe next formed The Renegades with the Higgs-trained Lloyd "Bread" McDonald, and George "Buddy" Haye. They began to record, but when Haye quit in 1966, the group recruited two new members and took a new name, The Wailing Souls. Pipe and Bread would be perennial members as the group experienced other line-up changes. For example, in 1974, names from the past, Joe Higgs and Buddy Haye, would join for a brief time. Original Black Uhuru member Garth Dennis would serve a stint though the early 1980s. Across all their line-ups, The Wailing Souls have recorded about 70 singles and over 20 albums, the last in 2006. And although some of the latter took stylistic chances, along with Burning Spear, live performances from The Wailing Souls are keeping the sound of vintage roots reggae alive decades past its heyday.

The Wailing Souls' self-produced 1977 track 'Bredda Gravalicious' is perhaps their best and most respected track. It's a bounty of heavy roots sounds, featuring a tough, horn-filled riddim loaded with dread descending minor-key melodies, deliciously strident roots harmonies and a tart, burning lead vocal from Pipe, with lyrics enriched with Jamaican folk sayings. As he often does, his voice resembles a tarter, more constricted Bob Marley, owing to nature and a common voice coach in Joe Higgs. A local variation on "avaricious", the title translates to "greedy man". He is "too damn craven [greedy]". To illustrate the error of greed, the lyrics rely heavily on the Jamaican parable of the greedy dog, who, upon seeing his reflection in the water, loses the bone in his mouth when he tries to snatch what he thinks is another. Another folk saying, "High seat kill Miss Thomas' puss [cat]", warns against pretensions. With every aspect of 'Bredda Gravalicious' so strong and dread, it became the signature song for this venerable vocal group and is a great roots reggae song by any measure. It can be heard on The Wailing Souls' *Wild Suspense* album, the CD edition of which also contains an instrumental dub version.

The Viceroys and Tommy McCook: *'Slogan On The Wall'/'Tenor On The Call'*
A disco-mix joining of The Viceroys' fine single, 'Slogan On The Wall', with Tommy McCook's equally fine sax cut of the riddim and a dub version proves that,

in Jamaica, adding one plus one plus one can equal ten. Combining these sides makes them bigger and better than playing them separately.

A distinctive stutter-step drum roll opens a fine, creative reggae riddim. The electric keyboard would be considered the lead instrument, were it not for the elaborate drum work that steals the spotlight. It comes courtesy of the only man who could play quite like that, Sly Dunbar. Muscular bass, reggae pulse rhythm guitar lightly treated with dub and tambourine complete an introspective riddim that is expert and efficient. Neither headliner has been heard, yet the song is already great.

The Viceroys enter with a deep roots vocal sound, singing about political graffiti that would deceive the Rastas and lead them astray. Resigned to their situation, they sound serious almost to the point of being dire, singing in unison throughout in a naturalistic, non-virtuoso harmony. The lack of flash and the way they follow the bass make the vocals blend into the riddim rather than stand out from it. A moody dread groove is thus established. More than the sum of its fine parts, the song has already reached critical mass, yet it's about to get greater.

Two minutes in, a double-length instrumental version is spliced into the vocal version. This is an unusual approach to a disco-mix, where adding an additional version to the end is the norm, but it proves to be the optimal approach. A moderate application of dub appears and makes the riddim bounce along previously unheard dimensions, deepening the groove. Four minutes in, a long, smoky, relaxed sax solo unfurls. It's unhurried and confident and quite excellent, as well it should be. That's because it's played by former Skatalites leader and sax-master Tommy McCook, who by this point in his career is reggae's elder statesman of brass. Whereas The Viceroys followed the melody of the bass line, McCook masterfully steps out and provides his own countermelody. He's grounded at the start, but as his performance nears its conclusion, he grows expansive. By the time he finishes, with dub enhancing his final moments, McCook has plowed a groove deeper than the Marianas Trench. Though originally the single's B-side, quality-wise there is nothing secondary about it. You will be hard pressed to find a better song-length reggae saxophone performance than this one. (I tried, and couldn't.)

For the final minute, the conclusion of the Viceroys' vocal version is heard, nicely book-ending the dub and sax versions of this 9-minute epic. This fine specimen of roots reggae, dub, reggae saxophone and demonstration of the benefits of the disco-mix can be heard on the compilation CD, *Nice Up The Dance: Studio One Disco-mixes*.

Prince Alla: *'Stone'*

Keith Blake was born in 1950 in the Greenwich Farm neighborhood of Kingston. He was first exposed to music at the church that was right next door to his home, where his grandmother sang in the choir. But a greater inspiration came when a fourteen-year-old Blake would walk over to nearby Trench Town and hear The Wailers and others singing *a yard*. He would begin recording with Joe Gibbs in

1968, first as a member of vocal group The Leaders and then as a solo singer. He would enjoy his greatest success as a solo roots singer, adopting the name Prince Allah (he has also recorded as Ras Allah). In spite of this name, he is a devout Rasta rather than a Muslim, which perhaps led him to eventually change the spelling of his name to Prince Alla.

'Stone', produced in 1977 by Bert Brown, may be Alla's best song. Opening with the sound of an explosion, he sings of a stone that is on its way to "mash down Rome" – to destroy what the Rastas view as the symbolic seat of Babylon. Accordingly, the riddim travels with a sense of mission. Though it's very musical, it's in an urgent, no-nonsense mode. It makes the song strong and inescapable as a plummeting meteor. Alla has a fine voice, and here he sings with the conviction of a patriot singing his national anthem. This is fierce roots reggae.

Alla would return to this riddim, re-voicing it as 'Black Rose', drawing from a Barrington Levy song of the same name and on The Abyssinians' 'Satta Amassa Ganna'. It's nearly as good as 'Stone'. Both tracks can be heard on the Prince Alla CD collection called *Only Love Can Conquer*.

Justin Hinds & The Dominoes: *'Weeping Eyes'*
Justin Hinds became well known in Jamaica from his 1964 ska hit, 'Carry Go Bring Come', a song that is still loved today. Thus launched, his career spanned the ska, rock steady and roots reggae eras, including some international cross-over success at the end of his career.

Born in 1942 in Ocho Rios, the teenaged Hinds was a lover of R&B, as were his friends, Dennis Sinclair and Junior Dixon. They formed a vocal group and named it after one of their idols, Fats Domino. But Hinds's distinctively Jamaican voice didn't sound like Fats or any other R&B singer – he sounded like reggae. After informal performances in town, Hinds, then seventeen, followed the advice to head for Kingston to further his career. For whatever reason, he failed an audition for Coxsone Dodd. He next found himself queued in a line of hopefuls auditioning for Duke Reid in the street. Witnessing the brusque dismissals of other audition-ees and finding this set-up disrespectful, Hinds walked away. But an intermediary brought him back for a proper audition – indoors and backed by a Skatalites line-up that included Baba Brooks. In the space of that day, Hinds was discovered, sang with a band for the first time, cut his first record – 'Carry Go Bring Come' – and gave us one of the biggest hits of the ska era. He would record a long string of sin-gles for Reid, as the combination of his country-accented voice, lyrics that included Jamaican folk sayings and Bible references, along with Reid's production and back-ing from The Skatalites, proved to be a sure-fire formula. Unusually for any reggae singer or producer, Hinds worked exclusively for Reid until the latter's death in 1975. He then worked with a number of other producers, but because he had no stomach for the money quarrels that were all but inevitable in the Jamaican music business, there would be gaps in Hinds's recording career. The last album to bear the Justin Hinds & The Dominoes name was 1984's *Travel With Love*, though the two Dominoes had long since departed, leaving Hinds with the group name, as was the case for Toots & The Maytals and Bob Marley & The Wailers. He would work on a variety of projects in several bands right up to his passing in 2005 after a short battle with lung cancer. This included his participation in the Nyabinghi group Wingless Angels, who recorded two albums for producer Keith Richards of The Rolling Stones.

'Weeping Eyes', a song from the *Travel With Love* album, was produced by Leroy Pierson and Robert Schoenfeld. It's a wonderful remake of 'Wipe Your Weeping Eyes', a song Hinds first recorded in 1978 for producer Sonia Pottinger. Whereas the original rendition was an okay, if unremarkable, entry in Hinds's catalog, the remake is stupendously languorous, even by reggae standards. And in this approach, the song finds its voice.

Hinds works from a vantage point that is particular to reggae, and most especially to roots. The antithesis of flashy, he sounds like a sage acquaintance who is calm and comfortable in sharing wisdom that comes from a lifetime of experience. He reminds us to follow the wise and the meek rather than the foolish and proud. If someone has erred in this confusing life, it's not too late for them. They need only dry their eyes and reflect before going forward again. Backing Hinds, the instrumental Wailers (with changes to the guitar ranks) create a riddim that is special. Every bit as relaxed and erudite as Hinds, it's the perfect vehicle for his song. It's rich with Carlton Barrett's fat drum rolls and multiple lazy keyboards. It's crowned by the warm glow of Chinna Smith's lead electric slide guitar with a strong Hawaiian feel. With that, two languid sounds from islands in different oceans come together beautifully. The Justin Hinds *Travel With Love* CD is currently out of print, but having been internationally released on the USA-based Nighthawk Records label, tracking down a used copy would not be terribly difficult and well worth the effort.

The Gladiators: *'Stick A Bush'*

The controlled dignity of The Gladiators' 'The Race' and 'Rearrange' is contrasted by the madcap fun of their 1978 Tony Robinson-produced track, 'Stick A Bush'. The title refers to an old Jamaican folk saying: "Every hoe have dem sticker bush", or every tool or task has its special challenges. But there is also a humorous ribald interpretation, in which the hoe is a male anatomical symbol, while the sticker bush represents a female anatomical obstruction, and we'll leave it at that. Some additional lyrics indicate that The Gladiators seem to be leaning towards the latter meaning, as the boisterous reggae, dominated by uncouth synthesizer, flows. Then comes a stanza of additional folk sayings. They seem have something of a work theme, but by the last one, helpfully informing us that the sun rises in the east and sets in the west, we're left wondering what any of this has to do with a hoe, a sticker bush, or anything else for that matter.

So what's it really all about? Probably not very much, but the song's exuberance carries you along without really caring. 'Stick A Bush' can be heard on a number of Gladiators collections. U-Roy recorded a great DJ version called 'Herbman Skanking', a song described later in this book (page 420).

Al Campbell: *'Take A Ride'*
Al Campbell's 1978 voicing of this respected Studio One riddim may be the best version, though others might argue for Johnny Osbourne's 'Truths And Rights' (a song described in the chapter on this artist; page 542). For that reason, the riddim is known by both of these songs' names. But Campbell is unlikely to care whether his version is deemed best, as he is not actually the singer. A mix-up with another singer named Al led to a labeling error that was never corrected.

The riddim's melody, as led by organ, is deeply melancholy. Even the naturally happy Lone Ranger in his version, 'Automatic', with all his ebullience and a generous application of fun Studio One dub, can't raise this, the saddest of all riddims, above the level of bitter-sweet. Other Al seizes upon this and provides a vocal brimming with sadness. His voice shows emotional wear around its edges, cracking as if he's on the verge of tears. It's heartbreaking to hear him urge his brethren to good spirits, even as he sounds to be suffering himself. No music other than roots reggae comes from this emotional vantage point. Sounding marginally less sad, Campbell (implicitly) advocates adopting Rastafarianism to stay on the right path for the titular ride he's advocating. Heartrending but not hopeless, this *sufferas* song can be heard on Heartbeat Records' Studio One compilation CD called *When Rhythm Was King*.

Inner Circle: *'We A Rockers'*
Quite the antithesis of the previous song, the reggae anthem, 'We A Rockers' by Inner Circle, is an irresistibly upbeat roots track. And how could it not be, with Jacob Miller at his merriest on lead vocals? After opening with a bit of dramatic imagery, "Dreadlocks flying t'rough the air", the song settles into a reggae love fest. Miller proclaims his roots reggae credentials, and asks if we love him for them. In fine voice and with such a positive outlook, how can we not? And he loves everyone back, generously bestowing the song's titular accolade in this genial, inclusive song. Inner Circle matches Miller with a riddim and backing vocals that are rootsy and accessible. An undercurrent of shaken tambourine, bells and guitar leads gives the riddim something extra – a bright shimmer that makes the song even more inviting. 'We A Rockers' was featured in the soundtrack of the movie *Rockers* and appeared on numerous compilations both before and after the movie's 1978 release. Did Inner Circle (and for that matter its progeny, Third World) deliberately make their music accessible? Sure. Does that take away from a song like 'We A Rockers'? Not in the least.

Jacob Miller: *'Deck The Halls'*
Produced by Errol Thompson in 1978, 'Deck The Halls' is indeed Jacob Miller's rendition of the classic Christmas carol. It comes from an album alternatively called *Ital Christmas* or *Natty Christmas* that Miller recorded with a DJ named Ray "Weatherman" I.

Miller has updated the lyrics. He explains that in Jamaica, Christmas is for everyone: young and old, Rasta and not. But the good tidings Miller has in mind are distinctively Rasta-flavored rather than traditional. The cover of the *Ital Christmas* LP makes this clear with its painting of a Christmas-ornamented ganja plant standing over a collection of presents that include pipes and spliffs. And when the cover was changed for CD release, it featured an illustration of Miller dressed as Santa Claus holding a big bag, not of toys, but of ganja. So it comes as no surprise to hear of Miller decking the halls, not with boughs of holly, but with "lots of collie", along with other non-traditional lyrics about lighting a pipe and getting red. Yes, this promises to be the most intoxicating reggae Christmas celebration since golden-age mento star Lord Lebby's boozy 'Jingle Bells Calypso' (a song described previously in this book; page 36) two decades earlier.

This approach to decking the halls inspires Miller. He blends the *tra-la-las* with his trademark staccato-stutter scatting. Brimming with good cheer, he reaches operatic heights of drama, when he sings of "licking" (lighting) his pipe. He's so passionate, you can't help but enjoy his fervor. The Fatman Riddim Section band also gives a fine performance. Sly Dunbar casually supplies a fiendishly creative rhythm by emphasizing a place in between the beats. Ian Lewis's bass dances around it, providing a cubist rendition of the 'Deck The Halls' melody, while an organ amiably carries the complete melody. Though not as well remembered as many of his songs, 'Deck The Halls' is a great piece of Christmas reggae that features one of the finest vocals of Jacob Miller's too-short career. A strong instrumental dub version called 'Unemployment Rock', credited to Inner Circle & The Fatman Riddim Section, can be heard on the CD collection called *Heavyweight Dub/Killer Dub*.

Cornel Campbell and Ranking Dread: *'Bandulu/Hard Time'*
In the late 1970s, Campbell, with DJ Ranking Dread (Winston Brown) in tow, released a wonderfully gloomy disco-mix 12-inch single in 'Bandulu/Hard Time', produced by W. Thompson (better known as Dr. Alimantado) and Bunny Lee. The song has interesting genetics originating in Jamaica and elsewhere. The riddim is derivative of Black Uhuru's uber-dread 'Shine Eye Gal'. The lyrics and melody are based on the old American folk song, 'Tom Dooley', that was popularized by The Kingston Trio in 1958.

After a brisk drum tattoo from Sly Dunbar, the descending dread bass line from his partner Robbie Shakespeare sets the riddim's heavy dread groove. Intensity is built by splashes of dub, smart flourishes from Dunbar, occasional Syndrums accents, and a stealthy change from piano to reverbed guitar for the reggae chop. Campbell sings sorrowfully to the *bandulu* (a Jamaican term for criminal), addressing him directly. He adapts the classic chorus from 'Tom Dooley', but here, it's the bandulu, not Tom Dooley, who must hang his head. As in 'Tom Dooley', the bandulu is sentenced to hang. But whereas Tom Dooley's crime was murdering his love in a triangle gone tragically wrong, Bandulu, after falling in with the wrong crowd, winds up robbing a woman and in the process "kill[ing] that poor policeman". Campbell's vocal is typically fine, as he adjusts and improves on the melody. In some renditions, 'Tom Dooley' could sound more celebratory than cautionary, but Campbell's minor-key melody leaves little room for such ambiguity. Nor do his lyrics, with their account of the hanging and its emphasis on taking a lesson from the downfall of the bandulu.

As Campbell sings the chorus one more time, Ranking Dread enters the disco-mix with a rather unimpressive demonstration of the DJ's technique of rolling syllables. He gets to chanting, and the performance improves greatly. Working off the descending bass line, he relays a grim tale filled with depressing detail that actually makes 'Bandulu' sound like a party song by comparison, especially considering how the hallmark of the reggae DJ is upbeat excitement and good vibes. He marvels at the number of calamities that have befallen him, and then lists them: he lost his house in a fire, his wife was run over, he's lost his job and must now turn to theft to survive. Drop-out/in underlines each crisis as it's uttered. He's so down, he really couldn't quite finish writing the chorus, leaving himself instructions instead: "The hard time, live me life alone, the hard time, rhyme, rhyme." It is unknown how much of this is autobiographical, but it is known that Dread would soon quit the music business and become one of Jamaica's most murderous gangsters. He fled to the UK, where he continued his criminal activity, and would become known as the most dangerous foreign national in the country. Eventually he was extradited to Jamaica, where he died in prison in 1996. Ironically, it was a fate not so different from the one Cornel Campbell sang about in 'Bandulu'. 'Bandulu/Hard Time' is available on the Cornel Campbell collection *I Shall Not Remove*.

Pablo Moses: *'Revolutionary Step'; 'Dubbing Is A Must'; 'Music Is My Desire'*
Pablo Moses possesses an archetypical roots reggae voice: reedy, delicate, wise and full of feeling. He was born Pableto Henry, in 1948 in Kingston or in Manchester Parish, depending on the source. Though he made music informally from the time he was in school, he was the antithesis of Jamaica's star *youth singers*, not recording until he was twenty-seven. It was then that he released the 1976 LP, *Revolutionary Dream*, the first of his eleven internationally released albums. These albums were *strictly roots, mon*, as Pablo took a dim view on dancehall and/ or slack music. At the time of this writing, he has plans on the drawing-board for several more albums.

These three songs come from Moses's second and best album, from 1980, *A Song*. It was lavishly produced by Geoffrey Chung, and has Moses backed by a host of roots luminaries too numerous to name. Though the CD is out of print in most places, it is available on digital music services. In France the CD is available with three bonus track dub versions of the album's best three songs.

Opening with a single pulse of dub, 'Revolutionary Step' is an accomplished piece of roots reggae. Backed by Marley-like female backing vocals, Moses's roots singing is a study in how someone can simultaneously sound wispy and strong, wistful and rousing. He describes all the good that one gets from doing the titular dance to reggae, such as forward social progress, love, and a rejection of drug use. Meanwhile, the backing music balances a powerful horn line with a danceable bass line. It's a big band, and everyone contributes to a beautiful piece of roots that equally serves head and feet. A double-length, nearly entirely instrumental, dub version on the French CD manages to turn the song inside out while putting the bass in the driver's seat.

There are many reggae songs that celebrate reggae, but 'Dubbing Is A Must' is a more specific love letter. In it, Moses nicely captures the passion Jamaicans felt towards the new style of reggae by calling dub a "special treat" and, in the titular refrain, stating that reggae music should always end with dub. As we have seen, another way Jamaicans celebrated this music was with a dance called the rub-a-dub. It had nothing to do with three men in a tub and everything to do with erotically rubbing together while dancing to reggae, especially to dub that's stripped down to just drum and bass. With a key change complementing the shift in subject, Moses acknowledges this by telling men that they will maximize love if they dance closely with their woman.

A lively organ spider-dances throughout the track that is alive with incidental percussion, as timbales (unusually for reggae), whistles and bells dot the landscape. Then, as the chorus promised, the song indeed ends with dub. Pablo drops out as echo bathes the backing vocalists, creating a new chorus of "reggae music-ic-ic ... dub-ub-ub-ub".

The B-side of the single release of 'Dubbing Is A Must', naturally, is a dub version. It has never been compiled on LP or CD, but this falls short of tragedy because, disappointingly, this is a just okay dub version at best. The French CD includes a 12-inch version. Rather than a disco-mix, it's a longer dub remix with extra percussion and dub throughout. It too is okay, but again it's disappointing that a great song about dub fails to elicit a great dub version.

Having already memorably sung about dancing to reggae and about dub, Moses broadens the topic a bit in 'Music Is My Desire'. It's a jazzy roots reggae meditation on his love of making music. The instrumentation is layered. Guitar, bass and drum provide a fine skeleton, fleshed out by guitar and organ, and a Nyah hand drum that pleasingly dapples the riddim. Layered atop is an electric piano that is so prominently featured, it effectively shares the spotlight with

Moses. It provides a varied array of tasty jazzy riffs and runs, each rhythmically and melodically catchy in the Jamaican jazz way. (It's not clear from the credits which of the album's three keyboardists, Earl "Wya" Lindo, Geoffrey Chung or Robbie Lyn, is responsible for this fine playing.) Moses sings unhurriedly but emphatically, as we learn about his titular statement. Not only does he love music, it's something he truly needs Apparently, his father wanted him to have a career as an engineer. He appreciated his father's concern, "but never try to be what someone else want you to be". Nor did he ever want to be a rich merchant. All he wanted was to play music every day. Listening to this song, as fine a piece of jazzy roots reggae as can be found, we can be glad Moses stuck to his convictions. The French CD includes a dub version called 'Dub Is My Desire'. By banishing almost all of the vocals and electric piano, the song is unexpectedly transformed into a tough, lean, driving dub-fueled instrumental, which is the best of the three bonus tracks. There was also a mix of 'Music Is My Desire' that is only heard on its 12-inch single release. This version is a minute longer, with additional jamming at the song's end and a rougher, rootsier mix. It's a potential bonus track, which the record label that eventually brings this CD to wider availability should keep in mind.

Third World: *'Uptown Rebel'*

Third World was formed in 1973 when several musicians defected from Inner Circle to form a new band. Rather than just a vocal group or a backing band, by combining both they were a complete, self-contained unit. While roots reggae was correctly considered to be the music of Jamaica's poor, every generalization has its limits: Third World was actually comprised of "uptown" musicians. They specialized in a brand of polished reggae that quickly found cross-over success with a string of albums released internationally on Island Records. (In a term I never cared for, they called their sound "roots with quality".) By the mid-1980s, they had progressed (regressed?) from international reggae to something closer to contemporary American R&B. This was best exemplified by their hit, 'Love Me With A Sense Of Purpose'. It sounded more like Prince or Billy Ocean than reggae. Though some roots purists considered even their early music to be too smooth and overly mannered, this was not true of all their tracks, and the group's talent could hardly be denied.

A case in point was 'Uptown Rebel'. It's polished *and* rootsy. A great song, it sounds different from any other roots reggae, but definitely part of it. It's an autobiographical story, in which lead vocalist William "Bunny Rugs" Clarke proclaims his Rastafarian faith to his family over dinner. There is so much crying, he compares it to a funeral. Even the vegetarian *ital* diet of the Rasta is rejected as sinning. But then common ground is found, as the "seasoning" he brings to the meal – likely to be a reference to a particular herb associated with the Rasta – is rather hypocritically quite welcomed.

Hearty-voiced Bunny Rugs's tough but refined lead is supported by instrumentation and backing vocals that could be described in the same way. The song ends with a long dub section over which Clarke chants his devotion to his beliefs and his appreciation of reggae music, while guitarist Steven "Cat" Coore jams on viola. Call it uptown or internationalized if you must, but even the fussiest roots purist couldn't fault this song.

Israel Vibration: *'Survive'; 'We A De Rasta'; 'Unconquered People'; 'Possibilities'*
Israel Vibration is a roots vocal group that has overcome a great deal. The trio is comprised of Cecil "Skeleton" (or "Skelly", both nicknames thanks to his bony visage) Spence, Albert "Apple" Craig (who ran away from the discipline of The Alpha Boys School) and Lascelle "Wiss" Bulgin. All three members are handicapped by polio and initially met as children in a Kingston rehabilitation clinic. They make a striking sight, three dreadlocked men supported by crutches. For these devout but indigent Rastas, in an unusual occurrence, a Rasta organization financed their first single in 1977. It was a hit, launching the group into stardom. They would soon be opening in concert for the island's biggest stars and secure an album deal with British EMI. (For this reason, Israel Vibration is album-focused, releasing an unusually small number of singles.) They compare well with the qualities that made two of Jamaica's greatest vocal groups special. Like the Bob/Peter/Bunny line-up of The Wailers, Israel Vibration is the only other vocal group where three members write and sing lead vocal on their own songs. And like the Congos, they are purveyors of the distinctive, wispy vocal style that roots fans prize. The group has survived to the present day through break-ups, reunions and partial reunions, having released over 20 albums and an additional quantity of solo albums.

All four of these tracks come from Israel Vibration's second LP, *Unconquered People*, produced by Tommy Cowan in 1980. The backing band is the instrumental Wailers, and both groups sound as if they were born for each other, inspiring great music from each.

'Survive' features a languid but unusually erudite skanking roots groove. Smart sax from Dean Fraser and piano are out front over a riddim led by the drums and bass of the Barrett brothers. A variety of additional percussion and reggae chop guitar are all that's needed to complete a fine riddim. With Wiss singing lead, Israel Vibration's vocals fall right in as they sing about Rastafari and perseverance in the face of poverty. This is brought home right from the opening line, where Wiss tells God that he has only him, and that's all he needs to survive. The song could not be rootsier, and with vocals, bass, sax and piano each playing complementary melodies to one another, it couldn't be more melodic.

'We A De The Rasta' is more aggressive than 'Survive', propelled by a riddim that's well appointed by keyboards (clavichord is featured, along with piano and organ), busy creative bass and drums, a flanged guitar chop, Nyabinghi hand drum and other percussion. With Apple providing heartfelt lead roots vocals, it's anthemic as Israel Vibration proclaims their faith with a sustained, controlled passion that builds throughout the song.

The title track 'Unconquered People' opens beautifully with lead singer Wiss chanting to Jah to send rain. Underneath is another keyboard-filled arrangement that's distinguished by its somewhat prickly sound and a featured harpsichord. Rain serves as the central symbol of all Jah provides in this spiritual track. At its climax, an invocation unfolds as Wiss chants a litany of Jah's blessings, ending again with rain. That these feelings led Israel Vibration to create this recording is another blessing.

'Possibilities', with lead vocals from Skelly, is a warning to the unrighteous. He challenges them to consider what they would do if their homes were burning, as a symbol for divine retribution, with a chorus of "Where you gonna run when your house on fire?" The arrangement is a bit sparser than that heard in the previous songs, allowing drummer Carlton Barrett's creativity on snare and hi-hat to come to the fore. An electronic drum adds righteous dub lightning strikes. The always reliable, strident yet delicate, Israel Vibration harmonies are particularly good on this track, with each line fraying away in a slow rough tremolo that is pure roots reggae.

The Mighty Diamonds: *'Pass The Kouchie'*

The Mighty Diamond's 'Pass The Kouchie', produced by Augustus "Gussie" Clarke in 1981, is a good example of how a classic riddim from decades earlier could be remade in a newer style with no loss of integrity. Far more unusually, it also shows how a Jamaican reggae hit could be turned into an internationally popular reggae hit when played by children. But more important than either is the fact that 'Pass The Kouchie' is a flat-out great roots reggae song.

It's based on an updated recutting of the ever-popular 'Full Up' riddim (a song described earlier; page 172). Whereas the original crackled with the particular sharpness of Studio One early reggae, this recut of the riddim recasts it as languid roots reggae. One key to this transformation is how the stabbing organ notes of the original are replaced with relaxed horns that slowly gather strength. These long notes take on extra meaning as they are coupled with the sound of someone taking long draws of ganja smoke, prefacing the subject of the song.

The Mighty Diamonds sing an exceptionally tuneful song. The verse finds lead singer Donald "Tabby" Shaw going for a walk one pleasant June day. He passes a dreadlocks camp as backing vocalists Bunny Simpson and Judge Ferguson quietly observe, perhaps with envy, that they have "leaf". Then the camp begins a session of ganja smoking, sitting in a circle, they sing as they pass the "kouchie" (water pipe) to the person on the left, making sure the kouchie doesn't go out, lest they displease Jah, and giving the song its chorus. Like the melodies and the story, the vocals are generous and soothing. In all ways, 'Pass The Kouchie' is a ganja song that's generous and mindful not to harsh your buzz.

A huge hit, 'Pass The Kouchie' appears on a number of CD collections. It was versioned, and other kouchie songs were soon recorded to this riddim. The Diamonds themselves returned to re-voice the riddim, recording a song called 'Pass The Knowledge' that lacked the magic of 'Pass The Kouchie'. There was also the unlikely international hit from the UK in 1982. Musical Youth was composed of four schoolboys who sang and played their own instruments. Though they were UK-based, they had Jamaica in their DNA. Two of the boys were the sons of former Technique Frederick Waite. Cleverly sidestepping controversy, their version was retitled 'Pass The Dutchie'. Rhyming with kouchie, "dutchie" refers to a cooking pot. It held the number 1 spot in the UK for three weeks running.

Rita Marley: *'One Draw'*

And speaking of ganja songs ... 'One Draw', Rita Marley's infamous paean to marijuana was produced by Asley "Grub" Cooper and Rickey Walters in 1981.

Alpharita Constantia Anderson was born in 1946, in Cuba. Her mother was Cuban and her father, a musician, was Jamaican. The family moved to Jamaica while Rita was very young. Just as Bob Marley was famously teased as a child for his light hue, his future wife was teased for being dark, Jamaica being so conscious of skin tone. Rita sang at home and at school. She formed a harmony group called The Soulettes with her cousin, Constantine Walker, and a friend, Precious Gifford. The Wailers, new stars then, would walk past Rita's yard on their way to Studio One. One day, the fledgling trio approached Bob, Bunny and Peter and auditioned on the spot. This led to about 30 singles at Studio One usually credited to the group, but sometimes listing Rita as a solo artist. In addition to this work and her extensive work with her husband, Rita would record another three dozen Soulette or solo sides and better than a dozen solo albums, with her last studio work coming in the first half of the 2000s. Today, she lives with her extended family in Ghana, where she is active in charitable causes and is called Nana Afua Abodea 1.

'One Draw' was her biggest hit, and though there are many fine reggae songs about marijuana, none sounds so totally, giddily stoned as 'One Draw'. It was not uncommon in reggae to hear a simplified arrangement employed when the lead singer was a woman. Such is the case for 'One Draw'. But rather than condescending, as this practice would often appear, here it sounds non-taxing and tipsy. Notice the simplified beat, influenced by American disco music of the day, and the prominent frothy, loopy synthesizer. And just in case someone is slow to pick up these musical cues, the lyrics open with Rita wailing that she wants to get high.

Sounding sweet and happy, Rita goes on to describe getting high, feeling good, dancing to music and invites you to "come and rock with me". Not since 'Cutting Wood' (a song described previously in this book; page 306) two decades earlier has she sounded this innocent and/or seductive. On its original 7-inch single release, the song is over and already great. But on its 12-inch extended mix single release, it's only beginning.

On this mix, the riddim continues as a teacher and students Smokey, Herby and 'Milla, act out a classroom drama, DJ style. The prim and proper teacher asks the children how they spent their holidays. Herby explains he learned about farming. Teacher sounds impressed, but then a piece of the song's chorus drops in to identify the crop as sensimellia and disapproval is heard. Teacher then calls on Smokey. Breaking into full-blown DJ delivery, Smokey chants an explanation that the paper in his workbook gave him other ideas. He gleefully describes using a page to construct a spliff to enjoy some sensimellia. 'Mellia describes studying music, rhythm, dancing and sensimellia, and how that makes 'sens'. Lest we miss it, the pun is sold with an exaggerated burst of dub echo. From there, the narrative gets a bit vague, with two possible interpretations. First, that the teacher remains clueless. Second, with the dropped-in chorus attributed to her, that she takes one draw and sings a celebration of how high she is. In either event, this play-acting makes for a unique disco-mix, elevating 'One Draw' to classic status. Though the Jamaican government quickly moved to ban the song, it was a number 1 hit there and popular beyond its shores. 'One Draw' is available on a number of CD compilations. Just make sure you choose one with the 7-minute plus extended mix.

Mikey Dread: 'World War Three'

Port Antonio's Michael "Mikey Dread" Campbell is a reggae renaissance man. He is a singer, DJ, producer and dub-master. He collaborated with the UK punk rock band The Clash, and made their good reggae better. He was a disc jockey on Jamaican radio with his show, *Dread At The Controls*, and hosted reggae television programs in the UK. The title track from his 1982 album, *World War Three*, is a standout song from him. It packs a sonic one-two punch. There's a riddim with a wonderfully swampy sound, as busy instrumentation is made thick and murky with a surfeit of dub. Atop of this is Dread's wonderfully nasal DJing in a fine and thoughtful performance. He warns of a third world war born of racial struggles and calls for harmony and acceptance. For example, he explains that while other hairstyles are accepted by society, dreadlocks still draw scorn. He does so with consideration and poetry, in perhaps the best discussion of this issue in any reggae song. These lyrics distinctively chanted atop a dub-juiced backing make 'World War Three' a notable roots reggae song.

Israel Vibration: 'Why You So Craven'

'Why You So Craven' is the title song from Israel Vibration's third LP, released in 1982. It features a different sound from the 'Unconquered People' tracks of two years before . This is not surprising, considering that there's a new producer (Henry "Junjo" Lawes) and backing band (Chinna Smith's High Times Band). Close listening lends credence to the rumor that internal strife led Apple to bring in vocal group The Tartans to replace Skelton and Wiss for backing vocals. Right from the aggressive drum roll that kicks off the track, the music is more muscular and direct, with a martial beat and tough horn lines. The sound suits the song, as Apple reprimands the "craven", which in Jamaica means greedy. Rather than angry or righteous, Apple sounds personally aggrieved at the poor behavior of those who have plenty and still prey on the poor. Cuttingly, he calls greed "dirty" and warns that the craven will be excluded from heaven. Reggae has other fine anti-craven songs (The Wailers' 'Craven Choke Puppy', The Wailing Souls' 'Bredda Gravalicious' and Israel Vibration's own 'Greedy Dog' are three examples described elsewhere in this book; pages 199, 392, 407), but none are more powerfully expressed than this one. Add to this the fine melodies he fashions and the nail-on-the-head backing instrumentation, and Apple has added another great roots reggae song to Israel Vibration's résumé.

Don Carlos: *'White Squall'; 'Music Crave'*
Roots singer Don Carlos was born in 1952 in the Waterhouse section of Kingston that was notorious for its toughness and its namesake style singing that he adopted. Born Euvin Spencer, friends and family combined to rename him; his mother was fond of calling him Carlos, but his friends called him Don. In 1982, when he recorded these tracks for his Robert Palmer-produced, Sly & Robbie-backed *Harvest Time* album, he was the once and future lead singer of Black Uhuru. Though not necessarily his most popular, these two songs may be the Waterhouse singer's best in a career that produced about 45 singles and more than 35 albums, the last coming in 2010.

'White Squall' features a pointed riddim, starring Sly Dunbar, who is impressive here even for Sly Dunbar. Listen to the stutter-step beat he plays on the snare, to his educated right foot as he alters the beat of the bass drum and to how he varies his playing as the song progresses. Also, listen to how the picked guitar with its mento banjo heritage plays off the drum pattern. So does the bass line, as it melodically supports Carlos's vocal. That's real good reggae, Sly & Robbie style. Completed by piano, rhythm guitar and additional percussion, the backing is both spiky and sweet, like a prickly pear.

'White Squall' starts as an autobiographical tale of hardships faced during a storm, when Carlos is left without any food for a day, feeling hungry and angry. This leads to a broader social concern, as he wonders what it's like for people who live a life in that state, concluding that we should not be so quick to judge such people. Carlos makes this song about hunger food for thought, and the band ensures it's palatable.

'Music Crave' is musically in the same vein as 'White Squall'. Dunbar's elaborate drum work again effectively co-stars with the singer. (But it's in another version of this riddim, 'Straight To The Government' by Papa Tullo, a song described later in this book, on page 437, where his drums are most easily heard and best enjoyed.) The biggest difference is the electric piano that is prominently featured. Working with the bass, it creates a strong melodic platform for Carlos to build upon. He uses it for a song about going to a dance, which is rich in detail. In this slice of life, Carlos shares all he is hoping for in the night ahead:

> A music crave, I want to rave tonight
> A music crave, I just can't be satisfied
> First thing I've got to do is
> find a corner to control
> then send for the girl that I adore
>
> She gonna rave with I, oh yes
> 'till broad daylight, oh yes
> Because music crave
> we a want reggae
>
> The dance well tight
> I hope they don't wreck no fight
> I want to enjoy myself
> right in the night
>
> Mister operator,
> I love the selection you playing
> It make me feel irie
> You make feel sweet

These simple dancehall sentiments lie comfortably atop the sophisticated reggae riddim. Interestingly, this is just about the time when dancehall reggae dawned, with lyrics that left the heavy concerns of roots reggae behind, while musically a syncopated and more danceable reggae would emerge. If Carlos had pitched this song with its dancehall lyrics a year later, it probably would have been matched to a simpler dancehall backing. Not that this would have been a bad thing, but happily we have 'Music Crave' just as it is.

John Holt: *'Police In Helicopter'*

Dating from 1983, 'Police In Helicopter' is a departure for John Holt, who was well known for the eminent geniality of his rock steady love songs as lead singer of The Paragons and as a solo artist. This song is militant by comparison, but that does not stop it from being a great song in its own right.

Producer Henry "Junjo" Lawes and backing band The Roots Radics are largely responsible, with the dubby but lean and tough roots riddim they provide. The snare drum and strong, marching bass line are direct and loud in the mix to the point of assault. One guitar anchors the reggae chop while another entertains with reggae picking and slurred phrases, the latter providing the song with a sonic hook. There's evidence here of the tough syncopation that characterized the sound of early dancehall. As we will see later in this book, it's a sound that Junjo and The Radics launched.

Holt matches this with a song describing escalating tensions between marijuana growers and a Jamaican government that is using its resources to locate and burn marijuana fields. Holt adopts a world-weary singing style for this song, sounding depressed and desperate. Yet, in another example of how Jamaicans turn pain into music, this downwardly turned vocal is remarkably catchy. He wistfully pleads and ultimately warns:

> We don't trouble your banana, we don't trouble your corn.
> We don't trouble your pimento, we don't trouble you at all.
> So if you continue to burn up the herbs, we gonna burn down the cane fields

'Police In Helicopter' represents a new but fully realized sound for John Holt and another notch in an already impressive three-decade-long string of hits.

The Wailing Souls: *'Shark Attack'*
'Shark Attack' is a track from The Wailing Souls' 1992 album, *All Around The World*, produced by Richard Feldman. As the album's title tips off, this is an unabashedly internationalized reggae affair, hoping to open more ears than those of traditional reggae fans. 'Shark Attack' stands out from the set, as a surprisingly strong hard-rocking piece of reggae.

The Wailing Souls excite with aggressive roots vocals as they liken Babylon's oppression to the titular bad happening. Feldman uses a kitchen-sink approach to arrangement, giving the song a rock-fortified reggae sound. In addition to aggressive reggae sounds, there's a guitar opening that bridges dub and Pink Floyd's echo explorations, lots of synthesized horns, female backing vocals and many a hard rock guitar power chord. The song was supported by a MTV-ready video and a strong live performance (with DJ Red Fox) on the popular American television show, *The Tonight Show With Jay Leno*. Yet the enjoyable fusion of 'Shark Attack' failed to achieve the overseas popularity it was intended – and deserved – to garner.

Israel Vibration: *'Greedy Dog'*
'Greedy Dog' appears on Israel Vibration's 1998 album, *Strength Of My Life*, produced by Dr. Dread and Israel Vibration. It's an example of roots still going strong even as reggae was well into the ragga era. This was achieved by the trio reuniting and using the tough (and by now) veteran backing band, The Roots Radics. They stretch Israel Vibration beyond their languid reggae comfort zone with a fast-paced, urgent roots backing. It features a Nyah hand drum and bright piano, but the star instrument is the melodica, which has never sounded more like an accordion than the way it's played here. It enriches the song by giving it an unusual European air.

Israel Vibration rides the riddim's torrid pace without losing the pungent roots qualities that make their vocals special. Lead singer Wiss drops the normal verse-chorus-verse approach for a continuous roll of lyrics that brings an immediacy to the song. He describes the exploitation and oppression of the Rasta, peaking with a defiant refusal to "bow down low". He then uses the same two folk tales that were heard in The Wailing Souls' 'Bredda Gravalicious', concerning the greedy dog dropping his bone and the cat killed by sitting in a high seat not intended for it. It's such a pleasure to hear Wiss's distinctive voice covering this familiar ground that these similarities are forgiven by the listener (though Wailing Souls' reaction is unknown). And when Skelly and Apple juice their harmonies with an undulation of pitch, you can't help but feel, twenty years past the peak of their popularity, that Israel Vibration is ageless and roots reggae is timeless.

Chezidek: *'Inna Di Road'*
Chezidek was born Desbert Johnson, in 1973, in Saint Ann Parish, well after the birth of roots reggae. He originally billed himself as Mel-Chezidek, the name of an obscure Old Testament figure (usually spelled Melchizedek) that has been interpreted variously. Perhaps because this name had also been used as an alias by guitarist Chinna Smith, he would soon shorten it. He enjoyed success as a sound system performer near home, but left Saint Ann for Kingston to record. He did so first in 2002 for producer Phillip "Fattis" Burrell. Chezidek is one of a number of singers who kept the flame of roots reggae burning in the face of the dancehall hurricane. He eschews slack and gun-love lyrics as well as ragga riddims (almost always) for a more traditional reggae sound. He has released six albums.

The title track of his 2007 album *Inna Di Road* is impressive. It uses producer Bobby Konders' 'Jah Love' riddim, a reverent recut of that from Yabby You's 1974 track, 'Warn The Nation'. As per its roots reggae origins, it features lead organ, a Nyabinghi drummer and drop-out/in. But at the same time, it has some modern elements, with keyboard bass, splashes of synthesized percussion and, complementing Chezidek's vocals, threatening samples of Robert De Niro as Al Capone from the 1987 film *The Untouchables* ("I want him DEAD! I want his family DEAD! I want his house burned to the GROUND!"). It's a fine, driving riddim that was versioned by many. But only Chezidek *killed it*, unleashing his finest vocal to date and heartfelt anti-violence lyrics, making it the ultimate anti-rude boy song.

He opens with a wordless falsetto workout that serves as a teaser for the astounding vocal performance to come. Chezidek displays a keen sense of and an acrobatic approach to melody, taking advantage of the multi-octave span of his expressive voice. This includes surprising leaps to a higher octave, sometimes dropping right back down after one word, other times working his way back down. It's a unique performance that stays richly rewarding even after repeated listens. He is appalled by the violence on Jamaica's streets, where blood is so common it "run like river", people live in fear and the innocent too often fall victim. The government is no help, leaving Chezidek to beg Selassie I for help. This dramatically wrought song ends with all the instrumentation dropping out and leaving Chezidek to repeat the chorus all alone. 'Inna Di Road' is the best roots song in a long time.

44 Big Youth

Manley Augustus Buchanan, better known as Big Youth, was born in 1949 in Kingston's Trench Town. Jah Yout', as he is affectionately called, is one of reggae's greatest DJs and one of roots reggae's greatest performers, DJing Rasta themes with unbridled enthusiasm and unmatched creativity. He is a charismatic figure, with stones in the Rastafarian colors of red, green and gold set into the front teeth of his typically smiling, always dreadlock-framed face.

His stage name comes from the fact that he was a big-for-his-age child. An alternative story is that the teenaged Buchanan was called "Youth" by his older co-workers when he landed a job as an auto mechanic at the age of fourteen. It was also then that one day he noticed how good the echo in a large room made his voice sound. The apple falling onto Isaac Newton's head and Archimedes stepping into his filled bathtub are history's only equivalent eureka moments. He would first pursue a career as a dancehall DJ, where a microphone, powerful amps and massive speakers would outdo the effect of the large room. He got his big break by impressing the DJ I-Roy, who brought Youth onto the mic at King Tubby's sound system. By 1971, he had worked his way to stardom at the Tippertone Sound, and he embarked on a recording career about a year later. Though not amongst the first DJs to record (U-Roy and Dennis Alcapone were already recording stars when he was starting out), Big Youth was different, and an influence on every DJ who followed.

What made him so different? Whereas previous DJ recording stars did most of their best work chanting to rock steady riddims, timing and predilection would find Big Youth choosing heavier pre-roots and roots reggae riddims, often featuring a heady dose of dub. Commensurately different were both his lyrics and delivery. Many of his best songs explored Rasta and *suffera* themes, as opposed to the lighter fare previous DJs favored. His voice has a resonance that brought to mind a picture of vocal cords coated with a thick layer of ganja resin. He used a lot of patois, but his words are never difficult to understand. He accented his songs with multiple trademark exclamations, such as *good gosh!*, *move-ya!*, *huuuuuh!*, as well as an assortment of distinctive cries, shouts and screams. His chanting had a swing to it that went beyond what was inherent in the chanting of other DJs. And his performances were bolder. The emotional pull of a song could elicit an unexpected creative leap in his chanting, reminiscent of how a jazz soloist might be moved to take a chance while improvising. All of these features made Big Youth's best records freer, heavier and dreader than any DJ music that came before, and little that came after. He would record over 150 singles and just shy of 20 albums, the last in 2006. Below is the cream of Jah Yout's crop. Each is readily available on Big Youth collections and reggae compilations, except where noted.

'Cool Breeze'

Big Youth's 'Cool Breeze' was produced by Derrick Harriott in 1972. It's a DJ version of a song Harriott produced in 1967, 'Stop That Train' by the rock steady vocal duo Keith [Rowe] & Tex [Dixon]. (Two notes on this song. It's different from The Wailers track of the same name. And it was a cover of an all-but-forgotten 1965 ska track by The Spanishtonians.) Though there was nothing wrong per se with Keith & Tex's easy-going but staid vocals, the amiable rock steady riddim would prove to have better value as a framework for DJing. In 1971, it provided Scotty with an internationally released DJ hit in 'Draw Your Brakes', a song described in the next chapter (page 428). Both it and Big Youth's version make the original version sound dull by comparison.

'Cool Breeze' is enriched by dub. This is tipped right from Youth's dub-haloed spoken introduction in which he references the recent movie *Shaft*. Then, bold applications of drop-out/in add excitement. The riddim, with its distinctive Western-sounding guitar hook, is heard. But suddenly, all the instrumentation drops out, leaving Keith & Tex to sing a cappella their famous chorus about their woman leaving them and boarding a train. The mix flips, Keith & Tex vanish and the instrumentation is dropped back in, as Youth assumes vocal duties. He works off the narrative of the original version, though the reason for catching the train is turned on its head. Keith & Rex wanted to see their departing girl. Youth chants instead about wanting to get away from a cheating one. And he does so with a swing to his chanting that no other DJ can match. But the dub drama is not over yet, as Youth pauses for three syllables of Keith & Tex. They are fancifully altered, so that the beginning and end of each syllable is cleanly lopped off, leaving only three beats of alien voice-sound. This exciting dub technique would prove to be influential. It became a favorite tool in Lee Perry's Black Ark bag of dub tricks in the later part of the 1970s. (The technique would be taken to its logical conclusion in the progressive rock of David Byrne and Brian Eno, on their 1981 song 'Red House'.) At this point of the song, Youth's DJing becomes looser as he jams with the riddim, and before you know it, you are listening not to words, but to the sound of his voice, like a solo instrument playing a new kind of jazz. Meanwhile, choruses of Keith & Tex's *la las* are dub-reduced to an abrupt solitary *la*, giving 'Cool Breeze' another piece of reductionist avant-garde ear-candy, *dubwise*.

'Screaming Target'

'Screaming Target' was produced by Augustus "Gussie" Clarke in 1973. It's a version of the riddim from K. C. White's 1972 single, 'No No No', itself a cover of Dawn Penn's 1967 hit, 'You Don't Love Me' (a song described later in this book; page 586). The recut riddim is distinguished from the original by the presence of a biting rhythm guitar that counterbalances the song's gentle rock steady piano. Youth's version famously opens with a wildly enthusiastic conversation between him and a friend, filled with patois, slang and screams. The subject of all this excitement? As in the intro of 'Cool Breeze', Youth find a character in a current movie to be noteworthy. He explains that after viewing both at Kingston's Carib Theater, he thinks *Screaming Target* must be ranked higher than the more popular *Dirty Harry*. He supports this view by screaming a number of times to launch the song of that name.

Just after Youth's first scream, the riddim's syncopated introduction comes crashing in. It drops out, leaving just a stub of K. C. White's titular vocal all alone. This cacophonous musical collage is of a type that can only be savored on reggae DJ records, and may never have been heard before this record. The body of the song begins, and Youth rides it with ease. He leaves the discussion of movies behind and amiably holds court on a variety of topics, punctuating with assorted exclamations, including the occasional return of the scream. So does White's titular refrain of "no no no ..." return, its long soft syllables contrasting with the DJ's staccato chanting. The lovely piano solo is another welcome holdover from White's version. It elicits additional shouting from Youth in this classic of DJ pandemonium.

Big Youth returned to this riddim with 'Screaming Target's B-side, 'Concrete Jungle'. It's nice to hear Youth ride 'No No No' a second time, as long as you don't hold it to the standard of the vastly better 'Screaming Target'.

'Can You Keep A Secret'
Produced in 1973 by Sonia Pottinger, 'Can You Keep A Secret' uses the riddim from Keith Hudson's 'Melody Maker' that was also used for Horace Andy's 'Don't Think About Me' (both songs previously described elsewhere in this book; pages 315 and 580). Unlike Andy's version, Big Youth performs over an intact version of Hudson's semi-instrumental song, adding his DJing to its wordless singing.

Amidst the moody guitar and harmonica, Youth enters and invokes God, sounding surprised at something. He goes on, jamming with the riddim, creating a free-form introduction that's filled with comments, exclamations, snatches of chanting and his trademark resinous screeches – one of the most immediately recognizable sounds in all of reggae. This briefly coalesces into order as we learn that litter is what had Youth surprised, but the subject is quickly abandoned. He next asks us to keep a secret, though the nature of the secret is unclear. This is because, as the song progresses, his chanting gains steam, building in intensity, but discarding narrative in the process. As Youth nears his peak, he is so frenzied, narrative fails him entirely. Exclamations of *good-gosh* take over. Then the song climaxes with a series of loud pants followed by a big resonant screech of *alright!*, topped off with an deluxe version of one of his trademark exclamations, an ecstatic *good, good, good, good, good gosh!*.

'Can You Keep A Secret' serves as a demonstration of Big Youth's unique instrument. His vocal creativity and emotional intensity are such that he can forgo narrative, even forgo words, and still tell a story that holds us entranced.

'Riverton City'

Jah Youth's 1974 self-produced 'Riverton City' is an *irie* travelogue. In it, a relaxed Big Youth mentions more Jamaican towns than any song since the old mento song, 'Names Of Funny Places'. It opens with Youth chanting "Kingston capital!" and reciting the opening of 'Old King Cole'. (It was not at all uncommon for DJs to fall back on a few lines of a nursery rhyme, an old mento song, or anything else from their past that hit their stream of consciousness when at the microphone.) He goes on to describe a lazy day trip with friends (Leroy, Barry and bredda [brother] Mike). This includes going to the country and looking at rainbows, with irie Youth reminding us that a pot of gold could be in the offing. With a second track of Big Youth, he is heard to inject a steady stream of commentary and exclamations over his chanting, including the full palette of his trademark resonant shouts and cries. At one point, a pleased-sounding Youth is moved to sing, rather than DJ, choosing the popular American song, 'Hush, Hush, Sweet Charlotte'. The riddim itself also has the feel of a relaxed journey. It's easy-going and a little funky, anchored by rumbling bass, organ and sharp saxophone answered by trebly piano phrases. (It's under-versioned, but it would have been nice to hear others have a go at such a pleasing riddim.) All of these relaxed vibes make the song a special pleasure. 'Riverton City' is the perfect soundtrack for the next time you and friends take a ride for the sake of taking a ride.

'Love Jah Jah Children'

Produced by George "Phil Pratt" Phillips in 1975, Big Youth's 'Love Jah Jah Children' adds layers of dread to a dubbed version of Al Campbell's melancholy 'Going The Wrong Way' (a song previously described in this book; page 385), making a heavy song even heavier.

It opens with Youth sounding like a philosopher-prophet, as he proclaims the perfection of God's work and warns of the imminence of his judgment. Over Campbell's opening wordless wailing, as dub churns the riddim, this is arresting. Campbell's vocal begins in earnest, and Youth begins to chant over it, unable to wait for it to echo away. The bass makes a belated entrance and mixed louder than on Campbell's version, fulfilling its potential as the lynchpin of a whole lot of dread.

Jah Youth launches and has much to say about the need for righteous behavior, love and protecting children from Babylon. He uses the bass as his anchor as he gives an unusual and emotional performance. Each of his lines quivers with intensity and ends with a stylized stuttering sob. His melody is slightly dissonant and the timing is slightly peculiar. At the same time, he plays with alliteration. All of this adds weight to his performance, which amounts to not only a triumphant *sufferas* song but a sound poem as well. Mid-song, he pauses. The emotional peak of Campbell's vocal is dropped in, adorned with dub. Youth uses it as a springboard to chanting with even greater intensity as he envisions African repatriation and its resulting unity. By then, DJing has been elevated to an address from a tribal elder. This great Big Youth track has been overlooked by all the Big Youth CD collections that are currently in print, but it can be heard on producer Phil Pratt's CD compilation called *Phil Pratt Thing*, released on the Pressure Sounds label.

'Keep Your Dread'

DJing from Big Youth and dub from producer George "Phil Pratt" Phillips make 1975's 'Keep Your Dread' a very heavy piece of roots reggae. It opens with a dub-reduced backing of just rhythm guitar and organ as Youth speak-chants a litany of injustices that slavery has inflicted on Jamaica's black population. He concludes with the startling notion that their ability to love may have been destroyed. At that dramatic moment, the guitar and organ drop out, and bass and drums drop in. With this flip of the dub-master's wrist, the riddim is suddenly recognized as one familiar from Ken Boothe's 'Artibella' and Ernest Ranglin's 'Surfin'' (both songs previously described in this book; pages 139 and 180). But this dread DJ version sounds little like either the rock steady hit or the guitar showcase that these other songs are. Male backing vocalists (possibly Youth himself) begin to sing a one-line sound poem built around the title that follows the bass and continues unchanged throughout the song. Youth chants in between its lines, also taking cues from the bass. This makes his delivery more rhythmically structured than is his norm, all the better to drive home the song's roots message. He urges his listeners to remain Rasta and learn about African culture as the only means to survive in Babylon, a place of great confusion. A heavy dread delivery of a roots message over a dub-enhanced version of a classic riddim makes 'Keep Your Dread' a head-swimmingly potent song.

'Wolf In Sheep's Clothing (Version 1)'

Like 'Keep Your Dread' from the same year, the self-produced 'Wolf In Sheep's Clothing (Version 1)' finds Big Youth dealing with Rasta issues with a heavy dread performance. But the rhythmically structured chanting of the other song is nowhere to be heard. This time around, Youth is loose and swinging.

The riddim comes from singer Desmond Young's song, 'Warning'. It's a strong spikey roots reggae riddim, with a powerful bass line, tart horns and gritty lead guitar out front, while sweet piano and creative reggae drums round things out. Young gave his all, but fell short of surmounting it. Big Youth, on the other hand, lopes right up to the top. He opens with a segment of speak-chanting, musing how a fool denies the existence of God. A shift of drop-out/in serves to signal him to get down to business. Chanting to the bass, he addresses the titular subject with a freedom, expressiveness and intensity that are akin to a jazz solo. He has complete control of melody, rhythm, intensity, texture and timing. He uses pauses and skipped beats, and colors parts of the song with edgy laughter or pained sounds. Although Big Youth influenced a generation of DJs, none could approach this aspect of his skill set.

He decries the titular dreadlocked men who look like Rastas, but, in fact, use their appearance to prey on true Rastas. He confronts them, telling them that they are dead to him and to be gone – "remove ya". A frequently used expression by Youth, he declares it here as if he's delivering the wrath of God. He describes how life should instead be harmonious and happy. He grooves for a time on the phrase, "black harmony", repeating it as if it's sweet on his lips. His closing couplet deplores the bad name these wolves give true Rastas, concluding with a shiver. Wolves in sheep's clothing may be a vexing problem for the Rasta community. But here, they are *chanted down* by no less than the world's only Rasta reggae jazz poet DJ, 100% on his game.

Also readily available is 'Wolf In Sheep's Clothing (Version 2)'. Not a dub version, it's instead Youth re-voicing the same version of the riddim, continuing the same themes. It features a good, if more casual, performance.

'Jim Screechy' (aka 'Jim Squeechy'; aka 'Jim Squashey')
The self-produced 1976 track 'Jim Screechy' finds Big Youth riding 'Stalag 17' (a riddim described earlier in this book; page 312) and it's a match made in heaven. This version of the riddim is altered from the original Ansel Collins/ Sound Dimension version. Dub is applied to the saxophone, guitar and drums. Horns are heard less frequently and Ansel Collins's organ is completely dropped out. This makes for the best of several dub mixes of the riddim, and serves to give Youth more room to move. And he uses it all, saying a great deal, though the theme defies easy summarization.

Jah Youth cautions Jamaica's black population against being ungrateful in life, warning against spitting in the sky. He advocates friendship and love. He introduces himself as "Jim Screechy", a DJ and smoker of marijuana. He pays tribute to jazz giant John Coltrane and his album, *A Love Supreme*. Rastafarian views are explored, decrying birth control and the trickery of politicians and the church, listing several denominations of the latter. The song ends with chanted praise for reggae singers of the ghetto (which accounts for most of them), complimenting them as cool cats and superstars. He should know; he's one of them and the description fits him as well.

Even as he runs through these barely related subjects, he chants with burning enthusiasm and his unique expressiveness. Phrases pop out to surprise and compel. Shaping his delivery to his passion, he recalls the jazz great he praises. Virtuosic, creative and free, Big Youth's chanting was like a new form of bebop. Hanging this performance on a dubwise version of one of the greatest of all reggae riddims, 'Jim Screechy' manages to be greater than the sum of its outstanding parts. The track blazes.

Though a live version of 'Jim Screechy' is also available, the studio track is the recommended rendition. Big Youth had previously voiced the "Stalag" riddim for the 1974 track 'All Nations Bow'. Though not as incendiary as 'Jim Screechy', any time Jah Youth rides the 'Stalag' riddim, it's worth a listen.

45 More great DJ songs

Of course, great DJ tracks did not begin or end with Big Youth, as the songs below attest. They are by a wide variety of practitioners of the DJ's trade. The DJ story is picked up in Chapter 53, "More great dancehall" (pages 548–77).

Early DJ sounds

King Sporty: *'Dr. Ring Ding'*
King Stitt: *'Dr. Ring Ding'; 'Iron Bar'*
'Dr. Ring Ding', the instrumental Skatalites ska scorcher produced by Coxsone Dodd, has already been discussed in the chapter on this group (page 84). Two DJ versions of this track, also Dodd-produced, give us a glimpse of how the sound system DJ moved from just introducing records to becoming part of the music.

A version of 'Dr. Ring Ding' that is found on CD collections by both Roland Alphonso and Jackie Mittoo includes the early DJ stylings of King Sporty. He was born less flamboyantly as Noel Williams (sharing his real name with that of golden-age mento star, Lord Lebby) in Port Antonio, in 1943. He began recording by adding rhythmic mouth sounds to ska songs by a variety of artists. By 1968, he had begun to release records under his own name, racking up at least 30 singles and an album through to the early 1980s. But then, he moved primarily into production of reggae and disco music.

First heard is an added introduction of a ringing phone being answered by an operator (rumored to be Rita Marley), who takes a call for Dr. Ring Ding. The song begins, and Sporty adds an antediluvian DJ performance to the track. This consists mostly of *chika chika* rhythm sounds, the likes of which he voiced on several Wailers ska songs, such as 'Lonesome Track'. When Moore's trumpet solo begins, Sporty is moved to yell *yeah!* In this way, sound system DJs began to interject themselves into the records they introduced.

Then there is the version credited to King Stitt, as heard on the CD called *Dance Hall '63 Featuring King Stitt* (released not in 1963, but in 1993). Stitt recreates vintage dancehall sounds by performing in his early DJ style over a spate of oldies. King Stitt is a colorful character, even by reggae standards. Second only to Count Machuki, Stitt helped originate the practice of the dancehall DJ adding his voice to the records he played. He was inspired (as his contemporaries all were) by the jive-talking American disc jockeys whose broadcasts could be picked up in Jamaica. Born Winston Spark, in 1940, in Kingston, he had two different stage names, both of them descriptive. First was "King Stitt", with Stitt coming from a childhood nickname and King being earned, when he won the first DJ competition at a big dance called The Crowning of King Street. His second stage name, "The Ugly One", comes from the fact that Stitt was born with a facial deformity, affecting his eyes and most seriously his mouth. It also affected his voice, giving his distinctively thick enunciation. Yet none of this stopped Stitt from being the first DJ King. (Reggae has rather direct nicknames for performers who are physically different. Other examples include the albino DJ Yellowman, percussionist Skully, who was named after his large forehead, Israel Vibration's similarly named Skelly, light-skinned, rodent-resembling Red Rat and singer/producer "Niney the Observer", who would have just been "The Observer", if he hadn't at some time earlier lost a thumb.) In 1957 Stitt began his DJ career at Sir Coxsone's Downbeat sound, moving to Jack Ruby's in 1968 when Dodd left the sound system business. Along the way he counted one Ewart Beckford as a fan, influencing the man who would soon be known as U-Roy. In 1970, he began to record singles for producer Clancy Eccles. By 1971, he began to operate his own sound system, King Stitt Disco. Stitt would record about 30 singles, the last in 1972, and two albums, a compilation and the aforementioned 1993 release. In 2011, Stitt passed away after battling prostate cancer and diabetes. He occasionally performed live, right to the end.

King Stitt's version of 'Dr. Ring Ding' starts with the King Sporty version, sans the phone and operator introduction. Stitt replaces it with a spoken piece introducing the record and extolling Sir Coxsone's sound system. The music begins and Stitt begins to interject various phrases throughout the song, such as *here we go!,ya-hoo! and ooh la la!,* as well as assorted whoops and hollers. Stitt's casual, unassuming delivery is an enjoyable, if unlikely, match for the red-hot virtuoso ska underneath. Led by U-Roy, DJs would build upon the style heard here. It would evolve from interjections of genial nonsense to full-fledged storytelling, acting as the lead instrument for the length of the song.

Another particularly good song on *Dance Hall '63* is an excellent ska instrumental rendition of the old mento song 'Iron Bar'. It's such a rousing performance, Stitt couldn't help but sing along with this classic Jamaican folk song. (Harry Belafonte couldn't help but take its melody, set it to new lyrics and enjoy a hit with 'Jamaica Farewell'.) The original single was credited either to the obscure Billy Cooke & His Group or to household name Tommy McCook. Jazz trumpeter Cooke was a bandmate of McCook's prior to ska, and both are likely heard on this track. Its inclusion in Stitt's collection is fortuitous. Outside of tracking down the original 45-rpm single, this is the only place the song can be heard.

U-Roy

Though not the first DJ to find popularity at the dance by adding commentary to the records he played, U-Roy was the first to have hit records doing so. Working off the riddims of rock steady hits, U-Roy's first records would cause a sensation. At one point, he held four of the top five spots in the Jamaican charts. It's not hard to see why. First was the novelty of the DJs' sound system antics being transported to vinyl in a new type of version. Second was the fact that U-Roy's song-length performances were more sophisticated than just a collection of shouted interjections. These early records were the halfway point between the DJ shouters who came before and the fluid chanting that would soon define the genre. U-Roy's artistic and commercial success would resound through reggae, right up to the ragga DJs who dominate reggae today. And he would show early American rappers that a beat and something to say is all you need to make compelling music – a singing voice and a band were not necessarily required. It's no wonder that this pioneer would come to be respectfully referred to as "Daddy U-Roy" or "The Originator" by his fans. The Jamaican government would also recognize U-Roy's importance, awarding him the Order of Distinction in 2007, the only DJ to be so honored. But perhaps the greatest measure of his influence is the number of DJs with tribute names who would follow, such as U-Brown, U-Black, I-Roy, New Roy, Nu Roy and U-Roy Junior.

U-Roy was born Ewart Beckford, in 1942, in Kingston, his unusual stage name being explained as a mispronunciation of his given name. He began DJing in 1961 for sound systems famous and forgotten. First was Doctor Dickie's Dynamic, moving on to Sir George The Atomic, Sir Mike The Musical Thunderstorm and, around 1967, King Tubby's Home Town Hi-Fi. He would leave Tubby briefly to work for Sir Coxsone's Downbeat in 1969, but soon returned. It was there that U-Roy had access to Tubby's versions of hit Treasure Isle riddims with the vocals dubbed out, making it easier to supplement the music with his banter. Paragon's lead singer John Holt, was at the dancehall one night and could not believe the crowd's response to U-Roy's DJing over the instrumental version of his group's hit, 'Wear You To The Ball'. Holt convinced Reid to allow U-Roy to record a performance of this, resulting in U-Roy's huge 1969 hit landmark DJ record, 'Wake The Town'. It contained a spoken introduction that may be the greatest of all self-referential reggae lyrics. He ebulliently announces the record with, "Wake the town and tell the people 'bout the musical disc coming your way". Many more records and hits would follow, both for Reid, with whom U-Roy worked until the producer's passing, and then for others. In all, U-Roy released about 120 singles and 26 albums, the last coming in 2013. He still performs around the world. Completing a circle, he started his own sound system, King Stur Gav, in the late 1970s, launching several significant DJ careers, including those of Ranking Joe, Charlie Chaplin and Josey Wales.

Though he is sometimes only remembered for his early work on Treasure Isle riddims that sounded so revolutionary when first released, a number of U-Roy's later songs are, to my ears, more accomplished and more timeless.

'Big Boy And Teacher' (aka 'What Is Catty')
'Big Boy And Teacher', from 1970, is a rule-breaking song for U-Roy. For one thing, he sang the track instead of DJing it. For another, Duke Reid provided a

gritty reggae riddim rather than the sparkling rock steady he is famous for. What could have inspired such a bizarro-world track with these two giants playing out of position? Apparently, it was the lure of Chin's Calypso Sextet's 1950 naughty mento hit, 'Big Boy And Teacher' (a song described in the chapter on this group; page 63). The result is a reverent reggae cover of a golden-age mento song, with an unusually accurate reading of the lyrics compared to many other examples of such. The man who popularized DJing as a new way to vocalize a record proves himself to be an acceptable singer. He's well supported not only by the riddim, but by a chorus of sexy female backing vocalists with a touch of Jamaican folk in their harmonies. Complete with *meow* sounds and a dirty guitar solo mid-song, U-Roy's rendition of 'Big Boy And Teacher' proves to be as much fun as the original. It can be heard on the *Trojan X-Rated Box Set*.

'Herbman Skanking'

'Herbman Skanking', produced by Tony Robinson in 1978, is a DJ version of 'Stick A Bush', a song by The Gladiators previously described in this book (page 395). The Glads' version is an exceptionally fun piece of roots reggae, but U-Roy puts the fun-meter off the scale. He adds new lyrics to the start of the song, portraying himself as a well-stocked ganja man visiting from Negril. The Gladiators are then dropped in from the original version, recounting the folk saying about hoes and sticker bushes. It's as if U-Roy is repurposing this Jamaican proverb to describe marijuana farming. The Glads are unexpectedly cut off at the first word of the verse and "Well ..." echoes for a very long time before it's finally out of earshot. This sets the stage for the reintroduction of U-Roy, amiably riding the rumbling, bopping bass line. He chants about the titular dance and, picking up from Peter Tosh's hit, 'Legalize It', from two years earlier, he recommends that marijuana be legalized, volunteering to provide advertising. The Glads' chorus returns, and U-Roy chants around and over it, as he is now rolling. His chanting is fluid, pulling wordless syllables from the air as the beat requires. Even with additional flashes of The Gladiators' vocals echoing by, the song has been fully appropriated by U-Roy. This automatic good time can be heard on U-Roy's 1978 *Jah Son Of Africa* album.

'Every Knee Shall Bow'

U-Roy's 'Every Knee Shall Bow' is voiced to a dub version of the riddim from Johnny Clarke's song of the same name, both produced by Bunny Lee in 1978. Between U-Roy's performance and the dub mix Lee provides, Clarke's version pales. It's a song that further establishes U-Roy's versatility. He *rocks the mic*, riding an especially *hard* roots reggae riddim that is made even tougher with aggressive dub effects – a far cry from the softer rock steady sounds with which he made his name.

With a thicket of echoed drum roll, the riddim bursts onto the field. Atop of it, chanting with greater intensity than his norm, rides U-Roy. He opens by adapting

Romans 14:11, a passage of the New Testament favored by the Rastas: "Every knee shall bow to me, and every tongue shall confess to God." U-Roy saturates it with emotion and rhythm, setting the tone for his performance. Rock-slide bass makes a delayed entrance and dub echo explodes like landmines, as the riddim rolls out surprises right past its false ending. U-Roy not only hangs tough, he thrives, bringing surprises of his own such as key changes, wordless chanting, pauses, cries, and dramatic exclamations ("How you mean!?") and quoting Bob Marley & The Wailers' 'Black Man Redemption', a Jamaican hit of the time. It's an impressive DJ performance; U-Roy was never as hard-hitting before or since. 'Every Knee Shall Bow' can be heard on any number of U-Roy collections and reggae compilations.

Trinity

Trinity was born Wade "Junior" Brammer, in 1954, in Kingston. He attended the Alpha Cottage School for Boys, adding his name to the incredible list of talented Alpha Boys who would make their mark on Jamaica music. He began recording in 1972, initially using the name Prince Glen. Following in his footsteps, his younger brother, Robert, is the DJ known as Clint Eastwood.

Trinity is perhaps the greatest of the many Big Youth-influenced DJs. But what makes him unique is his delightfully loopy style. On some of his best records, he comes off as more than a little eccentric. While all DJs tend to digress as they fill a record with their rapid-fire patter, Trinity's digressions often bordered on the outré, enlivening the proceedings. Some of his records open as if multiple versions of the riddim have crashed into one another, a sound that is awesome in every sense of the word.

Trinity was a very prolific DJ, recording hundreds of single sides and second halves of disco-mixes. (Over 250 have been documented, but the actual number is likely to be higher.) He also recorded 27 albums up to 1993, and then another in 2013. His most famous song, the 1977 hit, 'Three Piece Suit', inspired a storm of similar records from other artists. But it was not his best. Not when the great tracks below can be heard.

'School Days'
Produced by Jo Jo Hookim in 1976, 'School Days' is unrelated to the Toots & The Maytals song or the one by Chuck Berry, for that matter, – that share the same name. In it, we encounter a Trinity who is composed and domestic, in contrast to the wild performances described in the next two songs.

The riddim was originally recorded in 1970 as 'Roy Richards' Freedom Blues', produced by Coxsone Dodd. Around 1975, it was remembered, recut and recharged by the Sly & Robbie-led Revolutionaries as a vehicle for Tappa Zukie's DJ hit, 'MPLA'. The recut is a mighty piece of reggae with state-of-the-art musicianship. The glorious hook of an introductory melody from 'Freedom Blues' is brought forward, but is now played by the band rather than sung. An improved bass line gives the hook a melodic and rhythmic counterpoint, each strengthening the other. For Trinity's version, Hookim made the riddim more vivid with dub. And it's as if all this evolution was predestined for the moment that Trinity went into the Channel One studio to voice 'School Days'.

A drum roll announces the song, and dubby horns, organ and rhythm guitar sound the famous MPLA melody, providing Trinity with a swirling backdrop. He opens with a piece of play-acting, as he ushers his son off to school:

> Junior!
> Yes me father?
> Where you is?
> In the bath, cleaning me teeth, sir.
> Don't you know seven o'clock gone, understand that you should go to school?
> Yes, sir.
> Well, 'urry!
>
> Music and lyrics: Wade Brammer (aka Trinity) © 1979 by Roba
> Music Verlag GMBH, Hamburg. Reproduced with kind permission.

This concluded, the body of the song begins with an off-the-beat shift of drop-out/in. Simultaneously, the instruments previously heard disappear, as bass and drums appear in their place, and Trinity begins to chant. With a tight adherence to the beat, he amiably muses about school. He tells his son that school will keep him from becoming a fool and, for that matter, keep him from Hell. (His attitude to the subject is quite unlike several songs by The Wailers described earlier in this book (pages 199, 200) that indicted Jamaica's educational system as an oppressive tool of Babylon.) More than that, Trinity feels that going to school will save his son from some nightmare imagery he describes, the extent of the strangeness in this otherwise domesticated Trinity song. The riddim continues, with dub reducing the organ and guitar to intervals, while the horns are abridged to occasional echoing bleats. Trinity begins to mix in lyrics from the Christian hymn 'All Things Bright and Beautiful', including the well-known phrase "all creatures great and small". He sounds sincere and is surprisingly affecting, when he chants how good Fridays are at school. Trinity would be as entertaining again, but never in such a grounded way. 'School Days' can be heard on the compilation CD, *Channel One Well Charged*, which also contains the single's dub B-side, 'School Days Version'. This subtraction dub removes much of the vocals, allowing you to better enjoy the dub version of the MPLA riddim.

'Mr. Bassie'

Trinity's DJ version of Horace Andy's 'Mr. Bassie' (a song described previously in this book; page 388) was produced by Errol Thompson and Joe Gibbs in 1977. Kicking off with a brief asymmetrical drum roll, it opens riotously. As a swirling organ plays the familiar Mr. Bassie melody, we find Trinity engaged in a very enthusiastic dialog with another *dreadie* that is as incomprehensible as anything ever put to reggae vinyl. It begins with an exchange of greetings ("Hail, Trinity!" "Ites, dreadie!"); as it continues, the patois deepens, sounding less and less like English. Suddenly, someone is singing the opening lines of 'Mr. Bassie' in a decidedly non-virtuoso style, as Trinity asks if we are listening to the singer's words. Then dub grips the riddim. The singer vanishes and Trinity provides a sustained "Yeah". The body of the riddim begins and it's heavy and swinging. Trinity begins to chant in earnest. All this happens in less than 30 seconds, during which time the song dances on the precipice of chaos, much to the delight of fans of dub and DJ.

The riddim coalesces into a Grand Canyon-deep groove, with a river of dub running through it. A start-and-stop bass line is joined by drums playing a hypnotic pattern of rim shots, with ever-increasing amounts of reverb, and delicate cymbal taps. There's little else other than dropped-in snatches of organ and dub guitar strikes that echo or flash with reverb. Trinity cuts through this like a barracuda. Though his lyrics are largely eccentric free association, they are delivered with such relish that the performance has a powerful allure. He chants to Mr. Bassie about dancing to his playing and of liking his face. Not wanting anyone to feel left out, he also commends in crazy rhymes those who play drums, piano and "rhythm gits" (guitar). He employs one of his favorite digressions, a biblical reference to loaves of bread and fishes, and how the "wicked in the valley dem shakin'". His chanting is deeply rhythmic throughout, spiked with an array of gasps, throat noises and tongue clicks, as echo further embellishes his performance.

It's hard to resist the one-two punch of Trinity at his crazy best riding a deep dub-groove riddim. Though I wouldn't recommend this as anyone's first reggae song, it's like a double serving of caviar for any fan of DJ and dub. It can be heard on the CD reissue of Trinity's 1977 album, *Three Piece Suit*.

'No Galfriend'
Produced by Jo Jo Hookim in 1978, Trinity's 'No Galfriend' is a good demonstration of him at his most eccentric, not to mention the versatility of a good riddim. The latter originally served in 1975 as the backing for Ernest Wilson's deeply introspective 'I Know Myself', and notably again in 1978 for the champagne brunch reggae-jazz of Sly & Robbie's 'A Who Say' (both songs are described previously in this book; pages 386 and 367). Neither version does anything to prepare you for the crazy, chaotic DJ romp of 'No Galfriend'.

In it, we find Trinity is wallowing in self-pity, lamenting the romantic predicament of the title. His chanting is rife with emotion. He frequently digresses from this topic to muse on other subjects, either loosely related to the song's theme, or not at all. Some are rather inappropriate, making him seem a bit more than eccentric, though less than deranged. Add a dub-filled production, and we have a track that's so bursting at the seams with entertainment, it borders on chaos. It's a sound that would be alien to anyone other than a reggae fan who feasts on such an overstuffed concoction.

It opens with Trinity singing about poor Johnny and his lack of a soul. But before this can be explained, the subject is left behind in a splash of echo guitar. This ushers a drop-in of Ernest Wilson's vocal, with Trinity adding commentary, agreeing with the singer. Wilson exits the song permanently, his last syllable dissolving into echo, and the body of the song begins. Trinity digs right in with a whining chant to say that, unlike all his friends, he is in the titular situation. He rides the riddim, expanding on his loneliness, as echo and other dub effects bloom all around him.

Unfortunately for Trinity, it's easy to see why he is alone. For example, he casually asks a friend for the loan of his girlfriend, sounding desperate and creepy. And I'm not sure if this is a spiritual or medical situation, or what this has to do with dating, but Trinity points out that he has a parasite that he has to get rid of. As richly delivered as the couplet is, it does little to make Trinity's case for marketability on the dating scene. Nor is the assertion that he looks like and lives like a "predator" something he should highlight in his online dating profile. (This was before the Arnold Schwarzenegger movie *Predator*, eliminating that possible explanation.) Trinity finds time to throw in couplets from two Jamaican folk/mento songs, 'Sly Mongoose' and 'Brown Skin Gal'. These have little to do with the subject at hand, but are delivered with emphasis as if they are critical points. But Trinity's turmoil is our gain. His over-the-top emotion and strangeness, along with the fine dub version of a great riddim, make 'No Galfriend' a treat. But apparently this song was too much for a digital medium to hold, so to hear it, you will have to track down the 1978 LP *Three Piece Chicken & Chips (One For One)*, by Ranking Trevor & Trinity, an album in which, as the parenthetical portion of the title indicates, the two DJs alternate tracks *clash style*, rather than collaborate on them.

Eek-A-Mouse

The name tips you off to the fact that there may not be a bigger character in reggae than the man called Eek-A-Mouse. But it still does not prepare you for the sight or the sound of him.

Ripton Joseph Hylton was born in 1957 in Kingston. After he gave up betting on a favored racehorse on which he frequently lost money, the horse, named Eek-A-Mouse, promptly won its next race. The horse may have taken Hylton's money, but Hylton took its memorable name. Not that Eek needed it to stand out. That was assured by his 6'6" height, making him the tallest of all reggae performers – something he frequently refers to in his songs,. Like the mento greats of decades before him, he is a natural storyteller, and his best songs are richly observed. But in his singing he is quite unlike anyone who came before. Eek is a sharp, nasal-toned *sing-jay* (halfway between a singer and a DJ) with something extra: his own language of singing he calls "Amharic slurring". Like Waterhouse warbling, it sounds multicultural, with Eek himself at different times describing it as being Ethiopian, Chinese or Native American. But it is unlike Waterhouse in that it is more playful than pained. It can take the form of a short accent, a multisyllabic outburst, or an entire stanza. Few have tried to imitate it.

Under his real name and sans any Amharic slurring, he released a pair of 1975 singles that sank like stones. He continued as a live sound system DJ and rebooted his recording career in 1979, when, with his novel new name and singing style, he found immediate success. Eek has recorded fifteen albums, the last one from a live set in 2011, and enjoys popularity in Jamaica as well as overseas. His live shows are further enlivened with Eek's penchant for wearing costumes. In the annals of reggae, The Mouse, as he is affectionately called, is truly a singular character with a singular sound.

'Virgin Girl' (aka 'Wa Do Dem')

In 1981, Eek had a hit so nice he recorded it twice with different names for different producers. It's an amusing tale in which Eek professes his love. The fact that she is a virgin is mentioned but not explored. Instead, the focus is on the fact that the tallest man in reggae is dating a short woman. They can't go for a walk in public without being laughed at. "Wa do dem" means "Why must they do that?"

But neither studio rendition can hold a candle to the live rendition found on the 1982 album, *Reggae Sunsplash '81: A Tribute to Bob Marley*. (Sunsplash was Jamaica's reggae answer to Woodstock, held every year from 1978 to 1985 and a number of times thereafter.) Eek's spoken introduction alone would have been worth the price of admission. In just about 12 seconds, he introduces himself, informs you of his height, suggests a dubious ethnomusicology for his singing style (Chinese Apache Indian), gives you a generous sample of said style (uncorking the longest and gnarliest of Amharic slurring phrases), and asks for your approval, flashing his profile for your consideration . It has to be heard to be believed. He then launches into a relaxed rambling rendition of the song, loaded with Amharic slurring over ripping live instrumentation, as he proves himself to be a great storyteller, a great live performer and reggae's greatest Chinese Apache Indian.

'Ganja Smuggling'

The next year, 'Ganja Smuggling', a good Eek-A-Mouse song from 1982, was also outshone by a live Sunsplash rendition. It can be heard on the 1984 album, *Eek-A-Mouse And Michigan & Smiley, Live At Reggae Sunsplash*. It includes another incredible spoken introduction. First, he gives a language lesson, translating between patois and proper English for all the tourists who have come to Jamaica for Sunsplash. He then explains that he is a singer, not a DJ, and concludes with a demonstration of how his Amharic slurring makes his singing unique. The crowd erupts in response.

With these important points established, he then launches into the song, well supported by The Sagittarius band, replete with trombone and dub. With great verve, he sings a series of engaging verses and supplies blocks of Amharic slurring for the chorus. In just a few lines, the act of ganja smuggling is described in rich detail: the day and time, the muddy harvest, moving the ganja into town, then onto a plane, and the size of the financial reward. Perhaps to justify his actions, he devotes even more lyrics to an equally detailed description of his bad memories of childhood poverty. Two vivid and engaging tales for the price of one, told by one of reggae's most unique vocalists in peak form, 'Ganja Smuggling' is a great song and a great live reggae performance.

'Peeni Walli' (aka 'Fireflies')

'Peeni Walli' was produced by Anthony and Ronald Welch in 1981. It's a briskly told story of a traffic accident and trip to the hospital. A motorcyclist knocks Eek off his bicycle in front of oncoming traffic. Dazed, he sees "peeni walli", the Jamaican name for fireflies. He's surrounded by a throng of people, looking down at him, reminding him of a funeral. And he ponders how that could have been the outcome, if not for his relationship with Jah. One of the throng speculates on the accident's cause, but it's hard for a non-Jamaican to understand: "Hard the long youth ha' look 'pon a fat gal", meaning *I heard the tall youth happened to look at a fat girl (and got hit)*. Eek neither accepts nor denies this explanation.

The Mouse employs a variety of sharp Amharic slurring accents and exclamations of "hey mon!" to emphasize his story. The Welches make a good match by pairing Eek's sharp nasal delivery with fuzzy-toned lead rock guitar as the featured instrument. Sly & Robbie provide drums and bass, assuring a great rhythm and musical good time. A dramatic autobiographical story, singularly delivered, and fine instrumentation make 'Peeni Walli' another winner from The Mouse. It can be heard on the CD compilation, *The Very Best Of Eek-A-Mouse*.

'Terrorist In The City'

Produced by Linval Thompson in 1983, Eek-A-Mouse's 'Terrorist In The City' is an alluring piece of dubby trance reggae. Thompson features the dub technique of using a single reverbed keyboard chord repeated unchanged – at sometimes odd intervals – to build a retrograde drone. It's a fine complement to the murmuring chanting Eek employs for the track. The few lyrics, concerning random murder in Kingston, hardly matter, as Eek's performance is far more about sound than words. His voice, soaked in reverb and digital delay, rich in Amharic slurring and frequent shifts into falsetto, melts into the riddim. Like Augustus Pablo's melodica, here Eek's vocal is an exotic lead instrument in the fabric of the dub. The result is hypnotic.

'Terrorist In The City' can be found on three albums, but in different forms. 'The Mouse And The Man' features a mix with less dub and is therefore not recommended. *The Very Best Of Eek-A-Mouse* has the preferred mix. But if it isn't enough for you, there is also a 12-inch mix on the CD called *Most Wanted: Eek-A-Mouse* that nicely extends the preferred mix with an okay instrumental dub version. Be aware that Eek's similarly named 'Too Much Terrorist In The City' is a different song altogether.

'Local Fisherman'

'Local Fisherman' appears on Eek-A-Mouse's self-produced 1996 album, *Black Cowboy*. It's an ambitious song with a number of unexpected elements that each succeed fully as The Mouse demonstrates surprising versatility.

His vocal is a complete departure from what we've come to expect from him. He sings rather than DJs, his voice is in a lower register than normal (as is the case for many songs on this album) and his sharp nasal sound and flourishes of Amharic slurring are nowhere to be found. The instrumental backing is also surprising. It features an energetic, simplified beat that harkens back to the pre-ska double-struck mento rhythm. Carried by the drums, there is no sign of the typical reggae chop, while the busy bass and guitar have a calypso inflection. Trebly staccato piano, other keyboards and mournful backing vocals finish the unusual riddim. This, along with the storytelling lyrics with references to Jamaica's past, would have allowed this song to be placed in the chapter on mento-reggae.

The lyrics are serious and carefully considered. Eek provides a multifaceted look at how changing economic conditions are affecting Jamaica. This includes industrialized agri-business's impact on the small farmer, how the devaluation of the Jamaican dollar exacerbated class struggle, and how housing schemes create class separation. Eek uses two voices to tell his story. One is the voice of the cynical rich. This voice has the harshest disdain for Jamaica's poor, hoping they will busy themselves by killing one another and leave him alone. This is in stark contrast to Eek's second voice, that of a humanist who shows concern for various folk. This voice tells mento-like stories about the local fisherman, grandpa, child, farmer, Rastaman and an ailing rural woman who has to walk a mile to the well. Her story gives the song its chorus, with its mento-like melody and lyrics. Each of these figures suffers from the social ills of the growing economic divide. All Eek can do is lament about the good old days of Jamaica, when it "used to nice". He recalls this gentler time populated by comedy stage act Bim & Bam, Muma Louise (as he affectionately calls the beloved poet, folklorist, linguist, comedian, storyteller, songwriter, singer and star of stage, radio and television, Louise Bennett) and Mas Ran (Randolph "Ranny" Williams, Bennett's fellow folklorist and for a time her performing partner). In 'Local Fisherman', Eek-A-Mouse has so much to say, he masterfully reshapes his delivery and accompanying music to create a great song unique to his or any other catalog.

Assorted other DJs

Scotty: *'Draw Your Brakes'*
David Scott, better known by the single name Scotty, was born in 1951 in West-moreland Parish, but was raised in Kingston. He formed a vocal trio called The Federals in 1967 and was discovered by producer Derrick Harriott. Together, they recorded a handful of singles from that year through 1969. The next year, line-up changes led to a new name, The Chosen Few, a group that recorded through the first half of the 1970s and again briefly in 1985. But very early in the group's existence, Scotty would depart to enter the burgeoning DJ game. His irrepress-ible style, inspired by Count Machuki but taken to outlandish extremes, resulted in immediate success and several classics of the genre. As we will see, one of these would give Scotty the distinction of having the first DJ record that was released overseas. In all, he recorded about two dozen singles from 1970 through 1973. Then a move to Florida seems to have derailed his career, in spite of his staying musically active there, even opening his own recording studio. Scotty was work-ing on new recordings when prostate cancer took his life prematurely in 2003.

In 1971, Derrick Harriott produced Scotty's 'Draw Your Brakes', a DJ version of Keith & Tex's 'Stop That Train' (a song discussed in the chapter on Big Youth; page 411). Chosen as the only DJ song to be included in the sterling 1972 soundtrack of *The Harder They Come*, it would be the first DJ song that many overseas reggae fans would ever hear. How it must have sounded to those uninitiated ears!

Consider the song's chanted a cappella opening. Scotty sounds interesting, but the meaning is impenetrable, as most of the words are unfamiliar local terms. Author Steve Cotler was curious enough to research a translation (available at www.stevecotler.com) and has allowed its use here. Scotty is describing a man wresting away another man's girlfriend and having sex with her. It sets up Keith & Tex's story of being left by a lover.

The riddim begins, opening with Lyn Taitt's classic Western-sounding bluesy guitar riff. (When it later returns, Scotty is moved to comment how well suited it is for such a sad song.) Then comes Keith & Tex's opening chorus. During a pause in the singing, Scotty interjects in his irrepressible way. The appearance of an added voice to a record, which talks directly to the listener and urges on the original recorded vocal track, must have sounded quite strange to anyone not familiar with DJ reggae. So, too, what happens next. The singers drop out, leav-ing Scotty to get to work. He starts his rapid-fire, overly emphatic, commentary worrying for Keith & Tex, who are losing their girl. He is so upset that he can't stop the train for them. Scotty says that he is crying. With his hyperexpressive youth-ful voice, singsong delivery and a profusion of exclamations, Scotty certainly was unlike anything overseas listeners had ever heard before. To Jamaican ears, it was yet another superlative DJ record.

For another dose of Scotty working a fine rock steady riddim, check out 'I Worry', his version of singer Derrick Harriott's 'Do I Worry'. Available on the

Scotty CD compilation called *Unbelievable Sounds*, it includes more classic Lyn Taitt guitar and an astounding throat cry from Scotty to justify your attention.

Lorna Bennett: *'Breakfast In Bed'*
Scotty & Lorna Bennett: *'Skank In Bed'*
Lorna Bennett was born in 1952 in the rural Saint Elizabeth Parish. She loved music from a very early age and benefited from the exposure to her brother's collection of records by the world's top recording stars. She came to the attention of producer Geoffrey Chung when she was working as a nightclub singer at the age of eighteen. Bennett went on to record about sixteen singles and an album throughout the 1970s while concentrating on completing law school at the same time. She would continue to sing semi-professionally and return to recording a number of times up to the present day.

Another brother gave her a copy of Dusty Springfield's 1969 hit ballad 'Breakfast in Bed', challenging her by saying, "I bet you can't sing this". She could. Bennett brought the song to Chung, a session was arranged and the resulting song was a hit in 1972. Although a number of singers have since recorded the song, no one did it as sexily as Bennett, whose playfully seductive vocal makes even more of the lyrics than Springfield's smoky slow burn. The riddim is equally playful from its opening spill of drums. A vivacious, bouncing bass line, horns and organ are all featured, as guitar chips the reggae chop. This great song is as beloved today as it was when it was first released.

And when Scotty recorded his DJ version, 'Skank In Bed' in the same year, he gave us a DJ version that was as good as, if not better than, Bennett's beloved original. It was definitely wilder. The familiar instrumentation begins, but rather than hearing Lorna Bennett coo, Scotty busts onto the scene and holds court. Getting everyone's attention with a high-pitched noise, he introduces both the song and Lorna Bennett in a single gleeful, colorful, breathless, run-on sentence. With that, Bennett's vocal from the original begins, and Scotty answers Lorna, commenting on what she's singing. He's all over the map, topically and sonically, but is always appealing. Certainly, there's enough here to recommend this as a great song. But Scotty, in lieu of an instrumental solo, famously provides something mid-song that's completely unexpected. He gasps in shock and halts the recording session by yelling *"Cut"*. The problem is that there is a hanger-on in the studio, a boy who is unhelpfully singing along. Talking, no longer performing, Scotty gives the boy a dressing-down. He sarcastically asks if he can play an instrument, taking him through a list. The answer to each is "No, sir". The boy is then heard trying to appease Scotty, and asking to be given a chance. This makes Scotty even angrier, and he summarily throws the boy out of the studio. Without pause, he calls, "Riddim, come forward!" And with that, Scotty, who a moment ago sounded every bit the temperamental star having a tantrum, resumes the song, sounding as irie as ever, the incident over and forgotten. Was it real or was it staged? It's hard to be sure of anything other than that it works as a novel DJ technique to spice up a version. Other in-studio altercations from other artists would follow.

Both versions are available on numerous CD collections. Lorna Bennett recorded a remake that just can't touch the original, but it's difficult to find and it's unlikely that anyone will wind up with it accidentally. Let's give Scotty the last word on 'Skank In Bed': "I would tell you about this musical disc . . . good God, it's great!"

Ernest Wilson: *'Why Oh Why'*
Dub Specialist: *'Where Eagles Dwell'*
Lone Ranger: *'Noah In The Ark'*
Lightning struck three times for Lone Ranger's 'Noah In The Ark', as a great Studio One riddim begat a great example of Studio One dub that begat a great DJ version. Let's take them in that order.

The riddim is best known and named for singer Ernest Wilson's song, 'Why Oh Why'. This is a fine, *upful* song with a passionate vocal. Wilson imploringly asks why we can't live together, decrying the violence that occurs instead. Meanwhile, a riddim filled with frenetic energy roils underneath. Fil Callender's busy drums are on the spot, and there's a bass line that's all sinew and melody. Like steam fittings popping from too much pressure, Syndrum accents whistle and squirt. (Though much of the riddim's base sounds like it's from the late 1960s, there were no Syndrums in 1969. So at least some of it was added years later, as was often done by producer Coxsone Dodd.) *Chika-chika* and a second rhythm guitar along with supporting piano further fill the riddim, and the production is burnished with dub. Another vocal performance from a different version bleeds through accidentally, deliberately or ambivalently. It helps rather than hurts, adding yet something more to a production that is already full to the brim. And that's before considering the two lead elements.

The horn riff that opens, closes and provides a mid-song break steals the riddim. Of the many thousands of appealing horn riffs heard in reggae songs, this one stands out. It's a simple see-sawing melody played in unison on trumpet and trombone. They produce a mouth-watering harmony that is orange-sweet but lime-tart, bordering on the sound of Mexican mariachi horns. For his part, Wilson does not get distracted by the riddim's crowded energy. He stays totally composed, singing with long-drawn-out notes, following the path of bass for his melodic direction. And he nicely bookends his vocal with the soulful falsetto singing that opens and closes the song. Ernest Wilson's 'Why Oh Why' can be heard on the compilation CD, *When Rhythm Was King*, released on the Heartbeat label. The single's dub version B-side, called 'Why Oh Why Version' can be heard on the Heartbeat Records CD called *Studio One Presents Version Dread Dub Specialist*.

Though Wilson's version has some dub, there's a much better dub version of the riddim. 'Where Eagles Dwell' is often billed to Lone Ranger, even though it's completely instrumental. Other times, it is more accurately billed to Dub Specialist, the generic artist name Coxsone Dodd used for dub from Studio One. The classic Studio One dub sound works wonders here. Adding reverb to the abundance of rim shots does more to sharpen and vitalize the sound of drums and the overall rhythm of the song than one might imagine possible before hearing the result. It adds a dimension to the riddim, making it go from flat to suddenly standing out like a bas-relief. Additional reverb and the subtle use of drop-out/in further gild the riddim, allowing peek-a-boo views of instruments that were previously buried in the mix. The Syndrums heard in the original are gone and are not missed here, while, wisely, the horns are left completely intact. This is a premier example of Studio One dub.

Lone Ranger DJs atop this version for his song, 'Noah In The Ark'. Lone Ranger was born Anthony Waldron in Jamaica, but spent a good part of his childhood in the UK before returning and settling in Kingston. He spent a brief time as part of a vocal trio before breaking out as a DJ, developing his skills by chanting along with records by U-Roy and Big Youth. He began recording in 1977, and although he did not work with Dodd exclusively, he was heavily associated with Studio One. A DJ in the classic mold, his chanting style was unfailingly enthusiastic, sharp and welcome. He would punctuate his chants with his trademark exclamation of *right!* After a time, he popularized interjections of frog *ribbit*s and pig *oink*s, a practice that was imitated by other DJs, and even by Bob Marley in 'Punky Reggae Party'. He recorded more than 50 singles and nine albums, the last coming in 2002. Ranger still occasionally performs live.

His performance on 'Noah In The Ark' comes forth fully formed. An excited Ranger jumps in before the brief introductory drum roll is complete. He's energized not just by the excellent riddim, but by his own custom admixture of the Old and New Testaments. He sets things up with his opening, excitedly mentioning the Bible, Genesis 7, and Noah and the Ark. What comes next is the most enthusiastic and craziest Bible lesson you will ever receive. It begins by recounting the story of Noah gathering pairs of animals, the Flood, and the 40 days of the Ark's journey. So far, so good, but then things get strange. Despite Jesus' total absence from the Old Testament, and a difference of several thousand years, he makes frequent appearances in this story. Ranger explains that Jesus brought the storm because of man's disobedience and tells how Jesus led Noah through the waters. The deity picture grows even more complex as later in the journey Jah provides a rainbow. Ranger's chanting is as incisive as the dub-sharpened drums, complete with percussive rolling *r*s, cooing sounds and other verbal noises. The song ends with Ranger chanting peacefully over the great horn riff. By then, no doubt remains that his ebullience and DJ skills take precedent over any notion of accepted theological accuracy.

'Noah In The Ark' was released on Ranger's 1979 Coxsone Dodd-produced album, *On The Other Side Of Dub*, rather than ever appearing on a single. A show-case album pairing dub and DJ versions of riddims, this also includes 'Where Eagles Dwell'. 'Noah In The Ark' should not be confused with a later, inferior remake with the shorter title 'Noah's Ark'.

Dillinger: *'Jah Love'*
The man called Dillinger was born in 1953 in Kingston and given the less dramatic name of Lester Bullock. He was a successful sound system DJ working under the name of Dennis Alcapone Junior when Lee Perry asked him to record. This stage name was a tribute to one of the most successful of all early DJs, Dennis Alcapone. (Such tribute names were not uncommon in reggae, with trombonist Vin Gordon similarly being billed Don Drummond Junior early in his career, not to mention a U-Roy Junior who would have failed a paternity test. Gangster names were popular too, with examples such as Louie Lepke, Don Corleone, Jack Ruby, Luciano and Jessie James.) Perry didn't think either of the DJ's names would do, so he gave him a new one, a gangster name of his own. And so Dillinger and his recording career were born.

Dillinger's chanting style is fluid, with a plaintive quality that gives him an intriguing emotional intensity. He is best known for his cross-over hit, the funky disco-reggae hybrid, 'Cocaine In My Brain', though the two songs described below are certainly far better. He should not be confused with the dancehall singer from South Africa called Black Dillinger, who appeared on the scene in 2007, adding to the confusion with a similarly named song called 'Jah Jah Love'.

'Jah Love' was produced by Bunny Lee around 1977. Though Dillinger is out front and doing fine, equal credit must go to Lee for creating a perfect balance of singer, DJ, instrumental and dub that creates a rich roots reggae groove. Dillinger opens the song with a dub-hazed spoken introduction, explaining that because he is learning to speak Amharic, his Rasta cultural enlightenment will allow him to stand up to Babylon's "baton stick" without fear. (Substitute "truncheon" for "baton stick" if you are British, and "nightstick" if you are American.)

The music begins, featuring roots singer Linval Thompson from his version of the riddim, called 'Twelve Tribes Of Israel'. In an atypical but successful production move by Lee, rather than just a line or two of the singer's performance, a generous portion is heard before Dillinger comes in. One can see why the producer was reluctant to drop out Thompson's dynamic vocal sooner. He moves from free-styling exhortations answered by sparse guitar strums, to a wordless rhythmic refrain that gives the song a hook, to lyrics about the Old Testament that dovetail with Dillinger's theme. Having said his extended piece, the singer dissolves into a cloud of echo, from which Dillinger emerges, holding the mic. He begins to chant, resuming the lyrics from his spoken introduction. He then lists the varieties of Rasta that are learning Amharic, and goes off on various digressions. He idiosyncratically raises the intensity of the song by bending the melody of his chanting slightly out of tune, a variation of his trademark plaintiveness. Though it started strong, the song only gathers force as it progresses, and Dillinger doesn't so much ride the riddim as be propelled by it. Dubby bits of Thompson's vocal begin to drop in with increasing frequency, and by the end of the song, he and Dillinger are essentially duetting. 'Jah Love' is available on several Dillinger CD collections, typically presented as a disco-mix with an appended horns cut that uses the melody of Dave Brubeck's jazz hit, 'Take Five'.

Dillinger: 'Flat Foot Hustling'

Dillinger's 'Flat Foot Hustling', produced by Niney The Observer in 1977, takes its riddim from Dennis Brown's 'Have No Fear', also produced by Niney that year. If Dillinger shared the spotlight in 'Jah Love', here it's fixed solely on him. His chanting is so distinctive and his lyrics so attention-grabbing, even a recurring drop in of Brown's vocal, a fine riddim with a superlative bass line and a rich, dub-filled mix all wind up supporting the DJ.

He opens by chanting matter-of-factly about his father, whom he revered and who "died with a shovel in his hand", tipping us off that this will be an auto-biographical song. In fact, Dillinger will address three generations of his family. Dennis Brown is dropped in briefly, and over him Dillinger freestyles a warm-up, sounding like Big Youth. He then launches his story. Chanting intensely and with his plaintiveness tilted towards melancholy, he describes his parents' fathers, both of whom were Cuban. His maternal grandfather was a hustler and his paternal grandfather was a *scuffler* (someone who frequently got into fights). He goes on to explain that he's a product of both, and offers recollections of his own hustles, being careful not to include anything incriminating. He then reminisces about his youth, remembering the excitement of having some small change in his pocket and going to the corner store. And there's a long foray into the Jamaican folk song 'Linstead Market', a song that he no doubt first heard as a boy. With so many personal recollections chanted in a sorrowful style, the song has the strong feel of a confession, even though specific details are omitted. Combining this with a fine dub riddim that includes appearances from Dennis Brown makes Dillinger's 'Flat Foot Hustling' an undeniably great song. It's available on several Dillinger CD collections.

Errol Scorcher: 'Tourist Season'

Errol Scorcher was born Errol Archer, in 1956 in Saint Catherine Parish. He recorded from the mid-1970s through 1983, releasing about 50 singles and two albums, plus two more in combination with other artists. Reports of his murder in 1982 proved to be only rumor. Scorch was recording in preparation for a come-back when, at the start of 2012, he died of a brain aneurism.

He lives up to his name with the energetic and exciting 'Tourist Season'. Produced by Dudley "Manzie" Swaby in 1978, it's a great DJ version of a dub-happy recut of the riddim from Horace Andy's 'Fever'. But the riddim is not immediately recognizable as such; being totally bereft of the vocal and almost all of its distinctive organ melody, the ascending peppy bass line pops into prominence.

The song opens with a big dub splat – a rapidly echoing drum strike followed by two and a half notes cropped from the bass line. These instruments give over to a duet between dubbed organ and guitar chop, over which Scorcher chants an introduction: "Special requests to all tourists ...". Anticipation builds, and Manzie responds by throwing big dub levers. The dueling instruments vanish, and at the same moment in their place appear drums, a Nyah hand drum and a *wicked*, ascending, inside-out bass line, whose power was masked on Andy's version. Scorch launches into the body of the song, as further satisfying drop-out/in shifts await.

With his non-virtuoso DJing and very nasal voice, Scorcher comes off as a highly likable everyman. He chants about tourists and Jamaica in general. He then moves his tale to a particular tourist he encountered named Claire. He goes with her to the beach, where she suggestively asks him to rub her with sun lotion. The story is chanted in time to a guitar chop, flashing with reverb, which adds emphasis to the telling. Things don't go perfectly for Scorcher, but in the end he brags about her being there the next morning to give him "coffee in my favorite cup". Again, his story is highlighted by dub effects, this time landing on the drums. At the end of the song, the drums, percussion, bass, guitar and organ are all heard simultaneously, briefly united for the first time.

Though a well-remembered track, it does not appear to have been collected on LP or CD, making the original 45-rpm single release on the Ja-Man label the only way to acquire it. To reward anyone who goes through the effort, the single's B-side, called 'Version', is an enjoyable dub of the song with a lot of dropout applied. This version allows an X-ray view of the song's impressive skeleton – the bass and two-piece drum section. If you cannot track 'Tourist Season' down, I suggest as a consolation prize another DJ's version of this riddim. General Echo's 'International Year Of The Child', available on his CD *Teacher Fi Di Class*, is nearly as good of a song.

I-Roy: *'Package Deal'*

Roy Samuel Reid was born in 1949 in Saint Thomas Parish. He moved to Kingston when he was in his teens to attend school. He was working as an accountant for the government when he decided to run his own sound system, Turbo Sonic Sound, and established a weekly dance called Soul Bunny. His skills as a DJ were soon noticed, and he was first recruited by a bigger sound system, then offered an opportunity to record by producer Harry Mudie in 1970. It was Mudie who renamed him I-Roy in tribute to/imitation of the groundbreakingly successful DJ recording star U-Roy. I-Roy quickly found success as a recording artist and ledgers were permanently put aside for microphones.

I-Roy would go on to be a top DJ throughout the 1970s, even enjoying popularity in the UK as well as Jamaica. Leaving Mudie because of a financial dispute, he worked prolifically with a variety of producers. This is an understatement, as he released records with no fewer than sixteen different producers in 1973. In all, he would rack up about 25 albums, and least 200 single sides, the last coming in 1990. But for someone with so much going for him, his life would end in an unexpected series of tragedies. He became ill, destitute and homeless. Caring for a mentally retarded son added to the emotional and financial strain. When a second son was killed in prison in 1999, it may have been the final straw, as I-Roy died a month later of heart failure.

'Package Deal', I-Roy's best song, was released on his 1978 *World On Fire* LP. It can be considered a sleeper, as it was not one of his hits and has not been released on CD. However, it was considered worthy of inclusion on the 1983 I-Roy best-of LP called *Crucial Cuts*. Other than Big Youth's 'Riverton City', it's hard to imagine a DJ song that is so *irie*. That goes not only for I-Roy's performance, but for The Revolutionaries' fine riddim and the perfect application of dub that producer I-Roy sees to.

The riddim is welcoming and sweet, but highly creative, as the reggae of the late 1970s often was. Dub makes it a kaleidoscope of elements that shift in and out. As Sly Dunbar plays an inverted heartbeat drum rhythm, sweet rock steady piano phrases, cute martial snare tattoos, happy guitar leads, prancing snatches of organ, tambourine, guitar chords flashing with reverb, and expert applications of echo rotate in and out. Meanwhile, Robbie Shakespeare's bass line charms. The only other versions of the riddim are found on I-Roy LPs. A sax cut, called 'Andy Capp', is found on the I-Roy dub album *Cancer*. Its dub version, 'It's Alright', is also found on *World On Fire*. With uninspired sax completely supplanting I-Roy's performance, neither of these versions compares to 'Package Deal'.

In story and delivery 'Package Deal' is I-Roy's most endearing performance. It's the most detailed account of a date in any reggae song. But first he opens with spoken words of wisdom that, once untangled from patois, roughly translate as: "Be careful, valued friend, you can't just listen to what a woman says, you have to understand them." He then launches into his story, chanting disarmingly, as he describes a package deal of trials, tribulations and triumphs when he brings Imogene to a dance. She's a big, heavy girl, and wearing white. When she dances she reminds I-Roy of a satellite. He smooths over his natural stridency, never sounding sweeter. Rather than DJing, he sings (quite pleasingly) the "It's all right" chorus. And even when he chants, he has never sounded more like a sing-jay, making sure you notice this by prefacing many of his lines by first stating, "Singing ...".

He can't help but admire the other women at the dance, noting the color of their clothes and giving individual praise to each. When he turns his attention back to his date and asks what she'd like, Imogene proves to be demanding, asking for a costly meal of roast fish. Even after he buys her two wenchman (a type of snapper), the date continues to be a frustrating one. For example, she chides I-Roy for smoking marijuana. And later, when he tries to kiss her while dancing, she wanders away. But, as I-Roy promised, *it's alright,* and the song does have a happy ending. He finds Imogene back by the fish vendors and, ultimately, they rub-a-dub throughout the night. 'Package Deal' stands as a must-have DJ song. Let's hope that it appears on CD and on digital download services very soon so that more people can find themselves singing "It's alright" throughout their day.

Ranking Trevor: *'Masculine Gender'*
As he did for a generation of music-minded Jamaican youth, U-Roy had an impact on young Trevor Grant of Waterhouse. Born in 1960, he was nine when U-Roy's first song became a hit. He was inspired, and before too long would embark on a musical career of his own as a sound system DJ, admittedly copying U-Roy's approach to melody and overall style. He was established enough at the age of fourteen to begin recording in 1975 for producer Jo Jo Hookim.

His honorific of "Ranking" would set a trend for reggae artists, giving us many who rank, famous and otherwise. There is Ranking Ann, Ranking Barnabas, Ranking Buckers, Ranking Bukas, Ranking Caretaker, Ranking Courage, Ranking Devon, Ranking Dread, Ranking Fisheye, Ranking Jango, Ranking Jerry, Ranking Jessy, Ranking Joe, Ranking King, Ranking Lover, Ranking Mangum, Ranking Prendigras, Ranking Purple, Ranking Reuben, Ranking Roger, Ranking Scroo, Ranking Slackness, Ranking Spanner, Ranking Starkey, Ranking Superstar (an infrequent pseudonym used by Trevor) and Ranking Toyan. There is also Papa Ranking, Peter Ranking and Squidly Rankin. And that's not to mention Cutty Ranks, Delly Ranx, Gappy Ranks, Mikey Ranks, Echo Ranks, Shabba Ranks and the other such named.

The Original Ranking, as he is sometimes called, is known for his thick-throated voice that, instead of slowing him down, adds character to his chanting. He would record steadily through 1983, releasing about 60 singles and four albums, plus one shared with other artists. By 2012, he was a long-time resident of Great Britain, where he continued to perform live, until a traffic accident in Jamaica took his life.

'Masculine Gender', Trevor's DJ version of the 'Drifter' riddim (a song described in the chapter on Dennis Brown; page 333) was produced by Jo Jo Hookim in 1978. It appeared on Trevor's album of that year, called *In Fine Style.* Some years after the song's release, Trevor appeared in a video for the song. It includes all four requirements for a fun reggae video: a low budget, the artist nattily attired, a pretty girl and people dancing in a record store.

Trevor ropes you in right from the start. As the introduction to a fine dub version of the 'Drifter' riddim unspools, he studs it with a series of dub-enhanced throat noises – *uh-uhs* placed in the spaces between horn lines. This unlikely hook had a group of my friends walking around, uttering "uh-uh" at every turn for weeks after we first heard this song. Suddenly, the horns come to an echoing halt, Trevor exclaims, "Say so!", and the song takes full wing. Bass is belatedly heard, and Trevor chants to it. Then, after a guitar chop echoes off into the distance, reverb-soaked drums drop in. This oft-versioned riddim has never sounded better.

Though I've enjoyed this song hundreds of times since its release, I have to admit I have no idea what it's about. Colorful phrases flow, not one seemingly related to any other. Whatever it's all about, it's quite meaningful to Trevor, judging by the zeal of his delivery. His syrup-thick chanting is often tilted just a tick off-key, but that only serves to make him sound more interesting. Mid-song, there's a brief bongo solo that inspires him to jam by unleashing a stream of additional *uh-uhs*. A classic riddim, wonderfully dubbed, with a talented and eccentric DJ performance atop, pretty much guarantees "you bound to surrender" to 'Masculine Gender'. It's a track that is overdue for release on CD.

Ranking Trevor: '*Brown Skin Girl Rub-A-Dub*'
Ranking Trevor's 'Brown Skin Girl Rub-A-Dub' is the second half of a 1980 disco-mix single anchored by roots singer and producer Linval Thompson's 'Brown Skin Girl'. Thompson's half of the record is a perfectly good love song (unrelated to the Jamaican folk song of the same name) with a memorable bass line. But it does little to prepare you for the incomparably deep, dark, heavy dub DJ groove of Trevor's version. Carving it took four mighty implements working together. First is a reggae bass line that is so obese, you may have to reinforce your woofers. Second is an interesting drum pattern that challenges you to stay off your feet. It's slightly mechanical, foreshadowing the shift to dancehall soon to come. Third is the arrangement and its shrewd application of dub that milks every drop of potential from the riddim. Note, for example, how it compresses the guitar and keyboard to a grindy undertone. Fourth is Trevor's very rhythmic chanting in a voice that's thicker than molasses, regularly emitting a *waa!* as punctuation. As is the case in Thompson's song, Trevor is attracted to the titular woman. This is made very evident by the zeal of his performance, as well as the reference to his erection. But his vocal is far more about the sound of his chanting and its contribution to the groove than what he says.

Though Thompson's version is available on CD, Trevor's superior version is not. Record companies mean well, so how can this be? Perhaps the issue is that the medium's microscopic grooves (and the minute zeros and ones of a digital file) aren't capable of holding music this big. Until this is resolved, there's the 12-inch single, released on the UK-based Black Joy label.

Papa Tullo: '*Sweet Reggae Music*'; '*Straight To The Government*'
Though he was the best of the new generation of DJs who emerged at the start of the 1980s, there is little biographical information available on Everald Norman

Crawford, better known as Papa Tullo. This was not helped by a situation reminiscent of that of the little-known reggae drummer Fil Callender and his numerous billings. Papa Tullo was also known as Pappa Tollo, Poppa Tollo, Tullo T, Tulloch T and just Tullo, diffusing the greater fame he deserved and might otherwise have found. Unlike the larger-than-life DJ characters such as Scotty, Big Youth or Trinity, Papa Tullo comes off as a regular guy with a regular Jamaican voice, albeit one that happens to have great DJ skills, a very positive personality and a wonderfully enthusiastic delivery. An example of the latter is his catchphrase, "Well, watch out mon!", heard in so many of his songs. Throughout the 1980s, Tullo recorded more than 40 singles or DJ portions of disco-mixes and three albums, plus two more albums in *clash* style, on which he shared the tracks with other DJs.

Here are two must-hear Papa Tullo tracks, produced by Robert "Flacko" Palmer in 1981. Both were collected on a 1983 LP called *Straight To The Government*, which, although it has never been released on CD, is intermittently in print on vinyl and available at reggae specialty stores. Blow the dust off your turntable and enjoy.

'Sweet Reggae Music' is a joyride of a song. Of the many self-celebrating reggae songs that have been recorded, none can match it for its unbridled enthusiasm. The opening flow of dub drums barely concludes before Tullo is chanting a mile a minute over an introduction of dub-kissed horns and lead guitar. The body of the song begins, and Tullo slows down enough to get into the riddim's groove. And a good one it is, anchored by Sly & Robbie, with dub well applied all over and throughout. A grumbling start-and-stop bass line is in the driver's seat, and Tullo chants to it in melodic and rhythmic counterpoint. A honking sax and a reverbed guitar continually switch off playing the reggae chop, a simple detail of arrangement that adds depth to the sound. Lead guitar phrases, percussion and the horn theme heard in the song's introduction come and go and return *dubwise*.

Early on, Tullo makes pro-reggae and pro-music observations, suggesting that reggae is too sweet to be denied and that a dislike of music could only be explained as an illness. He chants genially about other issues. The riddim then begins to throw things at Tullo, and he seizes these challenges like an expert running an obstacle course. For example, the bass line briefly simplifies to an insistent note played three times, and Tullo adeptly rides the change, using the triplet as a springboard to conclude a line about reggae: "It make you *jump and twist*". These vocal calisthenics inspire him to boast about his physical fitness, including his ability to leap over a bottomless pit. Later, Sly snaps off one of his patented one-handed snare rolls to introduce a section that is predominantly just drum and bass. Tullo reacts by turning up the intensity of his chanting as he changes subject. He directs girls on how to take the lead when dancing with their boyfriends. Matching the backing music of the moment, part of this instruction is to follow the bass. As the song nears its end, following a section of especially sweet chanting, Tullo changes it up yet again. Seized by his passion for the subject, he moves to a more staccato delivery with a tighter rhythm, rolling his *rs*, as his lyrics become stream-of-consciousness run-on sentences. He should be exhausted, but he ends the song with great joy, enthusiasm and DJ virtuosity right through the song's fade-out.

The excellent riddim of 'Sweet Reggae Music' is under-versioned. The only other example I've heard is 'Jah Is Watching You' by roots singer Lacksley Castell, in disco-mix format with a modest dub version appended. It's good, but never having been released on LP or CD, is not necessarily worth seeking out. Save the effort for Tullo's LP.

'Straight To The Government' is a more somber song than 'Sweet Reggae Music', though no less impressive. It's a rent song, a theme that has resulted in a number of memorable reggae and mento songs already covered in this book. In this example, Tullo indicts the government as well as his landlord, referring to them as "Mister Government Man and his henchman, Mister Rent Man". In mento, rent woes were a source of wry humor, while in roots reggae the tone was more serious. But never has the protagonist been so disillusioned as here. Tullo equates the government man to a *sam fi man* – a con man:

> Say dat the government man, him a sell sam fi.
> Him sell a come me yard and then he tell pure lie.
> You can't a fe loan, they say you can't yet apply.
> And when dem left your yard, said dem a leave you a cry.
> © Blue Moon Music. Reproduced with permission,

His family circumstances are very bad, with a wife and five young children that are hungry. He begs for mercy, and promises to pay when he can. But this plea must have fallen on deaf ears, as an angry Tullo tells them that if they don't repent, they will wind up in Hell.

Serious stuff, but Tullo keeps it from being grim. Perhaps realizing how well the song was progressing, Tullo can't help but digress from his narrative for some requisite DJ self-aggrandizement and to enthuse about reggae. And he enlivens his performance with the playful DJ technique of percussively rolling nonsense syllables like an elaboration of rolled *r*s. These *bom-bom-bru-ro-ley u-ro-ley u-ro-ley*s help lighten the mood. Also playful are the reverbed inhaled gasps with which he sometimes ends his sentences – a DJ/dub punctuation mark. But make no mistake, even with these elements, this is a serious roots DJ performance. Matching it in tone and quality is another fine riddim from Sly & Robbie. This time it's Dunbar's drums rather than Shakespeare's bass that is most out front. He opens with a roll that reggae fans would recognize as Sly in less than a second. He then plays a devious bass drum-led rhythm that provides a fine framework for his frequent and varied rolls. There is little guitar but no horns or additional percussion. Instead, the riddim is filled out by keyboards. An electric piano is featured and its grounded stateliness supports Tullo's righteousness. Meanwhile, odd bent notes from a synthesizer whimper, echoing Tullo's distress.

This excellent riddim was also voiced by roots singer Lacksley Castell in the similarly themed 'Government Man' on the latter's 1982 CD collection, *Morning Glory*. This is a good song, but a better one to the same riddim is 'Music Crave' by roots singer Don Carlos, available on his 1982 CD, *Harvest Time*, and a variety of reggae CD compilations.

Papa Tullo: *'Girls Of Today'*
Produced by Henry "Junjo" Lawes in 1981, 'Girls Of Today' is an irresistible Papa Tullo song. It's the story of his less-than-ideal relationship with Rosie. When he calls, she won't talk to him. Worse, she smokes cigarettes rather than collie. He concludes that she just isn't *irie*.

The skanking, dubby riddim opens with a keening organ that's so trebly, it sounds like a tea-kettle. Over this, Tullo provides an impressive demonstration of the "fast-talk" DJ style. Though this would become quite popular with some DJs in the mid-1980s, it was rare for Tullo to take this approach. Also unusual for Tullo is the inclusion of some slack lyrics that explicitly describe a very fretful sexual encounter. Tullo shouldn't have expected anything else from Rosie. She expresses her unhappiness at every stage of the physical act, ultimately asking "if I sterilize it, Oh Lord!" Though explicit, these details are provided in the service of story-telling. Aided by clever rhymes, he prances through this adult content, just as his overall delivery prances through the riddim.

Junjo's dub engineers, Scientist and Barnabas, make the riddim dubby and spare. It stays engaging, with a rotation minimalistic dub piano, picked guitar and the keening organ changing to provide a mincing rhythmic strut that puts extra skank into the riddim. 'Girls Of Today' can be heard on the compilation album, *Whole New Generation Of DJ* that recently made its belated CD debut.

Clint Eastwood & General Saint: *'Can't Take Another World War'; 'Talk About Run'*
Clint Eastwood & General Saint are a DJ duo with a name that sounds like a compound mixed metaphor. Clint Eastwood was born Robert Brammer, the brother of another DJ, Trinity. General Saint was born Winston Hislop. Eastwood was well established on the scene, having already released more than 60 singles and seven albums, when the two came together in 1981. Saint had little résumé to speak of, but his nasal voice proved to be the perfect complement to Eastwood's rounded tones. Success followed with two internationally released albums. But within a few years, the team would separate as the two DJs pursued their solo careers. Both of these songs come from their 1981 album, *Two Bad D.J.*, produced by Chris Cracknell and Henry "Junjo" Lawes, with dub engineering from Barnabas and Scientist.

'Can't Take Another World War' is built on an interesting case of versioning. This track takes not so much the riddim of Johnny Osbourne's 'Love Is Universal' (a song described in the chapter on this artist; page 546) as just its drum and bass, dispensing with all other instruments and its sax-led lovers' rock sound. The producer and dub-master then alter the bass to make it more harmonic for a spacey effect. Laid over this are rocket noises and sci-fi-sounding keyboards and slide guitar that could have come from a Pink Floyd record. This completes the riddim's extreme makeover from lovers' rock to space reggae. It provides the right backing for Eastwood & Saint's song: an expression of anxiety over the arms race then in the news. They chant melodically in unison throughout, with the occasional burst of humorous histrionics that contributes greatly to this enjoyable, if unlikely, song.

'Talk About Run' is a cover of the 1962 Lord Kitchener calypso hit, 'Love In The Cemetery'. It quickly entered the mento repertoire, with King Barou, The Hiltonaires and others recording renditions. Here, it makes its reggae debut, sounding as if it was written for the flamboyant pair to chant over a dub backing. It's about an ill-advised romantic session in a graveyard that proves to be haunted. But where Kitchener was composed in telling the story, Eastwood & Saint are hysterical. When a ghost points out that Saint and his girl are kissing while on its grave, Saint describes his titular reaction: he ran so hard, he almost wound up breaking his head. "Kiss me neck!" he declares, using a Jamaican exclamation of surprise. There is no further mention of Saint's date, whom he must have abandoned in the cemetery after the worst date ever.

Michigan & Smiley: *'Diseases'; 'Sugar Daddy'*
Yellowman: *'Zungguzungguguzungguzeng'*
The DJ duo of Papa Michigan (Anthony Fairclough) and General Smiley (Erroll Bennett) appeared on the scene in 1978. Recording together until 1983, they had their share of hits. They released four albums over this time and have reunited occasionally since to record several more, the last coming in 1995. One of their biggest hits was the infamous 'Diseases', produced by Henry "Junjo" Lawes in 1981. This was a rather misguided song that grimly lists the diseases that Jah will inflict on the unrighteous. Unfortunately, in this song, the unrighteous are primarily defined as women who choose to wear pants (British, trousers) rather than dresses and indulge in other vanities. Thankfully, I guess, Michigan & Smiley find more deserving parties to smite with illness as the song progresses. The odd subject matter and the two DJs direly intoning a litany of serious diseases ending in -*itis* that automatically rhyme, over a fine upbeat riddim, proved to be a combination that caught the reggae fans' fancy. It can be heard on a number of reggae CD collections.

That riddim originally appeared in 'Mad Mad', a 1967 rock steady song by Alton Ellis that was produced by Coxsone Dodd. In 1977, trumpet player Bobby Ellis recorded an excellent instrumental version called 'Stormy Weather'. It jettisoned some chord changes that sound dated, and replaced the good bass line of the original with a contemporary high-stepping one. And it brought a rock steady brightness to languid reggae – a specialty of producer Sonia Pottinger. Ellis's version was the basis for 'Diseases', but not before it was further updated. The riddim's finest feature, its salutatory horns phrase, is brought forward, translated to guitar, while bubble-up organ, a dub production and Syndrum accents were added to complete the revision, now known as the 'Diseases' riddim. It provided a perfect vehicle for numerous DJs to ply their trade, making it more popular than at any other point in its fifteen-year life.

In 1983, Michigan & Smiley returned to the updated riddim for another hit with the Dr. Dread-produced 'Sugar Daddy'. Atoning for 'Diseases', they lighten up, show us a good time, and all is forgiven. The duo take turns at complaining that the other is more popular and detail their own virtues, ranging from the plausible (dreamy eyes) to the highly improbable (commander-in-chief of the armed forces). The song's vocal hook comes when Michigan & Smiley make the leap from DJs to singers with a ramshackle chorus introducing themselves, without injuring anyone too badly. Backing band The Roots Radics provide an engaging recut of the riddim. The simple bongo solo that opens the song and later makes a return gives the song another hook. The 'Mad Mad' riddim's refrain, originally heard on horns, then translated to guitar, on 'Diseases', is still a focal point for this version. First, it's given a mellowed-out, opened-up read on guitar. Then it's elaborated on when horns make their belated entrance. This playful DJ track can be heard on the Michigan & Smiley CD of the same name.

Yellowman was another DJ to jump on this riddim, riding it like a champion and also scoring a 1983 hit with the Junjo-produced 'Zungguzungguguzungguzeng'. The ascent of Yellowman, arguably the biggest reggae star in the period immediately after Bob Marley's death, could not have been more unlikely. He was born Winston Foster, in 1956 in Negril. Perhaps because he was an albino, a condition that is derided in Jamaica, he was abandoned as an infant and brought up in an orphanage. He later attended the famous Alpha Cottage School for Boys. Boldly embracing his albinism, he broke into DJing, christening himself Yellowman and, in case anyone was missing the point, dressing in a yellow suit. Apologizing to no one, he adopted a persona of confidence and braggadocio, frequently DJing about his conquests of women, sometimes with explicit slackness. This persona and his considerable stage charisma made him a sensation. He began recording in 1979, cranking out albums at an alarming rate. Prolific by any standard, in 1982 alone he released seven albums plus eight more in collaboration with other DJs. In 1984, he recorded an album for CBS Records – the only DJ album released on a major label. In all, he would release more than 50 albums, the last coming in 2005. Overcoming much and succeeding greatly, he would promote himself to "King Yellow". Yet his biggest challenges lay ahead. He was diagnosed as having cancer of the jaw in 1986 and was given a poor prognosis but, with the removal of a portion of his jawbone, he recovered. He then fought skin cancer in the early 1990s. In spite of this, he still performs today. Though the story of reggae is filled with performers who overcame great obstacles, none triumphed over as many as Yellowman.

On 'Zungguzungguguzungguzeng', King Yellow provides a melange of good vibes, folk wisdom, self-promotion, girl problems and anti-violence/pro-ganja sentiments. Perhaps the best line comes from Yellow's observation that his voice is not the norm for a DJ. He chants in a round-toned baritone, whereas most other DJs work in a higher register and often with a nasal voice. He equates this to the sonic differences between tinny AM and fuller-sounding FM radio disc-jockeys. A disco-mix of 'Zungguzungguguzungguzeng' with a dub version can be heard on the Yellowman CD of the same name. Be careful not to accidentally wind up with Yellow's lesser 1993 ragga remake of the song.

Yellowman: *'Morning Ride'*
The preferred rendition of 'Morning Ride' was produced in the early 1980s by Lloyd Campbell and is heard on the Yellowman LP, *One In A Million*. It's not to be confused with the not-as-good remake Yellow did for producer Henry "Junjo" Lawes a short time later that appears on several collections. This rendition stays true to its title, as both Yellowman and the riddim conjure up the pleasurable befuddled buzz of trying to function immediately upon waking. Yellow's delivery sounds like he rolled out of bed and straight to the microphone. The riddim (taken from Burning Spear's 'Black Disciples') is subdued, completely dominated by a somnolent bass line which is followed in turns by drowsy piano, guitar and, saved for the song's end, horns. There's lots of dub, courtesy of engineer Scientist, here creating the sensation of shaking off a dream. After describing the double-entendre virtues of the titular bus/sex ride (it's typically a good ride and may be the longest ride), Yellowman sleepwalks through a number of other topics, never failing for a moment to ride the riddim, no matter how early the hour. A good dub version of the riddim that continues the sleepy feeling, 'Swell Headed' by The Revolutionaries, can be heard on the CD compilation called *Drum Sound – More Gems From The Channel One Dub Room 1974 To 1980*.

Jim Brown: *'Jam It Up Tight'*
Prince Jazzbo & Jim Brown: *'Kechi Shubi'*
The DJ born Paul Sinclair adopted the stage name Jim Brown, before eventually changing it to Jim Nastic. Though far from prolific, Brown is remembered fondly for his DJ versions of classic Studio One riddims that he recorded in the late 1970s and early 1980s. (Two fine examples are 'See Him Deh' to the "Lecture" riddim and 'Minister For Ganja', recorded as a DJ duo with Rapper Robert to the "Full Up" riddim.) Brown's last work was an album in 2001, again for Dodd. Unfortunately for him, this Jim Brown is sometimes confused with another (in)famous Jamaican who adopted the name, that is, Lester Coke, head of the notorious drug gang, the Shower Posse, who would die in a fire in Kingston's General Penitentiary in the 1990s.

Appearing on its two best songs, Brown steals the show on the 1982 Studio One LP *Battle Of The DJs – Dance Hall Style*. As the title indicates, this set of performances from a group of DJs (ranging from stars of the genre to the unheard of) is recorded as it might have been performed live at the dance, with a parcel of DJs crowding around the mic, waiting for their turn to perform.

Brown's 'Jam It Up Tight' is set to a Coxsone Dodd recut of the riddim from the Duke Reid-produced 'Ba Ba Boom' by The Jamaicans (a song described earlier in this book; page 125). Once Brown begins to chant in his affable, enthusiastic style, the song becomes something of a communal performance. Unable to contain themselves, the other DJs shout encouragement, yell exclamations, pound on the nearest surface and generally react noisily. Encouraged rather than distracted, Brown chants about his place in dancehall, his style, and how he's a dandy. The other DJs never let up and he namechecks them at the end of the song, resulting in an even bigger outburst of this uniquely Jamaican racket.

Ketchy shubby is a Jamaican-rules version of cricket, with faster play and shorter matches. It provides the title ('Kechi Shubi') for Brown's duet with another DJ on the scene, the more nasal-sounding Prince Jazzbo. Born Linval Carter, though often referred to by his colorful nickname, "The Croaking Lizard", Prince Jazzbo also worked with Dodd, but later had a successful association with producer Lee Perry. He passed away in 2013 of lung cancer at the age of sixty-two. The song makes use of a classic Studio One riddim, a version of Vin Gordon's 'Heavenless' (a song described previously in this book; page 173). It's so roughly dubbed that you can picture an engineer yanking the faders rhythmically as the levels change. The song opens with some dancehall chaos. A female civilian provides a spoken introduction as the assembly of DJs again creates its particular commotion with all manner of chattering and yelling. Jazzbo opens with exaggerated sounds of inhaling ganja, and someone plays percussion on a bottle. Adding to the chaos, the song does not have a theme, instead jumping from one subject to another. In the end, it's Jazzbo who wins the prize for the most random personal revelation, explaining that he's country-born and "can drive a big back hoe".

Both songs are a ton of fun, and a reminder that while DJ reggae is recorded music for those outside of Jamaica, for dancehall-loving Jamaicans it's a music that is best enjoyed live. Perhaps Dodd's estate will one day release this LP (hopefully retaining the cover painting by Jamaal Pete) on CD.

Three DJs ride "Stalag"

The Technique's crucial instrumental 'Stalag 17' and Big Youth's DJ version of its riddim have been previously described in this book (pages 312 and 415). Each produced by Winston Riley in the late 1970s or early 1980s, the following are three more examples of how the "Stalag" riddim could inspire DJs and producers to the heights of their disciplines.

Sister Nancy: *'Bam Bam'*

Sister Nancy was born Ophlin Russell-Myers, in 1962 in Kingston. She had four-teen brothers and sisters, and her elder brother Robert preceded her into the DJ game as Brigadier Jerry. She began recording in 1980, and over the next few years she released just shy of 20 singles, one LP, and a portion of another with two other DJs. In the 2000s, her recording career restarted, working with overseas produc-ers in UK jungle and drum and bass reggae-influenced club music styles. Although not prolific, she did record a classic song in 'Bam Bam'. And as one of a very few successful female reggae DJs at the start of the 1980s, she helped pave the way for ragga stars Lady Saw, Tanya Stephens, Lady G and the rest.

Here's the recipe for Nancy's 'Bam Bam', a beloved song whose popularity has endured through the decades: start with a slab of great riddim, artfully fileted with dub. A fine DJ performance is the sauce and the chorus of a classic from Toots & The Maytals is a garnish. Serve it again and again.

Dub gives 'Bam Bam' a graduated opening. For the song's introduction, only the horn line is pulled from the riddim, with all else dropped out. Sister Nancy soon joins, her entire vocal performance treated with echo so that every word is heard twice. This gives the song a supreme bounciness, and serves to soften Nancy's typically astringent delivery. The body of the song begins, and now the only instrument heard is a honking sax, bleating on each beat. It's soon accented with occasional flashing guitar chords lit with reverb. When struck, these chords emphasize whatever Nancy is saying with bold, italics and underline. A notch of bass and drums is heard, teasing their belated entrance. They arrive, but at the expense of the sax, as drop-out/in continues to enliven the riddim throughout, windows rhythmically opening and closing on each instrument as per the pro-ducer's expertise. At no point is the entire instrumental arrangement from 'Stalag 17' heard. The original riddim was great, but here expert dub manipulates it into a therapeutic brain massage.

Meanwhile, for your consideration, Nancy chants about herself in a good example of a common DJ theme, the self-introduction. She provides the listener with some biographical information, musing on the source of her talent and her career intentions:

> Some a dem ask me where me get it [her ambition to be a DJ] from.
> I told dem, 'No know, it's from creation'...
> Me born and me grow in a Kingston 6.
> I Nancy write the priceless lyrics ...
> I never trouble no one,
> I'm a lady, I'm not a man,
> MC is my ambition,
> I come fe nice up Jamaica.

'Bam Bam' can be heard on Sister Nancy's CD *One Two* and on several reggae compilations CDs.

Lone Ranger: *'Fe Mi Woman A De Bes'*
Lone Ranger's take on 'Stalag' is sometimes less phonetically titled 'Fi Me Woman A The Best'. Like 'Bam Bam', it features a graduated opening and a dub mix, a fact that Ranger comments on: "Me have to play it in a rub a dub style". But it's a different dub mix from that of Sister Nancy's song. Rather than being persistent, echo only occasionally visits Ranger's voice, as it jumps around to various instruments. More of the horn section is heard, as are oddball organ chords not heard in 'Bam Bam'. The overall result is a tougher dub mix than the moonwalk of Nancy's song.

Ranger's performance is all enthusiasm and energy. He opens with über-rhythmic fast-talk chanting over an echoing drum strike. As the body of the song enters in phases, he chants down the bass, even before the bass is heard. He covers a variety of topics before focusing on the titular theme:

> Aye, aye, me say the girl no tell lie ...
> Yes, yes, fe me 'oman a de best in a any contest ...
> Me like how she kiss, me like how she caress.
> Me like when she play with every hair in on me chest.
> © Westbury Music Ltd. Reproduced with permission.

He further explains that she is unlike other girls from up North. Apparently, these girls like to gamble, whether it's the track or the numbers game "peaka peow". "You have fe lick dem with a coconut bow", he explains – strike them with a bowl made from half a coconut. All along, he punctuates affirmatively with his trademark raspy exclamations of *right!* Ranger's 'Fe Mi Woman A De Bes' is a bracing DJ performance, another great drink from the deep 'Stalag' well. It can be heard on his CD, *Rosemarie Meet DJ Daddy*.

General Echo: *'Arleen'*
General Echo was born Earl Anthony Robinson, in 1955 in Kingston. After working at such sound systems as Gemini, Stereo Phonic and Ray Symbolic, he started one of his own called Tone Hi Fi. He began recording in the late 1970s and although not nearly as prolific as many other DJs, he had his share of memorable songs. This was in large part due to the cool his chanting exuded, befitting his cool stage name. Notoriously, some of his records were explicitly *slack*, sometimes recorded under the pseudonym of Ranking Slackness, but none of his best songs are in this style. He recorded 28 singles and five albums, plus one more shared with another DJ, but his career was cut tragically short in 1980. In Kingston, the police pulled over the car in which he, Flux, the selector of his sound system, and Leon "Big John" Johns, owner of the Stereo Phonic sound, were traveling. For reasons still unresolved, the police shot all three men dead.

Producer Riley took a totally different tack with the Stalag riddim on General Echo's 'Arleen', and another classic version was born. Dub effects are used minimally, except for the fact that most of the instruments are completely dropped out. Gone are the horn lines, honking sax and rhythm guitar. Long gone are the hot organ and guitar solos. Everything is gone except bass, drum and the DJ. This minimalistic arrangement is perhaps the only three-piece reggae vocal song ever recorded (though, towards the end of the song, organ pokes its head out for the briefest of moments, then realizing it's not needed, vanishes). But not only does the song not suffer for it –on the contrary, 'Arleen' is superb. A DJ chanting over a tricky, swinging rhythm section sounds as if Jamaicans had crashed a 1950s beatnik coffee house in the USA to create a Jamaican form of beat poetry. *"Cool, daddy-o." "Ites."*

Rather than being pressed to do more by such an austere arrangement, Echo stays composed. In fact, he oozes cool, as he calmly and clearly chants in a soft lilting cadence that borders on singing. Listen to how he effortlessly ratchets up the intensity by emphasizing the first syllable of the song's famous droning refrain, "Arleen-a was a dream". Sounding not quite like any other, this is a masterful DJ performance. The song is about Echo's young girlfriend, who is more interested in food than in the General: as "every time me check her, she cook sardine". He also makes comments on the song itself: "This rub-a-dub hard, the people love it so." At one point these two subjects collide:

> When we take her out, she wouldn't stop eating.
> Lord you should have hear her ask me for bean:
> 'One little beans, two little beans, t'ree little beans and a more bass please'.
>
> © Westbury Music Ltd. Reproduced with permission.

'Arleen' can be heard on several CD compilations. Not yet compiled is the original 45-rpm single's dub version B-side that dropped out most of Echo's vocal. The resulting drum and bass track is perfect for aspiring DJs everywhere. Also uncollected is Echo's far less successful re-voicing of a fuller version of the same riddim called 'Flora Lee'.

46 Bob Marley & The Wailers, Part 7: The internationally released LPs

Chris Blackwell is a white Jamaican of upper-class background. As a young man working at the island's resorts, he became interested in recording local music. A jazz LP in 1960 was the first release on his new Island Records label. It starred Bermudan pianist Lance Haywood, who had been performing at a Jamaican resort, on one side, and Jamaican guitarist Ernest Ranglin on the other. Island's first big success came in 1964 with Millie Small's pop-ska cover of 'My Boy Lollypop', arranged by Ranglin. It reached no.2 in both the US and UK charts, giving Blackwell an entrée to overseas markets. By the early 1970s, when The Wailers began their association with Island, it was a thriving reggae label internationally as well as at home and had branched out as a force in UK rock and folk, with numerous successful album releases. The association between The Wailers and Blackwell was not planned. The group appeared in his London office in 1972 after an ill-fated UK tour organized by JAD left them essentially abandoned in England. At this, their first meeting, The Wailers so impressed Blackwell that he sent them away with a large cash advance to record an LP of new material for his label. Blackwell no doubt recognized a potential replacement for his most internationally successful reggae star, Jimmy Cliff, who had recently left him. He could not have dreamt the full impact – artistic, financial or cultural – of what ultimately would come of this deal.

Supposedly, Blackwell's associates told him that he had thrown the money away and would receive nothing in return. They could not have been more wrong, as The Wailers quickly delivered an album, *Catch A Fire*, with which Chris Blackwell would succeed where other great producers had failed, breaking The Wailers overseas. As subsequent Wailers LPs appeared with Island, Bob Marley & The Wailers became superstars around the world. Blackwell accomplished this by avoiding mistakes that Leslie Kong and JAD made. And he had some tricks up his sleeve that none of The Wailers' Jamaican producers would have considered.

He gave The Wailers complete control of the sessions, without trying to influence the direction of the music, not even making an appearance. The group had the freedom to choose their own backing band rather than having non-Jamaican sessions musicians foisted on them, as JAD too often had done. They cherry-picked The Upsetters, stealing them away from Lee Perry and making them members of the group. In Jamaica's Dynamic Sounds, they were able to choose a studio where they felt comfortable rather than being forced to work overseas as was often the case with JAD. Although the album came together quickly, they were able to work at their own pace, unlike the rushed Kong sessions. The result was an LP that was 100 per cent pure, unadulterated, cutting-edge Jamaican reggae. There was no sign of the compromised or diluted sounds that Kong and JAD used to entice non-Jamaicans. Nor did Blackwell ask them to tamp down the lyrical content, which ranged from (most frequently) serious roots reggae sentiments to love songs. (However, although Rasta themes were evident, the band abstained for now from naming Jah or Rastafarianism, perhaps afraid that they might alienate international audiences.) The result was an excellent Wailers album of nine very strong and varied songs.

But this was only half of the Island equation, since The Wailers' work with Lee Perry had already proved that strong, unadulterated material was not enough to break the group overseas. Blackwell made additions to the master tapes specifically to appeal to fans in the USA and the UK. But rather than funk up the music for the soul fans who just weren't biting, or watering it down for pop fans who preferred local product, Blackwell instead targeted the white rock fans who were buying Island's rock and folk LPs. The label had established a cachet of cool, and so its fans were open to the next new progressive rock or exotic folk sound that Island would make available. Blackwell knew that, for these fans, outstanding lead guitar would give The Wailers' music instant credibility, as rock fans of this period lived and died by lead guitar. It opened their ears, and they found that they liked the reggae that poured in. Excellent, tasteful, simpatico rock guitar was added to several songs, and it proved to be the Trojan horse for the reggae's international invasion.

Catch A Fire was both an artistic success and a cross-over success. It launched the years of Bob Marley & The Wailers' international popularity that continues unabated today, decades after his death. *Catch A Fire* and the Island albums that followed would be unrivaled in popularity by any other reggae release.

Within a few LPs, the sound on these releases would develop into the brightest, most colorful of all The Wailers' music. Bass and drums and lead vocals provided the body of the music, while a big band of guitars, keyboards, horns, backing vocals and percussion splayed out like incandescent peacock feathers, with dub sometimes making them luminescent. Though it has become fashionable to call the Lee Perry sessions The Wailers' best body of work, I just don't see them as better than the Island material, which is more varied in sound, bigger in size and more consistent. Taken as a whole, the eight international albums (there were also live releases and a posthumous collection) contain numerous great tracks, more than a few classic songs, some others that were good, and nary a one that could be called a bad song. But along the way, Bunny Wailer and Peter Tosh would leave The Wailers forever.

Catch A Fire

Many consider 1973's *Catch A Fire* to be Bob Marley's best album. It's easy to understand why. Added to The Wailers' usual array of musical riches, *Catch A Fire* showcases both a Bob Marley whose singing and songwriting had fully matured and a revolutionary instrumental arrangement.

Though his singing always possessed a vibrancy of spirit and great charisma, young Bob at Studio One didn't always have command of his voice. But his control grew over time. From the point of *Catch A Fire* through to the end of his career, Bob demonstrated complete mastery of his voice, never taking a single errant step again. This matured technique, combined with his emotional range and an endless reserve of intensity that he could tap at will as needed, made him exceptionally expressive and one of reggae's very best singers. This special combination of skills set Bob apart from the many other Jamaican singers who sounded similar to him, such as his contemporaries Albert Griffiths of The Gladiators, Pipe Matthews of The Wailing Souls and (at times) Lee Perry. The same is true for those who came after, including his sons and the various singers that replaced him posthumously in The Wailers Band, each of whom carries on his legacy. All are good singers in their own right, but none as good as Bob Marley.

Of the album's nine tracks, five are new and four are remakes of varying levels of success. Marley has seven lead vocals, Tosh has two and (reminiscent of the Kong-produced LP), Bunny has none. (He would have to wait for the follow-up album, *Burnin'*, released later the same year.) *Catch A Fire* and its follow-up, *Burnin'*, are devoid of horns, and it is the only one of the Island albums without a second percussionist (with one track an exception). This could have been a purely artistic decision, Bob just not wanting to work with those sounds at that time. (His last album, *Uprising*, also had no horns, but it is one of his best.) Or it could have been a logistical one, as The Wailers wanted to turn over the album quickly and be able to perform it live. Using other musicians would have made both more difficult. Or it could have been a financial one, with The Wailers wanting to be frugal with their cash advance. Or it could have been a commercial decision, with The Wailers wanting to sound more like a rock band. Whatever the reason or combination of reasons, the music did not suffer from the lack of horns and extra percussion, as the incomparable Barrett brothers and keyboards and guitars from Jamaica and elsewhere were all the backing The Wailers would need.

'Concrete Jungle'

The album's opener is a remake of 'Concrete Jungle'. But the brisk, tart, horn-filled self-produced 1971 original is reborn here as a stunning roots-rock classic. It's introduced with a moody instrumental jam from organ, rhythm guitar, clavichord, drums and the sparsest of bass lines, courtesy of guest bassist Robbie Shakespeare. The clavichord is played by UK sessions man John "Rabbit" Bundrick, who previously worked with The Wailers as part of their non-Jamaican backing band for the JAD sessions and was overdubbed onto the original master tapes by Blackwell. It establishes an instrument that would figure in Bob's music to the end of his career, would become a defining element of Peter Tosh's post-Wailers sound, and would henceforth become an ingredient in the sound of roots reggae in general. Suddenly, a filigreed guitar solo rises up into the mix. As it slows to an ascending series of notes on the verge of feedback, the rhythm guitar begins to play lead, and the two lines intertwine. This world-class guitar is played by Wayne Perkins, a session guitarist attached to the Muscle Shoals Studio in Alabama, the second of two musicians overdubbed by Blackwell. With rock fans' attention well in hand, the body of the song begins.

The song has a deliberate pace that suits Bob's lead vocal. It gives him room to fully express anguish, working his idiosyncratic quivering vibrato, and turning on the intensity as the lyrics demand. He sings of being trapped in an oppressive concrete jungle, denied a better life. This was a smart choice of a remake. Without any reference to the nature of the oppression or to a specific place, the concrete jungle can be any dangerous aspect of any city, making the song immediately relevant to urbanites around the world. Wailers fans were by now long accustomed to hearing stellar backing vocals in song after song. Yet Bunny and Peter somehow raise their game on 'Concrete Jungle'. With lines in varied pitches, sometimes singing with an edge never displayed outside of this particular song, they add to its considerable drama.

Mid-song, Wayne Perkins is heard again as he provides a masterful guitar solo with expert touches of sustain and distortion, while piano is added to the backing. It's amazing how well suited his work is to the song, especially considering that he had never heard reggae before Blackwell played him the master tape at the session. Bob loved Perkin's work. Purists may quibble, but they'd be wrong. Perkins proves to be an artistic collaborator rather than anything resembling a cheap commercial ploy. He makes a great song even greater. So great, it would have had a major influence on international reggae, essentially launching it as a sub-style. Bob Marley & The Wailers from this point forward, as was true for Peter Tosh, Black Uhuru, Steel Pulse and any other reggae artist who had aspirations of cross-over success, were sure to include rock lead guitar in their music, especially when they toured overseas.

'Slave Driver'

Though a number of previous Wailers songs ('African Herbsman', 'Crazy Baldhead', 'Soul Captives', '400 Years', etc.) broached the subject of slavery, 'Slave Driver' confronts the subject head on. Bob explores the pain felt by history's African slaves: He brings this around to the lasting aftermath on the black slave-descended population of Jamaica. This message of revolution, the strongest of The Wailers' career, is something that would have turned the cross-over dreams of Leslie Kong and JAD into nightmares. But Blackwell wisely did not bat an eye, recognizing that 'Slave Driver' is a great Wailers song,

Bob is well supported by backing vocals from Peter and Bunny that somehow manage to be simultaneously pretty and dread. A lean, tough, organ-led instrumental arrangement chock-full of flinty rhythm guitar is not far removed from the Lee Perry-produced sides of a few years earlier. And with 'Slave Driver', the purist that fretted about 'Concrete Jungle' was instantly mollified. The new fan was further impressed by the seriousness and sound of pure roots reggae.

'400 Years'; 'Stop That Train'

Peter has two lead vocals on *Catch A Fire*, and both are remakes of previously recorded songs. Faithful remakes, but not identical. The original Perry-produced '400 Years' bristled with anger, while here it's more of a lament. Nor did the original enjoy backing vocals this lush, nor did it have clavichord and understated synthesizer from Rabbit Bundrick. Though not necessarily better, it's every bit as good as the original, the listener's mood at the moment determining which is best. 'Stop That Train', a song originally recorded for Leslie Kong, trades that rendition's merry rock steady backing for a slower, stately, gospel-reggae arrangement that better suits the song. This surprising and successful return to a form that The Wailers previously had trouble mastering proved to be the last gospel song they would record, closing that uneven chapter on a positive note.

'Baby We've Got A Date' (aka 'Rock It Baby')

After four serious songs, the lovers' rock of 'Baby We've Got A Date' marks a shift in the album's tone, kicking off a string of three tracks about love and making love. Although the Wailers' middle-period love songs sometimes eluded greatness, this (the first love song of their international years) and those that followed, were considerably stronger.

The lyrics are perhaps the simplest of Bob's career. Sounding genuinely excited, he's looking forward to his date and assures his love that they will have a good time. He is accompanied by a seductively plush arrangement. On their way to becoming two-thirds of the greatest replacement vocal group in the history of music, Rita Marley and Marcia Griffiths bring their backing vocals to supplement those of Bunny and Peter. The song alternatives between rootsier male and voluptuous female choruses rather than combining the four voices. The instrumentation adds to the sweetness with something extra as well. Easy-going Hawaiian slide guitar played by Perkins is the lead instrument, backed by reggae drums, organ, rhythm guitar and Bunny on bass.

'Stir It Up'

The final of four remakes on *Catch A Fire* is a new rendition of their self-produced rock steady track, 'Stir It Up'. This song about making love features the unusual rhythm section of Sparrow Martin on drums and Robbie Shakespeare on bass. (Robbie's playing here and on 'Concrete Jungle' marks the extent of the great Sly & Robbie's involvement in the creation of Bob Marley's music. They would also go on to provide posthumous overdubs on some incomplete Bob Marley & The Wailers material and would also be heavily involved in the post-break-up solo careers of Peter Tosh and Bunny Wailer.)

This is the weakest of the album's remakes, as this rendition does not compare well to the original. The slower pace is part of the problem, but this time, Black-well's overdubbing hurts rather than helps – a fact that he has since admitted. Perkins's guitar is uninspired and an overbearing synthesizer track quickly wears thin and today sounds dated. For a song called 'Stir It Up' that celebrates sex, no one sounds very excited. Stick to the original rendition with its sprightly vocals and full-of-life arrangement.

'Kinky Reggae'
In the saucy 'Kinky Reggae', ladies' man Bob has it both ways. His mischievous vocal revels in the sexy goings on around him, couched in a series of crazy double entendres that he delivers with relish. But being a good Rasta, he rejects it all in the end. Yet he describes his departure as a "hit and run" and may otherwise clue us in that he didn't totally distance himself from it all. The band provides a solid backing that conveys a sly wink. Most notable is drummer Carlton Barrett. Sub-dued on the album up to this point, here he is able to air it out in his inimitable style, unleashing a variety of tumbling rolls and fills while maintaining a loose groove for the rest of the band to follow.

'No More Trouble'
The album turns serious again for its final two tracks. The impressive 'No More Trouble' is a sober, dramatic plea to choose love over conflict, to help those in need and to stay positive. This is emotionally expressed in the titular chorus. Later in the song, Bob surprises with a couplet where he shows the limits of his tolerance. He pleads that people not speak to him negatively or tell him of their conflicts, demanding positivity instead. Rita and Marcia are again included in the backing vocals, this time singing in unison with Bunny and Peter. The instrumentation is tough and dignified with Bundrick's clavinet out front, working off "Family Man" Barrett's weighty bass line. 'No More Trouble' is creative roots reggae with an intensity held at low boil.

'Midnight Ravers'
Catch A Fire closes with the dramatically ominous 'Midnight Ravers'. In it, Bob describes a nightmare vision of a smoke filled world with people that can't be fully seen and masses of supernatural chariots. Never before or since would Bob's lyrics be so fantastical. The meaning of this song has been subject to much speculation. But putting aside the nightmare imagery, the references to "people swinging" and the title may offer an explanation. Bob may be reacting to nightlife activities of the fast company he had been recently exposed to in his travels to Sweden and England in his work for JAD. (The same experiences may have also inspired 'Kinky

Reggae', but there he shook it off with a wink.) Strategic applications of reverb on Bob's vocal and spooky organ lines support his frightening story. The backing is dread roots reggae, suitably bass-heavy, complete with the return of Seeco Patterson and his Nyabinghi hand drum, with no sign of Bundrick or Perkins. 'Midnight Ravers' gives the album a closer as strong and distinctive as its famous opener.

'Ravers Version', the B-side of the song's original single release is of note. A radical dub, it strips away most of the song, leaving not much more than just bass and drum. It gives the listener another way to appreciate the melodic, rhythmic and compositional talents of the Barrett brothers. Surprisingly, it has never been compiled on LP or CD.

Deluxe Edition tracks
In 2001, Island Records released the two-CD *Catch A Fire Deluxe Edition*. It adds two songs ('High Tide Or Low Tide' and 'All Day All Night') that had been recorded for but were omitted from the album. It also includes "The Unreleased Jamaican Versions" of the original album's nine tracks. These are the mixes that were delivered to Blackwell before he applied the overdubs that helped create the *Catch A Fire* that is known and loved worldwide.

'High Tide Or Low Tide' is a very pretty R&B ballad, perhaps the softest ballad of The Wailers' entire career. There was room on the vinyl LP and the track has merit. But it might have sounded out of place on the more vigorous and more Jamaican-sounding *Catch A Fire*, making its delayed debut understandable. The reggae love song 'All Day All Night' is a good but flawed track, accounting for its omission. But its eventual release is welcome. Though it threatens to founder at its start, the ship is quickly righted. And at its peak, there's a stunning section where Bob, Bunny and Peter each take turns singing the same proclamation of love that's a joy to hear.

The "Unreleased Jamaican Versions" can differ greatly or minutely from the album mixes. Where they differ, they may be as good, better or worse than the album mix. Some sound complete, while others sound nearly finished, but waiting for a final application of studio polish. They give us the opportunity to hear not only the album before Blackwell's overdubs, but also some instrumentation that was scrubbed from the finished album and, surprisingly, an occasional alternative vocal take.

Most interesting – no surprise – is 'Concrete Jungle' sans its famous overdubs. Yet it survives as a surprisingly different rootsier track that is nearly as enjoyable as the album mix. Replacing Perkins's guitar and Bundrick's clavichord and piano is a mournful acoustic guitar that was completely excised on the album mix. Past the halfway point, unexpectedly, different lead and backing vocal tracks are heard, with some different lyrics too. And where there was a guitar solo, the vocals continue uninterrupted in this mix. This release gives fans of the classic rendition of 'Concrete Jungle' an exciting alternate way to hear the song, and provides the purists with what they wanted to hear when the album was originally released twenty-eight years earlier.

The Jamaican Versions' mix of 'Baby We've Got A Date' loses its lushness, as not only is Perkins's Hawaiian guitar not yet part of the mix, but neither are Rita Marley and Marcia Griffiths. Point goes to the album mix. 'Stir It Up' is relieved of its sludgy layer of overdubbed guitar and synthesizer and reveals a sparse arrangement that includes some simple rhythm piano and picked guitar that were dropped by Blackwell. Point to this mix, though it still does not top the 1967 rock steady original.

'No More Trouble' sounds sparse and airy in the Jamaican Versions' mix, lacking Bundrick's dominating clavinet. Suddenly, the bass is the instrument of focus. More alternative vocals are heard, including a bit of Peter and Bunny that was excised from the album mix. And since this mix is more than a minute longer, with some previously unheard lyrics, it gets the nod over the fine album mix. Also worth a listen is 'Kinky Reggae', which seems to be an entirely different take from the album rendition. New vocals with slightly different lyrics and new instrumentation are heard throughout. It's good, but does not topple the album mix.

Some may prefer the Jamaican Versions' rootsier take of '400 Years'. It loses the synthesized harpsichord and Bundrick's other keyboards, and returns Jamaican keyboard tracks for a less international sound. Though the difference is more subtle, the same is true for 'Stop That Train', with both its gospel and roots aspects coming across more directly. Both mixes of 'Slave Driver' are just about identical. Both mixes of 'Midnight Ravers' are nearly identical, except for the levels and the reverb used to add drama to the vocals on the album mix.

Burnin'

The similarly named follow-up to *Catch A Fire*, which appeared in the same year, *Burnin'* is the final chapter in the fruitful collaboration between Bob Marley, Peter Tosh and Bunny Wailer. Following its completion, Peter and Bunny would leave The Wailers to pursue their successful solo careers, leaving Bob the sole original member and standard-bearer of the revered Wailers name. Taken with *Catch A Fire*, *Burnin'* is viewed by many as the pinnacle of The Wailers' ten-year partnership. But closer examination shows that in spite of some peaks that reach very high, *Burnin'* lacks the consistency of *Catch A Fire*.

Of *Burnin'*'s ten tracks, Bunny gets two songs for his international lead vocal debut, and Peter has one. However, the addition of three bonus tracks to later CD editions of *Burnin'* doubled their contributions. A 2004 double-CD Deluxe Edition of *Burnin'* added two more bonus tracks (alternative recordings of 'Get Up, Stand Up'), along with a live show from 1973.

In *Catch A Fire*, we saw Bob in several roles: the advocate for social justice, the lover, the revolutionary, the *suffera* and the introspect. On *Burnin'*, Bob the lover is absent, while another aspect of Bob Marley is introduced to international audiences, and in no uncertain terms: the Rastaman. (Two final aspects would wait until the next album, *Natty Dread*: life-of-the-party Bob is introduced and, on the opposite side of the coin, Bob's brief foray into militancy.) Some Bob Marley fans seem to value only some of his aspects, while others enjoy all equally.

Burning' has less of an internationalized sound than its predecessor. Providing hand percussion on a number of songs, Seeco Patterson is back in the fold, and to stay. Perkins and Bundrick were not involved with *Burnin'*, nor would they record with Bob again. (But their legacy would continue. Bundrick's influence is heard in the continued use of clavichord on *Burnin'* and thereafter. And Perkins's influence would be heard on the next album, *Natty Dread* and thereafter, as Bob added a lead guitarist with rock leanings to the instrumental Wailers.) Also gone are the future I-Threes who guested on the previous album. But this situation would change drastically on the next album and thereafter. Half of *Burnin'*'s ten tracks are remakes. But it was three uncompromising great new songs, the first three described below, that are the most memorable on the album.

'Get Up, Stand Up'

A red-hot drum roll with a precision that could only come from Carlton Barrett opens the album and sets the tone for 'Get Up, Stand Up'. It's revolution time, as The Wailers provide the world with a universal protest song. It's fueled by the fiery lead vocals from two Wailers, and a militant instrumental arrangement. Nothing this incendiary had ever been heard in reggae, and very little outside of it.

The backing is lean, athletic, aggressive reggae, made spiky with Seeco Patterson's incidental percussion. Only the jazzy electric piano that plays off the bass line does anything to soften the sound, perhaps being there to keep the track from totally combusting. Co-authors Bob and Peter share lead vocals and harmonize on the chorus. Both contribute a great vocal performance, as Marley takes two verses and Tosh comes in for the third, like a secret weapon held in reserve. And although Marley was burning like a firebrand, Tosh's anger is white-hot. The effect is of two revolutionaries working in collaboration. It's riveting.

(Uncharacteristically, Bunny is nowhere to be heard, making this a rare Bob-Peter duet. Collectors are familiar with an out-take from the session with harmonies from Bunny. But they amounted to surprisingly little and only seemed to add fat to the lean, muscular song. Wisely, they were omitted, leaving a lean, mean, two-headed Wailers beast.)

With its universally known rallying-call chorus, to get up and stand up for your rights, the song would quickly become an anthem against any tyranny or institutional injustice. That one verse contained a strong Rasta rejection of the Christianity of Babylon did not prove to be problematic. The song closes with both Bob and Peter bouncing off each other on the chorus. The Wailers would never again sound as fierce as they do here. Bob, Peter and even Bunny would each subsequently record their own solo renditions of 'Get Up, Stand Up'. But although these renditions were good, none could match the original – the only song that features Bob Marley and Peter Tosh pushing each other to greater heights of Rasta revolution.

The Deluxe Edition of *Burnin'* contains two additional recordings of 'Get Up, Stand Up'. The first is an alternative take, perhaps a demo, with a slower pace and an energy level that does not match that of the original. The second, another mix of the album cut that had been considered for release as a single, is more interesting. Bob's vocal is from a different take, bursting with energy and with some different lyrics. Peter's vocal is the same as on the album rendition, but the different mix reveals previously buried parts of his performance. Though it does not surpass the original, it's a most enjoyable alternative mix.

'I Shot The Sheriff'
'I Shot The Sheriff' is a brisk and sinewy song that cuts like a ratchet knife. The band provides a flinty, slightly funky reggae backing, with a twisty descending organ-led riff that's the song's tent pole. And under the tent, The Wailers unleash a superb performance. Bob is anguished as he describes being backed into a corner by the sheriff's escalating hatred for him. The band provides a taut, tough reggae backing. But it's Bunny and Peter's backing vocals that threaten to steal the song with their soul-by-way-of-Jamaica harmonies. They've been this soulful before, but never so cuttingly sharp. Hear how they alternate between words and wordlessness. Hear how Peter drops down low from falsetto, and back to falsetto again. And hear Bunny; always hear Bunny.

'I Shot The Sheriff' is a song of social justice with revolutionary undertones. On the surface it seems to be a simple story of self-defense. Bob must shoot the sheriff who is about to murder him without cause. But the sheriff is also a symbol of deliberate systemic oppression or worse, as shown by his destruction every time Bob "plants a seed". Bob is matter of fact about the shooting. Its inevitability is expressed by the Jamaican folk saying about the well bucket that works every day until the day it doesn't, already familiar for its inclusion in The Ethiopians' 'Everything Crash' (a song previously described in the chapter on these singers; page 164). Bob then explodes, stuttering as he sings the song's title. Whether this is a cry of agony or ecstasy is up to the listeners to decide. While pondering this, they can enjoy the song's extended jamming instrumental run-out. The guitars and keyboards fade out, leaving only drum and bass, treating many non-Jamaicans to their first taste of dub.

In 1975, a live rendition of 'I Shot The Sheriff' appeared on the Bob Marley & The Wailers *Live!* concert album and greatly surpassed the *Burnin'* rendition in popularity. Though this slow-burning rendition is great in its own right, it can't match the vocal fireworks or the intensity of the original rendition. The live rendition's popularity was no doubt boosted by Eric Clapton's 1974 cover of the song that gave him an unlikely number 1 hit. Credit him for recognizing the song and being able to turn it into a radio-friendly melange of funk, rock and reggae. But don't over-credit him – Clapton's cover just can't compare to The Wailers' searing original or the rendition on *Live!*

'Rastaman Chant'

Bob exposes an international audience to Rastafarianism for the first time on *Burnin'*, and does so unequivocally. The album's closer (before it was later lengthened with CD bonus tracks), 'Rastaman Chant' was the first Nyabinghi-reggae song the Wailers had recorded since the late 1960s and the first time that "Rasta" appeared in the title of a Wailers song since the 1966 Studio One single, 'Rasta Shook Them Up'. The three Wailers and Seeco Patterson prove effective as a Nyabinghi drum troupe. Their playing is combined with reggae bass, drums and keyboards. The song is chant-sung in the Nyabinghi way, with Bob singing lead, sometimes in unison with Bunny and Peter's spiritual, rootsy harmonies. As often in Nyabinghi songs, a combination of Rasta sentiments and expressions with those from traditional American spirituals is heard.

With 'Rastaman Chant', The Wailers continue their small but consistently fine string of Nyabinghi songs. Its inclusion on *Burnin'*, along with the album's inner sleeve that humanizes dreadlocked Rastas and the back-cover image of a dreadlocked Bob drawing off a spliff (remember, the similar image on the cover of *Catch A Fire* was not that album's original jacket, but one that came later), signals a firm end to The Wailers suppressing expressions of their faith to international audiences.

'Burnin' And Lootin''

Also opening with nightmare imagery, the song that gives the album its name, "Burnin' And Lootin'", is reminiscent of *Catch A Fire*'s "No More Trouble". Bob envisions the oppression of Babylon as one step away from a Kafkaesque nightmare of imprisonment by unrecognizable uniformed fascists. He warns of the responses in the title. And although he softens this by targeting the burning at illusion and pollution, clearly, this is another song by Bob in his revolutionary aspect. But he's a reluctant revolutionary, sounding mournful rather than taking any pleasure in what he describes. The low-key instrumentation that simmers echoes these strong, sorrowful feelings.

'Pass It On'; 'Hallelujah Time'; 'Reincarnated Souls'; 'Oppressed Song'

On these four tracks, Bunny Wailer unveils his own brand of pastoral roots reggae that not only sounds like no one else, it sounds unlike any previous Bunny Wailer song. It's characterized by gentle melodies, sometimes diffuse but always positive and spiritual lyrics; an organic feel that is suited for acoustic instruments, even if they are not always employed, and an idyllic calm. This style of reggae answers the previously unasked question, "What would Jesus do, if he recorded roots?"

A remake of 'Pass It On' is almost unrecognizable from the original self-produced rendition, with different verses and no sign of the earlier recording's stridency. Bunny makes an appeal for good behavior and helping others rather than engaging in selfishness, as Nyah hand drums and electric piano are featured. A slightly different mix of 'Pass It On' can be heard on the soundtrack album for the movie *Countryman*. 'Hallelujah Time' soothingly addresses broad spiritual and earthly matters. As the second song on the album, it served as a firebreak between 'Get Up, Stand Up' and 'I Shot The Sheriff'. Bonus track 'Reincarnated Souls' features diffuse spiritual lyrics and a touch of funk. Another bonus track, 'The Oppressed Song', is quite good. It describes the journey of the *suffera*, forced into bad behavior, on to the more enlightened life of Rastaman. It is the only solo vocal performance on the expanded *Burnin'*, and the only song with acoustic guitar.

Bunny included renditions of 'Reincarnated Souls' and 'Oppressed Song' on his first solo album, the largely pastoral *Blackheart Man*, in 1976. Sadly, Bunny's finest pastoral reggae song, 'Searching For Love' (a song described in the Bunny Wailer chapter of this book; page 515) has never appeared on CD.

'Put It On'; 'Small Axe'; 'Duppy Conqueror'; 'No Sympathy'
Including the CD bonus track 'No Sympathy', *Burnin'* has four remakes each of songs previously recorded for Lee Perry. Unlike the remakes on *Catch A Fire*, little attention is given to updating or improving these songs, and, as a result, they are the weakest tracks on either album. They are similarly arranged to the Perry-produced renditions, but performed in an overly deliberate manner that does not compare well to the fresher, more exciting originals. 'Put It On' sounds especially pedantic, while 'Duppy Conqueror' sounds tired. Tosh's 'No Sympathy' suffers from an overdone synthesizer track that is even more obtrusive than that heard on *Catch A Fire*'s 'Stir It Up'. Only 'Small Axe' can compare to its original rendition. But it's bettered by an alternative take from these sessions that's included on the *Countryman* soundtrack. Thankfully, remakes on subsequent albums, though varied in quality, abandoned this uninspiring overly deliberate approach.

'One Foundation'
Tosh calls for putting aside divisiveness in favor of togetherness as the pathway to love. Though certainly not a bad song, the gospel-tinged 'One Foundation' is not special instrumentally, vocally and lyrically. Other than his portion of 'Get Up, Stand Up', this is Tosh's only new composition on The Wailers' international albums. It would be his only song from this time that Tosh would leave behind and not remake in his solo career.

Live show
The second CD in the Deluxe Edition of *Burnin'* finds The Wailers playing a twelve-song, 79-minute show in Leeds, England, on November 23, 1973. It's an interest-

ing performance, as it captures the music of The Wailers stripped down to its barest essentials. First, Bunny is not present, leaving just Bob and Peter to handle the vocals. And besides the Barrett brothers, the band consists only of Earl "Wya" Lindo on keyboard and Peter and Bob on guitars. But even with this, the minimal possible Wailers line-up, the music holds up surprisingly well. Bob reveals himself to be an energetic and charismatic live performer. Tosh's prowess on rhythm guitar can be easily appreciated. The songs are long, since most open with jams. The band loses control of 'Midnight Ravers'. But at the opposite extreme, the 13.30-minute 'Lively Up Yourself' is impressive. At one point, Bob starts improvising new lyrics. Later, he works in those of 'Rastaman Chant' and uses those as a jumping-off point to improvise additional new lyrics.

Natty Dread

Peter Tosh and Bunny Wailer would leave the Wailers after *Burnin'* to concentrate on their solo careers. Like Bob, Peter released a string of albums geared for the international audience, while Bunny's albums seemed largely focused on a local audience. Accordingly, Tosh would tour the world frequently, but Bunny did so less often. Though neither would ever again appear on a Bob Marley recording (with one very minor exception on *Confrontation*), they did occasionally perform live with him as late as 1975.

Their departure gave Bob the need/opportunity to alter The Wailers' overall sound for his 1974 album, *Natty Dread*. The first order of business was to replace the departed Wailers. Rather than try to find sound-alike backing singers who could only pale in comparison, he wisely went a different route and assembled a female vocal group that never once tried to sound like the departed Wailers. He called them The I-Threes, a name that loosely translates to Selassie I's three, or God's three. Each was an established reggae singer. Rita Marley, Bob's wife (and de facto sometimes Wailer), was joined by Marcia Griffiths and Judy Mowatt. Griffiths had a decade-long musical relationship with Bob, starting with 'Oh My Darling', a duet she recorded with him at Studio One in 1964, and guesting on *Catch A Fire*. The new-to-The-Wailers Judy Mowatt completed the trio. They had worked together once before, in 1971, when Rita recruited Griffiths and Mowatt as her backing singers for a well-received nightclub performance, where the three women clicked.

The I-Threes were strictly a backing unit, always singing together in harmony, never one stepping out from the group to take a lead. However, The I-Threes did record a handful of singles of their own, the best being 'Many Are Called', produced by Lee Perry and Bob Marley in 1978. (That and Bob Marley & The Wailers' 'Smile Jamaica (Fast Version)' are the only two tracks from the broad body of work from the extended Wailers family to feature Perry's Black Ark sound.) Though by no means the first female vocalists to back a reggae singer, their dignified gospel-fueled harmonies and stately presence were unlike anything that had come before.

And with their lush and feminine sound, even fans of the original Wailers could not deny that The I-Threes made Bob Marley's music prettier. They were amazingly consistent, never once hurting a Bob Marley & The Wailers song with so much as a single errant note. They greatly influenced the perception of what reggae should sound like for fans outside of Jamaica. As a result, similar female backing vocalists became de rigueur for non-Jamaican international reggae stars such as Lucky Dube of South Africa, Alpha Blondy of the Ivory Coast, Nasio Fontaine of Dominica, and others. (But not for Matisyahu of New York's Hasidic community, as the religious beliefs he adopted in his teens prohibit him from performing with women.) After all, The I-Threes did what no other vocal group could do – they successfully replaced the backing vocals of Peter Tosh and Bunny Wailer.

Horns returned on *Natty Dread*, ending their exile from *Catch A Fire* and *Burnin'*. Four hornsmen are heard, anchored by former Skatalite Tommy McCook on sax, along with the great trombonist and former Wailers collaborator Vin Gordon, plus relative newcomers Glen DaCosta, also on sax, and Dave Madden on trumpet, both from the Zap Pow band. They would anchor the horn section for Bob Marley & The Wailers for the remainder of Bob's career, with Gordon eventually replaced by Ronald "Nambo" Robinson and McCook by Dean Fraser. Al Anderson joined the band, bringing rock lead guitar in-house, fulfilling the role that once required overdubs from Wayne Perkins. (Though black and dreadlocked, Anderson was in fact an American rather than the Jamaican he was often assumed to be.) The album also features guest harmonica, played by white American Lee Jaffe, an instrument that had not featured in The Wailers' music since their ska days. But, unlike the happy harmonica of ska and mento, Jaffe's harmonica was strictly blues. (Other white musicians had played on Wailers sessions before, such as Rabbit Bundrick and Wayne Perkins, but Lee Jaffe was less of a supplementary player for two reasons. First, he played live with The Wailers on at least one occasion. Second, after a live performance, he was told that he was a Wailer by no less than Bunny Wailer.) Even with this greater sonic palette, and perhaps because of the emotions over the break-up of the vocal Wailers, apart from two songs, *Natty Dread* stands out as an unusually low-key, moody and sometimes dour Wailers album. Only one song, 'Lively Up Yourself', provides a ray of happiness. Perhaps this is why it is seldom argued for as being the best Wailers album.

The departure of Peter and Bunny not only caused changes to The Wailers' sound, but changed the meaning of that venerable name. Though The Wailers had broken up, the name was too established and valuable to be decommissioned. The act was now called "Bob Marley & The Wailers", effectively moving the designation "The Wailers" to Bob's backing band. That is why you can still see The Wailers live today, the name having been passed down to bassist and band leader "Family Man" Barrett, even though the presence of Bob, Bunny, Peter, Rita Marley, Junior Braithwaite, Dream Walker, The I-Threes or any other member of The Wailers vocal group is long a thing of the past.

'Lively Up Yourself'

Jamaican fans had already met Bob's life-of-the-party aspect in middle-period songs like 'Soul Shakedown Party' and the original, self-produced rendition of 'Lively Up Yourself'. International audiences were introduced by *Natty Dread*'s remake of the latter song, one of two remakes on the album. It's a major upgrade of the original, as the crowded sound of the earlier recording is opened up and given plenty of room to move. And that's important in a song where it's party time. Opening with an elated whoop and Tarzan cry from Bob, in a few words, he irresistibly implores us to join him and dance (though double entendres allow for him being interested in more than just dancing). So get up and skank with Bob to great bass work from Aston Barrett, with its ascending and descending clusters interspersed with swollen gaps of no notes at all. To a typically fine Carlton Barrett and to Seeco's tambourine and slapstick that spice the sound. To Al Anderson's tasty lead runs that are threaded through the song. To the horn section that makes a delayed entrance and follows the melody of the bass. To the sax solo that makes the song bigger. To The I-Threes, who effortlessly follow the template provided by Peter and Bunny's original, but sound more joyful. A quintessential reggae party platter, 'Lively Up Yourself' was already an important part of live Bob Marley & The Wailers concerts when *Natty Dread* was released, and would remain in the set through his final tour.

A good dub version of 'Lively Up Yourself' is available on the digital download album called *Bob Marley & The Wailers In Dub, Vol. 1*. It features the pleasure of two different vocal tracks from Bob.

'No Woman No Cry'

'No Woman No Cry' is one of a few Wailers songs that experimented with using a drum machine instead of a live drummer, foreshadowing the digitalization and mechanization of the dancehall to come in the next decade. But this is only one odd aspect of this track. The recording of Bob's vocal sounds like it was speeded up. The I-Threes are not present; instead the backing vocals sound as if they were provided by band members. This recording may have been a demo that was deemed strong enough not to need re-recording. Another unusual feature of the song is its uncertain authorship. Vincent "Tata" Ford is credited as co-author. He is also credited with 'Positive Vibration', 'Roots, Rock, Reggae' and 'Crazy Baldhead' on the 1976 album, *Rastaman Vibration*. Opinions differ on whether Ford, a friend of Bob's from his Trench Town days, was actually a songwriter or the recipient of Bob's generosity. There are other songs on *Natty Dread* with similarly questionable authorship attribution,which lends credence to the latter explanation.

Whoever the author really is, he filled 'No Woman No Cry' with slice-of-life reminiscences of life in Trench Town. This impoverished government housing project built in Kingston in the 1950s is where the Wailers' families settled and the group came together. One doesn't have to be from Trench Town to identify with the song's message: that happy memories of friends can overcome today's sad-ness, especially when Bob breaks into the famous chorus of "Everything's gonna be alright", repeated like a mantra, positive and reassuring. It's the first of a string of universally affirmative messages that turn up in his songs from this point forward. Immediately relatable and so emotionally conveyed, such lyrics are an important ingredient in Bob Marley's enormous cross-cultural, world-wide appeal.

An odd recording with great lyrics, the potential of 'No Woman, No Cry' as an unequivocally great song was fulfilled in the hit concert rendition that would soon appear on the Bob Marley & The Wailers 1976 album, *Live!*

'Them Belly Full (But We Hungry)'

The blues-tinged 'Them Belly Full (But We Hungry)' is one of the most vivid of Bob's *sufferas* songs. He sounds wounded as he opens the song by singing the title's theme of inequality and hunger. He dips into the wisdom of Jamaican folk sayings to elaborate: "rain fall, but dutty [dirt] tough", literally, it's finally raining but the earth is still too hard to plant. Or, even a good thing can be too little, too late. Bob also sings, "a pot cook, but the food no 'nough". (These lyrics were influ-enced by Louise Bennett's poem, 'Dutty Tough'. In addition to the folk saying of the title, her poem also includes a line about a cooking pot not having enough.)

When Bob sings in unison with The I-Threes, "Oh, what a tribulation!", you feel it. Then, a second chorus is heard, and it's extraordinary. Though he sounds no less pained, Bob describes dancing to reggae as a balm for life's most serious problems:

> We're gonna dance to Jah music, dance.
> Forget your troubles and dance.
> Forget your sorrows and dance.
> Forget your sickness and dance.
> Forget your weakness and dance.
> > 'Them Belly Full (But We Hungry)' by Carleton Barrett and Lecon
> > Cogill. © 1974 Blue Mountain Music Ltd o/b/o Fifty-Six Hope Road
> > Music Ltd and Blackwell Fuller Music Publishing LLC. Copyright
> > renewed. All rights reserved. Used by permission.

The I-Threes join in to emphasize every time Bob sings "dance", magnifying the insistence and the already strong emotions. Meanwhile, Seeco's Nyah hand drum percolates softly as horns and guitar join on an insistent reggae chop, creating a soft mandate. In 'Them Belly Full', Bob accomplishes true magic as he nourishes the needy and infirmwith the power of his music.

'Rebel Music' (aka 'Three O'Clock Roadblock')

Replete with harmonica from Lee Jaffe, the bluesy 'Rebel Music' is as emotional as 'Them Belly Full'. But rather than providing comfort for those in need, Bob is frustrated with, and pushes back against, the institutional oppression of the Rastas. He bemoans the curfews (the subject also arose on 'Burnin' And Lootin''), the need to carry identification papers and confrontations with the police at their roadblocks, all of which curtail his freedom. Amidst all these controls, as a Rastaman, Bob is particularly agonized that he must discard his ganja, giving the song a highlight. Another comes when Bob challenges the police by not producing his birth certificate. Mid-song, he takes a breather. The I-Threes continue to sing the chorus and Al Anderson provides a subdued wah-wah guitar solo, helping to stretch 'Rebel Music' to nearly 7 minutes, unusually long for a Wailers track, and their longest to date. When Bob returns, it's with a yodeling rebel yell, a cry of pain that ends with his idiosyncratic quivering vibrato that gives the song yet another highlight. The contrast between Bob's wailing and The I-Threes' soothing creates a special richness, and they would use this powerful dynamic again and again in other songs.

Two good dub versions of 'Rebel Music', released on Jamaican singles, have yet to be compiled on LP or CD. A different mix featuring piano and less harmonica can be heard on the soundtrack for the *Countryman* movie. It might have been the better mix outright, if not for the fact that it's much shorter than the original.

'So Jah S'eh'
With an exceptional lead vocal, rich Rasta lyrics and an unusual arrangement, 'So Jah S'eh' is an overlooked gem amongst Bob Marley & The Wailers' many hits. The song's carefully wrought intro finds a horn section playing a melody that recalls that of 'No More Trouble', exchanging lines with jazzy saxophone, while drum machine, bass and guitar provide a rhythmic framework. The body of the song begins, and the melody changes as sax is replaced by lead guitar runs that glow warm like vacuum tubes. The minimal backing vocals are handled by keyboardist Tyrone Downie, as The I-Threes are not present for the second of two songs on the album. Whether he is the cause or the effect of their absence, Bob fills the song up with memorable vocal work; his singing is introspective, yet overflowing with intense zeal.

Bob appeals to the listeners to follow Jah's direction to unite and take care of one another. One moment, he employs down-home reasoning, musing that if dogs and cats can get along, why can't people do the same? The next, he adapts Psalm 37:25: "I not seen the righteous forsaken, nor his seed begging bread". (Marley's friend Dennis Brown was impressed enough to write a song with the same name and to use the same Bible adaptation as its climax, as described in the chapter on this artist; page 331.) Three times, Bob builds to a peak of controlled intensity, each time reaching greater emotional heights than the time before, and sometimes breaking into chanting. Even in the run of international albums where his vocals were so consistently strong, this ardent meditation on Jah togetherness is a standout Bob Marley vocal.

'Natty Dread'

The song that gives the album its name turns out to be something of a lyrical lightweight. Bob sings verses advocating Rasta, but many of them are chosen more for the sound of the words than to be especially descriptive. The chorus consists of Bob counting up, skanking his way from First Street to Seventh Street. Meanwhile, The I-Threes' backing vocals consist of a trebly repetition of the song's title. Like the vocals, the arrangement is pleasant, if unremarkable, featuring an engaging horn line and a Nyabinghi drum. Though something of a trifle, 'Natty Dread' is still an enjoyable musical stroll.

'Bend Down Low'

A funky recut of 'Bend Down Low' is the second of two remakes on *Natty Dread*. It compares well to the JAD rendition, but it can't approach the crackling self-produced rock steady original.

'Talkin' Blues'; 'Revolution'

'Talkin' Blues' is another of the album's bluesy *sufferas* songs. But in spite of some memorable imagery, Bob has told this story better many times before and would do in the future. And the band has done better bluesy reggae arrangements than on this somewhat dour harmonica-strewn outing. At one point, Bob sings about bombing a church. The church is seen as an agency of Babylon's oppression, but the line is jarring, and the song is downbeat.

The fiery 'Revolution' comes off somewhat better musically and with its strong horn lines and Nyah drumming is somewhat more upbeat than 'Talkin' Blues'. Vocal high points include Bob, well supported by The I-Threes, singing of bringing lightning and brimstone, and his interesting, emotionally ambiguous, falsetto during the song's fade-out. But overall, like 'Talkin' Blues', 'Revolution' proves to be an unspecial Bob Marley & The Wailers song with controversial lyrics. Roger Steffens and Leroy Jodie Pierson reveal in *Bob Marley & The Wailers – The Definitive Discography* (2005, p. 80) that Chris Blackwell forced Bob to rewrite some of the more militant lyrics. One wonders what was cut, if the disturbing lines about paralyzing and killing the weak at the time of conception were left in. Even if these lines were describing the action of the oppressors, as is likely, this ugly lyric is jarring.

It is interesting to note that Peter Tosh is often called the militant Wailer. An analogy that has grown popular calls him The Wailers' Malcolm X to Bob's more peaceful Martin Luther King. But although his tone could be angrier and was more critical than his Wailers bredren, Tosh's lyrics never were as militant as on these two Bob Marley songs. Bob's cross-over from revolutionary to militant would always be controversial, exciting some and dismaying others. I take a dim view of these lyrics on the grounds that they are leaden compared to his better work, and I find it telling that they appear in songs that are substandard overall.

It's as if Bob's commitment to militancy was only strong enough to be used as a bolster for a weak song, but not strong enough to be included in his better material. Whether it was due to continued pressure from the record label, fewer weak songs that needed to be juiced in this way, or a change of heart, Bob's brief foray into militancy would end here. And it would have no impact on his ability to write powerful songs that demanded social justice while dealing with difficult realities. As a *suffera*, coming from the point of view of a victim rather than that of a would-be victimizer places him on higher moral and artistic ground.

'Am-A-Do'

Later CD editions of *Natty Dread* include the bonus track 'Am-A-Do', a leftover song from the album's sessions. It's not hard to see why this song, not fully developed, had originally been left on the cutting-room floor, but it's not a bad thing that it was eventually reclaimed. It's a simple love/sex song, as the chorus, "Am-do you" means, "I am going to do you".

Live!

Live! was recorded at The Lyceum Theatre in London on July 18, 1975, with the same band as is heard on *Natty Dread*, minus horns and harmonica. Still, the sound is magnitudes richer than the Spartan arrangement of the previously discussed 1973 live performance. The songs are unrushed, clocking in at between 4:30 and 7:30 minutes in length. The original LP and CD editions presented seven songs, but the CD was eventually upgraded with an additional song, 'Kinky Reggae'. (Nine other songs were performed that evening, so perhaps a two-CD edition of *Live!* is in our future.) *Live!* shows Bob Marley & The Wailers to be a stronger live act than ever. By this point, Bob's enormous charisma as a performer was undeniable, and both The I-Threes and the instrument Wailers are every bit as good live as in the studio. And the 2,000-seat Lyceum gives this performance an intimacy that was lost in later concerts, held in much larger venues. All of the songs are drawn from the three internationally released albums except 'Trench Town Rock', which both revives an oldie from their self-produced, middle-period days and previews a remake to come on their next studio album. *Live!* solidified Bob Marley & The Wailers' international popularity, with 'I Shot The Sheriff' and 'No Woman No Cry' garnering significant rock radio airplay in the USA and UK to provide the ultimate commercial to see them in concert.

There is nothing wrong with the version of 'I Shot The Sheriff' heard here, except that it undeservedly became more popular than the incisive *Burnin'* version. The intensity of the original version is dialed down a few notches, though Bob explodes nicely at the end. An improved arrangement of 'No Woman No Cry' features the beautiful gospel-influenced singing of The I-Threes, as this song blooms into a reggae hymn. The refrain of "everything's gonna be alright" inspires one of several sing-alongs, as the song is elevated to a communion. And a harpsichord solo at the end of the track is the icing on a fine slice of cake. The audience goes wild for 'Lively Up Yourself' and another sing-along breaks out. 'Get Up, Stand Up' also loses some of the intensity from the *Burnin'* rendition, but it still has a lot to offer. Reggae guitar picking is heard to good effect, and a wordless call-and-response between Bob and The I-Threes would be an obvious influence on Sting, lead singer of the reggae-influenced British new wave band The Police.

An interlude

'Rainbow Country'; 'Natural Mystic'
Before starting work on their next album, in 1975, Bob Marley, with the band basically intact but sans The I-Threes, reunited with producer Lee Perry for a short session. They recorded two new songs at Perry's studio. But they don't sound much like either The Wailers' previous work for Perry, or the amazing music soon to come that featured Perry's Black Ark sound, or Bob's international album music. Though once difficult to obtain, both songs have since been included in numerous Bob Marley & The Wailers CD collections.

'Rainbow Country' would be reworked into 'Roots, Rock, Reggae' on the following year's *Rastaman Vibration* album. 'Natural Mystic' would be given a makeover on the *Exodus* album the year after that. Here, both songs feature tart staccato lines from a horn section, busy bass lines, The Wailers' penultimate dalliances with a drum machine, and adequate but uninspired vocals from Bob. There are no backing vocals on 'Rainbow Country', and male backing vocalists on 'Natural Mystic'. The latter is clearly the better of the two tracks, but neither compares especially well to either their remakes to come or past glories with Perry.

Rastaman Vibration

After *Natty Dread*, Bob sets things *upfull and right* with his 1976 album, *Rastaman Vibration*. Banished from this album and on forward were downbeat songs with militant sentiments. Instead, the mood of the album's ten songs is positive, even when dealing with strife. As Bob makes abundantly clear on the opening track, the Rastaman vibration is a positive one. Also gone is the uneven quality of the last two albums, as there are no weak songs on *Rastaman Vibration*. The four remakes of songs old and quite recent are each is given new life.

Just as it was for Bob's songwriting, the instrumental sound brightens from *Rastaman Vibration* onward. It's a more Jamaican sound, bursting with reggae creativity as compared to the blues-fixated *Natty Dread*. (Probably not coincidentally, it's the first of the Island albums in which Chris Blackwell did not share the production credit with Bob Marley.) Harmonica is retired (other than on one song years later). The bass is mixed louder. Modest but effective dub reverb and dropout/in are in play. (No doubt contributing to these sonic changes was the presence of Lee Perry in the control room. Although he was not listed as a producer, he did have input into the album's vibrant sound.) The heartbeat pulse reggae chop is the prevailing beat, largely pushing out the more elaborate rhythm guitar work so often heard in The Wailers' middle period right through *Natty Dread*. (By the next album, *Exodus*, this shift would be complete.) And it's on this album that the Barrett brothers come into the peak of their powers, fully realizing the style they are most remembered for. Aston's masculine, melodic, stop-and-go lines are the epitome of reggae bass. A model of efficiency, his playing is powerful yet understated, providing the music with an unbreakable spine. Carlton studs the album with sharp rolls and fills, more abundant and creative than ever before. His playing is so unlike anything heard in rock and distinctive enough in reggae to be a sub-style of reggae drumming, with Carlton as its only successful practitioner. The Barrett brothers reside in a pantheon of reggae rhythm sections that would only be shared with Sly Dunbar & Robbie Shakespeare. Tyrone Downie provides the album with a pleasing breathy synthesizer sound that is frequently heard, along with organ and piano. It sometimes appears where horns might have been used. Horns are used on just on a few songs. Donald Kinsey replaces fellow American Al Anderson on lead guitar (though Anderson would make appearances on later albums in the string.). Kinsey tends to wait for his moments to play lead, rather than threading his work throughout a song, as Al Anderson did. And by this album, Seeco Patterson's incidental percussion is a nearly constant presence throughout the music.

Rastaman Vibration is a controversial album, as many consider it solid, prime Bob Marley & The Wailers, while, surprisingly, others have tagged it as weak. I'm firmly in the camp of the former, to the point where I can't account for the latter view. It's an upbeat set that's strong and consistent, filled with wonderful songs, and sports a great sound. And I'm supported by *Rastaman Vibration* being the highest-charting of Bob's albums in both the UK and the USA. In 2002, a two-CD Deluxe Edition of *Rastaman Vibration* appeared with all manner of bonus material. Raising the track count from ten to twenty-two, it makes a great collection greater, if less consistent.

'Positive Vibration'
Rastaman Vibration opens with 'Positive Vibration', whose lyrics give the album its name. Its sound is rich and alive right from Carlton Barrett's opening drum sculpture. Processed guitar plays the heartbeat reggae chop, supplemented by a synthesized organ that pumps rhythmically like breath. These elements have Lee Perry's fingerprints on them, sounding like a preview of what was soon to come from his Black Ark studio. Seeco Paterson's hand drums are held back for a delayed entrance, giving the song a roots afterburner. Keyboardist Tyrone Downie, singing in his best Peter Tosh baritone, and The I-Threes take turns providing Bob with backing vocals. It all contributes to vibrant reggae music, fresh and open to the point of sounding alfresco. It's a perfect platform for Bob's *upful* message.

Bob proclaims the Rastaman's vibe to be a positive one: about God, peace and helping others, rejecting disunity and wickedness. His singing is empathetic and self-confident, and his approach is conversational. It's as if he has found a wonderful truth that he is dying to share with us. His ideas are well supported by affirmations from The I-Threes, and underscored at one point by a dub guitar drop-out. Bob exits before the song's long fade-out, deputizing Tyrone Downie to sing in his place. Downie repeatedly asks if we are "picking up" – whether we are assimilating Bob's message – as The I-Threes sing praises to Jah. This great song leaves the listener hungry for more Bob and more positive Rastaman vibrations. Happily, the album is very quick to deliver these.

'Roots, Rock, Reggae'
'Roots, Rock, Reggae' is a simple song about the role of reggae in positive Rasta vibrations. It's a remake of 'Rainbow Country', a song from the previous year's brief session with Lee Perry. About half the lyrics of 'Rainbow Country' are thrown out, along with the clipped delivery, strident horns and drum machine. Instead, 'Roots, Rock, Reggae' is a fluent reggae, featuring a sometimes double-tracked Bob harmonizing with himself, The I-Threes enjoying themselves, playful keyboards, short, sweet rock guitar riffs, Tommy McCook sax, incidental percussion and more, all skanking around the reggae chop maypole.

Bob sings about wanting to hear some reggae and how dancing to it makes him free. Printed with commas as it is, the song's title is over-punctuated, since Bob was describing his current international sound as "roots rock reggae". He says how he wants more people to hear it, calling for his music to be played on black R&B radio so that black non-Jamaicans can be exposed to reggae, in the way that white album rock radio served its listeners. Extra bait was provided by Tommy McCook dishing wonderful soulful sax all over the track, yet Bob's wish would go largely unfulfilled within his lifetime. Generally, the song was a chart success, being the only Bob Marley single to chart in the USA, reaching no.51.

'Johnny Was'
'Johnny Was' is the odd duck of the album. It's a soulful R&B reggae ballad, as Bob tries to meet his targeted audience halfway to the goal he described on 'Roots, Rock, Reggae'. And it marks a shift to more serious concerns, as the album's only sad song.

It presents the other side of the coin to all the pro-rude boy songs that previously came from The Wailers (and to the gun songs soon to become so popular in dancehall) in the story of an innocent bystander killed by gunplay. Though it's not stated, the song is commonly believed to be specifically about the tragic death of Trevor Wilson, the younger brother of reggae star Delroy Wilson, ironically the author of The Slickers' classic rude boy song 'Johnny Too Bad'. But it was equally relevant to any of the growing number of innocent victims of guns in Jamaica, and beyond. 'Johnny Was' features some very soulful singing from Bob and The I-Threes, bluesy guitar licks and The Wailers' last use of a drum machine.

'Cry To Me'

'Cry To Me' is another remake, but the first from the international years that reached back to The Wailers' Studio One days. This song about romantic betrayal is transformed from a ska classic into languid reggae. A shimmering melange of keyboards, guitars and incidental percussion takes the place of the original's horns. Though good, it's not necessarily the best example of such a transformation, nor is it one of Bob's better vocals on the album. As a result, you may find yourself missing the original's distinctive horns and red-hot singing by Bob, Peter and Bunny.

'Want More'

Just because the Rastaman vibration is a positive one, this doesn't preclude Bob from righteous fury when events demand. 'Want More' finds him denouncing unnamed backstabbers. Though the perpetrators are unnamed and the details of the transgression remain unknown, Bob is provoked to give them a blistering dressing-down, his anger and disgust palpable. He is one of the few singers able to convey the full range of human emotion in his singing. Here, strong negative emotions intensify his performance, heightening a great song.

Bob comes to this from a place of power, backed with tough, confident music. A prowling riddim that's more dubby, lean and dread than any other on *Rastaman Vibration* is heard. Guitars are featured, with lead runs, a sinewy mid-song solo and elaborate strummed rhythm phrases. The latter is very reminiscent of Peter Tosh's signature style, raising the possibility that the song is a veiled attack on his former bandmate. Though the lyrics are few, they work as a series of hooks, with many lines that can stand alone memorably. Especially those made ominous with a halo of echo and those where The I-Threes jump in late to harmonize. As the song nears its end, all vocals drop out, leaving a section of dub. The I-Threes return to sing the opening refrain to fade-out, adding to the song's reggae intensity.

'Want More' is Bob Marley in a nutshell: using negative situations as fuel for his song craft; with singing that fully conveys the emotion of his sentiments; while seeing to expert musical backing, arrangement and production. It's a set of skills that produced a body of work unparalleled in reggae and rarely matched anywhere else.

'Crazy Baldhead'

Like 'Roots, Rock, Reggae', 'Crazy Baldhead' features a skanking riddim with reggae chop guitar front and center. But this time, instead of a celebration, there's a dread mood in this war dance about Rasta revolution. It's dominated by heady work from the rhythm section. Aston provides a bass line with masterfully dropped notes in yet another example of his less-is-more magic. Carlton brings complex hi-hat work and the occasional patented Carlton Barrett extended roll, giving the song its introduction. Guitars and keyboards build a skank that's high stepping, yet down and dirty. Ominous wordless vocals from The I-Threes add to the dread.

Bob enters by marshaling his quivering vibrato for a pair of warbling shrieks, upping the dread moodiness. His voice is treated with reverb, adding force to his call to chase the titular non-Rasta oppressors out of town. Bob gives a litany of their crimes as justification, including slavery, theft, general disrespect, imposed religion, education that indoctrinates, political deceit and corruption.

The song has even more to recommend it. Bob's talent for scat singing, last heard on an alternative version of 'Kaya' for producer Lee Perry during The Wailers' middle period, adds greatly. A mid-song interval of dub, in which the vocals and guitar drop out as oddball knocks and whistles are heard, does the same for the dread arrangement.

A minimalistic dub version of 'Crazy Baldhead' that ratchets the dread even higher can be heard on the digital download album, *Bob Marley & The Wailers In Dub, Vol. 1*.

'Who The Cap Fit'
'Who The Cap Fit' is a remake of The Wailers' middle-period Lee Perry-produced song, 'Man To Man'. It's lush with keyboards and languid, differing from the spiky, brisk original rendition. Unlike the fully realized original rendition of 'Cry To Me' that resulted in a good but less than revelatory remake, 'Man To Man' was a song ripe for further development, and the remake is a triumph. The new arrangement allows the song to come into its own.

It's a song about betrayal, a theme that has already cropped up twice before on the album. Though its lyrics are typically vague as to the identity of the betrayers, it's often taken to be about the record producers The Wailers had worked under in the past. Taking their musical careers very seriously, when they were financially cheated or otherwise mishandled, The Wailers felt betrayed in a very deep and lasting way. (Surviving member Bunny Wailer is openly aggrieved about this even today, and he started a blog in 2011 to further air these issues.)

'Who The Cap Fit' is rich in Jamaican folk sayings and expressions; "Who the cap fit, let him wear it", has its closest American equivalents in "If it looks like a duck, swims like a duck, and quacks like a duck, it's probably a duck" and "Where there's smoke, there's fire". To " su-su" is to gossip. "Me throw me corn but me no call no fowl", a folk saying we've also seen in Larry Marshall's song, 'Throw Me Corn', is a criticism of someone who goes through the cost and effort of putting out food for their chickens, but then neglects to call them to feed.

This last line comes from a second chorus that, as we have seen, was edited out from 'Man To Man' for reasons unknown (though it can be heard in a less common alternative mix). On 'Who The Cap Fit', it's fully developed and is a delight. Heard three times with mounting intensity from Bob, each phrase is gorgeously mirrored with a response from The I-Threes that includes mock chicken clucks. Even for the biggest fans of 'Man To Man', this chorus elevates 'Who The Cap Fit' as the superior rendition.

'Night Shift'

The fourth and final remake on *Rastaman Vibration* is 'Night Shift', a new rendition of 'It's Alright', another middle-period song that was produced by Lee Perry. Here, the high energy of the original carries over as a funk-reggae vamp is recast as a creative reggae skank. The creativity flows from the song's first moments, an elaborate tumbling drum roll that sounds like it's skidding downstairs on its heels, only to land on its feet. From there, the reggae bubbles, with Carlton again providing busy hi-hat work while Aston's bass line alternates between busy and sparse. Guitar and piano join to provide the reggae chop, while additional keyboards are laid on top. The I-Threes trade Bunny and Peter's tough, longing, soulful backing vocals for something far more soothing.

Lyrically, 'It's Alright' is based on one of the jobs Bob held when he moved to the USA for a time in 1966 to join his mother. This experience comes into greater focus on the remake, with its more descriptive title and new lyrics. Also coming in clearer are the double entendres that give a second meaning for working all night.

The new arrangement gives Bob more freedom than the staccato delivery required by the original's vamp; funky and enjoyable as its James Brown-esque stream of interjections were, the vocal is more satisfying on the remake. The James Brown influence is the only funk aspect from the original rendition to carry over. Unlike The Wailers' middle period, when admiration could result in imitation, by now Brown's rough, slurred delivery and guttural exclamations are fully assimilated into Bob's singing. Yet, even when he's channeling Brown, the sound is purely Bob Marley. With these changes, 'Night Shift' beats 'It's Alright' as the better rendition, though you can choose to play either song without any complaints from me.

'War'; 'War (Alternate Mix)'

The lyrics of 'War' were adapted by Marley from a speech that Haile Selassie delivered to the United Nations on October 4, 1963. The emperor of Ethiopia eloquently and powerfully put forth the notion that racial inequality and prejudice are incompatible with world peace. Specifically, as long as racially oppressive regimes operated in Angola, Mozambique and South Africa, there would be war. Turning Jah Rastafari's address to the nations of the world into a roots reggae song was a great risk for Bob Marley & The Wailers. They rose to the occasion.

A brief introduction that finds a horn section jamming with a simple bass line sets a heavy tribal groove. The horns vanish as the body of the song begins. Bob chant-sings Selassie's words, sounding powerful and righteous. So does the band.

The bass line serves as a lead. It's joined by a processed guitar chop, drums and Nyah drum in a dread Rasta march. Additional elements are added gradually: The I-Threes repeatedly chant the song's title, the horns return and hand drum takes a more prominent role in perhaps Seeco Patterson's finest performance. Empowered by Selassie I's words and this fine backing, Bob gets into a deep groove. He is controlled and dignified, maintaining a slow burn, choosing his moments to cut loose, once on the chorus and then again on the song's fade-out.

And speaking of the song's fade-out, it turns out that the recording of 'War' that had for decades been enjoyed as a Bob Marley & The Wailers classic was, in fact, incomplete. The Deluxe Edition of *Rastaman Vibration* includes an unreleased alternative mix that restores 40 seconds and the song's final stanza that had been truncated. In it, Bob becomes markedly more anguished and reaches a fiery peak. It's an unprecedented situation – a song whose climax was trimmed away before its release. Yet Bob must have been accepting of the song's shortening. He had ample opportunity to return these lyrics to live renditions of 'War', but did not choose to do so.

With lyrics by Jah Rastafari himself, set to music by reggae's greatest talent, Bob Marley & The Wailers, 'War' is a roots reggae song that is as great as its pedigree. It's a powerful piece of music, a righteous *chant down* not of Bob's personal oppressors or of oppression faced by Rastafarians in Jamaica, but of oppression and injustice on a geopolitical scale. Surprisingly, a dub version of 'War' has never been heard.

'Rat Race'

Overshadowed by the juggernaut 'War', *Rastaman Vibration* closes with a fine song of a different nature, the down-and-dirty 'Rat Race'. Opening with a guttural *Huuhh!*, Bob decries those who contribute to a situation where gang violence born of politics runs rampant in the streets. This is distasteful to Bob. As a Kingstonian, he saw his share of this violence and gangsterism. And as a Rastafarian, he shuns the politics of Babylon. So strong is his disgust that even children's songs aren't safe. For the chorus of 'Rat Race', Bob borrows the structure of the old Jamaican folk song 'Chi Chi Bud, Oh'. This simple song chants the names of various birds ("buds") whose songs ("chi chi") are heard in Jamaica: But in 'Rat Race', chanting in the same cadence, he catalogs the varieties of a different type of creature – the contributors to this violence. He lists hooligans, gorgons (in this context, it's someone who is very powerful) and guinea-gogs (underworld bigwigs, which we know thanks to Roger Steffens and Leroy Jodie Pierson [2005, p. 88]) and shames them as a disgrace.

'Rat Race' features an often double-tracked Bob, close harmonies between Bob and The I-Threes, strong lines from the horn section that are mournful or uplifting by turn, distinctive woodblocks from Seeco and an absolutely devious bass line from Aston.

In a situation similar to 'War', the song ends on the album version before the lyrics do, and collectors know of a mix that goes on almost a minute longer, in which Bob catalogs additional political creatures in Jamaican slang. And as was the case with 'War', the complete mix is desirable. There is also an alternative take of the song released as a single that was as good as the album take, which also has the full complement of lyrics. Let's hope that one, if not both, of these recordings (not to mention their dub versions) are soon released.

Rastaman Vibration Deluxe Edition bonus tracks

Twenty bonus tracks fill out the 2003 two-CD Deluxe Edition of *Rastaman Vibration*. Best of all is the inclusion of 'Jah Live' and 'Smile Jamaica', two topical Jamaican singles from this time, along with their dub B-sides. Also included are both sides of a planned single from the album that was never released, four alternative mixes (including the aforementioned untruncated mix of 'War'), plus ten live tracks from the tour that suppported *Rastaman Vibration*'s release.

'Jah Live'; 'Concrete'
Co-produced by Bob and Lee Perry, 'Jah Live' was famously recorded during the *Rastaman Vibration* sessions for rush release in Jamaica as a single on Bob's Tuff Gong label. It's an extraordinary record – a response to the news of Haile Selassie's death. As such, it's the first time in history that a song about the death of a religious deity was recorded at the time of the event.

With a reverent tone and a soothing sound held at a low-key bubble, Bob Marley & The Wailers bring succor to the Rastafarians. Bob tells them that in spite of the news, Jah in fact lives, dismissing the foolishness that Jah could die. He refers to his audience as his children, like a religious elder, comforting the unsure in his certainty. It's apparent that some of the lyrics were written on the spot, in a rush. But this only adds to the song's immediacy. Like Bob, The I-Threes are at their most comforting, especially with their reassuring chorus and their heavenly wordless harmonies. A mellow guitar solo from Al Anderson shows that rock guitar is now a fully legitimate component of the music of Bob Marley & The Wailers. Not just something to attract non-Jamaicans, it's equally suitable for this, the most Jamaican of releases.

The single's B-side dub version, 'Concrete', is made mystical by the administrations of the producers. It opens with an added yodeling cry from Bob reminiscent of the one that opens 'Crazy Baldhead'. Then, one of the better Bob Marley & The Wailers dubs is heard. There's lots of drop-out/in and several impressive swells of echo, adding gravity to an already substantial song. It ends with an oscillating sound effect as if a flying saucer was also interested in what Bob is describing.

'Smile Jamaica, Part One'; 'Smile Jamaica, Part Two'
Like 'Jah Live', 'Smile Jamaica' was released as a single in Jamaica in response to local events. An upcoming election had exacerbated politically driven street vio-

lence in Kingston to a point close to civil war. Also like 'Jah Live', Bob Marley and Lee Perry co-produced both sides of the single. They also did so on an entirely different rendition of 'Smile Jamaica', referred to as the "fast version", recorded around the same time. (More on that version later in this chapter.)

'Smile Jamaica' features a big band with a horn section and male backing vocals joining those of The I-Threes. These singers were recruited from Bob's camp: Antonio "Gilly" Gilbert, an old friend then employed as Bob's cook, was joined by Neville Garrick, the graphics artist who designed many classic Bob Marley & The Wailers album jackets.

Emotionally, 'Smile Jamaica' is an unusually conflicted song. The instrumental opening is bitter-sweet, as horns strive to elevate the mood. In the chorus, Bob sings about not being able to shake off a malaise, but then remembers that he should be happy just because he's in Jamaica. But there is a forced happiness in his vocals. And when he asks Jamaicans to get things together, he sounds like he's begging, where you would normally expect him to inspire. Even the horns have made a turn to melancholy. His spirits rise as he praises the people and their ability to enjoy themselves and to dance to reggae, but not for long. It's as if he is trying to convince himself as much as his audience that current conditions present anything to smile about. 'Smile Jamaica' is a rare glimpse at perhaps the most inspiring songwriter of his time up against a problem that he struggles to address. And it's a problem that nearly cost Marley his life.

In addition to this single, a huge 'Smile Jamaica' concert was planned for Kingston, with Bob Marley & The Wailers, Third World, Bunny Wailer, Peter Tosh and Burning Spear all set to perform. But Bob's good intentions became politicized as the show came to be seen as a campaign rally for Michael Manley of the socialist People's National Party. Though it was never proven, and a number of other reasons have been suggested, this was likely the impetus for a nearly successful assassination attempt at Bob's home three days before the concert. "*Oh, what a rat race,*" indeed. Bob and Rita, along with others present, were wounded by gunfire, but all survived. Though Bunny Wailer, Peter Tosh and Burning Spear opted out, the performance by Bob Marley & The Wailers went on. Immediately after the show, Bob, his family, his band and entourage would decamp to London for the next year and a half. Two albums, *Exodus*, released in 1977, and *Kaya*, released in 1978, were recorded there during that time.

The single's dub version B-side is called 'Smile Jamaica, Part Two'. It's largely instrumental, with modest applications of drop-out/in and reverb.

'Roots, Rock, Reggae' (unreleased single mix); 'Roots, Rock, Dub' (unreleased single mix)
This alternative mix differs most notably from the album track in having more of Tommy McCook's sax. This includes a brief, previously unheard, solo over a section of dropped-out vocal. Hearing more of the former Skatalite playing atop this reggae skank easily validates the release of this mix.

The dub side of the unreleased mix uses reverb, a touch of echo and lots of drop-out/in, with Bob completely dropped out of the version. It adds an opening muted picked guitar, extra percussion and sax, all not heard elsewhere. The result is an enjoyable dub version, even without Bob.

'Want More' (alternate mix); 'Crazy Baldhead' (alternate mix); 'Johnny Was' (alternate mix)
All three of these tracks sound like earlier working mixes rather than mixes considered for eventual release. None is as good as the rendition on the album. 'Want More' features lots of fluid blues-rock leads that replace the guitars heard on the album mix, as well as some of The I-Threes vocals. 'Crazy Baldhead' features an annoying, out-of-place synthesizer that was wisely abandoned for the album release. 'Johnny Was' features a simple live drum track instead of a drum machine, and additional, but crude, guitar and percussion.

'Live At The Roxy' (May 26, 1976)

Ten tracks out of the twelve played at this wonderfully unhurried performance fill out the Deluxe Edition of *Rastaman Vibration*. The band is intact, except, as is the norm for live Bob Marley & The Wailers concerts outside of Jamaica, there are no horns. Compared to his performance on *Live!*, Bob is more out front here, with The I-Threes and the instrumental Wailers in more of a supporting role. Some tracks feature touches of simulated dub, adding drama. The crowd is as enthusiastic as the one heard on *Live!*, perhaps more so, as instead of coalescing into sing-alongs, there's a lot of frenzied screaming. The songs are rather faithful readings of the originals, with a few exceptions. Bob goes a little wild mid-song in 'Lively Up Yourself', as he typically did in live performances of the song. Perhaps feeling obligated to bring something new rather than just repeating the popular rendition on *Live!*, 'I Shot The Sherriff' is elaborated and funkier, but it is no better for it. A long rendition of 'Rat Race', featuring a slightly altered rhythm, is the pleasant surprise of the set.

In 2003, Island Records released a two-CD set called *Live At The Roxy, Hollywood, California, May 26, 1976 – The Complete Concert*. In addition to the ten tracks heard on the *Rastaman Vibration* Deluxe Edition, the two other tracks from the performance are included. The first is 'Positive Vibration', which does not start strong, but gains strength as it progresses. The other is a monster of a track: 'Get Up, Stand Up'/'No More Trouble'/'War'. This 24-minute epic medley jam starts with the three songs in the title. Then Bob improvises a new song that could have been called 'Let's Move, Let The Rhythm Groove', before returning to 'Get Up, Stand Up' to conclude the track. (Hearing this unreleased song surrounded by familiar tracks is reminiscent of hearing 'Dewdrops' in the middle of Bob's mid-period acoustic medley.) This track makes having *Live At The Roxy – The Complete Concert* necessary even for owners of *Rastaman Vibration Deluxe Edition*.

Exodus

Bob Marley's next album, *Exodus*, was released in 1977. This great album had an albatross hung around its neck at the end of 1999 when *Time* magazine named it as the best album of the century ("The Best of the Century", *Time*, December 31, 1999). Two of the runners-up were *Kind Of Blue* by Miles Davis and *Are You Experienced?* by Jimi Hendrix. *Time* gave two reasons for its choice. First, that *Exodus* gave a worldwide voice to the Third World. While this is true, it's also true for other internationally released Bob Marley & The Wailers albums. Secondly, "Every song is a classic, from the messages of love to the anthems of revolution". Well, not so fast. While I'm thrilled that *Time* chose a Bob Marley release for this honor, I consider several of his albums to be better than *Exodus*. By *Time*'s own criteria, *Catch A Fire*, *Uprising* or *Rastaman Vibration* would have been more deserving of their praise. (So would *Songs Of Freedom*, but a career-spanning four-CD collection would probably be cheating.) *Exodus* does have some classics (as each of his albums does), but it's just not his best set. Nor is it helped by Bob being audibly congested on some tracks, as if he had a head cold. Two years after *Time*'s proclamation, a two-CD Deluxe Edition of *Exodus* would be released, with two tracks in particular bringing it closer to deserving the honor it had received.

The post-break-up sound that reached full maturity on *Rastaman Vibration* would continue here and beyond, proving itself to be endlessly malleable to Bob's prodigious songwriting. The band is the same as on *Rastaman Vibration*, with the exception of the departure of lead guitarist Donald Kinsey, who would go on to work extensively with Peter Tosh. Replacing him is Junior Marvin (born Donald Hanson Marvin Kerr Richards, Junior), who should not be confused with the reggae singer Junior Murvin, the first Jamaican to fill the lead guitar role originally created by Wayne Perkins. Bob took an interesting approach to this album that is less noticeable on its CD version. On *Exodus*'s original LP release, side 1 featured edgy, heavy, serious songs about Rasta and revolution, while side 2 was a collection of lighter fare, mostly party and love songs. Each side includes one remake.

'Natural Mystic'

Exodus opens strongly with a remake of 'Natural Mystic', a song originally recorded with Lee Perry in their brief 1975 session. The remake is made of sinew and smoke, rendering the punchy horn-driven original clumsy by comparison. A droning reggae vamp fades in over time, as the song slowly marches towards us through the mist. A typically crisp Carlton Barrett drum roll announces the body of the song, the key changes, and Bob is conjured into being. Deep bass studded with a Nyabinghi bass drum resonates the chest cavity while mercurial guitar leads run to the head. A horn section and piano join towards the end to embellish the droning groove.

Bob's vocal is spacey and detached, all the more so for the absence of The I-Threes. The lyrics are ominous, but opaque. Simple phrases grab the attention and draw you in, even if they are not explained. Likewise, the titular subject is not clearly defined. But we can understand that the song is describing the coming of Armageddon, which the Rasta can sense "blowing through the air", a phrase reminiscent of Bob Dylan's answer that was blowing in the wind.

A memorable deep roots meditation, 'Natural Mystic' was well suited for a dub version. Yet none appears to have been created. However, a different – and very good – alternative mix of 'Natural Mystic' can be heard on the soundtrack album for the movie *Countryman*. Amongst its many changes is an opening that includes the sound of tree frogs chirping in the Jamaican night, extra guitar and additional horns that are the missing link between the 1975 original and the *Exodus* rendition.

'So Much Things To Say'

'So Much Things To Say' uses the device of overstuffing the song with lyrics to mimic those who have so many negative things to say about Rasta. This has Bob rushing at times to fit in *his* many words on many topics. They include Rasta belief, political corruption, a folk saying, the injustices done to historical figures (Jesus Christ, Marcus Garvey and nineteenth-century Jamaican revolutionary Paul Bogle) and even finds room for some *bla bla bla* mock lyrics. It's difficult to take this all in, and Bob has covered the same subjects better in other songs. Ultimately, this hurried approach, along with Bob's nasal congestion, hurt the song's melody and the vocal performance, making 'So Much Things To Say' a curious but relatively weak song.

'Guiltiness'

'Guiltiness' follows without a pause. It's a condemnation of unnamed oppressors (or, in Rasta-speak, "downpressors"). Employing Psalm 127:2, Bob warns that they will ultimately, "eat the bread of sorrow". It's more musically developed and melodic than 'So Much Things To Say', but still unremarkable by Bob Marley & The Wailers standards.

'The Heathen'

Bob the revolutionary is heard from again in 'The Heathen', as he rallies the troops to prepare for battle. Victory is close with the titular adversaries' backs against the wall. Whether this revolution is physical or one of ideas is never made clear, but Rasta revolution was indeed eventually won, with music, not force. Rastafarianism is far more accepted in Jamaica today than it was up to Bob's time, due in no small part to him. The band provides another droning march, this time with a dystopian air of battle, touches of Hendrix-like guitar noise, a wild rock-guitar solo, and a lead synthesizer that manages to sound rootsy rather than out of place (as synthesizer occasionally does on Bob's Island albums).

'Exodus'

'Exodus' is about a familiar subject, the Rasta belief that repatriation to Africa is necessary for a better life. A roots staple, the last time The Wailers recorded a back-to-Africa song it was Bunny Wailer's 'Dreamland', though Peter Tosh's '400 Years' also visited this theme. 'Exodus' is the first Marley-penned example. His lyrics are clear-eyed and determined, as he exhorts Jamaicans not to accept their lives as they are when there can be a religious exodus to Africa. He then pleads to God for aid in the form of a Moses figure to lead the Rastas to their Zion.

All involved contribute to making 'Exodus' the most sonically powerful expression of this familiar Rasta theme. Appropriately, the music adopts an African aspect, giving it a polyrhythmic density not common to reggae. Listen to how the instruments enter one at a time – rhythm guitar, keyboard, piano, drums, horns, lead guitar, backing vocals, lead vocal, bass, Nyah drum – over the first half-minute of the song. At that point, it's reminiscent of the powerful 'War' from *Rastaman Vibration*. But it has more muscle, and is relentless, as every instrument is playing at its heaviest. Bob is on fire. The I-Threes are reinforced, as Tyrone Downie joins their harmonies. Near the song's end, the intensity is raised with swirling echo and repeated tribal chants of "Move!" Propulsive and with unprecedented tonnage for a reggae song, 'Exodus' rolls on unstoppable as a tank. With it, the original LP's serious Side 1 closed with a classic.

'Jammin''

The original LP's lighter side 2 opened with another Bob Marley & The Wailers classic, the warm, embracing 'Jammin''. It's a continuation of Bob's feel-good party music from songs like 'Soul Shakedown Party' and 'Lively Up Yourself', but it's also more. What exactly is *jammin'*? Partying? Loving? Making music? Respecting Jah Rastafari? After all, 'Jammin'' sounds like a party song, is sung like a love song, and reads like a Rasta song. Luckily, Bob slips in a key line to help us understand.

'Jammin'' opens joyfully with piano and bass playing the song's melody bolstered by bubble-up organ, puttering guitar, assorted percussion, and lots of great Carlton Barrett drumming. Bob gives a heroic vocal, powering his way through a bout of nasal congestion and The I-Threes sound especially precious. Living up to his surname, Robbie Shakespeare once described a good reggae arrangement as having a top that's well furnished, while the bottom makes your feet move. 'Jammin'' meets this criterion perfectly.

The party-time lyrics register first. But there are also a lot of reflective Rasta lyrics, including the exciting mid-song peak about God ruling all from his throne that brings the band to a standstill. And there is something more. Bob casually references the attempt on his life, and promises that bullets will not stop him from what he's doing. In this way, 'Jammin'' is Bob's brave proclamation that all that he does for his fans – sharing love, music, positive vibrations and the message of Jah – will continue unchanged in the face of nearly being assassinated. With a statement as fearless and positive as this, it's no wonder the music sounds like a celebration.

'Waiting In Vain'

'Waiting In Vain' is a ballad and a love song – Bob's first love song since 'Baby We've Got A Date' on *Catch A Fire*. But here, the love is unrequited, as Bob has been waiting in vain for years for the object of his desire. Its sophisticated arrangement, refined guitar solo and Bob's vulnerability result in a very smooth piece of lover's rock. And it is perhaps the most accessible song of his career, as this romantic, adult-oriented reggae couldn't offend even the most delicate of sensibilities. It's exactly the type of song that JAD would have died for about a decade earlier. It is also probably the finest love song that Bob would ever record. It inspired reggae covers and covers from overseas; Annie Lenox, Chrissie Hynde, Jimmy Buffett, jazz guitarist Lee Ritenour and others recorded renditions. But none can hold a candle to the original. Nor did Bob's various dub versions, remixes and alternative takes do anything to improve on the unbeatable album rendition.

'Turn Your Lights Down Low'

'Turn Your Lights Down Low' is another love song, and, as the title indicates, a more intimate one. But this time, Bob infuses contemporary R&B sounds into reggae, creating a slow-jam, reggae style. Although this doesn't work badly, following the accomplished, purely reggae 'Waiting In Vain', 'Turn Your Lights Down Low' does not come off as an especially strong song or focused performance.

'Three Little Birds'

'Three Little Birds' is famous for its universally affirmative chorus: "Don't worry about a thing, 'cause every little thing gonna be alright." The scant verse describes smiling at the sunrise while the titular birds sing. Positive vibes and reassurance have always been themes in Bob's songs and an ingredient in his wide appeal. But here, they are undiluted by any other aspect of his writing, like a bowl of sugar without the cereal. In response, the instrumental Wailers provide an adept but easy-going backing. A friendly buzzing keyboard is featured along with lovely slide guitar. And with Carlton Barrett clearly enjoying himself, so must all listeners. It's undoubtedly the sweetest and most innocent of any Bob Marley & The Wailers song. It's child-friendly and hard for adults to resist. This unabashed optimism was no doubt an influence on Bobby McFerrin's 1988 a cappella reggae novelty hit, 'Don't Worry, Be Happy', which reached no. 1. A pleasing, largely instrumental dub version of 'Three Little Birds' is available on the digital download album, *Bob Marley & The Wailers In Dub, Vol. 1*.

'One Love/People Get Ready'

Just as *Exodus* opens with a remake, it closes with another. 'One Love' dates back to the ska of The Wailers' Studio One days. For some reason, it gains a second title here, one that is a misnomer, as 'People Get Ready' (aka 'Freedom Time') is another song entirely. Unlike their last Studio One remake, 'Cry To Me' on *Rastaman Vibration*, the reggae of 'One Love' escapes the long shadow of its ska original. Here, the fully realized breakneck gospel-tinged ska of the original emerges transformed into relaxed, quaint, sun-soaked reggae that is equally realized. It's pleasing in its simplicity, complete with a piano introduction that conveys childlike innocence.

It's another song featuring that Bob Marley specialty, an inclusive, affirming chorus: "One love, one heart, let's get together and feel alright." Its appeal did not go unnoticed by those selling Jamaican tourism, and years after this rendition's release, the chorus of 'One Love' was used in a series of television commercials, urging "Come to Jamaica". With this, Bob Marley posthumously found himself pressed into the same tourist advocate role as the mento groups of the 1950s and 1960s. Needless to say, these commercials omitted the verses describing the behavior of sinners and the coming of Armageddon.

The available remixes do nothing to improve on the album track. Neither does the dub version on *Bob Marley & The Wailers In Dub, Vol. 1* that serves to show the effects of overdoing reverb on drums.

Exodus Deluxe Edition bonus tracks

In 2002, the two-CD Deluxe Edition of *Exodus* was released. It's filled out with handfuls of alternative renditions, dub versions, live tracks and, best of all, two classic non-album tracks, 'Roots' and 'Punky Reggae Party'.

'Roots'
'Roots' was recorded some months before the *Exodus* sessions began and would turn up as the B-side of the 'Waiting In Vain' single. It's hard to fathom why a place on the album could not be found for this mesmerizing roots reggae song. It would have only improved it. 'Roots' is a meditation on being Rasta: spare, dubby and mystical in sound. A meandering flute-like synthesizer gives the song a spacey feel. Carlton Barrett clearly enjoys the extra space the arrangement affords him, his drums painted with reverb. Aston Barrett provides Bob with a countermelody on bass. There is additional percussion and an assortment of other keyboards that bubble, shuffle and grind. But there is no guitar to be heard, and the instrument's absence feels like a song-length dub drop-out. On this artful frame, Bob and The I-Threes drape vocals that are, in the roots reggae way, introspective even as they are impassioned. Bob sings of surviving the *downpression* of Babylon, the danger of wolves in sheep's clothing and how none of them can keep him from his religion. In the song's central metaphor, he describes them as "dry wood", while other people, more vital, are likened to branches or leaves. Bob completes the metaphor by proclaiming himself as the roots. Having introduced roots reggae to the world outside of Jamaica, he's certainly entitled to say so.

Collectors also know of a dub version of uncertain origin sometimes called 'Roots Natty Roots'. Lots of drop-out makes this an ultra-sparse mix, with most of the keyboards replaced with wistful lead and rhythm guitar not heard on the original mix. This dub is a prime candidate for future CD release. Bunny Wailer recorded a bracing rendition of roots on his 1995 double-CD set called *Hall Of Fame: A Tribute To Bob Marley's 50th Anniversary*.

'Punky Reggae Party'; 'Punky Reggae Party' (dub)
It's party time with 'Punky Reggae Party' and what better way to celebrate than with a monster of a track? Previously, it had only been available as a single, either a shorter mix on 7-inch vinyl or, more commonly (and more desirably), longer mixes on different 12-inch single releases. It was a prized possession of any Bob Marley & The Wailers fan lucky enough to have a copy. The *Exodus Deluxe Edition* wisely chose to include it, and wisely chose to use the longest, most complete mix. Topping 9 minutes, it's the longest studio track Bob Marley recorded. With a big, atypical band, backing vocalists galore, a surprising subject and a tremendous two-part performance from Bob, there's not a single dull moment.

'Punky Reggae Party' is another collaboration with producer Lee Perry. His trademark creativity is heard literally in the first moment of the song, as its intro-duction opens with the sound of a sigh. Martial drums, a single note repeated on bass, dramatic piano and vocal teasers create a sense of promise. Good to their word, the body of the song begins and a torrent of fine reggae surges forth, with busy horns, male and female backing choruses, assorted keyboards, rhythm gui-tars, and a roots reggae rhythm section supplemented by both incidental hand percussion and Nyabinghi drum. The music bubbles untiringly at a galloping pace.

Bob recorded this track in London with a band consisting of members of Third World and British reggae band Aswad, sax men Headley Bennett and Cedric Brooks and others. Neither the instrumental Wailers nor The I-Threes were involved. But, as revealed by Dave Katz's definitive Lee Perry biography (Katz 2000: 310), Perry took the tapes home to Jamaica for a major overhaul. He replaced most, if not all, of these musicians' contributions with those of others. (Keyboardist Tyrone Downie is the only instrumental Wailer to be involved.) For example, the various male backing vocals come from Congo Watty Burnett and roots vocal group The Meditations, the latter of whom Bob would work with again. The resulting line-up creates reggae that measures up to the standard of The Wailers, while giving the song a somewhat different sound. The back-ing vocalists are notably playful and diverse. The female harmony chorus, sing-ing the scale, see-saws up and down. Watty Burnet supplies a bass chorus that repeats "punk, punk". The Meditations add dread drama with wordless descend-ing harmonies. Perry's production is also fine but atypical. Not only is there no sign of the Black Ark sound that he was spectacularly employing at this time, but the song is completely free of dub.

'Punky Reggae Party' is another of Bob's topical singles, but this one is not about events impacting Jamaicans. Instead, he is moved to sing about the connections between reggae and the UK's burgeoning punk music scene. Musically open-minded, punk fans and bands were often reggae fans too. A large portion of the initial fan base for UK reggae band Steel Pulse were punk fans, helping to launch the group. And it was commonplace for punk bands to try their hand at reggae. Shortly after this song's release, "Two Tone Ska" – also referred to as ska's second wave – would explode in the UK. This fusion of punk rock with ska rhythms would prove to be artistically and commercially successful, as the punky reggae party was carried forward by bands such as The Specials, Madness, The Selector and others.

But the punk-reggae connection ran even deeper than a love of Jamaican music. The performers and fans were from the poorer classes of their respective countries, disenfranchised by economic conditions. Their appearance marked them as rebels outside their societies' preferred norms, and they faced scorn and worse. These parallels are not missed by Bob, who covers these issues even as he devotes most of the lyrics to imagining the titular party. He namechecks a number of top punk bands that will be in attendance along with The Wailers and The Maytals. Who won't be there? "Boring old farts", says Bob, as he gets with the spirit of punk.

This is already a great song, but we haven't even gotten to its best feature. Near the 5-minute mark, Bob begins his celebrated extended scat. Whenever Bob graces one of his songs with a few bars of his scat singing, it's always a treat. This is the mother lode. He jams and grooves, punctuating with the occasional James Brownian grunt. Several minutes in, he starts oinking, a true punky reggae move. Following Lone Ranger, DJs had begun to spice their chants with animal-sound exclamations such as *oink!* and *ribbit!* But it was unprecedented for Bob – or any other singer – to thus dip into the DJs' bag of tricks. The scat continues its impressively varied flow for 4:30 minutes, as both the marathon scat and Bob's biggest and most playful song comes to an end.

The dub version, for all of its promise, is uninteresting. It has the vocals dropping out and back in a few times and there's some reverb. Some pressings of the 12-inch single had a more interesting, though shorter, dub version with oddball percussion overdubs. That might have been a better choice for inclusion here.

'Keep On Moving'; 'Keep On Moving' (dub)
'Keep On Moving' is the Curtis Mayfield song that The Wailers covered, versioned and recut with Lee Perry in the early 1970s. This rendition was recorded at the same London session that yielded 'Punky Reggae Party'. It's an adequate if unremarkable rendition of the song that makes it hard not to miss Bob, Bunny and Peter taking turns with the lead. But just as the song would be expected to end, it takes a surprising turn as Bob introduces new lyrics. He essentially speak-sings a letter

home to Rita, including specific regards to son Ziggy and to Auntie, a promise to resend a check to replace one lost in the mail, a mention of a planned big show, and his hopes for a brighter future for the children of Africa. For this reason, this rendition is sometimes called the "postcard version". It's reminiscent of The Who's song, 'Postcard', but the message here is so personal, it was probably intended as a truly personal postcard rather than conceived for release. Bob was known for his unrelenting work ethic, constantly recording, performing or rehearsing. Here, he apparently recorded a song when anyone else in the world would have written or picked up a phone. The dub version is crazy, pulsating with echo and rattling percussion, and does not sound as if it came from a Jamaican producer.

'Waiting In Vain' (alternative version); 'Jammin'' (long version); 'Jammin'' (dub version)
A different take of 'Waiting In Vain' is nearly as good, but not quite, as the album version. A piano solo is heard mid-song, bumping the guitar solo to later, in this longer rendition.

Another rendition of 'Jammin'' is taken from a previously released disco-mix single. It atypically appends the dub version at the start of the mix rather than at the end. The dub portion is largely instrumental, with some echoing vocals dropped in. When the non-dub version is heard, The I-Threes are held in reserve until late in the track. The lead piano that memorably helped to set up the song's melody on the album rendition is not heard here. It's a toss-up between this and the original rendition, making it a good bonus track. Also included is the disco-mix's B-side, an unremarkable, shorter and nearly instrumental dub version.

'Exodus' (dub version); 'Exodus Advertisement'
The dub version of 'Exodus' originally appeared as the B-side of its single release. It's a 3-minute instrumental slab of the original recording. That's a disappointment, as a good dub-master could have worked wonders with such a densely layered arrangement. 'Exodus Advertisement' begins with a short excerpt of the song that is abruptly interrupted by a gong, ushering in a laughing Bob Marley, who introduces 'Exodus' and sends salutations. The gong strikes again, Bob introduces 'Waiting In Vain', and a short segment of that song is heard.

Live at the Rainbow Theatre, London (June 4, 1977)
Five live tracks from the Exodus tour round out the Deluxe Edition of *Exodus*. The entire show would later become available on DVD. 'The Heathen' stretches out to three times the original's length, expanding with a roots jam that gives the song additional power. 'Crazy Baldhead' is presented as a medley with the yet-to-be-released 'Running Away', and 'War' is similarly blended with 'No More Trouble'. 'Jammin'' and a nearly 12-minute 'Exodus' complete this sample of another fine Bob Marley & The Wailers live performance.

Kaya

Released in 1978, *Kaya* is drawn from London sessions that also yielded the *Exodus* album released the previous year. Like *Exodus*, the original LP release of *Kaya* was something of a two-sided coin. The first side does not equivocate. It's a ride on billowing clouds of ganja smoke, as dub-happy songs focus on herb, love or both. The second side features more serious songs, recorded with far less dub. The sound throughout both sides is bright, right down to the profusion of incidental percussion, like sparks from a fire. From *Kaya* on forward, Seeco Patterson would be even more prominently featured in the mix as he spiced the sound with a variety of hand percussion.

Three of *Kaya*'s songs are remakes, each drawn from The Wailers' mid-period sessions with Lee Perry. Just as *Exodus* has been overrated, *Kaya* is sometimes an underrated album. Perhaps this is because there are only two overtly Rasta songs, and some fans may use this aspect as the sole yardstick of Bob's music. But weighing each aspect of Bob's diverse songwriting equally, and considering the quality of the songs and sound, *Kaya* should be reckoned as one of the best Bob Marley & The Wailers albums.

'Easy Skanking'

'Easy Skanking' is the very sound of relaxation, setting the tone for side 1 of *Kaya*'s original LP release. Though skanking most literally refers to dancing to a particular reggae beat or that beat itself, here it more broadly describes moving through life. And Bob advises us to take a most relaxed approach. A good portion of the lyrics explain the importance of ganja for this easy skanking. Ganja will give a lift, aid in the enjoyment of music, and help in dealing with reality. This reveals something of Bob's – and Rasta – beliefs about marijuana. It's not a way to escape reality, but a way to better bring it into focus. Later we learn more as Bob chooses ganja as his wine. Rastafarians view ganja as being the biblical sacrament rather than wine, as they forgo alcohol altogether.

Not surprisingly, both Bob and The I-Threes sound sumptuously relaxed. Likewise, the instrumental Wailers seem to be the first and foremost adherents of Bob's advice. The reggae is delivered with an easy touch that shields against harshing your buzz. Even the production adds to the feel with a stereo sound stage opened wide and incidental percussion tickling each ear.

'Kaya'

The marijuana theme continues into the album's second song and title track. Bob sings about being high and feeling great in his remake of The Wailers' first ganja song, 'Kaya', as originally recorded in their middle period with Lee Perry. It's fairly faithful to the original, though a goofy synthesizer, undoubtedly intended to sound stoned, replaces buzzed acoustic guitar, and not for the better. But this rendition does percolate nicely, and is kissed by a bright dubby sunshine. The vocals are stronger here than on the original, but some may prefer the earlier rendition's quirky, stoned-sounding singing. So which is the best rendition is open to debate. What is certain is that this one fits perfectly on the album and keeps the easy vibes flowing.

'Is This Love'

'Is This Love' is the follow-up to the popular love song on *Exodus*, 'Waiting In Vain'. Keeping with the album's established tone, there is no angst this time around. It's a simple declaration of love, with Bob sounding a bit vulnerable. But The I-Threes' harmonies are encouraging, while the band further bolsters Bob's declarations. Horn lines and acoustic and electric guitars are featured, as the band creates a bouncy reggae groove that's hard to resist.

All of this contributes to what would prove to be another internationally successful piece of lovers' rock for Bob. It reached no. 9 on the UK charts, perhaps aided by female record buyers – listen to the decidedly female shift in screaming when Bob introduces it on the *Live Forever* CD. And, as was the case for 'Waiting In Vain', 'Is This Love' was covered by a number of non-Jamaican singers. Carly Simon had some success with her cover recorded with Sly & Robbie. Rihanna, Brazil's Gilberto Gil, blues-rocker Pat Travers and other also took a turn.

'Sun Is Shining'

'Sun Is Shining', the album's second remake of a middle-period song originally recorded with Lee Perry, elevates an already great song into the realm of a Bob Marley & The Wailers classic. No other Marley song better captures the sensation of being high on ganja, with the Jamaican sun beating down on you, in throbbing waves of dub.

It opens creatively with a simultaneous guitar and bass note. The guitar abruptly ceases and is replaced by a burst of trebly piano that plays off the bass before it soon vanishes for the remainder of the track. But it's the processed rhythm guitar that is the song's secret weapon. It double-strums the rhythm, simulating dub echo while recalling the rural mento beat that helped give birth to reggae. It's played in a hypnotic cycle of chords that seems to grow heavier as it repeats. Double-tracked with one per stereo channel, it makes the sound 3D, especially when one is wearing headphones. Meanwhile, Aston Barrett plays a bass line that intuitively locates and massages a pleasure center deep inside the brain. Brother Carlton plays creative drums that contribute greatly to the song's stoned air. He employs a pattern whose woody sound is complemented by cowbell. Lead guitar returns to wander about, alternating between muted reggae picking and bluesy runs, and provides a mid-song solo. A late-to-the-party organ jams with the guitar. Dub heightens the music. Early on, there's a surprise dose, as bass and vocals drop out when incidental percussion appears: reverbed triangle in one ear and a ratcheting sound in the other. Bass re-enters with a flourish, then come vocals, while the percussion remains. Later, a second drop-out/in session is heard, further enriching this, the dubbiest of all Bob Marley & The Wailers international album tracks.

After an opening with a brief scat, we are greeted with the familiar feel-good sentiments about weather so good it makes Bob want to dance. Then the lyrics get giddy before meandering off to list the days of the week, for no apparent reason. This rendition adds some new lyrics that stay true to the song's ganja vibe, as Bob sounds dazed and confused and The I-Threes sound blissed out. This rendition of 'Sun Is Shining' is a rare example of a Bob Marley & The Wailers classic that is strong in every way except for the lyrics. But if the lyrics were focused differently, the song just wouldn't have been the same.

Surprisingly, a dub version of *Kaya*'s 'Sun Is Shining' has never been released. But just such a track was recorded and is circulated on the collectors' circuit. It's based on a mix that was so different it may be considered an alternative take. There are enough odd touches to raise the possibility that Lee Perry was the producer. It's crying out for release on CD.

'Satisfy My Soul'

'Satisfy My Soul' is another remake, but not of 'Satisfy My Soul Jah Jah' nor of 'Satisfy My Soul Babe'. In another misnomer, it's in fact a new rendition of 'Don't Rock My Boat', a song The Wailers self-produced in 1968. They subsequently recut it several times for producer Lee Perry at the start of the 1970s, usually with Bob as a solo vocalist. Further complicating the name game, one of the Perry renditions was instead titled 'I Like It Like This'.

It's a love song to a woman whom Bob equates to a sweepstake prize. He is so content, his only fear is that his love might change the status quo of their relationship, accounting for the earlier title. In keeping with the theme of the album's preceding songs, he sneaks in a ganja lyric that was not part of the earlier renditions. This remake differs in sound from its sparser, more direct predecessors. Here the song is more relaxed and cushiony, with prominent horns, a soft dub section and The I-Threes providing comfort. It's strictly a matter of choice, or one's mood for the day, which rendition is best.

'She's Gone'

The first song on side 2 of the original LP release of *Kaya*, 'She's Gone', signals a change of tone. It's another love song, but an unhappy one. Bob alternates between melancholy and pain in this song of abandoned love. He goes on to allude that his star lifestyle was the cause of the rift. On *Exodus*'s 'Three Little Birds', birds were harbingers of joy. But here, a mockingbird becomes a symbol of regret. The instrumental Wailers are restrained and The I-Threes sound solemn. Not one to wallow in self-pity, 'She's Gone' makes its point and is done in less than 2:30 minutes, the shortest song in Bob's string of internationally released albums.

Though not a bad song, it is fair to call it a minor one. A longer dub version can be heard on *Bob Marley & The Wailers In Dub, Vol. 1*. It features a surfeit of dub effects plus a very different arrangement, with a jazzy opening, horns and organ not heard on the original.

'Misty Morning'

Played in unison by the three-piece section of Gordon, DaCosta and Madden, 'Misty Morning' opens with a big, ascending horn line that sounds set to conquer the world. Rousing horns continue to dominate the instrumentation, with acoustic guitar providing a sonic counterpoint. Meanwhile, Carlton's drumming is especially generous as he breaks off many a fine roll. He's supplemented by a Nyah hand drum and other assorted hand instruments for a sound that is percussively rich. Brother Ashton's staccato bass line is playful, and shines through as the lead instrument during a mid-song span where the horns take a break.

Bob marries an emotional vocal to this powerful instrumentation, with typically strong melodies and memorable lyrics. But befitting the title, the song is a cypher, its lyrics never giving us enough to construct a clear story. There are pained demands to "straighten out", but it's not clear whether they are being made by Bob or directed towards him. A couplet about jumping into the water is memorable, yet there are several equally plausible meanings to it. Likewise, the musing on philosophy, which is described as being both light and heavy, is memorable and poetic, but does little to explain the song. Nor do typically fine backing vocals from The I-Threes add any clues. Keeping us totally in the dark does not impact on what is still a very strong song. The final mystery of 'Misty Morning' is why it was never played live, nor was a dub or other version ever released.

'Crisis'; 'Running Away'

'Crisis' and 'Running Away' are two songs in which Bob alters his singing to portray a character, but neither makes for a great vocal performance. Though both skank nicely, neither is one of the better songs on *Kaya*.

'Crisis' is the first of two Rasta songs on the album. In it Bob speaks directly to those who are chronically disheartened – those for whom the "sun never shines". This is the antithesis of the good feelings of 'Sun Is Shining'. Bob asks them not to forsake God no matter how bad things are. He also takes on the politicians he holds responsible for people dying. While doing so, he references the old American folk song, 'The House Of The Rising Sun', about a life-ruining New Orleans brothel. It's an interesting way to paint these politicians as corrupt. And, in the process, he circles back again to the sun as the song's central metaphor. Bob adopts the skanking beat 'Crisis', sometimes affecting a nervous, harried singing style to portray someone who is having a crisis. The riddim features one of the few touches of dub to infiltrate from side 1. But the overall sound is somber rather than giddy, right down to the grounded electric piano solo from Tyrone Downie. A less-than-crucial single B-side dub version of 'Crisis' with no vocals and extra lead guitar has eluded CD release to this point.

'Running Away' is a dark, mysterious song about an indeterminate interpersonal conflict, bringing 'Misty Morning' to mind. The sound is portentous as the Barrett brothers toil and an electric guitar gnashes. Somber electric piano is heard again, and is the lead instrument here. Guitars and horns do nothing to brighten the mood. Bob sings to a mysterious estranged party about the futility of their actions. Mid-song, he adopts a mocking voice that sounds like criticisms from an elderly relative, as the reggae roils. By the end of the song, he changes the point of view to that of the runner, who offers a defense of needing to leave problems behind, as Bob increases the mocking tone. It has been suggested that this song is Bob's veiled criticism of those who accused him of running away from Jamaica after the assassination attempt. It could also be about relationship problems that Bob was having with Rita at that time, leading Rita to move out.

The song includes a pair of nods to Wailers music of years past. Rare for this decade of Bob Marley & The Wailers music, 'Running Away' features a brief trombone solo, played by Vin Gordon. Bob enjoys this blast from the past, joining in with scat singing. Also reaching back to the previous decade is the couplet, "Everyman thinketh his burden is the heaviest. But who feels it knows it, Lord." Both lines were prominently featured in the mid-1960s Wailers track, 'Who Feels It Knows It'. But that was a Bunny Wailer song, recorded while Bob was away in Delaware. This creates yet another possible interpretation: 'Running Away' may be a belated reaction to the split-up of the original Wailers.

'Time Will Tell'
The album closes with its second of two Rasta songs, the great 'Time Will Tell'. It's the first Bob Marley & The Wailers Nyabinghi-reggae track since *Catch A Fire*'s 'Rastaman Chant', but not their last, as 'Babylon System' would later appear on the *Survival* album.

Nyabinghi drums, with the big bass drum thundering quietly on the first beat of each four, are on equal footing with idyllic reggae. There are assorted keyboards, but the reggae instrumentation is led by sparkling acoustic guitar, reminiscent of The Wailers' 1967 Nyah instrumental, 'Lyrical Satirical I'. Even with the occasional synthesizer line, the sound is largely acoustic and idyllic in a way that is reminiscent of the Bunny Wailer-led Wailers songs from 1973. As the song progresses, it fills out with even more keyboards and guitars.

'Time Will Tell' is conventionally sung rather than chanted (as Nyah music typically is). Bob's focus is the exploitation of the people by Babylon. He addresses the dichotomy that Jamaica is an island of great natural beauty but made ugly by oppression for all but a few. He sounds introspective and at peace. He sings in harmony, but not with The I-Threes, who are not heard on this track, but with his double-tracked self. It's a rare treat to hear two Bob Marleys harmonizing for the length of a song. The soul-steadying sound of Nyabinghi drums, bright acoustic guitar and double Bobs all contribute to a serene song of power and beauty.

A different take of 'Time Will Tell' that is quite striking can be heard on the *Countryman* movie soundtrack album. This shorter minimalistic rendition is dirge-like, ending with Bob singing over quiet heartbeat Nyabinghi drums in what sounds like a Nyah funeral march.

'Smile Jamaica' (fast version disco-mix)

Included as a bonus track on later CD editions of *Kaya* is a disco-mix of the "fast version" of 'Smile Jamaica'. The "slow version", recorded at the same time, appeared as part of the bonus material on the Deluxe Edition of *Rastaman Vibration*. With producer Lee Perry at the helm, it's no great surprise that two renditions of the song were released. When he was The Wailers' producer in the early 1970s, releasing multiple takes of a song, similar or different, was common practice for him.

The two renditions of 'Smile Jamaica' are different in more than their tempos. The sad sounds of the slow version are banished by the energetic, upbeat "steppers" drum pattern, with its insistent equal sounding of each beat. The band line-up is smaller, with Aston Barrett supplying guitar and some keyboards in addition to bass. Gone are the other rendition's horns and male vocals. Filling out the sound are the sonics of a Lee Perry Black Ark production – over-saturated cymbals and flanged rhythm guitar. Perhaps because of the urgency to get this topical record quickly released, it sounds less realized than better examples of the Black Ark art. Even the appended dub version of the disco-mix is quite tame. But the song is notable as the only intersection between Lee Perry's Black Ark sound and the music of Bob Marley. Bob's high-energy, scat-charged performance also differs greatly from the other rendition and its emotionally conflicted delivery. Here, his singing is a powerful tonic, and is truer to the intent of the song – to *big up* the people of Jamaica at a time when they most needed encouragement and support. With the two renditions of this fine, important song so different from one another, it's easy to see why both were released. And the Bob Marley & The Wailers catalog is better for it.

Babylon By Bus

In 1979, Bob Marley & The Wailers released *Babylon By Bus*, a double-LP live collection culled from four European shows from the previous year's Kaya tour. All of its songs are familiar from the internationally released albums, along with a performance of the single, 'Punky Reggae Party'. It's his first concert release since the revered *Live!*, and Bob now had a bigger repertoire to bring to the high standard set by the earlier album. Although some of the songs met this standard, others did not. Several songs are short and some of them sound rushed and perfunctory (most of all 'Stir It Up'). When this was the case, the songs seemed to lack the performers' full presence, and are denied the sultry richness of a live Bob Marley & The Wailers performance. But there is still a lot to like on *Babylon By Bus*. 'Punky Reggae Party' is a surprise inclusion, and a wise one. The audience is thrilled and roars a sing-along to The Mediations' wordless chorus, inspiring Bob to greater heights (though there is no sign of the famous scat). 'Rat Race's missing lyrics are heard. As 'Kinky Reggae' progresses, you can hear the song loosen Bob up. A jammed-out 'Exodus' is another of the set's high points.

Kaya Deluxe Edition live show

In 2013, the expanded *Kaya* Deluxe Edition was released. It was enhanced with a second disc with thirteen tracks from a July 7, 1979, live show from Rotterdam, in the Netherlands. Though this is the same tour that gave us *Babylon By Bus*, and both sets feature the same number of tracks, there are differences. The Rotterdam set leans more towards the hits, with the inclusion of 'No Woman No Cry', 'Get Up, Stand Up' and 'I Shot The Sherriff'. None of these songs appeared on *Babylon By Bus*, perhaps because they were already so associated with the previous concert release, *Live!* And Rotterdam trades the excitement of 'Punky Reggae Party' for 'Easy Skankin'', another song not often performed live. But overall, *Babylon By Bus* is the sharper set, as you would expect from an album that cherry-picked the best performances from multiple shows on the tour.

Two interludes upon returning home

Their fruitful sessions as exiles in England would come to an end when Bob and company returned to Jamaica in 1978. One of their first sessions at home was with producer Lee Perry, echoing the session with him in 1975. Again, Bob brought along the instrumental Wailers but not the The I-Threes. And again, the session was short, resulting in two songs. 'Who Colt The Game' and 'I Know A Place' would see eventual release on various collections, sometimes with over-dubs, as they sounded more like demos than tracks intended for release. 'Who Colt The Game' has underdeveloped instrumentation but a feisty vocal from Bob. As he later did in 'Bad Card', he uses cards, and here dominoes as well, to describe his conflicts with Babylon. 'I Know A Place' finds Bob offering solace to the disen-franchised, with a possible double entendre that may have been unintentional, judging by the rest of the lyrics. Its instrumentation is somewhat more developed than on the other song, but the pop-style keyboards (later overdubbed) were not necessarily the best way to finish the track.

'Jammin''' (live, from the One Love Peace Concert)
Bob Marley & The Wailers' first concert after ending their exile in London was a big one – the One Love Peace Concert of April 22, 1978. The concert was conceived as a symbolic plea to end the political strife that had grown to near

civil-war proportions in Kingston. More than a dozen top acts performed, with returning sons Bob Marley & The Wailers headlining. The soundtrack CD of the 2012 film documentary *Marley* includes the climax of the show, a performance of 'Jammin''. The performance is intense, Bob's especially. By sheer force of will, he works himself into a state, chanting, trying to channel the power of Jah to bring an end to the fighting. It does not sound quite like any other vocal in Bob's career. It compels the two party heads and bitter enemies, Michael Manley and Edward Seaga, to take the stage and join hands with Bob in a dramatic show of peace and a demonstration of the power of Bob Marley's music.

Survival

Released in 1979, *Survival* is a departure from *Kaya* in many ways. It lacks any of the happy love, ganja or party songs that characterized half the earlier album. 'One Drop', 'Africa Unite' and 'Ride Natty Ride' are the only songs on *Survival* that approach joyfulness in any way. On two songs, Bob sounds world-weary, adding to the somber mood. This makes *Survival* the most serious Bob Marley & The Wailers album. Even the sometimes dour *Natty Dread* had the joyful 'Lively Up Yourself' and the warm 'No Woman No Cry' to lighten the mood. Here Bob had *so much things to say* on Rasta and revolution that this would be his first album that did not include any remakes. Work on a remake of 'Soul Shakedown Party' was abandoned early in favor of new songs. On a roll, his next and final album, *Uprising*, would also only feature new songs.

The sound of *Survival* is bigger than on *Kaya* or any of the albums that came before. For one thing, several songs on this album feature a horn section that is unusually large for reggae. With up to eight players, it tops even The Skatalites for sheer size. Headly Bennett, Nambo Robinson and Dean Fraser are joined by five US sessions players, who, without blaring, produce a brassier, more melded sound than was typical for a Jamaican horn section. One of these players was American trombonist Melba Liston, giving her the distinction of being the only female instrumentalist to play on a Bob Marley & The Wailers session. The big section suits *Survival*'s return to heavy, horn-filled slabs of revolutionary reggae, last heard in songs like 'War' and 'Exodus'. Also making the sound bigger are the male backing vocals, led by keyboard player Tyrone Downie along with guitarist Al Anderson and keyboard player Earl "Wya" Lindo. At times, they are as prominent as The I-Threes. With this and the large quantity of lyrics Bob wrote for himself, The I-Threes sound a bit crowded at times on the album.

Even more adjustments were made to *Survival*'s sound. You will have to search to hear any rock guitar leads; only 'Top Rankin'' features this instrument. This makes *Survival* the most lead-guitar-free Bob Marley & The Wailers album other than *Burnin'*. One song, 'Ride Natty Ride', features the return of Lee Jaffe and harmonica, last heard on *Natty Dread*. A drier, less Jamaican sound is featured. The album is nearly dub-free, recalling the earliest albums in the string. It's well produced, but certain flourishes, and how the drums are recorded, recall the work of a top rock producer of the time rather than something from a Jamaican producer. The drum sound is further altered by Carlton Barrett's absence for a good portion of the album. Most often reggae's other drummer named Carlton, Carlton "Santa" Davis, fills in, as does Mikey "Boo" Richards.

There are no songs that are less than good on *Survival*. But few are outstanding and some are rather unremarkable. This makes it a consistent album, though not one of Bob Marley & The Wailers' best, especially if compared to the previous one, *Kaya*, and the upcoming *Uprising*. *Survival* opens with its most introspective song and closes with its most rousing.

'So Much Trouble In The World'

Survival begins with a unique Bob Marley & The Wailers song, the gentle and sorrowful 'So Much Trouble In The World'. It opens with a snippet of studio chatter, Bob wanting more drums. He gets just that as Carlton Barrett's miniature introduction kicks off the song. It's a precise, highly expert and polished approach to making reggae, one we've already heard on *Exodus*'s 'Waiting In Vain'. And on the next album, *Uprising*, 'We And Dem' and 'Work' would also be fashioned in this same carefully wrought style of the instrumental Wailers' craft.

Sorrowful synthesized flute plays lead over a backing of lilting strummed acoustic guitars. A layer beneath, drums, percussion, bass and keyboards bubble darkly, counterbalancing the brightness of the guitar. Atop it all, Bob sounds introspective and sorrowful. He is humbly thankful for the dawn of each new day. But he is bothered by governments' focus on such things as the space programs and weapons development, while ignoring the needs and abilities of the people. To make this last point, he revives his favorite Bible-based metaphor that uses the cornerstone as a symbol of unjust rejection (as previously discussed in The Wailers' middle-period song, 'Corner Stone'; page 219). Bob is well supported by The I-Threes, including a memorable wordless chorus with a recriminating descending melody that speaks more than words. Who other than Bob Marley would open an album with a lament for the world's problems? And who else could make it such an appealing song?

Available only on collections ranging from the arguably to the undoubtedly illicit, 'So Much Trouble Dub' is one of the better dub versions from Bob Marley & The Wailers' international album era. This simple instrumental version gets a lot of mileage by taking advantage of the song's polyrhythmic backing with a few clever applications of drop-out/in and some modest echo and reverb. Hopefully, this recording will turn up as a bonus track on a future edition of *Survival*.

'Zimbabwe'

'Zimbabwe' is a song more notable for its subject matter than its music; growling roots reggae made spikey with percussion (dig that cowbell!). It marks the return of Bob the revolutionary in his most politically specific song.

As he did when he set Haile Selassie's speech to the United Nations to music in 'War', Bob expands his concern from the oppression of black people in Jamaica to those in other nations. But unlike 'War', where Bob is so fiery, here he sounds world-weary. It opens with him singing about basic human rights, but the song's focus soon moves to Zimbabwe and the freedom fighters who were trying to wrest control of the country from a colonial government. They would soon triumph, and Bob Marley & The Wailers would provide the entertainment at Zimbabwe's independence celebrations, all costs paid by Bob. Amidst Bob's exhortations to victory (backed by a male chorus for a strong, soldierly sound), a surprising concern is given voice. The Rasta distrust of government seems to extend even to the revolutionaries. That concern and Bob's weary tone would ultimately prove prescient in light of the many serious problems that have emerged in Zimbabwe since the freedom fighters took power. Unfortunately, Marley can no longer provide much-needed musical succor for its citizens.

'Top Rankin''
'Top Rankin'' is another exploration of some of Bob's favorite themes: the need for unity, and how fussing and fighting not only is counterproductive, it plays into the oppressors' hands. Bob's vocals are emphatic but he sounds weary to the point of exhaustion, and the instrumental Wailers are uninspired. But all is not lost. The lyrics, melody and production (with a touch of dub rare for the album) all perk up nicely on the chorus, where Bob sings of love for his brothers and sisters. Instrumentally, Santa Davis provides fine drum work anchoring the song on the third beat of every four, and (also rare for this album) there are blues-rock guitar riffs. But the instrumental highlight is the album's first appearance of horns. The surprising sound of the expanded horn section brings much-needed punch to 'Top Rankin''.

'Babylon System'
'Babylon System' is the final Nyabinghi-reggae that Bob Marley would record (though the upcoming 'Redemption Song' would sometimes be performed in this style in concert), as he and The I-Threes *chant down Babylon one more time*. Organ, guitars and bass join Nyabinghi drums led by Seeco Patterson. Though the song lacks the chanted Nyabinghi vocals of 'Rastaman Chant' or the sparkle of 'Time Will Tell', the lyrics are more powerful than on either of these previous Nyah-reggae songs. Bob pushes back hard at Babylon's institutions, which exploit rather than accept the Rasta. He concludes by employing a favorite Rasta metaphor that equates Babylon to vampires. That all of this censure can be contained in such a pleasant-sounding song (The I-Threes sound especially pretty here) is a dichotomy that roots reggae fans are well familiar with and fully appreciate.

'Survival'
The album's title track is a teeming reggae song. It opens with the trebly combination of The I-Threes singing playful *ohs* over a restrained chart from the

large horn section and long quivering organ notes. It sounds like the band is pacing in its cage, waiting for release. Joining with a series of *yeahs*, Bob throws the door open, and the body of the song begins. Briefly, it's just Bob and the rhythm instruments led by a bustling bass line. The horns soon return, followed by organ swells, followed by male backing vocals that are quickly augmented by The I-Threes, as the song reaches its fullness. Along with the typical guitars, keyboards and percussion, this may be the biggest band to ever record a Bob Marley & The Wailers song.

In the song's opening, hypocrites, one of Bob's favorite targets, wilt under a blistering attack on those who only pay lip service to the suffering of others. He sings of the need to adopt the teachings of Rastafari as a means of survival, not just from oppression in Jamaica, but also, again broadening to global concerns, nuclear weapons. He works an impressive comparison between Jamaica's haves and have-nots. He also draws parallels between Rastas living in Babylon and stories from the Bible. Daniel surviving the lion's den after being cast there for his religious beliefs is referenced. So are Shadrach, Meshach and Abednego, whose faith kept them from burning when they were cast into a furnace for their refusal to follow the king's religion. But it's Bob who is on fire and his strong vocals are the very sound of moral authority as he covers all this ground. And then he softens his tone but not his intensity when he introduces a second chorus, using Rasta terms in an appeal to women ("sistren") and children ("I-dren"). By the force of Bob's outsized vocal performance, 'Survival' is one of the best songs on the album.

'Africa Unite'
'Africa Unite' is the second of two songs on *Survival* concerning Africa. But whereas 'Zimbabwe' was about that country's specific political situation, 'Africa Unite' covers more general Rasta themes. Bob muses on unity for Africans and those of African descent. And although it's not explicit, he calls for repatriation, making this his first song with a back-to-Africa theme since 'Exodus'. But unlike 'Exodus', it's an easy-going song, and one of the more relaxed tracks on *Survival*. This is immediately evident as Bob enters with a light-hearted scat over a sweet alto sax solo from Dean Fraser. Piano, flute (albeit synthesized) and percolating reggae guitar picking are also heard, giving the song a somewhat idyllic roots reggae feel. Bob sounds thoughtful but at peace as he explores the song's titular theme. Only in the closing refrain does he interject an anxious note: "Unite for it's later than you think." And in the song's final moments, Bob revisits a favorite symbol for the second of three cornerstone references on *Survival*.

'One Drop'; 'One Dub'
The upbeat 'One Drop' is Bob's first album track about reggae since 'Roots Rock Reggae' on *Rastaman Vibration* (though both single sides, 'Punky Reggae Party'

and, to a lesser degree, 'Roots', were partially about the subject). It takes its name from the reggae sub-rhythm on display here. Bob likens the rhythm to a heartbeat and praises it as a revolutionary force against a system that causes hunger, starvation and death. The power of the reggae and the power of Jah have him secure in his confidence. Wailing Wailer Bob provides the song with a rough keening vocal, as male and female backing choruses lend support.

'One Drop' has one of the few suggestions of dub on the album, and demands a proper dub version. Thankfully, one exists, since the single's B-side, 'One Dub', is the only dub version chosen for inclusion on the career-spanning Bob Marley & The Wailers box-set, *Songs Of Freedom*. This nearly instrumental version modestly dips into the whole classic dub toolkit, as reverb, echo and drop-out/in are in effect. (Who knew there was piano under the organ in the song's opening?) The riddim of 'One Drop' enjoyed further life when, in the mid-1990s, a faithful remake of its instrumentation became the basis of a dancehall riddim, with multiple dancehall stars each having a go at it with songs of their own.

'Ride Natty Ride'; 'Ride Natty Ride' (12-inch)
'Ride Natty Ride' is a song of revolution, focused on Rasta's triumph over the societal systems that are stacked against it. Instrumental highlights include an idiosyncratic drum intro from Carlton Barrett, trombone and harmonica exchanging phrases, and percussion that imitates the sound of clopping horse hooves, giving life to the song's title. It's a wordy song in which Bob does not take as much as a mid-song pause. In one long verse, he revisits his favorite Bible metaphor about the cornerstone. In the song's climax, he describes politicians trying to smooth things over with a speech. This is summarily rejected as the need for self-reliance is recognized and preferred.

Sometimes more is more and the 12-inch version included as a bonus track in later editions of the *Survival* CD is the preferred version. Rather than a disco-mix, it's a longer cut of the song that has the effect of giving Bob the time necessary to fully get the song off his chest. And there's a touch of dub that, although minimal, is enough to make the sound superior to the bone-dry, dub-free album rendition. Collectors also know of a good, mostly instrumental, dub mix called 'Ride Dis Ya Dub' that has not been collected on LP or CD.

'Ambush In The Night'
On 'Ambush In The Night', Bob appears to be dealing with the attempt on his life, although that was a daytime attack. He blames the ambush on a failed government that causes desperation, so that brothers turn on brothers. He attributes his survival to Jah. He doesn't sound defiant or aggrieved, just tired. And the instrumental Wailers come up with a rather casual backing. Horns help prop it up, and although this is not quite a bad song, it is the weakest on the album. Considering the subject, it's a song that deserved more from all involved parties.

'Wake Up And Live'

Survival goes out with a bang rather than a whimper with 'Wake Up And Live'. Even more than in the title track, Bob makes full use of this, his largest-ever band. The big horn section flexes its muscle, at times providing two overlapping horn lines, plus a long mid-song sax solo from Dean Fraser. Meanwhile, a male backing chorus again supplements The I-Threes. And an African talking drum is heard, the instrument's only appearance in a Bob Marley & The Wailers song. The guest rhythm section finds Mikey Boo on drums and Val Douglas on bass, with Aston Barrett providing guitar instead of bass. Douglas makes the most of his opportunity, enlivening the song with spaced clusters of deep notes, playful runs and the occasional triplet of a high note.

Unlike the similarly arranged title track, here Bob does not feel the need to match the big sound with a surfeit of lyrics. Instead he takes his time and brings slow-burn righteous intensity to the song. He implores Jamaicans to build something better than the exploitative system they live under today. He says they can do so through unity, persistence and numbers. He uses the Jamaican proverb, "one, one coco fill a basket", a call for patience and persistence, as gathering coco (a type of sweet potato) one at a time will eventually lead you to meet your goal. Imploring his people to do better, he revisits the road as a symbol of peril, familiar to us from such songs as 'Simmer Down', 'Trouble On The Road Again' and 'Caution'. Bob's deliberate pace allows him to more fully inhabit the song. When he urges his people to "rise", that word is sustained so long and strong, it could raise the dead. Mid-song, he starts to groove with James Brown-esque cries. He announces Dean Fraser's sax solo with "Breakdown!" and embellishes it with squeals and exhortations.

This is an excellent, fully charged reggae track, but when it appeared as a single, we learned that it was incomplete. That's because the B-side, called 'Wake Up And Live Part 2', was a previously unheard segment of the song where Bob adopts a softer tone. This suggested that the album track was edited, with this portion being excised. Confirmation came when a mix called 'Wake Up And Live Parts 1 & 2' appeared as a bonus track on later CD editions of the 1986 Bob Marley & The Wailers best-of collection called *Rebel Music*. The song was then finally complete, with 1:45 minutes restored to its length, yielding a nearly 7-minute slab of powerful reggae in the process.

Uprising

Released in 1980, *Uprising* is the final album by Bob Marley & The Wailers before Bob's death from cancer a year later. Although he was already battling the disease, it did not stop *Uprising* from being one of his very best albums. (This brings back to mind the Wailers/Beatles comparison, as the final album The Beatles recorded, *Abbey Road*, was one of their very best.)

Uprising is as different from *Survival* as *Survival* was from *Kaya*. The storm of horns has passed, and *Uprising* is the first Bob Marley & The Wailers album without horns since *Burnin'*. The surge of male vocals is reduced. Although they are featured on two songs, they are not as prominent nor do they sound as militaristic as they did on the previous album. The fine but non-Jamaican-sounding production of *Survival* is gone, replaced with the welcome return of dub (most frequently in the form of strategically applied reverb on the drums). Lead guitar is back in effect, though not to a great extent. Bob's songs have fewer lyrics than on *Survival*. This and the sparser arrangements allow room for Bob's natural playfulness to come to the fore, grooving as he repeats lines. Likewise, The I-Threes, who were sometimes crowded on *Survival*, are again given room to breathe.

The subject matter is mostly serious, though there is a joyous love song of sorts and a mischievous song in 'Could You Be Loved' and 'Bad Card' respectively. Some songs are uncharacteristically hopeless, downbeat lyrically, if not musically. This may have been due to the realities of Bob's illness setting in. But this is not to say that *Uprising* is a downbeat album. It's considerably brighter than *Survival*, and there are instances of religious ecstasy. And the album closes on a most positive note. It's an exceptionally strong set, filled with great tracks and classics, with perhaps two songs falling below this high standard. The nine songs are once again all originals. With his last two albums free of remakes, and considering the strength of *Uprising* in particular, we are led to the conclusion that Bob's songwriting gifts were only growing stronger, and the heart-rending realization that his death undoubtedly deprived us of an untold number of additional great songs.

Uprising has a diverse mix of reggae styles. One song is a solo acoustic performance and another is influenced by the disco music phenomenon, each resulting in a classic track. There are Rasta themes, plus a nod back to gospel. Some songs are loosely constructed, while several others ('We And Dem', 'Work', and 'Zion Train') are built of reggae that ticks with the precision of a metronome, as the instrumental Wailers shine. Carlton Barrett is back on drums for all but one track, where Santa Davis again fills in. As good as Santa is, the album is better for Barrett's return. Brother Aston provides a brilliant bass line for each song, something that fans of Bob Marley & The Wailers have now come to expect. Guitarists Junior Marvin and Al Anderson and keyboardists Tyrone Downie and Wya Lindo continue to fill the songs with music. With great assurance, they add their parts exactly where they should, handing off to and interacting with the other instruments like the well-oiled reggae machine they are. The music continues to be percussively rich, with Carlton's drum prowess enhanced with dub and supplemented by multiple tracks of incidental percussion from Seeco Patterson. Seeco's contributions are well chosen and out front, such as the pretty bell in 'Pimper's Paradise' or funky double-struck cowbell in 'Zion Train'.

That Bob's swansong album is such a strong one makes his passing all the more tragic. How many other great albums would he have released? Would he have embraced dancehall? Would dancehall not have eclipsed roots? Would he have created entirely new styles of reggae? What great Bob Marley & The Wailers classic songs – never written, never recorded – would there have been? We can only wonder. And we can console ourselves in the abundance of great recordings he gave us during his thirty-six years of life and nearly twenty years of recording.

'Coming In From The Cold'

Uprising opens winningly with 'Coming In From The Cold'. It bristles with life, right from its creative introduction: an acoustic guitar strums a rhythm while quirky electric guitar chords are splattered atop. A fat, loud drum roll from guest drummer Santa Davis then launches the body of the song. Aston Barrett's bass is in the driver's seat, inheriting the melody and rhythm established by the introductory guitars. Keyboards fill the song, as clean rock steady piano, grimy clavichord, a touch of organ and strange squeaking synthesizer notes are heard. The only further sign of guitar is the processed reggae chop that is joined by piano. Seeco quietly adds a touch of Nyah drumming. It adds up to a satisfyingly crunchy, unsinkably buoyant reggae riddim.

Bob enters dancingly, repeating lines to his heart's content and the betterment of the song. He wants his audience to know that he is singing directly to them, repeating "It's you I'm talking to". Now that he has your attention, the message is one of encouragement for anyone who is feeling down. This includes a saying originally attributed to Alexander Graham Bell: "When one door closes, another opens". He sings of life being sweet, as Jamaicans are coming in from the cold. By that he means they are living in unity (no doubt under Jah, though this is implied rather than stated) and ignoring the pressures of society. A male chorus (that by some accounts is said to include the august presence of Joe Higgs) and The I-Threes take turns harmonizing with or answering Bob. When they all come together, it sounds like a Jamaican folk choir. These vocals, taken with the piano and the opening acoustic guitar, give the song a bit of a rural undercurrent. The music is great, the message positive, everyone seems to be enjoying themselves, and the listener is swept up by a tidal wave of good vibrations.

A 12-inch mix of 'Coming In From The Cold' was included as a bonus track on later editions of the *Uprising* CD. It's something of a backwards disco-mix, with a dub version seamlessly added to the start of the recording rather than the end. There is an extra organ track up front, as drop-out/in are well utilized, having the effect of making the rhythm chunkier. A single application of echo sets up a big drop-out, as hand drums are moved up in the mix, all making for a fine bonus track. The original single B-side dub version is better, with the reverb and dropout you would expect to hear on a Bob Marley & The Wailers dub, but with more echo than most. This, one of the best Bob Marley & The Wailers dubs, is champing at the bit to be released on CD.

'Real Situation'

'Real Situation' is a merry little song about the inevitability that global politics will result in the destruction of the world. Bob has never been direr than here when he concludes, "... there ain't no use." There is nothing wrong with the jaunty reggae backing and The I-Threes' backing vocals, other than the fact that they are jaunty. A more introspective sound is called for, such as the sad reggae of *Survival*'s similarly themed and vastly superior 'So Much Trouble In The World'. On one line, Bob noticeably stumbles and recovers. You get the impression that he didn't care enough about the song to do another take. This oxymoron of a song is as close as *Uprising* comes to having a weak track.

'Bad Card'

The pace slows down in 'Bad Card' for Bob's dubbiest song since *Kaya*'s 'Sun Is Shining'. A descending cycle of long chords played by piano and organ over busy hi-hat work provides the song with a brief but suspense-building introduction. What follows is some fine, reverb-rich, skanking reggae, bouncy and elastic, bubbling with life. An altered electric guitar chops a rhythm that is doubled by piano, as the drums emphasize the third beat of each four with a reverb-enlivened rim shot. The bass line dances all over this rhythm, swinging between mirroring and elaborating on the melody of Bob's vocal.

Bob sings of an adversary who would rather that Bob wasn't around. The song may very well be about Bob's moving himself, his family, entourage and hangers-on into a house in one of Kingston's better neighborhoods. But reggae and Jah give him strength, even as lies are being told about him. As he did in 'Who Colt The Game', he uses cards as an analogy for their conflict. Stung by the bad cards of rejection and defamation played by his neighbor, but buoyed up by his love of reggae, Bob makes an ebullient proclamation of his next move:

> I want to disturb my neighbor, 'cause I'm feeling so right.
> I want to turn up my disco – blow them to full watts tonight.
> In a rub-a-dub style, in a rub-a-dub style.
> 'Bad Card', by Bob Marley. © 1980 Blue Mountain Music Ltd o/b/o
> Fifty-six Hope Road Music Ltd and Blackwell Fuller Music Publishing
> LLC. Copyright renewed. All rights reserved. Used by permission.

A night-time, full-volume dose of righteous dub is Bob's response.

The I-Threes sound ecstatic as they sing in unison with Bob. Then comes a surprise change in the bass line and key. A more serious sound is briefly heard as Bob includes a couplet about God in his palace, as if not wanting to ignore the inspiration for this music. Having paid his respects, the song returns to normal. In 'Bad Card', secure in his beliefs, bolstered by reggae, and armed with a loud stereo, Bob lifts himself and his listeners past antagonism.

The original single release of 'Bad Card' included a dub version on the B-side called 'Rub A Dub Style'. With some extra rhythm guitar, reverb and dropout/in, it reveals how inside-out in the reggae way the riddim of 'Bad Card' is. It's one of the better dub versions of a Bob Marley & The Wailers song, but to date it has not seen LP or CD release. One can only hope that this gross oversight will be rectified sometime soon. Collectors also know of a never officially released variant mix with drop-out hitting just as Bob sings, "In a rub-a-dub style". If just for that, this version is also worthy of release.

'We And Dem' (aka 'We And Them'); 'Work'

'We And Them' and 'Work' are both fine, brooding reggae songs. As loose and elastic as 'Coming In From The Cold' is, these songs are tightly arranged and precisely executed, with a lineage from songs like 'Waiting In Vain' and 'So Much Trouble In The World'. They show what a crack session outfit Bob Marley & The Wailers have become. Detailed, ordered and expert, the resulting reggae whirrs like a Swiss timepiece, giving us songs that are handsome, accessible and bursting with music. It's unfortunate that neither dub versions nor alternative mixes of these songs have ever been released, depriving us of X-ray views of their intricate inner workings.

'We And Dem' finds Bob unhappy about how those in power treat innocent people badly. He feels cut off and helpless, and offers no solution other than hoping for divine retribution. This makes 'We And Dem' bring the despondent 'Real Situation' to mind. But the heavier tone, more carefully considered arrangement, touches of dub, vocal richness and fine melodies all make 'We And Dem' a vastly better song. Hypnotic bass leads and builds a trance. Keyboard or guitar occasionally borrows the lead from the bass. When the subject turns to God, the male chorus and The I-Threes combine to create what sounds like a full church choir. This makes for the most dramatic use of male backing vocals heard in a Wailers song since Peter and Bunny departed. For Bob's part, he manages to be both introspective and playful. For a mid-song break, he scats over an electric guitar solo as Carlton airs it out on drums. At the end of the song, instruments drop out and male and female choruses make exchanges without Bob, as 'We And Dem' takes advantage of the embarrassment of riches that Bob Marley & The Wailers possess.

'Work' does not have a lot of lyrics, but Bob feels each word in this dramatic and urgent song. The verse urges working together under God. The chorus shifts the meaning to the work week, as Bob provides a fluid, bluesy countdown from Monday to Friday. It's much more musically satisfying than the listing of days in the remade 'Kaya' or the 1st Street to 7th Street count-up of 'Natty Dread'. Bob sings with beautiful anguish, as blues guitar runs are added to the weave of this guitar-rich track. It ends with the pained realization that "every day is work". Meanwhile, the music has subtly grown more industrious with percussion that alludes to the title. Carlton Barrett and Seeco Patterson play like a single multi-limbed percussion creature. At the fade-out, Bob improvises additional lyrics about work, recalling an earlier song, 'Nightshift'. 'Work' serves as the perfect anthem for anyone struggling through their work week.

'Zion Train'

'Zion Train' is an updating of the traditional gospel train spirituals that have always populated Jamaican music, such as The Wailers' own 'This Train'. Though the lyrics would not be out of place in a gospel arrangement, a gentle, melodic, dub-kissed reggae that achieves a quiet majesty is heard instead. Perhaps out of respect for the song's gospel roots, Bob does not make any direct reference to Jah or Rastafari, but he does inform the song with Rasta themes. This includes anti-materialism, black history, supporting one another, and watching one's own behavior. Bob takes a hackneyed expression, "Where there's the will, there's always the way" and he and The I-Threes deliver it with so much passion, it sounds new and undeniably true.

The vocals are superb, right from the entry of Bob and The I-Threes singing in unison. Bob emphasizes various lines either by allowing a roughness to his voice that is particular to this song, or by ending with vibrato. With the ultra-dense arrangements of *Survival* now in the past, The I-Threes can spread their wings in full and fitting gospel splendor. And they provide the song with a fine conclusion by playfully simulating drop-out in the final recitation of the chorus, as vocals play dub hide-and-seek with cowbell. As with 'Work', guitar is prominent throughout 'Zion Train', right from the song's opening soft jam. But, once again, the percussion stands out. Carlton Barrett's ingenious, dub-enriched playing, Seeco Patterson's roots hand drum and a variety of incidental percussion (cowbell, vibraslap, simulated train whistles and shakers) keep the music interesting all the way through.

An alternative mix called 'Zion Express' was released as a 12-inch single. It has never been collected on CD, though to no great loss, as it compensates for the lack of The I-Threes with a train-whistle sound effect – an obviously bad trade.

'Pimper's Paradise'

When 'Pimper's Paradise' was released, its title caused some surprise. This was well before the word 'pimp' was commonly heard in rap music, making the pimp a folk hero, and before the word was subsequently accepted in its vernacular meaning of 'to garishly over-accessorize'. Contrary to all this, Bob's song is serious and anti-pimp. He explores the partying lifestyle, a subject he has previously visited with 'Kinky Reggae' and 'Midnight Ravers'. He describes a girl on the scene, a model with a cocaine problem, who sadly becomes the titular subject. He also promises that the pimp will get his just deserts from Jah's retribution. Cautionary tales for women have antecedents in reggae that go back to golden-age mento (for example, Chin's Calypso Sextet's 'Look Before You Leap'). But here, the stakes are higher. The song has a sophisticated R&B reggae feel, somewhat similar to 'Johnny Was' on *Catch A Fire*. A sparse arrangement features breathy synthesizer as lead instrument and creative bass that drives the song. This combination of subject and sound has made 'Pimper's Paradise' a popular track with fans. But not popular enough with Marley for him to have released a dub version or alternative mix, or to have performed it live.

'Could You Be Loved'; 'Could You Be Loved' (12-inch mix)
By injecting elements of the then-popular disco music into reggae, Bob created 'Could You Be Loved', a world-music hit that blended reggae, disco and funk along with accents from Nigeria and Brazil. It opens with a disco jam between funk guitar and the distinctive sound of a Cuíca friction drum, making its way from Brazilian samba to Jamaican reggae. Then reggae crashes the party as the body of the song begins. But it's reggae with a simplified disco beat – most instruments sounding equally on each beat, while the bass roams restlessly across the rhythm. Funky clavichord and the continuation of the intro's funk guitar co-serve as lead instruments. They are supported by a metronomic reggae guitar chop, tinkling piano and claves. The latter, accenting the first beat of four, adds peaks of reggae brightness to the already sunny sound. The I-Threes sing rare stanzas unaccompanied by Bob, instantly broadening the song's sound. In one verse, they reprise the proverb about only appreciating water when the well fails to provide it, first heard in a Wailers song in the Peter Tosh-led Studio One track, 'When The Well Runs Dry', and then remade by Tosh as 'Till Your Well Runs Dry' for his first solo album, *Legalize It*, in 1976. This all results in a vibrant, ebullient piece of music, even by Bob Marley & The Wailers standards. If all disco music was this engaging, it would have been revered by music lovers as much as it was by the dancing masses.

Many take the apparently light-hearted 'Could You Be Loved' to be a love song. A closer look at the lyrics shows this to be correct, but it is an atypical example. Although it also touches on loving others and loving God, the song is primarily about self-acceptance – having love for yourself, in spite of your imperfections and in the face of systemic criticism from society. At one point, Bob lashes out at those who believe otherwise, telling them to go to Hell, in a rare instance of righteous anger displacing poetry.

What a great piece of dance music 'Could You Be Loved' is! A successful multicultural fusion with a sunshine- bright sound and a powerful affirmative message hidden like a Trojan Horse in what appears to be a love song. If only there was a way to hear more of it ...

Included as a bonus track in later editions of the *Uprising* CD is the 12-inch mix of 'Could You Be Loved'. A longer mix by a minute and a half, this is the preferred version, as it contains some mid-song music that was omitted on the album mix. There's a delicious break, with a guitar and keyboard jamming over bass and drums, that bridges American funk and African Highlife music. And Bob has an extra couplet, in which he urges us to dance. All of this makes a fine world-music dance song even worldlier and more danceable. It also makes clear that if Bob Marley & The Wailers had wanted to, they had the chops and the versatility to leave reggae behind and succeed as a funk band or as a world-music outfit. Few would argue that they were wrong not to do so.

'Forever Loving Jah'

'Forever Loving Jah' opens promisingly as Bob unveils a wailing variation of his scat singing over dub reggae. But after that, there's a lot that's okay but nothing great in the song. It's a hymn of devotion, with Bob singing about how his faith shields him against criticism and bad treatment, adapting Bible quotes to make his case. (One such quote, "Thou hast hid these things from the wise and prudent, and hast revealed them unto babes" [Matthew 11:25], previously appeared in the Wailers' Studio One song, 'Rudie'.)

But these are sentiments that he's expressed before in better songs. And although the chorus is fine, Bob's vocal and melody in the verse are not up to his high standard. The arrangement is also a mixed bag. There are (no surprise) creative drums and percussion, and (no surprise) good bass. And there's a measure of dub on the drums and on the bouncing rhythm guitar that leaves trails. But these elements do not coalesce into especially strong music. Like 'Real Situation', 'Forever Loving Jah' is not a bad song, but not quite of the caliber of the rest of this strong album.

A nicely stripped-down dub version of 'Forever Loving Jah' is available on the digital download album called *Bob Marley & The Wailers In Dub, Vol. 1*. Drawn from a different take at a slightly slower tempo and keying off the droning bass line, it's a somnolent dub. Collectors also know of a better instrumental dub version of the album rendition that has never been legitimately released. It would be a fine addition to a future edition of *Uprising* or for a collection of Bob Marley & The Wailers dub versions.

'Redemption Song'; 'Redemption Song' (band version)

Though a number of impromptu acoustic performances by Bob Marley (and by Peter Tosh as well) were posthumously issued, these were never intended for release. Far better is 'Redemption Song', the only official Bob Marley solo performance. With no other singers or musicians, just Bob accompanying himself with acoustic guitar strummed in simple folk style, it's the simplest and most intimate of any Bob Marley song. Yet, it's a powerful and classic performance. The closing track of the album, it serves as an antidote to the uncharacteristic hopelessness heard earlier on 'Real Situation' and 'We And Dem'. Bob describes troubling issues, such as Jamaica's legacy of slavery (with a Marcus Garvey quote: "Emancipate yourselves from mental slavery"), the assassination of leaders and fearful nuclear technology. Yet, in the face of these things, by God's strength, he will move "forward in this generation triumphantly". Jah has re-energized his positive outlook.

'Redemption Song' features as fine a melody and as heartfelt a vocal as Bob has ever recorded. With nothing to distract you, every bit of vibrato, every exclamation, every shift in intensity and every turn of melody that is a Bob Marley vocal can be fully appreciated here. His voice grabs hold as he draws you into his words.

In this chapter, we have seen that one of Bob's specialties is to insert a line that speaks directly to his audience, as we saw in "Coming In From The Cold". Here he takes this to the next level, tearing down the wall between audience and performer, and lays his heart bare by asking the listeners to help him sing. And with this, the last song on the last album that Bob would live to release, he does more than give hope. He redeems.

Later editions of the *Uprising* CD include the bonus track 'Redemption Song (Band Version)'. On this rendition, Bob has the full backing of the instrumental Wailers, though not of The I-Threes. But it does not improve on the album version. The nothing-special instrumentation only serves to constrain Bob's vocal and blunts the emotional impact of the song. Also released (though not yet collected on CD) was a 12-inch disco-mix of the band version that featured an appended dub version and an overlay of Nyabinghi drums. It improves on the 'Band Version', but still does not compare to the naked emotion of the album rendition. Sometimes when he performed it live, Bob would start with a solo performance, then add the accompaniment of Nyabinghi drums and then finish with the full band's backing (though still sans The I-Threes), for an enjoyable performance of the song that manages to encompass all three studio renditions.

Uprising Live: Dortmund, Germany, June 13, 1980

The year 2014 saw the release of *Uprising Live*, a two-CD and DVD package. It presents a June 13, 1980 show from Dortmund, Germany, with not bad – but not great – sound quality. Distinguishing itself from other Bob Marley & The Wailers concert recordings, it opens with a brief set from The I-Threes where they perform two Judy Mowatt songs and one each by Marcia Griffiths and Rita Marley. Then comes a track called 'Marley Chant' in which the band vamps on the 'Stalag' riddim (a song previously described in this book; page 312), while Tyrone Downie repeatedly chants 'Marley'. A nineteen-song set follows.

Live Forever: The Stanley Theatre, Pittsburgh, PA, September 23, 1980

In 2011, Island Records released a double-CD recording of Bob Marley's last live show, a twenty-song set from Pittsburgh's Stanley Theatre on September 23, 1980. Bob was so ill before the show, Rita begged him to cancel, calling Bob's mother to enlist her support. Yet neither the quality of his voice nor the level of his focus betray any hint of illness. On the contrary, he gives a very strong performance. If anything, it's the guitars and keyboards that were not as sharp as usual that night. 'Crazy Baldhead' is especially strong and 'Zimbabwe' benefits from an improved arrangement. Bob's heartfelt performance, his situation and the poignant lyrics all magnify one another in 'No Woman No Cry'. The same holds true of the aforementioned 'Redemption Song'. Only 'Coming In From The Cold' fails to get off the ground.

Confrontation

Confrontation was posthumously cobbled together in 1983 from a handful of songs recorded after the *Uprising* sessions, leftovers from other earlier sessions and a few previously released but uncollected singles. For this reason, it's the only Bob Marley & The Wailers album where none of its songs were ever performed live. Two of the new songs are good. They feature the return of the three-man horn section to the otherwise unchanged band, but a return to dub-free production. The other new songs sound incomplete and unintended for release. As for the older songs, it's easy to see why most were originally bypassed. Some were not up to the standard of the album they were originally recorded for or were unfinished works in progress. As a result, the quality of *Confrontation* is uneven, especially when considering the consistency of the albums that came before. (This brings us back again to the Wailers/Beatles comparison. The Beatles' *Let It Be* was released post-break-up and is often considered a substandard album for the group. Though perhaps a disappointing swansong, *Let It Be* is certainly a stronger set than *Confrontation*.)

The first two songs described below are from the sessions after *Uprising*. They could have sat comfortably on any Bob Marley & The Wailers album. Much of the remainder, like so much posthumously released material by major artists, is second-rate.

'Buffalo Soldier'; 'Buffalo Soldier' (12-inch mix)
More than two years after Bob's death, 'Buffalo Soldier' was released as a single. It was a hit in the UK, reaching the no. 4 spot to achieve the highest-ever chart position for a Bob Marley single there. This was due to Bob's joyous singing, with his memorable chorus of "*woy, yoy, yoy!*", sweet I-Threes vocals and uplifting horns all providing relief for the sad fact of Bob's untimely death. 'Buffalo soldiers' are what the Cheyenne Indians called the first regiments of black soldiers that the US government formed. Their fighting ability was highly respected, and the name was a badge of honor that was for a time applied to all black soldiers in the US Army. Bob equates their story of having to fight to survive to that of the Rasta in Jamaica. With this, Bob was expanding his purview, bridging the Rasta experience to the heritage of Americans of African descent. And, as only he could, he did so in an irresistibly buoyant song.

The CD bonus track 'Buffalo Soldier' (12-inch mix) is taken from the disco-mix single release. It opens with The I-Threes adding a crazy *ooh-we, ooh-we* hill-billy chorus that instantly makes this the desired mix. The appended dub version has few effects, saving some bold drop-out/in for its ending. Not included on the CD is this single's B-side, 'Buffalo Dub'. Not a great loss, as its dub is tamer than the A-side's dub portion. At the opposite extreme is the totally overdone, non-Jamaican-sounding 'Buffalo Soldier Electronic Mix', which has also not been compiled on CD, at no great loss. There is also the fast-paced rendition of 'Buffalo Soldier' that Bob cut around the same time, with different musicians, for producer King Sporty. It is available on some collections, but sounds like a demo rather than a recording intended for release.

'Trench Town'
Other than 'Buffalo Soldier', 'Trench Town' is the only finished-sounding song from Bob's final recording session of mid-1980. In it, he returns to the topic of the impoverished Kingston neighborhood of his teens, where The Wailers came together. He last visited the subject on The Wailers' 1971 self-produced single, 'Trench Town Rock'. Perhaps this explains Bunny Wailer's participation on 'Trench Town', providing a Nyah hand drum, the only time he (or Peter Tosh) recorded with Marley after leaving The Wailers in 1973. Bunny had always revered his Wailers bandmate and his legacy. This could be seen in his three CDs-worth of Bob Marley tributes. In sharp contrast, Peter Tosh, although he continued his musical and personal relationships with Bunny, unfortunately came to resent Bob for his success.

Though they share a subject, the sound of 'Trench Town Rock' and 'Trench Town' is different. Where the older song was funky and celebratory, 'Trench Town' is introspective and wistful. It's dominated by the most serene horn lines ever to grace a Bob Marley & The Wailers song, and all else follows suit. The lyrics begin with Bob going to Cane River to bathe. He then rests, and has a vision. He dreamily recounts the marvel that the reggae music of the poor, Rastafarian inhabitants of Trench Town was able to set the people free. He mocks the belief of Jamaica's upper class that Trench Town could never produce anything of value. It's no wonder that at the end of the song, as Bob gets into a groove, he concludes with the demand that we pay tribute to the place where roots reggae was born.

A 12-inch disco-mix of 'Trench Town' was released, and it absolutely should have been included as a bonus track on *Confrontation*, as was done for 'Buffalo Soldier'. It's a better mix, featuring a dubbier production, less keyboard, more percussion (including a more easily heard Bunny Wailer), a touch of synthesizer, a sax solo and an extended ending, where Bob grooves for longer before it seamlessly segues into a peaceful instrumental dub version. The 12-inch single's B-side, called 'Dub In Trench Town', is similar in sound to the dub portion of the A-side, but with vocals dropped out/in.

'Chant Down Babylon'; 'Jump Nyabinghi'; 'Stiff Necked Fools'
These three songs constitute the balance of Bob's final session. Each would normally have been developed further or rejected for release. As they are, they sound (sadly, understandably) incomplete.

In 'Chant Down Babylon', Bob is all too prescient as he sings of doing the titular chant "one more time". He explains that reggae music is the key to defeating Babylon's evil. It's not a bad song, but the instrumentation, lyrics and melody would all have benefited from additional development.

Having already chanted down Babylon, Bob next wants to bring down Jericho's walls, on 'Jump Nyabinghi'. If the intention was to eventually turn this into a Nyabinghi-style song, nothing of that sound is present, the prominent synthesizer being particularly out of place. Yet Bob feels empowered, as some of his favorite things are occurring: togetherness, people trying to better themselves, dancing, and herb smoking.

'Stiff Necked Fools', a dressing-down of Babylon, reprises and expands on the Bible quotes previously used in the mid-period Wailers track, 'Wisdom'. This is far from the most pleasant-sounding Bob Marley & The Wailers song, with Bob laying down a strident vocal sans The I-Threes over a synthesizer-led backing.

'Rastaman Live Up'; 'Blackman Redemption'
Both 'Rastaman Live Up' and 'Blackman Redemption' are roots reggae songs that were originally recorded at the beginning of the *Survival* sessions, but not released. Bob then re-recorded the songs with the male roots vocal group The Mediations instead of The I-Threes, and they were released as a pair of Jamaican singles at the end of the 1970s. The renditions on *Confrontation* feature the The I-Threes. Yet, at points, some traces of The Mediations' vocal bleeds through, pointing to a doctored mix. That's fine, but the singles (not to mention their dub version B-sides, or perhaps their 12-inch disco-mixes) should have been included on *Confrontation* as bonus tracks. Though, of course, The I-Threes are fine, anyone familiar with the singles can't help but miss the strident roots harmonies of The Mediations and other aspects of the single mixes.

'Rastaman Live Up' is an upbeat pep talk about maintaining righteous Rasta beliefs and behavior, or *living up*. It's a message that Bob has delivered many times before, but rarely as ebulliently. As is often the case when he discusses Rasta, the song is rich in heady Bible language, covering creation, meditation and Armageddon. The backing is crunchy roots reggae with fine work from the Barrett brothers, and tasty little rock guitar leads throughout.

The Mediations mix is different from the album mix in a number of ways, and almost all of them are improvements. There's an introduction completely omitted from the album mix, with a wild jam led by a ripping guitar lead and a crazy piece of scat vocals from Bob. The arrangement is rootsier with reggae guitar picking and Nyabinghi drum not heard on the album. And there's a liberal application of reverb on the drums compared to the album's dry mix. Whereas The I-Threes sound nice but staid on the album mix, The Mediations provide an edgier, more exciting sound, and have more of an impact on the song. Their slightly harsh roots harmonies are in stark contrast to The I-Threes, who never once uttered a dissonant note, and this proves to be a nice change of pace for Bob Marley & The Wailers fans. Only the shorter length that robs us of some final lyrics, including Bob's fade-out exhortation against giving up, prevents the single from being the unequivocally superior rendition. But it's certainly the more exciting one, making the album rendition sound disconcertingly smoothed-over by comparison.

'Blackman Redemption', like 'Rastaman Live Up', is an uplifting message to the Rasta, but a more pensive one. In this, Bob's earlier redemption song, the central message is clear, though the lyrics are diffuse. Sounding at peace, Bob explains that Jah will redeem his followers. The band and backing vocals are equally serene. The single rendition, though different, is not as divergent from the album mix as is the case for 'Rastaman Live Up'. In fact, The Mediations can be clearly heard at times, poking through The I-Threes' vocals. The album mix has more keyboards and the single mix has more horns. But the single mix is longer this time, including an extended fade-out and some modest dub towards the track's end, making it preferable to the album track.

'I Know'

'I Know', recorded during *Rastaman Vibration* sessions, is the oldest track on *Confrontation*. With Bob gone, what was once deemed inadequate for release is suddenly pressed into action, and released as a single to boot. It's another R&B-reggae hybrid with some good lyrics about Jah providing comfort during the hardships of life. It's not a great Bob Marley & The Wailers song – uh oh: lead synthesizer! – but certainly good enough to warrant a belated release. Both sides of the 'I Know' 12-inch single remain uncompiled on CD, but the dub is very tame, and neither side adds much to the album mix.

'Give Thanks And Praises'; 'Mix Up, Mix Up'

'Give Thanks And Praises' was recorded during the *Uprising* sessions. It's a devotional song, as Bob sings about all he owes Jah. Unlike some songs on *Confrontation*, this sounds like a completed song rather than a demo. But an unusually subdued vocal from Bob and a somewhat underdeveloped melody caused it to be held back until called upon for *Confrontation*.

On the other hand, from a session between *Survival* and *Uprising*, 'Mix Up, Mix Up' sounds like a demo of a song that was abandoned. That's a shame because it features some interesting lyrics with enough ideas to fill two songs. Making the title a pun, Bob equates time spent (mixing) in a recording studio to life, as good things and bad can occur in each. In one line, he sings of the importance of recording new material rather than versioning. The song also has autobiograph-ical lyrics, but it does not reveal anything we didn't already know. There is an oblique conflict involving music-making, in which Bob sounds put upon and dis-gusted. Someone has him angry enough to drop the f-bomb. As interesting as this freewheeling vocal is, it's a rather informal performance and does not sound as if it was intended for release. The same goes for an underdeveloped instru-mental track in which lead synthesizer is relied on once again as a crutch and/or placeholder.

Additional songs and mixes on posthumous albums

Island Records followed *Confrontation* with other posthumous album releases. To differing degrees, these included recordings that were not available elsewhere.

Legend *and* Rebel Music
No Bob Marley album would be as famous as *Legend*, the 1984 best-of collection that drew from Bob Marley & The Wailers' international years. It went through several different song listings and mixes as it moved from LP and cassette, to CD, to double-CD. Along the way, it sold a staggering twenty million copies, secur-ing Bob Marley's place as one of music's true international superstars. Unfortu-nately, the original LP edition and some others thereafter featured mixes that were altered in 1984. We are not talking about overdubbing a studio out-take to complete a song for release. We're talking about an outside agency taking a major artist's best work and altering it posthumously to "make it better". Before you point a finger at the label, in 2013 came *Legend Remixed*, a more radical alteration that stripped away reggae elements for club music sounds, made with the full participation of Bob's sons, Ziggy and Stephen. The label and Bob's estate would say it was to expand Bob's legacy, bringing his music to new and younger audi-ences. Cynics see nothing but exploitation and greed. Wailers purists don't care about the motives, they just cringe at the results.

Naturally, Island issued a follow-up drawn from the same pool of recordings, with *Rebel Music* being released in 1986. It also contained two live tracks, the first appearance on LP of 'Roots', plus a non-Jamaican-sounding remix of the title track that is strangled by its emphasis on harmonica.

Talkin' Blues
In 1991 Island followed *Rebel Music* with *Talkin' Blues*, a strange concoction of an album that was expanded on CD. It intermixes eight brief segments taken from a long interview with Bob conducted by Dermot Hussey in 1975 with ten live tracks from 1973, plus three studio out-takes from 1974 and a live track from 1975.

'Am-A-Do', one of the three studio out-takes, has already been discussed (page 466), since it was added as a bonus track to a later edition of the *Natty Dread* CD. An alternative, shorter mix of 'Bend Down Low' from the *Natty Dread* album features a different vocal from Bob and replaces several keyboard tracks with flute. Bob is not the flautist, even though the interview segment that precedes the song gives that impression, with Bob demonstrating that he plays a bit. An alternative mix of 'Talkin' Blues' is longer, with additional lyrics at the end. It does away with harmonica and acoustic guitar and moves a tremolo guitar up in the mix with additional lead guitar at spots. The 1975 live rendition of 'I Shot The Sheriff' comes from the night before the version on the *Live!* Album was recorded. It's a longer and hotter performance.

The meat of the CD is the ten-track live October 1973 performance in a nearly empty studio in Sausalito, across the Golden Gate Bridge from San Francisco. Bunny Wailer, who had earlier quit the tour, was replaced by Jamaican music veteran and Wailers mentor Joe Higgs. In addition to the expected *Catch A Fire* and *Burnin'* tracks, The Wailers performed four earlier tracks, including 'Walk The Proud Land', otherwise known as 'Rude Boy' or 'Rebel's Hop'. The performance is flawless, but with all due respect to the late Joe Higgs, it is impossible not to miss Bunny Wailer in this context.

Songs Of Freedom

In 1992, Island Records released *Songs Of Freedom*. This four-CD box-set served as the first and only career-spanning Bob Marley compilation, surpassing *Legend* in scope, size and quality, if not in units sold. As was the case with the box-set boom of the time, *Songs Of Freedom* was a combination of best-of and rarities. Some of these rarities have already been discussed in this book. The rest are described below.

'Iron Lion Zion' is an out-take from the *Burnin'* sessions. It was completed for this collection, scrubbing Bunny and Peter from the track and replacing them with The I-Threes. After a wobbly intro, a propulsive reggae backing with bracing vocals from Bob is heard. His story is exciting, as he is being chased as a fugitive and threatened by the gun-filled political strife of Jamaica. The song's title explains his deliverance: he will be iron-strong like a lion – a symbol of Haile Selassie – in the Rasta's holy land of Africa. Though underdeveloped instrumentation smacks of an abandoned track, a spirited vocal and rousing lyrics from Bob save this bracing romp. His fans happy with the first new Bob Marley single in ten years, it rose to no. 5 in the UK.

'Why Should I', a self-produced track from 1971 that The Wailers abandoned has been resuscitated here. New instrumentation is created while Peter and Bunny are again removed from the mix in favor of newly recorded vocals from The I-Threes. The song meanders, trying to cover too much lyrical ground, and Bob never develops much of a melody. It could have remained in the vault.

'Waiting In Vain (Advert Mix)' recalls 'Exodus Advertisement'. Both open with a gong being struck and a laughing greeting from Bob. But this is a full-length track rather than a 60-second commercial. 'Exodus (12" Mix)' is actually a bit shorter than the album cut and sounds an awful lot like the album mix, but it is claimed to be different. 'Three Little Birds (Alt Mix)' is clearly different from the album rendition, with different guitar and keyboard and a touch of dub added to the mix. So is 'One Love/People Get Ready (12" Mix)'. It's a disco-mix with some dub added to the first half, followed by a full dub version. 'Is This Love (Horns Mix)' is self-explanatory, as no small amount of horns are added to the otherwise familiar mix.

Additional compilations

The box-set's 1995 follow-up, *Natural Mystic – The Legend Lives On*, unfortunately resumes the practice of altering familiar tracks. This practice would continue and broaden. At the height of the ambient remix trend, in 1997, Island released *Dreams of Freedom – Ambient Translations Of Bob Marley In Dub*. In a play for the heads and/or wallets of ambient fans, the music of Bob Marley & The Wailers is made into a construction set from which producer Bill Laswell creates an album of tracks radically remixed in a non-Jamaican style. In 1999, Island Records released *Chant Down Babylon*, turning its attention to the minds and/or wallets of hip-hop fans. Bob's songs are remixed with hip-hop music, or turned into duets with star hip-hop singers and rappers. In 2005 *Africa Unite: The Singles Collection* was released. Some familiar songs, sometimes in their shortened-for-45-rpm format are gathered in a play for the hearts and/or wallets of completists. Once again, several classics are retooled by celebrity remixers. Also included is 'Slogans', a studio out-take from the *Uprising* sessions with a melody at times similar to that of 'No Woman No Cry'. In it, Bob rejects the political slogans that appear in graffiti all over Kingston's walls, as a symbol of strife. As the song nears its end, he denounces Jamaica's churches: "No more sweet talk from-a pulpit, no more sweet talk from the hypocrites." The instrumentation is not bad for a revived out-take, bolstered by guest Eric Clapton's guitar lines that figure prominently. In 2009, Island released *B Is For Bob*, a Bob Marley collection aimed squarely at the developing minds and/or piggybanks of children. Bob's eldest son Ziggy supervised the child-friendly remixing. Perhaps next will be *Bob Marley & The Whalers: Weeping And Whaling* – an album of Bob's hits remixed with contemporary oceanic music's top whale-song artists, as Island Records turns its attention to the massive hearts and/or ambergris of the planet's largest mammals.

Coda: 'No Woman No Cry'

Of the very many tributes to Bob Marley that were recorded after his passing, one stands out. It was part of Bunny Wailer's Youth Consciousness Festival performance in Kingston on December 27, 1982. Bunny orchestrated an impromptu, heartfelt collaboration on 'No Woman No Cry'. It's a fitting choice, as this song is about positive memories overcoming the day's sadness. Before he begins his emotional reading of the song, he calls Marcia Griffiths and Judy Mowatt on stage to join him, his voice bathed in echo and reverb, the very personification of dub. Bunny sings lead until, surprisingly, Jimmy Cliff (who had recorded a cover of this song in 1976) joins to take over for a time. It's a treat as he adds his famously powerful voice to the proceedings, altering the lyrics a bit to make them more personal, while Bunny responds with various exhortations. As Cliff is finishing, Bunny happily exclaims, "Brother Peter!", as Peter Tosh takes the stage, adding his voice to the chorus, along with Bunny, Marcia and Judy. An unrehearsed Peter then takes lead and improvises an expansion of Bob's verse. Bunny answers by repeatedly chanting his love for Bob. The song closes with another chorus, with all three taking turns out front, the boundaries between lead and backing vocals having crumbled. The concert served as the basis for Bunny Wailer's *Live!* album, but this song was not included. This could have been due to its 10-minute length, or because the spontaneous collaboration is a bit rough around the edges. Whatever the reason, release of this moving performance – a true *moment* in reggae – is overdue.

The song also serves as this book's coda to the story of Bob Marley's unparalleled career, and a segue to the post-Wailers careers of Bunny Wailer and Peter Tosh, which are covered in the next two chapters.

47 Bunny Wailer, after The Wailers

Bunny Wailer has one of the best and probably the most beautiful voice in the history of reggae. No other reggae singer has his technical prowess or accomplishments as both a lead singer and a backing vocalist. Nor does any other reggae singer have his combination of spirituality and cool. Bunny Wailer's speaking voice carries more music than many other vocalists' singing. He could read the contents of a binary file aloud and make it sound interesting.

In addition to the body of work he participated in as a member of The Wailers, Bunny also created some great self-produced tracks after departing the group at the end of 1973. As you will see, these included new songs, Wailers remakes and the occasional cover of another artist's song. When remaking a Wailers song, unlike Bob and Peter, Bunny didn't limit himself to his own songs but openly celebrated the songwriting of his bandmates. He has recorded three tribute CDs of Bob Marley remakes and the *Bunny Wailer Sings The Wailers* album, as well as other Wailer remakes on various albums.

In his solo career, he released nearly 100 singles and about 26 albums from 1976 through 2013. Unlike Marley and Tosh, other than his first album, which was released on Island Records, these were primarily intended for the Jamaican market and did not feature an internationalized sound. Several of his best songs were released as singles on his Solomonic label and have not yet been collected on LP, CD or for digital music services. For an artist of his stature, and as the surviving standard-bearer of the original Wailers, this neglect is difficult to fathom. In 2010, this situation was somewhat relieved by these singles being re-released, albeit in Japan only, but available to the rest of the world from there. The Jamaican government honored Bunny in 2012, when they awarded him The Order of Jamaica. The diverse entries below are the best songs of Bunny Wailer's post-Wailers solo career.

'Arab Oil Weapon'
'Arab Oil Weapon' was recorded in 1972 around the same time that Bunny and The Wailers were recording *Catch A Fire*. His band is the instrumental Wailers, augmented by a two-piece horn section (unlike *Catch A Fire*, which did not use horns), guitar, melodica and other keyboards from Peter Tosh and backing vocals from future I-Threes Rita Marley and Judy Mowatt. They grace Bunny's song with a tart sound and a crunchy rhythm. Ashton Barrett's bass line continuously roams towards and then diverges from – but always supports – Bunny's melody. The missing I-Three is not missed, least of all when Bunny joins Rita and Judy in har-

mony, in a rare combination of Wailers voices. The overall sound addresses the question of what would The Wailers have sounded like if it had been Bob rather than Bunny who departed, leaving Bunny and Peter to carry on with The I-Threes and the band. The answer? Excellent.

It's an interesting Bunny Wailer composition, featuring a great vocal in which Bunny reaches to the upper extremes of his range. Loaded with Rasta prophecy and Bible references, Bunny is at his most oblique. But he seems to be saying that oil-supply manipulation is yet another sign of Babylon's ruinous behaviour, and as a result man's final day is on the horizon. His interaction with The I-Threes is a joy to hear. Rita and Judy provide Bunny with beautiful high harmonies on the chorus, and powerfully sound key phrases for him in the verse. Not that he *needs* any vocal support, being Bunny Wailer. Listen to how he jumps up an octave to add emphasis to important phrases. And listen to how expressive he is when he sings about having his mind blown by the song's events. If only there were many more Wailer/Wailers tracks like this. At least, as we will soon see, it was not the only one.

'Arab Oil Weapon' was originally released as a single in 1974. It gained a higher profile in 1981 when it was released by the USA-based Nighthawk label as a single and on a compilation LP called *Wiser Dread*. The LP version was a disco-mix with a modest dub version appended. In 2003, it saw its CD release on the Bunny Wailer collection called *War And Peace*. But this CD went quickly out of print and the fine 'Arab Oil Weapon' is currently unavailable on CD. It's one of the aforementioned singles re-released in Japan, and can be acquired from specialty reggae retailers.

'Searching For Love'
Recorded around 1973, 'Searching For Love' is an extraordinarily good song with much to recommend it. For one thing, it may be the most contented reggae song ever recorded. And that is saying a lot, when you consider just how laid-back much of reggae is. It is also the most fully realized piece of pastoral reggae that Bunny would record, besting the sound he explored on such songs as 'Pass It On', 'Halle-lujah Time', 'Reincarnated Souls' and 'Oppressed Song'. He would never approach these idyllic heights again. Like 'Arab Oil Weapon', this is another instance of Bunny being backed by the instrumental Wailers, The I-Threes, and Peter Tosh helping out on melodica, piano and a blithely strummed reggae chop guitar. A trio of great hornsmen is heard, with Tommy McCook on flute, Vin Gordon on trombone and Bobby Ellis on trumpet. Tyrone Downie adds subdued organ, but just a touch, aware that any more would hurt the perfect but fragile scene. In their idyll, this marvelous combination of Wailers talent is a delight.

The song opens pleasingly with a languid reggae riddim from the Barrett brothers, Tosh's relaxed guitar and piano, and a laid-back theme played in the unlikely-except-in-reggae harmony of flute and trombone. The theme is joined and elaborated on by muted trumpet. Bunny adds his voice and he is answered with contented piano phrases like affirmations from above. The I-Threes' backing chorus (with Bunny sometimes joining in) ranges from pleased to ecstatic. Tosh's melodica makes a belated entrance to take a prominent position in the song.

Surrounded by this idyll, singing in a soulful falsetto, Bunny sounds serenely happy and utterly fulfilled. What has put him in this state? The title both informs and misleads. This is a love song, but one of religious love rather than romantic. As a paean to God, Bunny states that he wants the sound to be joyous. He succeeds absolutely. Familiar Wailers entreaties for togetherness and an end to fussing and fighting are heard, beautifully sung and presented as a prayer, complete with kneeling. This all amounts to perhaps the most beautiful song to come from a Wailer, and one that could best provide the soundtrack for nirvana. No other song by Bunny or anyone else captures its unique feel.

Released as a single, 'Searching For Love' has never been made part of a CD. In 1983, an extended mix appeared on the short-lived compilation LP called *Knotty Vision*, released on the Nighthawk label. This is a longer cut of the single's vocal side capped off with a brief instrumental reprise from the single's dub version B-side (alternately entitled 'Must Search' or 'Must Skank'). The single came back in print in Japan in 2010. Though it will cost far more than you would expect to pay for a new 45-rpm, the song is, as they say in Jamaica, *crucial*.

'Armagideon' (aka 'Armagedon')

There is no more regal figure in reggae than Bunny Wailer. How he carries himself, his elaborate stage attire, his accomplishments and his status as the last surviving Wailer all contribute to this. Furthermore, it's how some of his songs give credence to one of the proposed origins of the word "reggae" – that it comes from an African word that means "king's music". This is most evident in 'Armagideon', a track from Bunny's first solo album *Blackheart Man*, released in 1976.

A drum tattoo announces a regal introduction. Piano and bass in unison trade back and forth with majestic roots reggae horn lines. It sounds like the heralding of a biblical king's entrance. The king arrives, as Bunny's vocal begins, multitracked to provide himself with harmony. He sounds noble and authoritative as he warns that Babylon's evil is the cause of war, bringing us towards Armageddon. But he assures us that righteousness will triumph, and evil will be hellbound. To make his case, the song is loaded with depictions of good battling evil, history, Bible quotes, hope, retribution and more, all through the lens of Rasta belief, as it grows in length to 7 minutes. Bunny is most powerful as he sings of biblical creation and Armageddon. Equally powerful, but in a quieter way, is Bunny's emotional refrain about the world's troubles.

He is again backed by the instrumental Wailers band, sounding stately, to which he adds his own Nyah hand drumming. Peter Tosh is back again to provide guitar and his best-ever melodica performance that adds greatly to the multilayered arrangement. Prophetic, exotic, authoritative and grand, 'Armagideon' may be the single most majestic song in all of reggae.

Three dub versions of the track have been released. 'Armageddon Dub' can be heard on Bunny's CD dub collection, *Dubd'sco*. It's alright, but somehow this source material should have resulted in a more revelatory dub. Better, though shorter, are the two versions Bunny released as a single on his Solomonic label. The A-side, called 'Anti-Apartheid', is instrumental and features more of Tosh's plaintive melodica in place of vocals. Bunny billed this track not to himself but to Peter Tosh & Solomonic Reggae Star, the latter being the name he assigned to his band. The B-side, called 'Solidarity', is a dub version of the vocal track that he credits to Solomonic Reggae Star. It's better than 'Armageddon Dub', but still conservative, shunning echo, and falls short of revelatory. Never collected on LP or CD, the single is available as a Japanese import.

'Burial'

'Funeral', one of Peter Tosh's classic Rasta declarations, gets covered as 'Burial' on Bunny's strong 1981 LP, *Bunny Wailer Sings The Wailers*. (Though many consider his debut album *Blackheart Man* to be his masterpiece album, many others, myself included, prefer *Sings The Wailers*.) After the song's opening funeral march is heard, a sparse yet fat reggae jam bursts forth. The riddim consists primarily of Sly Dunbar's drums, a Robbie Shakespeare bass line so fat that it *bus' dem pants* and Earl "Chinna" Smith's dub rhythm guitar moonwalk bouncing all over the track. An undertone of rhythm organ drops in part of the time and if you hear an occasional isolated honk from sax, you're not going crazy. Bunny is typically fine, his emotional vocal on equal footing with the riddim in this ensemble piece. That is the case, until each time Bunny sings the refrain, "I said, dem want *I*", his voice cracking with intensity, reminding us who's the star of this show. A very good dub version of the track can be heard on Bunny's album called *Dubd'sco Vol 2*.

'Rise And Shine'

'Rise And Shine' is a track from Bunny's 1988 album, *Liberation*. But before that, there was the fine but often forgotten original rendition, as released on 12-inch single in 1981, that has never been collected on LP or CD. The song laments the oppression, suffering and the legacy of slavery felt by Jamaica's poor black population, but assures the oppressed that they will inevitably overcome. The two renditions are equally good, but take strikingly different approaches to the subject.

Befitting the title, the dreamy dub and somnolent pace of the 1981 original sounds as if all involved are just waking up. Bunny sings from the vantage of the verse about being oppressed, sounding mournful and injured, though not yet defeated, making this rendition a *sufferas* song. It's another great Bunny Wailer track that is thankfully being re-pressed in Japan and is therefore available again.

In the faster-paced, dub-free *Liberation* rendition, he comes from the vantage of the titular chorus, sounding upbeat and ready to triumph over adversity. As on several other tracks on *Liberation*, this rendition includes a dramatic spoken-word introduction from Bunny. Over drum kit and Nyah drum, with dub underlining key words, he's emphatic and intense. One at a time, bass, organ, piano, rhythm and picked guitars enter the song. A huge descending horn line joins to launch the body of the song. And even though he's reciting a litany of the mistreatments and injustice inflicted on those individuals who were enslaved, in Bunny's hands, it's a song of victory.

'Dog War'

'Dog War' is a surprising and very musically satisfying 1990 Bunny Wailer cover of a Toots & The Maytals song from 1964 (as described in the chapter on this artist; page 154). The excitement and joy of the original are recaptured in Bunny's rendition, which brings the wild ska mayhem of the original all the way forward to mechanized dancehall. Sequenced Pocomania-influenced drums, keyboard, bass and big synthesized swooping sounds join natural piano, a trumpet solo and percussion (including bird whistles that recall the jungle sounds of the original). Staying faithful to all the idiosyncrasies that made Toots & The Maytals' vocal performance so great, Bunny seems to be having a fine time, as one reggae giant is channeled by another. He does tweak the lyrics a bit, extolling dance (as this is a dancehall track) and liberation (as Bunny is a Rastaman). Bunny's 'Dog War' is so different from the original, but still undoubtedly the same song, carried effortlessly as he leaps across styles and decades of Jamaican music. 'Dog War' first appeared on the out-of-print Bunny Wailer LP and CD, *Gumption*, as well as on his anthology CD, *Retrospective*. Bunny would never again cover a Toots song, but in 2004 he would guest star with Toots on the duet called 'Take A Trip'.

'Bend Down Low'

An ebullient remake of the Wailers' 'Bend Down Low' is the highpoint of Bunny's 1995 release, *Hall Of Fame – A Tribute To Bob Marley's 50th Anniversary*. This two-CD, 50-song collection is only one of three albums that Bunny dedicated to revisiting the music of The Wailers, not to mention the Wailers covers that appear on his other albums.

'Bend Down Low' was originally recorded by The Wailers as a striding rock steady song. They remade it as a bluesy ballad and as funky roots reggae. Bunny once again changes the song's stylistic clothing as dancehall-style mechanization dominates the instrumental sound. But the baby isn't thrown out with the bathwater. The tempo and energy level recall the original rock steady rendition, even as the manic synthesizer lines fly by. To it, Bunny adds an exhilarating vocal performance. He's ebullient throughout, accompanying himself via multi-tracking.

When the chorus is heard, the multiple tracks of his voice jam with one another, working the blues. Twice heard, this multi-Bunny chorus puts the song over the moon.

'Love Fire'

The 1977 'Love Fire' is a remake of The Wailers' Wail'n Soul'm single, 'Fire Fire'. What started as a Peter Tosh rock steady song that repurposed the melody of a Jamaican folk song becomes a one-of-a-kind mighty reggae soul-review jam from Bunny Wailer.

With a big sound and an unhurried approach, the song's many elements are each allowed to make an impact. It's swollen with lots of electric piano, busy drums from Leroy "Horsemouth" Wallace, a brassy whiskey-soaked horn section, synthesizer horn lines, a sax solo from Tommy McCook, a trombone solo from Nambo Robinson and gospel-influenced backing vocals that include Bunny and Peter Tosh, the latter also supplying guitar. Relishing the relaxed, big backing, Bunny is at ease. He gets the most out of every word, singing expressively as always and, here, extra soulfully. He ranges from full-voiced bawdiness to an angelic falsetto. He adds to Tosh's lyrics and includes a long section of wordless singing. The result is an immersive song that feels much longer than its 5-minute length. Ecstatic and exhausting, it's like no other song in The Wailers' catalog. Originally released as a single and included on Bunny's 1979 LP, *In I Father's House*, 'Love Fire' can now be heard as a bonus track on his *Liberation* CD. Its less-remarkable dub version, called 'Burning Dub', is now out of print.

'Here In Jamaica'

Things come full circle for Bunny Wailer with his 1995 song, 'Here In Jamaica'. It's a cover of Lord Lebby's golden-age mento classic, 'Etheopia'. Bunny, who previously (three times) had recorded the most popular of all Jamaican back-to-Africa songs, 'Dreamland', now records a cover of the first such song. And he even works in a reference to Marcus Garvey, the father of African repatriation thought in Jamaica. The music is a hybrid, with guitar and drums bearing the mechanical angularity of early dancehall while the hand drum rallies the earthier tones of roots reggae, and, for that matter, of the rural mento original. Bunny honors Lebby as he carefully navigates the wonderfully twisty melody that is such an important part of the song. But he updates many of the lyrics to describe the deteriorating conditions in Jamaica, where 'you either bite the bullet or get flat' – get shot or quickly hit the deck – and where it doesn't pay to die because of the unaffordability of a cemetery plot. This gives the song new topical reasons for repatriation. In Lebby's original, a return to Africa was seen as a spiritual utopia. In Bunny's cover, this is still true, but it's also a practical matter of survival. Hearing Bunny Wailer sing and update a simpatico mento classic is a treat. It can be heard on his 1995 CD, *Crucial! Roots Classics*.

48 Peter Tosh, after The Wailers

Upon departing The Wailers, Peter Tosh embarked on a highly successful solo career that included a string of self-produced internationally successful albums and world tours. With these, he became the world's second-biggest-ever reggae star, and its biggest after Bob Marley's death. Regrettably, Peter's career and life would also be cut short when aged forty-three he was shot by a gunman – said to have been a childhood friend – during a home invasion robbery on September 11, 1987. In his post-Wailers career, he released over 50 singles and seven studio albums between 1975 and 1987, plus several more live albums.

Peter Tosh possessed reggae's greatest baritone – one of its most immediately recognizable voices. Though he benefited from The Wailers, he did not really need them, as he proved himself to be a fine front man, live and in the studio. His songs ranged from hard rocking to gentle, from down-to-earth to majestic, from soft-spoken to fiery. He would occasionally improvise passages of chant-talk-singing, invariably giving the song added gravity.

As we saw during our discussion of the Wailers' *Burnin'* and *Natty Dread* albums, Bob Marley's persona consisted of a variety of aspects, which was one of the secrets of his broad appeal. By comparison, Bunny Wailer skewed towards the positive, peaceful and spiritual. But Peter Tosh leaned towards the provoca-tive. Peter was not unaware of this, stating in interviews, to paraphrase, that his music was not for smiling. This extended beyond music. Tosh was a wicked punster, with a ready vocabulary of sardonic word substitutions, such as "Chris Whiteworse" for "Chris Blackwell". A list of forty examples is included in the liner notes of the Peter Tosh box-set, *Honorary Citizen*. At the One Love Peace Concert, where headliner Bob Marley and other top reggae acts tried to end a near-civil war in Jamaica, Tosh took the opportunity to deliver a lecture to the prime min-ister, who was present. But it was the disparaging comments about Bob Marley Tosh made in interviews that may be the ultimate demonstration of just how far he was willing to provoke.

This brings us back to the Beatles/Wailers comparison that was begun in the first chapter on Bob Marley & The Wailers (pages 90–110) and concludes here, in the final chapter on a Wailer. The Wailers had a John, a Paul, a George and two Ringos. Bob can be compared to Paul McCartney, both populists who reached so many people and were never afraid of a good love song. Bunny Wailer can be likened to George Harrison, often referred to as the spiritual Beatle. The acerbic Peter Tosh matches John Lennon, right down to the unkind comments Lennon would make about former bandmate McCartney. And original Wailer Junior

Braithwaite, and later Rita Marley, were the group's Ringo Starrs. They were valuable contributors to the group's success, but never having written a song, and providing less in the way of lead vocals, not to the same degree as the others.

Just as was true for Bunny Wailer, some of Tosh's early solo recordings utilized the instrumental Wailers as his backing band. But soon he would have a band of his own, which he named Word Sound and Power. Originally, it was anchored by the newly formed partnership of Sly & Robbie. Later, when Sly & Robbie left Tosh to join Black Uhuru, the band was anchored by Santa Davis on drums and Fully Fullwood on bass. Their international roots reggae was characterized by frequent use of clavichord (sometimes played by Tosh) and Tosh's distinctive rhythm guitar phrases. Rock guitar was liberally applied, helping to ensure that Tosh would be the most popular post-Bob Marley reggae act of rock fans worldwide. The result on any given song could be a busy, funky roots reggae sound, or a hard rock roots reggae sound, or both simultaneously. Dub was not employed by producer Tosh and the bass was mixed low for reggae, both further internationalizing away from a Jamaican sound. This is in contrast to Peter live, where on one occasion at The Ritz in New York City, he chanted "the bass, the bass, the bass is the heart of reggae", over and over, to a loud, otherwise unaccompanied Robbie Shakespeare bass line. In 2012, the Jamaican government posthumously awarded Peter Tosh the Order of Merit.

Peter Tosh has more than a few great post-Wailers songs. They are a combination of Wailers remakes and newly written tracks. They include some of his biggest hits as well as several under-the-radar classics.

Legalize It

'Legalize It'; 'Igziabeher' (aka 'Let Jah Be Praised')
Peter Tosh's first solo LP, 1976's *Legalize It*, was equally divided between new songs and remakes of Wailers songs. Two of each are great, giving a good album its four best tracks.

The title track of *Legalize It* is the first of two Peter Tosh pro-marijuana anthems that are amongst his most famous post-Wailers originals. (The other, 'Bush Doctor', is described later in this chapter.) It's a thoughtful meditation on the subject, with Tosh sounding quite relaxed and probably *red*, his voice bathed in reverb to boot. Meanwhile, the instrumental Wailers set a quiet, steady, introspective groove with a puttering Nyabinghi drum panning back and forth across the stereo field. Backing vocalists Rita Marley and Marcia Griffiths are also on hand for an interesting cocktail of Wailers talent. But with Tosh's clavichord prominent and processing applied to the backing vocals, 'Legalize It' sounds distinctly more like a post-Wailers Peter Tosh song than Peter Tosh backed by Bob Marley's post-breakup band.

Tosh opens with the famous chorus, calling for legalization rather than condemnation of ganja, and promising to provide advertising. He proceeds to do just that. He lists ganja's many names and its popularity with various important professions. He lists some of ganja's health benefits, including as a curative for the flu, asthma, tuberculosis, and even umara combosis (though it's not exactly clear what this last ailment is). Finally, he lists endorsements from the animal kingdom, listing birds, ants, fowls and goats as fans. In the face of this quiet persuasion the Jamaican government banned the song from radio. Tosh would soon counter by continuing the argument with the more forceful 'Bush Doctor'.

'Igziabeher' is the second great original on *Legalize It*. It sounds like nothing so much as a reggae soundtrack to God's creation of the heavens and earth. A sharp Carlton Barrett drum roll announces as dramatic a piano and organ as have ever been heard in a reggae song. Tyrone Downie's piano is lush and yearning in a way that is outside the norm of reggae piano. He supports it with dramatic sustained organ chords. Other keyboards, rhythm and lead guitars and a portentous bass line complete a riddim that skanks ominously. Without the benefit or need of backing singers, Tosh sings about 'Igziabeher', Amharic for God, with great authority and reverence. The lyrics are filled with Amharic phrases and adapted Bible passages, giving the song heavy Rasta gravitas. One such adaptation comes from Psalm 104:14: "He causeth the grass to grow for the cattle and herb for the service of man." Mid-song, Al Anderson provides a muted guitar solo that Tosh follows with some spoken-sung vocals that raise the drama. This reaches its peak at the song's conclusion, as Tosh invokes end-of-world lightning, earthquakes and hellfire, as the sound of winds and thunder are heard, and the instrumentation increases in intensity. 'Igziabeher' is perhaps Tosh's most ambitious song. It succeeds fully, giving us a reggae song quite unlike any other.

In 2009, the umpteenth Peter Tosh best-of collection, *The Ultimate Peter Tosh Experience*, included 'Let Jah Be Praised (ShaJahShoka Dub Plate)', an alternative mix of 'Igziabeher'. The piano and organ are gone, replaced by other keyboard tracks, giving the song a stripped-down, more down-to-earth sound. While not as impressive as 'Igziabeher', it's enjoyable in its own right. Either way, you can enjoy the fine drums of Carlton Barrett, one of reggae's very best. In 1987 he was ambushed in front of his home, shot in the head from behind in a murder orchestrated by his wife and her lover. Five months later, Peter Tosh would meet a similar fate.

'Burial'; 'No Sympathy'
The familiar funerary horn introduction signals the return of a Wailers favorite, 'Burial', one of two great remakes on *Legalize It*. This rendition features a revised, mournful melody that suits the subject. Tosh's vocal shows a controlled intensity that was characteristic of his matured post-Wailers leads. Like Bob Marley, his mastery grew from The Wailers' ska day into the 1970s. (Bunny Wailer's voice, on the other hand, seems to have emerged fully formed.) Peter leads the instrumental Wailers on clavinet and rhythm guitar for a crunchy-funky reggae sound

that characterized much of his post-Wailers music. Though Bunny Wailer, Judy Mowatt and Rita Marley provide backing vocals on the album, here they sound like they come from Tosh himself. As he occasionally did at this stage of his career, at one point he seems to be improvising new lyrics on the spot. With 'Burial', Tosh succeeds in remaking a great old Wailers song into a great new Peter Tosh song.

You might not expect trading backing vocals from The Wailers for blues guitar licks to be a wise exchange. Yet, on the remake of 'No Sympathy', it somehow makes for a better rendition of the song than any previous one. The bluesy sound (guitar courtesy of Donald Kinsey) is truer to the dejected mood of the song, just as a solo vocal is truer to lyrics that describe alienation. Tosh is miserable and needs support from those close to him, but his friends have let him down. With this approach, Tosh inhabits the song as never before, and 'My Sympathy' finally reaches its potential. The lyrics were made sadly prophetic when, in the following decade, Tosh was murdered by an old friend.

Equal Rights

'Downpressor Man'

In 1977, Tosh released his second solo album, *Equal Rights*. Like *Legalize It*, it's a solid collection of remakes and new songs, with standouts of both kinds. But no song on the album loomed as large as the remake of 'Downpressor Man', Tosh's longest-ever studio track at 6:30 minutes. It had its beginnings as the traditional American spiritual 'Sinner Man', which The Wailers recorded as ska during their time at Studio One, with Peter and Bunny Wailer singing lead in unison. Tosh later recorded it as 'Oppressor Man', and then as the superior 'Downpressor', during The Wailers' varied middle period. Here, the song is expanded to an epic.

With each rendition, the song's tempo slowed from its ska beginnings. Now, Tosh reins it in to a devilishly slow roots reggae burn. The Sly & Robbie-anchored band simmers with prominent Nyabinghi hand drum, rock-style bluesy guitar leads, bubble-up organ and the expected Peter Tosh funky clavichord. Bunny Wailer is on hand to add backing vocals, the secret sauce that has been delighting reggae fans in general and Wailers fans in particular for well over a decade.

Tosh rides this groove with an outstanding vocal performance. He is moved to add some new lyrics about the callous rich, who drink champagne as they laugh at the poor, sung in a mocking voice, complete with haughty laughter. This is already a great song, when after 4 minutes, Tosh turns it on its head. He begins to wail the lyrics, stepping out from the song's structure. In response, organ and backing vocals drop out and a touch of reverb enlivens the drums in a rare application of dub. He works himself into a chant, improvising new lyrics, jamming with the bass. This unexpected and musically exciting turn runs for more than 2 minutes until the song's end, elevating what would have already been a great Peter Tosh song to something even better.

'Get Up, Stand Up'; 'Stepping Razor'

Two other remakes on *Equal Rights* stand out. A sinewy rendition of 'Get Up, Stand Up' with a revised rhythm is very good in its own right, even if no rendition could possibly top the one-two punch of a fiery Marley and an acerbic Tosh exchanging verses on the *Burnin'* original. One line of the song vexed the US record labels, and Tosh had to twice bowdlerize the song. On *Burnin'* we hear Tosh singing about being sick and tired of "your -ism scism game", Tosh's Rasta-speak term for Babylon's practice of prejudicially dividing people. But in live renditions of the song from that time, we learn that Tosh's intended lyric was "your bullshit game". This remake finds Tosh now singing, "this game of technology", again softening the language for acceptance by CBS Records. But in live performances at this time, he returned to the most uncompromised version of the lyrics.

Tosh had already recorded a fine rock steady rendition of the Joe Higgs-penned 'Stepping Razor' while with The Wailers. Here, he converts easy-going rock steady to a classic of hard rock reggae. It opens with a ripping guitar solo assault, as Al Anderson cuts loose and hardly lets up for the duration. This helps set an aggressive tone that's well suited to the song's swaggering, threatening lyrics, as Tosh warns that he's a dangerous man. Tosh ups the ante with additional violent lyrics that were not found in the earlier rendition, delivered as only Peter Tosh can. He warns bullies that he will treat them to a meal where they'll "drink lead soup" (with "brick crackers") and more. And he breaks into a section of rapid speak-singing, heavy in patois and accent, which ends with Tosh threatening to wipe the smile off an adversary's face by hurting him. The aggressive lyrics and rock guitar give hard rock fans a double-door entrée into reggae. Before they know it, they're enjoying the exotic fare of Sly Dunbar's creative drumming and lyrics rich in such unfamiliar terms as *duppie, chuckie* and *bull bucka*.

'I Am That I Am'; 'African'

The previously described remakes were not the only standout songs on *Equal Rights*. Two new songs showed Peter Tosh, though never the songwriting machine that Bob Marley was, continuing to write fine new material. The introspective 'I Am That I Am' is a call for acceptance of oneself and of one another. Though the verses are sometimes gritty, the chorus – a simple statement of self-affirmation – stands as elegant and gentle as anything Tosh ever recorded. The arrangement from the instrumental Wailers follows suit with a handsome collection of keyboards (harpsichord, clavinet, organ and electric piano) played by Tosh and Tyrone Downie, and Bunny Wailer again adds his voice for harmony. At the end of the song, Tosh proclaims his resolve by chant-talk-singing an expansion of the chorus that draws on figures and images from the Bible. Performed in a voice of absolute authority, it's like nothing so much as religious invocation.

'African' is a simple, upbeat song of solidarity. Tosh reminds all people worldwide of African descent that, regardless of complexion or religion, irrespective of the city, country or Jamaican parish of their birth, they are African. The straightforward reggae comes from the instrumental Wailers but with Robbie Shakespeare on bass and a two-piece horn section. And as producer, Tosh remembers that bass should be prominent in the mix of a reggae song and turns it up. More than thirty years later, Peter's son, Andrew Tosh, recorded an affecting acoustic rendition of this song. It's the best track on his 2010 album, *Legacy – An Acoustic Tribute To Peter Tosh*.

Songs on other albums

'Oh Bumbo Klaat'
In 1979 and 1981 came *Mystic Man* and *Wanted Dread And Alive*, two albums filled with good songs such as 'Coming In Hot' and 'Rastafari Is', but only 'Oh Bumbo Klaat' is a standout. Tosh's verses describe strife and oppression. His chorus intones what are Jamaica's two most infamous and most unsavory curses: "Bumbo klaat! (translates to vagina clot/cloth – meaning sanitary napkin) and "Raas klaat" (ass cloth/clot – meaning toilet paper), both carrying the implication of being soiled. At the conclusion of the song, Tosh explains how Jah told him to invoke these curse words to combat evil. Taking street language and reclaiming it is not shocking coming from the wordplay-loving and provocative Peter Tosh. Reggae's resident punsmith also popularized "shitstem" for "political system", "shituation" for "bad situation" and "politricks" for "politics". But his notorious employment of these terms would prove to have little impact on reggae beyond this song.

The song features a matter-of-fact vocal with a see-sawing melody from Tosh, a Sly & Robbie-led band, a three-piece male backing chorus (featuring two of The Tamlins) and a four-piece horn section that provides the song with a fine, twisty countermelody. Or you may choose a live rendition of the track with the shortened title of 'Bumbo Klaat', culled from a 1981 single and included on the Peter Tosh *Honorary Citizen* box collection. The band is different, anchored by the rhythm section of Fully Fullwood and Santa Davis, and includes the former Soulette and replacement Wailer Constantine "Dream" Walker on backing vocals and percussion. It's a smaller band, without horns, as rasping guitar power chords take over for the countermelody. Matching this sound and befitting the coarse lyrics, Peter's voice is unusually rough and raspy here. It's a recording that can help you imagine what Peter Tosh would have sounded like if he had lived long enough to try his hand as a ragga singer.

'Bush Doctor'; '(You Gotta Walk And) Don't Look Back'
Tosh's 1978 album, *Bush Doctor*, was his first and only on The Rolling Stones' new eponymous record label. Separate contributions from Rolling Stones Mick Jagger and Keith Richards each contributed to the creation of a Peter Tosh classic.

Like 'Legalize It', 'Bush Doctor' argues for the legalization of marijuana, but takes a different approach musically. Whereas Tosh mused introspectively on the earlier song, here he delivers a full-blooded, hard-rocking appeal. Adding greatly to the assault, Keith Richards provides down-and-dirty guitar throughout, including a brief mid-song solo.

An oblong-shaped drum intro, immediately identifiable as the distinctive work of Sly Dunbar, kicks things off. Over a fine introductory jam, Tosh famously intones the US Surgeon General's warning against cigarette smoking, ready to put forward the case for an alternative. The body of the song begins and Tosh throws down the gauntlet, singing in a full-blooded voice to demand that marijuana be legalized in Jamaica. The female backing vocalists coo support and a big band cooks up a bustling, creative international roots reggae sound. Sly & Robbie stretch out, as organ, synthesizer and clavinet, incidental hand percussion and the grittiest rock guitar to ever grace a reggae song are heard. As he did in 'Legalize It', Tosh argues the health benefits of ganja, and proclaims himself a bush doctor – a purveyor and expert in the medicinal properties of Jamaica's botanicals. He adds the economic and social benefits of legalization to his argument. Surprisingly, in neither song does he bring religion into the debate to any great degree.

As great as 'Bush Doctor' is, you have the option of a bigger, better spliff. Later CD editions of the album include 'Bush Doctor (Long Version)' as a bonus track. It features a bassier mix that is longer all around, including some extra lyrics and an extended Keith Richards guitar solo.

'Don't Look Back' is a remake of Tosh's fine but often forgotten Temptations cover from The Wailers' Studio One days. But what was a terse sub-2-minute soulful ska track has been blown wide open into a looser reggae-flavored R&B jam of almost triple the length. Tosh is supported by a big band with lead synthesizer, horns, female backing vocalists, a sax solo, and most importantly of all, Mick Jagger in a great guest turn. He shares the lead with Tosh, exchanging verses and bringing an unlikely ragged harmony to the chorus. This makes 'Don't Look Back' an exceptionally fun listen. After all, what other song lets us hear two iconic voices, one from rock and one from reggae, performing together? The fun continues right up to the song's run-out, with the two playfully exchanging improvised lines. A dub version of the song is included as another *Bush Doctor* CD bonus track.

'I'm The Toughest'; 'Soon Come'

Bush Doctor also features two remakes of note. 'I'm The Toughest' dates back to The Wailers' Studio One era. In this remake, Tosh delivers a mature read fittingly filled with adult-oriented sax from Saint Lucian session man Luther François. The result is a song especially well-suited for the international audiences that either never heard or wouldn't know quite what to make of the wilder (and ultimately superior) original rendition.

'Soon Come' is a remake of a song from The Wailers' album sessions with producer Leslie Kong. Horns, rock guitar from Donald Kinsey and fine drums from Sly Dunbar are on equal footing. They bolster Tosh, who is frustrated at a woman who is always late. (The title is a Jamaican expression for the promise of a short wait that typically turns out to be a long one. An expression with that kind of irony is right up Tosh's alley.) Different but as good as the original rendition, this remake is bested by the CD bonus track called 'Soon Come (Long Version)'. Not only is it longer, with more of everything, but it adds an extended drum introduction from Sly Dunbar to the top of the song and features a bassier mix.

'Johnny B Goode'

Tosh's 1983 album, *Mama Africa*, included good but unexciting remakes of two of Tosh's Wailers classics, 'Maga Dog' and 'Stop That Train'. But it's another cover – an unexpected one – that provides the album with its only great song.

A stripped-down roots reggae riddim is spiced with Nyabinghi hand drum, additional percussion and bird whistle. A horn line enters, bringing a heavy melody that completes the grounded roots sound. Tosh begins to sing with great intensity, and although they're tweaked to better suit him, there is something familiar about the words and melody. Suddenly, it snaps into focus that Tosh is singing an earnest *dread* cover of Chuck Berry's classic, 'Johnny B Goode'. Dread piano joins prominently in the mix, as do female backing vocalists, filling out the sound. Rock guitar riffs from Donald Kinsey appear as per the lyrics. Mid-song, Tosh unleashes Kinsey, the man he would introduce as "the reggae Frankenstein" in his live performances, and he rocks out with a monster solo. He reprises the solo at the song's end to fade-out, with Tosh cutting loose as well.

When asked if he chose this cover because of an affinity with Chuck Berry's song, with candor rare for a star but not for Tosh, he answered, 'No, man, strictly for commercial reasons.' But that does nothing to lessen the fact that the song succeeds on many levels: as roots reggae, as reggae-rock fusion, as a reggae cover, as a Peter Tosh song, and, to Tosh's point, a cross-over hit. The *Mama Africa* CD includes as a bonus track a 12-inch remix of 'Johnny B Goode', but the album mix is preferred. While the remix is longer, it doesn't add much of any great value and does away with the album mix's strong ending.

'Vampire'

Tosh first recorded 'Vampire' as a 1976 single that was eventually collected on a CD compilation (exaggeratedly) called *The Ultimate Peter Tosh Experience*. Its dub version B-side, entitled 'Dracula' was compiled on the Peter Tosh *Honorary Citizen* box-set. It's another example of a favored Rasta metaphor that likens Babylon's exploitation of Jamaica to the bloodsucking of vampires. We have discussed other examples of this analogy fueling fine roots reggae songs, including 'Babylon System' by Bob Marley, and songs called 'Vampire' by Black Uhuru and Devon Irons (see pages 494, 358, and 280). The lyrics mostly describe the bad doings of the titular subject, yet 'Vampire' is a fun song. Perhaps it's Tosh's horror-movie moaning and the ghostly rattling of chains that opens the song. Or Tosh's prefacing every couplet with "Oh no!" But mostly it's because Tosh seems to be enjoying himself, as does a Sly & Robbie-led band. 'Vampire' gives The Wailers a sequel to 'Mister Brown' and another entry for a possible Halloween reggae compilation.

A remake of 'Vampire' is the one standout track on Tosh's final studio album, 1987's *No Nuclear War*. True to form, it opens with horror-movie sounds as wolf howls and rattling of chains are heard. But nothing prepares you for Tosh's vocal. He is unexpectedly *joyous*, so powerfully so, the instrumentation is held back for a time, allowing you to better enjoy him supported only by backing vocals. The instrumentation drops in but Tosh never flags. And with a Peter Tosh vocal so filled with joy that it could slay vampires more effectively than wooden stakes, silver bullets or a torrent of holy water, we conclude the chapter on Peter Tosh and the story of The Wailers' legacy of great songs.

49 Great dub poetry

We have already discussed how the advent of DJ reggae would pave the way for yet another new style. Dub poetry, a more serious offshoot of DJ, would begin to be recorded at the end of the 1970s. Its rhythmic chant-speak delivery owes much to that of the DJ. But the dub poets' songs are more formally composed and more serious in tone. The DJ's improvisations, topic jumping, catchphrases and sound effects have no place in the work of a dub poet. Riddims were newly created for the dub poetry, unlike the DJ's heavy use of versions. That is, when musical backing was employed. Dub poetry was sometimes performed solo, with no backing at all, something unique in reggae. As we will see, dub poetry has another distinction. It's the first style of reggae that was born outside of Jamaica.

Linton Kwesi Johnson

Linton Kwesi Johnson (LKJ) was born in Clarendon in 1952 and emigrated to London when he was eleven. Johnson had published several volumes of poetry before he began to record. Dennis "Blackbeard" Bovell became his keyboardist, bandleader, producer and dub-master. Perhaps their similar backgrounds were responsible for their obvious creative synergy. Bovell was born in Barbados in 1953 and moved to London when he was twelve. Together, their work became one of the triumvirate of great British reggae, along with Steel Pulse and Black Slate. But whereas the other two created reggae in the familiar international roots style, LKJ would create something new.

His poems often described the bitter racism, violence and oppression experienced by the West Indian minority in England. This made them perfect as lyrics for reggae, and Johnson began to record in 1978 with Bovell providing the backing. But Johnson did not sing, nor did he possess a DJ's playful, fluid chanting skills. Instead he recited his poems seriously with a rhythmic chanted delivery in his unabashed Jamaica-by-way-of-London accent. And although many of his themes were familiar to roots reggae, there was no talk of Jah. Johnson was not a Rasta, but an atheist, making him a rare secular reggae performer.

Johnson paved the way for (and in some cases gave direct support to) other Jamaican poets, at home or abroad, to move from printed word and live recitation to recorded dub poetry. Soon, recordings by such poets as Mikey Smith, Oku Onuora and Mutabaruka would appear. Depending on the poet and the poem, dub poetry could represent the most radical social leanings expressed in reggae.

Johnson would release a dozen albums between 1978 and 2002, including four live and three dub albums. All of his tracks, including his best as described below, are readily available on CD. In many of his recordings, the poem ends before the song. Not a problem, since Bovell and The Dub Band, as he called the large group he led, played a bold, confident brand of reggae, with impeccable playing and production. Although it carries a slightly internationalized flavor, being recorded in Britain with Jamaican and non-Jamaican musicians, it was still undoubtedly creative, unadulterated roots reggae. Bovell wisely put all instruments on an equal footing, a balanced arrangement that prevented distractions from LKJ's speak-chanted poetry. Some of the dub versions Bovell created from these tracks are recommended in the 'More great dub' chapter of this book (pages 291–8).

'Fight Dem Back'

In 'Fight Dem Back', Johnson unleashes a strong counterattack against racists who brag of their intention to physically harm England's minorities. Responding in kind, in the gravely intoned chorus, LKJ vows to break their empty heads. The music is as strong as the words. The multilayered riddim struts its stuff with rousing horn lines, a descending picked guitar riff, strummed guitar flourishes, a trombone solo and more. It's shocking to hear a well-considered argument for explicit violence set to excellent reggae, but that is very much a part of the dub poetry experience.

'Sonny's Lettah [Anti-Sus Poem]'

'Sonny's Lettah [Anti-Sus Poem]' is another explicitly violent LKJ song. Over a bluesy reggae backing, complete with jailhouse harmonica, LKJ reads back a letter Sonny's written in prison to his mother. He is full of regret, having failed in his promise to look after his little brother. Arrested and beaten by the police for no reason, his brother has been a victim of England's controversial sus law that allowed a person to be arrested because of a mere suspicion of guilt. Johnson rhythmically chants a litany of blows and injuries received by his brother from police batons. Unable not to get involved, Johnson fought back, with another chanted blow-by-blow account of his violent reprisal. He ends the letter by revealing that he's been charged with murdering a policeman, and asks his mother to stay positive and brave. An emotional and violent story set to excellent reggae, 'Sonny's Lettah' is a classic piece of dub poetry.

'Reggae Sounds'

In 'Reggae Sounds', one of Johnson's most famous poems, the sound of reggae is described as being born of painful Jamaican history, and as a wellspring of revolution. Its first two stanzas impress with a poet's description of the sound of reggae, mixing the literal and the symbolic, performed in a way that redoubles the meaning of the words. Passages of carefully chosen syllables provide a work that is as much a sound poem as a word poem to stunning effect. The Dub Band enters with the sparsest of dub backings, and slowly builds a fine groove worthy of the lyrics. Reggae inspires a poem, and the poem returns the favor by seeding a great piece of reggae and a prime example of dub poetry.

Other great LKJ songs
There are other LKJ songs in the same vein that are nearly as good. For example, in 'It Noh Funny', Johnson expresses concern for youths who choose risky behavior over school, while The Dub Band provides a peppy reggae backing. Similar issues are considered in 'Want Fi Go Rave', with Johnson chanting to a galloping backing. 'Reggae Fi Peach' is the sad story of the death of Blair Peach at the hands of the Special Patrol Group of the Metropolitan (London) Police during an anti-Nazi rally in West London in 1979, recited over a rousing reggae track. The dub version, 'Peach Dub', sounds like the requiem it is.

Other great dub poetry

Michael Smith: *'Mi Cyaan Believe It'*
Michael "Mikey" Smith was born in 1954 in Kingston and began to write poems in in his mid-teens. 'Mi Cyaan Believe It' is the title track of his 1982 LP, produced by Linton Kwesi Johnson. Though performed a cappella with no backing music at all, it remains one of the most potent performances a dub poet has ever recorded. Smith makes observations about family, work woes, police beatings for smoking ganja, housing conditions, the 1977 Orange Street fire and the violent eviction of a thousand tenants from the impoverished Rema neighborhood of Kingston that preceded it. His reading is rhythmic but remarkably fluid, masterfully twisting the beat to best suit what he's saying. He plays roles. He ranges from whisper to scream. LKJ called Smith, 'the quintessential performance poet, with an actor's sense of the dramatic and a musician's acute sense of rhythm". [Jamaican Gleaner, November 3, 2002] Sadly, a year after his first and only album was released, Smith was murdered in Kingston after a political rally, the motive widely believed to be his activism. Also sad is the fact that this LP was never released on CD and is not currently in print.

Louise Bennett: *'Colonizing In Reverse'*
As mentioned in an earlier chapter (page 427), Louise Bennett was a beloved Jamaican poet, folklorist, linguist, comedian, storyteller, songwriter, singer and star of Jamaican stage, radio and television. So much so, she is the very personification of black Jamaican culture. "Miss Lou", as she was affectionately called, was born in 1919 in Kingston. She began performing in the mid-1940s. Her recording career began with singles and albums in the early 1950s in folk and urban mento styles. She released nine albums in a variety of styles and about the same number of single sides. The first of two books of her poems was published in 1966. Though college-educated, she did not shy away from using patois in her poetry. Instead, she embraced and celebrated its use, to paraphrase, not as a corruption of English,

but an enrichment of it. The government made her a member of the Order Of Jamaica in 1974 and the island's Cultural Ambassador, and honored her again as a Member of the Order of Merit in 2001. In 2006, she passed away in Toronto, Canada, where she had moved a decade earlier (to a city which long had a large Jamaican immigrant population). Though Jamaica misses the irreplaceable Miss Lou, they can take solace in the fact that, living past her mid-eighties, she enjoyed a much longer life than most performers discussed in this book.

In 1983, Bennett released an album (now available on CD) called *Yes M' Dear – Miss Lou Live*. Among the songs and spoken observations, she recites her poem, 'Colonizing In Reverse', without any accompaniment. She does so with the rhythmic delivery, self-awareness and sly edge of the dub poet. The subject is the same one that gave us a number of fine golden-age mento and reggae songs: the wave of emigration from Jamaica to the UK. England might have colonized Jamaica in the seventeenth century, but now, she wryly notes, the waves of Jamaicans migrating to England may have the effect of her title.

Mutabaruka: '*The Monkey*'

Dub poet Mutabaruka released a string of nine LPs from 1982 to 2002. He is currently Jamaica's top reggae disc jockey on IRIE FM. 'The Monkey' is from his last CD, the 2002 self-produced *Life Squared*. It shrewdly opens with the banjo introduction from Lord Flea's similarly named mento song. He then updates New Orleans R&B singer Dave Bartholomew's 1957 song, 'The Monkey Speaks Its Mind'. This song, in which monkeys observe and puzzle over human behavior, made an impact in Jamaica at the time. Mento band Chin's Calypso Sextet recorded a very similar song called 'Monkey Opinion' in the same year, while others also covered it. The backing is trombone-dominated reggae with the occasional banjo riff. Though Mutabaruka has recorded many good tracks, there is something special about hearing him recite modern dub poetry while keeping an eye fixed on Jamaica's musical past. And if that's not enough, the CD also includes a more purely mento-backed version of the track, called 'Monkey (Mento Mix)'.

50 Great Jamaica Jazz

Just as dub poetry arose at the end of the 1970s to expand the sound of reggae, so did another new reggae sub-style appear in the 1990s. It was then that Jamaica Jazz came into being, as jazz was re-infused into ska and reggae with exciting results.

Strong jazz musicianship has long enriched Jamaica's music. This is obvious to anyone who has ever heard The Skatalites, but the story begins much earlier than that. As early as the 1920s, 78-rpm singles with jazz interpretations of Jamaican folk songs were being recorded, most prominently by the Trinidad-born singer-bandleader Sam Manning, who sometimes used Jamaican musicians. Manning continued to record Jamaican songs into the 1940s. At the start of the 1950s, such recordings came home. The first record released on MRS, Jamaica's first label, was not rural mento, though this style would soon follow. Instead, it was a vocal jazz rendition of a medley of four Jamaican folk songs performed by native sons Lord Fly (Rupert Linly Lyon) and Dan Williams And His Orchestra. (Singer/actor Grace Jones is Williams's granddaughter.) Throughout the golden age of mento and into the 1960s, not only would rural mento be recorded, but so would its more polished, urban, jazz-based cousin.

Jamaica's jazz musicians next participated on the Jamaican R&B records of the late 1950s and early 1960s. They jammed with Nyabinghi drum troupes. They played the newly founded ska, expanding it from R&B with an inverted beat to something far more exciting and sometimes wondrous. Though jazz was less overt in rock steady and reggae than in ska, it was never far from the surface. But by the time dancehall became the predominant style, there was less jazz influence in reggae than ever before. Perhaps in a reaction to this, in 1993, unabashed jazz lover Coxsone Dodd produced an album called *Reggae Au Go Jazz*. It combined reggae and jazz to different extents on twelve instrumental tracks. Coming together in various tracks were different combinations of Jamaican jazz trumpeter Roy "Bubbles" Burrowes, US tenor sax players Clifford Jordan and Charles Davis, Jamaican guitarist Ernest Ranglin, keyboard great and former Skatalite Jackie Mittoo, Studio One sessions drummer Fil Callender and even pioneering Nyabinghi percussionist Count Ossie amongst others. But somehow, although there were some acceptable tracks, the set didn't quite jell. Perhaps this was in part because Dodd relied on the versioning technique of mixing new jazz instrumentation with existing Studio One recordings. That which had served him so well in ska, rock steady and reggae failed to ignite Jamaica Jazz. But the idea of re-infusing jazz into reggae using Jamaican and non-Jamaican talent was too good to be abandoned and others would soon run with this to greater success.

One of these was the big band known as Jazz Jamaica or The Jazz Jamaica All Stars, assembled by double bassist (and nephew of Ernest Ranglin) Gary Crosby. They released four albums, the first also in 1993 and the last in 2005. Their repertoire included ska and reggae classics, jazz standards, an album of Motown covers (complete with vocals – an exception for this largely instrumental genre) and more. For the first time since ska, reggae with stand-up rather than electric bass was featured. The style thus launched, great Jamaica Jazz would soon follow, easily acquired today on CD.

Ernest Ranglin: *Below The Bassline*

It should come as no surprise that the eminently qualified Ernest Ranglin, virtuoso jazz guitarist and master reggae musician and arranger, recorded the first completely successful Jamaica Jazz album. It most certainly helped that the album's pianist and producer was the equally talented and well-known Jamaican musician, Monty Alexander. Born in 1944 in Kingston, Alexander started playing piano as a child. Seeing visiting US jazz greats perform at Kingston's Carib Theatre had a huge impact on him. By the 1950s, he would begin to record sessions and formed a band, The Cyclones. By the early 1960s, The Cyclones, or Monty & The Cyclones, had released almost a dozen Coxsone Dodd-produced singles, covering a melange of R&B, ska and jazz styles. Just as he started recording in Jamaica, Alexander left for the USA. There, he would quickly achieve greatness, soon finding himself playing with Frank Sinatra, Charlie Parker and other jazz luminaries. He would be listed in the top five of Gene Rizzo's 2005 book, *The Fifty Greatest Jazz Piano Players of All Time* (Rizzo, 2005: p. 19). But Alexander would never forget the music of his homeland, returning to it in different ways throughout his career. Nor would Jamaica forget him. In 2000, the Jamaican government awarded him the title of Commander in the Order of Distinction.

Below The Bassline, released in 1996, gets the recipe right. It starts with Ranglin and Alexander, plus august Skatalite Roland Alphonso guesting on sax for one song. They're joined by an American jazz rhythm section and second keyboardist for a set of instrumental jazz-reggae renditions of well-chosen reggae classics, plus three new Ernest Ranglin compositions. The arrangements work just as they are supposed to – as both jazz and as reggae. Naturally, fine solos abound. Though all of the renditions of reggae songs are fine, the first five discussed below are especially good. (Each of the five originals are described elsewhere in this book; pages 288, 180, 251, 318, and 157.)

'Congo Man Chant' opens with a jazz drum groove, as Alexander's piano, guitar and bass transformatively take up the melody of The Congos' Black Ark Nyabinghi-reggae song. A jazz updating of Ranglin's own reggae classic, 'Surfin'', finds the classic bass line well carried by stand-up bass. And somehow, piano solos add greatly to Ranglin's answer to the surf guitar instrumental. 'King Tubby Meets The Rockers' is a fine jazzy interpretation of Augustus Pablo's 'King Tubbys Meets Rockers Uptown'. Piano wanders about and simulates dub echo as Ranglin shows off his massive chops (as could be said about every song here). 'Satta Amassa Ganna', The Abyssinians' Rastafarian ode to African repatriation, receives a light touch, in keeping with the feel of the introspective original. Monty solos on melodica. The jazz take on '54-46 (Was My Number)' is just as spirited as the original by Toots & The Maytals. 'Ball Of Fire' is a ska-leaning, sometimes skanking, remake of a Skatalites song, and Roland Alphonso is on hand to play sax. It's long and jamming, leaning more towards jazz than reggae. 'Black Disciples', a Burning Spear song with a memorable bass line, provides perfect fodder for a jazz exploration. 'None Shall Escape The Judgment', a Johnny Clarke song, receives a jazz-reggae makeover without losing the high-energy insistence of the original. 'Bourbon Street Skank' is a new reggae composition from Ranglin that all parties involved seem to be enjoying. The same can be said of the more low-key 'Below The Bassline'. A third new composition, 'Nana's Chalk Pipe', is engaging but has little reggae to it at all.

Dean Fraser: *Big Up!*

The same year, reggae saxophone player Dean Fraser released the self-produced *Big Up!*, in which Jamaican musicians and American jazz musicians again combined their talents to produce a strong album of instrumental Jamaica Jazz.

Dean Ivanhoe Fraser is reggae's top sax man of his generation. He recorded more prolifically than any post-Skatalites sax player, appearing on countless hundreds of tracks and recording about 35 albums of his own. He was born in 1955 in Kingston and began playing the clarinet at age twelve. He switched to sax at fifteen, inspired by such Jamaican sax greats as Skatalites Tommy McCook and Ronald Alphonso, as well as Cedric Brooks and Glen DaCosta. As many Jamaican singers and instrumentalists did, Fraser started on the hotel circuit, playing in such bands as The Sonny Bradshaw Seven. Jacob Miller was an early supporter and helped the young musician, whom he called "Youth Sax", cross over to the reggae session scene. By the end of the 1970s he began to appear on reggae tracks, and by the 1980s, he was Jamaica's top sax sessions man, playing with Bob Marley and just about everyone else. In fact, if you hear saxophone on a dancehall record, it's probably him. He appeared on numerous such tracks even as the style had become otherwise completely electronic, and horns were mostly being passed over. His fine and prolific musicianship earned Fraser the Musgrave Medal from the Jamaican government in 1993.

On *Big Up!*, Fraser took an interesting approach to Jamaica Jazz. He had two drummers play simultaneously: reggae's Sly Dunbar and jazz's Idris Muhammad. Fraser had no problem in finding another seven reggae classics to cherry-pick for Jamaica Jazz makeovers. (Once again, the original renditions of the first five songs below are described elsewhere in this book; pages 84, 170, 354, 140, 130.) On these tracks, *Big Up!* achieves a more even balance of reggae and jazz, while *Below The Bassline* was a bit more jazz-leaning by comparison. The set is rounded out by two new jazz numbers.

The Skatalites' 'Dick Tracy', revitalized as a ska-reggae-jazz scorcher, launches the album. 'Big Up/Armageddon Time' starts off with a straight jazz introduction, and then turns on its heels to become an extended jazz-reggae jam on Willie Williams's vocal take on the most versioned of riddims, 'Real Rock'. Keyboards play a simulation of dub. The heavy dread of Black Uhuru's 'Shine Eye Girl' is in no way weakened by an infusion of jazz, as Fraser's sax takes over the role previously held by lead singer Michael Rose. Touches of real and simulated dub are heard and everyone solos on this, the album's longest track. After a short jazz intro, 'Have Mercy' proves to actually be the Gladiators' 'Rearrange', whose riddim is better known from The Cables' 'Baby Why'. 'Minstrel & Queen', originally recorded by the US Motown group The Impressions and covered as 'Queen Majesty' by The Techniques, and Culture's 'Natty Never Get Weary' give the band the opportunity to show its softer side. 'None A Jah Jah Children No Cry', a Nyabinghi song by Ras Michael, takes advantage of the natural simpatico that has long existed between Nyabinghi music and jazz. 'Bank Of The River', a jazz original by bassist and future member of the reconstituted Skatalites Kevin Batchelor, does not really have much in the way of reggae to it. Neither does 'African Elation', an original from Fraser.

More great Jamaica Jazz

Ernest Ranglin's cover of Keith & Tex's 'Stop That Train', found on his otherwise non-Jamaica Jazz 1998 album, *Memories Of Barber Mack*, would have fit nicely on *Below The Bassline*. It features one of the greatest of Ranglin's many virtuoso solos. More than thirty years after their heyday, all the surviving Skatalites along with Ernest Ranglin reunited in 1998 for an album called *Ball Of Fire*. The line-up is filled out with talent from the USA, and the music, mostly remakes of Skatalites hits, can certainly be classified Jamaica Jazz. In 1999, Monty Alexander released *Stir It Up*, a Jamaica Jazz album of Bob Marley covers. In 2004 Alexander and Ranglin released *Rocksteady*, another love letter to classic reggae songs from a jazz point of view. Toots guests on a rendition of his 'Pressure Drop'. And check out the playfulness on the renditions of Dave and Ansel Collins's 'Double Barrel' and The Skatalites' 'Confucius'. Monty Alexander released his second album of Bob Marley material in 2006, *Concrete Jungle*, with a number of tracks featuring vocals. He has orchestrated a number of incredible concerts combining mento, ska, reggae and jazz in every way imaginable. Let's hope these are released on CD, or better yet DVD, sometime soon.

51 Barrington Levy and the birth of dancehall

Barrington Levy was born in 1964 in Kingston, but grew up in Clarendon Parish. A youthful music fan, he was especially fond of Dennis Brown, The Jackson Five and Michael Jackson. He first made a record around 1975 in a short-lived group called the Mighty Multitude that included a cousin of his. A year later, as a grizzled veteran of two sides, at fourteen years of age he decided to go solo. He initially found success as a sound system performer. He then recorded a handful of undistinguished singles for various producers, sounding like the *youth singer* he was. Things took an abrupt change for the better when he began recording for Henry "Junjo" Lawes.

Junjo was born in 1960 in Kingston, growing up at an especially rough time in a particularly bad neighborhood. Two reggae producers would prove to be his salvation. He was mentored away from *badness* by Bunny Lee, and after trying his hand in a vocal trio, he moved to production, working with Linville Thompson. By the end of the 1970s, he began producing on his own, choosing to employ a hot new band on the scene, The Roots Radics. Anchored by Errol "Flabba" Holt on bass and Eric "Bingy Bunny" Lamont on guitar, The Radics offered the first new competition to Sly & Robbie since the latter teamed up in 1974. They featured a new sound: one tougher, leaner and more directly to the point than either the uber-creative Sly & Robbie or the roots gold standard, the Barrett brothers-led instrumental Wailers. While working for Junjo, The Radics began to create riddims that emphasized a simplified, syncopated rhythm that was perfect for the dancehall. This was the start of dancehall growing into a stylistically different genre of reggae, rather than just a lyrical subject.

By now, Levy's voice had lost any last vestige of baby fat, and something special emerged. In many ways it was an archetypical reggae voice: high, nasal, expressive, melodic and sweet. But perfectly suited to dancehall, it was a powerful voice. Even his Waterhouse-influenced undulating wordless flourishes were delivered with greater force than was typical for Waterhouse singing, sounding more like a call to party than something more emotional. And Levy had a strong sense of how to write songs that used his voice to its best advantage. With these tools, his singing amounted to a clarion call signaling a move away from the quieter, more introspective roots reggae delivery that was then so popular, announcing the emergence of dancehall reggae.

Junjo now had all the pieces in place, and the first Barrington Levy-voiced Roots Radics-backed track he produced, 'A Yah We Deh', can be considered the first dancehall song. A hit, it led to more songs from this aggregation, and soon additional producers, singers and musicians joined the party, as dancehall grew to challenge and ultimately overtake roots as the most popular style of reggae. After going through several seismic shifts, resulting in the ragga of today, dancehall would come to dominate reggae.

Junjo would go on to be a highly successful producer, working with numerous singers and DJs (perhaps most famously with Yellowman) on his Volcano label. Sadly, the badness he strove to avoid would catch up with him in 1999. While visiting London, he was killed in a drive-by shooting. The Roots Radics would enjoy great popularity as the top dancehall backing band. (Sly & Robbie were also successful in this new style, but the instrumental Wailers never made this stylistic move.) The band effectively ended in 1994 when Lamont died from prostate cancer. By then, much of ragga was being created with digital tools rather than with musical instruments.

Happily, Barrington Levy is still going strong with a new album planned and frequent live performances. He already has over 25 albums and over 100 singles under his belt. He influenced a generation of dancehall singers. Though many sound similar to him, none can match the strength of his voice. He would earn the moniker "The Mellow Canary", a well-intentioned name, but a bit passive for the man with a voice so powerful that it helped launch a new style of reggae.

'A Yah We Deh'

As mentioned above, 1979's 'A Yah We Deh' was the first collaboration between Levy, producer Junjo Lawes and The Roots Radics. With all three legs of the stool bringing something new to the song, it can be considered the first example of dancehall as a musically separate style of reggae. It's a sleek and exciting song, propelled by mechanized drumming, most probably a live drummer imitating the sequenced sound of a drum machine. And although all else in the riddim is familiar from the reggae that came before (including roots lyrics, rippling picked guitar fills, guitar leads bleeding all over the track, urgent organ stabs and the double-struck rhythm that dates back to mento), the simple, driving drum pattern shapes these elements differently from what came before.

Much the same can be said about Levy's vocals, even though he is singing about roots reggae concerns. Although voices this strong and high had been heard before in reggae (Desmond Dekker and Jimmy Cliff come immediately to mind), Levy has an immediacy here that sets him apart from any singer who came before him. He is perfectly suited to ride the exciting new riddim and the overall results are electrifying. A fine song in its own right, it's also a fascinating view of roots reggae beginning to be streamlined and modernized into something new.

A 6:30-minute disco-mix with an appended dub version is available on several Barrington Levy CDs, and is the recommended version. A different and better dub version entitled 'A Yah We Deh Dub' is also available on Barrington Levy and King

Tubby CD collections. It trades most of the vocals, organ and guitar for sharply structured horn lines. Another vocal version of this riddim, the curious 'Tribute To Bobby', is described later in this book (page 585).

'Here I Come'

On 'Here I Come', a dancehall classic from the 1984 album of the same name, Levy opens his pipes to sing about a demanding young woman. She insists on having children with Levy, only to promptly dump them on him to run off for a wilder lifestyle. Bad for Levy, but good for his fans, as he reacts with great emotion. He shows his pain by his custom brand of Waterhouse warbling, a stanza of which opens the song. Later, he moves to righteous anger. Yet so powerful is his voice, no matter what emotion he is expressing, it's felt as pure exuberance. And he's not so upset that he can't work in a brief advertisement for producer Junjo's Volcano sound system, as well as a proclamation of his popularity with women. He draws these disparate observations together with the famous chorus about being broader than Broadway.

The Roots Radics and producer Paul "Jah Screw" Love crystallize the further forking off of dancehall from roots. The beat is simplified and exaggeratedly syncopated, all the better for dancing. With far fewer subtleties than any reggae that came before, it's not difficult to see how this sound would soon lead to fully machine-generated riddims.

'Here I Come' was a hit, and is available on numerous reggae compilations and Barrington Levy collections. Naturally, Levy recorded several remakes, though none tops the excitement of the original. He also recorded a revoicing of the riddim, called 'Black Roses'. It's good, but lacks the drama of 'Here I Come'. One remake with the shortened title of 'Come' has revised lyrics that stay focused on the story of the demanding woman. There's a wonderful live rendition of 'Come', sometimes titled 'Here I Come' or 'She Give Me Love', rattling around on the internet. It opens a cappella, and when the band joins in briefly, Levy orders them to stop. By its conclusion, his solo chant drives the audience wild. A pox on the next Barrington Levy compilation that does not include this rendition.

'Under Mi Sensi'

Like 'Here I Come', 'Under Mi Sensi' is a collaboration with The Roots Radics and producer Jah Screw that resulted in a big 1984 hit for Levy, spawning remakes and live versions. Its popularity is easy to understand. The riddim is agreeable, traipsing along as deliberate drums, reverbed rolls, metronomic rhythm guitar and sweet yet mechanized lead guitar runs dab it with dancehall colors. The lyrics are engaging, as Levy sings about police harassment over ganja. This common occurrence is a familiar theme to reggae fans, with Gregory Isaacs's 'Mr Cop', Bob Marley & The Wailers' 'Three O'Clock Roadblock' and Toots & The Maytals' '54-46 (Was My Number)' being examples found in this book (pages 341, 463, and 157).

The story opens with Levy performing and smoking at the Volcano sound system. But soon, policemen intervene. Levy tries to talk his way out of the mess, claiming that he was smoking "shag" – loose tobacco. When that fails, he tries to reason with the policeman, pointing out that although the officer may not like ganja smokers, it brings money into Jamaica. The police rebuttal is a beating that starts with a split lip.

This richly detailed story is conveyed by dancehall's best set of pipes. Once again, even as he tells of his anguish, the strength of his singing makes the song upbeat. Especially as he peppers the song with a second vocal track of enthusiastic expressions of self-commentary, such as *Oh, no! Oh-whoh-ho-ho!, Oh well!, Seen?, Hey!, I like it!,* etc. Providing such play-by-play reporting on his own story is the icing on the cake, making an already enjoyable song even more fun. The original rendition, as heard on Levy's *Here I Come* album, is preferred to the many others that followed.

Robin Hood

Barrington Levy's 1980 album, *Robin Hood*, was another collaboration between Levy, foundation dancehall backing band The Roots Radics, and the style's pioneering producer, Henry "Junjo" Lawes. But, surprisingly, dancehall's mechanization, syncopation and simplification are nowhere to be heard, as Junjo guides them in a different and ambitious direction. *Robin Hood* has a big and creative reggae sound, rich with dub (due to Junjo's use of dub-master Scientist as his engineer) and horns. The sound is so big, it would have overpowered a lesser singer, but not the mighty Barrington Levy. Love songs dominated the set, yet the music was too heady and heavy to be considered straight lovers' rock. Nor did it sound exactly like roots reggae, and it lacked any of the style's lyrical concerns. Neither did it sound much like the internationally released albums from Bob Marley, Peter Tosh, Toots & The Maytals, Black Uhuru or Third World from the same time. *Robin Hood* is a reminder that all involved were completely capable of creating exciting new reggae sounds in addition to dancehall. Public demand, however, would dictate that they work mostly in the latter arena.

In addition to the superb tracks below, the title track is quite good too, memorable for its creative drumming and the lyric, "If life was something that money could buy, the rich would live and the poor would die". (It was re-voiced by Levy as 'Warm And Sunny Day' on a 1980 single, though it does not warrant the effort to locate a copy.) 'Many Changes In Life' is very good as well. But the three tracks below, overflowing with dub and emotion, are inspired.

'Gonna Tell Your Girlfriend'
In 'Gonna Tell Your Girlfriend', Levy is wounded by an unfaithful woman. He learns that the girl he loves has other lovers. He is so devastated, he compares his mental state to being mixed in a blender. His delivery is unusually slow and

bluesy, allowing him to fully portray his anguish, his natural ebullience held at bay. He takes the time to repeat words in a line, adding emphasis to their meaning, wailing wordlessly, working his vibrato and Waterhouse warbling. He sings over an arrangement that is typical for the album. Prominent reverb-kissed trebly horns bleat ominously, as creative drum work is supplemented by surprise accents from various hand percussion instruments. Meanwhile, groaning guitar and piano provide a dark undercurrent. Even without an overt application of dub effects, the sound is dreamily dubby, carrying Levy like a leaf in a stream.

'Why Did You Leave Me'

The self-explanatory 'Why Did You Leave Me' finds Levy's romantic affairs still in turmoil. But unlike 'Gonna Tell Your Girlfriend', rather than being overwhelmed, Levy is just sad. He expresses this with another unhurried performance that is strewn with cries of pain, soulfully wailing in the reggae way. The song reaches a peak with his dub-enhanced cry, "Why did you do this to me?!"

The underlying riddim is suitably dark, as the absence of horns moves bass into the fore. Scientist's heady application of dub keeps the sound heavy throughout with all manner of reverb, drop-out, splashes of echo, an extended ending and more. And, as dub can do, it's used to add drama to the vocal performance. But rather than ejecting portions of the vocal track, as was typical on dub version B-sides, here dub complements Levy's fine vocal without sacrificing a syllable. Never has despair sounded so heady.

'Rock And Come In'

In a change of mood from the previous two songs, 'Rock And Come In' is absolutely joyous. Levy is excited about a well-dressed girl, especially as she passes a series of tests. She is over sixteen, the age of consent in Jamaica. She prefers natty dreads over baldheads, and civilians over police. There is even more to celebrate, as Levy goes to the movies, and is granted admission by a simple kindness, even though he doesn't have enough money for a ticket. In 'Rock And Come In', everything is coming up Barrington, and the listener reaps the benefits. He demonstrates his joy by merrily elongating syllables and by oscillating a vowel between two notes, sometimes for a dozen iterations. No singer has ever gotten more out of the word "in", as Levy's nineteen-syllable rendition threatens to become the listener's preferred pronunciation. The instrumental arrangement is dominated by trebly horns in elaborate descending lines and creative drums and percussion, over an undertone of piano, grinding guitar and touches of dub. An example of the latter is how bass and drums are dropped out, leaving only Levy's high voice and a corkscrew horn line supported by guitar and piano for an orgy of treble with no low-register content at all. That is, until the bass and drums are slapped back in, the aural playfulness adding to the happiness of this track.

52 Johnny Osbourne

Errol "Johnny" Osbourne was born in 1948 in the Jones Town section of Kingston and would become another in the long line of notable reggae stars who received their musical education from the Alpha Cottage School for Boys. He started his recording career in the late 1960s as a member of two vocal groups. First came The Wildcats, but they had little to show for their work other than one single in 1969, the fast-paced early reggae of 'All I Have Is Love'. (Though they shared a name, it was a different song from Gregory Isaacs's first hit.) Greater success was achieved as a member of The Sensations, who released two popular songs in 1969 produced by Winston Riley. 'Come Back Darling' straddled the rock steady of the recent past and the roots reggae soon to come. 'Warrior' featured a nascent roots reggae sound. Osbourne then moved to Toronto, Canada, for a period of years, working with local bands. After his return to Jamaica in the latter part of the 1970s, he would henceforth work as a solo artist, and, as was his greatest wish, he began a residency at Studio One with Coxsone Dodd. Osbourne could shape his versatile singing equally well to a variety of styles, and while his was not one of Jamaica's virtuoso voices, it was one that was unfailingly likable. At Studio One he recorded roots, lovers' rock, soulful reggae and began to flirt with dancehall reggae, the style that he is most associated with. As the decade turned over, so did Osbourne's sound. His 1980 album *Fally Lover*, with producer Henry "Junjo" Lawes and The Roots Radics band signaled a break from Dodd and Studio One sounds. The rhythm was simplified, and the roots lyrics were left behind. Even though Junjo's engineer Barnabas brought a dub aspect to the proceedings, the sound was clearly early dancehall. Working next with Prince Jammy, the die would be cast. Johnny Osbourne will be remembered as one of dancehall's foundation singers, though truth be told, he was that and more.

'Truths And Rights'
From Osbourne's 1979 Coxsone Dodd-produced album of the same name, the highly respected 'Truths And Rights' is the best roots song from his work at Studio One. It's set to the melancholy 'Take A Ride' riddim, named for the Al Campbell song described earlier in this book (page 396). A serious riddim, it spurs equally serious lyrics from Osbourne, and a vocal that is disciplined compared to some of his dancehall hits.

After chanting the song's title, he gets down to business with a stanza of Bible language. This rivets the listener's attention, as something obviously serious is being conveyed. Osbourne's central theme is that the inalienable truths of human rights should be taught to children. Ruining whatever small chance this song had to serve as a lullaby, he advises children to pray every night, as the next day may bring "sudden destruction". As I said, this is a serious song.

Female backing singers, applying their voices sparingly, support Osbourne attractively. A new, dubby, propulsive drum track with rapid-fire hi-hat work and dub on the rhythm guitar distinguish this version of the riddim from that of Al Campbell's original. But the riddim's strongest features, its melodic bass line and the organ riff of unmatched sorrow, are intact. At the song's end, Osbourne's vocals are briefly double-tracked as he jams with himself and the backing vocalists, giving it a fine conclusion. Stick to the rendition on the album of the same name to avoid a later, lesser remake.

'Murderer'; 'Murderer Version'

In 1981, at Studio One, Osbourne voiced a version of the classic 1968 Vin Gordon instrumental, 'Heavenless' (a song described earlier in this book; page 173), calling his song 'Murderer'. Dodd gives the riddim a tune-up for Osbourne's use. The trombone and strummed guitar are reduced in the mix, while the bass is much louder. The saxophone, trumpet and picked guitar are completely dropped, while an oddball keyboard track and delectable dub effects on the drums are newly added. Though these modifications are significant, what's completely unchanged is the overall nature of this eccentric and irresistible riddim.

Osbourne's singing honors the riddim's era, being merry and melodic in the rock steady way. And the mixed-gender folk-style backing singers are so mannered and upbeat, they could fit on a Harry Belafonte record (other than for the fact that they are limited to chanting the song's title and for the big aurora of dub reverb Dodd casts around them). 'Murderer' is a rude boy song, though the term is never used. Osbourne lists the subject's many crimes, which include murder, decried as being against God and against love. At one point, the uniquely reggae nature of the session inspires Osbourne to digress in a uniquely reggae way. He sings a couplet that comments on the very session he's recording: he is commenting on how he is versioning a version! This break from the song's narrative is the lyrical equivalent of Fil Callender's dub-enhanced oddball drum fills and Vin Gordon's loopy trombone playing. All three are reggae caviar.

'Murderer' can be heard on the CD collection, *Studio One Rude Boy*, released on the Soul Jazz label. The original 45-rpm single release on the Coxsone label extended the fun with 'Murderer Version', a dub version B-side. It opens with a mix of riddim that's different from that of the A-side. Then vocals are dropped in and out, as various instruments appear, take a bow, and are ushered off stage. Some of these instruments were scarcely heard on the single's A-side, if at all, and this drop-in/out action propels the version. Surprisingly, no Johnny Osbourne or Studio One compilation has collected this version on CD. But since the single is relatively easy to find in reggae specialty shops, an eventual CD release seems likely. Also in 1981, Osbourne would re-voice this riddim, with some extra guitar, as 'Unity', giving us a good, but not as good, follow-up. In 1988, Bunny Wailer recorded a rendition of the song, substituting 'Serious Thing' for 'Murderer' in both title and lyrics, the spiritual Wailer mindful not to celebrate *badness*. In 1994, Ini Kamozi adapted the chorus of 'Murderer' into his hit, 'Here Comes The Hot-stepper'. 'Murderer' should not be confused with another (quite good) Johnny Osbourne song, the dancehall track 'Musical Murder'.

'Back Off' (aka 'Back Off Ringcraft'); 'Rock And Come On Ya'
In the early 1980s, Osbourne released two excellent disco-mix singles, produced by Linval Thompson; in each one he hands off the riddim to DJ Papa Tullo. On both tracks, Osbourne brings a great performance that Tullo matches in a complementary way. In that respect, these disco-mixes demonstrate the possibilities of this uniquely Jamaican type of record. So much so that it's unthinkable to listen to the original Osbourne tracks sans Tullo's performance, or the other way around.

In 1981, Johnny Osbourne recorded an unusual and memorable song in 'Back Off', in which Papa Tullo responded inventively and, as is always the case with him, appealingly. Producer Thompson combines these performances optimally, while his engineer, Scientist, creates an eerie dub-soaked sound. The result is a thoroughly entertaining 7-minute reggae track that stays engaging from beginning to end.

The riddim is lean and dread. After reggae's one-millionth creative opening drum phrase, a trance is established by spacey organ lines, guitar chords assigned varying degrees of dread importance with dub, and semi-melodic wood blocks, sounding extra-woody with reverb. To this, Osbourne brings an unusual but thoroughly enjoyable vocal. His singing is rhythmically clipped, and he sounds distant and detached. Especially with the dub backing, he appears in a trance. Osbourne gives the titular warning to anyone coming at him with "ring craft". Rather than just referring to boxing skills, the lyrics give some indication that this term may also be referring to the DJ skills of his rivals. (Perhaps supporting this interpretation is the fact that his backing band is called The Ring Craft Posse.) He chants a list of his adversaries' failings, being detached and unimpressed. The chorus and verse are so similar, they give Osbourne's performance a strange relentlessness.

Then comes the DJ version, welded on with a bead of dub. The mix is subtly changed, with reverb now emphasizing the snare drum rather than the rhythm guitar. Tullo contrasts perfectly with Osbourne. Whereas the singer was detached and rhythmically restricted, Tullo is lively and free-flowing. He *chants down* the wicked with Rasta righteousness and expert DJ skills, playfully rolling his *r*s, as the syllables pour off his tongue. He ties his vocal to the bass line, making that instrument stand out more than it does in Osbourne's take. As his performance builds to a peak, so the rhythm of his chanting grows more complex. The producer surprises us by dropping in a block of vocals from Osbourne's version, making this disco-mix sound like one continuous, complex song rather than two joined versions. Tullo returns, but with a different melody and subject, as he's moved to comment about how good this very record is for dancing! He adds more praise, but he is too excited to be clearly understood, the fast syllables collapsing into one another. He then picks up Osbourne's vocal, but in a looser, swinging style. The song concludes with Tullo calling for togetherness over a dub-fattened bass line, as 'Back Off' closes on its only non-adversarial note.

A track that good calls for more, and luckily there is a dub version called either 'Ring Craft Dub' or 'Craftsman Dub'. It features a new chanted introduction from Papa Tullo, but is mostly instrumental, with modest dub effects and more guitar that the original. Osbourne's 1997 CD, *Nightfall Showcase* has 'Back Off' and 'Ring Craft Dub', but the version of 'Back Off' is not the disco-mix version, so Tullo is not heard. Surprisingly, a nearly three-decade-old 12-inch single is currently the only place to hear 'Back Off' in its fondly remembered full splendor. At least it is easier to find than many such specimens, as this popular record was released internationally on the Greensleeves label.

Unavailability worsens to the point of criminal neglect with the second Osbourne/Tullo disco-mix, because the 1982 'Rock And Come On Ya' is even harder to locate. All that's available on CD is an Osbourne-only mix that is pitched much faster than the disco-mix single. As of today, the only way to hear this song as God intended is to track down the original 12-inch single on the UK-based Black Joy label.

Whereas 'Back Off' is foreboding and confrontational, 'Rock And Come On Ya' is friendly and inviting. The Roots Radics provide a lovably droopy version of the 'Drifter' riddim led by a bass line that is so burly and busy, you wouldn't want to be next to it on the dance floor. A guitar plays the riddim's melody as it was sounded by horns in Dennis Walk's original rendition and by keyboards in Dennis Brown's hit remake. Piano sweetens the sound, dub deepens it, and deliberate drums take a step towards the dawning of dancehall. Keeping with the latter, the lyrics are about a dance.

Osbourne sings in a regular-guy voice that is so easy-going, he doesn't bother to enunciate clearly all the time. It's chock-full of good-natured, conversational expressions about going to a dance, wanting to see you there, dancing with daughters (in an equivalent to the American 'babes') and so on. You'd have to work pretty hard to resist Osborne's good vibes and high dancehall hopes.

The riddim abruptly restarts. Papa and Tullo enter with some fast talking that contrasts nicely with Osbourne's relaxed delivery. Then, all the instrumentation drops out except bass and dubbed drums, as Tullo begins to expertly ride the rhythm, chanting enthusiastically as he is wont to do. He is less focused than on 'Back Off': this is a DJ performance of the crazy melange of topics variety – his stream of consciousness is channeled unfettered to his mouth. We hear a variety of philosophical axioms, accounts of his DJ skills, a digression about a romantic rival, another about a crime where the police are called, comments about his wardrobe, his preferred food seasonings and even a laundry tip. And it wouldn't be a proper Papa Tullo song without at least one interjection of his trademark exclamation, "Well, watch out, mon!" Having said his piece(s), at the song's end, Tullo swings the subject around to that of Osbourne's song, chanting about the dance to wrap up this most amiable disco-mix.

'In Your Eyes'; 'Love Is Universal'
There are two standout tracks on Osbourne's 1982 album, *Never Stop Fighting*. Though produced by Junjo Lawes, this is not a dancehall affair. Instead, it's an album of lovers' rock songs, but especially on these two tracks, with Junjo's use of Scientist as his mixer, the music is unusually dubby for this variety of reggae, bringing a dreamy quality to the tracks. In this way, it's a continuation of the sound that Junjo and The Radics crafted for Barrington Levy's *Robin Hook* album two years earlier (as described in the chapter on this artist; page 540).

'In Your Eyes' uses the melody from Dennis Reid's 1978 song, 'By The Look', but definitely not its lyrics. Where Reid's song was a condemnation of an unfaithful lover, Osbourne is head-over-heels in love. Where Reid calls his lover a devil, Osbourne equates his to starlight and ecstasy. His fine vocal switches between romantic crooning and breaks of rhythmic chanting that verge on sing-jay style. Lush, romantic piano supports the lovers' rock vibe, while dub brings the heady feel of infatuation. Listen, for example, to how Scientist, in one of his trademark moves, reshapes bass notes into swollen toroids as the song progresses, sounding here like something from a dream.

'Love Is Universal' takes things even further. Osbourne sings movingly about romantic love, and family love as well. This time around, sax rather than piano prominently brings the romantic vibes. The droning bass line and the surfeit of dub, complete with a short dub section appended disco-mix-style to the end of the track, remind us what a heady sensation love can be. This dreamy riddim was commandeered and retrofitted for the science-fiction DJ song, 'Can't Take Another World War' by Clint Eastwood & General Saint (a song described earlier in this book; page 440) for a version that couldn't sound any more different.

'Budy Bye'
Johnny Osbourne's 'Budy Bye' is perhaps the greatest of the nearly 200 (and counting) versions of this previously discussed (page 30), revolutionary, Casio-born 'Sleng Teng' riddim. It can be heard along with Wayne Smith's original and thirteen other versions on the 1985 CD *Riddim Driven: Sleng Teng Extravaganza*, on the VP label.

With simple, celebratory lyrics it's unequivocally upbeat, danceable dancehall reggae. The riddim may be in "computer style", but there is also lot of good old-fashioned dub. At points, the vocal is treated with echo, while keyboard chords bounce with echo so festively, it's the sonic equivalent of party balloons being released from the ceiling. The keyboard-generated bass – big and fat as monster truck tires, yet nimble – as well as the other keyboards, drop out/in throughout, further enlivening the party riddim.

Osbourne sounds like he's in a great mood, ready to make the scene, as he sings about having a No.1 song. He mixes a melodic delivery with blocks of DJ-style fast rhythmic chanting. Mid-song, he breaks into 'Frère Jacques', modifying the lyrics to fit his story. All of this is singalong ready, especially when Osbourne leads a rousing call and response of *whoh!*s and *yeah!*s. 'Budy Bye' has been the perfect party record from the day it was released up to today.

53 More great dancehall

Presented chronologically, here are more great dancehall songs, which represent the full range of styles, subjects and sounds that this genre of reggae offers.

Papa Levi: *'Mi God Mi King'*
Phillip Levi was born in England of Jamaican parentage. He came up as a DJ in the UK sound system scene, most famously at Saxon Sound. To someone in the USA or UK, his accent might sound Jamaican, but elements of a British accent would be immediately detected by a Jamaican. But none of these *a foreign* aspects did anything to hurt the reggae of Levi's 1981 song, 'Mi God Mi King', or keep it from achieving popularity in Jamaica as well as the UK. He would go on to record three albums.

Levi is aided by a riddim from Sly & Robbie. They create an absolutely *wicked* dancehall reduction of Vin Gordon's great instrumental, 'Heavenless', a song previously discussed in this book (page 173). It keys in on the original's bass melody, while each instrument adopts a mechanized approach. The result is a riddim that sounded up-to-the-minute modern, but with strong ties to a past classic. Interestingly, as we have previously seen, in the same year, producer Coxsone Dodd and singer Johnny Osbourne blew the dust off the original cut of 'Heavenless' for Osbourne's 'Murderer'. So in the same year, 'Heavenless' was versioned radically and conservatively, both resulting in a great new version.

The riddim is matched with an equally exciting vocal. Levi starts off conventionally, as he chants amiably about himself, Jah and reggae, while taking on slavery, racism and guns. But near the song's halfway point, he shifts gears and begins chanting in the fast-talk style of DJing, cranking out a high rate of words per minute. While other DJs used this technique to spice their performances, Levi sustains his rhythmic staccato chanting for championship durations. Words fly by, as any subject becomes grist for this mill working at double-time. At the end of the song, he drops back to regular-speed DJing, and can be forgiven for sounding self-satisfied.

'Mi God Mi King' is available in a number of different mixes and configurations. The preferred sparer mix is found on a 12-inch single on the Mango label, boosted with a long dub version that brings the song to a massive 12 minutes in length. Hopefully, this mix will appear on CD sometime very soon.

Tenor Saw: *'Ring The Alarm'*
Half Pint: *'Crazy Girl'*
Here are two great early dancehall tracks, each using a different modernization of the great "Stalag" riddim. "Stalag" was previously described in this book (page

312), as were four DJ versions of its riddim that established its vibrancy. These two songs demonstrate its renewability. Both are readily available on multiple CDs.

Tenor Saw's 'Ring The Alarm' was produced in 1985 by Winston Riley, the producer of the original 'Stalag' riddim. Here, he keeps some of the tracks from the original recording, removes the horns and solos, and replaces some of the drums with electric ones. This nudged the riddim towards the more direct and mechanized sound of the day's dancehall.

Singer Tenor Saw was born Clive Bright in Kingston, in 1966. The first part of his stage pseudonym was descriptive, as he sang in a relaxed, appealing tenor croon. The second reflected the trend in which for a time dancehall performers named themselves after tools. (There was also Lady Saw, Pliers, Pinchers, Screwdriver and Spanner Banner, who, if he had been American, would no doubt have been called Wrench Banner.) A newcomer, Saw had begun to record just a year earlier, impressing immediately with his fine Jamaican voice. Sadly, at the entirely too early age of twenty-two, Saw would die when struck by a car in Houston, Texas, but not before he had recorded eight albums, most often dividing the tracks with another singer in clash-style.

Saw rides the riddim like he owns it. He tells of competing in a big dance with four sound systems. His sound system is so superior that an alarm is rung to warn of the others' demise. In his excitement, he reaches back to a line from 'Hold 'Im Joe', a song from the mento repertoire, as he recounts his victory. The completely pleasing 'Ring The Alarm' is the biggest hit and best song of Tenor Saw's short but respected career.

In 1986, producers Errol "John" Marshall and Errol "Myre" Lewis recut the 'Stalag' riddim, taking it several steps further down the road to the digital domain for Half Pint's "Crazy Girl". The drums, bass and picked guitar all feature a heavily mechanized sound. These three instruments are treated with lots of dub echo and drop-out/in. At one point, the beat becomes simplified and syncopated, a favorite device that distinguished early dancehall from roots, and provided a song with its dance floor highlight. The intricate drum and bass work that was at the heart of every previous version of 'Stalag' is now simplified away. Yet somehow 'Stalag' still thrives, successfully recast as a heavy dancehall riddim. And it suits Half Pint fine.

Half Pint was born Lindon Andrew Roberts, in 1961, in Kingston. His stage name comes from a childhood nickname, earned, no surprise, by his small physical stature. Like so many of his predecessors, he began singing in church and school choirs. From there, he became a sound system singer, no doubt influenced by the singing of Barrington Levy, as many of his contemporaries were. He became a recording artist in 1983, and his first (or second, depending on the source) song, 'Winsome', would be adapted by The Rolling Stones for their 1987 reggae song, 'Too Rude'. In spite of taking a decade-long break from music for most of the 1990s, Half Pint has recorded about twenty albums and is still active today.

His voice powerful and his delivery playful, adorned in echo, Half Pint sounds great on 'Crazy Girl'. He questions his girlfriend's sanity, when despite his love and financial generosity, she runs off with another man. He uses popular adages to admonish her into changing her mind, such as biting the hand that feeds you and the goose that lays the golden egg. Likewise, he employs Jamaican folk sayings that are by now familiar to readers of this book: not wanting water until the well runs dry, and "those who want don't get, while those that get, don't want". But there is no indication that this admonishment, as well expressed as it is, has the desired effect. 'Crazy Girl' is available as a disco-mix with an appended sax cut, and in remade renditions in collaboration with other artists. But the vocal performance on the original rendition can't be beat and this is the only version you need. It can be found on several Half Pint albums.

Pinchers: *'Mass Out'*
Delroy Thompson was born in 1965 in Kingston. He was bitten by the sound system bug as a young teen and began recording not long thereafter in 1986. Like other dancehall singers of his generation, his vocals were influenced by Barrington Levy, though Pinchers is more of a sing-jay. Also like other dancehall singers of his generation, he took his stage name from a tool. To date, he has recorded about fourteen albums, a number of which are in *clash style* with another singer (including one with Pliers that somehow passed on using *Toolbox* as its title). His son, Kemar Thompson, is perhaps dancehall reggae's only second-generation recording artist (the earlier roots reggae by comparison has many), working under the stage name of Jr. Pinchers.

Though it's not his only hit, the Philip "Fatis" Burrell-produced 'Mass Out' is Pinchers' greatest song. This amazingly buoyant piece of 1987 dancehall is stripped down to digital drums, bass and sheafs of flinty guitar strums that shoot sparks everywhere. Occasional echo doubles an already hurried beat. Sweet-voiced Pinchers has no problem riding this bristly riddim, mixing it up along the way. He employs singing, a touch of Waterhouse warbling, chanting and flourishes of fast-talk DJ style. And, as if all this was not enough to engage you, he employs play-acting to better tell his story. Pinchers begins to flirt with a young woman. Assuming her voice, the singer responds by praising his own song "Greetings". Pinchers explains that it's not his song, but was instead recorded by Half Pint. His own current hit is 'Lift It Up Again'. But all is not lost, as she responds most emphatically to the mention of this song with "I like the way it moooves me!" Every time he sings as the woman, it's an instant hook in this little slice of life. But when he sings this refrain, it's completely irresistible. Rather than trying to resist the irresistible, find 'Mass Out' on the Pinchers and Frankie Paul combination CD, *Dance Hall Duo*, or on several dancehall compilations.

Gregory Peck: *'Pocoman Jam'*
The DJ called Gregory Peck (born Gregory Williamson) was by no means a big name or a prolific artist. (Why Gregory Peck? Popular stars and characters were sometimes the inspiration for reggae singers' stage names. Other examples include Clint Eastwood, Charlie Chaplin, John Wayne, Lee Van Cleef, Jim Brown, Tony Curtis, Josey Wales, Dirty Harry, Red Fox, Lone Ranger, Kojak, Barnabas Collins, Top Cat, and even King Kong.) But in 1990, his 'Pocoman Jam' put him on the map with a textbook example of the pre-reggae Pocomania folk rhythm making its way into dancehall. This was a sea change for reggae. The reggae beat that had defined the music since the days of mento was supplanted. Not by something new and from overseas, as had happened in the Jamaican R&B craze of the early 1960s, but by something as old and essentially Jamaican as mento. This opened the door for dancehall to feature all manner of non-reggae musical elements, greatly broadening its sound, and coming to be called *ragga*.

Pocomania was typically played with sticks on a single drum with a fife accompaniment. In America, this might conjure images of 'Yankee Doodle' being played by a limping military trio, but the Poco sound is far more energetic and rooted in African rhythms, with a distinctive intricate shuffling beat. Though ignored on CD, one sample of Pocomania, called 'Drum And Fife', can be heard on the LP *From The Grassroots Of Jamaica*, which, as previously described, can be acquired with only modest difficulty.

Pocomania-influenced rhythms were always around in reggae. For example, such songs already described in this book include the R&B of Toots & The Maytals' 'Treating Me Bad', the ska of Baba Brooks's 'Bank To Bank' and the late 1970s reggae of Nora Dean's 'Play Me A Love Song' (pages 155, 113, 243). But credit the team of Steely & Clevie with the masterstroke of bringing a much fuller measure of the Poco rhythm into dancehall. Keyboardist Wycliffe "Steely" Johnson was a session man with a diverse background, including membership in The Roots Radics. Drummer Cleveland "Clevie" Browne also did sessions and had an interest in the possibilities of drum-machine technology. They first worked together at Lee Perry's studio at the end of the 1970s and would later form a partnership, coming into their own in the dancehall era. Reminiscent of Sly & Robbie, Steely & Clevie provided backing for various artists by playing on, arranging and producing numerous records. In 2009, Clevie died from multiple health problems at the age of forty-seven.

Pocomania drum patterns, accompanied by a one-note bass line that thrums on the first and third beat, and nodding to the sound of a rumba box and/or the playing of a Nyabinghi bass drum, dominate on 'Pocoman Jam'. Bright keyboards complete the riddim in lieu of a Pocomania fife. Piano is joined by a synthesizer that sounds like a banjo riffing wildly in yet another modern dancehall nod to early Jamaica music.

In simple lyrics, Peck celebrates the Poco sound and encourages us to dance to it. Mid-song, as the other instruments step back to give it room, the Poco drum cuts loose, and Peck urges it and prospective dancers on. The song succeeds fully as dancehall reggae, exhilarating by pulling Pocomania from Jamaica's past to become a vibrant part of reggae's future. Uncountable other songs and riddims henceforth would feature a Pocomania beat. 'Pocoman Jam' can be heard on VP Records' dancehall collection *Strictly The Best. Volume 1*, helping to kick off this highly successful series, which at the time of writing was up to volume 51 and counting.

Junior Reid: *'One Blood'*
Like his inspiration, Dennis Brown, the Waterhouse-born Delroy "Junior" Reid is yet another reggae star who began his career as a *youth singer*. He recorded his first singles in 1978 at age thirteen, often billed as Little Junior Reid, but soon outgrew the "Little". He recorded in the roots and early dancehall styles, working for such famous producers as Augustus Pablo and Prince Jammy. In 1986, he replaced fellow Waterhouse singer Michael Rose as lead singer in Black Uhuru, at that time the biggest reggae act in the world. (Inheriting the crown from Bob Marley, Peter Tosh had stopped touring several years earlier and would release his final album, the lackluster *Mama Africa*, in 1987. This left only Steel Pulse to compete with Black Uhuru for worldwide reggae ticket sales.) Though not nearly as consistently good as they were in their prime, the Reid-led Black Uhuru did record several memorable tracks, as described in the chapter on this group (pages 344–65). But after two years, Reid quit Uhuru, opting to restart his successful solo career, usually producing his own records. He would seem to be a favorite of overseas rock, R&B and hip-hop stars, judging by all the samplings of and collaborations with him. Additionally, in 1997, he recorded *Living Legend*, an album that featured a cadre of hip-hop guest stars, and followed it a year later with a second volume. He remains active today, with about 20 albums under his belt thus far.

Reid's 1989 song, 'One Blood', would give him his biggest hit. He shows acumen as a producer in the way he ramps up the arrangement from just voice to full buzz-saw ragga power. He also expertly combines traditional reggae conventions with the new possibilities of ragga. An a cappella introduction, rich with Waterhouse inflections, opens the song ominously, warning of vampires. The fat keyboard bass can't keep from revving it a few times rather than sitting idle. The body of the song is announced reggae-style with a flurry of drums, albeit electronic ones. Reid's first couplet is backed just by a hi-hat-led, machine-produced reggae drum pattern, as the keyboard bass plays in the start-and-stop reggae way. His next couplet is announced by the first blast of a dubby horn sample that is heard throughout the song. It ushers in a replacement drum track with an exciting Pocomania-based dancehall rhythm, the simpler drum track revealed to be a ruse. Dropout and dropin are worked to enliven the riddim. The third couplet brings a traditional reggae rhythm guitar chop that is soon to be processed by all kinds of dub effects. All the players have now been introduced, but the producer keeps the arrangement dynamic right to the song's end.

Reid's impassioned vocal is equally engaging. For most of the song, he presents a litany of different Rasta sects, racial backgrounds, professions, Jamaican neighborhoods, cities and nations, in order to deliver a message of pan-human unity. Putting his Waterhouse skills to use, he boosts the emotional content on two lines in particular, as he muses on blood. First, how blood makes us all the same and, second, on blood as a symptom of strife. With these lines in particular, Reid soars over the impressive ragga landscape he's built.

'One Blood' was popular enough to spawn remixes, a Spanish-language version and more than one collaboration with rap acts by way of sampling. But these can't beat the original rendition as found on the album of the same name.

Junior Reid: *'Banana Boatman'*
Junior Reid's 'Banana Boatman' is a self-produced track from his 1991 album *Long Road*. It's a sonic heir to 'One Blood', but by comparison is another increment towards ragga and away from traditional reggae conventions. The riddim is again anchored by fat keyboard bass (that is held in reserve for a dub-style delayed entrance) and electronically generated drums playing a Pocomania pattern, delivered with machine-gun precision. But here, there's no sign of reggae rhythm guitar or horns. Instead, big fills and swoops from a synthesizer provide a modern, nocturnal-sounding lead instrument. Only when the synth does the occasional drop-out/in swap with piano is there an organic sound other than Reid's vocal. The result is a dark, taut pressure cooker of a ragga riddim that bolsters Reid's story. He sings emphatically of a ragga-muffin (as ragga singers are fond of calling themselves) who leaves Jamaica under difficult circumstances. Not having a passport, he secures passage on a banana boat. Yet he rises to great success. There are few details, as Reid keeps the result vague enough to make success as a ragga performer or as a gangster equally acceptable interpretations, though the darkness of the riddim points to the latter. Either way, the fine riddim draws you in and Reid's lyrics and vocal keep you locked up, making 'Banana Boatman' stand out from the pack.

General Degree: *'Granny'*
Producer Haldane "Danny" Browne, born in 1960 in Kingston, is responsible for several highly creative ragga riddims described in this chapter. His first productions were in the mid-1980s, but his career took off in the early 1990s, establishing the Main Street Records label in the process. Danny had four other brothers who were active in music, most notably the late Cleveland Browne of Steely & Clevie fame.

Born Cardiff Butt in Manchester Parish around 1970, the DJ called General Degree was new on the scene when, in 1992, he recorded the number 1 hit, 'Granny'. Its popularity is easy to understand, as it's probably the funniest reggae song ever recorded. Degree would go on to record eight albums, including one in combination style.

Browne sets Degree up nicely with an exceptionally playful riddim. Traditional reggae and ragga elements are combined, so the Pocomania-influenced drums are complemented by a classic see-sawing reggae bass line (albeit probably played on a keyboard). A winking keyboard manages to say a lot with little effort. Jaunty and uncluttered, it inspires Degree to a big performance. He provides the voices of two characters: himself and a convincing imitation of his obstreperous old grandmother. Showing that this is a country granny, she threatens that she may have to leave Jamaica to move to Kingston! Yes, granny steals the show.

Degree marvels at how miserable granny is, as her responses bear this out. Then, as the bass kicks in, granny rides the rhythm! What is she chanting about? Various granny concerns, such as a very detailed account of how expensive food is these days, folk sayings, incomplete chores and losing her false teeth. But mostly, she complains about Degree. Ultimately, she beats up her disobedient grandson, threatening that a hearse will have to be called. While mento singers lampooned societal norms, ska and rock steady singers criticized the wrongdoings of the rude boys, roots singers stood up to institutional oppression, and Bob Marley faced down injustice on a geopolitical scale, Degree is utterly defeated by his grandmother.

'Granny' can be heard on the General Degree album of the same name that features two other Granny-voiced songs, 'Granny Granny Cry' and 'Granny Walk An' Rock'. Something about Danny Browne's riddim brought out a creatively humorous performance from a second dancehall singer. Papa San sustains his entire performance of 'Maddy Maddy Cry' as a man in a state of hysterics, barely comprehensible as he cries over his problems, yet never failing to ride the rhythm. He sounds like nothing so much as the late American comedian Andy Kaufman's crying conga player routine. Papa San's song is available on several dancehall compilation albums.

Shaggy: *'Oh Carolina'*
The Kingston-raised, New York City-based dancehall DJ Shaggy (Orville Burrell) has the incongruous distinction of being the only artist in this book who has served as a United States Marine. Though born in 1968 in Jamaica, he migrated to Brooklyn to join his family when he was eighteen. In rapid succession over the space of no more than two years, he would take singing lessons, perform at local sound systems, join the Marines, and, during breaks from service, begin to record, enjoying a bit of local success. After completing his active service in Kuwait, he recorded his sample-rich dancehall rendition of The Folkes Brothers' classic, 'Oh Carolina' (a song described previously in this book; page 72). It would launch Shaggy into international stardom, as it was a hit in the UK and Europe, and charted in the USA as well. Other worldwide hits would follow, making the argument for Shaggy being the biggest dancehall star in the world. It's no mystery why. Shaggy has a rich baritone, and when he wants to add emphasis, he can

switch to a growly, throaty singing style (reminiscent of Big Youth's resin-coated vocal cord richness). His voice is clearly a Jamaican one, but every word can be clearly understood by non-Jamaican ears. And his hits are good-natured fun. Shaggy comes off as happy, highly likable and wanting to entertain, right down to his name. This is miles away from the controversial *hard* (tough guy) stance and gangsta lyrics that would take a prominent place in dancehall, and the antithesis of the gay-hate lyrics that would tarnish the genre's reputation across the globe. Some of Shaggy's hits used samples from American hits, boosting their international accessibility and resulted in what could be called a subgenre of international pop-ragga, a province that is solely his own. But Jamaica did not embrace him like overseas audiences did, preferring dancehall stars closer to home with greater street cred. Shaggy has recorded ten albums since 1993, and an equal number of compilation albums.

'Oh Carolina', Shaggy's star-making hit, appeared on his 1993 debut CD, *Pure Pleasure*, as produced by Shaun "Sting International" Pizzonia. In a bold but highly successful gambit, it's a savvy dancehall rendition of the Folkes Brothers' seminal pre-ska hit. Just as the original famously succeeds in combining Jamaican R&B and Nyabinghi drumming, Shaggy's remake famously succeeds in combining the major elements of the Folkes' song with ragga – plus Henry Mancini's 'Peter Gunn Theme' thrown in for good measure. John Folkes's song has proven to be a melting-pot of styles, countries and decades.

Although there's a great deal of updating here, Shaggy and Sting International astutely avoid throwing the baby out with the bathwater. The song is grounded by opening with a sample of the entire piano, maracas and handclap introduction of the original. Just at the point where the original would hit you with an eruption of *doo-wop* vocals and Nyah drums, Shaggy's rendition erupts with colorful dancehall elements: synthesizer and keyboard bass, conga drums, a bell that sounds like it was borrowed from an amusement park and Shaggy's DJ chanting. He changes the lyrics from a come-back-to-me song to an angst-free one about a girl whom men love to watch dance. The backing vocals follow suit, as the wordless *doo-wop* chorus of the original is changed to a call for Carolina to dance. A sax appears to play the familiar swoops of the 'Peter Gunn Theme' and suddenly we realize that the keyboard bass was halfway there all along. More percussion, sax and backing vocal interjections are heard, but Shaggy is clearly the main attraction. He alters his voice and the intensity of his delivery as he makes a modern ragga celebration of one of reggae's historic songs.

Shaggy: *'Bedroom Bounty Hunter'*

Shaggy's 'Bedroom Bounty Hunter', another track from *Pure Pleasure* produced by Sting International, features riotous ragga creativity from all involved. It's a demented addled ragga rendition of the tango, with the melody played on what sounds like a synthesized accordion. But it's the drums that dominate and define the riddim. They are like a ragga updating of rock steady Studio One drummer Fil Callender's drum style that slings oddball strikes and flourishes, nailing the beat at the last possible moment. Where Studio One used dub to enhance the sound of these trick shots, Sting International uses a broad palette of digital drum sounds to accomplish the same in the ragga idiom. Bass and swatches of picked guitar restricted to a single note complete the riddim.

To match this madness, Shaggy sing-jays in a higher register than his norm and affects an overwrought approach. What is he trying to convey amidst all this intensity? He wants to ensure that you are fully aware of his bedroom prowess. A cooing, panting female vocalist supplies validating responses lest there be any doubt. The lyrics are somewhat *slack* for Shaggy in this ribald ragga rollercoaster ride.

Sly & Robbie: *'Murder She Wrote Riddim'*
Chaka Demus & Pliers: *'Murder She Wrote'*
Pliers: *'Bam Bam'*
Six countries across both hemispheres come into play in the story of the 1994 international dancehall hit, 'Murder She Wrote'. The story begins with producers/bandleaders Sly & Robbie being exposed to contemporary Bhangra music while in London. (Or, perhaps more accurately, just Sly, as Robbie is not heard, and his name is sometimes missing from the production credits.) Bhangra is a popular dance music with a centuries-old history in the Punjab region that includes North India and Pakistan. The producers rightly suspected that they could use this beat for a fresh new dancehall riddim.

As it would come to be known, the 'Murder She Wrote' riddim created a *wicked* polyrhythmic dancehall groove with just a few instruments, interlocking diabolically at odd time signatures. There is a seven-note bass line played on a guitar's low notes that's repeated unaltered throughout the song. Triplets of flinty rhythm guitar likewise continue unaltered. Three drums are heard. The first is a digital equivalent of a snare, playing the modified shuffle beat that is a key component of the sound of Bhangra. Second is the digital equivalent of a hand-held percussion instrument, playing at the fastest tempo of any instrument here. The third is a bass drum that sounds thunderously on the first beat, injecting an element of Nyabinghi to the world-music mixture. Taken together, these instruments create an exciting sound that would forever make the Bhangra beat part of the dancehall vocabulary. And cultural exchange went both ways, as remixes of 'Murder She Wrote' would soon appear for the Bhangra market. Branching off all of this was the creation of Reggaeton – a Spanish-language music originating in Puerto Rico that based its signature rhythms on the 'Murder She Wrote' riddim and the variations that followed. Reggaeton took over the charts in every Spanish-speaking country and beyond in the early 2000s, as the combination of Spanish-language rap vocals over the Punjab-by-way-of-Jamaica rhythms proved to be too much to resist. Meanwhile, in Jamaica, 'The Murder She Wrote' riddim was heavily versioned, and influenced sound-alike riddims that would follow for years to come.

Chaka Demus was born John Taylor, in 1965, in Kingston. The DJ began recording in 1985, but success did not come easily. The same could be said for singer Pliers, born Everton Bonner in 1963, in Kingston. In spite of having two brothers in the industry, Richie Spice and Spanner Banner, success at first eluded him. Even a 1988 song with a catchy melody and provocative lyrics called 'Murder We Wrote' was ignored, perhaps because of its uninspired riddim. After performing at the same show in 1991, the two decided to work as a duo. The combination of a bluff-voiced DJ with a gruff blustery delivery and a sweet-sounding singer with a smooth easy falsetto turned out to be a winning combination. Within a year, they were scoring hits. And in 1994, the pair salvaged Pliers's earlier song, performed it over Sly's Bhangra-influenced riddim, and with the tweaked title of 'Murder She Wrote', all involved had an international smash hit.

As great as the riddim is, Chaka Demus & Pliers were indispensable in putting the song over. Handling most of the verses, when Demus gets rolling, the words tumble out and pile up in a way that can sometimes make him hard to understand, leaving just the blunt force of his enthusiasm to carry the listener along. In complete but complementary contrast, Pliers handles the chorus with long, easy notes in his clear, soothing voice. That is, except when he turns the tables on Demus and breaks into fast rhythmic chanting of his own, suddenly a DJ rather than singer, adding to the riches of their combined talents. Together, they tell the story of Maxine, whose beauty belies her lax morals that include an annual abortion.

'Murder She Wrote' can be heard on the single riddim collection CD called *Bam Bam It's Murder*. It includes some other notable versions, each with the riddim slightly altered. The best is Pliers's faithful cover of Toots & The Maytals' 'Bam Bam' (a song described in the chapter on these artists; page 156). Singing sweetly, he drops Toots's song into the riddim, and, lo and behold, it fits beautifully. The delayed introduction of the rhythm guitar makes for a softer sound initially. Skullman (Paul Bartley) DJs a version called 'Je-Taime'. He's endearing with his crazy stuttering vibrato and his breaks into French with an exaggerated quiver, no doubt intended to magnify his romantic appeal. This version starts only with the rhythm guitar, and is enlivened by modest drop-out/in throughout, with the bass drum never heard. Nardo Ranks performs 'Them A Bleach', a song that picks up a topic first sung about forty years earlier in the great mento single 'Glamour Girl' by Harold Richardson (a song previously described in the chapter on this group; page 43). He rallies woman to accept their natural skin tone and blames Buju Banton's 1992 hit, 'Love Me Browning', for the renewed popularization of skin lightening. (Dancehall star Vybz Kartel obviously took a different view. While awaiting trial on a murder charge, he found time to plan the release of his own line of skin-bleaching products. He is also the only dancehall star with his own line of condoms. It is unclear how his guilty verdict in 2014 will impact his music career and other endeavors.)

Chaka Demus & Pliers would make a fine return to a modified version of the riddim with their 2006 'My Girl'. Not only is the riddim updated, but the sound is further altered by double-tracking each vocalist. It can be heard on the Sly & Robbie album called *Rhythm Doubles*. The album also includes a strong track by TOK, called 'Sunshine', to the same riddim.

Shaggy: 'Boombastic'

In 1995, Shaggy had another international hit with the title track from his third album, *Boombastic*. In the ragga way, producers Robert Livingston and Sting International concoct novel elements to hang on the riddim's slow-burn shuffling drum and bass. There's synthesized fuzz guitar that makes the riddim rich in faux heavy-metal power chords. Providing a counterpoint, they're answered by a piano note that's ominous when sounded seven times. It recalls the minimalistic piano heard in Boogie Down Productions' classic 1980s rap song, 'The Bridge Is Over'. Further ragga spice comes from odd sustained percussion sounds and rhythmically triggered samples of a woman speaking and cooing. When the piano temporarily switches to rhythm, it instantly gives the song a pre-ragga reggae grounding.

Over this, Shaggy begins with a spoken introduction, announcing himself as a "boombastic fantastic romantic lover". Apparently, "romantic" and "fantastic" and all other existing words fell short, so Shaggy had to create a superlative of his own to fully describe his prowess. Riding the drums, Shaggy struts, prowls and growls. He is very cool and in control, in stark contrast to the overheated approach he used in his similarly themed 'Bedroom Bounty Hunter'. He gives his love interest numerous examples of why they should be together. They are like bun and cheese, like rice and peas, making reference to both Jamaica's traditional Easter treat and a Sunday meal.

Shaggy: 'Gal Yu A Pepper'

The wild ragga of 'Gal Yu A Pepper' is another strong track from the *Boombastic* CD, again produced by Robert Livingston and Sting International. It's about a girl who is so hot she's likened to the ultra-hot Jamaican scotch bonnet pepper. But Shaggy seems to be pronouncing it as a "scorch bottom pepper", appropriate for an after-effect that chili pepper fans are familiar with. It's unknown whether this pun is intentional or not.

This is a feverish ragga track teeming with the creativity that ragga fans demand and technology makes possible. The riddim consists primarily of percussion and percussive sounds. There are digital interpretations of recognizable drum sounds and other percussion that only exists in the digital domain. There is no bass line to speak of, unless you are willing to greatly broaden the definition; then there are two. First is the sound of a bass drum and a bass guitar note merging for a deep pumping effect. Second is the big plucked bedspring that pogos madly through the track, juicing its already high energy level. Various synthesizer phrases are sprinkled about, sounding more influenced by videogames than reggae. And there is also a single syllable of backing vocals with a chorus of male voices rhythmically exclaiming, *Whoei!*

Somehow, this modern riddim inspires Shaggy to kick it old-school. In a nasal chant, he gives a motor-mouthed DJ performance that nicely builds to a peak. It could have come from a DJ record from two decades past.

Cutty Ranks: *'A Who Seh Me Dun (Wake The Man)'; 'Limb By Limb'*
Philip Thomas was born in 1965 in Kingston, where he worked as a butcher before he became a DJ. His stage name, Cutty Ranks, then, translates to *the butcher who is a good enough DJ to be ranked.* His success on the mic began as a young teenager, ensuring that his future would be as Cutty Ranks rather than cutting flanks. As the title of his 1986 debut single, *Gunman Lyrics*, tips us off, Ranks was one of the first reggae DJs to move to harsher, violent lyrics. Whether celebrating, decrying, or ambivalent towards the subject, wry, unflinching descriptions of violence and murder have always been part of Jamaican music. We have already seen examples in this book, from the folk/mento standard 'Penny Reel', to the ska of Bob Marley & The Wailers' 'Mister Chatterbox', to the rock steady of Prince Buster's 'Too Hot', to the reggae of Johnny Osbourne's 'Murderer'. But in dancehall, further stimulated by the overseas advent of gangsta rap, violent lyrics would become more prevalent, explicit and celebratory. Cutty helps usher in this change. Though his blunt voice always contained the element of a wink, he nonetheless routinely gleefully describes shooting and maiming as a means to vanquish his adversaries. He has recorded eight albums to date, plus four more in combination style, dividing the tracks with another artist.

The 1996 Courtney Cole-produced 'A Who Seh Me Dun' finds Cutty exploring a favorite topic. With a wicked smile, he imagines the violent demise of rival DJs by his own hands. Meanwhile, producer Cole creates equal mayhem with the riddim. The commonly available mix toggles between the 'Murder She Wrote' riddim and a second, darker one. (There is also a version set solely to 'Murder She Wrote', but it packs less of a punch, and is not worth searching for.) In what could have been a mess, Cole's gambit works, and suits Cutty's song well, making for an exciting record. The mix is lean, leaving room for a clutter of samples that allow Cutty to shout, laugh, comment and encourage as he DJs his story. He opens with some general threats, including that, as a former butcher, he knows how to chop things up. Before long, he gets much more specific, as he boxes with Admiral until his rival is deafened, uses his electric chair to end Grindsman, and dispatches Buju Banton with dynamite. 'A Who Seh Me Dun' is pure Cutty Ranks. It's available on the VP Records CD collection called *Cutty Ranks Reggae Anthology – Limb By Limb.*

The collection's musically and thematically similar title track is also great in the Cutty Ranks way. Produced by Fashion (the team of John MacGillivray and Chris Lane) in 1993, 'Limb By Limb' engages with another mutation of the 'Murder She Wrote' riddim. This time, a bass line is newly added, and out of the blue the out-sized keyboard hook familiar from 'Action', the Terror Fabulous & Nadine Suther-land pop-ragga hit of the same year, is dropped in. Cutty is accompanied by a cartoon voice that interjects urgings to murder. He seems inclined to listen. The song is a litany of merrily described shootings, maimings and killings of Cutty's enemies. Though they are not named, there are hints that his adversaries are again his rival DJs, as he promises to take a hacksaw to their tongues. Amidst the bedlam, he works in funeral-related quotes from The Wailers' 'Burial' and Prince Buster's 'Too Hot' (two songs previously described in this book; pages 517 and 122), giving the song an impressive pedigree for a threat of murder.

Buju Banton & Red Rat: *'Love Dem Bad'*
Buju Banton is a massively popular dancehall star in Jamaica. He was born Mark Anthony Myrie in 1973, in the Salt Lane section of Kingston made famous in a folk/mento song, 'Salt Lane Gal'. The first part of his stage name comes from a childhood nickname. The big, round breadfruit is also called a "buju", so here it means chubby. He takes the second name, as well as his gruff, gravelly deliv-ery from Burro Banton, a DJ whom Buju admired. But, being so popular (and infamous), he has achieved single-name status, with reggae fans in Jamaica and abroad knowing exactly who is being talked about when they hear the name "Buju".

Buju was a youth performer of the dancehall variety, beginning to chant at sound systems at the age of twelve and first recording at fourteen. By eighteen, he was breaking records with a string of number 1 hits, and released his first of the ten albums he's recorded to date. And he was already embroiled in contro-versy. His 1992 hit, 'Love Me Browning', was taken to mean that he preferred brown-skinned girls to those with dark skin. He was able to make amends with a follow-up song, 'Love Black Woman'. But later lyrical controversy was not so easily dismissed. In 1993, 'Boom Bye Bye', recorded when he was fifteen, was released. Yes, he was young, and, yes, the song was said to have been a reaction to a pedo-phile rape then in the news. But there's no getting around the fact that this is an exceptionally ugly song, with Buju gleefully describing shooting "batty men", as gays are called in Jamaica, in the head. An apology of sorts followed, and by 1995 Buju had moved to more mature, socially conscious lyrics. But he defiantly continued to perform the song live on occasion. This opened the door for more dancehall gay-hate lyrics, ruining the reputation of the genre for many world-wide, though not in Jamaica. Bigger troubles would follow. In 2009, Buju was arrested in Miami for possession of and intent to sell a large quantity of cocaine and possessing a firearm in furtherance of drug-trafficking crime. He was found guilty in 2011 and was sentenced to ten years in prison. As tends to happen for a beloved performer, back home in Jamaica this news was met with either forgiveness or the belief that Buju was set up.

It's a totally different story for Buju's one-off partner on 'Love Dem Bad', Red Rat. Rather than being embroiled in lyrical controversy, Red Rat is as light-hearted a dancehall performer as they come. In contrast to Buju's tough sound, Red Rat uniquely sounds like an adolescent, though with an insistence and whine that makes him sound even younger. Wallace Wilson Junior was born in 1978 in Saint Ann Parish. Wallace Wilson Senior was a sessions guitarist best known for playing for Byron Lee's Dragonaires and, for a time, with The Dynamites, including their session on Paul Simon's 'Mother And Child Reunion'. In another example of how physical anomalies make for good reggae nicknames, the light-skinned performer took his unusual stage name from DJ General Degree, who helpfully volunteered, "You're red [light-skinned for a black] and you look like a rat". He would adopt a wild hairstyle that accentuated this look, but soon grew out of both. Having older brothers who performed on Jamaica's hotel circuit, Junior's first stage performance (of The Jackson Five's 'ABC') came at the age of four. He began to record in 1995, growing into an appealing and flamboyant performer, with a unique voice. His trademark exclamation, *ohhh nnnooo!*, never fails to invoke empathy. Red Rat has released three albums to date.

Producer Donovan Germain was born in Kingston in 1952, and spent part of the 1970s in New York, pursuing his education. While there, he also ran a Brooklyn record shop. This led to working in distribution for several Jamaican producers, and greater exposure to the industry. He began to produce records in 1978. Though his first work was in the roots reggae of the day, it was as a ragga producer that he made his greatest impact. He started his own label, Penthouse, in 1988.

Germain's 1997 production of Buju Banton & Red Rat on 'Love Dem Bad' results in a joy of a ragga track. The riddim features a rotation of colorful ragga instruments in different combinations while a simple drum track provides an anchor. There's a bright strummed guitar phrase, a deliciously high keyboard bass line, a synthesizer guitar line and a high-energy bass drum that kicks the riddim into a higher gear every time it's deployed. The ragga carousel makes a fine ride for both Buju and Red Rat. They sound like two friends exchanging thoughts on the joys of women. Both DJs are *on*, making the collaboration potent. And their contrasting sonics make the performance even richer. Buju features short syllables, a gruff demeanor and a mature, gravelly baritone. Red Rat features longer syllables, a friendly demeanor and a youthful, nasal soprano. As the DJs trade comments enthusing about women, and ragga instruments cycle underneath, 'Love Dem Bad' is a richly rewarding song. As a bonus, the song ends with Buju unexpectedly dropping the gravel from his voice to kick a chant old-school style, sounding like a DJ from decades past. 'Love Dem Bad' is included on several Buju Banton & Red Rat CDs.

Red Rat & Goofy: *'Big Man Little Yute'*

The same year, Red Rat recorded a second great woman-focused DJ duet, this time with the dancehall sing-jay called Goofy. Produced by Dannie Browne, it's called 'Big Man Little Yute'.

Goofy was born Chad Simpson in 1974, in Kingston. A music-lover from an early age, and determined to work in the field, by the age of twelve he was DJing block parties. Favoring sometimes frivolous lyrics, he adopted the stage name of Goofy. He continued to develop his skills as he waited to be discovered. This happened in 1996, when ragga producer Danny Browne first recorded him. Goofy has recorded two albums to date, the second under his new moniker, Mr. G.

'Big Man Little Yute' finds Goofy providing Red Rat a different kind of sonic foil than the one Buju did in 'Love Dem Bad'. Goofy has a penchant for breaking into dramatic singing, sometimes with operatic grandiosity. This bombastic delivery makes him a perfect foil for Red Rat, who sounds more humble, like a precocious teen amid voice change. Especially here, where instead of sharing an admiration of girls, as on the last song, the two are competing for the affections of the same woman, fighting it out in words.

The overtly dramatic ragga riddim, with a melody that pitches back and forth like a frenzied tango, sets the tone for the song's theatrics. A slinging drum track anchors, as a crazed keyboard, synth guitar, keyboard bass, wordless backing vocals and more are juggled by Browne for maximum effect. Atop it, Red Rat and Goofy exchange lines politely (mostly) taking each other apart, as they argue whether an unnamed girl wants an older man in Goofy or a younger one in Red Rat. In one memorable exchange, Red Rat proclaims that he is more desirable because he's slim. Goofy pounces on this, arguing that she prefers muscles, with a ready rhyme about joining a gym. Things just escalate from there, as they insult each other's virility, ability to hold alcohol and member size with the mercilessness of romantic rivals. With two disparate voices and all this drama, 'Big Man Little Yute' comes off like nothing so much as a dancehall opera. It can and should be heard on the album *Oh No It's Red Rat*, which also contains 'Love Dem Bad'.

Jeremy Harding: *'Play Ground'*
Beenie Man: *'Who Am I'*

Producer Jeremy Harding was born in Kingston around 1969 and attended music school, concentrating on the guitar. While continuing his studies in Montreal, he began to work as a disc jockey, then in managing and producing local talent. In the late 1990s, he returned to Jamaica, bringing his production skills with him. He hit the ground running, as one of his first riddims, 'Play Ground', was huge. He explained his success in ragga production as due to his taking a different approach from that of a traditional reggae producer. Rather than primarily focusing on the work of the instrumentalists, he utilized his sampling and record-spinning acumen, while keeping an ear open to hip-hop production. As Sean Paul's first producer, Harding would also serve as his manager of fifteen years.

Harding's 1997 riddim, 'Play Ground', is as great as it is misnamed. Any expectation of a light-hearted children-at-play sound is quickly dispelled, by a disquieting opening of echoing guitar scratching. Then, the gates of Hell open wide and from them emerges – a tuba? This is ragga, where what spices up a riddim is only limited by the producer's imagination. Sinister and inspired, this synthesized tuba riff helps define the riddim. So does the four-beat percussion hook that sounds like banging on a tin pan.

Beenie Man's tough but melodic sing-jay style has made him one of ragga's biggest stars. He was born Anthony Moses Davis, in 1973, in the rough Waterhouse section of Kingston that has produced more than its share of reggae singers. He has been a star most of his life. Knowing from before he started school that he wanted to be a DJ, he was discovered as a young child when he won a talent show. He began recording at age eight, unprecedented even by the reggae tradition of *youth singers*. This explains his stage name, which literally means "little man". But there's nothing small about the career of this popular dancehall star who is frequently lauded as the "don dada" (literally, the "boss daddy") of dancehall. Unfortunately, he is another of the genre's stars who has trafficked in anti-gay lyrics, harming his international appeal. His response to the controversy is a tangle of explanations, excuses, apologies and retractions. Beenie Man has released about 25 albums to date.

On his song, 'Who Am I', Beenie Man brings to 'Play Ground' different deliveries for chorus and verse. It's a performance that would require two lesser dancehall stars to match. He melodically sings the mid-tempo chorus, while sheaves of words spill out of him for the rapid-pace verses. The song is a response to Missy Elliott's rap hit 'The Rain'. One line caused raised eyebrows in Jamaica. "How can I make love to a fellow? In a rush, pass mi the keys to my truck" was heard by many to be "How can I make love to a fellow in a rush? Pass me the keys to my truck". Ironically, a totally gratuitous anti-gay lyric was misconstrued by many as Beenie Man's coming out. And those are some of the easier to understand lyrics, as the verses are a tumble of heavy patois, Jamaican terms and gusto that makes it hard to glean an answer to the titular question. Suffice it to say, Beenie wants you to know that he has great love-making prowess, complete with an outrageous list of tool analogies. Yet, although he treats girls well, he still gets dumped. But no matter, because the girls are pursuing him. Along the way, he is moved to work in a segment of the famous Cuban song, 'Guantanamera' for no apparent reason other than that he wanted to.

'Who Am I' is perhaps best heard on the 1997 single-riddim CD called *No Fear* released on VP Records, since some of the ten additional versions of 'Play Ground' are quite good. Spragga Benz explains that he's a 'Strong Performer', chanting over various degrees of drop-out. General B's 'Scream' and Merciless's 'Work Dem' impress with their exuberance. Seal Paul's hit, 'Infiltrate', and Mr. Vegas's 'Hand In The Air' each give 'Play Ground' a good ride by adopting the sinister tone of the riddim.

Danny Browne: '*Filthy*'
Beenie Man: '*Let Him Go*'
Mr. Vegas: '*Heads High*'

In 1998, Danny Browne's "Filthy" riddim gave Mr. Vegas and Beenie Man each a big hit while providing a springboard for good versions from other dancehall stars. The riddim sounds like it was carved out of the 'Murder She Wrote' riddim with a grab-bag of eccentric ragga percussion sounds thrown in. Though more percussive than 'Murder She Wrote', 'Filthy' was also more minimalistic, giving the vocalists ample room to work their melodies and words. And work they did.

Beenie Man sing-jays 'Let Him Go' (not The Wailers song) in his full, slightly raspy voice. He's melodic, upbeat and assertive, qualities that are taken up by the male backing singers who chant the titular refrain. Once again, his heavy accent, patois and use of Jamaican terms, not to mention the mocking tone he occasionally affects, make his lyrics difficult for non-Jamaicans to understand. That's a shame because they're missing out on free relationship advice. Women are advised to dump unfaithful boyfriends, accounting for the song's title. Men are advised to appreciate the women they have instead of looking elsewhere. They should show their love by being romantic. His advice then extends to the more physical aspects of a relationship, advising men to be ready to perform. He also advocates against giving oral sex. (Coming from Rasta religious belief, it's a theme Mr. Vegas would expand on in his version, as we will soon see.) If only all unsolicited advice was chanted so well to a music like this.

Mr. Vegas was born Clifford Smith, in 1974 in Kingston. His stage name did not come from his musical style or any high-rolling ways. Instead, it came from a cousin's teasing remark, equating Smith's soccer-playing skills to those of the go-go dancers from a local club called Las Vegas. Vegas had decided on music from an early age, and his name can be included in the rolls of reggae performers who began their careers before they were teenagers. He was originally a singer, until an incident famously put a stop to this. In a fight over ownership of a master tape, Vegas's jaw was smashed by a crowbar and had to be wired together. Before it was fully healed, Vegas heard Beenie Man's 'Who Am I' on the radio. Inspired, he forced the doctor to remove the wiring so he could voice a version. But with his jaw movement constrained, he had to adopt a new sing-jay style. The song 'Nike Air (Hands In The Air)' was a success, and his new style would long outlast the injury. Mr. Vegas has recorded eight albums. Health issues and a desire to lead a more religious and family-oriented life led him to announce his semi-retirement in 2008, releasing only a handful of singles until he made a big return with a rare-for-reggae double-CD release in 2012, and more CDs in 2013 and 2014.

Though always fine, Vegas's vocals have never been more alluring than on 'Heads High', where all of his best qualities are on full display. His voice is high, sweet and strong, with a lineage back to Barrington Levy, and before that to Desmond Dekker and Jimmy Cliff. But Vegas has a darting quality that makes his melodies bend at interesting angles. As Beenie did on 'Let Him Go', Vegas offers free relationship advice. He speaks literally as well as figuratively when he sings the titular refrain. The song is an anthem rallying young women to reject requests for oral sex from their boyfriends. 'Heads High' is music's only explicit anti-blow job international hit. Reggae has a long tradition of songs that look askance at oral sex. Two songs already discussed in this book (pages 61 and 364) are examples of this: Chin's Calypso Sextet's classic golden-age mento hit 'Night Food' and Black Uhuru's roots dub track, 'Sodom'. As the title of the latter indicates, religious views fuel these beliefs. 'Sycamore Tree' by dancehall star Lady Saw, set to the bouncing 'Joyride' riddim, is another notable example of a *no bow* anthem. It's based on the folk song 'Under The Coconut Tree', but Saw is dealing with a very different proposal from the marriage proposal of the older song.

Beenie Man's 'Let Him Go' is available on a number of Beenie Man and dancehall compilation CDs. 'Heads High' can be found on the Mr. Vegas album of that name in two mixes. The album mix emphasizes oddball ragga percussion, while 'Head High (Kill 'Em With It Re-Mix)', is longer and better. Its sound is closer to 'Let Him Go', with percussion that owes more to the 'Murder She Wrote' riddim.

Not surprisingly, sharing a riddim and having overlapping themes, both songs are highly complementary. Dancehall fans are familiar with a great megamix of the 'Filthy' riddim anchored by these two versions that also incorporates prime pieces of several other dancehall stars' versions, such as 'Ease Off Breeze Off', a strong entry from Lady G and the enjoyable 'Traffic Blocking' by General Degree. This makes for a long track that crackles with excitement throughout. Unfortunately, it does not seem to have ever been officially released. Nor has there ever been a single riddim CD collection for 'Filthy' – surprising considering some of the lesser riddims that have received this treatment. Let's hope this is soon addressed so that the megamix and other good versions of 'Filthy' can be easily enjoyed.

Dave Kelly: *'Bruk Out'*
Lady Saw: *'Oh Yeah'*
Bounty Killer: *'Caan Believe Mi Eyes'*
One of the most recognizable voices in dancehall belongs to Lady Saw. Marion Hall was born in 1972 in Saint Mary Parish, but moved to Kingston as a child. There, she discovered she enjoyed singing in church, as well as writing songs. She began to perform at sound systems at the age of fifteen, more as a singer than a DJ then. She has given two accounts of how she chose a stage name. First, it was to honor dancehall singer Tenor Saw, who was a big influence on her before she moved to DJing. Second, it indicated the way she could cut down her male competition. She released her first album in 1994. In both her success and her approach, Lady Saw is a groundbreaking female figure in dancehall. Though by no means the first female DJ, she was the first female ragga star. And she was the first woman in reggae to embrace explicit *slack* lyrics, releasing a number of sexually

frank songs that, coming from a woman, caused a sensation. But ultimately it was her DJing skills, and not slackness, that made her popular. Unusually incisive in words and style, Saw typically has something of interest to say and says it in an interesting way. Her 2002 guest-spot on 'Underneath It All', a song by reggae-influenced US rock group No Doubt, gave Lady Saw a distinction. The song won a Grammy for best performance by a duo or group, making Saw the only woman in reggae to have won one of these awards. In 2013, Lady Saw announced that she was turning away from the negativity of dancehall and towards the church and a career in gospel. But in 2014, she released her tenth reggae album.

Dave Kelly was born in 1969, in Kingston. He began his career as an engineer at Bob Marley's Tuff Gong studio in the late 1980s, advancing to producer at Penthouse, the label of top ragga producer Donovan Germain. Kelly would soon go on to be a top ragga producer in his own right, and start his own label, Madhouse. His 1993 international ragga hit, 'Action', by Terror Fabulous and Nadine Sutherland, was an early feather in his cap.

Lady Saw's 1998 song, 'Oh Yeah', is set to Kelly's 'Bruk Out', a dark undertow of a ragga riddim. It's made up of digitally generated bass and percussion, slithering lead synthesizer and a male voice that occasionally states the riddim's name. It glides sleekly and threateningly as a shark. Describing the material gains of a sexual relationship (Versace, a bedroom set, a Montero jeep, an apartment, etc.), Saw gives a three-headed performance. First comes a spoken-chanted opening, dense with accent and patois, difficult to understand, but clearly confrontational. Second is the chorus, which Saw sings-jays, circling the rhythm like a second shark. Third is the DJed verse, where Saw demonstrates her bold, rich rhythmic chanting, nailing the riddim to the wall. It's one of her finest performances, and can be enjoyed for her lyrics, her sound, or both. 'Oh Yeah' is to be found on Saw's album, *99 Ways*, as well as on several dancehall compilation CDs.

Kingston's Bounty Killer was born in 1972, the same year as Lady Saw, making it a good year for the ragga to come. Rodney Basil Price performed for a short time as "Bounty Hunter", but by the time he upped the ante with his stage name, as Bounty Killer, he was well on his way to becoming one of ragga's biggest stars. He was born into dancehall. His father operated the Black Scorpio sound system, where Rodney first chanted on the mic at the age of nine. But it was talent, not nepotism, that would make him a success. He sounds like no one else, chanting in a thick baritone voice (free of the gravelly rasp that characterizes Buju and others), thick with patois, street terms and slurred-together words, all seeming to come from a place of deep, dark annoyance. Who else would have a catchphrase like Bounty's "Cross, angry, miserable" (the last pronounced *me-so-rebel*).

No one in dancehall personified gun lyrics as much as Bounty Killer. This started with one of his first records, 'Coppershot', recorded at King Jammy's at the start of the 1990s. Jammy was put off by the violent lyrics that celebrated the shooting of adversaries and declined to release the song. He gave it away to another label that released it in 1992, giving Bounty one of his first hits. Though he was not the sole purveyor of gun songs in reggae or rap, they would flow from him like a fountain. To date, he has released no fewer than eight songs with "gun" in the title, with many more at least mentioning the subject. Unlike Cutty Ranks, there was no hint of a smile in any of Bounty's gun lyrics. We can only wonder what effect having been shot as an innocent bystander at age fourteen while returning home from school had on all this. As if this does not make him controversial enough, he is another dancehall star who drew international condemnation for lyrics describing violence and murder against gays. Though it hurt his record sales and ability to perform overseas, it all served to increase his street cred in Jamaica. Since 1993, Bounty Killer has released twelve albums.

Bounty plumbs the inky depths of 'Bruk Out' in his version, 'Caan Believe Mi Eye'. Sounding richly displeased, as only he can, Bounty can't believe his eyes about a tangle of issues. These include the number of gays in Jamaica, that gangsters and gays could be friends, that gangsters would wear tight pants and use hair products and bleaching cream, and other assorted gangster and gun business. Obviously, this song is no love letter to Jamaica's gays. Though there are no calls for explicit violence, there is an air of hostility, right down to the male backing vocalists who aggressively chant the titular refrain. 'Bruk Out' is a great ragga riddim and Bounty nails it as well as Lady Saw did. But the intolerance it portrays badly mars what is otherwise a great track.

Richie Stephens: *'Winner'*
Mr. Vegas: *'Everywhere I Go'*
Though they were immensely popular subjects, not every great ragga song from this time was about sex or violence. Take, for example, the title track of Richie Stephens's 1998 album, *Winner*, that couldn't be more different.

Richard Frederick Freeman Stephenson III was born in 1966, in Westmoreland Parish. He first recorded as part of the UK's R&B group, Soul II Soul, of 'Back to Life' fame. But by the time he joined in 1992, the group's hit-making and Grammy-winning days were behind them, and they would soon break up. Undaunted, Stephens would move into dancehall reggae and prove his talent as both a singer and producer. He has recorded ten albums to date.

In 'Winner', Stephens describes how his abilities, positive attitude, support from his family and belief in God have allowed him to triumph over poverty and racial prejudice. Though it's every bit as affirmative as any roots reggae song, this is dancehall, so these sentiments are presented as a reason to party. Stephens is in fine voice and he delivers a mighty vocal that is infectious and upbeat throughout. He matches this with a riddim that is just as rousing (and provides his own backing vocals for good measure). Opening with a burble of synth percussion sound, it centers on a drum beat that sounds like the Pocomania rhythm restricted to being played with one hand. It's fleshed out by an assortment of bustling keyboards and a traditional reggae bass line. 'Winner' is a song that lives up to its name.

Though nearly as great, Mr. Vegas's version of the 'Winner' riddim, 'Everywhere I Go', is a very different song from Stephens's. Vegas's melodic DJing is hyper-rhythmic, bounding along with a staccato flow of words and nonsense syllables. Though the outcome is equally upbeat, this contrasts greatly with Stephens's orderly singing that's filled with long syllables. Also in contrast are Vegas's lyrics. Instead of a family-values message, he tells us – complete with a few *slack* touches – that everywhere he goes, he's in demand with women, especially when he's performing. Two versions, so different, but both so full of life. Play them back-to-back for one of the greatest disco-mixes that never existed. 'Everywhere I Go' is available on Vegas's *Heads High* album.

Steven "Lenky" Marsden: *'Diwali'*
Sean Paul: *'Get Busy'*
TOK: *'Galang Gal'*
Sean Paul is a top dancehall star with a foot in each of the Jamaican and international arenas. He was born Sean Paul Ryan Francis Henriques in 1973, in Kingston, though he spent a portion of his childhood in Saint Andrew Parish. His gene pool is broad, with grandparents coming from such ethnically diverse backgrounds as African, English, Chinese and Sephardic Jewish Portuguese, all by way of Jamaica. As the national motto says, "Out of Many, One People". His family is talented. His mother was accomplished both as a swimmer and as a painter. His grandfather and father both played for Jamaica's national water polo team. Paul followed in the latter, competing through his teens, until at twenty-one he began to concentrate on his musical career. He became interested in DJing and started to write songs. He admittedly was influenced by the style of Supercat – the DJ who scored a huge hit in 1986 with 'Boops'. Supercat would make a thinly veiled reference to Paul's similar sound background in his 2004 song, 'Reggae Matic'. Paul's first recording, 'Baby Girl Don't Cry', appeared in 1999, followed by the first of six albums in 2000. With his always cool, articulate sing-jay delivery, and showing no interest in homophobic or violent lyrics, Paul had great cross-over potential. And in 2003, this potential was fulfilled, as his 'Get Busy' became a monster international ragga hit.

Producer Steven "Lenky" Marsden was born in 1968 in Kingston to a musical family. He began studying piano at the age of thirteen. He climbed the same ladder as many Jamaican musicians. From talent shows, he worked his way up to the hotel circuit, to reggae backing bands, then on to studio sessions. In addition to his keyboard skills, his songwriting abilities made him in demand by top ragga producers. (In fact, in 2003, he would win awards for best song and songwriter of the year from the American Society of Composers, Authors & Publishers/Performing Rights Society.) He capitalized on his growing successes by starting his own label in 1996, working as a producer and developing new vocal talent.

In 2002, he created a riddim called 'Diwali', after the Indian Festival of Light. Befitting its name, it is exotic even for ragga. The rhythm is composed of a hypnotic pattern of handclaps supplemented by a synthesized hi-hat cymbal and a one-note bass line. Atop of this, synthesized strings are sawn and plucked to give us mysterious melodies. Every sound is familiar but a bit alien at the same time. The closest comparison comes not from Jamaica, but from the David Byrne and Brian Eno groundbreaking, pan-cultural altered-sound album, *My Life In The Bush Of Ghosts*. But whereas *Bush Of Ghosts* used 1981 recording technology to make conventional instruments sound familiar yet strange, decades later, Lenky is able to achieve the same exotic effect working in the digital domain.

'Diwali' didn't just put Lenky on the map, it put him all over it at once. It was so intoxicating that three versions of 'Diwali' charted simultaneously on *Billboard*'s top ten, a feat no other riddim has matched. In addition to Sean Paul's number 1, 'Get Busy', there was also 'No Letting Go' by Wayne Wonder and Lumidee's 'Never Leave You'. (The latter, to a stripped-down version of 'Diwali', has a distinction of its own. Lumidee is a Harlem-born American R&B singer of Puerto Rican descent. This makes her song the first and only instance when versioning has provided an international hit for either a non-Jamaican or a non-reggae performer.) This opened doors for Lenky, who would go on to work with such big names as Madonna, Janet Jackson, Christina Aguilera, Britney Spears and Timbaland, in addition to his ragga work.

The lyrics of Sean Paul's 'Get Busy' are dancehall pure and simple. In his cool, confidant style, Paul DJs about wanting to see women dance to his music and how women want to be with him. The song opens and closes with a hook as Paul rides 'Diwali' tight, chanting a list of women he commands to dance. His serious tone leverages the strangeness of the riddim and makes this hook mesmerizing. There's something familiar about a part of Paul's melody – a similarity to the Bee Gees' 'Staying Alive'. It wouldn't be the first reggae track to borrow from this song, Sly & Robbie's instrumental 'Oriental Taxi', a song previously described in this book (page 368), being another example. It's just another way that Paul effectively turns the exotic 'Diwali' riddim into a great party song.

TOK (short for Touch Of Klass) is a four-man *dancehall crew* consisting of singers Alistaire "Alexx" McCalla and Xavier "Flexx" Davidson, and DJs Roshaun "Bay-C" Clarke and Craig "Craigy T" Thompson. They came together in 1992 while still in school and began by performing R&B at parties. They moved up to the hotel circuit while coming into a more Jamaican sound. Talent shows gained them further exposure, and in 1996 they found themselves recording their first single, 'Hit Them High', for producers Sly & Robbie. It flopped, and TOK moved on. In 1998 they recorded 'Hardcore Lover', a collaboration with the red-hot Lady Saw that was based on Stevie Wonder's 'Part Time Lover'. It was a hit, launching the crew's career. With four very good, very diverse dancehall voices, hits of their own would quickly follow. To date, they have recorded three albums plus two solo albums.

In 2002, TOK recorded 'Galang Gal', their fine version of 'Diwali'. Even more than Sean Paul in 'Get Busy', TOK creates a song that leverages the exotic mysteriousness inherent in the riddim even as the lyrics are down to earth. Each member takes a turn with the lead and each contributes something interesting to the overall sound. Though they provide new lyrics, TOK borrows aspects of two folk/mento songs, giving their track deep genetics. The melody and structure of 'Mandeville Road' is used, though the lyrics are new. And the subject and part of the title of 'Galag Gully' are employed, as both songs are about admiring a woman. The song begins, and the chanted patois over the 'Diwali' riddim sounds like a religious invocation from a lost continent. But the story is down to earth, as TOK salute a woman they admire for her figure (her bustline gets a *big up*) and wardrobe. She inspires jealousy and failed imitators:

> Cut eye [dirty looks], cut eye can't cut you in two
> Penny, penny can't buy your shoe
> 'Nuff a dem a follow, but dem see what you a do
> Dem try copy copy, but nah come close to you.
>
> © Westbury Music Ltd

The famous chorus of 'Mandeville Road' that describes the hard labor of breaking up rocks ("Bruk dem one by one, galang [go on] boy, bruk dem two by two ...") is adapted as a tribute to how the woman deals with her rivals:

> Whop dem one by one, galang gal
> Top dem two by two, galang gal
> Drop dem three by three, galang gal
> From you know say, you hotter than she.
>
> © Westbury Music Ltd

An exceptionally strong dancehall crew performance, repurposed mento songs, a mento eye for detailed observation and a state-of-the-art ragga riddim all complement one another. And a great song that is simultaneously fun and stunningly exotic is born. Both 'Galang Gal' and Sean Paul's 'Get Busy' are readily available on multiple CDs.

Sizzla: *'Subterranean Homesick Blues'*

The popular dancehall sing-jay Sizzla (Miguel Orlando Collins) was born in 1976 to religious Rastafarian parents. He would grow up to become a member of the strict Bobo Shanti sect of Rastafari, outwardly recognizable by their colorful turbans and robes, often living apart in religious communities. He began his career as a performer at the Caveman Hi-Fi sound system, recording his first song in 1995, with his first hits coming later that year. The prolific Sizzla has released 70 albums since that time. His delivery is wild and can sound undisciplined, in a popular style that he shares with his contemporaries like Capelton, and which can be traced all the way back to golden-age mento star Lord Power.

But Sizzla sounds anything but undisciplined on his 2004 cover of the 1965 Bob Dylan song, 'Subterranean Homesick Blues'. When I first heard it, though there was something maddeningly familiar in its words and cadence, the voice and music were so out of context, it took time for recognition to click. Once it did, I was delighted, as Sizzla's unlikely rendition is an inspired choice and a triumph for the DJ. Producer Gary "Doctor Dread" Himelfarb provides an exceedingly springy dancehall riddim featuring ranging, funky reggae bass and moon-bounce organ. Sizzla enters, laughing with gusto, as if he is relishing the dual challenges of riding this bouncing riddim while delivering Dylan's torrent of rapid-fire lyrics. Charged up, he freestyles a few lines and then gets down to chanting. He fully meets the challenges of the song, riding it like a bronco buster.

Dylan's idiosyncratic cadences translate nicely to DJ chant. Likewise his anti-establishment sentiments – a song with so much to say about distrusting the government is a natural for reggae. Perhaps this is why Sizzla is careful to be reverent. He does not miss a line and takes few liberties, though he is unable to keep from working in a marijuana and a gun reference. 'Subterranean Homesick Blues' is the standout song on the album called *Is It Rolling, Bob?: A Reggae Tribute to Bob Dylan*. Be sure to play it to any fan of dancehall and Bob Dylan.

Louie Culture: *'Donkey Back'*
Lewin Brown was born in 1968 in Portland Parish. He began DJing while still in school, adopting the second half of his stage name in homage to his mentor, the DJ called Bobby Culture. As you would expect, both were *cultural* DJs, meaning that even though they were dancehall artists, their songs frequently centered on Rastafarian beliefs and roots reggae issues, while eschewing the sex and violence lyrics of some dancehall. His first record was a duo with another DJ in 1986, but it flopped and Louie's partner left Jamaica. Going solo and working with a variety of producers, Louie would find success around 1992 and released his first of two albums in 1994.

His 2004 song, 'Donkey Back', aided by producer M. "Justice" Halsall, expands the notion of a cultural DJ to include the music's cultural heritage. Though TOK's 'Galong Gal' (described above; page 570) and other dancehall songs flirted with the notion, 'Donkey Back' boldly and quite brilliantly blends Jamaica's newest recorded music, dancehall, with its oldest, mento. This was not the only mento-dancehall riddim. Others include 'Chaka Chaka' (described below) from the same year, Steely & Clevie's 'Nine Night' from 2001 and Arif Cooper's 'National Pride' in 2009.

'Donkey Back' is a delightful romp, with music that perfectly mixes the old and new. The riddim is mechanized and synthesized, as dancehall was at that time. But the instruments consist of a banjo, strumming and riffing with mechanical precision, a synthesized fife and a bass line simple enough to have emerged from a rumba box. The drum rhythm is a simplified Pocomania pattern. Rather than sounding pedantic in any way, the riddim absolutely pops with vitality. Its only downside is that Halsall didn't version it, so other performers could ride this donkey's back.

Culture's lyrics also work as a mix of the old and the new. On the surface, it's a mento-esque story of a donkey in the tradition of such songs as 'Hold 'Im Joe'. In this case, Culture warns about loading on one coconut too many, cautioning against putting "too much pressure on the donkey's back" (giving us a Jamaican variation on the straw that broke the camel's back) and against other mistreatment. But then a second meaning emerges with:

> Early this morning, the donkey get away
> Free so free, the donkey start bray
> You hear what him say?
> 'No I'm not coming back your way
> I've got to find a place where I can kneel and pray
> Got to find a place where I can romp and play
> Got to find a place where I can have my say.

With this, Culture turns the donkey into a symbol for Jamaica's oppressed. Suddenly, the donkey becomes a Trojan horse for dreams of Rasta freedom, the sentiment never more sweetly expressed. This mento-dancehall fusion should be heard by all fans of Jamaican music. It's available on Louis Culture's 2004 album, *The Uprising*.

Dane "Fire Links" Johnson: *'Chaka Chaka'*
Alaine: *'No No No'*
Tanya Stephens: *'Bleach Pon It'*
Ragga producer Dane "Fire Links" Johnson was active for several years in the middle of the 2000s. In 2004, he produced the mento-dancehall riddim called 'Chaka Chaka'. Like 'Donkey Back', it blends the organic musical textures of Jamaica's oldest recorded music with the up-to-the-minute sound manipulation of its newest. But rather than sounding forced in any way, the result is an ecstatically happy marriage. A computer-crafted ragga rhythm approximates a galloping mento beat. It's layered with mechanically dispensed banjo picking, natural harmonica, a rumba box-friendly keyboard–bass line and synthesized fiddle swoops, each brimming with high-energy glee.

Sweet-voiced Alaine Laughton was born in 1978 in New Jersey, but moved to Jamaica when she was three. She was a successful child actor, appearing in several movies, the most famous being 1988's *Clara's Heart*, with Whoopi Goldberg. As an adult, she was a successful investment banker in the USA. But in 2004, she abandoned corporate life to return to Jamaica and concentrate on her singing career. 'No No No' finds Alaine tapping into 'Chaka Chaka's happy energy to deliver a peppy break-up song. It shares the title and some lyrics with another song described in this book (page 586) about the end of love, Dawn Penn's 'You Don't Love Me'. But where Penn's is a bluesy song of defeat, Alaine's is a happy unburdening as she recounts the romantic mistreatment of her now former lover, ignoring his pleas for another chance.

Vivienne Tanya Stephenson was born in 1973 in Kingston but lived all over the island when growing up. After success on the mic at various sound systems, she released her first record, 'Is This For Real' in 1993. By 1996, she had secured a spot as one of dancehall's top female stars. Stephens has a tough, blunt, in-your-face style that works especially well in this song about sexual confrontation. And she is never afraid to get *slack* to illustrate her point. In a welcome change, she has bravely condemned violence against gays in her song 'Do You Still Care'. And in interviews, she has taken dancehall stars who write hate lyrics to task. Tanya Stephens has released seven albums to date.

Like Alaine's song, Tanya Stephens's 'Bleach Pon It' is about relationship dissatisfaction, set to the 'Chaka Chaka' riddim. But the similarities end there, as Stephens's slack song puts Alaine's brave but wholesome 'No No No' in danger of fainting. Stephens is concerned that what she brings to the bedroom should be matched by her prospective lovers, stated in no uncertain terms. To put it as politely as I can, if you are going to take matters into your own hands, you'd better know what you are doing, otherwise she will have to show you how. She praises her own equipment and warns against empty boasts from men about theirs. Her sexual bragging goes beyond outrageous, as she warns that her *rough ride* "might make you vomit". Now, even with a history of reggae songs celebrating the women with the *rough ride* that dates all the way back to the mid-1950s and Chin's Calypso Sextet's infamous 'Rough Rider', that's quite a warning. Sweet talk this isn't, but she's far from done. In fact, she's on a roll. In one patois-filled blue streak, she equates her sexual performance to an atomic bomb, saying that she could engage the X-Men, that she deserves an Olympic gold medal, and so on. Stephens certainly didn't invent explicit slack lyrics. But rarely, if ever, has slackness been so colorfully expressed. In the 1950s, golden-age mento's best songwriters, E. F. Williams of Chin's and Count Lasher, were pressured by the government to put a stop to their winking double-entendre songs. If any of these parties were alive to hear 'Bleach Pon It' – sung by a woman no less – and performed over an electro-mento ragga backing, they'd probably have been knocked off their chairs. For another good Tanya Stephens song, check her 'Buss Back Skettel', her version of the difficult-to-ride 'Hard Drive' riddim. It can be heard on the single-riddim collection called *Hard Drive Part 2* on the Greensleeves label. 'No No No' and 'On Bleach Pon It' can be found along with eighteen other versions on the single-riddim CD called *Chaka Chaka*, released on the Fire Links label.

Voicemail: *'Jamaican Jiggas'*
Voicemail (not to be confused with Busy Signal, another dancehall artist) is a dance-hall crew that came together at the end of the 1990s. They were originally a five-piece outfit, having met at a talent show. But they would not find success until they pared down to three members: Craig Jackson, Kevin Blaire and Oniel Edwards (the son of reggae singer and producer Rupie Edwards). They recorded their first record, 'Never Really Want To Let You Go', in 2003, and have recorded three albums to date.

In 2005 producer Robert Livingston constructed a fine updating of the riddim from Keith & Tex's 1967 rock steady gem, 'Stop That Train'. (Songs by Scotty and Big Youth on this riddim have already been described in this book; pages 428 and 411.) Calling the riddim "Return", he included samples of the original, including its centerpiece, Lyn Taitt's guitar riff that was inspired by the American Westerns then so popular at Kingston's movie theaters. Four decades later, the riff has lost none of its power as a hook. 'Return' is fleshed out with updated reggae guitar, organ, bass and drums. The only purely ragga sound is the ominous synthesizer stabs that paint 'Return' with a darker vibe than that of 'Stop That Train'.

'Jamaican Jiggas' gets half its title from a term popularized by rap star Jay Z, so it's no shock that the song features *gangsta* lyrics, Jamaican style. It opens with the three members of Voicemail singing the chorus in unison, warning of death for those who would impede their success. They then take turns sing-jaying the verse and there are further threats to informers and warnings of having a "tool" [gun]. But there is great energy in the performance and a finesse to the lyrics that elevate the song above what can be a dreary subject. Consider how well constructed is the stanza about an informer who didn't heed a warning and its wordplay on the Jamaican dish, jerk [spiced] chicken. It's reprehensibly violent, but there's artistry in its telling. In a terrible irony all too familiar to gangsta rap fans, in 2010, Edwards was robbed and shot at his home, and died several weeks later at the age of thirty-six.

Another good version of the "Return" riddim is the rousing 'Stand Up' by Shaggy. Just as the riddim recalls the reggae of the past, so do Shaggy's lyrics with their stand-up-for-your-rights theme. Both songs and more can be heard on a VP Records CD from 2005, *Riddim Driven – Return To Big Street.*

Lady G: *'Run Him'*
Ce'Cile: *'She She'*
Mr. Easy: *'Club Tonight'*
Mr. Vegas: *'Herb Tree'; 'Yuh A Di Wife'*
Producer Nigel Davey's riddim, 'The Return Of Mudd Up', hit the scene in 2006. It's more of a sequel than a revival of the previous decade's popular 'Mudd Up' ragga riddim, and an improvement on it. It's a merry, candy-colored piece of ragga that sometimes veers towards a traditional reggae rhythm even as it nods to Trinidad with calypso guitar strumming and steel drum keyboards. Numerous dancehall artists enjoyed a good ride on this fun ragga wave. Several second-tier

players outdid most of the bigger names that took a turn. That is, except for Mr. Vegas, who chalked up not one but two fine versions of the riddim.

The Spanish Town-born sing-jay Lady G (Janice Fyffe) has recorded about 45 songs, solo or with another artist, since the end of the 1980s. She has enjoyed success even as she stood by her morals and ignored pressure to record *slackness*. In 'Run Him', she amplifies the positive energy of riddim, with a song empowering women. She cheerfully recommends the rubbish truck as the solution to being saddled with a worthless man. As she catalogs the man's failings (no skills, doesn't provide financially, doesn't help around the house, weak sexually, isn't faithful, etc.), the girl-power-supporting vocalist exhorts, "Run him!", meaning, "get rid of him". She also points out that in the circumstances dumping the man can't be considered cruel (the last word pronounced with two syllables, as in *krew-el*).

Unlike most dancehall stars who came out of the poverty of Kingston's ghettos (Sean Paul being another notable exception), sexy sing-jay Ce'Cile (Cecile Claudine Charlton) is from a prominent family in Mandeville, where her grandfather was the mayor. She has recorded three albums and approximately 25 singles since 2000. 'She She', her go at 'The Return Of Mudd Up' riddim is a frothy song that pokes fun at easy women. She's clever without having to resort to explicitness, creating colorful turns of phrase. Many of her lines end with the final syllable jumping to a high register and gaining harmony through multi-tracking. It's a fun device that gives an already appealing song a persistent hook.

Sing-jay Mr. Easy (Ian Dyer) was born in the rural parish of Trelawny in Jamaica's Cockpit Country. Like many country boys, he moved to the city as a child, but in this case the city was New York rather than Kingston. He has recorded one album and appeared on about 25 singles since 1989. 'Club Tonight' is well sung and its cheerful vibe perfectly matches the riddim. It genuinely conveys the excitement of going out to party. We hear about dressing well, VIP status, buying rounds of beer for his friends, and of the attractive ladies at the club. And, although Easy isn't breaking any new ground here, it's hard to resist a good dancehall song about going out to dance.

With his version of 'The Return Of Mudd Up', called 'Herb Tree', Mr. Vegas shows that legalize-marijuana songs didn't end in the roots era. Vegas imagines the convenience, if legalization were to happen, of being able to smoke at any point for the rest of his life. He chants about ganja being the "healing of the nation", a familiar phrase from roots reggae. (It's based on a Bible passage from Revelations 22:2 that states, "The leaves of the tree were for the healing of the nation ...". In 1978, Jacob Miller used it for his popular legalize-marijuana anthem, 'Healing Of The Nation'. Peter Tosh helped popularize the expression in various interviews, and would use it in his 1979 song 'Buk-In-Hamm Palace'.) Vegas sounds both skilled and stoned, as the cadence of his chanting impressively follows the riddim's loopy, wheezy synthesizer to a T. He chants of the positive effect of ganja on his DJing, and, if this song is any indication, he's right.

Vegas takes a different approach to his second voicing of 'Return Of Mudd Up', called 'Yuh A Di Wife'. His voice is double-tracked to harmonize with himself for the entire song. This gives the song an unusual vocal sound, both edgy and rich. It fits his lyrics about marital discord and sets the song apart from all other versions of the riddim. These five tracks and fifteen more versions can be heard on the 2006 Greensleeves single-riddim CD, *The Return Of Mudd-Up*.

Mr. Vegas: *'Gangsta Confession'*

Set to producer Delroy "Delly Ranks" Foster's 'Gangtaz Prayer' rhythm, Mr. Vegas's 2007 song, 'Gangsta Confession', is a compelling rude boy melodrama and as explicitly violent as any reggae song recorded. Not surprising for a song and a riddim with alternative spellings for "gangster", its introduction features strains of gangsta rap. The tone set, the purely ragga body of the riddim begins. Three instruments are heard. Programmed drums bring a Pocomania-derived beat. Shifting keyboards with touches of ominous dub echo bring a traditional reggae sound. So does an enormous bass line, albeit played on a keyboard. It's a lean and hungry riddim, the tone oscillating between galloping aggression and mournful regret, fully befitting the lyrics.

Vegas rides the riddim tight, his chanting adhering to the spikey drum beat, except when singing the long notes of the chorus of "we pray". Rude boy songs have been pro-, anti- or ambivalent about their subject. Here, the sentiments are more complex, putting the listener in several conflicting minds. Vegas titillates with an explicit description of responding to violence with greater violence, as he kills adversaries who tried to kill his friend. But there is poetry in the lyrics. He uses a ready vocabulary of patois and repurposed street terms, as formerly innocent words gain dark new meanings. "Crown" means "head", so "lick off your crown" means 'blow off your head'. A "puppy" is a young adversary. To "wet" is to make bloody. "My chrome" and "big thing" are his guns. To "Flintstone" is to run in place when trying to run for your life. And "leave dem breathless" here means murder. At the same time, Vegas can be pitied. The account of his actions is presented as a confession to God. (In this way, the song is reminiscent of another song previously described in this book, the stunning though largely forgotten 'Rude Boy Prayer'; page 134.) He begs forgiveness and eventual entry to heaven, desperately trying to explain his actions.

This is one of Mr. Vegas's best performances and certainly the best voicing of the 'Gangtaz Prayer' riddim. But somehow, instead of releasing the track just described on CD, Vegas put it out under the name 'Gangsta Prayer', with inferior, less-Jamaican backing music. Don't settle for this when reggae specialty shops can help you acquire the original single on the Pure Music label. (Its flipside is the like-minded 'Violate The Link' by Chino, also set to the 'Gangtaz Prayer' rhythm.) It's worth the effort for what may very well be the last great rude boy song.

54 Coda: More great songs, but difficult to categorize

Presented chronologically, here are some more great reggae songs that don't slot into any of the preceding chapters. Each one is great in its own right, and it would be a shame to miss even one of them. What better way to end this book than with a handful of unique reggae gems?

The Gaylads: *'Africa'*
Not unusually for a Jamaican vocal group, The Gaylads' history has a lot of moving parts. Winston & Bibby (Winston Delano Stewart and Harris "B. B." Seaton) were a not-unsuccessful duo who recorded R&B and ska at Studio One starting in 1962. But greater success would follow, when in 1964 they added Maurice Roberts and called themselves The Gaylads. Mid-decade, Seaton left to form BB & The Astronauts, but would return to The Gaylads in time for the rock steady era. Before the decade was over, they had recorded in a variety of styles for such producers as Coxsone Dodd, Sonia Pottinger, Lee Perry and Leslie Kong. (This included an unusual album produced by Dodd in 1967 of mostly mento songs set to a calypso backing.) Stewart departed in 1968 for a solo career, leaving Seaton and Roberts to carry on as a duo, still enjoying success. They would resume work as a trio, with former Paragon Howard Barrett amongst those who were deputized as Gaylads. Seaton began recording with The Conscious Minds, counting Ken Boothe as another member, and moved into production. He would leave the Gaylads around 1972. Roberts retained the Gaylads name and continued intermittently with returning and substitute members. At one point, the group was renamed Psalms, best known under that moniker for providing backing vocals for Bunny Wailer, both in the studio and live. In all, The Gaylads recorded over 150 singles and three albums.

'Africa', an unusual song produced by Coxsone Dodd in 1967, may be the crowning jewel in The Gaylads' story. It's an adaption of 'Tabu', a haunting African-influenced piece of jazz exotica recorded by Trinidadian bandleader Cyril X. Diaz in 1958, but based on an older Cuban song. Featuring haunting wordless chanting, Latin and African hand drums (the latter not so very different from Nyabinghi) and a dramatically serious vibe, 'Tabu' is dread in its own way. It inspires The Gaylads to a unique reggae song. They repurpose the haunting melody and the African vibe of the original by adding back-to-Africa lyrics, making their song an exotic Rasta hymn.

It opens similarly to the original with a dark jazz introduction led by heavy horns. The body of the song emerges as wordless vocals, serious melodies and hand drums are hung over a ska rhythm. The lyrics begin, sung in the careful manner of rock steady. As is typical for a back-to-Africa song, the continent is idealized as a place of plenty and freedom. These sentiments are interspersed with returns to wordless singing, and the occasional outburst of faux jungle noises. 'Africa' can be called strong ska, odd but wonderful rock steady, an early roots classic, a great reggae cover or multi-island reggae exotica. You'll get no argument from me, as long as you qualify it as great.

In 1973, Dennis Brown had a hit with his rendition of 'Africa', but even the Prince of Reggae could not surpass The Gaylads' rendition. In 1975, Ras Michael transformed it into a sprawling Nyabinghi-reggae recording with greater success. Called 'Zion Land', it was described earlier in this book (page 329). The Gaylads' 'Africa' can be found on their compilation CD, *Ska Days*,

John Holt & The Paragons: *'I've Got To Get Away' (aka 'Quiet Place'; aka 'Man Next Store')*
'Quiet Place' was self-produced by The Paragons in 1968. They may have been influenced by the lyrically similar but musically different 'A Quiet Place', recorded by the smooth American R&B crooner Garnet Mimms in 1964. John Holt and company sing about a bad living arrangement, thanks to close-quarters ghetto housing and the intolerable man next door:

> He gets in so late at nights, always a fuss and fight, all through the night.
> I've got to get away from here. This is not a place for me to stay.
> I've got to take my family, and find a quiet place.
> Hear the pots and pans they fall. Bang, against the wall. No rest at all.
> I've got to get away!
>
> © Westbury Music Ltd

The stress of the situation etches every aspect of the song with tension. It's a terse 2 minutes long, and too harried for a mid-song solo. The lead and backing vocals have an anxiety that was not hinted at on the group's rock steady hits. The pressure-cooker backing music has a busy arrangement with fast hi-hat work as the guitar chop sounds with metronomic insistence. The only relief comes from a melodic piano, but it's overwhelmed by the other instruments. In 'Quiet Place', one of life's small problems grows intolerable, eliciting an exciting song that does not sound quite like anything else from the reggae canon. It will be immediately loved by anyone who has ever had to put up with a chronically noisy neighbor.

Several DJs have used the intensity of this song as a springboard for exciting versions of their own. Doctor Alimantado's 'Poison Flour' and Dave Barker's boisterous 'I've Got To Get Away' are two good examples. Dennis Brown and Horace

Andy have covered the song, as have the reggae-influenced UK punk group The Slits. The original rendition is available on several CD collections.

Errol Dunkley: *'A Little Way Different'*

Singer Errol Dunkley was born in 1951 in Kingston, and recorded his first single at age fourteen. This was when producer Prince Buster released 'My Queen', billed to Gaynor & Errol, Gaynor being the sax-playing Alpha Boy, Bobby Gaynair. But Dunkley's first hit wouldn't come until the 1967 rock steady of the Joe Gibbs-produced 'You're Gonna Need Me'. He enjoyed a cross-over hit in the UK with a 1979 rendition of John Holt's 'OK Fred' and followed up the next year with another song that charted there. Dunkley would release over 120 singles and twelve albums, recording steadily through 1983 and intermittently to 2001.

In 1972, Dunkley and producer Sonia Pottinger loaded 'A Little Way Different' with so much goodness, impossible contradictions arise. It's exceptionally sweet, yet very tart. It's bright as the sun, yet carries a sad bluesy feel. Dunkley sounds like he is celebrating, yet he's mournful. It's clearly rock steady, yet it's clearly reggae proper. This yields a unique mood-ring of a song that is suitable for whatever humor the listener is in.

The last contradiction can be easily explained, as the producer was known to favor the orderliness and sweetness of rock steady well into the reggae era. So the careful craftsmanship of rock steady is fully evident, even as each instrument leaks reggae creativity into the song, as if they can't contain it any longer. Though every instrument is played impeccably, special note should be made of the fine, archetypically Jamaican horn line sounded in unison by trombone and trumpet. It straddles the rock steady of the past and the roots reggae to come. Special note should also be made of how the organ excitedly dances around the horn line. And how the piano complements the organ. And how creative the bass and drums are. Well, it turns out that every instrument deserves special note.

Errol Dunkley is just terrific with his quintessential Jamaican strong nasal voice. Befitting the musical backing, he sings with a restraint that comes from rock steady cool, but with deep emotion and a vibrato more associated with roots reggae. The lyrics also straddle these styles. Celebrating individuality, they would be at home in rock steady. But then they also foreshadow the socially conscious lyrics that would become so popular in roots reggae as Dunkley asks not to be judged by his race or religion. The cascade of "*no*"s that follow this last lyric are conveyed so emotionally, they give the song its peak. This is Dunkley's finest vocal performance, miles away from the *youth singer* sound of a number of his well-known records. It's available on a number of compilations. But be careful not to confuse it with a 1977 remake for producer Dennis Bovell that, while not bad, is not nearly as good.

Horace Andy & Earl Flute: *'Don't Think About Me (I'm Alright)'*
In 1973, producer Keith Hudson nicely set up Horace Andy with a longer version of the riddim from his classic pseudo-instrumental, 'Melody Maker' (a song described previously in this book; page 315) and with a simpatico backing singer in Earl Flute. Andy responded in kind, and the result is the great record called 'Don't Think About Me'.

The evocative wordless vocals, harmonica and guitar tracks from 'Melody Maker' are dropped out here, effectively eliminating the defining Western atmosphere of the original version. This leaves a brooding bass line to set the tone, and Andy delivers an unusually moody song. The titular refrain is delivered as a reprimand, as Andy would rather you not concern yourself with him. At first he seems defensive, but as the song goes on, he sounds downright paranoid. In this context, Andy's natural vibrato comes off as fueled by anxiety, while the mellower Flute serves as a calming influence, trying to sooth a troubled psyche. With many syllables drawn long, the vocals contrast pleasingly with the short rumbling bass-note clusters that dominate the riddim. This makes the song a sonic treat in addition to a gallery of edgy sentiments. The odd but wonderful 'Don't Think About Me' is available on several CD compilations.

Marcia Griffiths: *'Children At Play'*
We have already seen how Marcia Griffiths made a guest appearance on Wailers records in the 1960s, and became a member of The I-Threes in the 1970s. There, she was an important component of the Bob Marley & The Wailers sound through to the start of the 1980s, when Bob's death ended this amalgamation of talent. But her career began before she recorded with The Wailers, and would continue after their time in a long and respected career.

Marcia Llyneth Griffiths was born in 1949 in Kingston, and enjoyed singing in church. In 1964, she was discovered while singing at home by Philip "Boasie" James of the popular Jamaican R&B duo, The Blues Busters, who was visiting a neighbor of the Griffiths. He ushered her to a talent show, where she was backed by Byron Lee & The Dragonaires. This led to the start of her recording career a year later at Studio One, where she recorded ska and soul, as a solo artist or occasionally as a duo with a male singer ('Oh My Darling', with Bob Marley, being an example of the latter). She scored her first hit in 1968 with 'Feel Like Jumping', set to the '54-46' riddim that Toots & The Maytals had made famous a year earlier. Before she joined Marley's The I-Threes, she collaborated with another Bob – Bob Andy. Bob & Marcia were a successful duo, releasing about two dozen single sides from 1969 to 1972, and enjoying two pop-reggae hits in the UK. They also recorded four albums, two in the second half of the 1970s upon resuming their collaboration. After Marley's death, Griffiths resumed her solo career, which continued into dancehall, amassing about 70 singles and thirteen albums. One of her later hits would make her a staple of American weddings, where the Electric

Slide is danced to her song, 'Electric Boogie', a dance-reggae-rap hybrid produced by Bunny Wailer. With a career this long and diverse, and having achieved success as a solo singer, in duos, and in a vocal group, it's no wonder Marcia Griffiths is called "the first lady of reggae" and "the queen of reggae". The Jamaican government was not able to make either of these honorifics official, but it did bestow the Order of Distinction on her in 1994, and then upgraded it to Commander class in 2014.

Produced by Lloyd Charmers in 1974, Marcia Griffiths's 'Children At Play' has a particular vibe that makes it unique in the reggae canon. The band strikes a sophisticated, sultry, low-key pop-soul groove. Shimmering electric piano is out front, and a shuffle drum beat is supplemented by a simmering hand drum, soul rhythm guitar and bass. Almost everything enjoys a dose of reverb. Griffiths wades right in with a great vocal performance. She's in a zone, singing with a singular air of contentedness, as she ruminates on how good it is to be reunited with her children and man after a day of work. Sounding completely fulfilled, she paints a picture of an evening outdoors as she and her man enjoy the sight of their children at play. A pure celebration of family that's completely devoid of angst in any form, it's an absolute pleasure to listen to. It can be heard on her CD collection, *Play Me Sweet And Nice*, as well as on the *Trojan Reggae Sisters Box Set*.

The Heptones: *'Country Boy'*
Produced by Harry "Harry J" Johnson in 1975, The Heptones' 'Country Boy' is a difficult song to categorize. It certainly isn't the smooth rock steady for which The Heptones made their name. Nor is it the roots reggae that they later recorded. The backing band is the instrumental Wailers, and although they are excellent as ever, the song does not sound like anything from the Bob Marley canon. There's a lilting rural feel to this song, but it couldn't be considered mento-reggae.

The Heptones are atypical as well. Their vocals, though tremendous, have never sounded quite like this at any other point in their prolific career. Rather than the tight, often smooth, soulful harmonies they are known for, here they've opened up with a rich and rangy, strident-yet-sweet rural Jamaican edge. Especially irresistible are the verses sweetly chanted over striding piano.

The lyrics are the key to defining the song. They begin with the Heptones emphatically assuring us that this is a true story. They describe the titular figure carrying on around town, firing his gun and brandishing a ratchet. As depicted in the film, *The Harder They Come*, the influx of rural poor into Kingston helped fuel the rude boy phenomenon. Here, The Heptones give us a song from the point of view of the city's natives. They are unimpressed, complaining that the rude boy is a bumpkin. He doesn't know his way about the city and probably doesn't even know what a light post (lamp post) is. More than fearsome, he's just in the way. 'Country Boy', then, is best described as a rural reggae rude boy song that turns the phenomenon on its head, lyrically and musically. As great as it is unusual, it should not be missed, especially since it's available on numerous reggae compilations and Heptones collections.

The Prophets & Trinity: *'King Pharaoh's Plague'*
Tommy McCook: *'Plague Of Horn'*
Trinity and Dillinger: *'Jesus Dread'*
King Tubby: *'King Pharaoh Dub'*

Roots singer and producer Yabby You was born Vivian Jackson, in 1946, in Kingston. His was a childhood of poverty, malnutrition, health problems and hospital stays. His first record was 'Conquering Lion' in 1972 for King Tubby. It contained some introductory chanting to the effect of "ya be you" that was distinctive enough to give him his unusual stage name. He later explained that he heard angels sing this to him during a thunderstorm after a discussion on religion. Yabby would move into production by 1974, working with a number of top vocalists and instrumentalists. In spite of health problems, he was prolific, recording approximately 27 albums, but he died suddenly of a brain aneurism in 2010.

These four tracks from 1977 are versions of Yabby You's urgent roots reggae riddim, 'King Pharaoh's Plague'. Rather than disperse them around the book's roots, DJ and dub chapters, I decided to look at them together here, with a mind to turning them into a custom megamix.

Billed to The Prophets & Trinity (the former being the name Yabby gave his backing band), the riddim's namesake version is a disco-mix. It teams a roots vocal performance from Yabby that segues into Trinity's DJ version. (It's not to be confused with Yabby's similarly named but completely different song, 'Pharaoh's Plague'.) The song opens with the riddim's trademark: an exciting, hard-charging syncopated riff that is heard several times throughout the song. It's led by hot strummed electric guitar phrases answered by an equally hot organ riff. The guitar's chord progression is unusual, as the melody gets bent to an acute angle, then is released to snap back by the end of the phrase.

In his plaintive roots voice Yabby You sings about the titular Old Testament story. His focus is on how the rod of Jehovah will conquer the Pharaoh, causing Babylon to fall. When he sings of Pharaoh's scientists, he could be bringing the symbol of Pharaoh into the present time, or he could employing a Rasta use of "science" to mean black magic. Yabby wails, and the vocals are handed off to the DJ. Trinity enters, and sounds a bit annoyed, as he repeats "alright", as if to say, *relax, I'm here, I've got this covered.* Who but Trinity would enter a disco-mix like this? He then DJs on a variety of unrelated topics, including references to Rasta taking a train to Brazil and China, a pun (intentional or accidental) about a dog in the yard doing its duty, the *higgler* (street vendor) in the market, the fox in the forest, and more. As he lets flow his stream of consciousness, Trinity rides the riddim and its idiosyncratic kink with ease. And although what he says does not amount to much, it sounds good. For our deluxe megamix , let's truncate the song right after he proclaims, "Stand firm as a dread", since all that follows is repetition. It's a great segue for the next version.

Tommy McCook's sax cut is poorly named 'Plague Of Horn'. If this is a plague, let it become a pandemic. The riddim and sax are dappled with dub, as McCook lays down a theme that's strong and limber. Once established, he digresses from it, occasionally touching on the abstract. He builds to a groaning wail that is immediately recognizable as Tommy McCook, one of the greatest sounds in all of reggae. His performance compares favorably with his version of the Viceroy's 'Slogan On The Wall' riddim (a song described previously in this book; pages 392–3). That's no faint praise as it's one of the greatest performances in his long, unmatched career, and perhaps his last great performance. You'll want 'Plague Of Horn' in its entirety for your megamix.

Next comes another DJ version, called 'Jesus Dread', billed to Trinity and Dillinger. The billing might have been more accurately made to Trinity and Tommy McCook. Dillinger is only heard very briefly at the song's opening and conclusion. The version uses a dubbier mix of the McCook's sax cut, with lots of choice bits of sax left in. This time, instead of spewing random topics, Trinity chooses to chant praise of Yabby You. (The song's title is a nickname of Yabby's that comes from the fact that he is a Rasta who adamantly believes in the divinity of Jesus rather than Haile Selassie.) With this added to the end, our megamix has passed the 10-minute mark. If that doesn't satisfy your appetite for the 'King Pharaoh's Plague' riddim, you can tack on King Tubby's 'King Pharaoh Dub', a good version with different dub from that heard elsewhere. All four versions can be found on the two-disc Yabby You CD collection called *Jesus Dread*.

Lloyd & Devon: *'Push Push'*
More than a decade after their rock steady classic 'Red Bum Ball' (a song described previously in this book; page 140), Lloyd Robinson and Devon Russell reunited in 1979 to record another great but very different song. Produced by Coxsone Dodd, 'Push Push' is a jazz-disco-reggae-soul jam. It's a simmering stew of duetting soul falsetto vocals, electric piano, saxes (with a lead that sounds like the great Tommy McCook) and Syndrums. The "push, push" refrain simultaneously describes the righteous path to Rastafari while serving as sexy dance lyrics. The groove is too nice to end, so its dub version is appended in disco-mix fashion, doubling the enjoyment for dancers and listeners alike. It features a newly added reggae chop guitar flashing with effects and a bit of drop-in/out. The groove is so good that even though it tops 6 minutes, 'Push Push' still seems too short. It can be heard on the Soul Jazz Records compilation CD, *Studio One Disco Mix*.

Blood Sisters: *'Ring My Bell'*
Reggae has a long history of quickly covering hit songs from other genres in reggae style. Often, these come off as cheap knockoffs, at other times they fare

better. Occasionally, they exceed the original. A faithful reggae cover of Anita Ward's 1979 disco hit 'Ring My Bell' that was released the same year is one such example. It's by Blood Sisters, a name never heard from before or again, as produced by L. Laing and N. King, two more names whose legacy was confined to this one single. Too bad, as their record is a perfect blend of disco and reggae that's far more engaging than the original rendition.

The Blood Sisters do an adequate job imitating Ward's sexy, detached, falsetto vocals. And both renditions share Syndrums, the electronic drums that found a home in both the reggae and disco music of the day. Both songs have a four-on-the-floor beat (though the reggae beat is more elaborate, unsurprisingly, as disco sported the simplest beat of any dance music). The biggest difference is in the overall approach to making music. In the reggae rendition, every instrument is played distinctly and earnestly. For example, listen to the ominous trebly one-finger piano riff. The result is that this rendition is more genuinely musical than the over-produced disco original, which sounds as if it was extruded whole by a machine. Suitably, the Blood Sisters song was most commonly available as a disco-mix single. I wonder if any non-Jamaican dancers stumbled a bit on the dance floor as the song segued to its churning dub version. 'Ring My Bell' was rescued from obscurity by its inclusion on the Soul Jazz Records compilation CD called *Hustle! Reggae Disco*.

Delroy Pinnock and Dickey Dread & Mikey Ranks: *'I Want To Be'*
Why is this 1981 12-inch single in the difficult-to-categorize chapter? First, because it doesn't fit in a chapter on any one style of reggae. It's a lovers' rock song performed over dubby backing that's disco-mixed with a roots DJ version. Second, because it does not fit in a chapter on a famous producer, label or artist. It doesn't even come close. The record comes out of the London reggae scene, where it was released as a 12-inch single on the small S & G label, never appearing on an LP or CD. The singer, Delroy Pinnock, is an obscure name who recorded just a handful of songs. The DJ duo Dickey Dread and Mikey Ranks are even more obscure. This record seems to have been the extent to which either of them has recorded. And in case you thought things couldn't get even more obscure, the producer's name is not offered at all, other than the record being an S & G production.

So, why is this 1981 12-inch single in this book? Because, in spite of all involved being household names only in their own households, this is a great reggae song. It is truly nothing less than excellent.

Delroy Pinnock, a singer obviously influenced by Dennis Brown, movingly sings a proclamation of love that becomes a marriage proposal. He is occasionally double-tracked to harmonize with himself for added drama and is backed by a wall of roots reggae strong enough to stop a tank. With lots of dub as the mortar, there is rhythm piano, fat rumbling bass, a good if unfamiliar drummer, locked-in Nyabinghi hand drum, swoops from novelty whistle and a hint of guitar. The piano is so prominent, the character of the song utterly changes during the intervals where it's dropped out or echoed.

The riddim reaches its conclusion with a drum roll. Suddenly, everything is dropped out except bass, drums and new surging dub effects. DJs Dickey Dread and Mikey Ranks enter and begin to *reason* over an echoing cascade of dub piano. Their chant intensifies as they exchange positive affirmations, and as dub roils, until the song's run out.

It's a shame twice over that 'I Want To Be' has never been compiled on LP or CD. Not only is it a great record worthy of a wider audience, but it gives us an understanding of how deep the UK reggae scene was at that time, that such fine, unadulterated reggae could come from such obscure players there, matching the best from its star acts. Optimist that I am, no matter the circumstances, I believe a song this good can only be overlooked for so long. Amazed that it has not happened yet, I can only trust that it will soon be plucked from obscurity and put onto a compilation CD sometime very soon.

C. Livingston: *'Tribute To Bobby'*

Roots singer Carlton Livingston was born in 1962 in Saint Mary Parish. He learned to sing in church from his mother and sisters, who sang in the choir. In 1975, he became part-owner and performer on the Fantastic Three sound system, starting as a singer, becoming a DJ for a time and then returning to singing for good. His first recording was the roots reggae 'The Tale of Two Cities' in 1977. He has since released four albums and about 35 singles and is still actively recording today.

Livingston's 'Tribute To Bobby' was produced by Tad Dawkins and engineered by Scientist in 1980. As heard on the *Trojan Tribute To Bob Marley Box Set*, it's easily the shortest song described in this book, coming in at 75 seconds. But its brevity is due to a sleight of hand by the label. It's actually a tribute to a different Bob: one who was murdered at a dance. Trojan truncated the original track, losing key lyrics and leaving a song that could be easily construed as a celebration of Bob Marley. But regardless of whom it's about, you won't find a more enjoyable minute-and-a-quarter reggae song anywhere. Not when this one packs in a seminal dancehall riddim, mournful roots vocals and a fine dub segment in miniature.

Livingston sings over a dub version of the riddim from Barrington Levy's 'A Yah We Deh' (a song described earlier in this book; page 538). Sweet blues guitar runs co-exist with mechanized drums, while dub makes the riddim more interesting. At one point, dub processing briefly doubles the drum beat, creating a sizzling roll that a human would never play. With a sad melody full of long heartfelt notes, Livingston laments Bobby and celebrates his memory. As he does so, the guitar drops out, leaving only a stripped-down arrangement of voice, drum (which also drops out for a notch) and bass. Then, the dub-master expertly turns guitar strums into sonic skyrockets of echo to conclude the song, as a brief, beautiful firework show fills the aural sky in tribute to Bobby, whoever he may be.

Anyone interested in hearing the original recordings out of which Trojan carved this one will have to track down the 1980 compilation LP called *Soul To Soul Vol. 1* on the Tad's label. Presented there as a disco-mix with an appended dub version, it's six times longer than the Trojan edit. But not necessarily six times better, as Trojan served up the prime cut.

Dawn Penn: *'You Don't Love Me' (aka 'No No No')*
Born Dawn Pickering in 1952 in Kingston, Dawn Penn may not have been pro-lific, but she has a rock steady classic to her credit. She recorded her first songs for Prince Buster in 1966 but would soon move to Coxsone Dodd, and then on to other producers. She recorded about a dozen rock steady songs in all before leaving Jamaica and music by the new decade. But she returned to both in 1987, and has since released three albums.

Penn recorded her first rendition of 'You Don't Love Me' for Dodd in 1967. But many reggae fans would be surprised to learn that the song had a life before she took ownership of it. 'You Don't Love Me' was first recorded in 1961 as a rollicking, rocking, bluesy R&B track by American Delta bluesman Willie Cobbs. Cobbs's song is a fine performance with great integrity in that idiom. Yet producer Dodd, singer Penn and backing band Sound Dimension were able to translate it to rock steady with no loss of quality or integrity. It opens creatively with a distinctive syncopated introduction that sounds an urgent charge. Then a drum roll tumbles through molasses and is drawn out over the start of Penn's vocal, helping the musicians downshift to the slower rhythm of the body of the song. Penn sounds genuinely hurt and lost, describing being abandoned by her lover and left with no place to live. She makes 'You Don't Love Me' one of the saddest of all rock steady songs.

As is often the case with the style, piano is out front. But the instrumental spotlight is stolen by a mid-song trumpet solo by Dave Madden. He plays a wonderful bluesy theme, expanding on a bit of melody suggested by Cobb's original. Penn's vocal, the idiosyncratic opening and this solo would each be enough to make 'You Don't Love Me' great. Possessing all three makes it a rock steady classic. It can be heard on such Studio One collections as *Feel Like Jumping: Best Of Studio One Women* on the Heartbeat label in the USA and *Studio One Rockers* on the Soul Jazz label in the UK.

Penn's song proved difficult for other singers to resist. In 1972, K. C. White recorded a successful self-produced cover version, called 'No No No'. It repeats all the song's virtues, the trumpet solo translated nicely to piano, though one may miss Penn's voice. A version of its riddim is the basis for 'Screaming Target', Big Youth's famous DJ version of the riddim (a song described in the chapter on this artist; page 411). In 1979, amidst recording a string of deep roots singles that constituted the *Showcase* LP and the *Guess Who's Coming To Dinner* CD, Black Uhuru also recorded a cover of 'You Don't Love Me', also calling it 'No No No'. But it is not particularly effective either as a rendition of Penn's song or as a good Black Uhuru track. In the late 1980s, Marcia Griffiths recorded a faithful cover. But the best rendition of all was Penn's remake in 1992, as produced by Steely & Clevie.

In the remake, Penn's vocal is true to the original, but stronger. She still sounds sad, but no longer devastated. It's as if she is singing from the vantage point of retelling the story, knowing that she overcame the break-up. Likewise, the musicians can't hide their enthusiasm, obviously supporting Penn's new perspective and thrilled to be celebrating such a beloved riddim. Though faithful to everything good in the original, this recut is triumphant rather than pensive, and is tricked out with a variety of upgrades. It gives rock steady a modern digital sheen, yet avoids throwing out the piano with the bath water. The syncopated opening and drum roll take on a mechanized dancehall precision. A trumpet doesn't just play the famous solo, it swaggers through it, sounding every note lovingly. When it drops out, digital bass becomes the lead instrument until the trumpet returns to play through the solo a second time. A sample provides a new introduction in the form of U-Roy's famous 'Wake The Town' proclamation. Altered pieces of the sample are triggered throughout the song. And twenty-five years after the original, an admixture of the old and the new gives us a dancehall–rock steady rendition of 'You Don't Love Me' that bests the classic original.

This rendition charted in the USA and in Europe, reaching number 3 in the UK and number 1 in Jamaica. It spawned numerous remixes, appeared on motion picture soundtracks and was covered in Spanish. It was perhaps the biggest reggae hit of the decade. To be sure to get the best mix of this rendition, choose the cut entitled 'You Don't Love Me (No, No, No) (Extended Mix)', as found on Penn's 1994 album, *No No No*.

Damian Marley: *'More Justice'*
Damian Robert Nesta "Junior Gong" Marley is the only child of Bob Marley and Cindy Breakspeare, the Jamaican beauty queen crowned Miss World in 1976, who had a long love affair with Bob. Damian is just one of Bob Marley's sons to have followed in their father's footsteps as lead singers, with some already having had longer careers and lives than their father. Besides Damian, Ziggy, Stephen, Julian, Ky-Mani and Fabian have also all recorded. Additionally, daughter Cedella has recorded as a lead singer and, as has daughter Sharon, provided backing vocals for Ziggy and other brothers at various times. And in 2012, Ziggy's son, Daniel Bambaata Marley, followed by Stephen's son, Joseph "Jo Mersa" Marley, became the first third-generation Marleys to record. Others are waiting in the wings, already performing live. (And before we leave the subject of Wailers' offspring, Peter Tosh's sons, Andrew and Jawara (aka "Tosh 1"), as well as Bunny Wailer's son, Asadenaki Wailer, and daughter, Cen'C Love, have also recorded.)

All of Bob's sons have voices that are similar to (though none quite as good as) their father's. Damian is a bit different, sporting a rougher voice and a sing-jay delivery. This gives his better tracks exciting rhythmic charge, making them stand out from those of his extended family. This was evident on 'Old War Chant', a strong song on his 1996 debut album *Mr. Marley*, and again on his international 2005 hit 'Welcome To Jamrock', found on his album by that name. And better than either is 'More Justice', a song released in between on Damian's 2001 album *Halfway Tree*. He has recorded four albums to date, including one in collaboration with rap star NAS.

Produced by brother Stephen, 'More Justice' features a hard rocking sound without relying on lead guitar. Instead, urgent pacing, Vocoder-processed vocals, dub keyboards, hand drum, defiant roots lyrics and a tough, skilled sing-jay vocal performance contribute to the aggressive sound. With so many modern elements, 'More Justice' can be equally described as modern roots reggae, roots dancehall or contemporary international reggae.

The song opens plaintively with a talk-box effect, blending guitar sound with voice to bluesy effect. Damian starts chanting, his interaction with the bass becoming the song's rhythmic and melodic backbone. A certain level of intensity is established and maintained. Damian explains that God inspired him to be an outspoken roots performer. He goes on to describe the poor outcomes when politicians are more focused on keeping marijuana illegal than on the desperation of the poor. It's striking how little these issues have changed since his father sang of them decades before. It's equally striking how much Damian reminds us of Bob, even with his DJ delivery and modern backing.

Damian occasionally spikes the song's already high level of intensity by doubling the pace of his chanting. The excitement peaks when he brings the paperboy call of, "Extra, extra, read all about it" into his DJ chant. No song by a Marley offspring can match the originality or excitement of 'More Justice', as the Marley legacy is carried into the new millennium.

Bibliography

Linton Kwesi Johnson (2002). *Jamaican Gleaner*, November 3.

Dave Katz (2000). *Lee "Scratch" Perry, People Funny Boy.* Edinburgh: Payback Press.

Gene Rizzo (2005). *The Fifty Greatest Jazz Piano Players of All Time.* Milwaukee: Hal Leonard Books.

Roger Steffens and Leroy Jodie Pierson (2005). *Bob Marley and the Wailers: The Definitive Discography.* Cambridge, MA: Rounder Books.

Daniel Tannehill Neely (2008). *Mento, Jamaica's Original Music: Development, Tourism and the Nationalist Frame.* New York: New York University Press.

Time (1999). "The Best of the Century", December 31.

Michael Turner and Robert Schoenfeld (2004). *Roots Knotty Roots: The Discography of Jamaican Music.* Maryland Heights, MO: Nighthawk Records.

Michael E. Veal (2007). *Dub: Soundscapes and Shattered Songs in Jamaican Reggae.* Middletown, CT: Wesleyan University Press.

Index of names

Abrahams, Horace 52
Abyssinians, The 317
Aces, The 146
African Brothers, The 384
Agard, George Canic 136
Aitken, Laurel 114
Alaine 572
Alexander, Monty 534
Alphonso, Roland 76–8
Anderson, Alpharita Constantia 306, 403
Andy, Horace 387
Archer, Errol 433
Austin, Peter 135

Banton, Buju 560–1
Barrett Brothers, The 211–12
Barrett, Aston 211–12
Barrett, Carlton "Family Man" 211–12
Beckford, Ewart 418–19
Beckford, Stanley 299–300, 308
Bedasse, Alerth 60
Beenie Man 563
Bennett, Errol 441
Bennett, Lorna 429
Bennett, Louise 531
Big Youth 410
Biggs, Barry 381–2
Black Slate 370
Black Uhuru 344–5
Blackwell, Chris 448–9
Bleechers, The 257
Blood Sisters 583–4
Bonner, Everton 557
Boothe, Ken 138–9
Bovell, Dennis "Blackbeard" 529
Braithwaite, Franklin Delano Alexander
     "Junior" 94
Brammer, Robert 440
Brammer, Wade "Junior" 421
Bright, Clive 549
Brooks, Baba 111
Brooks, Cedric "Im" 326–7
Brown, Dennis 330–1
Brown, Hopeton 292
Brown, Jim 443
Brown, Lewin 571
Browne, Danny 553

Browne, Haldane "Danny" 553
Bryan, Karl "Cannonball" 313
Buchanan, Manley Augustus 410
Bullock, Lester 432
Bundrick, John "Rabbit" 450
Burnett, Watty 284
Burning Spear 321–2
Burrell, Orville 544–5
Butt, Cardiff 553

Cables, The 140–1
Callendar, Fil 169–70
Campbell, Al 385
Campbell, Cecil Eustace Bustamente 13,
     72–3, 119–20
Campbell, Cornel 382–3
Campbell, Naomi 117
Carlos, Don 405
Carter, Linval 444
Ce'Cile 575
Chaka Demus 557
Charlton, Cecile Claudine 575
Chezidek 408
Chin, Ivan 7–8
Chin's Calypso Sextet 60
Clarke, Johnny 390
Cliff, Jimmy 92, 232–3
Clive & Naomi 117
Collins, Bernard 317
Collins, Miguel Orlando 570
Congos, The 284
Count Lasher 55
Count Ossie 324–5
Count Owen 38
Crawford, Everald Norman 437–8
Crooks, Derrick 142, 227
Culture, Louie 571

Davis, Anthony Moses 563
Davis, Sangie 261
Dean, Nora 236–7
Dekker, Desmond 145–7
Dekker, George 136
Dillinger 432
Dillon, Leonard 162
Dillon, Phyllis 132
Dixon, Percy 307
Doctor Alimantado 391

Dodd, Clement "Coxsone" 13–14, 18, 24, 168–9
Donaldson, Eric 265
Dowe, Brent 230
Downer, Roland 325
Dread, Dickey 584
Dread, Mikey 404
Drummond, Don 76–7
Duke Reid 13, 17, 22, 123–4
Dunbar, Sly 344, 366–7
Dunkley, Errol 579
Dynamites, The 146

Eastwood, Clint 440
Edwards, Oniel 573–4
Eek-A-Mouse 424–5
Ellis, Alton 127–8
Emanuel, Owen 38
Ethiopians, The 162

Fairclough, Anthony 441
Folkes Brothers, The 72
Foster, Winston 442–3
Fraser, Dean 535
Freedom Singers, The 135
Fyffe, Janice 575

Gatherers, The 261
Gaylads, The 577
General Degree 553
General Echo 446
General Saint 440
Germain, Donovan 561
Gibson, Joel "Joe Gibbs" 227–8
Girl Wonder 306
Gladiators, The 141
Godfrey, Hugh 74
Goofy 562
Gordon, Henry "Raleigh" 153
Gordon, Joseph 40
Gordon, Vin 173
Grant, Boysie 48
Grant, Trevor 436
Griffiths, Marcia 580–1

Half Pint 549
Hall, Marion 565–6
Harding, Jeremy 562
Harriott, Derrick 70
Henriques, Sean Paul Ryan Francis 568
Henry, Slim 307
Heptones, The 144
Hibbert, Frederick Nathaniel "Toots" 153–4

Hibbert, Lennie 178
Higgs & Wilson 71
Higgs, Joe 71
Hiltonaires, The 306–7
Hinds, Justin & The Dominoes 394–5
Hinds, David 374–5
Hippy Boys, The 313
Hislop, Winston 440
Holt, Errol "Flabba" 537
Holt, John 129
Hudson, Keith 315
Hylton, Ripton Joseph 424–5

I-Roy 434
I-Threes, The 460–1
Inner Circle 396, 400
Isaacs, Gregory 338–9
Israel Vibration 401

J, Harry 143
Jackson, Clifton Courtney "Jackie" 124
Jah Lion 259
Jamaicans, The 125
Jazz Jamaica 534
Jazz Jamaica All Stars, The 534
Johnson, Dane "Fire Links" 572
Johnson, Desbert 408
Johnson, Harry Zephaniah 143
Johnson, Linton Kwesi 529–30
Johnson, Roydel "Congo Ashanti Roy" 284
Jolly Boys, The 309

Kelly, Dave 566
Killer, Bounty 566–7
King Barou 304
King Stitt 417–18
King Tubby 22, 291
Knibb, Lloyd 78
Knibbs, Arthur 46–7
Kong, Leslie 91–2, 207

Lady G 575
Lamont, Eric "Bingy Bunny" 537
Lara, Jennifer 186
Laughton, Alaine 572
Lawes, Henry "Junjo" 537–8
Lee, Bunny 314
Lee, Byron & The Dragonaires 115
Lee, Naaman 302
Levi, Phillip 548
Levy, Barrington 537–8
Lewis, Hopeton 132
Livingston, Carlton 585

LKJ 529–30
Llewellyn, Barry 144
Lone Ranger 431
Lord Composer 51
Lord Flea 50
Lord Lebby 35
Lord Messam 44–5
Lord Tanamo 40

Marley, Bob & The Wailers 90–2, 109, 189,
    201–2, 207–8, 211–12, 224, 448–9
Marley, Damian 587–8
Marley, Rita 306, 403
Marsden, Steven "Lenky" 568
Marshall, Larry 182
Mathias, Jerry 153
Maytones, The 390
McCook, Tommy 76–8
McKay, Freddie 125
Melodians, The 230
Messam, Charles Augustus 44–5
Michigan & Smiley 441
Mighty Diamonds, The 261
Miller, Jacob 388–9
Minott, Albert 310
Mittoo, Jackie 78, 175–6
Monty & The Cyclones 435
Morgan, Derrick 116
Morgan, Earl 144
Morris, Eric "Monty" 115
Moses, Pablo 399
Mr. Easy 575
Mr. Vegas 564
Mundle, Omri 51
Murvin, Junior 274–5
Mutabaruka 532
Myrie, Anthony 560–1
Mystic I 267
Myton, Cedric 284

Nash, Johnny 201
Nastic, Jim 443

Osbourne, Johnny 542

Pablo, Augustus 245–6
Papa Levi 548
Papa Tullo 437–8
Paragons, The 126–7
Parkins, Terrence 55
Paul, Sean 568
Peck, Gregory 551
Penn, Dawn 586

Perkins, Wayne 451
Perry, Lee "Scratch" 211–13, 255, 263–4
Pinchers 550
Pinnock, Delroy 584
Pioneers, The 227
Pliers 557
Plunkett, Robin 53
Pottinger, Sonia 136–7
Price, Rodney Basil 566–7
Prince Alla 393–4
Prince Brothers 301
Prince Buster 13, 72–3, 119–20
Prince Jazzbo 444
Prophets, The 582

Ranglin, Ernest 180
Ranking Dread 398
Ranking Trevor 436
Ranks, Cutty 559
Ranks, Mikey 584
Ras Michael 264–8
Red Rat 561
Reid, Arthur 13, 17, 22, 123–4
Reid, Junior 552
Reid, Roy Samuel 434
Revolutionaries, The 297–8
Richardson, Harold 42
Riley, Winston 130
Roberts, Lindon Andrew 549
Robinson, Earl Anthony 446
Robinson, Lloyd 140
Rodney, Winston 321–2
Romeo, Max 270–1
Roots Radics, The 537–8
Rose, Michael 344–5
Ruby, Jack 322
Ruddock, Osbourne 22, 291
Russell, Devon 140
Russell-Myers, Ophlin 445

Saw, Lady 565–6
Saw, Tenor 549
Scientist 292
Scorcher, Errol 433
Scotty 428
Shaggy 544–5
Shakespeare, Robbie 344, 366–7
Sibbles, Leroy 144
Silver Seas Calypso Band 305
Silvertones, The 136
Simms, Noel "Zoot" 135
Simpson, Chad 562
Sir Horace and His Merry Knights 52

Sister Nancy 445
Sizzla 570
Skatalites, The 76
Skully 135
Slickers, The 142
Slim & Sam 60
Sly & Robbie 344, 366–7
Smith, Clifford 564
Smith, Michael "Mikey" 531
Smykle, Paul "Groucho" 295
Soul Brothers, The 178–9
Sound Dimension 169–70
Spanishtonians, The 136
Spark, Winston 417–18
Steel Pulse 374–5
Stephens, Richie 567
Stephens, Tanya 573

Taitt, Lyn & The Jets 146
Taylor, John 557
Taylor, Stephen 162
Techniques, The 130
Tewari, Dada 88
Third World 400
Thomas, Norman 50
Thomas, Philip 559
Thompson, Delroy 550
Tinglin, Wesley 187
TOK 569
Toots & The Maytals 153–4
Tosh, Peter (Winston Hubert McIntosh) 93, 520–1
Trinity 421

U-Roy 418–19
Upsetters, The 211–13, 255, 263–4

Valentines, The 136
Versatiles, The 258
Viceroys, The 187
Voicemail 573–4

Wailer, Bunny (Neville O'Riley Livingston) 93, 514
Wailing Souls, The 392
Waldron, Anthony 431
Walker, Constantine "Vision" 102
Ware, Winston 136
Williams, Everard Franklyn 60
Williams, Noel 36
Williamson, Gregory 551
Wilson, Clive 117
Wilson, Delroy 185
Wilson, Ernest 386
Wilson, Roy 71
Wilson, Wallace 561
Winston & George 136

Yap, Justin 86
Yellowman 442–3
You, Yabby 582
Young, Desi 143

Index of songs

Note: Album names are italicized.

'007' (Desmond Dekker) 147–8
'1 Ruthland Close' (Augustus Pablo) 253–4
'54-46 (Was My Number)' (Toots & The Maytals) 157–8
'400 Years' (Bob Marley & The Wailers) 452

'A Food Wedding' (Chin's Calypso Sextet) 65
'A Ju Ju Wah' (Roland Downer & Count Ossie) 325
'A Little Way Different' (Errol Dunkley) 579
'A Who Say' (Sly & Robbie) 367–8
'A Who Seh Me Dun (Wake The Man)' (Cutty Ranks) 559
'A Yah We Deh' (Barrington Levi) 538
'Abortion' (Black Uhuru) 352
'Addis Ababa' (The Skatalites) 81
'Africa' (The Gaylads) 577–8
'Africa Unite' (Bob Marley & The Wailers) 495
'African' (Peter Tosh) 524–5
'African Teacher' (Burning Spear) 323
'Africans To Africa' (Black Slate) 371
'Ali Baba' (John Holt) 129–30
'All I Have Is Love' (Gregory Isaacs) 339
'Am-A-Do' (Bob Marley & The Wailers) 466
'Ambush In The Night' (Bob Marley & The Wailers) 496–7
'Answer Me My Darling' (Derrick Harriott) 70–1
'Arab Oil Weapon' (Bunny Wailer) 514–15
'Ark Of The Covenant' (The Congos) 287–8
'Arleen' (General Echo) 446–7
'Armagideon' (aka 'Armagedon') (Bunny Wailer) 516–17
'Artibella' (Ken Boothe) 138–40
'Artibella' (Michael Rose) 345–6
'Ay Ay Ay' (aka 'Angie La La') (Nora Dean) 241–2

'Ba Ba Boom' (The Jamaicans) 125–6
'Ba Ba Di Ya (Miss A Ram Goat)' (The Jolly Boys) 309–10
'Baby I Love You So' (Jacob Miller) 251–3
'Baby We've Got A Date (Rock It Baby)' (Bob Marley & The Wailers) 452
'Baby Why' (The Cables) 140–2
Babylon By Bus (Bob Marley & The Wailers) 490–1

'Babylon System' (Bob Marley & The Wailers) 495
'Babylon Too Rough' (Gregory Isaacs) 339–40
'Back Off' (aka 'Back Off Ringcraft') (Johnny Osbourne & Papa Tullo) 544–6
'Back To Base' (Sly & Robbie and Groucho Smykle) 295–6
'Bad Card' (Bob Marley & The Wailers) 500–1
'Bad Luck Natty' (Jah Lion) 258–60
'Bad Minded Woman' (Laurel Aitken) 114
'Bad To Worse' (The Ethiopians) 166–7
'Bam Bam' (Pliers) 556–7
'Bam Bam' (Sister Nancy) 445–6
'Bam Bam' (Toots & The Maytals) 156–7
Bam Bam It's Murder (various artists) 556–7
'Bam O Say; Take Us Back To Ethiopia' (Count Ossie) 325–6
'Banana Boatman' (Junior Reid) 553
'Banana' (Arthur Knibbs & Cecil Knott) 47–8
'Bandulu' (Cornel Campbell) 397–8
'Bank To Bank Part 1' (Baba Brooks) 113
'Bank To Bank, Part 2' (Baba Brooks) 113
'Barbwire' (Nora Dean) 238–40
'Bathroom Skank' (Lee Perry) 260
'Bedroom Bounty Hunter' (Shaggy) 555–6
'Bellevue Special' (The Skatalites) 89–90
'Belly Lick'/'Bargie' (Arthur Knibbs and Cecil Knott) 47–8
Below The Bassline (Ernest Ranglin) 534–5
'Bend Down Low' (Bob Marley & The Wailers) 194, 465
'Bend Down Low' (Bunny Wailer) 518
'Bendwood Dick' (Percy Dixon) 307
Best Of Bob Marley & The Wailers, The (Bob Marley & The Wailers) 207–10
'Big Boy And Teacher' (Chin's Calypso Sextet) 63
'Big Boy And Teacher' (U-Roy) 419–20
'Big Man Little Yute' (Red Rat & Goofy) 562
'Big Sid' (Chin's Calypso Sextet) 63–5
Big Up! (Dean Fraser) 535–6
'Big Youth Special' (Big Youth) 293–4
'Bird In Hand' (Lee Perry [as The Upsetters]) 266–7
'Black Liberation' (Dennis Brown) 333
'Black Man Message' (Big Youth) 293–4

Black Uhuru (Black Uhuru) 349–55
'Black Wa-Da-Da' (Burning Spear) 297
'Blackboard Jungle Dub (Version 1)' (Lee Perry) 260
'Blackman Redemption' (Bob Marley & The Wailers) 508–9
'Blam Blam Fever' (The Valentines) 136–7
'Bleach Pon It' (Tanya Stephens) 572–3
'Bluesy Baby II' (Sly & Robbie) 368
'Bodyguard' (Steel Pulse) 380
'Bondage And Slavery' (Black Slate) 371
'Book Of Rules' (The Heptones) 144
'Boom Boom' (Black Slate) 371
'Boombastic' (Shaggy) 558
'Born For A Purpose' (Doctor Alimantado) 391
'Born Free' (Michael Rose) 347
'Brain Smashing Dub' (Linton Kwesi Johnson) 294
'Breakfast In Bed' (Lorna Bennett) 429–30
'Bredda Gravalicious' (The Wailing Souls) 392
'Broadway Jungle' (Toots & The Maytals) 154–5
'Broom Weed' (Stanley Beckford) 308
'Brown Skin Gal' (Count Owen) 38–9
'Brown Skin Girl Rub-A-Dub' (Ranking Trevor) 437
'Bruk Out' (Dave Kelly) 565–7
'Budy Bye' (Johnny Osbourne) 546–7
'Buffalo Soldier' (Bob Marley & The Wailers) 506–7
'Buffalo Soldier' (12-inch mix) (Bob Marley & The Wailers) 506–7
'Bull Dog' (Count Owen) 39
'Bum Ball' (Sly & Robbie) 368
'Burial' (Bunny Wailer) 517
'Burial' (Peter Tosh) 522–3
Burnin' (Bob Marley & The Wailers) 455–60
'Burnin' And Lootin'' (Bob Marley & The Wailers) 458
'Bus Dem Shut' (Bob Marley & The Wailers) 195
'Bush Doctor' (Peter Tosh) 525–6

'Caan Believe Mi Eyes' (Bounty Killer) 565–7
'Calypso Cha Cha' (King Barou) 304
'Can You Keep A Secret' (Big Youth) 412–13
'Can't Come In' (The Congos) 286–7
'Can't Take Another World War' (Clint Eastwood & General Saint) 440–1
'Capo' (The Hippy Boys) 313
'Cassandra' (Dennis Brown) 332–3
'Cassava Piece' (Augustus Pablo) 251–3

Catch A Fire (Bob Marley & The Wailers) 449–55
'Caution' (Bob Marley & The Wailers) 208–9
'Chaka Chaka' (Dane Johnson) 572–3
'Chant A Psalm' (Steel Pulse) 376
'Chant Down Babylon' (Bob Marley & The Wailers) 508
'Charlie's Cow' (Silver Seas) 305
'Check Him Out' (The Bleechers) 257
'Cherry Oh Baby' (Eric Donaldson) 302–3
'Children At Play' (Marcia Griffiths) 580–1
Chill Out (Black Uhuru) 362–3
'Chinese Baby' (The Hiltonaires) 305–6
'Choice Of Music Part 2' (Jackie Mittoo) 176–7
'Christine Keeler' (The Skatalites) 82
'Clap The Barber' (Michael Rose) 346–7
'Cloak And Dagger' (Lee Perry [as The Upsetters]) 258–60
'Club Tonight' (Mr. Easy) 574–6
'Cocaine Cocaine' (Sly & Robbie) 367–8
'Coconut Rock' (aka 'Passing Through') (The Skatalites) 83–4
'Cold I Up' (Johnny Clarke) 390
'Colonizing In Reverse' (Louise Bennett) 531–2
'Come We Go Down To Unity'/'Old Lady Oh'/'Linstead Market' (Boysie Grant and Reynolds) 49–50
'Coming In From The Cold' (Bob Marley & The Wailers) 499
'Concrete' (Bob Marley & The Wailers) 474
'Concrete Jungle' (Bob Marley & The Wailers) 450–1
Confrontation (Bob Marley & The Wailers) 506–10
'Confucius' (The Skatalites) 87
'Congoman' (The Congos) 288–9
'Consider Me' (Jennifer Lara) 185–6
'Cool Breeze' (Big Youth) 411
'Coon Can' (Sly & Robbie) 369
'Could You Be Loved' (Bob Marley & The Wailers) 503
'Could You Be Loved' (12-inch mix) (Bob Marley & The Wailers) 503
'Country Boy' (The Heptones) 581
'Crawfish' (The Soul Brothers) 178–80
'Crazy Baldhead' (Bob Marley & The Wailers) 470–1
'Crazy Baldhead' (alternate mix) (Bob Marley & The Wailers) 476
'Crazy Girl' (Half Pint) 548–50
'Crinoline Incident' (Lord Tanamo) 41

'Crisis' (Bob Marley & The Wailers) 488–9
'Cross Over' (Junior Murvin) 283
'Cry To Me' (Bob Marley & The Wailers) 103, 470
'Cry Tough' (Alton Ellis) 127–9
'Cuss Cuss' (Lloyd Robinson) 229
'Cutting Wood' (Girl Wonder) 306

'Dada Beg Your Pardon' (Stanley Beckford) 300–1
Dance Hall '63 (King Stitt) 417–18
'Daphne's Be-Bop Walking' (Silver Seas Calypso Band) 305
'Deck The Halls' (Jacob Miller) 397
'Declaration Of Rights' (The Abyssinians) 319–20
'Denham Town' (Winston & George) 136–7
'Dentist Dub' (Lone Ranger) 297
'Dick Tracy' (The Skatalites) 84
'Dinah' (Joe Higgs) 113–14
'Dirty Harry' (Sly & Robbie) 367–8
'Disco Devil' (Lee Perry) 273
'Disco Jack' (Jackie Mittoo) 314–15
'Diseases' (Michigan & Smiley) 441–2
'Diwali' (Steven Marsden) 568–70
'Do You Still Love Me' (Bob Marley & The Wailers) 92
'Doctor Kinsey Report' (Lord Lebby) 35–6
'Dog War' (Bunny Wailer) 518
'Dog War' (Toots & The Maytals) 154–5
'Don D Lion' (aka 'Don De Lion') (The Skatalites) 80
'Donkey Back' (Louie Culture) 571–2
'Don't Call Me Daddy' (Derrick Morgan) 116–17
'Don't Ever Leave Me' (Bob Marley & The Wailers) 99
'Don't Fence Her In' (Harold Richardson & The Ticklers) 43–4
'Don't Fool Round Me Gal' (Count Lasher) 58–9
'Don't Mind Me' (Higgs & Wilson) 75
'Don't Tek It For A Joke'/'Rukumbine' (Lord Messam) 46
'Don't Think About Me (I'm Alright)' (Horace Andy) 580
'Downpressor Man' (Peter Tosh) 523–4
'Dr. Ring Ding' (King Sporty) 417–18
'Dr. Ring Ding' (King Stitt) 417–18
'Dr. Ring Ding' (The Skatalites) 84
'Draw Your Brakes' (Scotty) 428
'Dread Oppression' (The Mellodies) 385–6
'Dread Organ' (Big Youth) 293–4

'Dreadlocks In Moonlight' (Lee Perry) 264–5
'Dreamland' (Bob Marley & The Wailers) 108
'Drifter' (Dennis Brown) 333–4
'Drug Squad' (Steel Pulse) 375–6
'Drum Song' (Sound Dimension) 171–2
'Dry Up Your Tears' (Nora Dean) 243–4
Dub Factor (Black Uhuru) 362–4
'Dub Feeling' (Bob Marley & The Wailers) 197–8
'Dub In A Matthews Lane Arena' (Augustus Pablo) 248
'Dub Of Righteousness' (King Tubby) 291–2
'Dubbing Is A Must' (Pablo Moses) 398–400
'Duppy Conqueror' (Bob Marley & The Wailers) 216–17, 459

Earth Crisis (Steel Pulse) 378–80
'East Of The River Nile' (Augustus Pablo) 249–50
'Eastern Standard Time' (The Skatalites) 80–1
'Easy Skanking' (Bob Marley & The Wailers) 485
'Easy Snappin'' (Theophilus Beckford) 13–14
'Easy Task' (Junior Murvin) 280
'El Rockers Chapter 3' (Augustus Pablo) 253
'Empty Belly' (The Ethiopians) 167
'Endurance' (Black Uhuru) 358
Equal Rights (Peter Tosh) 523–5
'Etheopia' (Lord Lebby) 35–6
'Ethiopian Binghi Drums' (Augustus Pablo) 250
'Every Knee Shall Bow' (U-Roy) 420–1
'Everything Crash' (The Ethiopians) 164
'Everywhere I Go' (Mr. Vegas) 567–8
'Exodus' (Bob Marley & The Wailers) 479
'Exodus' (dub version) (Bob Marley & The Wailers) 484
'Exodus Advertisement' (Bob Marley & The Wailers) 484
Exodus (Bob Marley & The Wailers) 477–84
'Extra Classic' (Gregory Isaacs) 340

'False Teachin'' (Junior Murvin) 279–80
'Fat Fish' (Viceroys) 187–8
'Fe Mi Woman A De Bes' (Lone Ranger) 446
'Feel Alright' (Bob Marley & The Wailers) 197–8
'Fidel At The Control' (Inner Circle) 293
'Fidel Castro' (The Skatalites) 85
'Fight Dem Back' (Peter Tosh) 530
'Filthy' (Danny Browne) 564–5
'Fireflies' (Eek-A-Mouse) 426
'Fisherman' (The Congos) 285–6
'Fit You Haffe Fit' (Black Uhuru) 364–5

'Flat Foot Hustling' (Dillinger) 433

'Forever Dub' (Augustus Pablo) 250

'Forever Love' (Augustus Pablo) 250

'Forever Loving Jah' (Bob Marley & The Wailers) 504

'Forward With Jah Orthodox' (Mystic I) 267

'Four Days Of Love' (Harold Richardson & The Ticklers) 44

'Free Man' (aka 'Free') (The Ethiopians) 163

'Freedom Time' (Bob Marley & The Wailers) 194–5

'From Creation' (Lenny Hibbert) 177–8

'Fu Manchu' (Desmond Dekker) 152

'Full Up' (Sound Dimension) 172

'Funky Kingston' (Toots & The Maytals) 161

'Funny Dub' (Linton Kwesi Johnson) 294

'Fussing And Fighting' (Bob Marley & The Wailers) 218

'Gal A Gully/Matilda' (Lord Composer) 51–2

'Gal Yu A Pepper' (Shaggy) 559–60

'Galang Gal' (TOK) 568–70

'Gangsta Confession' (Mr. Vegas) 576

'Ganja Smuggling' (Eek-A-Mouse) 425–6

'General Penitentiary' (Black Uhuru) 351

'Get Busy' (Sean Paul) 568–70

'Get On The Right Track' (Phyllis Dillon & Hopeton Lewis) 132–3

'Get Up, Stand Up' (Bob Marley & The Wailers) 456–7

'Get Up, Stand Up' (Peter Tosh) 524

'Ghost, The' (Burning Spear) 296

'Girl Answer To Your Name' (Prince Buster) 121–2

'Girls Of Today' (Papa Tullo) 440

'Give Me A Ticket' (Bob Marley & The Wailers) 196

'Give Thanks And Praises' (Bob Marley & The Wailers) 509

'Glamour Gal' (Harold Richardson & The Ticklers) 43–4

'Going The Wrong Way' (Al Campbell) 385

'Gonna Tell Your Girlfriend' (Barrington Levi) 540–1

'Granny' (General Degree) 553–4

Great Expectation (The Jolly Boys) 310–11

'Greedy Dog' (Israel Vibration) 407–8

'Guess Who's Coming To Dinner' (Black Uhuru) 350–1

'Guess Who's Coming To Dinner' (Michael Rose) 346–7

Guess Who's Coming To Dinner (Black Uhuru) 349–55

'Guiltiness' (Bob Marley & The Wailers) 478

'Gun Fever' (The Valentines) 136–7

'Hallelujah Time' (Bob Marley & The Wailers) 458–9

'Hammer' (Bob Marley & The Wailers) 202

'Happiness' (Black Uhuru) 356–7

'Hard Time' (Ranking Dread) 397–8

'Harder They Come, The' (Jimmy Cliff) 233–4

'Heads High' (Mr. Vegas) 564–5

'Healing In The Balm Yard' (Harold Richardson & The Ticklers) 44

'Hear River Jordan' (Ras Michael) 267–8

Heart Of The Congos (The Congos) 284–9

'Heartaches' (Nora Dean) 237–8

'Heathen, The' (Bob Marley & The Wailers) 478

'Heaven And Earth' (The Skatalites) 85

'Heavenless' (Vin Gordon) 173–4

'Herb Tree' (Mr. Vegas) 574–6

'Herbman Skanking' (U-Roy) 420

'Here I Come' (Barrington Levi) 539

'Here In Jamaica' (Bunny Wailer) 519

'Hey Grandma' (Desmond Dekker) 150–1

'Hill and Gully Ride'/'Mandeville Road' (Lord Composer) 51–2

'Hold Tight' (The African Brothers) 384

'Holiday No.' (Lord Messam) 45–6

'Hool-A-Hoop Calypso' (Count Owen) 39–40

'House Of Dub Version' (Augustus Pablo) 249

'I Am That I Am' (Peter Tosh) 524

'I Chase The Devil' (Max Romeo) 273

'I Don't Know Why' (Delroy Wilson) 185–6

'I Don't Know Why (I Love You)' (Desi Young) 143

'I Know' (Bob Marley & The Wailers) 509

'I Know Myself' (Ernest Wilson) 386

'I Shot The Sheriff' (Bob Marley & The Wailers) 457

'I Stand Predominant' (Bob Marley & The Wailers) 107–8

'I Visited A Wedding' (Chin's Calypso Sextet) 65

'I Want To Be' (Delroy Pinnock, Dickey Dread & Mikey Ranks) 584–5

'I Was Appointed' (Junior Murvin) 281

'I'm Gonna Take Over Now' (The Ethiopians) 162–3

'I'm The Toughest' (Peter Tosh) 526–7

'I've Got To Get Away' (John Holt & The Paragons) 578

'Igziabeher' (aka 'Let Jah Be Praised') (Peter Tosh) 522

'In Your Eyes' (Johnny Osbourne) 546

'Independence Ska' (Baba Brooks) 111–12

'Inna Di Road' (Chezidek) 408

'Iron Bar' (King Stitt) 418

'Iron Bar Dub' (Linton Kwesi Johnson) 294

'Is This Love' (Bob Marley & The Wailers) 486

'Island In The Sun' (Count Owen) 39–40

'Islington Rock' (Augustus Pablo) 251

'Israelites' (Desmond Dekker) 148–9

'It Hurts To Be Alone' (Bob Marley & The Wailers) 99

'It Is Not Easy' (Desmond Dekker) 151

'It Mek' (aka 'A It Mek') (Desmond Dekker) 149–50

'It's You' (Toots & The Maytals) 155

'Jackpot' (The Pioneers) 227–9

'Jah Jah Me No Born Yah' (Cornel Campbell) 382–3

'Jah Light' (Augustus Pablo) 250

'Jah Light Version' (Augustus Pablo) 250

'Jah Live' (Bob Marley & The Wailers) 474

'Jah Love' (Dillinger) 432

'Jah Moulty Ital Sip' (Augustus Pablo) 249

'Jah No Dead' (Burning Spear) 322

'Jah Say Dub' (Augustus Pablo) 248

'Jailhouse' (Bob Marley & The Wailers) 104–5

'Jam It Up Tight' (Jim Brown) 443–4

'Jamaica Banana' (Count Lasher) 58–9

'Jamaican Jiggas' (Voicemail) 573

'Jamaican Mentos' (aka 'Mango Walk'/'Gi Me Back Me Shilling'/'Chichi Bud Oh'/'Hog In A My Mint Tea') (Lord Messam) 45–6

'Jammin'' (Bob Marley & The Wailers) 479

'Jammin'' (dub version) (Bob Marley & The Wailers) 484

'Jammin'' (live, from the One Love Peace Concert) (Bob Marley & The Wailers) 491

'Jammin'' (long version) (Bob Marley & The Wailers) 484

'Jesus Dread' (Trinity & Dillinger) 582–3

'Jim Screechy' (aka 'Jim Squeechy'; aka 'Jim Squashey') (Big Youth) 415

'Jingle Bells Calypso' (Lord Lebby) 36–7

'Joe Grazer' (Vin Gordon) 174–5

'Johnny B Goode' (Peter Tosh) 527

'Johnny Too Bad' (The Slickers) 142

'Johnny Was' (Bob Marley & The Wailers) 469

'Johnny Was' (alternate mix) (Bob Marley & The Wailers) 476

'Journey' (Black Uhuru) 361

'Judge Not' (Bob Marley & The Wailers) 92

'Juicy Oyster, The' (Chin's Calypso Sextet) 62–3

'Jumbie Jamboree' (Bob Marley & The Wailers) 102–3

'Jump Nyabinghi' (Bob Marley & The Wailers) 508

'Jumping Jehosophat' (Jackie Mittoo) 176–7

'Kaya' (Bob Marley & The Wailers) 485–6

Kaya (Bob Marley & The Wailers) 485–90

'Kechi Shubi' (Price Jazzbo & Jim Brown) 443–4

'Keep On Moving' (Bob Marley & The Wailers) 483–4

'Keep On Moving' (dub) (Bob Marley & The Wailers) 483–4

'Keep Your Dread' (Big Youth) 414

'King David' (Black Slate) 372

'King Dub' (Black Slate) 372

'King Pharaoh Dub' (King Tubby) 582–3

'King Pharaoh's Plague' (The Prophets) 582–3

'King Tubbys Meets Rockers Uptown' (Augustus Pablo) 251–3

'Kinky Reggae' (Bob Marley & The Wailers) 453

'Kunta Kinte (Version One)' (The Revolutionaries) 297–8

'Landlord And Tennant' (Max Romeo) 381

'Leaving To Zion' (Black Uhuru) 353

'Legalize Collie Herb' (Black Slate) 371

'Legalize It' (Peter Tosh) 521–2

Legalize It (Peter Tosh) 521–3

Legend (Bob Marley & The Wailers) 510

'Let Him Go' (Beenie Man) 564–5

'Let Him Go' (Bob Marley & The Wailers) 108

'Let Love In' (Dennis Brown) 335

'Let Me Tell You Boy' (Nora Dean) 242

'Let Off Supm' (Gregory Isaacs and Dennis Brown) 336

'Limb By Limb' (Cutty Ranks) 559–60

'Limbo' (Count Owen) 38–9

'Linstead Market' (Boysie Grant and Reynolds Calypso Clippers) 49–50

'Little Fist' (Lord Tanamo) 41–2

Live! (Bob Marley & The Wailers) 466

Live At The Roxy, Hollywood, California, May 26, 1976 (Bob Marley & The Wailers) 476

Live Forever (The Stanley Theatre, Pittsburgh, PA) (Bob Marley & The Wailers) 505–6

'Lively Up Yourself' (Bob Marley & The Wailers) 462

LKJ In Dub (Linton Kwesi Johnson) 294
'Local Fisherman' (Eek-A-Mouse) 427
'Long Shot' (The Pioneers) 227–9
'Long Shot Kick De Bucket' (The
    Pioneers) 227–9
'Love' (Bob Marley & The Wailers) 203
'Love' (Lord Flea) 50–1
'Love And Love Alone' (Lord Lebby) 37
'Love Dem Bad' (Buju Banton & Red
    Rat) 560–1
'Love Fire' (Bunny Wailer) 519
'Love In Sweet Jamaica' (Count Owen) 39
'Love Is A Treasure' (Freddie McKay) 125
'Love Is Universal' (Johnny Osbourne) 546
'Love Jah Jah Children' (Big Youth) 413
'Lucifer' (Junior Murvin) 280–1

'Mabrak' (The Abyssinians) 318–19
'Mabrat (Passin' Thru)' (Count Ossie) 326–7
'Magic Composer' (Lord Flea) 50–1
'Make Me Believe In You' (Devon Russell) 184
'Mama Look A Boo-Boo' (Slim Henry) 307
'Mambo Jamaica' (Sir Horace and His Merry
    Knights) 52–3
'Man In The Street' (The Skatalites) 82–3
'Man Next Store' (John Holt & The
    Paragons) 578
'Mango Time' (Count Lasher) 56
'Manny Oh' (Higgs & Wilson) 71–2
'Masculine Gender' (Ranking Trevor) 436–7
'Mass Out' (Pinchers) 550
'Mellow Mood' (Bob Marley & The
    Wailers) 202
'Melody Maker' (Keith Hudson) 315–16
'Mi Cyaan Believe It' (Mikey Smith) 531
'Mi God Mi King' (Papa Levi) 548
'Midnight Ravers' (Bob Marley & The
    Wailers) 453–4
'Mind Your Motion' (Black Slate) 371
'Mister, Give Me De Rent' (Lord Flea) 50–1
'Mister Bassie' (Sly & Robbie) 367–8
'Mister Brown' (aka 'Who Is Mister Brown?')
    (Bob Marley & The Wailers) 216–17
'Misty Morning' (Bob Marley & The
    Wailers) 488
'Mix Up, Mix Up' (Bob Marley & The
    Wailers) 509–10
'Mo-Bay Chinaman' (Count Lasher) 58–9
'Mojo Girl' (Nora Dean) 237
'Mondays' (Black Uhuru) 363
'Money Generator' (Karl Bryan) 328
'Money In My Pocket' (Dennis Brown) 334
'Money Trouble' (The Maytones) 390–1

'Monkey' (Lord Flea) 50–1
'Monkey, The' (Mutabaruka) 532
'More Justice' (Damian Marley) 587–8
'Morgan's Mento' (Sir Horace and His Merry
    Knights) 52–3
'Morning Ride' (Yellowman) 443
'Mr. Bassie' (Augustus Pablo) 253
'Mr. Bassie' (Horace Andy) 388
'Mr. Bassie' (Trinity) 422–3
'Mr. Cop' (Gregory Isaacs) 341–2
'Mr. Know It All' (Gregory Isaacs) 340–1
'Mr. Music' (Sly & Robbie) 367–8
'Murder She Wrote' (Chaka Demus &
    Pliers) 556–7
'Murderer' (Johnny Osbourne) 543–4
'Murderer Version' (Johnny Osbourne)
    543–4
'Music Crave' (Don Carlos) 405–6
'Music Is My Desire' (Pablo Moses) 398–400
'My Time' (Hugh Godfrey) 75

'Nana' (Count Owen) 39
'Nanny Goat' (Larry Marshall) 182–3
'Nanny's Corner' (The Skatalites) 85
'Natta Bay Road' (Count Lasher) 57
'Natty Dread' (Bob Marley & The Wailers) 465
Natty Dread (Bob Marley & The Wailers)
    460–6
'Natty Dread In A Greenwich Farm' (Cornel
    Campbell) 384–5
'Natural Mystic' (Bob Marley & The
    Wailers) 467, 477–8
'Natural Reggae Beat' (Black Uhuru) 352–3
'Natural Way' (Augustus Pablo) 253
'Nature Dub' (Augustus Pablo) 253
'Naughty Little Flea, The' (Boysie Grant and
    Reynolds Calypso Clippers) 49–50
'Naughty Little Flea, The' (Lord Flea) 50–1
'Nigger Whitie' (Sly & Robbie) 367–8
'Night Food' (Chin's Calypso Sextet) 61–2
'Night Shift' (Bob Marley & The Wailers)
    472
'No Baptism' (The Ethiopians) 165–6
'No Galfriend' (Trinity) 423–4
'No More Trouble' (Bob Marley & The
    Wailers) 453
'No No No' (Alaine) 572–3
'No Sympathy' (Bob Marley & The
    Wailers) 459
'No Sympathy' (Peter Tosh) 522–3
'No Time To Lose' (Nora Dean) 243–4
'No Woman No Cry' (Bob Marley & The
    Wailers) 462–3

'No Woman No Cry' (Bunny Wailer) 512
'Noah In The Ark' (Lone Ranger) 430–2
'Noisy Spring' (Boysie Grant and Reynolds Calypso Clippers) 49–50

'Oh Bumbo Klaat' (Peter Tosh) 525
'Oh Carolina' (Folkes Brothers) 72–3
'Oh Carolina' (Shaggy) 554–5
'Oh Yeah' (Lady Saw) 565–7
'Old Lady' (Prince Buster) 120–1
'On The Rocks' (Dennis Brown) 335–6
'One' (The Ethiopians) 165
'One Blood' (Junior Reid) 552–3
'One Cup Of Coffee' (Bob Marley & The Wailers) 92–3
'One Draw' (Rita Marley) 403–4
'One Drop' (Bob Marley & The Wailers) 495–6
'One Dub' (Bob Marley & The Wailers) 495–6
'One Foundation' (Bob Marley & The Wailers) 459
'One Love'/'People Get Ready' (Bob Marley & The Wailers) 480–1
'One Step Forward' (Max Romeo) 272–3
'Open The Door' (Clive & Naomi) 117–18
'Oppressed Song' (Bob Marley & The Wailers) 458–9
'Oriental Taxi' (Sly & Robbie) 368
'Originator' (Jimmy Cliff) 234
'Orthodox Dub' (Lee Perry [as The Upsetters]) 267
'Out De Fire' (Lord Flea) 50–1

'Package Deal' (I-Roy) 434–5
'Pass It On' (Bob Marley & The Wailers) 458–9
'Pass The Kouchie' (The Mighty Diamonds) 402–3
'Passing Through' (The Skatalites) 83–4
'Peace Begins Within' (Nora Dean) 242–3
'Peach Dub' (Linton Kwesi Johnson) 294
'Peeni Walli' (Eek-A-Mouse) 426
'Penny Reel' (Eric "Monty" Morris) 115–16
'People Funny Boy' (Lee Perry) 256
'People Get Ready' (Bob Marley & The Wailers) 194
'People Get Ready' (The Minstrels) 186–7
'Pimper's Paradise' (Bob Marley & The Wailers) 502
'Plague Of Horn' (Tommy McCook) 582–3
'Plastic Smile' (Black Uhuru) 354
'Play Ground' (Jeremy Harding) 562–3
'Play Me A Love Song' (Nora Dean) 243–4

'Pocoman Jam' (Gregory Peck) 551
'Police And Thieves' (Junior Murvin) 276–7
Police And Thieves (Augustus Pablo) 275–83
'Police In Helicopter' (John Holt) 406–7
'Pomps And Pride' (Toots & The Maytals) 160–1
'Poor Me Israelites' (Desmond Dekker) 148–9
'Positive' (Black Uhuru) 364–5
'Positive Vibration' (Bob Marley & The Wailers) 468–9
'Possibilities' (Israel Vibration) 401–2
'Poun' Paper' (Lord Messam) 46
'Pound Get A Blow' (Bob Marley & The Wailers) 195
'President Kennedy' (The Skatalites) 85
'Pressure Drop' (Toots & The Maytals) 158–9
'Problems' (Desmond Dekker) 151
'Pum Pum A Go Kill You' (aka 'Tonight') (Prince Buster) 120–1
'Punky Reggae Party' (Bob Marley & The Wailers) 482–3
'Punky Reggae Party (dub)' (Bob Marley & The Wailers) 482–3
'Push Push' (Black Uhuru) 357
'Push Push' (Lloyd & Devon) 583
'Put It On' (Bob Marley & The Wailers) 216–17, 459
'Pyaka' (Bob Marley & The Wailers) 195

'Queen Majesty' (The Techniques) 130–2
'Quiet Place' (John Holt & The Paragons) 578

'Race, The' (The Gladiators) 383–4
'Rainbow Country' (Bob Marley & The Wailers) 467
'Ram Jam' (Prince Brothers) 301–2
'Rasta Dub' (Black Slate) 372
'Rasta Fiesta' (Sly & Robbie) 368
'Rasta Reggae' (Black Slate) 372
'Rasta Shook Them Up' (Bob Marley & The Wailers) 107–8
'Rasta To The Hills' (Augustus Pablo) 249
'Rastaman Chant' (Bob Marley & The Wailers) 458
'Rastaman Live Up' (Bob Marley & The Wailers) 508–9
Rastaman Vibration (Bob Marley & The Wailers) 467–77
'Rat Race' (Bob Marley & The Wailers) 473–4
'Ravers' (Steel Pulse) 377
'Real Rock' (Sound Dimension) 170–1
'Real Situation' (Bob Marley & The Wailers) 500

'Rearrange' (The Gladiators) 140–2

Rebel Music (Bob Marley & The Wailers) 510

'Rebel Music' (aka 'Three O'Clock Roadblock') (Bob Marley & The Wailers) 463–4

'Rebel's Hop' (Bob Marley & The Wailers) 213–14

Red (Black Uhuru) 359–62

'Red Bum Ball' (Lloyd Robinson & Devon Russell) 140

'Redemption Song' (Bob Marley & The Wailers) 504–5

'Redemption Song' (band version) (Bob Marley & The Wailers) 504–5

'Reggae Fever' (Steel Pulse) 375

'Reggae Fever Dub Version' (Steel Pulse) 375

'Reggae Hit The Town' (The Ethiopians) 163–4

'Reggae On Broadway' (Bob Marley & The Wailers) 204

'Reggae Sounds' (Linton Kwesi Johnson) 530

'Rehab' (The Jolly Boys) 310

'Reincarnated Souls' (Bob Marley & The Wailers) 458–9

'Rent Crisis' (Max Romeo) 381

'Rent Man' (Max Romeo) 381

'Rent Man'/'Resident Area' (Black Uhuru and Jah Grundy) 347–8

'Rescue Jah Children' (Junior Murvin) 278

Return Of Mudd Up, The (various artists) 574–6

'Revolution' (Bob Marley & The Wailers) 465–6

'Revolutionary Step' (Pablo Moses) 398–400

'Ride Natty Ride' (Bob Marley & The Wailers) 496

'Ride Natty Ride' (12-inch) (Bob Marley & The Wailers) 496

'Right Track' (Phyllis Dillon & Hopeton Lewis) 132–3

'Ring My Bell' (The Blood Sisters) 583–4

'Ring The Alarm' (Tenor Saw) 548–50

'Ringo Rides' (aka 'Ringo') (The Skatalites) 86–7

'Rise And Shine' (Bunny Wailer) 517–18

'Rivers Of Babylon' (The Melodians) 230–1

'Riverton City' (Big Youth) 413

'Robusta Banana' (Count Lasher) 58–9

'Rock And Come In' (Barrington Levi) 541

'Rock And Come On Ya' (Johnny Osbourne and Papa Tullo) 544–6

'Rock On' (aka 'Rock Away') (Gregory Isaacs) 342

'Rockers Meets King Tubbys In A Firehouse' (Augustus Pablo) 247

Rockers Meets King Tubbys In A Firehouse (Augustus Pablo) 246–9

'Roll On Sweet Don' (The Skatalites) 85

'Roller Skates' (Steel Pulse) 379–80

'Roots' (Bob Marley & The Wailers) 481–2

'Roots, Rock, Dub' (unreleased single mix) (Bob Marley & The Wailers) 475–6

'Roots, Rock, Reggae' (Bob Marley & The Wailers) 469

'Roots, Rock, Reggae' (unreleased single mix) (Bob Marley & The Wailers) 475–6

'Roots Radical' (Jimmy Cliff) 235

'Roots Radical' (12-inch version) (Jimmy Cliff) 235

'Roots Train' (Junior Murvin) 275–6

'Round 7' (Scientist) 292–3

'Rude Boy' (Bob Marley & The Wailers) 103–4

'Rude Boy Prayer' (Alton Ellis, Peter Austin & Zoot Simms) 134–5

'Rudie' (Bob Marley & The Wailers) 104–5

'Rudie Gets Plenty' (The Spanishtonians) 136–7

'Rudie's In Court' (Derrick Morgan) 137–8

'Ruler, The' (Johnny Clarke) 390

'Rumours' (Gregory Isaacs) 342–3

'Run For Cover' (Lee Perry) 255

'Run Him' (Lady G) 574–6

'Running Away' (Bob Marley & The Wailers) 488–9

'Sam Fi Man' (Count Lasher) 55–6

'Same Thing You Gave To Daddy, The' (Nora Dean) 240

'Sammy Dead'/'Get Up Adina'/'Mr. Ramgoat, Oh' (Arthur Knibbs & Cecil Knott) 47–8

'Satisfy My Soul' (Bob Marley & The Wailers) 487

'Satta Amassa Ganna' (The Abyssinians) 318–19

'School Days' (Trinity) 421–2

'Screaming Targets' (Big Youth) 411–12

'Searching For Love' (Bunny Wailer) 515–16

'Selassie I Dub' (Augustus Pablo) 249

'Selassie Is The Chapel' (Bob Marley & The Wailers) 226

'Send Me That Love' (Bob Marley & The Wailers) 218–19

'Senegalese Market Place' (Sly & Robbie) 368

'Seventy Two Nations' (Ras Michael) 329

'Shake Shake Senora' (Lord Flea) 50–1

'Shanty Town' (Desmond Dekker) 147–8

'Shark Attack' (The Wailing Souls) 407

'Sharp Razor' (Lee Perry [as The Upsetters]) 258–60

'Shaw Park Blues' (Robin Plunkett & Shaw Park) 53–4

'She She' (Ce'Cile) 574–6

'She's Gone' (Bob Marley & The Wailers) 487

'Shenk I Sheck' (Baba Brooks) 112–13

'Shenk I Sheck' (Bobby Ellis) 313

'Shine Eye Gal' (Black Uhuru) 354–5

'Shocking Dub' (Linton Kwesi Johnson) 294

'Short Man Dub' (Augustus Pablo) 247

'Should I' (Dennis Brown) 332

Showcase (Black Uhuru) 349–55

'Sidewalk Doctor' (Jackie Mittoo) 177–8

'Silver Dollar' (The Skatalites) 79–80

'Simeon Tradition' (Augustus Pablo) 248–9

'Simmer Down' (Bob Marley & The Wailers) 95–6

Simple Sly Man (Sly & Robbie) 375–6

'Sinsemilla' (Black Uhuru) 358

Sinsemilla (Black Uhuru) 355–9

'Ska Jerk' (Bob Marley & The Wailers) 100

'Ska La Parisienne' (The Skatalites) 82

'Ska-Ra-Van' (The Skatalites) 87

'Skank In Bed' (Scotty & Lorna Bennett) 429–30

'Skull And Crossbones' (Sly & Robbie and Groucho Smykle) 295–6

'Skylarking' (Horace Andy) 387

'Slave' (Derrick Harriott) 76

'Slave Driver' (Bob Marley & The Wailers) 451

'Slide Mongoose' (Count Lasher) 56–7

'Slogan On The Wall' (The Viceroys) 392–3

Sly, Wicked And Slick (Sly & Robbie) 375–6

'Small Axe' (Bob Marley & The Wailers) 459

'Smile Jamaica' (fast version disco-mix) (Bob Marley & The Wailers) 490

'Smile Jamaica, Part One' (Bob Marley & The Wailers) 474–5

'Smile Jamaica, Part Two' (Bob Marley & The Wailers) 474–5

'Smiling' (The Skatalites) 88

'So Jah S'eh' (Bob Marley & The Wailers) 464

'So Jah Say' (Dennis Brown) 331

'So Long' (Count Ossie) 327

'So Much Things To Say' (Bob Marley & The Wailers) 478

'So Much Trouble In The World' (Bob Marley & The Wailers) 493

'Social Living' (Burning Spear) 322–3

'Soldering' (Stanley Beckford) 300

'Soldier Man' (Arthur Knibbs & Cecil Knott) 47–8

'Solomon' (Junior Murvin) 277–8

'Solus Market' (Boysie Grant and Reynolds Calypso Clippers) 49–50

'Some Like It Hot' (Dennis Brown) 335

'Son Of Jah Dub' (Augustus Pablo) 248

'Son Of Man Dub' (Augustus Pablo) 249

Songs Of Freedom (Bob Marley & The Wailers) 511

'Sonny's Lettah [Anti-Sus Poem]' (Linton Kwesi Johnson) 530

'Soon Come' (Peter Tosh) 527

'Soul Scorcher' (Karl Bryan) 313–14

'Soul Shakedown Party' (Bob Marley & The Wailers) 209

'Sounds And Pressure' (Hopeton Lewis) 134

Special (Jimmy Cliff) 234–5

'Sponji Reggae' (Black Uhuru) 360–1

'Stalag 17' (Technique All Stars/Ansel Collins) 312

'Stand Up' (Eric Donaldson) 265–6

Stanley Beckford Plays Mento (Stanley Beckford) 308

'Stay With Me' (Bob Marley & The Wailers) 203

'Steppin' Out' (Steel Pulse) 378–9

'Stepping Razor' (Peter Tosh) 524

'Stick A Bush' (The Gladiators) 395–6

'Stiff Necked Fools' (Bob Marley & The Wailers) 508

'Stir It Up' (Bob Marley & The Wailers) 196, 452–3

'Stone' (Prince Alla) 393–4

'Stop That Train' (Bob Marley & The Wailers) 452

'Straight To The Government' (Papa Tullo) 437–40

'Stylish Girls' (Tallawah Mento Band) 311

'Subterranean Homesick Blues' (Sizzla) 570–1

'Sugar Daddy' (Michigan & Smiley) 441–2

'Sun Is Shining' (Bob Marley & The Wailers) 217–18, 486–7

'Sunday Morning' (Bob Marley & The Wailers) 106–7

'Surfin'' (Ernest Ranglin) 180–1

'Survival' (Bob Marley & The Wailers) 495–6

Survival (Bob Marley & The Wailers) 492–7

'Survive' (Israel Vibration) 401–2

'Sweet And Dandy' (Toots & The Maytals) 159–60

'Sweet Charlie'/'Matty Rag'/'Nobody's Business' (Boysie Grant and Reynolds Calypso Clippers) 49–50

'Sweet Jamaica' (Lord Tanamo) 42

'Sweet Reggae Music' (Papa Tullo) 437–40
'Sweeter Than Sugar' (Naaman Lee) 302
Swingin' Calypsos (Lord Flea) 50–1

'Take A Ride' (Al Campbell) 396
'Take Her To Jamaica' (Count Owen) 38–9
'Take Me Back To Jamaica' (The Jolly
    Boys) 309
'Talk About It' (The Mighty Diamonds) 261
'Talk About Run' (Clint Eastwood & General
    Saint) 440–1
'Talkin' Blues' (Bob Marley & The
    Wailers) 465–6
Talking Blues (Bob Marley & The
    Wailers) 510–11
'Teacher Lick The Gal'/'Ada' (Arthur Knibbs &
    Cecil Knott) 47–8
'Tedious' (Junior Murvin) 278–9
'Tenement Yard' (Jacob Miller) 388–9
'Tenor On The Call' (Tommy McCook) 392–3
'Terrorist In The City' (Eek-A-Mouse) 426–7
'Thanks We Get, The' (The Versatiles) 258
'Thanksgiving Dub' (Black Slate) 372
'Them Belly Full (But We Hungry)' (Bob
    Marley & The Wailers) 463
'Thoroughfare' (The Skatalites) 80
'Three Little Birds' (Bob Marley & The
    Wailers) 480
'Throw Me Corn' (Larry Marshall) 183–4
'Tide Is High, The' (The Paragons) 125–7
'Time Will Tell' (Bob Marley & The
    Wailers) 489–90
'Too Hot' (Prince Buster) 122
'Top Rankin'' (Bob Marley & The Wailers) 495
'Tougher Than Tough' (Derrick Morgan)
    137–8
'Toughest, The' (Bob Marley & The
    Wailers) 107
'Tourist Season' (Errol Scorcher) 433–4
'Treat The Youths Right' (Jimmy Cliff) 235
'Treat The Youths Right' (12-inch version)
    (Jimmy Cliff) 235
'Treating Me Bad' (Toots & The Maytals)
    155–6
'Trek To England' (Count Lasher) 59
'Trench Town' (Bob Marley & The
    Wailers) 507
'Tribute To Bobby' (Carlton Livingston) 585–6
'Trodding' (Black Uhuru) 361
'Trouble Dub' (Bob Marley & The
    Wailers) 196–7
'Trouble On The Road Again' (Bob Marley &
    The Wailers) 196–7

True Democracy (Steel Pulse) 376–8
'Truths And Rights' (Johnny Osbourne) 542–3
'Tunnel One' (Tommy McCook) 181
'Turn Your Lights Down Low' (Bob Marley &
    The Wailers) 480
'Twin Seal Dub' (Augustus Pablo) 249

'Unconquered People' (Israel Vibration)
    401–2
'Under Mi Sensi' (Barrington Levi) 540–1
'Underground Root' (aka 'Underground') (Lee
    Perry [as The Upsetters]) 268–9
Uprising (Bob Marley & The Wailers)
    (album) 497–505
Uprising Live (Dortmund, Germany) (Bob
    Marley & The Wailers) 505
'Uptown Rebel' (Third World) 400–1
'Utterance' (Black Uhuru) 361–2

'Vampire' (Black Uhuru) 358–9
'Vampire' (Devon Irons) 280–1
'Vampire' (Peter Tosh) 527–8
'Vibrate On' (Augustus Pablo) 269–70
'Victorious Dub' (Linton Kwesi Johnson) 294
'Virgin Girl' (Eek-A-Mouse) 425

'Wa Do Dem' (Eek-A-Mouse) 425
'Waiting In Vain' (Bob Marley & The
    Wailers) 480
'Waiting In Vain' (alternative version) (Bob
    Marley & The Wailers) 484
'Wake Up And Live' (Bob Marley & The
    Wailers) 497
'Want More' (Bob Marley & The Wailers) 470
'Want More' (alternate mix) (Bob Marley &
    The Wailers) 476
'War' (Bob Marley & The Wailers) 472–3
'War (Alternate Mix)' (Bob Marley & The
    Wailers) 472–3
'War Ina Babylon' (Max Romeo) 271–2
'We A Rockers' (Inner Circle) 396
'We And Dem' (aka 'We And Them') (Bob
    Marley & The Wailers) 501
'We Are The Rasta' (Israel Vibration) 401–2
'Wear You To The Ball' (The Paragons) 125–7
'Wedding Bells' (Lord Tanamo) 41
'Weeping Eyes' (Justin Hinds & The
    Dominoes) 394–5
'What Goes Around Comes Around' (Bob
    Marley & The Wailers) 202–3
'What Is Catty' (U-Roy) 419–20
'Wheel' (The Congos) 290
'When I Fall In Love' (Ken Boothe) 138–40

'When I Fall In Love' (Sly & Robbie) 368
'When You Come America'; 'Cowhead'
  (Arthur Knibbs & Cecil Knott) 47–8
'Where Eagles Dwell' (Dub Specialist) 430–2
'Whip Them Jah' (Ranking Trevor) 253–4
'White Rum' (Sly & Robbie) 369
'White Squall' (Don Carlos) 405–6
'Who Am I' (Beenie Man) 562–3
'Who The Cap Fit' (Bob Marley & The
  Wailers) 471
'Why Did You Leave Me' (Barrington
  Levi) 541
'Why Oh Why' (Ernest Wilson) 430–2
'Why You So Craven' (Israel Vibration) 404–5
'Winner' (Richie Stephens) 567–8
'Wolf In Sheep's Clothing (Version 1)' (Big
  Youth) 414–15
'Wood For My Fire' (Black Uhuru) 347–8
'Words' (Sangie Davis) 261–2
'Words Of My Mouth' (The Gatherers) 261–2
'Words Of Wisdom' (Max Romeo) 327–8
Words Of Wisdom (Dennis Brown) 331–4
'Work' (Bob Marley & The Wailers) 501
'Work All Day' (Barry Biggs) 381–2
'Workin' In The Cornfield' (Junior
  Murvin) 281

'World War Three' (Mikey Dread) 404
'Worth His Weight In Gold (Rally Round)'
  (Steel Pulse) 377
'Wreck A Buddy' (Nora Dean) 240–1

'Ya Ho' (The Viceroys) 187–8
'You Don't Care' (Sly & Robbie) 368
'You Don't Care' (The Techniques) 130–2
'You Don't Love Me' (aka 'No No No)' (Dawn
  Penn) 586–7
'(You Gotta Walk And) Don't Look Back' (Peter
  Tosh) 526
'You'll Want Me Back' (The Techniques)
  130–2
'Youth Man' (The Congos) 289–90
'Youth Of Eglington' (Black Uhuru) 360
'Yoyo' (The Congos) 289–90
'Yuh A Di Wife' (Mr. Vegas) 574–6

'Zimbabwe' (Bob Marley & The Wailers) 493–4
'Zion Gate' (Horace Andy) 388–9
'Zion Is A Home' (Augustus Pablo) 247–8
'Zion Land' (Ras Michael) 329
'Zion Train' (Bob Marley & The Wailers) 502
'Zungguzungguguzungguzeng'
  (Yellowman) 441–3